Emotional Disturbance in Children
Theories & Methods for Teachers

Edited by
James L. Paul
University of North Carolina at Chapel Hill

Betty Cooper Epanchin
University of North Carolina at Chapel Hill
Wright School, Durham

Charles E. Merrill Publishing Company
A Bell & Howell Company
Columbus   Toronto   London   Sydney

Published by
Charles E. Merrill Publishing Co.
A Bell & Howell Company
Columbus, Ohio 43216

This book was set in Clearface Heavy Condensed and Baskerville.
Production Editor and Text Designer: Martha Morss
Cover Design Coordination: Will Chenoweth

Excerpt from *Winnie-the-Pooh* by A. A. Milne on page 424 reprinted with permission of E. P. Dutton & Co. Copyright © 1926, 1954.

Photo credits:

Cover photo, pp. 133, 160, 342, Strix Pix; pp. 15, 67, 194, 255, *Resource Teaching*, Charles E. Merrill, 1978; pp. 17, 42, 43, Susan Hartley; pp. 69, 382, Irma McNelia; p. 91, Larry Hamill; p. 103, Jerry Harvey; p. 221, Jean-Claude Lejeune; pp. 232, 285, 325, Marjorie McEachron, Cuyahoga County Board of Mental Retardation; pp. 247, 372, Harvey Phillips/Phillips Photo Illustrators; p. 274, Tom Hutchinson; pp. 307, 309, Celia Drake; p. 420, Constance Brown.

Copyright ©1982, by Bell & Howell Company. All rights reserved.
No part of this book may be reproduced in any form, electronic or mechanical, including photocopy, recording, or any information storage and retrieval system, without permission in writing from the publisher.

Library of Congress Catalog Card Number: 81–81628
International Standard Book Number: 0–675–09909–9

Printed in the United States of America

3 4 5 6 7 8 9 10—86 85 84

Foreword

"But what should I do on Monday?" This question looms before each new teacher of emotionally and behaviorally disordered students. Mainstream teachers also pose this question. And even the most experienced special teacher of distraught children searches for answers to this question, not just every Monday but every day and every hour.

Teachers seldom see a textbook as a path to solving the problems of what to do in the classroom. On the one hand, texts are criticized for being too theoretical; the general concepts presented are intriguing but are not useful when it comes to practice. On the other hand, texts are criticized for taking a cookbook approach. They read well in their specificity, and are popular, but teachers find that in their jobs they are continually confronted with new situations. Each child and each classroom is unique. So a bag of instant solutions to the "wrong" set of situations proves to be just as useless as a bag of theories.

The really useful textbook does not fit either of these types in format, or rather, it combines the best of both. It provides a theoretical framework that serves as a cognitive map of the discipline. The reader has a right to expect an honest review of the state of the art. An overview of theory is essential because the reality of the classroom is so variable. Each issue and situation in human affairs can be examined from many points of view, and there is no single path to success. With a broad understanding of theory the teacher has more paths to choose from.

While a theoretical foundation, then, is essential, the truth is, there are no theoretical classrooms, no theoretical children, and no theoretical schools. There are only real-life situations which call for a sequence of astute responses. Thus, the useful professional text offers a myriad of practical suggestions. Some people call this practical part the nitty-gritty, but this is an error. If all we do in the many hours of teaching is ad hoc responding to what confronts us at the point of decision, we are operating without a true awareness of our craft. Practical actions derive their meaning and orientation from our cognitive map which provides the theoretical base.

In addition to blending pragmatic suggestions and undergirding theory, the truly useful textbook presents information and concepts in an evenhanded and stimulating format. Such a book respects its readers. It doesn't talk pap and recognizes that each teacher must create his or her own unique style. Since teaching is a creative process, the text must avoid provincialism, indoctrination, and facile solutions, and offer instead analytical evaluations which encourage readers to apply their own reasoning and imagination to the problems it describes.

Given these difficulties of producing a really useful text, it is worth noting how this book has met the challenge. When the expertise needed requires a team of writers, as in this case, their work must be blended into a unified whole. The editors have achieved this unity without obscuring the dedication and excitement each contributing author has for his special area. Because of the conciseness of the substantive material, this book will be useful to both the new teacher and the seasoned professional. None of the writers talks down to the reader or offers homogenized platitudes and oversimple solutions. The "theory chapters" are attentive to application and the "practice chapters" give a sense of the concepts which direct a given procedure. This is a spare book, with overlap and redundancy cut clean. The concern for emotionally disturbed children and their families is evident in all the chapters. While the material definitely focuses on the elementary special education experience of disturbed students, this text will also be of use to those who plan to teach the very young or the adolescent.

No one underestimates the need for direct experience in learning to teach. But at the same time we also recognize that even many years of experience do not in themselves bring quality to one's professional practice. What is needed is experience which is guided by insight and reflection on the meaning of what we do. That is why the study and application of the material in this book will be a rewarding professional adventure for both new and longtime teachers.

William Morse

Preface

Educating emotionally disturbed children has been a major challenge to American schools. Until the last ten years, the research on these children and the philosophies of intervention focused primarily on understanding their needs and treating these children in clinical settings. Our knowledge of emotional disturbance has been mostly associated with the characteristics of the children themselves.

Some of the knowledge upon which treatments are built is based on well-conceived and carefully controlled research. Some of the knowledge is based on the successful experiences of professionals who work with these children in clinical settings. That is, our ideas about the nature of the problems of emotionally disturbed children have been those that made sense to the clinician. The interventions that seemed to work have been described in the literature and comprise a body of clinical knowledge transmitted through clinical training programs.

The major task for educators has been to understand the problems of emotional disturbance in ways that are relevant to the classroom. What impact does the understanding that a child is emotionally disturbed have on the teacher's approach in teaching the child in the classroom? How does emotional disturbance affect the child's performance as a student? The education of emotionally disturbed children must be guided, therefore, by sound principles of curriculum and educational practice as well as by our knowledge about the characteristics of these children.

The teaching of emotionally disturbed children, then, incorporates two major considerations: theories of behavior, that is, the nature of the problem, and theories of instruction, that is, the educational task. Teaching methods and behavior management strategies should be based on sound behavioral and instructional concepts.

Several important views or theories of emotional disturbance and behavior disorders have been developed. These views have varied in their appeal, to teachers and teacher trainers, as practical and helpful in guiding the planning and implementing of educational programs for these children. In a survey of public school programs for behaviorally disordered children, Kavale and Hirshoren (1980) found that, while a majority of programs consider their primary theoretical focus to be behavioral, the pragmatic approaches to treatment cover a wide variety of techniques from different theoretical models. They pointed out that "there is no evidence to support the superiority of any one theoretical approach over another" (p. 153), and that teachers take a utilitarian approach to meeting the needs of these children rather than adopt a single theoretical approach to the exclusion of others. The authors concluded that "university training programs should reflect a more eclectic stance by carefully synthesizing assorted theoretical components into a composite which meets the diverse pragmatic demands of public school programs for behaviorally disordered children" (p. 151).

The authors of this text have found a practical and eclectic perspective to be helpful in training teachers to work with these children. An eclectic

---

*Kavale, K. & Hirshoren, A. Public school and university teacher training programs for behaviorally disordered children: Are they compatible? *Behavior Disorders*, 1980, 5(3), 151–155.

perspective should not be regarded as a superficial one in which there is no in-depth understanding of particular views. Educational decisions based upon an eclectic perspective should be guided by a detailed knowledge of a number of subjects: child development, how behavior is learned and how it is changed, how concepts are acquired and how information is processed, how the child's affective qualities and character traits develop and how they affect the child's social behavior in different environments, and how different social environments work to enhance or impede the child's positive adaptation. In addition to knowing about children, the teacher must also understand the age- or grade-appropriate curriculum for the child with whom she or he is working, instructional planning and evaluation, and alternative teaching strategies and techniques. A sound eclectic orientation will help the teacher to understand the child in ways that lead to instructional planning and to make wise choices among appropriate instructional alternatives.

In the present text the major theories or views of behavior are presented and related to specific instructional methods that can be used by the teacher in the classroom. The authors do not claim to have reconciled the differing views covered herein or to have established a new eclectic program that incorporates the educationally relevant points of the various perspectives. Rather, the perspectives are reviewed with the educator in mind, and examples of educational approaches are presented that are practical and represent sound theoretical and philosophical principles.

Teachers should derive four benefits from this text. First, they should obtain an understanding of major theories and knowledge of the nature of the problem of emotional disturbance. Second, they should understand many practical curriculum concepts and instructional strategies that will assist them in teaching these children. Third, teachers should develop some appreciation of the relationships between theory and practice and, hence, become better equipped to plan and evaluate professional practices. Fourth, in acquiring a comprehensive framework that integrates several different perspectives teachers should be better able to relate to different professionals and parents in planning appropriate educational services for these children.

The text is divided into three sections. The introductory section provides an overview of the nature of emotional disturbance in children. The overview is presented in the philosophical and historical context of education. The nature of the professional services available to emotionally disturbed children and their families and the systems that deliver these services are also described in the introductory section.

In the second section, major theories of behavior and behavior deviation are presented. These include psychodynamic, organic, behavioral, ecological, sociological, and cultural theories. The practical implications of each of these perspectives for the classroom are emphasized.

The third section of the text deals with curriculum and teaching methods. In this section, specific instructional strategies and behavioral management techniques are described.

Acknowledgments

The editors wish to acknowledge the contributions of many of their colleagues in the development of this text. The editors assume sole responsibility for any deficiencies that may be identified in subsequent reviews of the text. Credit for the positive features of the text, however, they gladly share with those who helped make this work a reality.

As background for the approach taken in the text, the editors wish to acknowledge the very important scholarly work done by Professor William Rhodes and his staff and students at the University of Michigan in the Child Variance Project. Professor Rhodes and his colleagues at the University of Michigan organized and classified the vast literature on theories, interventions, and service delivery systems in the field of special education for emotionally disturbed and behaviorally disordered children. Without the guidance provided by that important work, the present work probably would not have been accomplished.

Some of those who contributed to the present text helped strengthen the overall conceptualization and organization of the material. Others assisted by critiquing individual chapters and making invaluable editorial suggestions for improving the substance and clarity of the writing. Others provided more specific technical assistance in the review of literature or in the production of the manuscript. The final product enjoys the collective benefits of all of these efforts.

The editors would first like to express their gratitude for the guidance, assistance, and encouragement they received from the outstanding professional staff at Charles E. Merrill Publishing Company. Marianne Taflinger provided the initial impetus for the book and contributed substantively to the idea and materially to the fulfillment of the idea. Vicki Knight engineered and carefully guided the production of the book. The creative leadership and enthusiasm provided by Marianne and Vicki made development of this text a very enjoyable and gratifying experience. Martha Morss did an outstanding job editing the manuscript, helping to balance the writing styles of the different authors and keep the writing at an introductory level, improving the clarity with which ideas are expressed, and overall helping us practice the principle of parsimony.

The authors are grateful for the professional reviews of the total manuscript. Professor Robert Rutherford read the first full draft of the manuscript and provided invaluable assistance and guidance in suggesting ways to improve the text. His editorial suggestions strengthened the entire manuscript.

The authors are especially indebted to Professor William Morse for his scholarly guidance in improving the text. Professor Morse reviewed the first complete draft of the book and the first major revision. His ideas improved the philosophy, technical and theoretical concepts, and the discussion of interventions.

Numerous colleagues and doctoral students read drafts of different portions of the manuscript and were extremely helpful in their suggestions for improving the material. These included William Bender, Linda Christensen, George Griffin, Carol Lachenman, Patricia Porter, Jane Stevens,

Bonnie Strickland, and Richard Yell. Nancy Creekmore made an important contribution in an extensive review of current literature. Alex Epanchin provided candid feedback and valuable support. Some of the masters students at the University of North Carolina and students in field-based courses read the manuscript and provided excellent suggestions for helping to keep the material at an introductory level. All of these contributions are gratefully acknowledged. The authors also wish to express their gratitude to Alice Isley, Anita Buie, Constance Lowe, and Sylvia Mewborn for their patient assistance in typing portions of the manuscript.

Above all the editors wish to express their gratitude to the chapter authors who worked so closely with us throughout the preparation of this text. The commitment of these colleagues to the development of a quality text, their individual standards of excellence, their patience with us when we asked again and again for revisions, not because there was any deficiency in their original work but because we were trying to achieve a well-integrated text, their good humor through it all, and most of all their own scholarship, which is reflected in their work, are deeply appreciated.

James L. Paul
Betty Cooper Epanchin

Contents

Section One
Introduction

1 Emotional Distubance in Children *James L. Paul*   3

  A Complex Problem 4
  Emotional Disturbance as an Educational Handicap 11
  The Emotionally Disturbed Child in the Classroom 14
  Different Roles—Different Views 19
  The Nature and Role of Theory 27
  An Eclectic Approach 29
  The Teacher as Decision Maker 30

2 Special Services for Emotionally Disturbed Children
James L. Paul   35

  Realities of Service Delivery 37
  History and Philosophy of Human Services 39
  Service Delivery Systems 49

3 Educational Services for Emotionally Disturbed Children
Mark D. Montgomery   59

The Development of Educational Services   61
The Regular Classroom Teacher   64
The Support Specialist   68
The Special Class   73
The Special School   78
Other Intervenors and Other Settings   79

4 Screening, Identification and Diagnosis   *Betty C. Epanchin*   87

Screening Techniques: Procedures and Problems   89
Identification and Diagnosis in Educational Settings   96
Diagnostic Evaluation in Mental Health Settings   106

Section Two
Perspectives

5 Psychodynamic Theory and Practice   *Charles Keith*   121

Normal Development: The Psychodynamic View   124
Emotional Disturbance and Learning: The Pyschodynamic View   131
Misconceptions about Psychodynamic Theory   138
Educational and Therapeutic Interventions   139

6 Organic Factors
Stephen R. Schroeder and Carolyn S. Schroeder   155

Organic Definitions of Emotional Disturbance   155
Biological Defect Theories   156
Developmental Theories of Brain Damage   164
Instructional Issues   171
Methodological Issues   174

7 Behavior Theory and Practice
Carolyn S. Schroeder and Stephen R. Schroeder   185

Elements of Behavioral Theory   188
Variables to be Assessed   193
Classification of Psychological Disorders   195
Classroom Intervention Strategies   197
Misconceptions about the Behavioral Approach to Treatment   205

8 Ecological Theory and Practice
Mark D. Montgomery and James L. Paul   213

Ecological Concepts   215
Ecological Research   217
Ecosystems: Units of Analysis   218

Ecological Disturbance 223
Ecological Interventions 225

9 Sociological Theory and Practice 243
Phillip C. Schlechty and James L. Paul

Social Control in the School 246
The Social Meaning of Behavior 248
Rules 249
The Problematic Nature of Rule Breaking 251
Labels 253
Practical Implications of the Sociological Perspective 258

10 Cultural Theory and Practice *Mark D. Montgomery* 269

Cultural Views of Disturbance 271
The Culture of the School 276
Cultural Aspects of Special Education 279
The Cultural View of Emotional Disturbance 281
Interventions from the Cultural Perspective 284
The Culture of the School: Prospects for Change 290

Section Three
Teaching Approaches

11 Curriculum Design and Educational Programming
Betty Cooper Epanchin and Virginia Dickens 297

Components of Educational Programming that Affect Curriculum 299
Individualizing Curriculum 305
Steps for Designing a Curriculum for Emotionally Disturbed Children 313

12 Behavior Management *Betty Cooper Epanchin* 321

Conditions for Effective Behavior Management 323
Preventing Behavior Problems 324
Enforcing Behavioral Expectations 331
Dealing with "Out-of-Control" Behavior 346

13 Educational Methods
Betty Cooper Epanchin and Virginia Dickens 353

Readiness 357
Language Arts 361
Listening 362
Speaking 365
Reading 369

Conceptual Writing 379
Handwriting 383
Spelling 385
Arithmetic 389
Choosing and Adapting Teaching Materials 395
Developing Teaching Sequences in Specific Academic Areas 396

14 Affective Education
Betty Cooper Epanchin and Lynne B. Monson   405

The Current Emphasis on Affective Education 407
Examples of Affective Curricula 408
Efficacy of Affective Curricula 417
Using Affective Curricula with Emotionally Disturbed Children 418

Section One

Introduction

THE EDUCATION of emotionally disturbed children as a professional area is less than two decades old. The development of this area has been very complex in part because the knowledge and skills from several different disciplines were needed. How to teach these children is an educational problem. But how to understand the needs of these children, in ways that lead to the development of classroom interventions, is a problem that requires the insights of several social and behavioral sciences.

Behavior occurs in two contexts. One is the psycho-organic context of the child. The child's developmental status, psychological needs and resources, and medical status, including neurological functioning, are important sources of information for understanding the child's behavior. Psychiatry, pediatrics, psychology, social work, neurology and nursing are among the important professional disciplines that help us understand children in these areas.

Another context that is relevant in understanding behavior is the environment in which the child is functioning. What are the cultural, physical and psychological resources available to the child? What opportunities, constraints and expectations exist? The professional helping disciplines have some sensitivity to environmental as well as physical and psychological contributions to behavior.

The education of emotionally disturbed children has, in the opinion of the authors, benefited most from viewing behavior as a product of the interaction of these two contexts. In order to teach these children, therefore, the teacher needs to be aware of the interaction of psychological, organic and environmental factors that affect the behavior and learning of children who are labeled *emotionally disturbed* or *behavior disordered*.

Many philosophical issues are involved in understanding and integrating the perspectives of different professional disciplines. It is important for the teacher to understand the relevant questions and to know where, or from whom, he can get assistance in understanding and planning an educational program for these children. While educational planning is an educational responsibility, the teacher must be able to work effectively with other professionals. The teacher needs to be able to use information from different professionals about the child's needs and abilities and integrate this information into an educational plan. As a professional, the teacher must also be able to contribute relevant information about the child's abilities and needs as a student to other professionals who may be working with the child or the family in a different setting. The ability to teach emotionally disturbed children effectively depends in part on the teacher's understanding of the nature of emotional disturbance and the philosophical and technical problems associated with defining, identifying, planning for and teaching these children.

In this section the history of concepts applied to these children and the philosophical issues involved in educational planning are discussed. The role of the teacher is examined with an emphasis on the legal, professional and political context of the public school. Approaches to screening, identification and diagnosis of the educational needs of emotionally disturbed children are discussed as a basis for educational planning. Section One provides the basis for Sections Two and Three which deal more specifically with understanding emotional disturbance and teaching emotionally disturbed children.

Section One includes the following chapters:

1 Emotional Disturbance in Children
2 Special Services for Emotionally Disturbed Children
3 Educational Services for Emotionally Disturbed Children
4 Screening, Identification and Diagnosis

1
Emotional Disturbance in Children

main points

1 Emotional disturbance is a complex problem. It is expressed differently in different settings. It affects and is affected by others with whom the child labeled disturbed interacts, and our knowledge of the causes and treatment is limited.

2 Professionals disagree about how to define emotional disturbance. No single definition is entirely satisfactory from an educational perspective.

3 The way a child is classified depends on the theoretical perspective being used and the purpose of the classification.

4 The prevalence of behavior disorders in the school-age population is estimated at 2%, although the range is from 0.1% to 30%.

5 Emotional disturbance can be viewed as a psychological disorder or a form of social deviance, but it is the educational consequences that are of primary concern to the teacher.

6 Parents, teachers and clinicians from mental health fields have different roles, interests, types of investment, and views of the problems of emotional disturbance in children.

7 Teachers benefit from an eclectic perspective in planning and implementing educational programs for emotionally disturbed children.

A Complex Problem

Emotional disturbance is one of the most complex problems in childhood. It does not take the form of a single, simple condition. Rather, it involves the total physical, psychological and social being of the child. Emotional disturbance may be manifested in problems of inappropriate behavior, faulty thinking, excessive variations in mood, depressed intellectual functioning, symptoms of physical illness, developmental lag in social and emotional maturity or underachievement. The ways in which emotionally disturbed children are noticeably different from their peers may be social, behavioral, psycho-organic or educational. *Emotional disturbance* is a label applied to many different patterns of characteristics.

Another reason why emotional disturbance is a complex problem is that not all of the professionals who label a child as emotionally disturbed agree on what constitutes disturbance. The patterns of characteristics vary with different children, and the assessment of those characteristics varies with

---

This chapter was written by **James L. Paul**, University of North Carolina at Chapel Hill.

different professionals who identify, diagnose and label these children. Different professionals have different approaches, philosophies, methods and languages for evaluating the child and drawing the conclusion that the child is emotionally disturbed.

The problem of emotional disturbance may be manifested in different ways in different settings. For example, a child's pattern of difficulty in the school may be such that the child is identified and labeled emotionally disturbed, but the same child may not be singled out as noticeably different in his home or neighborhood. The child may have more difficulty in his role as a student than as a son or brother or friend. The more seriously disturbed child is more likely to be noticeably different ("disturbed") in all of his roles in all of his environments.

Emotional disturbance in children is complex because of the many different ways it affects the life of the child, his family, his teachers, his school and his community. Whether the child is attacking the world around him or has psychologically left that world and created his own internal world, the child's interactions with others are difficult—not only for the child but for those around him. Emotional disturbance is acted out as a series of negative transactions and failures. Sorting out the roles of the different actors in each scene—the child himself, his teachers, parents, siblings, friends and neighbors—is difficult. The interactions change over time as the developmental needs and skills of the child and the expectations of others change. These changes alter the nature of the problems that must be addressed.

Our knowledge of the causes and treatment of serious emotional disturbance in children is very limited. While substantial gains have been made in our understanding of the problems of emotional disturbance in children during the past 15 years, there are still many things we do not understand about the various types of problems grouped under the label *emotional disturbance*.

As we look deeper into the problem of emotional disturbance the teacher should keep in mind the following:

1 The complexity is real, and no individual or group of individuals has all of the answers needed. The problems defy a single simplistic solution.
2 Teachers must understand the needs of emotionally disturbed children in a way that helps them provide an appropriate educational program in an appropriate setting.
3 Other professionals have points of view, knowledge and skills that can be helpful to the teacher.
4 The teacher needs to understand the perspectives of other professionals, value the contributions other professionals and parents can make, and be able to use their help.

Definition

Many definitions of emotional disturbance and behavior disorders in children have been proposed. No single definition, however, has been found to be adequate for the purposes of all of those who work with children identified as emotionally disturbed, or behavior disordered. (Hence the variety of terms used to describe this condition.) Psychiatric definitions, for example, which historically were applied to seriously disturbed children found in hospital and clinical settings, have been of limited value in defining emotional disturbance in educational settings. There are several reasons for this. First, children treated in special clinical settings are likely to represent a more restricted range of disturbances and to be more severely disturbed than most children needing special educational services in the public school. Second, the theoretical framework for psychiatric definitions is likely to be unfamiliar to teachers. Third, psychiatric definitions usually do not describe the disorder sufficiently in behavioral terms to suggest specific educational intervention approaches. Psychiatric approaches, however, as well as other approaches to defining, describing and explaining emotional disturbance, can be useful to teachers in planning educational programs if the teachers understand the theoretical perspective upon which the definition is based. Furthermore, the creative integration of several perspectives in defining emotional disturbance results in a richer professional foundation for understanding the complex social and emotional problems presented by these children and the educational consequences of those problems. Kauffman (1981) accurately observes that "the definition of behavior disorder or emotional disturbance is unavoidably a subjective matter" (p.14). He notes that those who disagree at a conceptual or theoretical level are not likely to agree upon a practical definition. The definition must serve the "purposes of the social agents who use them" (p. 15). Cullinan and Epstein (1979) point out that a definition can be useful in guiding the delivery of services through administrative channels, reflecting a particular theoretical position or describing a population for research purposes.

The various definitions of emotional disturbance in this text will be discussed in light of their educational relevance. Definitions are presented in the context of each perspective and the educational merits are examined. For an excellent discussion of definition see Wood and Lakin (1979).

The purpose of a definition of emotional disturbance in children in educational settings is to identify those children who have certain problems that interfere with their educational success. The definition should conversely assist decision makers in identifying children who are not emotionally disturbed. While no single definition of emotional disturbance has been found to be entirely adequate for identifying emotionally disturbed children for educational purposes in the public school, it is possible to describe criteria for a satisfactory definition.

1 The definition should relate to some theoretical formulation of the problem of emotional disturbance. This does not mean the definition has to relate exclusively to one theory; the definition can, in fact, have an eclectic orientation. The definition, however, should reflect a theoretical orientation and that orientation should be clear.
2 Assumptions regarding the settings in which the emotionally disturbed child is to be identified and educated should be specified.

3 A definition should apply to the child as a student (for school-age children), particularly the academic and social aspects of that role.
4 A definition of severe emotional disturbance should be interdisciplinary in nature.
5 A definition should exclude cultural difference as a criterion for disturbance; it should incorporate the concept of cultural pluralism, distinguishing cultural difference from psychopathology.
6 A definition should avoid indicting children, parents or social institutions as responsible for the disturbance. Broad generalizations regarding the etiology of emotional disturbance have not been well supported in the research literature. The problems of emotional disturbance are sufficiently complex that multiple correlates rather than single or specific causes are identified. Even in instances in which the etiology is known, that knowledge may be of little specific value to the teacher in developing an appropriate educational program for the child. It is important to recognize the interactive nature of the problems of emotional disturbance. The teacher needs to understand the variables that are involved in the child's difficulties in school and, as much as possible, the relationship between these variables.
7 The definition should specify the relationship between emotional disturbance and other disabilities, such as mental retardation and learning disabilities. In particular, the concept of severity must be incorporated in a definition. Algozzine, Schmid, and Conners (1978) differentiate two types of emotional distrubance in children. Type One is the milder form of emotional disturbance which may appear in school but not at home. Curriculum modifications may be sufficient in successfully educating these children. The more severe type of disturbance, Type Two, involves children who are disturbed and disturbing in different settings. Type Two disturbance is more pervasive and self-limiting in the lives of these children, and they are more likely to require a comprehensive clinical program. A definition should take the qualitative differences of these populations into account.
8 The definition must contain concepts that can be put into effect to facilitate measurement.
9 The definition should facilitate the process of identifying the child.

Part of the reason that there is not an agreed upon definition of emotional disturbance or behavior disorders is that there are so many theories of disturbance in use at the present time. Each theory has its own language, concepts, and definition. Wyne and O'Connor (1979), recognizing this difficulty, suggest three types of definition that illustrate the relationship between theoretical approach and definition of emotional disturbance:

1. Psychodynamic: Impairment of emotional growth during one or more of the states of ego development resulting in feelings of inadequacy, distrust of others, and hostility or withdrawal in reaction to anxiety.

2. Behavioral: Inadequate, inappropriate, or undesirable behaviors that are learned and that can be changed or eliminated by the use of applied behavior analysis.
3. Developmental/Ecological: All forms and degrees of behavioral deviance, irrespective of etiology, which result in behavioral-environmental maladaptation and personal-social alienation. (p. 316)

While no single definition satisfies all of the criteria and interests of different professionals working with emotionally disturbed children and takes into account the different theories applied to the understanding, treatment and education of emotionally disturbed children, the definition by Bowers (1969) has been most widely accepted by educators. This definition, which is included in the 1975 Amendments to the Equal Educational Opportunity Act and P.L. 94-142, is accepted by the U.S. Department of Education and many state departments of education. It defines a serious emotional handicap in children as behavior that is developmentally inappropriate or inadequate in educational settings as indicated by one or more of the following characteristics:

A. An inability to learn which cannot be explained by intellectual, sensory or health factors;
B. An inability to build or maintain satisfactory interpersonal relationships with peers or teachers;
C. Inappropriate types of behavior or feelings under normal circumstances;
D. A general or pervasive mood of unhappiness or depression;
E. A tendency to develop physical symptoms or fears associated with personal or school problems. (*Federal Register*, 1977, p. 42478)

The behavior must be of sufficient duration, frequency and intensity to call attention to the need for intervention on the child's behalf to insure her* educational success. The term does not include children who are socially maladjusted, unless it is determined that they are seriously emotionally handicapped. (P.L. 94-142 does include schizophrenia and autism in the definition.)

The concepts of duration, rate and intensity are particularly important. All children at some time engage in behaviors that are inappropriate or unexpected for their chronological age, since normative behavior is a statistical concept and some variance or deviation is expected and acceptable. Also, all children at some time act in ways that are inappropriate and unacceptable in specific social settings like the classroom. Emotionally disturbed children, however, violate age-appropriate and setting-specific norms at a rate that is significantly greater than the deviations of normal children, over a longer period of time and with greater intensity.

Historically, the professional literature has tended to associate the terms *emotional disturbance* and *social maladjustment* (Rhodes & Paul, 1978). It is not necessarily the case that emotionally disturbed children are socially malad-

---

*In this text, both "he" and "she" are used to refer to the emotionally disturbed child. While wholeheartedly supporting this democratic pronoun policy, the authors note that, by far, most of the children identified as emotionally disturbed are boys.

justed, or that socially maladjusted children are emotionally disturbed. Delinquent behavior and predelinquent behavior, for example, are considered to be forms of social maladjustment. Such behavior, however, may be primarily the result of the social or economic circumstances of the child's life rather than of a psychological disorder.

Grosenick and Huntze (1980), who collected information in a national needs analysis of behavior disorders, recommend deleting the exclusion of social maladjustment from the definition of emotional disturbance. They conclude that "there is no clearcut evidence or thought in the field which delineates the distinctions" between emotional disturbance and social maladjustment (p. 23). There are differences of opinion among professionals about this issue (Algozzine, 1980).

Grosenick and Huntze (1980) suggest substituting the term *behavior disorder* for *emotional disturbance*. They argue that the term *behavior disorder* could include the concept of social maladjustment and avoid some of the stigmatizing impact of the labeling and conceptual difficulties associated with the definitions of emotional disturbance. They, and others (Epstein, M. H., Cullinan, D. & Sabatino, D.A., 1977), point out, however, that most states label these children as emotionally disturbed and apply a wide range of definitions. Wood and Lakin (1979) note the variability of definitions used in research studies which has contributed to the confusion about the nature of behavior disorders and emotional disturbance.

In this text we will be concerned primarily, although not exclusively, with the nature and educational needs of emotionally disturbed and behavior disordered children in the elementary school. The reader should, however, find the chapters on social and ecological theory useful in examining some problems associated with social maladjustment.

Classification

Just as there are several theories and definitions of emotional disturbance and behavior disorders, there are also several systems for classifying behavior. The assumptions and values of a theoretical perspective are reflected in the codification of behavior. That is, each perspective has its own set of labels or vocabulary, concepts and definitions. The labels are applied to different behaviors or groups of behavior manifested by different children. Some perspectives incorporate the concept of etiology in the classification scheme while others recognize only manifest behavior. Each classification system has its own merits relative to its uses. That is, different professionals use perspectives and classification schemes that are appropriate to their particular professional responsibilities. Many common classification systems, such as DSM III and GAP (see Chapter 4) were developed for use in clinical settings. Quay (1972, 1975) and others have tried to develop more educationally relevant classifications. However, just as there is not a single definition or theoretical perspective that is entirely adequate for teachers, there has not been complete agreement on a single classification system to be used by teachers.

There are also many generic problems in labeling children that cut across different classification systems (Mercer, 1973). These are problems in the organization and administration of special services, especially the placement of children (see Chapters 2 and 3). Hobbs (1979) suggests that the difficulties involved in classifying children or behavior are so great that only interventions should be classified. This is a serious and promising proposal but not yet a reality. It is important to understand the uses and limitations of different systems. Changing or even doing away with labels and categories does not reduce the need for a clear diagnostic understanding of the child. Morse (1967) long ago cautioned against throwing out the diagnosis with the label. Classification will be discussed in Section 2 in the individual chapters on theory and in more detail in Chapter 4 in the context of screening, identification and diagnosis.

At the present time it is important for teachers to understand that there are different systems for classifying children. Each has its own utility, but a single system has not been accepted by all special educators.

Prevalence

Morse (1975) reviews survey reports and finds that from 0.1% to 30% of the school-age population have been considered behavior disordered. This wide variation in prevalence estimates is largely the result of differences in definition and criteria for behavior disorders. Wood and Zabel (1978) suggest that much of the variability in prevalence estimates is also due to differences in the ways in which the data are collected.

The U.S. Office of Education uses a 2% estimate of prevalence for behavior disorders. Kelly, Bullock, and Dykes (1977) report that teachers identified about 20% of their students as suffering from some kind of emotional disturbance. Morse & Coopchik (1979) point out that there is much evidence indicating that emotionally disturbed children are among the least adequately served in schools. The behavior of many of these children is not severe enough to fit state definitions. These children, as Kauffman (1980, 1981) points out, are largely unidentified and unserved. He notes that "statistics show that about 0.5%of school-age children are receiving special educational services as seriously emotionally disturbed, only about 1/4 of a very conservative estimate of prevalence" (1981, p. 58).

Morse and Coopchick (1979) suggest that at least 3% of the total student population are very seriously disturbed and need intensive help. Of the 2% to 3% of the school-age population considered to be seriously emotionally disturbed, 6% have a primary diagnosis of mental retardation and 7% have physical disabilities. They suggest that the remaining 87% of the 2% to 3% of the student population considered seriously emotionally disturbed are the "true socio-emotionally disturbed" (p. 60).

Morse and Coopchick (1979) classify the socio-emotionally disturbed into four categories: (a) reactive, (b), neurotic, (3) inadequate socialization and (d) psychotic.

Approximately 26% of the emotionally disturbed population are considered reactive, that is reacting to a crisis or chronically stressful situation. Circumstances external to the school are usually involved in precipitating the disturbance in these children. Examples of these circumstances are family conflict, divorce and moving. Another 26% of the seriously disturbed population are considered to be neurotic. These children have internalized the values of the culture, but there is a conflict between their impulses and their controls. These children know how to behave, but they lack the psychological skill and ability to behave appropriately. Often the conflict for these children stems from unconscious factors.

Another 27% of the seriously emotionally disturbed children are inadequately socialized. These are children who have character disorders, children who have not internalized the values of the culture. These children typically do not experience guilt. They engage in delinquent, impulsive and aggressive acts. Psychotics, the most seriously impaired group, make up 8% of the emotionally disturbed population. These children have serious communication disabilities, distort or fail to comprehend reality, and are unable to learn in the same way other children learn. There is considerable disagreement among professionals working with this specific group of children on etiology, treatment and prognosis. Indicative of the disagreement on etiology is the fact that many professionals now classify autism as a developmental disability rather than an emotional disorder (Schopler & Reichler, 1976). Morse and Coopchik (1979) include infantile autism and schizophrenia in the psychotic group.

Emotional Disturbance as an Educational Handicap

In providing an appropriate education for an emotionally disturbed child the teacher is concerned with the child's mental health and psychological well-being, the child's achievement and general success as a student, and the welfare of the classroom, including the integrity of the environment and the maintenance of normative procedures and activities in the environment. Since emotional disturbance has generally been viewed as a psychological disorder or a form of social deviance, an understanding of both psychological and social principles will help teachers meet the educational needs of emotionally disturbed children.

Psychodynamic, psychoneurological and behavioral theories (see Chapters 5–7) have made important contributions to the broad area of special education for emotionally disturbed and behavior-disordered children. During the past 15 years, however, special educators have become increasingly aware of the value of social theories in understanding the nature of emotional disturbance. Ecological, social and cultural theories (see Chapters 8–10) have viewed emotional disturbance more as a form of social deviance or a product of a mismatch between a person and the environment. Social theories have not been as prominent as psychological theories, in part because the mental health system, historically the primary service delivery system for emotionally disturbed children, conceptualized emotional disturbance as a psychological problem. Educators have a task that is different from the task of clinicians in mental health treatment settings. Therefore, as educators have assumed responsibility for teaching emotionally disturbed children, it has been necessary to expand the framework within which emotional disturbance is understood. Social and ecological theories have contributed to the growing conceptual and knowledge base of the special education of emotionally disturbed children. That these interactional views of disturbance have contributed to an educationally relevant understanding of disturbance is indicated by the growing professional and research literature in this area during the past 10 years.

Neither social nor psychological theories alone can guide educational programming for emotionally disturbed children. The teacher is specifically and uniquely concerned about emotional disturbance as an educational handicap. The psychological and social sides of the problem are important in helping the teacher understand the child and plan an appropriate educational program. The teacher, however, must view emotional disturbance in the context of the classroom in which specific problems occur and he must understand it in ways that lead to interventions appropriate to the classroom.

A classroom is a social setting in which certain prescribed activities occur. The teacher is in charge of activites in the classroom, and students are expected to participate in prescribed ways and achieve at certain levels. The expectations for students in a classroom are presumed to be appropriate to the age and developmental status of students in that classroom. While all of the students in the classroom may be approximately the same chronological age, however, they may not all be able to achieve at equal rates or to respond with equal proficiency to the demands made on them as students.

Many children have difficulty succeeding as students because of emotional problems. The relationship between the psychological status of a child and her performance of the social roles of a student, including achieving academically, is very complex. A few brief examples will illustrate the problem of emotional disturbance as an educational handicap.

In order for a child to be a successful student, she must be able to participate as a member of a group, her class. For some children successful group participation is almost impossible because of the high level of anxiety they experience as group members. Speaking in the group, taking one's turn, reading out loud, asking or responding to a question, or making a presentation to the class becomes a nightmare for some children. A child afraid of groups, or of speaking to a group, may try to disrupt the class in order to relieve his anxiety and ultimately get put somewhere else. If the child is asked to leave the room, the anxiety is reduced and the disruptive behavior is effectively rewarded. The next time the child is asked to verbally perform for the class, the teacher might well expect this disruptive behavior to occur again. In asking the child to leave the classroom, the teacher may not have punished the behavior or in any way reduced the likelihood that the behavior will occur again. Quite the contrary, he may have rewarded the behavior and increased the likelihood that, under similar circumstances in the future, the behavior will reoccur.

Students are constantly being evaluated. Test taking is a fundamental skill the child must develop if she is to succeed as a student. Being evaluated, however, has psychological implications for the child. If a child feels reasonably good about herself, is relatively secure and is fairly successful as a student, a test of her comprehension and retention of certain material presented in class may well be reliable. If, on the other hand, the child is extremely fearful, has very low self-esteem and is failing most of the time as a student, taking a test may well serve to increase her fear, elevate her anxiety and cause her to be angry and resentful. A child who experiences evaluation in this way is not going to apply her normal intellectual resources for analyzing, recalling and reporting appropriate responses to questions.

Being a good student requires the ability to attend. Attending has psychological and motor implications. For example, in order to attend to the teacher talking to the class, the child must be able to sit quietly at her seat. This means that motor impulses to fidget or to pester a neighbor must be inhibited. In order to effectively listen to and understand the teacher, the child must also be able to focus her attention on what he is saying. This means that the child must inhibit other psychological activities such as daydreaming or active fantasies.

The seriously emotionally disturbed child may not be able to control her attending behavior. Hallucinations, for example, of which the teacher may or may not be aware, may make the child's successful participation in a group learning experience almost impossible. Some children, who may or may not be emotionally disturbed, experience intrusive interference when trying to attend because of seizures. In the case of petit mal seizures, the teacher may or may not be aware of this cerebral activity that effectively negates all of his teaching during the seizure episode. A child who asks a question the teacher feels he has already clearly answered 10 minutes earlier in a presentation to the class was most likely not paying attention. The teacher's question, "Weren't you paying attention to what I just said?" or "Didn't you understand what I just said?" is understandable but not very helpful. The child may not have been attending because of a psychological process over which she had no control, such as hallucination or distractibility.

It is also possible, of course, that the question was not prompted by a lack of information or a desire to know the answer, but rather from a need to gain the teacher's individual attention. Attention-getting behavior may also be symptomatic of emotional disturbance. But to say that behavior has occurred simply to get attention is to explain nothing. Knowing why the child wanted individual attention and why she sought it in an inappropriate way, too often, or at an inappropriate time may help the teacher find a way to help the child meet this need in more appropriate ways.

The ability to attend is learned; it is acquired through practice over time. Norms related to attending change over time. As the child grows older, her attention span increases, her ability to inhibit inappropriate psychological or motor responses improves, and she can maintain an appropriate focus on relevant visual or auditory stimuli. The child's normative development in this area, however, relies on an intact central nervous system and emotional and intellectual resources in a relatively normal range.

Another requirement for the child's success in the student role is that she exhibit certain attitudes toward authority. The teacher is an authority figure and is in charge of the classroom. A child must be able to listen to, or in some instances read, understand and obey the teacher's instructions. The teacher provides a structure for the classroom. It is a complex social, psychological and instructional structure. The teacher makes decisions, for example, about the physical space, the structure of the curriculum, the materials, the schedule and activities for the day, rules governing appropriate behavior and consequences for inappropriate behavior. The teacher determines the emotional climate and the nature and quality of social activity in the classroom. This arrangement generally works because it is understood by students and by significant others outside the classroom that the teacher has authority and is in charge in the classroom.

This arrangement works for most but not all children. Some children have serious problems with authority. Some children, for example, have chronically resisted the authority structure of their own homes by defying their parents. Many of these children have a long-standing pattern of defiant and, consequently, disruptive behavior. These children are particularly upsetting to teachers because they challenge the teacher's role and threaten the order and composure of the classroom. Some of these children exhibit great and genuine anger while others seem to display little honest affect; in the latter case the child may be extraordinarily manipulative and able to exhibit the affect needed for the moment. These children are often able to identify weaknesses in the teacher and exploit them.

Children who over time defy the authority structure of the classroom, whether from neurotic needs, unreasonable emotional demands, anger or a defect of character, may be high risk for delinquency later in life. Robbins (1966), in a 30-year follow-up study, finds that the sociopathic child grows up into an unproductive and asocial adult. Children who refuse or fail to learn to live within the authority structure of the classroom may have difficulty with the authority structure of society. These are the children who are serious discipline problems in school and develop a reputation that follows them through school. These children reinforce and are reinforced by their reputation. Within this group, the children who are defiant and manipulative and seem to have little sense of right and wrong or guilt have, as a group, been least responsive to psychological treatment and educational remediation.

Impulse control is another important requirement or characteristic of a successful student. The child who is constantly out of her seat, who is always picking on her neighbor, who repeatedly gets into fights, who has temper tantrums or who exhibits some other disruptive behavior pattern probably has low impulse control. That is, she acts spontaneously, without analyzing the appropriateness of the response, alternative responses or the consequences of her response. Such children have been referred to as *stimulus bound* since they behave predictably in the presence of certain stimuli. They are very vulnerable in their peer group to being set up, teased and exploited as the group scapegoat or clown. A child who cannot inhibit impulses in the presence of certain stimuli is easily manipulated. Stimulus-bound behavior, however, is often the most easily extinguished. The teacher who understands how the child is behaving, and the prompts for and consequences of her behavior, will be able to systematically extinguish that behavior.

The Emotionally Disturbed Child in the Classroom

Emotionally disturbed children come to the attention of teachers either through the teacher's own observations in the classroom (this is usually the

In the past, teachers and parents were more concerned about disruptive behavior than other problem behaviors.

case) or when parents make the teacher aware of some special difficulty the child is having. In the past, a child was more likely to be identified as emotionally disturbed if she was creating a disturbance in the classroom. Defiance, inability to get along with other children, insensitivity to the needs of other children, lack of respect for classroom rules, hyperactivity, destruction of property and other social and behavioral offenses were more likely to be noted by the teacher and ultimately result in the child being labeled *emotionally disturbed*. Now, however, as a result of improved teacher education, increased public awareness of and sensitivity to the needs of handicapped persons and the implementation of P.L. 94-142, teachers are much more likely to be clinically astute and sensitive to the wide range of emotional needs of children. For example, the teacher is more likely to be aware of the special needs of an excessively shy and fearful child, who may not in any way disrupt the normal operation of the classroom or make the teacher uncomfortable. Teachers are now likely to be concerned about the child who has a self-defeating relationship with her peers and therefore becomes the clown or scapegoat in the group. In general, teachers are now more likely to understand the sociology of their classroom and the psychology of their instructional strategies. They are more likely to understand the way the classroom setting influences their own behavior, the curriculum, and the growth and development of children.

The heightened awareness of teachers to the wide range of issues involved in emotional disturbance in children is evident in teachers' remarks about their students. In the teacher's lounge, in teacher conferences, in parent-teacher conferences, in the cafeteria and outside the classroom, one hears comments like the following:

> I don't seem to be getting anywhere with Billy. I have tried everything I know but he seems terrified every time I go near him, and when I talk with him I have a feeling he doesn't hear or understand a thing I am saying.

> I spend most of my time controlling Jerry. He won't keep his hands to himself; I can't get him to stay in his seat; he is interrupting my lessons; and quiet work at his seat is simply out of the question.

> Mark is a real problem. He does all right in the classroom, but anytime we have an unstructured activity he picks a fight with the other kids. He has created trouble on the playground and in the lunchroom almost every day for the last two weeks.

> I'm really concerned about Mary; she just sits and stares out the window. She doesn't give me any problems in class, she does what I ask her to, and she is doing her work at a passing level, but she is performing far below her ability.

> Michael is a charmer and very smart, but he seems to enjoy misrepresenting the truth. He worries me; he's so manipulative and convincing. He doesn't seem to care about others at all.

Obviously, a single occurrence of disturbed behavior does not an emotionally disturbed child make. The behavioral themes running through these teacher comments are, of course, very familiar in the school. They indicate that something is going on with the child that is concerning or perhaps even upsetting the teacher.

The teacher who makes these kinds of comments usually is concerned about two things. First, he is thinking about what is typical or normal for children in the classroom. The child who is of concern to the teacher is in some important way different from her classmates, her developmental peers. Second, the teacher is thinking of the child herself. It may be that a certain behavior is new for this child; or it may be the duration and pattern of the child's behavior that has changed. Of course, it is not unusual for a child to have problems in school from time to time. One or two bad days does not an emotionally disturbed child make either. However, if unusual negative and unacceptable behavior continues, the persistence and consistency of the behavior will gain the teacher's attention. The teacher, then, is concerned about behavior that is exceptional for the individual child who manifests the behavior or that is exceptional in the social context of the classroom in which the behavior occurs.

Obviously, not all children identified by teachers as having or causing some kind of problem in the classroom become identified as emotionally disturbed. In some instances, the problem is acute and transient. While alarming at the time it occurs, the difficulty subsides in a reasonable period of time. Again, "reasonable" is defined by the teacher who has two norms in mind—the child and the class. The difficulty may pass without teacher intervention. An example of a transient disturbance that often passes without special teacher intervention is the otherwise well-adjusted child who becomes belligerent or very withdrawn because of anxiety over a serious conflict between his parents. The death of a family member is another source of anxiety or depression that may trigger a transient behavior problem in the classroom. When the disturbance in the family has subsided, or the child has found ways to psychologically cope with her feelings, the child's normal and acceptable behavior as a student returns. In the normal course of things, teachers provide support and encouragement for children through these difficult periods, and the trauma passes without receiving formal, institutional attention.

In other instances, an acute behavior problem is brief in duration because of the skillful intervention of a teacher. For example, say a child is creating a group disturbance at approximately 9:30 every morning. The regularity of the event will prompt the skillful teacher to question what is happening in the curriculum and classroom activities at that time each day. If the class started oral reading two weeks ago and about that time Billy started creating difficulties in the class, the teacher would begin to investigate possible difficulties in Billy's oral reading ability, or his anxiety about reading out loud in class. The teacher obviously has some leads to investigate

Nondisruptive behavior, often associated with acute or persistent depression, may also indicate emotional disturbance.

and, depending on his findings, he may use instructional or other intervention techniques to help Billy reduce his anxiety and succeed. The classroom disruption thus subsides, and a potentially chronic behavior problem is prevented.

The special educational needs of emotionally disturbed children come to the attention of teachers primarily when some unacceptable behavior is demonstrated. As noted earlier, the behavior may be unacceptable because it violates classroom norms or the norm for that particular child. Unacceptable behavior is not necessarily bad or offensive behavior. Offensive behavior usually refers to behavior that interferes with the normal routine activities of the classroom. Some behavior, however, such as excessive daydreaming or an unusual amount of sadness, may not interfere with the normal classroom activities but may arouse the teacher's concern for the child's psychological welfare which, of course, ultimately will affect the child's educational achievement.

There are two aspects of behavior that determine its acceptability in the classroom. One aspect is the quantity or amount of a particular behavior. The amount of a certain kind of behavior that is acceptable depends on the setting in which the behavior occurs, the teacher and the nature of the activity in progress. For example, the amount of talking that is acceptable is greater in a reading group where the meaning of a short story is being discussed than it is when the teacher is making a presentation of a basic arithmetic fact to the entire class.

Quality is another important aspect of behavior. That is, the timing and amount of a behavior may be appropriate, but the intensity and quality may be unacceptable. For example, a teacher may be leading a lesson on government and ask Michael to name the present governor of the state. Instead of giving the teacher the answer or telling her he does not know the answer, Michael says, "Leave me alone." Or take the example of Phyllis. As the students are preparing to go outside on a cold day, the teacher reminds Phyllis to button up her coat. Phyllis screams at the teacher, "Go to hell." Or consider Larry, who begins to cry when the teacher asks the class to clear all of the books off their desks, get out clean sheets of paper and well-sharpened pencils to prepare for a test.

Unlike the student who exhibits excessive or otherwise inappropriate behavior, such as frequently being out of her seat, fidgeting, or picking at her neighbor when the teacher is trying to get the class to do quiet seat work, or interrupting the teacher or other students who are talking in a class discussion, the child whose behavior is qualitatively unacceptable violates the norms of a setting. These include, but are not limited to, norms of authority, rules for conduct, and the intensity in teacher-student relationships that is tolerated. The qualitatively variant behaviors also are provocative and suggest to the teacher that something is wrong with the child.

The specific types of behavior described here either interfere with the normal operation of the classroom, or with the child's success as a student achieving in the classroom, or both. The child's behavioral, attitudinal or affective deviation may offend social or psychological norms, or standards. The identification and diagnosis of a child as emotionally disturbed, however, depends upon the nature, intensity and duration of the offense. A child is often considered to be emotionally disturbed when, in the absence of a primary diagnosis of mental retardation, neurological, sensory or other physical impairment, she cannot derive reasonable benefit from the normal curriculum in the regular classroom without making excessive demands on the teacher's time and energy as compared with other students. The problem of emotional disturbance in the classroom is characterized by its intractability, its resistance to modification by normal teacher intervention, and its persistence over time in the presence of reasonable variations in curriculum, classroom structure and routine.

Different Roles—Different Views

Just as different theoretical orientations give rise to different views of behavior and strategies for intervention, the type of involvement—personal, educational, or professional—one has with an emotionally disturbed child affects one's perception of the issues. Parents, teachers and clinicians each may have a different perspective. The teacher's concerns are specific to the task of educating the child, usually in the context of a group of children and in the administrative, legal and social context of a school. Parents and clinicians, however, often have different concerns, interests and responsibilities with respect to the child. The teacher is in a unique position because he can draw upon the technical perspective of clinical specialists and the personal perspective provided by parents.

Often different pictures or views of the child exist. They may all be correct but not all equally useful to the teacher. The teacher needs to recognize and accept these differences and can often be very helpful in harmonizing different interests. The views of clinicians and parents should be recognized, understood, respected and incorporated when possible in planning and programming for emotionally disturbed children. The orchestration of effective interventions for the child is best accomplished when there is mutual respect among teachers, parents and special clinical professionals working with or on behalf of the child.

Parents

The concerns of parents are, of course, extremely variable, as are the concerns of teachers and clinicians. Generalizations are therefore somewhat risky and can be misleading. Generally, however, the personal perspective of a parent of an emotionally disturbed child usually involves very strong feelings about the child and the problem. While the nature of these feelings and the central issues vary as much as the children (and parents) themselves vary, the feelings of the parents are likely to involve some combination of the following issues.

First of all, the parent often takes the role of an advocate who represents what he understands to be the best interests of the child. Depending on the nature of the child's problem, the parent's advocacy may well involve him with a large number of human services. If the parent is acting as an advocate, he must understand enough about the problem and about the human services system to get the child to the appropriate place for assistance. Each agency has a professional staff, and the staff has a particular view of emotional disturbance which the parent must confront. Sometimes there are waiting lists; sometimes the services are very expensive; sometimes parents are referred to an agency only to learn when they arrive that this agency does not have the appropriate service for their child and they are then referred to another service. Sometimes the parent never arrives at the right place at the right time, even though they have been acting on the advice of professionals in these agencies. Sometimes, after considerable expense, parents learn that no one is quite sure what to do with their child.

Acting as advocate for one's own child can be extremely frustrating. Very often the parent's feelings about the child, the problem and himself as a parent are compounded by feelings of resentment and anger acquired during the process of obtaining services for the child. Parents are sometimes referred to agencies that are unable to respond to their needs. They may pay for diagnostic assistance that does not lead to effective intervention; their child may acquire technical labels that do not seem to help the child acquire appropriate services. Parents are often expected to understand different professionals who do not seem to understand each other. These experiences can be devastating to parents who are saddened, bewildered and frightened by a child they cannot understand or control. These feelings are sometimes expressed in the form of anger which may appear to be an overreaction or an inappropriate response in a particular situation. Angry, frustrated, hurt, vulnerable parents sometimes become their own worst enemies. They sometimes lose hope and they quit believing in their ability to cope. They lack the energy to try again; their attitude, implied if not stated, becomes, "What's the difference, nobody knows what to do and no one really cares." Individuals in the service delivery system have a responsibility to communicate concern and to form an effective helping alliance with the parents. An effective service delivery would help many parents avoid this negative attitudinal trap.

Some service delivery systems, of course, are effectively integrated and coordinated with other human services. Some interdisciplinary teams function effectively. Some agencies have case management and tracking systems that are reasonably successful in preventing parents from getting lost in a bureaucratic maze of helping services. The system, however, continues to be very imperfect. When parents experience the organizational and philosophical defects of the human service delivery system, that experience exacerbates their sense of confusion and helplessness about their child's needs and problems.

Another reason why parents have strong feelings about their emotionally disturbed children is that they may see themselves in some way implicated in the child's disturbance, or in some instances as having caused the disturbance. One important view of disturbance is that it arises early in life out of and as a result of faulty nurturance. Autism, for example, until rather recently was considered to be caused by faulty mothering (Paluszny, 1979).

The view of the role of parents in the emotional difficulties of the child has changed in the past 20 years. For one thing, alternative conceptions of the problem of emotional disturbance have been accepted. Behavioral, social, ecological and psychoneurological conceptions have gained considerably more acceptance in the past 10 years; they are now seen as alternative views that contribute to our understanding of the complexity of the issues involved in emotionally disturbed children. In the past 20 years, emphasis has shifted from the psychodynamic view as the single or predominent view of emotional disturbance to the view that human behavior is extraordinarily complex and our knowledge, while increasing, remains very limited.

Accompanying and closely related to the broadening of professional and lay understanding of emotional disturbance has been the assumption of responsibility for the treatment and education of these children by a much wider professional group. Traditionally, emotionally disturbed children were considered to be primarily the responsibility of professionals in mental health. The problems of these children were understood, diagnosed and treated almost exclusively by mental health professionals, specifically psychiatrists, psychologists and social workers. During the past 20 years, however, public schools have assumed responsibility for the education of these children. This shift has meant that teachers have had to become knowledgeable about the problems of emotionally disturbed children and approaches to teaching them. Indeed, the service network available to these children has been expanded beyond public schools to include a wide variety of public and private agencies and child care workers.

Another important factor affecting the perceived and actual role of parents is the change in the focus of research on the relationship between the emotionally disturbed child and the parent. In the past five years, considerable research has addressed the hypothesis that it is the child's behavior affecting the parent rather than the parent's behavior affecting the child that accounts for the troubled parent-child interaction (Paul & Bell, 1981). There is considerable evidence accumulating that the difficulty is interactive and that emotionally disturbed and developmentally disabled children very early in life have a profound impact on their parents (Bell, 1977).

While our understanding of emotional disturbance in children and the professional services available to these children has increased considerably, the view that parents are in some way to blame for their child's difficulty is still not uncommon among parents of emotionally disturbed children. These parents often fear that they have failed as parents.

Low parent self-esteem and feelings of self-blame and guilt may be associated with feelings of resentment and anger toward the child. The child "has refused to respond," "has no gratitude" or "has no sympathy for our feelings at all." Guilt feelings are usually more socially acceptable to the parents than feelings of anger and resentment. Consequently, parents may or may not be aware of the full range of their feelings about their child. The parents may be worn out from interacting so intensely with their child and having failed in so many encounters with the child, or even from working with others to try to get help for the child. These parents are often depressed, and one wonders where they get energy for advocacy.

It is true that not all parents do what is best for their child. It is true that adults function on some continuum of mental health and that not all adults function equally well as parents. It is true that some parents contribute to serious problems for their children. It is not true, however, that emotional disturbance in children is a childhood disorder caused by parents.

In understanding the perspective of parents, it is important to appreciate the conscious intent of parents. In the author's experience, parents of these children, like parents of all children, are attempting to do the very best they can as parents, given the resources which they have. Sometimes the intellectual and emotional, as well as economic, resources of parents may be limited. They may not have, in a given instance, the resources necessary to cope with a particular child or a particular situation, but the intent is primarily to do the best they can for their child given their understanding of the child's needs and the resources which are available.

Teachers

The perspective of teachers is quite different. The teacher is concerned with the child as a student in his class. If there is a behavioral issue, the question is, how can the behavior be controlled so that the educational business of the classroom can proceed? The teacher *does* have a personal concern for the child, but he also has responsibility for certain tasks and these tasks affect his perspective and the nature of his interactions with the child.

The teacher is interested in more than simply controlling behavior; he is interested in teaching the child. If the child is not motivated to learn, how can he motivate her? If the child is failing in reading, how can he teach her to read? If the child is in the sixth grade and reading at a second grade level, where can he find materials for the child to read that would be appropriate to her level of interest? If the child is excessively shy or withdrawn, how can he help the child become comfortable participating? If the child has "a problem," how can he be sure that he will not contribute to the child's problem or make it worse?

A child who has low impulse control, who seems to be angry at the world, who seems to have no skills or interest in developing skills as a student, or who shows some other behavior disorder or evidence of emotional disturbance, is a challenge. Some of these behaviors are indeed very threatening to teachers. Behavior that seriously interferes with the teacher's control of his class is particularly threatening. Also, a teacher does not like to find himself unable to teach a child. A teacher is a professional whose professional self-image is directly affected by his ability to teach.

The teacher is concerned about the disturbed child in relation to the rest of the children for whom he has educational responsibility. Sometimes the teacher has difficulty making decisions about dividing his time and attention. Some emotionally disturbed children seem to have an almost limitless need for attention. A teacher, who may well understand some things he could do to assist the child beyond what he is doing, may feel resentful that one child is occupying more of his time than he feels can be justified in a classroom with 26 other children.

The teacher, then, sees the emotionally disturbed child as a student. He is concerned with that student's individual welfare, but he is also concerned with the collective welfare of his class. He is likely to approach the problem from the perspective of understanding and controlling the child's behavior in the classroom at a level where instruction is possible. Beyond this he is likely to focus on academic needs and curriculum decisions that will facilitate the child's academic achievement. In the following section the teacher's view will be further described in relation to the views of clinicians.

Clinicians

The mental health professionals involved directly in the psychological or psychiatric treatment of emotionally disturbed children are primarily psychiatrists, psychologists and social workers. While the teacher is concerned about consequences of a child's emotional conflict and wants to help the child achieve, the clinician is more likely to be concerned about the source of the child's emotional conflict, the nature and basis for the child's motivation, or lack of it. Because of his theoretical orientation and professional task, the clinician, therefore, is more likely to engage the child in a process to "work through" or resolve these difficulties. (The process will, of course, vary with the particular theoretical orientation of the teacher or of the clinician. It should be noted that there are different perspectives among clinicians as a group, just as there are among teachers and parents, which are just as important as the differences between these groups.) The clinician will have a very specific theoretical framework in which to analyze and understand the child's behavior.

The clinician is concerned with the specific nature of the emotional disturbance, its causes and treatment. The clinician is concerned with the psychopathology of the child and with effective treatment regimens designed to reduce or otherwise alter the behavior of the child.

The perspectives of clinicians and teachers differ in several important ways. One difference is that the teacher usually has a normative orientation to child growth, development and behavior. Most of the children with whom the regular classroom teacher works function within normal social, psychological and academic limits. The clinician, on the other hand, has more direct experience working with problems of behavioral and psychological deviance. Most of the clinician's professional time is spent with children who are characterized by some negative deviation from mentally healthy norms for adjustment and functioning. The sensitivities of the clinician and the teacher, therefore, are likely to be quite different, the teacher being more subject to surprise and "being offended." The teacher has a normative frame of reference while the clinician is more accustomed to dealing with deviant behavior.

The teacher's primary task is cultural transmission, helping the child learn and use information and develop skills considered important in this culture. The teacher, therefore, is primarily involved in the constructive intellectual and behavioral development of the child. The clinician, on the other hand, has professional responsibility for working with problems that exist, repairing emotional damage, healing psychological hurts, and correcting defective thought processes and conclusions about the self or the world. The clinician, therefore, has treatment goals whereas the teacher has teaching and educational goals.

Teachers work with students; clinicians work with patients. If all goes well, patients improve and get well; students learn, achieve and are promoted. The generic label for the role a child occupies is different in each case, and the child is treated differently. The expectations of the child and of the professional—teacher or therapist—are different. The clinician's standard is the child. Progress is measured in terms of the child's own level of functioning and the nature of the particular problem involved. The teacher's standard is the class and the universe of children of similar age. Children are expected to perform at certain grade levels, depending on their age.

The settings in which clinicians and teachers work are different. Clinicians work exclusively in a one-to-one or small-group situation. Teachers usually work with large groups. Even when they work on a one-to-one basis with a child, it is typically in the context of the larger group or class. Clinicians work with children on the basis of appointments. Teachers have responsibility for children for most of the day, five days a week. The behavior setting in which the teacher works is the classroom. The behavior setting in which the clinician works is more likely to be an office, a room in the clinic, or a room in the hospital.

When comparing the teacher's task and the clinician's task, it should be remembered that children who go or are taken to a clinician usually go voluntarily. Even if the parent takes the child against the child's will, the fact that the child goes to the clinician shows a recognition that a problem exists. A child goes to school, however, because she is required by law to attend. While the child may have other appropriate motives to attend school, the fact remains she cannot quit. There is certainly nothing built into the arrangement of schooling or the fact that the child attends school that encourages the child to recognize the existence of a problem and work constructively on it, apart from the general motive of avoiding failure, rejection and expulsion. The negative experience of failure and rejection and the positive experience of succeeding are sufficient to encourage most children to work to achieve academically. This is not necessarily the case for emotionally disturbed children. For some of these children the avoidance of failure does not appear to be motivating. For some disturbed children failure and rejection are so consistent with their low self-esteem and their concept of themselves as unloving, unworthy and incompetent that success may be a more dissonant experience than failure.

On the other hand, some disturbed children have suffered such serious ego injury that they cannot risk trying to succeed at anything. They fear failure and defend themselves against the pain of further rejection by not trying. To not try is to exert one's own will and to decide to not succeed. The apparent lack of motivation in some of these children is in reality a defensive strategy to avoid the risk of failure. The teacher is likely to understand this as a motivational problem. He can deal with it successfully if he can develop a trusting relationship in which the child is willing to take risks and in which the teacher can provide opportunities for the child to succeed. The teacher usually must offer small increments of challenge, minimize risks to the child, provide support and assurance, and praise approximations. This process of helping the child develop a concept of herself as an able student takes time and patience and can be a source of frustration to the teacher who must accept small gains made by the child. Sometimes the child seems to lose ground and the teacher cannot understand the reason for the apparent regression. The teacher has to persist and assume that the dynamic involved in the child's failure will change as the behavior changes.

The clinician, by contrast, is more likely to analyze the motivational problems, discover the dynamic involved and work directly on this in therapy. While the strategies vary considerably, the aim is generally the same.

Teachers and clinicians have different orientations to behavior. The teacher is likely to be primarily interested in manifest behavior and the "fit" of that behavior with expectations for social and academic performance in the classroom. Behavior may be viewed as intentional, primarily an act of the child's will which is expressed in a context of innate intellectual capacity on the one hand and teacher expectations and task requirements on the other hand. Behavior that does not fit the normative requirements and expectations in the classroom may be viewed by the teacher from a moral perspective, as good or bad, since it is a function of a child's will; or it may be viewed from the perspective of competence, as success or failure, since the child's capacity is involved. The teacher is more concerned with the consequences of behavior than with the psychological nature, origin and quality of the behavior.

The clinician, on the other hand, is more interested in how and why the behavior occurs as it does. The clinician is likely to be working with the reports of the behavior rather than with the behavior itself. The teacher deals directly with the behavior in the classroom. The clinician is frequently dealing with abstractions, memories of what occurred, reports of what occurred and interpretations of patterns of behavior. The clinician is more interested in a psychological assessment of the behavior: What motivates the behavior? What feelings and thoughts produce the behavior? What are the internal psychological consequences and effects of the behavior? A teacher is interested in the child's succeeding as a student at a level that corresponds generally with her ability. The clinician is interested in a psychologically healthy child whose intellectual and emotional resources can be expressed in a well-integrated, socially adjusted personality whose basic psychological needs are met. The interests of clinician and teacher are distinguished here in terms of primary interests. Both the clinician and the teacher are interested in psychologically healthy and happy children, and obviously success as a student is both primary evidence of, and a major source of nourishment for, the psychological health of the child. The clinician and teacher approach a mutual goal from different perspectives.

The clinician's agenda and the teacher's agenda, however, are different. The clinician's agenda and responsibility is to work with the experience of the child, that is, the child's behavior, feelings, and the content and process of the child's thinking. The clinician focuses on the primary affective and intellectual process of a child and is interested in the total social and psychological adjustment of the child. The teacher, on the other hand, has a more specific agenda with more givens. The teacher is interested in the child's success primarily as a student. He provides content and structure for the child's experience. The teacher takes as given his obligation to teach the child certain values, attitudes and skills, as well as specific subject matter. This agenda is based on the expectations the educational system has for all children at a certain age or grade level. The teacher, then, has certain obligations that accompany his relationship with the child as student. In the teacher-student relationship, the teacher has a responsibility to teach certain material to the child and the child, as a student, has a corresponding responsibility to learn that material.

Obviously, neither the teacher's nor the clinician's perspective is valid to the exclusion of the other. Special educators of emotionally disturbed children must often be prepared to understand and at times to reconcile the two perspectives. The special educator who works with emotionally disturbed children must combine some aspects of the clinician's perspective and the regular classroom teacher's perspective. The teacher's temperament as well as his skills will determine how successfully the two perspectives are combined.

The Central Role of the Teacher

The educational slogan, "Teach children not subjects," served a very useful purpose historically in calling attention to the fact that teachers must look beyond the content of what they are presenting if they are to be effective teachers. It helped open the door of the classroom by calling attention to the need for teachers to understand that their students are learners with varying styles and capacities for learning. It helped to shed new light on the child as a developing person, with her own social history and needs, her own abilities, her own strengths and weaknesses. The slogan both reflected and contributed to the development of a new educational philosophy and new educational theories.

This slogan was appropriate 40 or 50 years ago, but the behavioral and social sciences were developing and their relationship to education was being more fully explored. Out of this very important movement, lead by John Dewey and others, the important focus on individual differences emerged. The importance of individual student differences in education, which developing psychological theories have supported, has been recognized in educational philosophy and practice for more than 30 years. Psychological theories emphasizing individual differences, however, have been only partially translated into educational practices.

An important reason why these theories have been difficult to implement is that the teacher is not just dealing with individuals. He is dealing with a group, a class. Understanding the behavior and dynamics of groups, and how to work with and use groups, is a very basic and fundamental area of knowledge and skill for teachers. Unlike the clinician who selects a method or strategy to fit his agenda, the teacher works with the child on issues of individual adjustment, using the child's own experience and data. The teacher must select instructional strategies that take into account the demands of the classroom and the curriculum as well as the needs of the individual learner. The teacher must meet an obligation to the child and to the educational system. The teacher, for all practical purposes, takes as given the subject requirements and achievement level expectations for his grade. He must then develop instructional strategies that take into account the needs of children in his class and make possible their achievement at the expected level.

Parents have different roles with clinicians and teachers. With clinicians the parent is involved as a source of information, and sometimes as a receiver of advice about proper management of the child. Parents may be directly involved in a psychotherapeutic process in which the child's gains are acknowledged to have a direct relationship to the parent's gains. The relationship between a parent and a teacher is somewhat different. The focus is on the child's performance, his adjustment and achievement. The parent and teacher may collaborate in order to find the best approach to helping the child succeed as a student.

The relationship between teachers and parents is particularly important in view of the provisions of P.L. 94-142 which guarantees parents a right to participate in educational decisions about their children. The teacher has a very important central role in planning and implementing appropriate educational services for these children. Considering the complexity of the needs and the interdisciplinary challenge of educational programming for emotionally disturbed children, the teacher must be able to give and receive information to facilitate appropriate programming for the child. The teacher's relationship with other professionals, especially clinicians, and parents is often a very important factor in developing and implementing appropriate services. The teacher must be aware of the different needs and perspectives and the potential contribution of each of the individuals involved in planning and programming. Harmonizing and, when possible, reconciling the different perspectives in the interest of a common understanding and a consistent approach to the child is an important part of helping emotionally disturbed children.

The Nature and Role of Theory

Theory is important to the development of the area of special education for emotionally disturbed and behaviorally disordered children in guiding the development of knowledge, providing a basis for definition and guiding educational planning and practice. Theory, as a belief about the nature and working of something in which we are interested, provides an intellectual framework for reality. A theory must, however, meet certain technical requirements. It must be at least potentially subject to verification, and it must have a technical language in which terms are clearly and operationally defined. In addition to its technical requirements, a good theory has two additional features. First, it recognizes and builds upon existing knowledge. Second, it leads us to some understanding of the practical working of some part of the world. In other words, good theory is practical (Lewin, 1951).

Different types of theories serve different purposes. Rapoport (1970) suggests that there are three types of theories: (a) *deductive theory*, the logical system of mathematics which deals only with the conceptual level of reality and the proof of propositions, is determined by the validity of logical deductions rather than by correspondence with observable reality; (b) *predictive theory*, comprised of empirically based models of the real world, is subject to observable data-based proof and has as a primary purpose the discovery of the laws that operate in and control the real world; and (c) *heuristic theory*, which helps make sense out of something and, to that extent, explains it, does not predict anything and, therefore, does not enable one to control any aspect of reality.

Our progress in developing knowledge about emotionally disturbed children and how to work effectively with them relies in part on our development of theory. Many theories about human functioning are heuristic although some psychological theories purport to be predictive. Theories of intelligence, for example, are predictive. It is in the area of predictive theory that psychological science is developing.

Many psychological and social theories have been applied to the understanding and education of emotionally disturbed children. Unfortunately, these theories have not always met the criteria of good theory. Many theories have not, for example, always taken account of existing knowledge or alternative theories. Second, the theories applied have not always met the criteria of specifying variables and relationships between variables that are quantifiable and ultimately verifiable. Finally, theories applied to the education of emotionally disturbed children have not always had predictive appeal; that is, they have been heuristic in nature. Consequently, "theory" as a whole has suffered a great deal of criticism. Practitioners in particular have found theory irrelevant to the practical realities of education.

The role of theory as a guide for making educational decisions is important. The teacher is interested in the child's positive and constructive participation in class and in his educational achievement. If the teacher is confronted with behavior that interferes with or negates the child's positive psychological and social participation as a student in the class, he must make decisions about the meaning and significance of the behavior to the child and to the class. Based on his understanding of the behavior, he must make a decision about intervening. If he intervenes, he must decide what the nature and objective of the intervention will be. If, for example, in response to the teacher's direct request that he clean off his desk in preparation for the test, Jerry says, "Go to hell, you bitch," how should the teacher respond? If Mary is a new student in the school just entering the second grade and the teacher notices that Mary is masturbating during class, what should the teacher do?

As any teacher will tell you, you must "know the child," meaning that, in addition to knowing the child's age and academic ability, you must know something about the child's pattern of behavior, her history and, in some instances, what is going on in the child's personal life. The question remains, however, how does the teacher decide what he needs to know about a child? How does the teacher know if he knows enough? How does the teacher organize what he knows in some way that helps him make sense out of the behavior that is problematic in the classroom and make decisions about what, if anything, should be done about the behavior?

Teachers are guided in their day-to-day activities by theories of behavior and theories of instruction. In fact, according to a concept of theories developed by Argyris (1970), we all use different theories to guide our behavior. We operate from some premise, set of assumptions or theoretical framework in making decisions about our activities. The theories teachers use may or may not be conscious and well thought out. The theories may or may not be well founded in terms of existing research knowledge about human behavior and instructional strategies in the classroom. Some teachers are more informed than other teachers, and some teachers are more effective than other teachers, but all teachers make thousands of decisions about the meaning of the behavior of children and about their own behavior as a teacher in response to the child's behavior. These decisions are based on the teacher's theory. For example, a teacher sees Behavior A and decides that he simply wants to get rid of Behavior A, or to replace Behavior A with Behavior B. Based on the teacher's understanding of Behavior A, his objective, to get rid of Behavior A or to replace Behavior A with Behavior B, and his theory of behavior change, the teacher selects Strategy X. Strategy X is selected for the intervention because it is a part of, or can be made a part of, the teacher's behavior repertoire and he predicts that the objective will be accomplished by it. If the objective was accomplished, then the theory was a good one. This is not to say that the theory was more effective or efficient than another theory might have been, but the teacher will use it again because he was reinforced by the fact that it worked.

Numerous theories of behavior and deviance have been applied to understanding, treating and educating emotionally disturbed children. Some of these theories have been found to be more useful than others, and some have been found to be more efficient than others. Some are based on a more solid foundation of research knowledge than others.

This book reviews some of the most important theories that have been found useful in understanding and educating emotionally disturbed children. The theories have been selected because of and are reviewed primarily in terms of their practical merit and appeal to teachers. While no attempt has been made to expand existing theory or to develop new theory, we have attempted to place educational practice with emotionally disturbed children in a broad theoretical context. The applications of theory and the theoretical foundations of good practices are emphasized.

An Eclectic Approach

Throughout this book the terms *theories, views, perspectives, frames of reference* and *models* are used interchangeably. Although these terms do not have the same technical meaning, they have been used interchangeably in the special education literature. For example, the technical distinctions between a model and a theory and the technical problems associated with terminology have been discussed by Rhodes and Paul (1978). For the purpose of the present writing, however, the distinctions are not meaningful.

The basic issue is this: Human behavior is complex and there are several different definitive scientific and quasi-scientific ways to understand it. It is a mistake to argue that one perspective is correct and the others are incorrect, or that one is necessarily more correct than others. The various theories or perspectives are not mutually exclusive and, as the reader will discover in the chapters that follow, each perspective is useful to teachers in understanding emotional disturbance and in providing an educational program for emotionally disturbed children.

For the teacher the perspectives are part of the intellectual framework within which he works. The teacher's ability to understand the child's needs and plan and carry out interventions that respond to those needs is, in part, directly related to his ability to analyze the problem of disturbance from different perspectives. Maslow (1966) suggests that if one only has a hammer, one tends to treat everything like a nail. If a teacher has only been exposed to a psychodynamic perspective, he will tend to view the disturbance more in terms of the child's inner life, primary transactions and social history. On the other hand, if the teacher has only been exposed to a behavioral perspective, he will tend to view the problem more in terms of actions and their consequences. A focus on a single perspective obviously limits the teacher's ability to help the emotionally disturbed child.

The different perspectives presented in the chapters that follow are separated to facilitate analysis and discussion of different ways of thinking about the problems of emotional disturbance. They are not presented in this fashion to encourage the reader to think about emotional disturbance simply in terms of philosophical categories. Rather a teacher should be both flexible and critical in analyzing emotional disturbance. This is especially important when interventions are not working or when the teacher finds himself saying, "I just don't know what to do with Gregory; I have run out of ideas." Moreover, teachers need the assistance of other professionals in understanding the needs and developing educational services for disturbed children. An appreciation for the various perspectives and approaches to understanding emotional disturbance will help the teacher be a better "consumer" of related professional services in his work with these children.

The integration of the different perspectives begins as an intellectual task. The teacher must think about emotional disturbance as a problem or set of problems that can be seen through different lenses (Montgomery, September 1979), each having some value in suggesting how to plan and implement an educational program for the child. The curriculum, the approach to managing behavior and the educational methods used to help the child with a particular problem, reading for example, must reflect integration. Indeed all of the educational decisions the teacher must make and the educational program that must be described in the child's individual education program (IEP) should reflect an integrated framework or "critical eclecticism" (Hewett & Taylor, 1980).

The Teacher as Decision Maker

Some children cause themselves difficulty because they are psychologically unable to interact with others or to compete with their classmates academically. Other children present behavior problems for the teacher because they are defiant. Still other children present problems for other students in the class because they are disruptive. Many different combinations of problems for the child, the class and the teacher exist in the academic life of the student labeled *emotionally disturbed* or *behavior disordered*. No single perspective is sufficient to effectively and efficiently guide the teacher's understanding of all problems.

The teacher is a decision maker and a problem solver who must make decisions about the most appropriate educational methods, curriculum and approaches to behavior management in the classroom. Figure 1.1 outlines some of the relevant factors involved in the decisions teachers make. The

Decisions Teachers Make	Factors that Influence Decisions Teachers Make	
	Background of the Teacher	Conceptual Models for Viewing the Emotionally Disturbed Learner

1. Is there a problem?
2. What is the problem?
3. What interventions are available?
4. Which interventions best meet the child's particular needs?
5. Did the selected approach work?
	1. Values and philosophy
	    Of life
	    Of education
	2. Personality
	    Needs
	    Style
	3. Norms of the teaching setting
		1. Psychodynamic
		2. Organic
		3. Behavioral
		4. Ecological
		5. Sociological
		6. Cultural

1.1 Influences on Decision Making for the Teacher of Emotionally Disturbed Children

teacher must decide if there is a problem, the nature of the problem and what to do about it. These decisions are influenced and guided by personal values, personality and the professional context in which the teacher is working as well as his understanding of alternative conceptual models that he can use in understanding the child and how to work with her.

Since the teacher decides when a "problem" exists, the teacher must have some idea of what constitutes a problem before a specific problem occurs. Teachers have individual definitions of a problem, which differ in their concrete details and their theoretical sophistication. The teacher's definition of a problem is related to his view of classroom rules, his behavioral expectations, his values and philosophy, both personal and educational, as well as to his scientific knowledge of child behavior, learning and teaching.

Conceptual models or theories of emotional disturbance and behavior disorders are helpful to the teacher in understanding the problems of children labeled emotionally disturbed or behavior disordered. They are useful in giving the teacher a professional basis for deciding whether to intervene and in what way.

Emotional disturbance involves many factors that are expressed differently in each child and in each classroom. The teacher must make the most informed educational decision he can in each instance. There are no patent answers. He is guided by an understanding of several theoretical perspectives, each of which may be useful in helping him respond to a particular child. The teacher must also consider the norms of the teaching setting in which he is working. The primary conceptualization of the problems associated with a child or a child's "disturbance" in a public school, for example, is likely to be different from the way the problems are viewed in an educational program in an inpatient psychiatric treatment facility.

The teacher's own values and philosophy of education also affect his view of the child and what approach he chooses. The teacher is most likely to understand the child's needs and be guided in his interventions by perspectives that fit with his view of life and can be comfortably incorporated into his teaching style.

One or several perspectives may be most useful when the teacher plans for a specific child. All perspectives will be helpful when the teacher works with other helping professionals in planning for a child. These professionals may sometimes hold views that differ from those of the teacher. A basic understanding of alternative perspectives, however, will improve communication with other professionals in planning appropriate services for these children.

SUMMARY

Emotional disturbance is a label associated with many problems that affect a child's life. Professionals are not in agreement on a single definition, a label, the causes or the most appropriate way to conceptualize the problem. It is generally recognized that these children do not comprise a homogeneous group from an educational perspective. Estimates of the prevalence of the problem vary widely.

Parents, teachers and clinicians have different types of concerns about emotional disturbance because they have different roles and responsibilities in relation to the child. These differences must be recognized and the efforts of parents and professionals orchestrated if the child's best interests are to be served.

There are several different conceptual views or theories of emotional disturbance that are useful to the teacher in understanding the educational needs of these children. These views assist the teacher in making appropriate decisions about educational programming.

DISCUSSION QUESTIONS

1. What have been the barriers to developing an appropriate definition of emotional disturbance to be used in educational settings?
2. What is an educationally appropriate definition of emotional disturbance?
3. What are some of the examples of classroom problems associated with emotional disturbance in children?
4. What are some of the strategies for effectively harmonizing parent, clinical and educational perspectives?

REFERENCES

Algozzine, R., Schmid, R., & Conners, R. Toward an acceptable definition of emotional disturbance. *Behavior Disorders*, 1978, 4(1), 48–52.

Argyris, C. *Intervention theory and method: A behavioral science view.* Reading, Mass.: Addison-Wesley, 1970.

Bell, R. Q. Socialization findings re-examined. In R. Q. Bell & L. V. Harper (Eds.), *Child effects on adults.* New York: John Wiley & Sons, 1977.

Bowers, E. M. *Early identification of emotionally handicapped children in school.* Springfield, Ill.: Charles C Thomas, 1969.

Cullinan, D., & Epstein, M. H. *Administrative definitions of behavior disorders: Status and directions*. Paper presented at the Advanced Institute for Trainers of Teachers of Seriously Emotionally Disturbed Children and Youth, Charlottesville, Va., February 1979.

Epstein, M. H., Cullinan, D., & Sabatino, D. A. State definitions of behavior disorders. *Journal of Special Education*, 1977, *11*, 417–425.

Federal Register. Washington, D.C.: U.S. Government Printing Office, August 23, 1977.

Grosenick, J. K., & Huntze, S. L. *National needs analysis in behavior disorders: Severe behavior disorders*. Columbia: Department of Special Education, University of Missouri, 1980.

Hewett, F. M., & Taylor, F. D. *The Emotionally Disturbed Child in the Classroom* (2nd ed.). Boston, Mass.: Allyn & Bacon, 1980.

Hobbs, N. *Helping disturbed children: Psychological and ecological strategies, II; Project Re-ed, twenty years later*. Nashville, Tenn.: Center for the Study of Families and Children, Vanderbilt Institute for Puclic Policy Studies, Vanderbilt University, 1979.

Kauffman, J. M. Where special education for disturbed children is going: A personal view. *Exceptional Children*, 1980, *46*(7), 522–527.

Kauffman, J. M. *Characteristics of children's behavior disorders* (2nd ed.) Columbus, Ohio: Charles E. Merrill, 1981.

Kelley, T. J., Bullock, L. M., & Dykes, M. K. Behavioral disorders: Teacher's perceptions. *Exceptional Children*, 1977, *43*, 316–318.

Lewin, Kurt. *Field theory in social science: Selected theoretical papers* (D. Cartwright, Ed.). New York: Harper & Row, 1951.

Maslow, A. H. *The psychology of science*. New York: Harper & Row, 1966.

Mercer, J. *Labeling the mentally retarded*. Riverside, Calif.: University of California Press, 1973.

Montgomery, M. D. Personal communication, September 1979.

Morse, W. C. *Some approaches to meeting the needs of emotionally disturbed children in a public school setting*. Speech delivered at 19th Annual Conference of Exceptional Children, Charlotte, N.C., November 1967.

Morse, W. C. The education of socially maladjusted and emotionally disturbed children. In W. M. Cruickshank & G. O. Johnson (Eds.), *Education of Exceptional Children and Youth* (3rd ed.). Englewood Cliffs, N.J.: Prentice-Hall, 1975.

Morse, W. C., & Coopchik, H. Socioemotional impairment. In W. C. Morse (Ed.), *Humanistic teaching for exceptional children: An introduction to special education*. Syracuse, N.Y.: Syracuse University Press, 1979.

Paluszny, Maria J. *Autism*. Syracuse, N.Y.: Syracuse University Press, 1979.

Paul, J. L., & Beckman-Bell, P. Parent perspectives. In J. L. Paul (Ed.), *Understanding and working with parents of children with special needs*. New York: Holt, Rinehart & Winston, 1981.

Quay, H. C. Patterns of aggression, withdrawal and immaturity. In H. C. Quay & J. S. Werry (Eds.), *Psychopathological disorders of childhood*. New York: John Wiley & Sons, 1972.

Quay, H. C. Classification in the treatment of delinquency and antisocial behavior. In N. Hobbs (Ed.), *Issues in the classification of children* (Vol. 1). San Francisco, Calif.: Jossey-Bass, 1975.

Rapoport, A. *Modern systems theory: An outlook for coping with change*. Paper presented at the John Umstead Lectures, North Carolina Department of Mental Health, Raleigh, February 1970.

Rhodes, W. C., & Paul, J. L. *Emotionally disturbed and deviant children: New views and approaches*. Englewood Cliffs, N.J.: Prentice-Hall, 1978.

Robbins, L. *Deviant children grown up.* Baltimore, Md.: Williams & Wilkins, 1966.

Schopler, E., & Reichler, R. J. (Eds.). *Psychopathology and child development: Research and treatment.* New York: Plenum, 1976.

Wood, F. H., & Lakin, K. C. (Eds.). *Disturbing, disordered or disturbed? Perspectives on the definition of problem behavior in educational settings.* Minneapolis: Advanced Institute for Trainers of Teachers for Seriously Emotionally Disturbed Children and Youth, Department of Educational Studies, University of Minnesota, 1979.

Wood, F. H., & Lakin K. C. *Defining emotionally disturbed/behavior disordered populations for research purposes.* Paper presented at an Advanced Institute for Trainers of Teachers of Seriously Emotionally Disturbed Children and Youth, Charlottesville, Va., February 1979.

Wood, F. H., & Zabel, R. H. *Making sense of reports on the incidence of behavior disorders/emotional disturbance in school populations.* Minneapolis: University of Minnesota, 1978.

Wyne, M. D., & O'Connor, P. D. *Exceptional children: A developmental view.* Lexington, Mass.: D. C. Heath, 1979.

2

Special Services for Emotionally Disturbed Children

main points

1 Since the teacher is one among several professionals who works with emotionally disturbed or behaviorally disordered children and their families, she needs to know the services available and the other professionals who provide those services.

2 Sometimes the child receives help from more than one service delivery system. Since the systems are often large and complex and have problems communicating effectively with each other, cooperation between the systems and coordination of the services is extremely important.

3 The redefinition of emotional disturbance as a problem of behavior, learning or social interaction, which did not occur until the late 1960s and early 1970s, has made it possible to more effectively develop educational programs for these children.

4 Human service policies in the last decade have emphasized integrated community-based services, parent and child rights, and procedural safeguards to improve the systems' accountability in providing appropriate services.

5 While several important organizational changes, such as the development of state human resource agencies and governor-appointed developmental disability councils, have in some cases produced better-integrated program planning and service delivery, major barriers to well-integrated service delivery still exist.

6 The mental health system, the social welfare system, the legal-correctional system and the religious system may also be involved in providing services to the emotionally disturbed child. Communication between these systems is necessary to promote cooperative planning and continuity of services.

EMOTIONALLY DISTURBED children and their families receive services from professionals in several different disciplines. These professionals are employed by different agencies and institutions. Some services, such as a mental health clinic, are found in the community where the child lives, while others, such as a psychiatric hospital, may be far removed from the child's home. Some services, such as a special treatment center, are residential; others, such as a therapeutic day-care center, work with the child for several hours every weekday; and still others offer specialized treatment for an hour, one or more times a week.

Some services are primarily educational in nature while others focus on medical, psychological or social-welfare problems. Some offer service to the child on an individual basis while others work with the child in a group. Some service providers are interested in involving the parents in some way; others are not.

The teacher needs to understand the nature and quality of professional services available in the community and see herself as a part of the professional community. In this chapter generic human service systems that work with emotionally disturbed children and their families, and some of the professional issues involved in providing those services, are described. For a detailed and comprehensive discussion of service delivery systems the reader is referred to Rhodes & Head (1974). The emphasis here will be specifically on matters of interest to teachers.

Realities of Service Delivery

Special services for emotionally disturbed children vary in philosophy and approach. Which service is most appropriate depends on the child's age, the type of problem and the severity of the problem. Most emotionally disturbed children are served in their own community by professionals in public institutions and facilities. These basic services are frequently supplemented by specialized private professional services. Services vary in their geographic availability and cost. The cost may range from nothing to more than $75,000 per child per year, depending on the nature of the service and, in some instances, the ability of parents to pay. Quality and effectiveness of services also vary widely.

Children and their families often need more than one type of professional service, and these services involve more than one service delivery system. Coordination among the different services ranges from nonexistent to moderately effective. The ability of parents to understand and access appropriate services is equally varied. The one professional constant, in this complex myriad of services for all school-age emotionally disturbed children who are living in the community, is the teacher. The law (P. L. 94-142) requires that all children be provided a free, appropriate education in the least restrictive setting. This service is generally provided by the teacher.

Educators need not have a detailed understanding of the structure, organization, programs, policies and procedures of the various service deliv-

---

This chapter was written by **James L. Paul**, University of North Carolina at Chapel Hill.

ery systems. They should, however, be aware of the major systems that exist and the ways in which emotionally disturbed children in school may be involved with those systems. Teachers should be familiar with certain basic realities regarding the nature, operation and accessibility of human service systems.

1. Emotionally disturbed children sometimes come from families whose needs require the assistance of more than one helping system. Because of the complexity of the human service systems and the lack of information parents often have about those systems, they may need help obtaining and integrating information about different service delivery systems and accessing needed services in appropriate ways.
2. Because human service systems are large and complex, communication within and between these systems is often difficult. Coordination of services, therefore, requires the commitment of all involved. Different systems do not as a matter of routine coordinate their efforts. Interagency councils and other special efforts to coordinate services do not always work.
3. The teacher is not alone as a professional in working with the child. In the community are many allies whose skills can be drawn upon to assist in meeting the child's needs. Parents are likely to be the closest allies of the teacher; in most instances they are willing and able to be helpful. In all instances they have a right to be involved in educational decisions about their child. Volunteers, such as advocates who try to obtain services for the child, or "big brothers" or "big sisters" who work with children in camping, athletic or general social activities, can also be of help. These volunteers can frequently be accessed through social welfare and religious organizations and groups. In some instances other professionals may be working with the family or with the child through another system. At the discretion of the parents, or the courts, information may be exchanged between systems and cooperative alliances may be formed to better meet the needs of the child and his family.
4. Different views of emotional disturbance and behavior disorders exist in different service delivery systems. Frequently, the child in question may have committed several types of behavioral offenses and been diagnosed and labeled by more than one system. The teacher may find herself working with professionals with slightly different perspectives, definitions and technical vocabularies. When this occurs, the teacher needs to help others understand the realities of the classroom and visualize the child's behavior in that context. The teacher's position is not superior, however, and she should appreciate and learn from the perspectives of others, who are appraising the child's behavior in the context of the home or community.
5. A child's socioeconomic background may affect the evaluation of his difficulties in school and the services he and his family receive in the community. Opportunities for service may be limited if the child comes from a family of low socioeconomic status. The interrela-

tionship of a child's socioeconomic background, his emotional and social adjustment in school, and his academic achievement is complex and varies with each child.

The human service bureaucracies that seek to meet related human needs in our society are massive. Some of the difficulties of the different systems in working together are a product the size and complexity of the organizations through which the services are provided. Partly the difficulties stem from the different legislatively mandated missions of these systems.

History and Philosophy of Human Services

The 1960s and 1970s were decades of change in attitudes toward and opportunities available to emotionally disturbed children and their families. The changes were dramatic and extensive. Two important areas of change were the redefinition of the problem of emotional disturbance, and the reform of human service policies.

Redefinition of Emotional Disturbance

From early in the 1900s until the 1960s, the mental health system was viewed as having primary responsibility for the professional treatment of emotionally disturbed children. Research in the late 1950s indicated that the needs of these children were greater than conventional mental health strategies employed by traditional mental health professionals could handle (Albee, 1956). Too many children with too many needs confronted a system with limited professional resources and a highly specialized knowledge base. New concepts and procedures had to be developed and a new professional force trained. A new system had to be found to augment the services of the mental health system.

Educational philosophy and practices, the public school system and teachers became primary focuses during this period of inventive thinking about and new ways of working with emotionally disturbed children. Morse, Hobbs, Hewitt, Rhodes, Trippi and Bower, themselves psychologists by training, were among those who led the reform, building conceptual bridges from traditional mental health practices to new psycho-educational, behavioral and ecological approaches. These leaders, who successfully developed the argument that education provided an important alternative, were aided in their efforts by professionals from other disciplines. Szasz (1964), a psychiatrist, questioned the appropriateness of the whole concept of mental illness. He argued that the so-called mentally ill are not sick; rather, they have difficulty adjusting and coping with life. At the same time, Goffman (1961) and other sociologists were exposing the negative effects of large institutions and the stigmatizing effect of labels. Morse (1971) and others contributed to expanding concepts of school mental health.

The professional leadership for developing special services for emotionally disturbed children in public schools came from outside education, mostly from psychology. Problems of definition, instructional methods and curriculum, in part, came about because the basic questions, who are these children? and, what do we do with them? were addressed by different professional groups with different philosophies, technical languages and methods. The integration of emotionally disturbed children into the educational system has, therefore, involved integrating the orientations, technical languages and practices of different professional groups.

Alternatives to the view of emotional disturbance as child mental illness had to be developed. The medical view of emotional disturbance as an illness, and the attendant philosophy, technical language and professional practices, had to be reconsidered. During the sixties the medical view was broadened into a more interdisciplinary perspective, and education came to the fore as an important service alternative. If the educational system assumed direct responsibility for emotionally disturbed children, then the problems had to be explained in a way that teachers understood. The needs of these children had to be considered in light of the goals of education, teacher interventions, and the philosophical and organizational context of the classroom and the school.

In the late 1960s and early 1970s mental health and education professionals were defining emotional disturbance more in terms of problems of behavior, learning and social interaction and less in terms of internal psychological states. This shift in conceptualization placed the problems of emotional disturbance more appropriately in the domain of teachers. Teachers deal with social behavior, relationships between children in groups, and problems in learning. Unless specially trained to do so, teachers do not deal directly with defense mechanisms, problems of irrational fears and anxieties or attempt to "work through" problems in the child's social history. With the changing perspective alternative instructional strategies were developed and evaluated, some by trial and error and some by more systematic research. Teachers became primary intervenors, and the public school system came to be viewed by many as a primary service delivery system for emotionally disturbed children.

In addition to developing appropriate teaching methods and curricula, an appropriate administrative arrangement within the school for serving these children had to be worked out. These arrangements vary widely from school to school, from special classes for emotionally disturbed children to various arrangements under which the child stays in the regular classroom as much as possible. The latter include resources rooms, where the child can obtain special help as needed outside the regular classroom, and the use of crisis or helping teachers, consulting teachers, resource teachers and "teacher moms" to provide special help to the teacher of the child in the regular classroom. (Specific educational services are discussed by Montgomery in Chapter 3.)

Reform of Human Services Policies

Ideological and professional changes in understanding and providing services for emotionally disturbed children during the past two decades were part of a much wider change in special education and a much deeper change in the philosophies and laws governing human services for all handicapped children. These changes were largely the result of successful advocacy by parents within all three branches of government. Changes in the educational system were most dramatically affected by P.L. 94-142 which brought together the major principles of law articulated by the courts, where parents or parent organizations were litigants on behalf of their children, into a single instrument of law.

The provisions of P.L. 94-142 are pervasive in their implications for the delivery of educational services to emotionally disturbed children. (They will be described in the context of specific discussions in Section Three.) P.L. 94-142, however, has a larger social, economic and political context. The genesis of this law demonstrated that citizens, through their elected representatives, could make decisions about their rights and interests on matters of special concern to them. In our democratic society, this legislative process operates in conjunction with another social system equally vital to the welfare of the society, the judicial system. This system provides for the fair interpretation of law and protection of the legal rights and constitutionally guaranteed interests of individuals.

In the past 20 years, the parents of handicapped children have worked actively with the legislative and executive branches of government. In the last 10 years, however, they have worked more with the judicial branch, declaring, testing and securing certain rights to services for their children and appropriate roles for themselves. Their gains have affected the nature of services provided as well as the number of services available to their children.

The values of a society are revealed in the way it spends its money. In the United States the Congress must approve a budget to secure the services it values. Approving the allocation of resources is a fundamental responsibility of Congress, and decisions to establish priorities are made in the presence of limited resources. Major themes of congressional action upon which human service policies have been based include (a) emphasis on community-based services, (b) accountability of service delivery systems, (c) integration of services and (d) integration of training and human services.

Emphasis on community-based services. Since the late 1960s reduction of institutional dependency has been a national goal (Paul, Stedman, Neufeld, 1977). Programs for least restrictive placement, or mainstreaming, and deinstitutionalization reflect this goal. The individual's right to and ability to take advantage of community-based services has been espoused, while the process, benefits and ethics of special placement have been questioned.

The process by which handicapped children have been labeled and placed in special settings has come under harsh attack (Mercer, 1973). The test data upon which decisions have been made have been criticized for their cultural bias (Bailey & Harbin, 1980). Also, the influence of the child's cultural background and socioeconomic status on the identification and labeling of the child has been described, and the ways in which the poor and ethnic minorities are disadvantaged in this regard has been noted (Mercer & Lewis, 1978). The social stigma of labels, often inappropriately applied, and

Mildly handicapped children generally show greater social gains in special classes and greater academic gains in regular classes.

of special placements, often inappropriately made, have been reported extensively in the literature (Gove, 1975; Kitsuse, 1975; Becker, 1963).

The efficacy of special class placement has been evaluated and most research has indicated that academic gains are greater for handicapped children in regular classes while social gains are greater in the special class (Goldstein, Moss, & Jordon, 1965). Farther removed from the mainstream of society than the special class is the large institution, the psychiatric hospital for the mentally handicapped. Blatt (1966) and others note the plight and tragic circumstances of residents of some of these larger, often dehumanizing, understaffed, remote public facilities.

The ethics of separating a person from the mainstream of society by placing him in a facility or program that may, in fact, deprive him of opportunities afforded to others not so placed has been questioned. In some instances the individual's right is examined in relation to society's right. The belief that society's rights, or the rights of others, are being protected has in some instances been posited without demonstrable evidence. The constitutionally assured right to due process when a person is denied freedom, that is, placed in an institution against his will, has also been questioned. The law has determined that such a person has a right to due process, and that if he is placed he has a right to appropriate treatment. The principle that has been affirmed is that a person's rights and privileges as a citizen should not be limited because he is handicapped.

The rights of children to speak on their own behalf and to express preferences are often overlooked (Paul, Neufeld, & Pelosi, 1977). The belief

Though encouraged under P.L. 94-142, children's participation in IEP conferences to date has been negligible.

that adults know best is reflected in the way administrative decisions are typically made, with relatively little input from the child affected by those decisions. P.L. 94-142, for example, provides for children to contribute to their individual educational program plans. Evidence available at the present time, however, suggests that the participation of children in IEP conferences is slight (Gillespie, 1981).

The right of emotionally disturbed children to participate in educational planning is especially important given the nature of the problem of disturbance as some professionals see it. Rhodes (1980), for example, emphasizes the value of individual differences, which may be overlooked in planning educational programs designed to reduce differences.

> My own conviction is that these are differing views of reality and that there is no real consensus. I believe that certain children make life rocky for us and are more likely than others to upset the feeling of equilibrium in groups. I believe that some children hurt, and are hurt by others, that these hurts should be healed. I believe that there are gross physical differences among children and that some of these differences place limits on certain children doing certain things. But I do not think they should be made to change these differences, nor that we would even help to change them. I do believe we should help the child understand these differences, and, in most cases, come to cherish the very uniqueness expressed by this difference. (p. 259)

The right of the child to be different, however, must be balanced with the rights of others in the same setting and the rights of the institution. This balancing of the values and perspectives of individuals and institutions is crucial in integrating children who are different into settings defined as "normal" or "regular."

The philosophy of normalization (Wolfensberger & Zauha, 1973) has guided the movement toward deinstitutionalization and mainstreaming. To ensure that normalization works in the interest of handicapped individuals, many institutional and programmatic interventions have been developed. For example, community alternatives have been developed so that institutionalization is unnecessary for most seriously handicapped individuals while institutional services have been improved for those persons who need them. Community alternatives and services include but are not limited to group homes, foster homes, sheltered workshops, camping programs and re-education centers.

Mainstreaming, providing educational services in the least restrictive setting, is the movement in the educational system aimed at integrating all handicapped children as much as possible into the regular education program. Within the public schools, resource teachers, consulting teachers and other educational supports to regular class teachers have been used to minimize the inappropriate placement of handicapped children in special classes. The use of these supports protects the interests of the child who should not be placed in a special class. It also protects the interests of those who do require special class placement by reserving that limited resource for the children who truly need it.

Accountability of service delivery systems. One of the most important social themes of the last 10 years has been the accountability of public agencies. During the sixties the nation as a whole became aware of many social injustices. The rights of many American citizens were being denied, abridged, or compromised. The rights of Blacks, women, the poor, and later children and the handicapped came into national focus. In this social, political and legal context the accountability of human service systems became an important national issue. The accountability issue surfaced in four major areas: advocacy, individual program planning, program evaluation and parent rights.

The civil rights movement during the early sixties led the way for many different advocacy movements in the late 1960s and early 1970s, including advocacy for children and for the handicapped (Paul, et al., 1977). Different types of advocacy have emerged to represent the interests of vulnerable populations and their rights to appropriate human services. These include citizen advocacy (Wolfensberger & Zauha, 1973), in which volunteers organize to promote the rights and interests of individuals, advocacy within the system (Paul et al., 1977), in which formal advocate roles have been developed and funded within agencies to promote the rights of consumers of human services, and legal advocacy (Turnbull & Turnbull, 1977; 1978), in which individuals have pursued a more adversarial role in representing, in court where necessary, the legal rights and interests of individuals.

Advocates seek to understand the needs of individuals from their perspective rather than from the perspective of an agency that has a particular point of view and a particular service to offer. Advocates help individuals to obtain appropriate services, monitor the quality of the services and intervene as necessary to see that individuals receive appropriate and high-quality services for the duration of their need. Most advocacy groups have in common the goal of making human service delivery systems more responsive and more accountable to the users of those services.

One of the major aims of the accountability movement has been to recognize individual differences and to see that individual needs are appropriately addressed. Individual program planning became very important and was ultimately mandated by federal legislation. A number of plans have been required either by federal law or regulations: the individual education plan (IEP) was mandated by P.L. 94-142, the Education for all Handicapped Children Act; the individual habilitation plan (IHP) was mandated by the Developmentally Disabled Assistance and Bill of Rights Amendment, P.L. 94-103; the individual program plan (IPP) was required by the federal regulations developed for implementing Title XIX of the Social Security Act which mandated intermediate care facilities for the mentally retarded; individual treatment plans (ITP) were required by the Mikva Amendments of 1976 for children who are eligible for SSI benefits; and individual written rehabilitation plans (IWRP) were required by the Rehabilitation Amendment of 1973.

In the mid to late 1970s individual planning technologies developed rapidly to facilitate the implementation of these individual planning requirements. Some problems associated with individual planning have emerged, however, which work against the intent of the requirements. For one thing, developing and recording an individual plan takes an enormous amount of staff time. Some have claimed that the time consumed in planning may be taking important time away from service delivery and that, in the long run, the consumer's interest may not be served by excessive accountability requirements. Also, each service delivery system has developed its own individual planning format so that multiple plans (IHP, IEP, ITP and so forth) may exist for one individual who is receiving services from different systems. Those plans and services, in many instances, are not being effectively coordinated.

Individual planning and the specifying of the objectives of the services in a written plan increase the accountability of the agency to the individual consumer. While barriers to the development of effective and efficient accountability mechanisms do exist, these barriers can be overcome through improved organizational planning and development, such as better utilization of resources, more efficient planning technologies, staff development and a commitment within and among service agencies to the concept of accountability to individual clients.

Another manifestation of the commitment to accountability is the emphasis that has been placed on program evaluation. During the last decade program evaluation has been used to guide administrative and programmatic decisions during the life of the program and to provide a more objective basis upon which to make decisions about continuing or discontinuing a program. As a result of this emphasis evaluation technology has seen tremendous development during the past 10 years.

Another important aspect of the accountability movement is the recognition and guarantee of certain parent rights. For a more complete discussion of parents' rights, the roles and responsibilities of parents provided by P.L. 94-142, and the ways in which parents and teachers can work together effectively in the context of all of the provisions of P.L. 94-142, see Turnbull (1981) and Turnbull and Strickland (1981). Parent rights and responsibilities, provided for by P.L. 94-142, include the right to be involved in developing and ultimately approving the child's individual education program (IEP). Also included is the guarantee of procedural safeguards. In an extensive discussion of parent rights, Turnbull (1981) lists six procedural safeguards:

1 Parental consent must be obtained prior to a preplacement evaluation;
2 Parents have access to all records having to do with the identification, evaluation and placement of their child;
3 Parents have the right to have an independent evaluation by a certified or licensed examiner, who is not employed by the school system, and have that evaluation considered by the school in making its decision regarding what constitutes a free, appropriate public education;
4 Parents must be notified in writing by the school before initiating or changing the child's identification, evaluation or educational placement;
5 If a child is a ward of the state or his own parents are unknown or unavailable, the school must appoint a surrogate parent for the child; and
6 Parents have the right to initiate a due process hearing when they have complaints regarding the child's identification, evaluation, placement, or the appropriateness of his educational program. The school has the same right to initiate a due process hearing when problems exist in any of these areas which they are not able to resolve.

Some parents may not want to become involved with more than one service delivery system. Inconvenience, negative attitudes toward certain service delivery systems or a lack of information about services may limit parents' interest in having services coordinated. Confidentiality, too, though it protects the rights and interests of parents and children in these instances, may limit service agencies in providing integrated and comprehensive services.

Integration of services. A major aspect of the reform in human service policies has been the move toward integration of services. The passage of P.L. 88-164 in 1963 provided the impetus for the development of comprehensive community-based services and emphasized the importance of the relationships among human service agencies. Individuals and families have different kinds and combinations of needs which change over time. Human services, on the other hand, may be organized for individuals who are a certain age, such as preschool, or who have needs that fall into a certain category and have acquired a label, such as *mentally ill* or *mentally retarded*. Services are also organized according to the severity of the problem; for example, institutional services address the needs of the profoundly handicapped. The services of a certain agency do not always fit the unique pattern of needs of an individual or a family.

People do not always know how to access services or how to adjust when their service needs change. Individuals or families are said to "fall between the cracks" when their particular needs do not meet the criteria of available service delivery systems. For example, a child who is multiply handicapped and whose problems may include emotional disturbance and blindness or mental retardation and deafness may have difficulty finding an appropriate service. Services are available for the emotionally disturbed, or for the mentally retarded, or for the deaf, or for the blind. When the child has a combination of serious handicapping conditions such as these, however, he has often been viewed as someone else's problem.

Another problem is created when an individual outgrows a service. For example, the educational needs of an emotionally disturbed child in sixth grade may be appropriately met in a special class. When he gets to the seventh grade, however, such a class may not exist in his junior high school. Historically, a child in the unfortunate situation of having outgrown the appropriate services that were available has been placed in whatever program was available, in the absence of alternatives, regardless of whether the program was designed to meet his particular educational needs. This practice, of course, violates the letter and the spirit of present law (P.L. 94-142). Many organizational and programmatic problems remain, however, in coordinating services and providing continuity between services over time. Case management and client tracking strategies have been developed in many service systems to minimize these problems.

The human services systems have made attempts to address the problems of coordination and communication between service systems. Interagency planning councils were a very common response to these problems during the late sixties and the early seventies. The concept of the "single portal of entry" to the entire array of human services at the community level has been tried. Advocacy efforts both within and outside the service delivery system have addressed the problems of coordination, communication and the responsiveness of the human service delivery system.

One major strategy at the state level has been to organize state departments of human resources which incorporate under a single organizational umbrella the state's mental health, health and social services programs. The specific agencies and services that have been included under the human resources umbrella has varied from state to state.

At the national level a coalition of categorical disability groups has tried to obtain better political and economic support for services and to integrate the network of human services to better meet the needs of individuals. The developmental disabilities movement initially brought together the National Association for Retarded Citizens, the Epilepsy Foundation of America and the United Cerebral Palsy Association into an integrated and coordinated force to develop services for developmentally disabled citizens. These were later joined by the National Society for Autistic Children. The Developmental Disabilities Services and Facilities Construction Act, passed in 1970, contained several important provisions for assisting in this area. It provided for the formation of developmental disability councils at the state level in every state which, among other things, addressed the problems of coordination and integration in the planning of services. In 1975 the Developmentally Disabled Assistance and Bill of Rights Act created Protection and Advocacy (P & A) systems in each state for the developmentally disabled. While the developmental disabilities councils serve primarily a planning function, the P & A agencies serve primarily an advocacy function.

These various organizational interventions, which addressed the complex issues of services integration, have affected the human service systems as a whole rather than a particular categorical group, such as services for the emotionally disturbed. These efforts illustrate that service providers, policy makers, and legislators have recognized the problems involved in coordinating and integrating services and are committed to generating organizational solutions to the problem. There are still many philosophical and organizational barriers to the effective and efficient integration of services, however. A common view of the problems to be addressed does not exist. Moreover, existing services are resistant to change. Massive bureaucracies are involved; the inertia in these systems is considerable. Also, human service agencies in transition do not always have clear missions and objectives, and therefore accountability is difficult to enforce. Organizational integrity is compromised under these conditions, and a strong commitment from staff is difficult to obtain.

In addition to philosophical and organizational barriers, major problems related to the allocation of resources have emerged. Most service providers have pointed to the need for additional resources in order to provide more effective services and to coordinate their work with other agencies. The political and economic climate of the early 1980s is clearly encouraging reduced government spending. This reduction, especially at the federal level, will reduce services available for emotionally disturbed children and their families. Policy makers and legislators are more inclined to recommend the reallocation of existing resources, arguing that it is possible to use the resources we have more wisely. Within the larger context of resource allocation, support of basic and programmatic research, preventive programs and training must be balanced with support of direct services.

Integration of training and human services. An important theme in the reform of human services during the past 10 years has been a commitment to integrate training and service delivery activities more effectively. Historically, universities and colleges have been responsible for turning out a cadre of professionals to meet service needs in the community and leadership needs in areas of government concerned with human services. Training has generally proceeded on the assumption that the skills being taught are those in demand in the field. As the skills needed by professionals change with reforms in human services, training programs must keep pace.

Most of the teachers who are currently in the classroom will still be teaching in 1990. The new graduates of colleges and university teaching degree programs who enter the teaching profession will account for a relatively small percentage of the teacher force over the next decade. The small influx of teachers with up-to-date training is a particular problem in special education because policies governing services, knowledge about assessment, intervention, and program evaluation technologies, laws, and the professional responsibilities and roles of special educators have changed so rapidly. If new programs are to work effectively and if professional quality is to be maintained, then the professional training curriculum must reflect changing organizational realities.

To acquaint special education teachers with these realities, in-service training activities in schools have been intensified, and field-based training activities at universities and colleges have increased. In some instances, the degree-oriented training that has traditionally been conducted exclusively on university campuses, has been conducted on location, in schools. More emphasis has been placed on improved collegial relationships between professionals in the public schools and university and college faculty.

Many organizational, philosophical and resource problems remain to be addressed if training and service delivery systems are to be coordinated more effectively. These problems are now being addressed by both the training and the service delivery systems.

Service Delivery Systems

The mental health, social services, legal-correctional and religious service delivery systems provide the major services for emotionally disturbed children outside the public school (Rhodes & Head, 1974). In the following sections we will look at individual delivery systems and the perspectives, practices and roles of professionals who work in those systems as they are relevant to understanding services for emotionally disturbed children.

Mental Health System

The mental health system is a major component in the network of services for emotionally disturbed children. The mental health center, the child guidance clinic and the psychiatric hospital are the major institutions through which public mental health services are delivered. Important services are also provided by the private sector.

Typically seriously disturbed persons receive services from and reside in psychiatric hospitals, as *inpatients*, and less seriously disturbed persons receive services in the community mental health clinics on an *outpatient* basis; that is, they live at home and visit the clinic for specialized treatment. A continuum of services is presumed to exist which matches the continuum of needs of individuals. Services along the continuum vary in the intensity of the treatment and the restrictions imposed on the person (patient). The least restrictive service might be an outpatient service at a mental health center. The most restrictive and intense might be hospitalization with several therapeutic treatments such as psychotherapy, occupational therapy and milieu therapy.

Hospitalization has been reduced dramatically during the past 20 years primarily as a result of improvements in drugs affecting mental functioning and behavior. Persons who, prior to these advances, needed the structure and supervision provided in a hospital setting are now able to function in the community with the aid of medication. Hospitalization has also been reduced by changes in the philosophy and policies of mental health services. Since the middle of the sixties more and more mental health services have been provided in the community, reducing the need for and length of hospitalization. Because of the deinstitutionalization movement, new enabling legislation has been passed and additional community programs have been developed. Community programs now attempt to prevent hospitalization whenever feasible, and hospital services have been improved for those persons who need hospital care.

The need for the mental health and education systems to work closely and cooperatively to provide effective services for emotionally disturbed children and their families is extremely important. While arguments have been put forward to place primary professional responsibility with either mental health or education, both systems now generally recognize that the responsibility must be shared and that each system makes an important and necessary contribution to the education and treatment of emotionally disturbed children. Communication between the school and mental health services is so important that a new role, the liaison teacher, has been developed in some community mental health programs.

Several problems arise in coordinating mental health and educational services. Differences in philosophy and terminology, for example can make communication difficult. The personal nature of the information the mental health professional may have and the confidence in which that information is obtained and held may limit the communication between the two systems. Attitudes of mental health professionals toward teachers and schools and attitudes of teachers toward mental health professionals, if stereotyped or negative, can also inhibit effective coordination of services. The professional relationship between teachers and mental health professionals is very important in providing services for emotionally disturbed children and their families.

Professionals historically associated with the field of mental health have primarily been psychiatrists, psychologists and social workers. Teachers, occupational therapists, psychiatric nurses and others may also provide services within the mental health system. Our discussion will focus on those most likely to be involved in community mental health programs and, therefore, most likely to interact with teachers. Each type of professional contributes information that is used to make an informed judgment on the nature of a child's emotional disturbance, that is, a diagnosis. In the descriptions of professional roles that follow, the reader should recognize that the styles and patterns of functioning vary with the individual and the professional setting in which he works.

A psychiatrist is a medical doctor who specializes her training in psychiatry by completing a residency in some aspect of psychiatric practice such as child, adult, forensic or community psychiatry. The principal treatment strategies or interventions used by psychiatrists include psychotherapy, drugs, consultation and hospitalization. The psychiatrist is typically the senior member of a mental health treatment team or staff and is usually involved in primary or direct care.

The psychiatrist may provide secondary and also tertiary mental health interventions by consulting with or providing training for parents, teachers and other child care workers. These interventions have become an increasingly important preventive strategy in child mental health. For example, if a particular child is being treated by the psychiatrist and is on medication, communication between psychiatrist and teacher is critical. The psychiatrist needs information from the teacher regarding the child's functioning in the classroom and particularly any important changes in the child's functioning. Similarly, the teacher needs information from the psychiatrist regarding the child's special needs and approaches that are more likely to be successful in working with the child.

Psychodynamic theories used to explain human behavior and guide therapeutic interventions have been developed and tested by clinicians working, for the most part, with individual cases or small groups. The individual case is considered significant in developing and testing knowledge and in training clinicians.

Serious behavior deviation has been conceptualized by psychiatrists as mental illness. This view derives from the fact that psychiatry grew out of the tradition of medicine. The notion of deviance as mental illness has had profound implications for our views of emotional disturbance and our interventions.

The psychiatrist has clinical diagnostic responsibility in the determination of a person's ability to function. She basically collects, or causes to be collected, two kinds of information: medical information on a person's physical health and, depending upon the presenting symptoms, specialized technical data on a person's neurological functioning. Detailed neurological studies are usually conducted by a neurologist, a medical colleague of the psychiatrist. The psychiatrist, however, is frequently certified in neurology and may conduct at least part of the studies herself. At a minimum, a psychiatrist has enough understanding of the possible neurological implications of physical and behavioral symptoms to know when to obtain more detailed and sophisticated neurological studies, and how to interpret and use these data when they are obtained. In addition to medical data, the psychiatrist also collects information about the individual's psychological functioning. Her primary method for collecting this information is the psychiatric interview.

The clinical psychologist is also an important member of the traditional mental health team. A fully accredited, practicing clinical psychologist is a professional mental health specialist with a Ph.D. in psychology. As a member of the mental health team, the clinical psychologist has two important clinical functions. One function is to administer, score and interpret psychological tests designed to elicit information about a person's psychological status and functioning. The psychologist contributes her understanding of the person's functioning, derived from the test data, to the information collected by the psychiatrist and the social worker and any other data on the person's functioning that may have been collected by other professionals.

In addition to diagnosing, the psychologist can also provide treatment. The psychologist may either be a part of a treatment team or have the primary responsibility for the intervention. Individual and group psychotherapy are primary interventions used by clinical psychologists. Psychologists also frequently provide secondary and tertiary intervention by working with parents or consulting with or training teachers. The psychologist may help the teacher improve educational strategies for a particular child or develop a better general understanding of child mental health, behavior management, counseling students, classroom climate or working with parents.

The psychiatric social worker is another important member of the mental health team. She is more interested in the history of the problem and the social, especially family, contexts in which the problem has occurred. The social worker collects historical information primarily from the parents through interviews. She may also collect specific information on the child's functioning in different systems including the school. The social worker is interested in the trends and patterns in family interactions, in the roles the child and other family members play, in relation to the child's disturbance. The social worker contributes this information to the diagnostic team.

Like the psychiatrist and the psychologist, the social worker also provides treatment. This may involve individual psychotherapy with the child, group psychotherapy or work with parents in conjunction with another professional who is working with the child. Social workers also assume case management responsibilities in many instances.

Some social workers work primarily in the context of the school and are therefore referred to as school social workers. They assist children and families with problems that interfere with the child's success as a student. The school social worker often assumes a major liaison role with other agencies that may be, or should be, assisting the child and family.

Many social workers specialize in community organization. Community organization involves working with the various community agencies or systems involved in providing professional services and working with the resources in the public and private sectors of the community to ensure that effective mental health services, including prevention, are available. The social worker may work alone in a private practice or as a part of a mental health staff in a clinic or hospital. She may also serve as a consultant on individual cases and in program development. Social workers are accredited by the National Association of Social Workers (NASW). The primary professional degree required for accreditation is a master's degree in social work (MSW).

Social Welfare System

The social welfare system provides many different types of services, including protective services, adoption and foster care, aid to families of dependent children, day care, family planning, group homes, health services, emergency services, housing, transportation and employment services. These services are primarily for individuals and families that lack the financial resources to purchase necessary human services or otherwise meet basic needs.

The size and scope of the social welfare system has created some problems in the effective delivery of social services through this system. Communication within a given service and between services has been difficult due to the large size of the social welfare system (Unger, 1974). Coordination between programs has also been difficult, and case management has lacked consistency. One family may receive several different social services that may or may not be complementary. Often no one has assumed responsibility for coordinating or monitoring those services. The delivery of the service becomes fragmentary, inefficient and ineffective. Some children and their families have needs that do not neatly fit the services of any one particular service, and therefore do not get the full attention of any single service provider.

Case management systems have been developed and implemented in some places that are designed to track client service utilization and monitor service delivery. Sensitivity to the need for improved communication and coordination and the development of policies and technologies to support case management should reduce problems in this area.

Social welfare system policies have changed over time; public assistance or income maintenance has generally come to be separated from service programs (Unger, 1974). This should contribute to the effective management and quality of services available.

Services of the social welfare system are primarily intended for indigent individuals and families, rather than for individuals with particular handicapping conditions. While emotional disturbance is not uniquely a problem of the socioeconomically disadvantaged, the socioeconomic characteristics of children and families may color in some very subtle ways the way they are viewed and the services they receive. For example, Bloom, Whiteman, and Deutsch (1965) observe that children from poor families do not do as well in school as other children. While many factors contribute to adjustment and achievement in school, the child's emotional well-being, including his self-esteem, is very much involved in his success as a student. Well-trained teachers recognize the process and cyclical nature of school failure, lowered self-concept, reduced motivation and resistance to learning that may be expressed in inappropriate and disruptive behavior and academic failure. Whelan (1977) describes this phenomenon and the need for intervening to break the failure cycle by helping the child succeed. (Specific approaches are discussed by Dickens and Epanchin in Chapter 13.)

The socioeconomic characteristics of a child and family may also influence the nature of the services received. Hollingshead and Redlich (1958), who found higher proportions of mental illness among lower socioeconomic groups, also found that the treatment a person received was more related to his socioeconomic class than the nature of the problem. Individuals from lower socioeconomic groups who were mentally ill were more likely to be institutionalized in a public facility and to receive electric shock and drugs.

Middle-class individuals were more likely to receive psychotherapy and less likely to be institutionalized. Upper-class individuals were more likely to receive long-term psychoanalysis from a psychoanalyst on a private basis. While this study focused on adults, it illustrates that socioeconomic factors are likely to be involved in the treatment of emotional disturbance.

Lastly, socioeconomic factors have an impact on the process by which a person comes to the attention of a service delivery system. Mercer (1973) and others have described the process by which a mentally retarded child is labeled and placed in a special class. While the law now requires culture-fair assessment and due process in placement, it would be naive to assume that socioeconomic factors have been completely removed from the labeling process. Chapters 8, 9 and 10 describe the ways in which core culture (middle-class) norms are taught and enforced in the school, serving as the standard against which social and behavioral differences are measured.

The primary professional worker in the social welfare system is the social worker. Social casework and community organization skills are generally more relevant to the social worker's role in the social welfare system than psychiatric skills. In addition to the professional social worker, volunteers help children and families served by the social welfare system in important ways. Their services range widely from in-home assistance, such as tutoring, to transportation to and from schools or treatment centers.

Legal-Correctional System

While we will not directly address the problems of delinquency and social maladjustment, we will look briefly at the vast array of services provided by the legal-correctional system for dependent and neglected children and youth, as well as juvenile offenders. Some of these children and youth are emotionally disturbed. Many, if not most, of them may be high risk for developing emotional or behavioral problems.

The juvenile court operates at the county level under the leadership of a judge who acts as an administrator and magistrate. The court has responsibility for the treatment and protection of delinquent, dependent and neglected youth. Atkinson (1974) divides juvenile correctional treatment into the following areas: (1) correctional treatment, that is, long-term, institutional postdispositional (after sentencing) treatment, (2) probation and other postdispositional treatment activities, and (3) detention, including predispositional holding centers.

The juvenile court's authority is exercised primarily through the mental health and social welfare systems. The judge has considerable control over the services provided to children and youth who are under the jurisdiction of the court. She is often responsible for programs such as foster and adoption home placements, group boarding homes, residential and aftercare service for dependent and neglected children, probation services and the distribution of child welfare money.

As with the institutional services of the mental health and social welfare systems, the legal correctional system encompasses different views of the nature and causes of behavioral deviance. Increasingly deviance is viewed as a complex interaction of many social, economic and biological factors (Rhodes & Paul, 1978). Models of the child as an "innocent victim," genetically inferior, or "mean" by nature are being replaced by more scientific and humanistic (interactional and developmental) views of the problems of juvenile crime and delinquency in society. As a result, rehabilitation and education are increasingly important in a system that historically emphasized security and custodial functions to the exclusion of positive programming. Community services are being developed to reduce long-term institutionalization. Also, the schools have turned to community-based family services and educational and technical training programs in their efforts to reduce dropout rates and prevent delinquency.

The size of trained professional staffs of juvenile courts varies considerably. The social worker is frequently the primary professional providing juvenile court services. The correctional system often employs professionals from different clinical, corrective and educational disciplines. They may include forensic psychiatrists, psychologists, social workers, teachers, rehabilitation counselors, occupational therapists and others. If the child has been to juvenile court or if the court has for reasons of parental neglect assumed responsibility for providing services to the child, the teacher is most likely to interact with the juvenile court counselor or the probation officer. The training and professional backgrounds of these staff are extremely variable.

Religious System

Many professional services for emotionally disturbed children are provided by private sectarian-sponsored institutions and family and social service agencies. Pappenfort and Kilpatrick (1970) point out that 40.3% of the institutional programs for children are sponsored by sectarian organizations. Of the total number of dependent and neglected children in institutions, 57.1% are under sectarian sponsorship. Of particular relevance to teachers working with emotionally disturbed children, 48.5% of the institutions for emotionally disturbed children are sectarian-sponsored.

Petarsky (1974), in a review of the religious system and the delivery of human services, points out that, while sectarian-sponsored services comprise a considerable portion of the professional services available for children, their institutional services have declined dramatically in the last 30 years. This fact, of course, is in keeping with the movement toward deinstitutionalization and community-based alternatives observed in other service delivery systems. Petarsky points out that homemaker services, day foster care, therapeutic nurseries, foster homes and group homes have increased as large institutional programs have been reduced.

The full range of professional mental health, social service and educational disciplines are to be found in sectarian-sponsored services. Volunteers are also an important part of this system.

SUMMARY

The teacher of emotionally disturbed children needs to be aware of relevant services that exist in the community for these children and their families. The nature and quality of services vary widely from community to community.

Emotionally disturbed children often need more than one type of professional service, and it is essential that the services provided be coordinated so that the child and family receive maximum benefit and the community supports a minimum of duplication. In some instances teachers must work together with other professionals in planning and implementing services if coordination is to be effective.

The teacher sometimes has occasion to use a community service, for example, when a referral is indicated. Typically, the teacher cooperates with the special services staff of the school system rather than contacts the service directly. At other times the teacher is called upon to assist a community agency working with a child in his classroom or the child's family. In order to effectively use existing services or to offer assistance in planning, it is helpful for the teacher to have some understanding of current laws, policies and practices relating to services for emotionally disturbed children and their families. Specifically, the teacher should be aware of the mental health, social-welfare, legal-correctional and religious systems in the community and the services they provide.

There are many barriers to effectively integrating human services. Considerable progress has been made in human services integration, however, as the national human services policy has increasingly emphasized community-based services. The fiscal policies of the early eighties suggest that the efficient and effective integration and use of services will be increasingly important.

DISCUSSION QUESTIONS

1. What is the role of education in providing appropriate services for emotionally disturbed children and their families?
2. What are the barriers to effective interagency collaboration?
3. How have human service policy changes affected educational services for emotionally disturbed children?
4. Why is the teacher of emotionally disturbed children likely to communicate with professionals in other service systems?

REFERENCES

Albee, G. W. *Mental health manpower trends.* New York: Basic Books, 1956.

Atkinson, L. Treatment of deviance by the legal-correctional system. In W. C. Rhodes & S. Head (Eds.), *A study of child variance: Service delivery systems* (Vol. 3). Ann Arbor: University of Michigan Press, 1974.

Bailey, D. B., Jr., & Harbin, G. L. Nondiscriminatory evaluation. *Exceptional Children*, 1980, *46*(8).

Becker, H. *Outsiders: Studies in the sociology of deviance.* New York: Free Press, 1963.

Blatt, B. *Christmas in purgatory: A photographic essay on mental retardation.* Boston: Allyn & Bacon, 1966.

Bloom R., Whiteman, M., & Deutsch, M. Race and social class as separate factors related to social environment. *American Journal of Sociology*, 1965, *70*, 471–476.

Gillespie, E. *Student participation in the development of individualized education programs: Perspectives of parents and students.* Unpublished doctoral dissertation, University of North Carolina at Chapel Hill, 1981.

Goffman, E. *Asylums.* Garden City, N.Y.: Anchor Books, 1961.

Goldstein, H., Moss, J., & Jordon, L. *The efficacy of special class training on the development of mentally retarded children* (Cooperative Research Project No. 619). Washington, D.C.: U.S. Office of Education, Department of Health, Education and Welfare, 1965.

Gove, W. Labeling and mental illness: A critique. In W. Gove (Ed.), *The labeling of deviance: Evaluating a perspective.* New York: Halstead Press, 1975.

Hollingshead, A. B., & Redlich, F. C. *Social class and mental illness: A community study.* New York: John Wiley & Sons, 1958.

Kitsuse, J. The new conception of deviance and its critics. In W. Gove (Ed.), *The labeling of deviance: Evaluating a perspective.* New York: Halstead Press, 1975.

Mercer, J. R. *Labeling the mentally retarded.* Riverside, Calif.: University of California Press, 1973.

Mercer, J. R., & Lewis, J. F. *System of multi-cultural pluralistic assessment: Conceptual and technical manual.* Riverside, Calif.: Institute for Pluralistic Assessment Research and Training, 1978.

Morse, W. C. Crisis intervention in school, mental health and special classes for the disturbed. In N. J. Long, W. C. Morse & R. G. Newman (Eds.), *The education of children with problems* (2nd ed.). Belmont, Calif.: Wadsworth, 1971.

Pappenfort, D., & Kilpatrick, D. M. *A census of children's residential institutions in the United States, Puerto Rico and the Virgin Islands: 1966* (Vols. 1, 2, 4). Chicago: School of Social Services Administration, University of Chicago, 1970.

Paul, J. L., Neufeld, G. R., & Pelosi, J. W. *Child advocacy within the system.* Syracuse, N.Y.: Syracuse University Press, 1977.

Paul, J. L., Stedman, D. J., & Neufeld, G. R. *Deinstitutionalization: Program and policy development.* Syracuse, N.Y.: Syracuse University Press, 1977.

Petarsky, D. Treatment of deviance by religious institutions. In W. C. Rhodes & S. Head (Eds.), *A Study of child variance: Service delivery systems* (Vol. 3). Ann Arbor: University of Michigan Press, 1974.

Rhodes, W. C. Beyond theory and practice: Implications in programming for children with emotional disabilities. *Behavior Disorders,* 1980, *5* (4), 254–263.

Rhodes, W. C., & Head, S. *A study of child variance: Service delivery systems* (Vol. 3). Ann Arbor: University of Michigan Press, 1974.

Rhodes, W. C., & Paul, J. L. *Emotionally disturbed and deviant children: New view and approaches.* Englewood Cliffs, N.J.: Prentice-Hall, 1978.

Szasz, T. S. *The myth of mental illness.* New York: Hoeber-Harper, 1964.

Turnbull, A. P., & Strickland, B. Parents and the Educational System. In J. L. Paul (Ed.), *Understanding and working with parents of children with special needs.* New York: Holt, Rinehart & Winston, 1981.

Turnbull, H. R. Parents and the law. In J. L. Paul (Ed.), *Understanding and working with parents of children with special needs.* New York: Holt, Rinehart & Winston, 1981.

Turnbull, H. R., & Turnbull, A. P. Deinstitutionalization and the law. In J. L. Paul, D. J. Stedman & G. R. Neufeld (Eds.), *Deinstitutionalization: Program and policy development.* New York: Syracuse University Press, 1977.

Turnbull, H. R., & Turnbull, A. P. Procedural due process and the education of handicapped children. *Focus on Exceptional Children,* 1978, *9,* 1–12.

Unger, C. Treatment of deviance by the social welfare system. In W. C. Rhodes & S. Head (Eds.). *A study of child variance: Service delivery systems* (Vol. 3). Ann Arbor: University of Michigan Press, 1974.

Whelan, R. J. Human understanding of human behavior. In A. J. Pappanikou & J. L. Paul (Eds.), *Mainstreaming emotionally disturbed children*. Syracuse, N.Y.: Syracuse University Press, 1977.

Wolfensberger, W., & Zauha, H. *Citizen advocacy and protective services for the impaired and handicapped*. Washington, D.C.: National Institute on Mental Retardation, 1973.

3
Educational Services for Emotionally Disturbed Children

main points

1 The education of emotionally disturbed children is a relatively recent phenomenon.

2 A continuum of services is required by law to be available to the emotionally disturbed child.

3 Many emotionally disturbed children will be served in the regular classroom, with supportive services provided to the child or the teacher.

4 Many will be served in full- or part-time special classes.

5 Some will be educated in special day or residential schools.

6 Many intervenors, such as counselors, administrators and parents, may be involved in an educational program for the disturbed child.

7 A variety of settings, such as camps and open classrooms, have been utilized for the education of the disturbed child.

8 The individual needs of the child should be taken into account in selecting an educational program.

THIS CHAPTER presents an overview of the educational services available to emotionally disturbed children. The focus is not on the methods of interventions but rather on the types of settings within which those interventions, whether behavioral, psychodynamic, bio-medical or ecological, take place.

Educational services for disturbed children range from relatively low-intensity services for mildly disturbed children in regular classrooms, through resource services provided on an "as needed" basis, to more intensive services for seriously disturbed children in special classes and special schools. In addition, educational services are provided by persons other than teachers and in settings other than schools.

The educational system is the one system required to provide services for all children. All children, including the emotionally disturbed, are required by law to attend school. School is, therefore, different from the

---

This chapter was written by **Mark Montgomery**, University of North Carolina at Charlotte.

mental health center which is a resource only to those who choose to go. School is also different in that its primary focus is on the child who does not have a handicap, whereas the special human service delivery systems (see Chapter 2) focus primarily on the child or family with special needs. The school exists in a community and each community has a particular network of human services. Emotionally disturbed children and their familes often require more than one kind of professional service in the community. They are most appropriately served if those services are effectively coordinated in the community.

The Development of Educational Services

The special education of emotionally disturbed children is not even two decades old. Before the 1960s the notion that teachers could make a significant contribution to the growth and development of these children was, to many, heresy. Schooling was viewed as something that needed to wait until the child's emotional problems had been successfully treated. At that time, only 20 years ago, the staff members of a special school for emotionally disturbed children were suspected of practicing medicine without a license since emotional disturbance, or mental illness, was considered primarily a medical responsibility. At this same time, Project ReEducation (Chapter 8) was developed to evaluate the proposition that teachers could work effectively with emotionally disturbed children. Ironically, the students in this training program had to be placed in special residential treatment centers across this country, England, France, Scotland and Canada, because appropriate public school programs were not available for this purpose.

The experience of schools with children labeled emotionally disturbed is therefore relatively brief. To understand the events that led up to the school's assumption of educational responsibility for these children, a deeper historical perspective is required. For more on the history of special services see Kanner (1970).

Prior to the 19th century, emotional disturbance was largely considered to be a mystical phenomenon. That is, strange behavior was usually explained as the result of demonic possession in some form or other—a manifestation of evil. Children thus affected were shunned by the larger community, and often even by their parents. The notion of humanness was so narrow that children who were aggressive, hallucinatory or self-destructive were thought to be changelings, and no longer human at all, or under the influence of satanic forces, and probably forever lost to humanity.

It was not until the mid 1800s that much interest in the description and classification of various forms of disturbance arose. Scientists, particularly physicians, began to observe and describe very carefully the characteristics and behavior of "insane" children, constructing elaborate and detailed case studies. The prevalent feeling, even among scientists, was still that disturbed behavior was the result of evil in some form, although it was becoming obvious that it might manifest itself in a variety of ways.

Later in the century, various investigators began to posit other, more immediate causes of disturbance. Genetic inferiority, atmospheric conditions, dietary imbalances and the like were considered possible causes. There was still little attention given to treatment of the emotionally disturbed, let alone their education, since disturbance was generally thought to be irreversible.

The early 20th century was a time of greater optimism. Vigorous attempts were made to increase the specificity of diagnosis. Pinpointed diagnoses, it was thought, would eventually lead to prescription. Psychodynamic theory, with its emphasis on quasi-medical classifications, was in vogue. Freud's successes held the promise, long-awaited, of a cure for the emotionally disturbed.

The 1940s and 1950s saw increased attempts at direct bio-medical intervention, through drugs, electroshock and psychosurgery. At the same time, pioneer work was being conducted in a new area that would revolutionize the way in which emotionally disturbed children would be treated. The development of behavioral technology seemed to signal the end of the view of emotional disturbance as an irreversible problem.

The 1960s saw further developments in behavioral methods, and in the use of psychoactive drugs to reduce unwanted feelings and behaviors in emotionally disturbed children. Also, a variety of therapies were being developed and proposed by psychologists and counselors in the humanistic movement, as part of a general trend to free individuals of their "hang-ups." In 1964, Morse, Cutler and Fink published a report on *Public School Classes for the Emotionally Handicapped*. Among their findings: in 1962, only 30 states claimed to have public programs for emotionally handicapped children. In fact, only 306 such programs were in existence across the country, and many of these were to be found in institutions and hospitals. The authors estimated that there were perhaps 160 special programs for emotionally disturbed children in U.S. public schools.

In the late 1960s the issue of mainstreaming began to get a tremendous amount of attention. Dunn's landmark position paper (1968), written as he was stepping down as president of the Council for Exceptional Children, was one of many scholarly and popular articles on the subject (Christopolos & Renz, 1969; Lilly, 1970; Deno, 1970; Burrello, Tracy & Schultz, 1973). The issue centered around the benefits of integrated versus segregated settings for handicapped children. Some argued that integrating handicapped children into the mainstream would enhance their self-concepts and social development (Knoblock, 1973). Segregated settings, they said, were emotionally and socially stigmatizing to handicapped children (Jones, 1972).

Others were opposed to mainstreaming. Such a system, it was thought, would be unfair, not only to the handicapped children but to the nonhandicapped children and teachers who would be expected to help them become integrated. Some of the fears expressed were that classroom teachers would not modify the curriculum to be appropriate for handicapped children and that their nonhandicapped peers would not socially accept them (Kolstoe, 1972; Smith & Arkans, 1974).

As rhetoric gave way to research, a number of reports of mainstreaming programs began to appear in the literature. Most compared the academic gains or social adjustment of mildly handicapped (retarded, learning disabled, emotionally disturbed) children in integrated programs, that is, programs where the student spends much of his or her day in the regular classroom, with comparable groups of children in self-contained special classes (Vacc, 1972; Shotel, Iano & McGettigan, 1972; Iano, Ayers, Heller, McGettigan & Walker, 1974). The weight of the evidence from these studies seemed to support the mainstreaming concept, although methodological problems in this sort of research were immediately recognized (MacMillan, 1971; Nelson & Schmidt, 1970).

In 1975, when Public Law 94-142, the Education for All Handicapped Children Act, was signed by President Ford, mainstreaming became a legal rather than a research issue. Questions of efficacy were temporarily put aside. Instead, most special educators turned their attention to strategies for implementing mainstream programs. These strategies included in-service training for regular teachers (Harasymiw & Horne, 1976), the creation or refinement of supportive roles for special educators (Miller & Sabatino, 1978; Morse, 1980), and the development of new models for special class and resource room programs (Wiederholt, 1975; O'Connor, Stuck & Wyne, 1979; Hewett & Taylor, 1980).

The current challenge for special education is twofold. First, questions of efficacy, left unanswered in 1975, need to be reconsidered. Beyond that, they need to be recast to fit the times. No longer is it appropriate to think of special or regular class placement as the only alternative. Rather, the effectiveness of various programs at all levels of the continuum of services (regular class with support, part-time special class, full-time special class, special school, institution) needs to be measured.

In spite of the "zero reject" principle of P.L. 94-142, there remain a large number of emotionally disturbed children who are either not served or underserved. According to a study funded by the Office of Special Education (Grosenick & Huntze, 1980), approximately 741,000 emotionally disturbed children are unserved in the U.S. The authors go on to say that over $900 million is needed to meet the basic service needs in this area, and that even this amount will not address the problem of the underserved or inappropriately served. Thus, the second challenge for special education is to find ways to secure funds in difficult financial times, for more, better, and more cost-beneficial services.

Currently, every state in the United States, as well as the District of Columbia, Puerto Rico and American Samoa, offers special educational programs for emotionally disturbed children in the public schools. While incidence figures and definitions vary widely (Hirshoren & Heller, 1979), all states seem to recognize the need for specialized educational programming for these children.

P.L. 94-142 requires that each child identified as emotionally disturbed (e.g., behaviorally disordered, emotionally handicapped) be provided with an Individualized Education Plan. The IEP spells out the educational goals for the child, as well as the instructional services that will enable these goals to be attained. Besides academic goals, the IEP is to deal with socialization or behavioral goals, and to specify appropriate therapeutic intervention (see Chapter 14).

Another provision of P.L. 94-142 is that a full range of services be made available to children with special needs. This continuum of services is conceived as representing various levels of intensity and restrictiveness. Further, each child is to be placed in the "least restrictive" (most normal) setting that is appropriate to her needs. The typical programs at each level of the service continuum, which we will consider in this chapter, include the following:

1. *Regular classroom.* At this level, emotionally disturbed children are housed fully within the regular class, under the direction of a teacher. The children found here are the least problematic, although they will still have an IEP spelling out the kinds of services they will receive from the classroom teacher.
2. *Supportive services.* Here again the child is found in the regular classroom. In addition, however, the child or the teacher receives diagnostic counseling or consultation from a specially trained support person.
3. *Special class.* At this level of the continuum, the child leaves the classroom for all or part of the day. She receives direct instruction or therapy from a specially trained teacher.
4. *Special school.* Here the child goes to a school designed to meet the needs of seriously emotionally disturbed children.
5. *Institution.* In this most restrictive setting, the child has been placed in a corrective facility or mental hospital and receives an educational program in conjunction with other institutional services.

The Regular Classroom Teacher

Rationale for Service

With the passage of P.L. 94-142 and its requirement that handicapped children be served in the least restrictive alternative environment, regular class placement has become a real possibility for some emotionally disturbed children who had previously been excluded. Thus, the regular classroom teacher must be prepared to integrate at least some emotionally disturbed children into the mainstream of the school, with or without supportive services from specially trained therapists.

There are four ways in which the regular classroom teacher may be called upon to be the primary intervenor for emotionally disturbed children.

1. *Prevention.* Perhaps the most important function of the regular classroom teacher regarding intervention for the emotionally disturbed is prevention. The classroom teacher can, by making the classroom a healthy, productive, responsive place, help children deal with anxiety, frustration, hostility and maladaptive behavior. To the extent that this can be accomplished, the need for intervention by specialists is reduced.
2. *Referral.* Frequently the classroom teacher is the first to recognize the need for specialized intervention. It is incumbent on the teacher to be sensitive to the behavior and feelings of all students. It is important that the teacher know the procedures for making an informal or

formal referral for additional assessment or services when the need arises.
3. *Carrying out the IEP.* There is nothing in P.L. 94-142 that requires that the IEP be implemented by a specialist. The classroom teacher, therefore, may very well be the one to work toward the goals written down on that document. If the school-based committee has functioned properly, the regular teacher will have been involved in making decisions about placement and program for the child. Also, the committee, including the teacher, will have judged the teacher capable of carrying out the instructional objectives listed in the IEP.
4. *Coordinating services.* While the regular classroom teacher may be called upon to carry out the IEP alone, more commonly the IEP is a joint effort of the regular teacher and one or more specialists. If, as is often the case, the child has a regular class as a home base, then the classroom teacher will be managing the comings and goings of the child. Programmatic cooperation among the various professionals who serve the child, including the classroom teacher, is usually necessary.

Prevention

The most common conditions that may lead to educational disturbance in the classroom are academic frustration, confusion, isolation, boredom and intentional noncompliance. For each of these conditions the teacher can employ certain techniques that will help prevent emotional disturbance.

Academic frustration. It is not unusual for a child who is frustrated in his academic performance to strike out at the system. Children, after all, are not in school by choice; they are compelled to attend. If we add to that compulsion academic tasks that are unrealistically difficult, boring, or insulting, we are asking for trouble.

The most obvious way to reduce academic frustration is to make academic tasks appropriate for the child. Not only must the individual's cognitive ability be taken into consideration, but also various aspects of her learning style. There are two major approaches to this individualization of instruction. In the first, each child is assessed to yield information on abilities, aptitudes, modality preferences, and so forth. A profile is then compiled and a program is designed to meet these individual needs. In the second approach, the classroom is set up to allow students to select the kind and level of activity that best suits their needs.

Confusion. Children who are unsure of how they fit into the class, who are not clear about the allowable limits of classroom behavior, or who do not see consistencies in class rules and their enforcement are likely to attempt to find clarity. One of the ways in which some children try to clarify the classroom situation is to test the teacher.

In order for children to feel comfortable in the classroom, they must be aware of the structure and order that are required by the teacher. This structure makes the events in the classroom predictable for the child. One of the ways in which teachers establish this predictability is by making public the class rules. These rules should ideally be the result of discussion between the teacher and the students, allowing the latter to feel that they are active participants in establishing patterns of acceptable behavior. Public schedules of daily, weekly and monthly routines also make the environment more predictable to the students.

Isolation. Another typical response to unpleasant situations is withdrawal. It is not unusual to see children isolate themselves within classrooms, not feeling at home in the room. Not only does this isolation make these children difficult to teach, it sets up a potentially dangerous situation, one in which the child has no natural outlet for the normal emotions that need expression—anger, joy, fear, caring.

Providing students with opportunities to participate is an important means of preventing or reducing feelings of isolation. Steps toward this goal include displaying the work of children, making sure that all children are given a chance to answer and to ask questions, allowing natural play groups to develop, encouraging nonparticipators to join in, having children work in "teams," and using *ad hoc* rather than permanent groupings.

Boredom. All sorts of noncompliant behaviors result from boredom. Most of them (e.g., out of seat, punching, talking) are so typical as to cause teachers little concern. More unusual behaviors (e.g., head banging, stealing), however, may be attempts to add stimulation to an otherwise barren environment.

The teacher is responsible for providing activities for students that are relevant to their immediate lives and that promote active involvement. There is nothing wrong with making learning fun. It is when learning is seen as a chore that trouble starts. Variety can also help. Tasks that, when repeated interminably, could be boring can be made more interesting when introduced in a variety of ways. The reverse is also true. Activities that are interesting can become boring through constant repetition.

Intentional noncompliance. This is one that we don't like to talk about. While it may be true that "there are no bad kids," there are children who go out of their way to disrupt the flow of classroom activities. Whether this is disturbance, or a natural response to an unpleasant situation, cases do arise where, through subversion or confrontation, students attack the system.

A child will attack a system that she considers "bad." This is true for all of us. In order to elicit cooperation rather than confrontation, the wise teacher will attempt to be seen as one who has the interest of the child at heart.

Referral and Intervention

The teacher is often the one to begin the referral process, which leads to the ultimate certification of a child as emotionally disturbed. Once the referral has been made, the teacher is usually asked to give information to a school-based committee, which is responsible for writing the IEP, on the

Academic frustration can be reduced by adjusting learning tasks to the child's ability and learning style.

child's academic and social skills and behavior. With this in mind, the teacher can take several steps to become an integral part of this process.

1 *Keep records.* The classroom teacher should document observations of a child and the class situation that is causing concern. His records may take the form of anecdotal records, behavior checklists, samples of work and so forth (see Chapter 4). Not only will this information be important to the other members of the school-based committee, but it may help the teacher discover ways of dealing with the situation without going on with the referral process.
2 *Know the process.* A classroom teacher should become aware of the procedures used in the school and school system for referring, screening, assessing, placing and re-evaluating the child. The special educator or principal should be a source of this information.
3 *Try to solve the problem first.* The classroom teacher may be able to deal with the problem without a formal certification and placement. Toward this end the teacher should consult with others, read printed informational materials and use problem-solving skills in order to find a workable solution. Only after all of these fail should a teacher consider beginning the time-consuming process of legal certification.
4 *Participate actively in the screening.* During the time when the child is being screened and evaluated for special placement, the classroom teacher can be a vital member of the school-based committee. The classroom teacher, after all, has generally had the most contact with the child, and can provide the bulk of the information on classroom

behavior, academic strengths and needs, and relationships with classmates.
5. *Participate actively in writing the IEP*. Classroom reachers often feel a bit intimidated by the other members of the school-based committee—psychologists, specialists, administrators. It is important, however, that this feeling be overcome. The classroom teacher has expertise to bring to the situation which should allow him to participate as an equal with the rest of the committee. What is more, the classroom teacher is often the one who will be responsible for much of the child's instruction. Therefore, the teacher should contribute to the behavioral and academic goals and objectives selected by the committee.

Once a child has been certified as emotionally disturbed, she is placed in the least restrictive appropriate setting. Since this may be the regular classroom, the classroom teacher should be able to implement strategies for dealing with these children effectively. The exact nature of the interventions to be used in the classroom will be spelled out by the school-based committee and recorded on the child's IEP. The teacher needs to be sure of what the committee expects and should seek help from other members of the committee if there is a need for additional skills.

The Support Specialist

One of the trends in special education is toward more contact and, it is hoped, more cooperation between special and regular educators. Much of the impetus for this movement has come as a result of P.L. 94-142 and its requirement for handicapped children to be placed in the least restrictive appropriate setting. It is generally acknowledged that, if this setting is to be the regular classroom, teachers need supportive services as they attempt to deal effectively with the problems that these children may represent.

The Nature of Supportive Services

Several types of supportive services have been implemented.

1. *Diagnostic services.* In some cases, specially trained professionals have been made available to classroom teachers for providing them with diagnostic information that can be used for educational programming. They might, for instance, gather behavioral data or perform formal or informal educational assessments. As part of the school-based committee, these persons participate in writing the child's IEP.
2. *Consultative services.* The use of special educators by classroom teachers for help in dealing with learning and behavior problems is a growing phenomenon (Prouty, 1970; McKenzie, Egner, Knight, Perelman, Schneider & Garvin, 1970; Montgomery, 1978). Here the special educator attempts, through a variety of means, to assist the classroom teacher in developing those skills necessary to deal effectively with the emotionally disturbed child within the regular school

setting. For a more detailed description of the special educator as consultant, see Chapter 8.

3 *Crisis intervention.* A number of models have been developed for providing services to children in crisis (Redl, 1959; Morse, 1980). This typically involves short-term counseling or remediation, which is designed to enable the child to stay in the regular classroom to the maximum extent possible.

4 *Service broker.* The special educator is often in a position to act as a liaison between the school and other service agencies in the community. Acting as a broker for the school, the special teacher can contact such services and coordinate their efforts on behalf of the disturbed child.

A vital prerequisite for the support specialist is the development of a good working relationship with the rest of the school, particularly with the regular classroom teachers. While this is perhaps the most obvious requirement, it is also the most difficult to accomplish. Several facts of school life make real cooperation between the specialist and the classroom teacher extremely difficult.

The teacher and specialist have conflicting affiliations. The specialist, by and large, has been exposed to training that gives him an affiliation with a specific discipline and, in many cases, a specific therapy, program or theoretical orientation. The classroom teacher, on the other hand, typically has come through an eclectic teacher training program.

A fundamental truth of the culture and organization of the school is that each teacher has a territory within which he operates (Becker, 1953; Sara-

The support specialist works directly with the teacher on learning and behavior problems of children in their classes.

> ### The Crisis-Resource Teacher
>
> It was near the end of fourth period. Mrs. Green was in the Resource Room working with Tommy on a science reading assignment. Tommy had come to the room at the beginning of the period. His teacher had sent him there because he was disrupting the class. Mrs. Green tried to cool him off by talking about his behavior, helping him to see the situation clearly. She had then asked him to take out his science book, which he found difficult to read.
>
> They were making progress. Tommy was much more relaxed than he had been when he came in. Mrs. Green was able to get him to try the reading. With her help, Tommy was able to deal with a task that had upset him in the regular class. She was just about to ask Tommy to return to his class and try again when Sue came in.
>
> Sue had been in math class when she had become angry. She had yelled at one of her friends, cursed at the teacher when he tried to intervene, and stormed out of the class. She arrived at the Resource Room still puffing with anger. This was not unusual for Sue. At the beginning of the year, when the Crisis-Resource Room was established, she had learned that this was the place to go when she was mad, upset or depressed. It was better than always going to the assistant principal.
>
> Mrs. Green asked Tommy to go back to class and to come back the next day after fourth period, so she could check on his progress. She then turned her attention to Sue.

son, 1971; Waller, 1932). This territory is usually a classroom. Even in open schools where the physical space is not divided into recognizable units, there remains a psychological territory, within which a single teacher is dominant. It is a common phenomenon, by the way, for teachers in open schools to attempt to demarcate territory by the use of bookcases, movable partitions and other furniture (Rivlin & Rothenberg, 1976).

Along with territory, each teacher assumes ownership over a group of children. Teachers are used to referring to children as "my students," or "Mrs. Smith's kids." It is taken for granted that these children are the direct responsibility of one teacher. So-called team teaching arrangements are usually characterized by divided responsibility rather than shared responsibility (Bredo, 1977).

Teachers and specialists tend to have different views on what "help" is. Teachers generally define help in terms of material assistance (Lortie, 1975). Thus, teachers may ask for fewer students, relief from paperwork or money for materials. Less often, teachers might ask for help with "problem students." According to the ethos of the school, however, this help is asked for, never imposed. Teachers may maintain isolation, along with the autonomy that obtains, if they wish (Sarason, 1971).

This isolation puts specialists in a difficult position since they often are obliged to provide help to teachers who have not asked for it. One of the problems with professional helpers, from the teachers' point of view, is that "they (specialists) define help in terms of what the *teacher* can do with the

> **The Consulting Teacher**
>
> Mr. Ericson is a busy man. Although he has no scheduled classes, and is not responsible for the ongoing education of any specific children, he has one of the most demanding jobs in the school.
>
> As a school-based educational consultant, Mr. Ericson works with teachers on learning and behavior problems that they face in their classes. Teachers make referrals to Mr. Ericson, which he uses as the starting point for his service. He makes observations in classrooms, meets with the referring teachers, conducts series of experimental teaching sessions with the referred students, writes up "prescriptions" for the classroom teachers, does demonstration lessons in classes and follows up on the cases as the teachers deal with problem situations.
>
> His primary concern is for those children who have been certified as needing special education services but who are based in regular classrooms. By working directly with teachers, however, he is able also to have an impact on the education of noncertified children. Thus, as teachers become more skilled in dealing with school-related problems, they are able to handle a wider range of behaviors in their classrooms.
>
> A typical day for Mr. Ericson might be summed up this way: Before school—meet with a teacher to set up a series of experimental sessions with five children in her room; give a "prescription" to another teacher. Morning—carry out an experimental session with four children; observe a classroom to see how a referred child performs; follow up on prescriptions given to two teachers. Lunch—eat with a teacher and discuss the progress of one of her children. Afternoon—carry out two experimental sessions; give a demonstration lesson. After school—have a conference with a teacher to go over a prescription; attend a school-based committee meeting.

child" (Sarason, 1971, p. 157). Thus, they are seen as adding to, rather than subtracting from, the teacher's workload. From the specialists' point of view, indirect help may be the only kind they are able to give, either because of their training or their own workloads. The reluctance of teachers to accept this kind of assistance is seen as resistance to change (Abidin, 1975) or an abdication of professional responsibility (Montgomery, 1978).

Special Considerations

Given the teachers' wariness of supportive services, special attention to certain aspects of the school environment and teacher concerns will help to ensure the acceptance and success of the programs proposed by the special educator.

Establishing the program. The way in which a program is instituted will have a real effect on the way in which it is evaluated. To the maximum extent possible, the support of the school principal and the faculty should be sought for any program that redefines the role of the special educator within the school. Schools are mini-communities. The school community, incidentally, does not always include the special education supervisor. Support from this person, then, is not as vital as support from those within the school. Parents should be informed of the kind of service to be provided. A presentation at a PTA meeting will go a long way toward reducing the misconceptions that inevitably accompany any educational innovation.

Overcoming territoriality. There are three problems here. First, the perception of ownership of kids must be overcome. The classroom teacher is apt to think of the certified children as belonging to the specialist and the noncertified kids as being his own. One way to reduce this perception is for the specialist to refer to the certified children as the teacher's when discussing them with the teacher. The specialist must resist the temptation to claim ownership of any students.

A second problem is the territorial boundary that surrounds the regular classroom. The specialist's job requires violation of this territory in order to observe, demonstrate techniques and so on. Some of the steps that can be taken to reduce the inevitable tension that entering a class causes are (a) getting permission before visiting a class, (b) making frequent and brief visits, (c) not making eye contact with the teacher during class observations, (d) not writing anything down while in the classroom, (e) sitting down and staying put while there, and (f) finding an opportunity to compliment a teacher on something done during the visit.

The third problem is helping teachers to overcome their reluctance to invade the resource room territory. Teachers must be shown that the room is a resource for the entire school, that materials are available to them on loan, that a coffee pot for teachers' use is handy. The specialist can look for ways to attract teachers to the room. The more they are there, the less they are likely to feel that the room is the specialist's exclusive domain.

Providing service. Teachers are not used to interpreting consultation or crisis assistance as service. In talking with teachers, therefore, specialists need to make sure that teachers see them as valuable aids. The specialist can demonstrate his usefulness by providing materials to teachers, finding opportunities to listen to their concerns about the students, bringing together teachers with similar or complementary interests, or lending out professional books. By being the first one to school each day, the last to leave, and the busiest while there, the specialis can show teachers he works very hard to provide service. Apperance counts.

Job description. It is important for the special educator to have an official job description that spells out, in writing, the things that he is supposed to do and, just as importantly, the things that he is not allowed to do. The teacher's knowledge that the special educator is not allowed to tutor kids in reading, or work with noncertified children, for instance, takes a lot of pressure off the specialist and helps to maintain the integrity of the program.

Program evaluation. Program evaluation is necessary for three reasons. First, special educators need to be able to justify their programs as a valuable service—to supervisors, principals, parents and classroom teachers—even though they do not have regular classes. Second, this justification is important to the specialists themselves. Teachers, regular or special, have been conditioned to define their worth in terms of their direct effect, in the form of teaching, on students. In order for specialists to feel good about what they are doing, they need to keep records of the kinds of changes (in teachers as well as in students) that they are able to make. Finally, evaluation information is important to the specialist for making program decisions. By being in constant touch with the effects of the program, he has information that can be used to improve its services.

While such information might be as simple as a folder that includes an anecdotal record of behavior changes observed, comments by teachers, new methods or materials used by teachers, improvement in students' grades and records of school disciplinary action, some specific guidelines can assist the teacher in collecting information program evaluation.

1. *Delineate standards.* Examine the state and local guidelines governing the program; review the professional literature; discuss the program with the school principal, teachers, the special education supervisor and parents. Then delineate the standards that the program should meet.
2. *Conduct needs assessment.* Compare the existing program with the standards; ask others for their opinions. Describe the ways in which the program needs improvement (e.g., "More parental involvement is needed in writing and carrying out IEPs.").
3. *Establish goals.* Turn the needs into goal statements which generally describe what should happen (e.g., "Parents will become more involved in writing and carrying out IEPs.").
4. *Set objectives.* List specific, concrete steps that can be reasonably achieved by a given date (e.g., "By November 1, 198-, 60% of the parents of children in the ED program will have contributed specific suggestions to be included in their child's IEP.").
5. *Specify activities.* List the things that must be done in order to achieve each objective (e.g., "Make phone calls to all parents; send mailings home.").
6. *Document outcomes.* Keep records on the attainment of the stated objectives. Also helpful is information that compares the existing program with other, similar, programs, or compares this year's program with those in previous years (Tuckman, 1979).

The Special Class

There may always be some children who cannot be successfully maintained in the regular classroom, even with supportive services from a special education teacher. Within the area of emotional disturbance, this group would include children whose behavior is so disturbing to the class, or who are so impervious to ordinary management and instruction techniques, as to make a segregated, self-contained placement necessary.

> **The Full-Time Special Education Teacher**
>
> Mr. Newman is responsible for the ongoing education of seven elementary school students certified as "emotionally disturbed." Together with Mrs. Adams, an instructional aide, Mr. Newman provides instruction in all academic areas to the students.
>
> Mr. Newman's room is somewhat smaller than a regular classroom. In it are a number of learning centers, a reading corner, a time-out booth, and tables and chairs.
>
> Since the students are on several reading and math levels (third through sixth grade), Mr. Newman must have available a wide variety of materials. The specific academic goals for each student are spelled out in the IEPs.
>
> Also listed in the IEPs are the social and behavioral goals for each child. In order to reach these goals, Mr. Newman uses a combination of behavior modification and counseling techniques. Thus, there is a token economy, in which each student is reinforced with plastic tokens for appropriate behaviors. These tokens can be traded in at the end of the week for free time or for posters which Mr. Newman got free from a local record store. Besides the behavior modification program, Mr. Newman uses Class Meetings as a way of helping the kids deal with their frustration and anger. These meetings are also times for talking about current events, social skills and class rules.
>
> Five of the students in Mr. Newman's class are mainstreamed into certain subjects. That is, they join other regular classes for special subjects. Two of the boys have reading instruction in regular classes. Mr. Newman and the regular teachers meet every week or so to discuss the progress of the boys.

The special class has several advantages for providing services to seriously emotionally disturbed children. One of them is segregation. The special class, being separated from the rest of the school, can be designed in such a way as to allow the teacher to create a controlled, therapeutic environment. The curricular constraints and social milieu of the regular class can be replaced with a structure more relevant to the needs of the children. Smallness is another advantage. Typical special classes for the emotionally disturbed contain about 6 to 10 students. This small number of children allows the teacher to provide more intensive attention to the students. Also, most classes are provided with an instructional or therapeutic aide to maximize adult contact with the students. The theraeutic focus of the special class is another plus. Special classes, relieved of regular classroom demands, allow the teacher to give more time to therapeutic intervention than would be possible in supportive services programs.

Conscientious programs for the emotionally disturbed expect growth in children. This growth is accompanied by changes in the kinds of treatment needed, and in the structure of the program offered to the child. Some of the changes that are found in most special class programs are

> ### The Part-time Special Education Teacher
>
> Ms. Mays calls her room a Resource Room. There are 33 children certified as emotionally disturbed, learning disabled or mentally retarded that she works with each day.
>
> Children come to Ms. Mays in groups of four to six for remedial work in a variety of academic subjects. She groups the kids according to the specific skills that are listed on their IEPs. Thus she might work with one group on beginning consonant skills, another on two-place multiplication and a third on syllabication.
>
> The emotionally disturbed children on her roll are there because of frustration, anger or helplessness they have shown in attempting academic tasks. Ms. Mays tries to present the work in such a way that it is interesting and nonthreatening. Besides working with the children, Ms. Mays is responsible for coordinating each IEP. This includes doing educational assessments on each child, and conferring with their classroom teachers, in order to coordinate the two experiences.
>
> The Resource Room is the center of a great deal of activity. Children come and go, work at various stations in the room and are instructed by Ms. Mays or her aide. When no children are coming to work, Ms. Mays makes observations in classrooms, plans lessons, talks with teachers or tests children.

1. *From rigid to flexible scheduling.* Most programs plan for every minute of each child's day initially. As the child becomes more competent, greater flexibility is gradually introduced into the schedule.
2. *From external to internal control.* The child is heavily controlled, reinforced, planned for or supervised as she enters the program. With treatment she begins to take more responsibility for herself.
3. *From short-term to long-term goals.* Initially, the child may be working under a system that sets hour by hour, or perhaps daily, goals to work toward. The aim of most programs, however, is for the child to be able to operate with long-term goals, with rewards deferred for several days or even weeks.
4. *From segregation to integration.* Special classes by their very nature remove the emotionally disturbed child from the company of her peers. This, it is thought, is necessary in order to provide her with an environment consistent with her needs. As the child becomes more well-adjusted, however, and re-entry into the regular program becomes a possibility, both the child and the receiving classrooms need to be prepared for this eventuality. Such re-integration is, in the best situations, undertaken gradually and with the understanding of all those involved.

Most special classes have in common the characteristic of segregation and exclusiveness, but these classes vary in several respects. First, the degree to which the class adheres to a "program" varies a great deal. Some classes

> ### The "Engineered Classroom"
>
> This program, developed by Hewett (1967), is intended to help children move from primitive to more civilized forms of behavior. The classroom curriculum, and the physical space itself, is divided up into three areas: Order, Exploratory and Mastery. The Order Center is designed to increase children's ability to pay attention, to make responses and to follow directions. Materials include puzzles, worksheets and space in which to work. Group communication skills and exploratory skills are developed in the Exploratory Center, where listening activities and simple science experiments are conducted. Finally, the Mastery Center involves desk work, either in group seating arrangements or in booths set aside for individuals.
>
> An initial assessment is conducted to determine where on the hierarchy of skills (attention, response, order, exploratory, social, mastery, achievement) the child is performing. This assessment, updated periodically, is the basis of the child's IEP.

> ### The "Zoomer Class"
>
> Weinstein (1975) conceived of the Zoomer Class as a transitional environment between the ReEd (re-education) school (Chapter 8) and the regular classroom. Its purpose is to provide children returning to class with a setting where their academic skills will accelerate enough to allow them to catch up with their peers.
>
> The child from the ReEd school is matched with a child from the receiving classroom. These "buddies" spend the morning in the Zoomer Class, working on basic reading and arithmetic skills, and the afternoon in a regular class for special subjects (e.g., art, music, social studies). The ReEd child is eased into the classroom milieu by her buddy.
>
> Each morning, class begins with a group discussion in which the teacher and students decide on the morning's activities, bring up concerns and resolve problems. The children then spend 90 minutes on basic academic skills. They may work for 90 minutes straight or take breaks whenever desired, but 90 minutes of actual work must be accomplished each day. The remainder of the morning is spent on individual projects, library research, field trips or games.

are spin-offs of research programs, or run by adherents of a particular theory, approach or method, and therefore are structured according to strict programmatic guidelines. Most programs, on the other hand, are more eclectic in nature, combining ideas, strategies and materials from a variety of other programs.

Another way in which classrooms vary is in the relative emphasis placed on behavorial and affective goals. While many programs depend, to some

> ### Developmental Therapy
>
> This program, developed by Wood (1972), encourages disturbed children to interact positively with each other, their environment and, ultimately, the regular classroom. Each child's development is assessed according to five stages.
>
> The first stage, Responding to the Environment with Pleasure, is for children with profound problems in trusting the environment. The teacher's role is to help the children find satisfaction and pleasure in activity rather than withdrawal. Activities involve concrete experiences and are predictable, simple and familiar.
>
> Stage Two is called Responding to the Environment with Success. A Stage Two Child has at least expressive and receptive speech but generally has the basic competencies and organizing skills for learning. The teacher's role is an active one, not only involving the children but also holding limits while encouraging exploration.
>
> Stage Three, Learning Skills for Successful Group Participation, marks a shift from teacher-directed, extrinsic structure and control to the beginnings of child control and direction. The child has more skills, an improved appreciation of self and greater awareness of the group. The teacher's role is that of group leader, and much of her time is spent helping children see the relationship between actions and consequences.
>
> In Stage Four, Investing in Group Processes, the teacher is involved in helping children enlarge their capacities to function in natural environments. The teacher's role is that of counselor and group leader, providing necessary guidance, direction, feedback, support and sense of caring about the child.
>
> Stage Five, Applying Individual and Group Skills in New Situations, is for children in regular schools who have been "provisionally terminated" from the program. Here the role of the developmental therapy teacher is that of friend to the child and consultant to the regular school.
>
> The task of the teacher, then, is to enable each child to progress through these developmental stages by providing him or her with appropriate social and academic experiences.

degree, on behavioral or learning principles, interventions, such as counseling and role playing, vary considerably.

A third source of variance is the particular mix of therapy and instruction. Some programs are set up primarily as therapeutic environments, where the first point of intervention is the emotional or behavioral disturbance. Academic goals are secondary. Other classes are established as educational interventions. Academic success, it is thought, is, in itself, therapeutic.

The potential drawbacks to the self-contained class have been widely recognized since the mainstreaming movement took hold in the late 1960s. Critics of this traditional form of special service delivery have pointed out the negative effects of segregation and the stigmatizing that results from labeling. In addition, it is felt by many that special education has been a one-way street. That is, once children are labeled and segregated, there is a tendency to leave them in special classes. Adapting children to this special environment has often not prepared them to be integrated into the larger school program.

On the other hand, proponents of self-contained classes have argued that stigmatization is actually reduced by having children separated from their nonhandicapped peers. When these children are out of sight, their differences are not as visible, and therefore not as socially damaging as they would be in an integrated setting, where differences in learning and behavior are obvious to their classmates.

In considering the pros and cons of self-contained classes, the teacher should keep in mind the letter and spirit of P.L. 94-142. Self-contained classes should be only one of the options available to emotionally disturbed children. Other, less restrictive placements must also exist as alternatives. Placement in segregated classes should be made with caution. The potential harm caused by this placement should be carefully weighed against its anticipated benefits. Moreover, mechanisms for re-integration must be available. Not only should the special class curriculum prepare children for eventual placement in regular classes, perhaps supplemented by supportive services, but there must also be a real effort on the part of the professionals involved to actively seek this re-integration.

The Special School

Schools which are exclusively devoted to the education of the emotionally disturbed may be public or private. Since these facilities are intended for the few severely disturbed children within the population, only largest urban school systems, if any, have their own such schools. Typically, such a school serves the needs of children from several surrounding school districts.

The disadvantages of segregation of children in special schools—stigmatization, isolation, lack of interaction with nonhandicapped children—are thought to be balanced by several factors.

1 *Environmental control.* The school can be designed with the emotionally disturbed in mind. This might include special rooms for counseling sessions, isolation or observation. Classrooms in special schools tend to be smaller and offer fewer distractions.
2 *Resources.* Specially trained personnel are usually employed in such schools for academic and therapeutic activities. Psychologists, psychiatrists and other support staff are also available to a larger extent than in regular schools.
3 *Continuity.* The school's curriculum, discipline policies and so forth can be kept consistent to a degree not usually possible in regular school, where different demands may be made on emotionally disturbed and nonhandicapped children.
4 *Staff support.* The special school is a setting where teachers understand each others' concerns and give each other meaningful support to counteract the frequently debilitating frustrations and anxieties involved in teaching the emotionally disturbed.

The phenomenon of *teacher burnout* is of growing concern to professional educators (Kyriacou & Sutliffe, 1979). This problem is particularly acute among teachers of the emotionally disturbed (Grosenick & Huntze, 1980). These children are likely to present the teacher with the kinds of problems that threaten a teacher most seriously (e.g., physical aggression, sexual acting-out, self-mutilation). A study of student problems relating to teacher stress (Gesten, 1978) points out that problems that occur often enough to become part of the routine (talking out in class or running in the hall, for instance), and for which there can be routine remedies, are not sources of much stress. It is the unexpected or bizarre problem that creates, because of its novelty, a stressful situation.

The special school for the emotionally disturbed has two advantages in relationship to burnout. First, the teachers are more likely to understand each others' problems, thus reducing the isolation and loneliness that increase stress (Knoblock & Goldstein, 1971). Second, the special school may be a place where "novel" problems occur more frequently and, therefore, can be readily handled through routine solutions.

Special schools for the emotionally disturbed may be either residential or day schools. In the former, the child lives on the campus of the school. In this environment she usually receives educational services from teachers, as well as individual or group therapy from a trained counselor, psychologist or psychiatrist. In addition, specially trained counselors, often called the "cottage staff" or "houseparents," work with the children on social living skills.

A comprehensive treatment plan is developed for each child. This plan is developed and monitored by a team, including representatives of the educational, therapeutic and residential staff, during periodic meetings. The Individualized Education Plan which is required by law for all children in residential schools is part of the overall treatment plan.

Some such schools, the ReEd schools for instance, make specific efforts to include the child's family in the treatment plan. Regardless of whether such involvement is direct, through family therapy, or indirect, through liaison services from a social worker, most residential schools try to coordinate efforts with the community.

Special day schools, such as Mark Twain School (Laneve & the Mark Twain Staff, 1980), are nonresidential. Children come to these schools during regular school hours for academic or vocational instruction. Individual or group therapy may or may not be offered. Academic and social goals will be listed in the IEP, developed by the same kind of school-based committee that has this responsibility in regular schools.

Other Intervenors and Other Settings

Other Intervenors in the School Setting

Parents. Although parents of the emotionally disturbed have sometimes been considered to be part of the problem (Wright, 1959), the role of the parents in the treatment and education of the emotionally disturbed is gaining increased attention. Various programs have been developed to train parents to work cooperatively with the school in reducing disturbance (Barach, 1969; Kroth, 1975; Glenurick & Barocas, 1979; Brown, 1980). P.L. 94-142 has formalized the relationship between the parent and the school, requiring that parents be involved at each step of the way in the identification, assessment, placement and treatment of their child. Educators have a duty to use this relationship for the benefit of the child, to actively seek out parental participation and to inform parents of their legal rights as well as ways in which they might join with the school as partners in the education and treatment of their child.

The school counselor. The school counselor is often in a position to provide services to supplement academic intervention from the regular or special teacher. Many counselors offer crisis intervention and group or individual counseling for troubled children. In addition, some counselors provide workshops for teachers on topics such as management and counseling techniques, emotional development and career exploration. Some counselors conduct activities in the areas of values clarification and social relationships in classrooms upon request from teachers.

Counselors are often available to talk with parents about their child's school experience. This can be especially valuable in the case of an emotionally disturbed child, whose behavior may be as distressing to the parents as it is to the teacher.

Administrators. The school principal is often a valuable intervenor for emotionally disturbed children (Morse, 1971). Having major responsibility for disciplinary action, the principal can often work with the teacher to develop the child's self-discipline, as well as a more tolerant attitude among school faculty.

Aides. Some children require a great deal of individual attention, often more than the teacher can provide. In such situations the instructional aide can be a valuable resource. This paraprofessional can often develop a good, trusting relationship with the emotionally disturbed child, helping her to deal with the demands of the class and school (Donahue & Reing, 1966).

Special subject teachers. Art, music, physical education and the library have for a long time supplemented the academic program of the school. Increasingly, however, professionals in these fields have begun to develop specialized programs for children with special needs. Art, music, play and movement therapies are becoming more prevalent in treatment programs for emotionally disturbed children (Alexander, 1971; Ogletree, 1976). "Bibliotherapy," provided by the school librarian, media specialist or reading teacher, is another specialized program with therapeutic value (Rubin, 1978).

The career education teacher. The career and leisure time concerns of the emotionally disturbed child are receiving increased attention (Lamkin, 1980). Some schools have specially trained career education teachers who introduce children to career possibilities, consumer skills and leisure-time activities. These subjects are of immediate interest to children, including the emotionally disturbed, and provide the teacher with an opportunity to help the child in a variety of social, emotional and academic ways.

Educational Services in Other Settings

Mental hospitals. Educational services in mental or psychiatric hospitals are usually restricted to children and adolescents with severe forms of emotional disturbance, such as psychosis or autism. Ideally, placement in such an institution is the last resort for adolescents who have been placed in other less restrictive settings prior to institutionalization.

As an example of services offered by mental hospitals, the Austin State Hospital (Texas) includes a 54-bed Adolescent Unit for youngsters displaying psychotic behavior, along with some adolescents who are being evaluated by the staff. An educational component in the unit is responsible for the instruction of the residents who are considered able to benefit from such services. The educational program is a part of the overall treatment plan, which also involves individual or group therapy. Attempts are made to individualize the program for each resident and to coordinate the efforts with the local special education program. The average length of stay in the Adolescent Unit is about six weeks, after which time the resident returns to a less restrictive setting, such as a special school or a special class within a regular school (Northcutt & Tipton, 1978). A detailed description of a school within a children's hospital may be found in Murphy (1974).

The number of programs in institutional settings is decreasing due to the trend toward deinstitutionalization (Paul, Stedman & Neufeld, 1977). More and more, emotionally disturbed adolescents are being served in community-based programs, such as group homes, while attending special day schools or special classes in regular schools for academic and vocational instruction.

Outdoor education. A number of programs have been developed in the past several years, designed to provide services for emotionally disturbed children in outdoor settings (Behar & Stephans, 1978; Hung & Thelander, 1978). These programs can include everything from conducting classes in cabins rather than in classrooms to intensive experiences in wilderness camping. Outdoor education programs attempt to take the child away from the familiar context of the school, where a number of undesirable behaviors have been developed, and place him in a new environment. This shift in setting, it is hoped, enables the child to develop other, more desirable patterns of behavior.

The structured experiences in these settings are often designed to force children to engage in social behaviors, such as cooperation and trust, that were not established in the child's home or school environment. The wilderness setting also capitalizes on the concept of logical consequences, wherein the advantages of certain behaviors are obvious from their result.

While the long-term effectiveness of outdoor education for the emotionally disturbed has been questioned (Byers, 1979), many practitioners see promise in this approach.

Open education. Open classrooms for emotionally disturbed children have been advocated by Knoblock (1973) and others. Such classes, characterized by a student-centered structure, less authoritarianism and rigidity, more opportunity for individual expression and participation, and a greater sense of community are thought to be nourishing for all children, no less for the emotionally disturbed child. These conditions tend to prevent the need for inappropriate behavior while promoting a greater tolerance for such behaviors when they do occur.

SUMMARY

Selecting a placement for an emotionally disturbed child is a serious business. For this reason the selection should not be left up to one individual but rather should be agreed upon by the parents, school officials and various professionals involved in the case. In order to ensure that no placement will be maintained if it does not prove beneficial, the child's IEP is to be reviewed at least annually and a complete re-evaluation conducted at least every three years. If at any point the parent or the school officials feel that a different placement or program is needed, the case can be examined and a new program designed.

There does not seem to be an answer to the deceptively simple question, what is the best kind of program for emotionally disturbed children? Programs at all levels of the continuum offer evidence of their effectiveness. RE-ED schools claim success with their clientele, success which appears to hold up over time (Gamboa & Garrett, 1974). A study of special schools for emotionally disturbed children in Massachusetts (Stotsky, Browne & Philbrick, 1974) likewise found that most children had benefited from this experience. One factor that seems to make a difference in the long-term results of residential treatment is after-release services for the child and the family (Allerhand, Weber & Haug, 1966).

Efficacy studies comparing special classes with resource or supportive services have been equivocal (Sindelar & Deno, 1978). Due to a number of methodological problems (Cegelka & Tyler, 1970), claims that either the self-contained class or the resource room is the better service for all disturbed children are hard to make. Studies evaluating consultation services (McKenzie, 1972; Miller & Sabatino, 1978) seem to indicate the effectiveness of this kind of program for mildly handicapped children.

The key problem with efficacy studies is that they usually rely on group data; that is, they look at the way in which the children as a group respond to the program in question. Thus a given program might claim positive results with 80% of its children. Usually, however, there is no way of knowing beforehand whether or not an individual child will benefit from the program. Thus efficacy research is of questionable value for making placement decisions for individual children.

In short, no program can claim to be effective for all children. It is for this reason that federal law requires a "continuum of services" to be available to the child. Only through careful matching of the child's characteristics and needs with various programs can an appropriate placement be determined. In order to do this, the needs of the individual child, including current status, academic, social, physical and vocational needs, become goals for the IEP. Only after the goals for the child have been established should placement be considered. When placement is decided upon, the principle of least restriction should be taken into account. That is, the child is to be placed in a setting that is only as far away from the regular classroom as is deemed necessary in order to provide him or her with an appropriate array of services. Finally, the specific array of services, programs and therapies that are to be employed in the case should be designed for the benefit of the child, not, as too often happens, for the convenience of the school.

The key to appropriate programming is to understand the process spelled out in P.L. 94-142. When all parties work conscientiously to comply not only with the letter but the spirit of the law, an appropriate program is more likely to result.

DISCUSSION QUESTIONS

1. In what ways might special educational services to emotionally disturbed children be different in the year 2000?
2. How would you go about deciding, for an individual child, whether a special class or regular class with support placement would be better?
3. What are some ways in which parents could be encouraged to participate in developing and carrying out their child's educational program?
4. What would an ideal special class for emotionally disturbed children look like? How would it be furnished and equipped?

REFERENCES

Abidin, R. Negative effects of behavior consultation. *Journal of School Psychology*, 1975, *13*, 51–57.

Alexander, E. School centered play-therapy. In N. J. Long, W. C. Morse & R. G. Newman (Eds.), *Conflict in the classroom* (2nd ed.). Belmont, Calif.: Wadsworth, 1971.

Allerhand, M., Weber, R., & Haug, M. *Adaptation and adaptability: The Bellefaire follow-up study*. New York: Child Welfare League of America, 1966.

Barach, R. *The parent teacher partnership*. Reston, Va.: Council for Exceptional Children, 1969.

Becker, H. The teacher in the authority system of the public school. *Journal of Educational Sociology*, 1953, *27*, 128–141.

Behar, L., & Stephans, D. Wilderness camping: An evaluation of a residential treatment program for emotionally disturbed children. *American Journal of Orthopsychiatry*, 1978, *48*, 644–653.

Bredo, E. Collaborative relations among elementary school teachers. *Sociology of Education*, 1977, *50*, 300–309.

Brown, G. Parents in the classroom. In N. J. Long, W. C. Morse & R. G. Newman (Eds.), *Conflict in the classroom* (4th ed.). Belmont, Calif.: Wadsworth, 1980.

Burrello, M., Tracy, M., & Schultz, E. Special education as experimental education: A new conceptualization. *Exceptional Children*, 1973, *40*, 29–34.

Byers, E. Wilderness camping as a therapy for emotionally disturbed children: A critical review. *Exceptional Children*, 1979, *45*, 628–635.

Cegelka, W., & Tyler, J. The efficacy of special class placement for the mentally retarded in proper perspective. *Training School Bulletin*, 1970, *67*, 33–68.

Christopolos, F., & Renz, P. A critical examination of special education programs. *Journal of Special Education*, 1969, *3*, 371–379.

Deno, E. Special education as developmental capital. *Exceptional Children*, 1970, *37*, 229–237.

Donahue, G., & Reing, V. Teacher-moms help emotionally disturbed pupils. *Nation's Schools*, 1966, *78*, 50–52.

Dunn, L. M. Special education for the mildly retarded—is much of it justifiable? *Exceptional Children*, 1968, *35*, 5–22.

Gamboa, A., & Garrett, J. Re-education: A mental health service in an educational setting. *American Journal of Orthopsychiatry*, 1974, *44*, 450–453.

Gesten, E. Teachers' judgments of class-related and teaching-related problem situations. *Journal of Special Education*, 1978, *12*, 171–181.

Glenurick, D., & Barocas, R. Training impulsive children in verbal self-control by use of natural change agents. *Journal of Special Education*, 1979, *13*, 387–398.

Grosenick, J., & Huntze, S. *National needs analysis in behavior disorders*. Columbia, Mo.: University of Missouri, 1980.

Harasymiw, S., & Horne, M. Teacher attitude toward handicapped children and regular class integration. *Journal of Special Education*, 1976, *10*, 393–400.

Hewett, F. M. Educational engineering with emotionally disturbed children. *Exceptional Children*, 1967, *33*, 459–467.

Hewett, F. M., & Taylor, F. D. *The emotionally disturbed child in the classroom: The orchestration of success*. Boston: Allyn & Bacon, 1980.

Hirshoren, A., & Heller, O. Programs for adolescents with behavior disorders: The state of the art. *Journal of Special Education*, 1979, 13, 275–281.

Hung, D. W., & Thelander, M. J. Summer camp treatment program for autistic children. *Exceptional Children*, 1978, *44*, 534–536.

Iano. R., Ayers, D., Heller, H., McGettigan, J., & Walker, V. Sociometric status of retarded children in an integrative program. *Exceptional Children*, 1974, *40*, 267–271.

Jones, R. Labels and stigma in special education. *Exceptional Children*, 1972, *38*, 553–564.

Kanner, L. Emotionally disturbed children: A historical review. In L. A. Fass (Ed), *The emotionally disturbed child*. Springfield, Ill.: Charles C Thomas, 1970.

Knoblock, P. Open education for emotionally disturbed children. *Exceptional Children*, 1973, *39*, 358–366.

Knoblock, P., & Goldstein, A. *The lonely teacher*. Boston: Allyn & Bacon, 1971.

Kolstoe, O. Programs for the mildly retarded: A reply to critics. *Exceptional Children*, 1972, *39*, 51–56.

Kroth, R. *Communicating with parents of exceptional children*. Denver: Love, 1975.

Kyriacou, C., & Sutliffe, J. Teacher stress and satisfaction. *Educational Researcher*, 1979, *21*, 89–96.

Lamkin, J. *Getting started: Career education activities for exceptional students*. Reston, Va.: Council for Exceptional Children, 1980.

Laneve, R., & the Mark Twain Staff. Mark Twain School: A special public school. In N. J. Long, W. C. Morse & R. G. Newman (Eds.), *Conflict in the classroom* (4th ed.). Belmont, Calif.: Wadsworth, 1980.

Lilly, M. S. Special education: A teapot in a tempest. *Exceptional Children*, 1970, *37*, 43–49.

Lortie, E. *Schoolteacher*. Chicago: University of Chicago Press, 1975.

MacMillan, D. Special education for the mildly retarded: Servant or savant? *Focus on Exceptional Children*, 1971, *2*, 1–11.

McKenzie, H. Special education and counseling teachers. In F. U. Clark, D. R. Evans & L. A. Hamerlynck (Eds.), *Implementing behavioral programs for schools and clinics*. Champaign, Ill.: Research Press, 1972.

McKenzie, H., Egner, A., Knight, M., Perelman, P., Schneider, B., & Garvin, J. Training consulting teachers to assist elementary teachers in the management and education of handicapped children. *Exceptional Children*, 1970, *37*, 137–143.

Miller, T., & Sabatino, D. The evaluation of the teacher consultant model as an approach to mainstreaming. *Exceptional Children*, 1978, *45*, 86–91.

Montgomery, M. The special educator as consultant: Some strategies. *Teaching Exceptional Children*, 1978, *10*, 110–112.

Morse, W. *Classroom disturbance: The principal's dilemma.* Reston, Va.: Council for Exceptional Children, 1971.

Morse, W. The crisis or helping teacher. In N. J. Long, W. C. Morse & R. G. Newman (Eds.), *Conflict in the classroom* (4th ed.). Belmont, Calif.: Wadsworth, 1980.

Morse, W., Cutler, R., & Fink, A. *Public school classes for the emotionally handicapped: A research analysis.* Washington, D.C.: Council for Exceptional Children, 1964.

Murphy, L. *Growing up in Garden Court.* New York: Child Welfare League of America, 1974.

Nelson, C., & Schmidt, L. The question of the efficacy of special classes. *Exceptional Children*, 1970, *37*, 381–384.

Northcutt, J., & Tipton, G. Teaching severely mentally ill and emotionally disturbed adolescents. *Exceptional Children*, 1978, *45*, 18–23.

O'Connor, P., Stuck, G. B., & Wyne, M. Effects of a short-term intervention resource room program on task orientation and achievement. *Journal of Special Education*, 1979, *13* (4), 375–385.

Ogletree, E. J. Eurythmy: A therapeutic art of movement. *Journal of Special Education*, 1976, *10*, 305–319.

Paul J., Stedman, D., & Neufeld, R. (Eds.). *Deinstitutionalization: Program and policy development.* Syracuse, N.Y.: Syracuse University Press, 1977.

Prouty, R. Diagnostic teaching: A modest proposal. *Elementary School Journal*, 1970, *70*, 265–270.

Redl, F. The concept of the life space interview. *American Journal of Orthopsychiatry*, 1959, *29*, 1–18.

Rivlin, L., & Rothenberg, M. The use of space in open classrooms. In H. M. Proshansky, W. H. Ittelson & L. G. Rivlin (Eds.), *Environmental psychology* (2nd ed.). New York: Holt, Rinehart & Winston, 1976.

Rubin, R. *Using bibliotherapy: A guide to theory and practice.* Phoenix, Ariz.: Oryx Press, 1978.

Sarason, S. *The culture of the school and the problem of change.* Boston: Allyn & Bacon, 1971.

Shotel, J., Iano, R., & McGettigan, J. Teacher attitudes associated with the integration of handicapped children. *Exceptional Children*, 1972, *39*, 677–683.

Sindelar, P., & Deno, S. The effectiveness of resource programming. *Journal of Special Education*, 1978, *12*, 17–27.

Smith, J., & Arkans, J. Now more than ever: A case for the special class. *Exceptional Children*, 1974, *40*, 497–502.

Stotsky, B., Browne, T., & Philbrick, W. A study of outcome of special schooling of emotionally disturbed children. *Child Psychiatry and Human Development*, 1974, *4*, 131–150.

Tuckman, B. W. *Evaluating instructional programs.* Boston: Allyn & Bacon, 1979.

Vacc, N. Long-term effects of special class intervention for emotionally disturbed children. *Exceptional Children*, 1972, *39*, 15–22.

Waller, W. *The sociology of teaching.* New York: John Wiley & Sons, 1932.

Weinstein, L. The zoomer class: Initial results. In H. Dupont (Ed.), *Educating emotionally disturbed children* (2nd ed.). New York: Holt, Rinehart & Winston, 1975.

Wiederholt, J. L. Planning resource rooms for the mildly handicapped. In H. Dupont (Ed.), *Educating emotionally disturbed children* (2nd ed.). New York: Holt, Rinehart & Winston, 1975.

Wood, M. M. (Ed.), *The Rutland Center model for treating emotionally disturbed children.* Athens, Ga.: University of Georgia, 1972.

Wright, B. A. A new look at overprotection and dependency. *Exceptional Children*, 1959, *26*, 155–122.

4
Screening, Identification and Diagnosis

main points

1 Screening, identification and diagnosis are three separate stages in the process of labeling and evaluating emotionally disturbed children. Screening is the superficial procedure of locating children who *may* be emotionally disturbed. Identification involves certifying that a child's problems are indeed of sufficient magnitude that the label is justified. Diagnosis involves gathering data about the individual and his life circumstances so that an intervention can be prescribed.

2 The evaluation of children's social and emotional problems is a complex process that cannot be done properly or legally by one person. Because teachers, parents, clinicians and children often have different perceptions of emotional problems, the evaluation data should be based on observations of the child's behavior in different settings.

3 Each of the current techniques used to gather data on social, emotional and behavioral problems has limitations.

4 Diagnostic procedures and classification systems in clinical settings and those in educational settings often focus on somewhat different issues. Clinicians tend to be more concerned about the child's intrapsychic conflicts, his ability to form and maintain relationships and motivation to change. Educators tend to focus on how the child deviates from the norm educationally and behaviorally, and on what can be done to minimize his deviance.

SCREENING, identification and diagnosis are the procedures used by professionals to move from the nebulous position of questioning whether children have emotional problems to the more definitive position of prescribing an intervention. These procedures are complicated by several facts: definitions of emotional disturbance are diverse; the professionals who work with emotionally disturbed children differ in their techniques and philosophies; and the systems that serve this population emphasize different kinds of services. Nevertheless, education and mental health professionals do employ certain common procedures in order to locate emotionally disturbed children and to evaluate their problems so that treatment may be prescribed. Through these procedures, they try to answer the following questions:

1 How do we identify emotional disturbance in children?
2 Are the problems of these children of sufficient magnitude to warrant intervention?
3 What should be the nature of the intervention?

This chapter was written by **Betty C. Epanchin,** University of North Carolina at Chapel Hill.

Screening Techniques: Procedures and Problems

Screening involves surveying large numbers of children in order to locate those who may be in need of additional, specialized help. With school-age children, screening is usually done by a professional, most often the teacher. The term *screening* generally refers to quick, valid measurement activities that are administered systematically to large groups of children, although in some school systems referrals from teachers or other concerned adults may be the only form of screening used.

Within the past two decades more attention has been given to adequate screening procedures. The impetus for this seems to arise from two sources. The first of these is the belief that early detection and early intervention reduce the prevalence of emotional handicaps. As Lillie (1977) points out, "There is no specific evidence indicating that age one intervention is better than age two intervention, or that intervention at age two is better than at age three. What we do have are general indications . . . that the earlier the intervention, the more there is potential for improvement" (p. 20). The second force behind the development of screening programs is the mandate in P.L. 94-142 that each state develop a plan for identifying, locating and evaluating all children in the state who are handicapped and that each state develop a practical method for finding who is and who is not being served.

Preschool or early school screening programs are the most common type of screening program. All children who are entering the school system are screened for physical, intellectual, perceptual and emotional handicaps. Screening programs designed specifically to identify emotionally disturbed children usually require teachers, parents and children to complete brief questionnaires or ask teachers to identify children with various characteristics.

Teacher Ratings

Teachers are the people most frequently involved in screening for emotional disturbance in school-age children. Numerous studies have been conducted comparing teachers' ratings of children with a number of other measures: children's ratings of themselves (Harth & Glavin, 1971); direct observational data (Nelson, 1971); mothers' ratings (Glidewell & Swallow, 1968; Yellot, Liem & Cowen, 1969); and ratings of psychiatrists, psychologists and counselors (Bower, 1957). All have concluded that the use of teacher ratings in screening procedures is a valid practice.

Although the bulk of the literature supports the validity of using teacher judgment in screening procedures, there is evidence that teachers, as a group, have biases. For example, when comparing teacher referrals with pupil self-referrals, Davis (1978) found that teachers perceived only 12% of the girls as in need of help whereas 33% of the girls perceived themselves as needing help. Almost all of the referred females were having behavior problems. Teachers do not appear to perceive social withdrawl as problematic and, as a rule, are not inclined to refer withdrawn children for professional help or to seek special assistance in managing or instructing them (Cooke & Apolloni, 1976). For example, Kirschenbaum, Marsh, and Devoge

(1977) found that teacher referral was an adequate screening technique for learning and overt behavior problems, but moody, withdrawn children who presented no problems in the classroom were less likely to be referred for help. The results of a study by Harris, Drummond and Schultz (1977) also lend support to the above observation.

As a means of dealing with teacher bias some researchers have suggested that teachers should not be expected to rate such general characteristics as a child's adjustment; rather, they should be asked specific questions about school-related behavior.

> While the concept of adjustment is understood by teachers, its operational implementation is somewhat out of the frame of reference and functioning of teachers. Most feel that in rating "adjustment" they are attempting to fill the role of a psychiatrist somehow and rate the degrees of intrapsychic conflict and chaos in the minds of their students. Whatever adjustment is or means I would suggest that ratings asked of teachers stick to school-related behaviors which can be operationally defined and observed. Does the child get into fights? Can he pay attention when required? Does he learn to read? Is he in a blue funk? Does he get sick? Does he get hurt? Can he express an idea? (Bower, 1969, p. 96)

The use of behavior checklists is the most common procedure for obtaining teacher ratings or observations. They define behavior operationally and many have been developed for use in schools. The Children's Behavior Questionnaire (Rutter, 1967) is an example of this type of rating form. The questionnaire contains only 26 items. Some sample items are "Frequently fights with other children" and "Tends to be fearful of new things or new situations." Teachers indicate that the item either "Doesn't Apply," "Applies Somewhat" or "Certainly Applies." A total score is obtained which may be used to identify children needing more intensive evaluations. The Behavior Problem Checklist (Peterson & Quay, 1979) and the Walker Problem Behavior Identification Checklist (Walker, 1970) are two other well-known checklists.

Parent Ratings

Parents are another obvious source of information about a child's emotional and social development. Information from parents is gathered through interviews or through checklists or questionnaires. Parents are clearly an important source of information about the child; however, the accuracy of parents' observations has been questioned. Parents' responses on a questionnaire have been compared to direct observations of behavior, using a clinic-referred group and a control group of nonreferred children (Lobitz & Johnson, 1975). The correlations between the child-behavior variables and the scores from the parent questionnaire were negligible. Similar studies have lent support to the position that what parents report on child behavior rating scales and similar instruments has little relationship with behavior when it is observed by others (Peed, Roberts & Forehand, 1977). One obvious problem with using direct observations as the criterion for validating parental ratings is the observer's limited view of behavior. Unless observations are conducted on a continuous basis over a long period

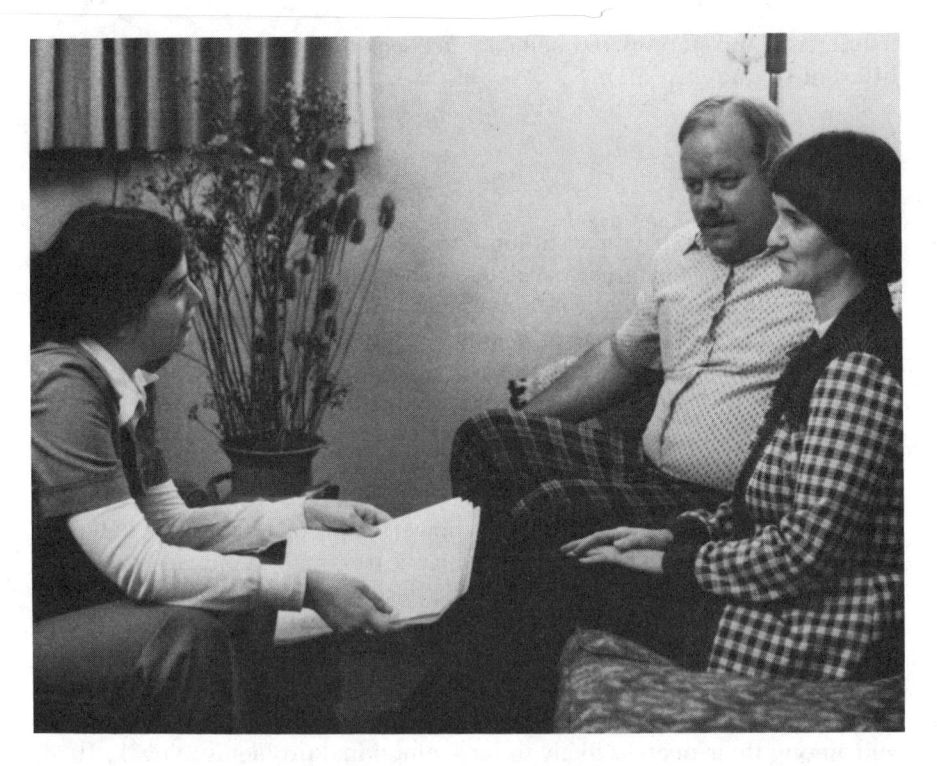

A social worker gathers information on a child's emotional and social development through an in-home interview with parents.

of time, observers may miss the times when the child's behavior is most difficult. Furthermore, the presence of an observer in the setting may significantly alter the child's behavior.

In spite of the questionable reliability of parent ratings, parents often have a major influence on referral. Shepherd, Oppenheim and Mitchell (1966) compared 50 children being treated in a child guidance clinic with a group of supposedly healthy children who were matched on the basis of sex, age and behavior. They concluded that the critical variable in determining which children are referred and which are not is the parents' level of tolerance for the behavior rather than the actual pathology of the behavior. The Louisville Behavior Checklist (Miller, 1977) is an example of a behavior checklist normed on parent ratings. It can be used as part of screening identification or diagnostic activities. It has 164 items, some of which describe socially desirable behaviors; thus it gathers information about both adaptive and deviant behavior. In addition it has a scale entitled Normal Irritability which is intended to be a gauge of parents' tolerance for troublesome behavior.

Perhaps the critical issue here is not whether parent reports are accurate but whether parent reports and teacher-observer-clinician reports match. Ross (1980) notes, "Marked differences in child behavior in different settings should be viewed as reflecting relatively good adaptive capacities. It is an indication that a child is profoundly disturbed when his or her bizarre mannerisms and stereotyped behavior are seen time and time again in vastly different settings" (p. 91).

Peer Ratings

Current research in psychology and education consistently indicates that children's social status correlates with adjustment in school as well as with academic achievement (Kaplan & Kaufman, 1978); therefore, peer ratings have been regarded as a logical method for screening for socio-emotional problems. Cowen, Pederson, Babigian, Izzo and Trost (1973) report the results of an 11-to-13-year follow-up on children "red-tagged" early in their school careers as being at greater risk for clinical behavior disorders. They found that, when compared to clinicians' predictions and teachers' ratings, peer ratings of social competence, using Bower's class play (Bower, 1969), were by far the most powerful predictor of later behavior disorders and the need for future psychiatric treatment. Long, Cook, Evans, Kerr, Linke, Neubauer and Payne (1962) also report that social acceptance scores are stable over time. Rolf (1976) provides evidence that children are able to differentiate vulnerable children from normal children quite competently.

Efforts have been made to learn more about how children distinguish who among their peers is likely to have emotional problems (Novak, 1974; Hoffman, Marsden & Kalter, 1977; Coie & Pennington, 1976). Generally the technique used has been to read descriptions of normal and disturbed behavior to children participating in the study. The subjects are then asked to rate the behavior of the child in the story. Results suggest that school children of all ages are able to identify personally noxious behavior, but young children (approximately ages 6 to 9 or 10) have trouble placing behavior in a normative framework. Around the ages of 9 or 10, children become less self-centered and are able to see noxious behavior as a sign of the child's problems rather than as personally directed.

Sociometric measures, which focus on interpersonal relationships in a group, are typically used to measure peer perceptions. They are essentially descriptive and their analytic potential is limited because one cannot determine from them *why* a pattern emerges (Gordon, 1966). Furthermore, the reliability of sociometric measures has been less than adequate for identification purposes (Greenwood, Walker & Hops, 1977). One reason is that over a short period of time groups of emotionally disturbed children had greater fluctuations in friendship choices than did groups of normal children (Davids & Parenti, 1958). Sociometric techniques, however, can be helpful as screening procedures and, if interpreted with caution, may also be helpful to the teacher in planning interventions. Two examples of techniques used in obtaining peer ratings are the L-J Sociometric Test and the "Guess Who" technique.

The L-J Sociometric Test (Long et al., 1962) is an example of a simple sociometric measure that attempts to measure social preference. It is intended for use in the classroom by the teacher. Administration procedures are straightforward. The teacher asks students to complete questions such

Screening, identification and diagnosis

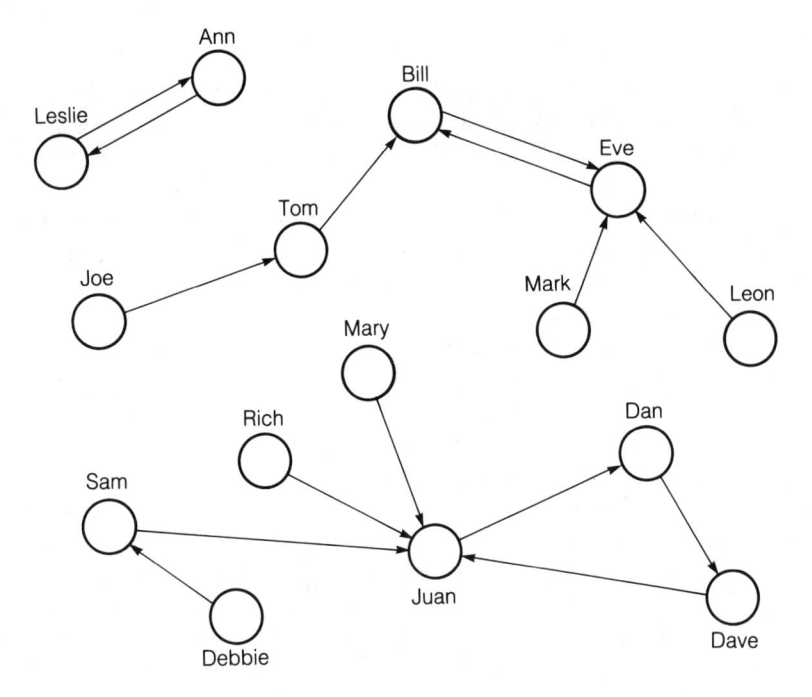

4.1 A Sociogram

as, "Write the names of three pupils in this classroom whom you like the most" and "Write the names of three pupils in this classroom whom you like the least."

Once the student selections are completed, the teacher transfers the choices to a matrix table, which gives a graphic picture of the social structure in the classroom. These data enable the teacher to determine who is most popular, who is rejected, who is isolated, who belongs to subgroups and so on. In a sociometric measure, questions may vary but they should be specific and reality-oriented. Obviously the way in which the question is worded will influence the type of responses received. If the question is, "We are going to form groups to complete projects. What three people would you like in your group?" children may choose, quite wisely, the most academically proficient students. The question, "Who in the class are your three favorite people?" is likely to elicit very different responses.

Another type of sociometric testing utilizes a questionnaire format frequently described as the "Guess Who" technique (Gordon, 1966). Students simply complete the questionnaire providing as many names as they wish. Typical items found on such measures are, "This person is always worried or scared and won't take a chance when something unexpected or unusual happens" and "This person is friendly, has lots of friends and is nice to everybody."

Data from the questionnaire can be analyzed in several ways. A student's choice of himself can be matched with others' choices of him or frequency of choices can be computed for positive and negative questions.

Self-Ratings

Another source of data about a child's adjustment is the child himself. After an extensive review of the literature Bower (1960) concluded that teacher ratings were "better predictors of maladjusted children when the resultant behavior was manifested overtly or acted out; self-descriptive data appeared to be better for evaluating that aspect of maladjustment which had to do with feelings, attitudes, and inner tensions of self" (p. 24). Self-concept and self-esteem measures have been used frequently as a means of identifying children who are dissatisified with themselves or who are unusually defensive and thus report no problematic feelings. The Piers-Harris Children's Self-Concept Scale (Piers & Harris, 1969), the Self-Observation Scales (Stenner & Katzenmeyer, 1974) and the Self-Esteem Inventory (Coopersmith, 1959) are examples of self-report measures.

The validity of children's self-reports has been studied in a variety of ways. Scores on self-concept measures have been correlated with scores on anxiety measures (Piers, 1969). As expected, a strong, negative relationship between positive self-regard and anxiety was found. Scores obtained on self-concept measures by clinically diagnosed groups and by normals have been compared with equivocal results. Bloom, Shea, and Eun (1979) and Wood and Johnson (1972) report that the behaviorally disordered children in their samples had significantly lower scores on self-report measures, but Piers (1969) reports a study in which emotionally disturbed boys scored within the average range. Scores on self-report measures have been compared with peer and teacher ratings, again with mixed results. Such findings should not be surprising nor should they necessarily be considered to invalidate self-report measures. After all, who can determine which is more accurate—a person's view of himself or another's view of him? Both are critical parts of the "total picture."

Multiple Ratings

Given the diverse nature of children's emotional problems and the psychometric limitations of various screening procedures, a number of researchers have concluded that different kinds of data about the child's development and adjustment are needed in order to accurately identify a child as emotionally disturbed. Peer ratings, teacher ratings and self-ratings, used in combination with achievement and age-grade relationships, have been very effective in separating emotionally disturbed children from others (Bower, 1960).

One instrument which samples perceptions from multiple raters is A Process for In-School Screening of Emotionally Handicapped Children (Lambert, Hartsough & Bower, 1979). Shea (1978) describes it as "the most popular and widely used device reported in the literature" (p. 76). It utilizes teacher ratings, peer ratings and self-report. Another example of the use of multiple ratings is found in the Behavior Rating Profile test battery (Brown & Hammill, 1978). Designed to provide an ecological evaluation of children's behaviors, it consists of parents' ratings of the child, teachers' ratings of the child, peer ratings and the child's self-ratings at home, at school and with peers.

When children's behavior is assessed by multiple measures, the individual scores usually contribute different but complementary information. If the teacher learns that Johnny has trouble in school but not at home and that Johnny feels relatively satisfied with himself except in relation to school work, the teacher has information that if confirmed through other techniques is valuable in planning an intervention. In addition, given the disparity among various types of screening procedures, the use of multiple measures increases the probability of locating specific types of problems. On the other hand, these instruments are time-consuming. Since more in-depth testing must be done before a child can be identified as emotionally disturbed, teachers may prefer to compile their own screening batteries from reliable but less time-consuming instruments.

Concerns about Screening Procedures

It is very easy to over-interpret the results of screening devices. Screening procedures are useful in bringing to light children that *may* be in need of help; they are not definitive tools for diagnosing. In practice, however, the careful distinction between screening and more in-depth evaluation is not always made. Teachers generally respond to the label *emotionally disturbed, emotionally handicapped, behavior disordered*, with lowered expectations of behavior. Hence, once a child is labeled, the risk of a negative self-fulfilling prophecy is increased.

Because the erroneous identification of children can have such negative effects, one must be very careful to minimize the number of *false positives*, that is, identification of nonhandicapped children, in a screening program. Likewise, one must be concerned about *false negatives*, handicapped children that were not identified. To overlook children who are in need of help is to allow the cycle of defeat and despair to grow even larger.

Research (Kirschenbaum, Marsh & Devoge, 1977) suggests that in systematic screening programs, more children in need of help are located than when referral procedures alone are used. However, as Adelman (1978) points out, the present technology of massive screening programs is not adequately developed to prevent large numbers of false positives: "The evidence does not support the efficacy of currently available predictive and identification procedures especially those already being used for massive screening of preschoolers and kindergartners" (p. 154).

On a more pragmatic level, screening programs have been criticized for identifying children in need of help when the possibility of providing services does not exist. Since many school systems already are having difficulty serving identified children, the uncovering of a large group of additional children needing help could overwhelm the system and be destructive for the child.

What then should one do? The usefulness of screening, even with its shortcomings, is upheld in the following comments by Hobbs (1975):

> Lacking a better alternative, screening programs are important to the nation's children. But it seems clear that procedures must be improved before confidence can be placed in this logical first step in the sequence of screening,

diagnosis, and treatment. Our best judgment is that the process should be truncated and screening omitted as soon as it becomes possible to provide adequate health maintenance services. All children should have periodic physical and psychological examinations by competent clinicians, preferably in treatment settings, with diagnosis and treatment ensuing as may be required. But until such time as comprehensive diagnostic and treatment programs can be provided, it would appear sensible to continue early screening programs, inadequate as they seem to be, and to invest in research to improve them. (p. 97)

Identification and Diagnosis in Educational Settings

Once a child has been located through screening or referral procedures as possibly needing additional, specialized services, more extensive evaluations are undertaken. Since the advent of P.L. 94-142, educational identification and evaluation procedures have become more uniform.

P.L. 94-142 is very specific about certain aspects of the evaluation procedures. It stipulates that a "full and individual evaluation of the child's educational needs" must be done prior to the child's placement in any special education program. With respect to tests used during the evaluation, the law requires that all tests and materials must

1. Be in the child's native language or other mode of communication
2. Have been validated for the specific purposes for which they are used
3. Be administered by trained personnel in conformance with instructions provided by their producer
4. Be tailored to assess specific areas of educational need

The law further specifies that no single procedure be used as the sole criterion in determining an appropriate educational program for a child and that all children be assessed in all areas related to the suspected disability. It specifically identifies social and emotional status as areas for assessment. It also mandates that the evaluation be conducted by a multidisciplinary team or group of persons, including at least one teacher or other specialist with knowledge in the area of suspected disability.

While individual school systems have their own unique evaluation practices, certain standard procedures are followed. The child is evaluated with individual psychological and educational tests; teacher and parent observations or ratings are obtained; and often, though not required, informal or formal observations are conducted in the child's setting. The child's behavior under various conditions and in different settings may be observed. The classroom setting and its characteristics may also be studied.

The information gathered during the evaluation procedures is compiled and reviewed by a multidisciplinary team before placement is determined. The task of this committee is to recommend placement as well as to monitor the ensuing IEP development. Diagnostic information gathered during the evaluation should be helpful in developing an IEP; therefore, a variety of evaluation techniques are usually employed.

These educational diagnostic procedures, guided in large part by legislative mandate, are somewhat different from those used in mental health settings. For example, because the educational system is based on group instruction, it is particularly important that the child conform or fit into the system. Lack of conformity, or deviance, poses particular management and instructional problems. The focus of diagnosis in educational settings, therefore, is first on determining whether the child is deviant by comparing him to his age mates and second on prescribing educational interventions that will help the child adapt to the student role. In order to formulate such a prescription, the diagnostician needs to gather information not only about the child but also about the classroom, the setting in which specific norms are established. In mental health settings diagnostic investigations focus on whether or not the child is experiencing intrapsychic conflict. Therapists are interested in helping the child acquire more adaptive ways of coping with stress; and the setting of primary concern is the family, not the classroom.

Another difference between the educational diagnostic process and the mental health diagnostic process is the scope of concern. In a mental health setting when clients seek help for problems, they sanction the therapist's inquiry into all areas of their lives. In school when a child is identified as having problems but neither he nor his family feels there is a problem, the school's legitimate focus is on the child's life in the school. The legitimacy of the school's concern with children's emotional and social problems stems from the school's societal role—to educate children.

Still another difference between educational and mental health diagnostics is in the content of the evaluation. In educational settings assessing motivation to change is not as critical as it is in mental health settings because teachers may provide external motivators until the child acquires his own positive sources of motivation. The teacher is with the child much of the day and can structure and organize the environment in order to optimize the child's functioning. Since clinicians do not have such direct control, they are very concerned about whether the child and his family understand the problem and are motivated to change. When the child is not motivated, the clinician's goals and techniques are blocked.

Diagnostic practices in both educational and mental health settings do have some common elements. In both settings, multiple sources of information are utilized because no one technique or professional can be relied upon to consistently obtain an objective understanding or representation of all facets of the problem. Also, psychological and educational tests that measure intellectual, perceptual-motor and language ability are included in both types of evaluations in order to rule out disabilities that are not emotional or social, as well as to gain important information about the child's cognitive and perceptual functioning.

Techniques and instruments frequently used for diagnostic purposes in educational settings include analysis of settings, direct observation of behavior, paper-and-pencil tests of personality, intelligence tests, perceptual-motor tests, tests of auditory and visual acuity and educational assessment. A brief critical summary of these techniques and instruments follows.

Analysis of Setting

Setting analysis, or the systematic analysis of the context in which behavior occurs, is included as a critical variable in an educational diagnosis because of the seductive influence that space, props, activities and time can have (Redl, 1966). The rationale for including an analysis of the classroom setting in an educational diagnosis stems from two sources: (a) it helps in determining to what extent the setting may be contributing to the problem, and (b) changing the setting or aspects of it may be a central component of the recommended intervention. For example, a child who is easily distracted and lacking in self-control may have great difficulty in a large, open, stimulating classroom that relies heavily on student initiation, whereas in a small, structured regular classroom this same child may adjust quite well. Looking at the child without also looking at the classroom setting would miss vital diagnostic information.

Approaches to gaining information about the classroom setting range from simple, direct observation, with or without the aid of setting analysis instruments, to very complex anthropological systems of observation. Since most of the instruments and observation systems show, at present, more promise for research purposes than for classroom use, only the simple observation approach will be described here. Further information about setting analysis instruments can be found in Moos (1979).

The properties in the classroom that should be considered during an informal, direct observation of a classroom include the following (Miller, 1979).

Total number of students and student-teacher ratio. A high student-teacher ratio may interfere with the teacher's ability to individualize instruction and may increase the stress on the teacher. This, in turn, may decrease teacher effectiveness. Having a large number of people in the classroom also increases the noise level and potential distractors.

Utilization of space. The arrangement of desks influences teacher-student interactional patterns. Desks in straight lines promote interaction primarily between the teacher and individual students whereas a semicircle or U-shaped desk arrangement fosters more student-to-student interaction. The individual child's needs should be considered in relation to the classroom arrangement.

Location of an individual child's desk is also important. The physical isolation of a child's desk from the group may contribute to social ostracism. Location near activity centers such as the pencil sharpener, the doorway or other children who serve as poor role models may be inviting trouble. If the location of the child's desk interferes with his vision or hearing, problems may result.

A final consideration in assessing the utilization of space is the location of the classroom in relation to the bathroom, playground, cafeteria and drinking fountains. For some children a walk down a long hallway several times a day, especially if they are unsupervised, is a source of major distractions and problems.

Props. The comfort, fit and type of desk are important. The size of the desk of course should be appropriate, but of equal importance is the type of desk. For hyperactive children a desk with a lift-up top or with chairs separate from the table may pose problems.

Other props which should be considered are carpets and bulletin boards. Carpets help reduce the noise level but also reduce the room flexibility. Art activities and other messy activities are hampered. Bulletin boards where work is displayed may be a source of embarrassment for the less able child and a source of overstimulation for distractible children.

Time. The scheduling of activities, both sequence and duration, is critical for some children. Some children need variation in activities in order to maintain their interest. Some children become discouraged and disruptive or despondent when activities are not long enough to allow them to finish. Other children get distracted or into trouble when too much time is allotted to an activity and no provision is made for fast workers. Many children function better and feel fresher at a certain time of the day, usually the morning. The most difficult and stressful activities should be scheduled when most of the children are at their best.

Direct Observation of Behavior

Another technique that has been demonstrated to be helpful in obtaining diagnostic information about the child's problem behavior is direct observation in the classroom. The importance of such information rests on the assumption that a person's behavior is always affected by the context in which it is evoked—a thesis developed by Mischel (1968). For example, a child in the classroom of a favorite teacher may strive to please; yet when a disliked substitute is teaching, that same child may join his cohorts in disruptive, uncooperative behavior. Should his parent or the principal walk into the room, that same child who was participating in a planned chorus of book dropping, may suddenly stop and go back to his work. Likewise, a child who enjoys math may behave quite differently in math class than in a class of lesser appeal.

Direct observations have the advantage of providing relatively precise, objective data about behavior. By describing overt behavior in behavioral terms, a biased perspective is minimized. Informal estimates or judgments of behavior by teachers, for instance, often do not correspond to the actual frequency of such behavior (Fitzgerald, 1979). Teachers tend to overestimate the magnitude of behaviors that are particularly troublesome to them, so their reports may be a measure of their tolerance for the particular behavior rather than a precise description of the problem. To avoid such biases, concrete, quantified descriptions of behavior are needed. For example, if Johnny has a reading problem, it is more accurate to say that he was out of his seat five times during a 30-minute reading period, or that 25% of the time during reading Johnny was behaving inappropriately, than to say he has a "lot of problems" during reading.

Some observation techniques are very structured and require considerable training in order to use them; others are less structured and require less training. All, however, involve careful, systematic observation and record keeping. Usually the stimuli (antecedents of behavior), the overt behavior and the environmental consequences are recorded.

An example of a structured observation system that requires training of the observer is the *Coping Analysis Schedule for Educational Settings* developed by Spaulding (1973). This scale consists of 13 categories in which overt, observable behavior can be classified. These categories may be grouped into larger categories, labeled "appropriate," "inappropriate" and "unacceptable"—judgments which are determined by the setting. For example, self-directed activity when it occurs with the teacher's sanction may be coded "5a" (appropriate). When the child should be involved in other activities, however, self-directed behavior might be coded as 5b (inappropriate).

Data from such an observation system yield information about the amount of time the child spends in various activities during specific periods of the day as well as what type of behavior preceded and followed categories of child behavior. Observations of a child's behavior may be coupled with observations of a teacher's behavior. When observations of both the child and teacher are conducted simultaneously, the results often have implications for intervention (Sibley, Abbott & Cooper, 1969). An intervention plan is often suggested on the basis of the baseline observation period.

These same categories can be used to sample the behavior of an entire classroom. The observer, after describing the setting, can go down the class roll recording each child's behavior at 10-second intervals. After recording for all children, the observer returns to the first child and begins the sequence again for the second 10-second interval. In this way each child is sampled several times during an observation session. The data are compiled in summary form, reflecting the composite behavior for a classroom setting. With such data, the teacher or diagnostician can determine, with confidence, that more children are distracted and disruptive during geography (lecture and group presentations) than during math (small work groups).

The obvious drawback to using this observational system in the classroom is the fact that a trained person must serve as an observer. The teacher could not possibly teach and record behavior simultaneously. Not only are such observers not readily available but funds for hiring them are limited. One solution to this problem has been for teachers, aides, parents, volunteers and other professionals, or the child himself, to learn the system.

An observation technique that requires virtually no observer training and that the teacher can use while teaching is a daily log. With this procedure the teacher pays close attention to the child in question and, as soon as possible, records her observations of the behavior and of the setting in which the behavior occurred. If kept systematically over time, a teacher log contains accurate descriptions of behavior in specific settings. When compiled, recurring patterns of behavior and progressive changes in behavior may be noted. While certainly more accessible, this technique also has its drawbacks. Subjectivity is involved in choosing what to report. Furthermore, the technique is time-consuming and somewhat cumbersome. Since this method is not easily quantified, patterns of behavior are not so readily observed as in the CASES observation technique.

Paper-and-Pencil Tests of Personality

In educational settings objective measures of personality functioning or of adjustment are more frequently used than are projective tests. Of the several different approaches to personality assessment, behavior rating scales are probably the most widely used although self-report instruments are also frequently used. Given the differences in self-perception versus other-perception, the combination of these two techniques seems most effective.

Behavior checklists and self-concept measures are used for screening as well as for diagnostic purposes. While some instruments, such as the Quay-Peterson and the Piers-Harris, may be used for both purposes most instruments have been developed either for screening or for diagnostic purposes. None are so technically adequate that they should be relied upon solely when making diagnostic decisions. A personality instrument that is useful for diagnostic purposes is the Burks' Behavior Rating Scales (Burks, 1977).

Intelligence Testing

Intelligence testing is usually included in a diagnostic evaluation because it can provide valuable information about both the child's cognitive abilities and the relationship between the child's emotional conflicts and intellectual functioning. For example, some children become distracted by items which conjure up aggressive fantasies. They give inferior, egocentric answers to such items whereas on neutral items their performance is adequate. Diagnosticians can learn a lot about both the content of fantasies and the stimuli which tend to trigger the fantasies. Additionally, overall intellectual ability may have considerable influence on the child's behavior. Excessive dependency in a youngster may stem more from mental retardation and inappropriate environmental expectations than from conflicts about assertion and independence.

Probably the most widely used intelligence test for children ages 6–16 is the Wechsler Intelligence Scale for Children—Revised (WISC–R) (Wechsler, 1974). This instrument, which is individually administered, consists of 12 subtests, 2 of which are optional. Clinicians obtain both global scores (Verbal IQ, Performance IQ and Full Scale IQ) and diagnostic information about particular skills and knowledge areas believed to reflect a person's intellectual ability. According to Salvia and Ysseldyke (1978) and Sattler (1974) the WISC–R is technically adequate and valid.

Another instrument gaining in popularity is the SOMPA, System of Multicultural Pluralistic Assessment, developed by Mercer and Lewis (1977). This system for estimating learning potential combines information about the child's sociocultural background, health and developmental history and adaptive behavior with the child's performance on the WISC–R. Within this framework children's performance on the WISC–R can be compared to children from similar sociocultural settings.

Other intelligence tests occasionally used both in clinical and educational settings include the Leiter International Performance Scale and the Arthur Adaptation (Leiter & Arthur, 1969), the Pictorial Test of Intelligence (French, 1964), and the Hiskey-Nebraska Test of Learning Aptitude (Hiskey, 1966). These are primarily used when testing nonverbal children. The Stanford-Binet Intelligence Scale (Terman & Merrill, 1960) and the McCarthy Scales of Children's Abilities (McCarthy, 1972) are other individually administered tests of intellectual functioning. Buros (1978) contains reviews and detailed descriptions of these instruments.

Perceptual-Motor Testing

Perceptual testing is frequently used to rule out other disabilities, most frequently those of organic origin (e.g., brain damage). The reliability of perceptual tests, however, has been questioned. According to Salvia and Ysseldyke (1978), "What the majority of the research has shown is that most perceptual motor tests are unreliable. We do not know what they measure because they do not measure anything consistently" (p. 303).

One of the most widely used of these tests is the Bender Visual Motor Gestalt Test (Bender, 1938). The test consists of nine geometric designs which the child is instructed to copy on a separate sheet of paper. It has not been empirically demonstrated that the test measures visual-motor perception or that it discriminates individual cases of brain injury, perceptual handicaps or emotional handicaps, yet the test is frequently used as a criterion in the differential diagnoses of children with these problems. Like many of the other similar tests, it provides a limited sample of perceptual-motor behavior. Other tests frequently used include the Developmental Test of Visual Perception (Frostig, Maslow, Lefever & Whittlesey, 1964), the Developmental Test of Visual-Motor Integration (VMI) (Beery & Buktenica, 1967) and the Purdue Perceptual-Motor Survey (Roach & Kephart, 1966).

Auditory and Visual Acuity

Vision and hearing difficulties can have a profound effect on the educational performance of children. The behavior of children with these difficulties often resembles the behavior of emotionally handicapped children. For example, children with visual difficulty frequently complain of headaches and dizziness; children with hearing difficulties often do not pay attention in school, do not respond consistently when people talk to them and frequently seem distracted or preoccupied.

Most schools routinely screen for visual acuity, that is, the clarity or sharpness with which a person sees. The Standard Snellen Wall Chart is the most commonly used screening test. Although it is a relatively effective screening instrument, it only assesses central visual acuity. Salvia and Ysseldyke (1978) provide a critical review as well as descriptions of screening devices for measuring other visual skills.

Most schools also screen for hearing difficulties. Depending on the school system, the screening is done by a school nurse, speech therapist, hearing therapist or other trained technician. Hearing ability is assessed with an electronic instrument called an audiometer. If a hearing loss is detected, the child is then referred to an ear doctor (otologist or otolaryngologist) for an otological evaluation or to a specialist in hearing evaluation and rehabilitation (audiologist) for a complete audiological evaluation.

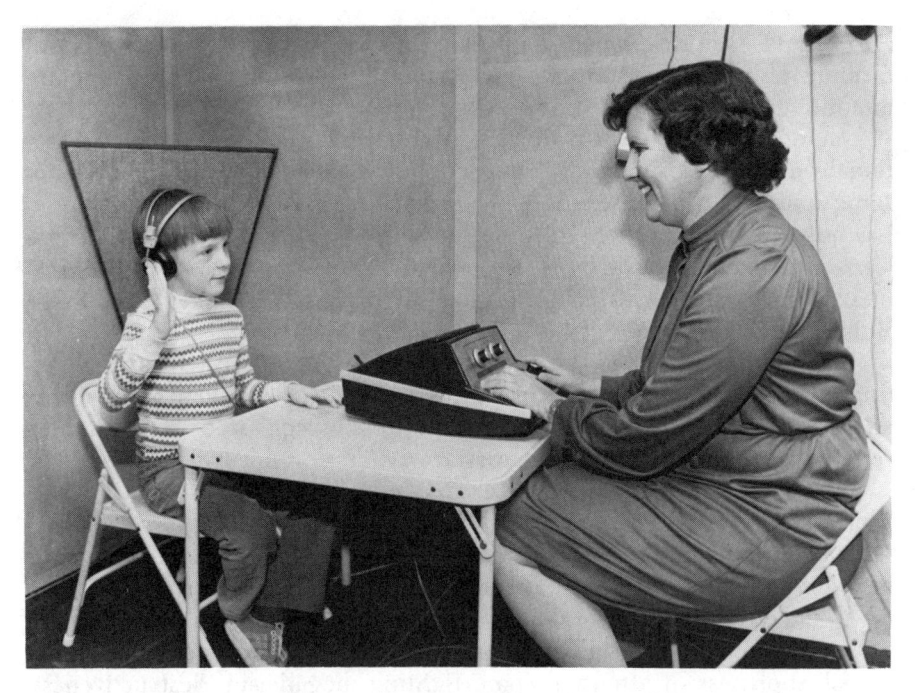

In most schools, children are routinely screened for hearing difficulties.

Educational Assessment

In educational settings one of the central diagnostic questions has to do with children's academic status. Teachers want to know whether the children are performing on a level consistent with their ability and their age mates. The answer to this question has diagnostic as well as prescriptive importance. If children are functioning on a significantly different level than their age mates, they may become bored, distracted or threatened, and these reactions may be expressed as a problem behavior.

Tests used to determine children's level of academic performance are generally norm-referenced diagnostic or achievement tests. Results of these tests yield hypothetical age and grade equivalencies which make possible cross-age and cross-grade comparisons.

When the teacher's primary concern is not how does a particular child compare to his classmates but rather how much progress the child has made or what specific skill should be taught next, a criterion-referenced test may be more useful. These tests consist of specific tasks requiring the use of certain skills listed in a developmental sequence. This format enables the teacher to identify the level at which the child is functioning and to measure the child's progress from one point to another. Some diagnostic norm-referenced tests also enable the teacher to determine the specific skills that the child has mastered and those for which the child needs remedial help.

Educational Classification Systems

No educational system for classifying emotional problems compares to those used in mental health settings. Hewett and Taylor (1980) and Wood

(1975) have each developed diagnostic classification systems. These classifications also have prescriptive properties, but both of these systems are intended for a specific education program.

In most states educators do classify children as learning disabled, emotionally disturbed or mentally retarded, but as Newman (1961) pointed out some time ago, the phrase emotional disturbance is a "portmanteau" term. It has no prescriptive value. In some states the qualifiers *mild, moderate* and *severe* are attached to the label *emotional disturbance* but there is little agreement on what the terms mean. (Olson, Algozzine & Schmid, 1980; Kelly, Bullock & Dykes, 1977).

Another approach to classification used frequently in educational settings consists of empirically determined categories derived from factor analyses of problem behaviors. With impressive consistency, researchers report that the two strongest factors are aggression and anxiety.

Aggression. While aggressive behavior is seen with almost every constellation of emotional problems, the type of aggression that consistently appears in factor analytic studies is frequently expressed in behavior that is disturbing to the enviroment. The salient behavorial characteristics of children in the aggression category include disobedience, inattentiveness, laziness in school, shortness of attention span, fighting, negativism, destructiveness, temper tantrums, irritability, restlessness, attention-seeking behavior, disruptiveness, boisterousness, irresponsibility, disobedience, uncooperativeness, hyperactivity, impertinence, physical and verbal aggression, daredevil behavior and bossiness. Many of these children lack social-interpersonal trust and therefore are hypersensitive to rejection and insincerity from others. For many of these children, school represents an alien, rejecting, hostile environment that offers few positive experiences. Instead, it is a place that highlights failure, that utilizes repressive, punitive measures to gain conformity and thereby robs these children of one of their primary coping mechanisms—controlling others as a defense against the fear of vulnerability. Also included in this group are children who have a strong identification with a subculture that devalues education. Loyalty to their peers is of paramount importance to many of these children. Almost all of these children respond to threats and emotional stress with hostility toward the environment. Some act out their hostility in overt aggressiveness; others express their hostility through more covert, passive-aggressive means. Regardless of the mode of expression, as Kauffman (1977) aptly puts it, these children create a great deal of "interpersonal nastiness" if their aggressive behavior is not controlled. These are the "disturbing" children.

Children who exhibit these behaviors frequently come from homes in which antisocial behavior and values are prevalent. Achenbach (1966) studied 191 children who exhibited behaviors similar to those described above; all came from families in which the parents were described as "resentful" or "indifferent." These families also had high frequencies of overt social problems, such as a criminal history, alcoholism, illegitimacy and unemployment. Achenbach concludes that these symptoms reflect a learning regime in the child's home that leads to antisocial behavior. Numerous studies have lent support to Achenbach's conclusion (Ross, 1980; Kauffman, 1977.)

Labels that have been attached to this cluster of aggressive behaviors include "conduct disorder" (Peterson, 1961), "unsocialized aggressive" (Hewett & Jenkins, 1946), "negatively organized" (Ross, 1966) and "externalizers" (Achenbach, 1966). Almost all of the behavior checklists have a subscale for aggression. Although the specific items or problem behaviors do vary from scale to scale, almost all report a strong factor that reflects aggressive, antisocial behavior.

Anxiety. The other pattern of disordered behavior that consistently appears in factor analytic studies is one that reflects anxiety, inhibition and social isolation. Although many people experience anxiety, they experience it, like aggression, with less intensity and frequency. Behaviors characteristic of this pattern include hypersensitivity, self-consciousness, fearfulness, social withdrawal, feelings of inferiority, lack of self-confidence, anxiousness, perfectionism, passivity, fear of strange adults, over-responsiveness to change, fear of physical hurt, slowness of speech, finger chewing, little smiling, limited verbal responsiveness, failure to speak when angered, social isolation and somatic complaints. Morse (1969), using the label *neurotic* to describe these children, suggests that the common element in this pattern of disordered behavior is a personal problem, an internalized unconscious conflict accompanied by a devalued perception of self. Children who exhibit many of these behaviors are usually the ones who suffer discomfort, not others in their environment. These children are the "disturbed" children.

Many of these anxious children do not have achievement problems, and in fact some may be over-achievers (Ross, 1966). Behaviors such as perfectionism, excessive need to please others and a fear of failure serve as motivators to achieve. Quay (1963) suggests that anxiety facilitates the acquisition of simple, conditioned responses but interferes with complex learning; hence initially and superficially such children may produce, but nevertheless the high level of anxiety does interfere by constricting the child's creative and integrative thinking.

Parents of anxious children seem to have different traits compared to parents of aggressive children. Achenbach (1966) reports that in a sample of 211 children in a psychiatric facility who fit this pattern (more girls than boys) most were living with both natural parents and their parents were described as "concerned." Furthermore, the parents had made relatively good social adjustments in their adult lives, and during their school years had experienced few overt problems (e.g. suspension, failure).

Labels that have been attached to this cluster of problem behaviors include "personality disorder" (Peterson, 1961), "over-inhibited" (Hewitt & Jenkins, 1946), "striving decompensated" (Ross, 1966) and "internalizers" (Achenbach, 1966). As with the aggression factor, most current behavior checklists have a neurotic, inhibition or anxiety subscale to account for the anxiety factor.

Although a large number of children can be appropriately classified in one of these two groups, not all children fit this dichotomy. In Achenbach's (1966) study, 31% of the 300 females were unclassified (that is, 60% of their problem behaviors did not fit in either category) and 35% of the males were unclassified. Many children display a variety of behavioral problems and thereby earn elevated scores on several behavioral dimensions. It is difficult to categorize such children.

Diagnostic Evaluation in Mental Health Settings

The traditional diagnostic evaluation in a mental health setting is carried out by the child psychiatrist, the clinical psychologist and the psychiatric social worker. In recent years other professionals have been included, such as pediatricians, neurologists, teachers, psychiatric nurses, occupational and physical therapists, and speech and hearing specialists. The purpose of the evaluation is to clarify the nature of the intrapsychic conflicts of the child and his family. In order to do this, the content of the evaluation focuses upon the following questions:

1 How long-standing is the problem? Did it appear recently in reaction to trauma or stress or has it been evolving since very early childhood?
2 What are the contributing factors? Are there neurological or psychological problems? Do the parents' personalities and stresses interact with the child's personality and stresses in counterproductive ways?
3 How severe are the problems? Does the child experience the problems frequently and intensely or do they arise during particularly stressful times?
4 How do the child and family organize themselves to deal with daily stresses? Do they run away literally or psychologically? Do they blame others? Are they very disorganized and unpredictable?
5 How amenable are the child and family to change? Do they have a fairly clear understanding of the problems or are they highly resistant to believing they have a part in the problem? Can they form a trusting relationship with a therapist or are they extremely guarded and aloof?

Traditionally these issues are explored by the psychiatrist in the clinical interview, by the psychologist in the testing sessions and by the social worker in the parent interviews.

Clinical Interviews with Latency-Age Children

The clinical interview typically is an unstructured interview in which the child is encouraged to express himself freely. Materials that elicit symbolic play are available, such as crayons, Play-Doh, finger paint, family dolls, doll houses, clay, puppets, play guns and play knives. The assumption is made that what the child chooses to do with the materials has preconscious and unconscious significance. The interviewer follows closely the symbolic meaning of the play while interacting with the child around the literal content.

The interview normally includes introductory activities, time for free play and a closing (Werkman, 1965). The introductory phase includes the meeting and the orientation activities both in the waiting room and in the office. During this phase the interviewer notes how the child greets new people and situations and how he deals with separations from his parents. The free play phase begins once the child gets involved in an activity. During this time the interviewer tries to facilitate the child's involvement in fantasy and the expression of affect and attitudes. Toward the end of the free play time the interviewer may use some projective techniques such as asking the child, "If you had three wishes, what would they be?" During the closing part of the session the interviewer discusses with the child her view of the child's problems and what she thinks should be done.

As soon as the child leaves, the interviewer records verbatim what transpired during the session. These data must then be summarized in a report, which should include the following topics: the child's relationship with the interviewer (trust, intimacy, warmth), the child's expression of affect, the child's ability to separate and the adequacy of the child's motor functioning, reality testing, coping mechanisms and judgment (Werkman, 1965). Werkman also suggests including a brief description of the content of material covered during the sessions.

The clinical interview has problems with reliability, validity, and interviewer bias and error. As Shepp (1979) points out, the interview is a "blunt instrument and it should not be used in attempting to cut fine slices" (p. 118). It remains a very popular technique, however, because it is direct and flexible and it gives the interviewer an opportunity to gauge how the child will be able to function in therapy.

Psychological Testing

As with the clinical interview, the primary goal of psychological testing is to establish the existence of underlying conflicts and to clarify the nature of these conflicts. One of the reasons psychological testing is so prevalent during diagnostic evaluations is that it is a shortcut to learning about the child's psyche (Kessler, 1966).

Typically the psychologist utilizes an array of instruments ranging from structured tests of intellectual and academic functioning to unstructured tests of personality. Intelligence tests, perceptual-motor inventories, tests of auditory and visual acuity and of oral language are administered by the psychologist in order to ensure that the child's odd or inappropriate behaviors are not caused primarily by conditions other than emotional disturbance, such as mental retardation, brain damage, visual or auditory impairment, or aphasia. Additionally, these tests provide corroborative data for personality assessment.

The personality tests used in clinical settings are usually projective in format although a few nonprojective, paper-and-pencil tests are also used. Projective tests have a subjective format. Ambiguous stimuli are presented to the child who is then expected to respond. Answers are viewed not as right or wrong but rather as a reflection of the child's opinions, beliefs, attitudes and feelings that typify his conscious or unconscious personality characteristics. In contrast, nonprojective personality tests rely on the conscious reports of the child or parent (and occasionally other adults significant in the child's life). Responses are scored in an objective, standardized fashion. Interpretation of the results is fairly standardized as well.

It has frequently been said that a test is only as good as the person using it. Nowhere is this dictum truer than in the area of personality testing, a realm of testing that relies heavily on clinical judgment. A test is a tool which helps the clinician make decisions—the test itself is not the decision maker.

The least structured of the widely used projective tests is the Rorschach Test (Rorschach, 1942). It consists of 10 white cards on which inkblots have been printed, of which 5 are achromatic, 2 are black and red, and 3 are multicolored. As each card is presented to the child, he is instructed to tell the examiner what it reminds him of and to explain why (that is, what characteristics of the inkblot provoked his response). Several scoring systems have been developed (Beck, 1944; Exner, 1974; Halpern, 1953; Klopfer & Kelley, 1942) but essentially all of them attempt to provide systematically obtained answers to the following questions: How does the child characteristically approach a problem? Does he look at the problem as a whole and then break it down into component parts, or does he look at the individual parts and build to a whole? Is he flexible, rigid, persevering, creative, and so on, in his approach to problem solving? How effectively does he use his intelligence? How well does he modulate his emotions?

Numerous studies done with the Rorschach Test have yielded mixed results. Proponents of the instrument find it clinically very useful while critics charge that it is subjective, unreliable and invalid. All agree that in order to use it, a psychologist must have a broad psychological background and extensive experience with the instrument itself.

Other projective tests frequently used with children in clinical settings are the Tasks of Emotional Development (TED) (Cohen & Weil, 1971), the Child's Apperception Test (CAT) (Bellak, 1954), the Blacky Test (Blum, 1950) and the Thematic Apperception Test (TAT) (Murray, 1943). All of these consist of a series of cards with pictures of situations designed to elicit reactions to developmental tasks. The Blacky and CAT use animals in the pictures whereas the TED and the TAT have people. The child is supposed to make up a story about each card. Theoretically, the child identifies with the central figure in the picture and creates a story that projects his own feelings about the situation. Content of the stories is analyzed using criteria such as the ones suggested by Bakwin and Bakwin (1960):

1 The type of individual with whom the child identifies
2 The needs manifested by the central figure
3 Influences exerted by the environment
4 The nature of the interaction between the central figure and external pressures
5 The outcome

Another form of projective testing is the sentence completion technique. The child simply finishes incomplete sentence stems such as "I would like to . . .", "I am ashamed of . . .", "I dream about . . ." and "My mother thinks I . . .". Hypothetically, the child will reveal feelings about himself and his life situation through his responses; however, since the technique is so direct and the intent so transparent, the results are not always very revealing. Children can easily give socially desirable responses, thereby concealing their own feelings.

Figure drawings are another projective technique that is widely used. Among the several approaches to this technique are "Draw a person," "Draw a person doing something," "Draw a house, tree and person" and "Draw your family." The child's drawing is presumed to provide an index of the child's self-perception. Clinical guidelines for interpreting the results are reported in Ogdon (1975), Hammer (1972) and Harris (1963).

Swenson (1968) reviewed 10 years of research on projective drawings and concluded that global ratings have a level of reliability suitable for most psychometric purposes. Many clinicians use this technique as an icebreaker because children generally enjoy the task and at times reveal important information about themselves.

An example of a nonprojective measure of personality is found in the Multidimensional Description of Child Personality (PIC) (Wirt, Lachar, Klinedinst & Sear, 1977). The authors of the PIC used the same methodological approach that was used in developing the Minnesota Multiphasic Personality Inventory (MMPI); that is, responses on normals are compared to responses on children with problems. The 600 items on the PIC are answered true or false by the parents.

Parent Interviews

Prior to or concurrent with the child's evaluation are the parent interviews, which may be conducted with the mother, the father or both parents together. During the diagnostic phase usually a minimum of two one-hour interviews are conducted to gather factual information about the child and family and to assess parental attitudes toward the child and family. The information sought during these interviews can be classified into the following categories (Kessler, 1966):

1 *Presenting problems.* These include the parents' understanding of the child's problems and information about duration of these problems.
2 *Current functioning.* The child's adjustment with the family, with other children, and in school is described. This information may indicate both additional symptoms of psychopathology as well as personality strengths of the child.
3 *History.* This includes information about the child's development and any unusual events that the parents recall.
4 *Family relationships.* These are roles played by the child in his family and roles played by other family members.
5 *Parental history.* Information about the parents' lives can provide valuable insights into their current behavior and attitudes.

While a skilled interviewer will cover all these topics and gather a great deal of information, she generally does so in an informal conversational manner. Clinicians generally view diagnostic sessions as the initial phase of treatment. Subscribing to the belief that it is useless to get the facts and lose the case, care is taken not to push the parents too much. If parents indicate a reluctance to discuss a topic, their resistance is usually respected. As treatment progresses, additional diagnostic information is gathered and resistances are explored when a better relationship has developed between client and therapist.

Systems of Classification

Once the data have been collected, the results are shared with other members of the professional team. A diagnosis is determined and treatment plans are recommended. Among the many systems for classifying psychopathology, the two prevailing systems in mental health settings are the system delineated in the third edition of the *Diagnostic and Statistical Manual of Mental Disorders* of the American Psychiatric Association, better known simply as the DSM III, and the *Classification System of Psychopathological Disorders in Childhood* proposed by the Group for the Advancement of Psychiatry, or simply the GAP. These two systems represent somewhat different approaches to diagnosis.

The DSM III is a classification system for adults as well as for children that is descriptive and atheoretical with regard to etiology. Rather than hypothesize how or why the disturbance came to be, the DSM III attempts to describe comprehensibly the manifestations of the disorder. It utilizes a "multi-axial" system which provides for systematic coding of more information than was included in previous systems. Operational criteria to be used in determining a diagnosis have been specified for most of the disorders, and information is provided about age at onset, course of development of the disorder, typical degree of impairment, expected complications, predisposing factors and sex ratio.

One of the major problems with diagnostic systems has been the lack of uniformity in the use of diagnoses. By including such specific descriptive information, the DSM III represents a significant effort to overcome this problem. Since its publication in 1980, there has been little time to research the inter-rater reliability of clinicians' diagnoses using the DSM III. Critics of the DSM III charge that it lacks prescriptive value because it deals only with the overt, behavioral, or symptomatic, level.

The GAP system was designed specifically for children's psychiatric disorders and is based upon the psychodynamic view of disturbance. Heavy emphasis is placed upon developmental issues and the nature of intrapsychic conflicts. The major categories and primary characteristics of each are

1 *Healthy responses*. These are defined as age- or stage-appropriate in intellectual, social, emotional, personal and adaptive functioning. Examples of problematic behaviors which might be so classified are separation anxiety in preschool children, a normal developmental crisis, and depression and mourning following the death of a loved animal.
2 *Reactive disorders*. These are disturbances that are primarily a reaction to an event or situation. The problematic behavior is seen as a manifestation of a predominantly conscious conflict between the child's drives and feelings and his social environment. An example of a reactive disorder is a young child, suddenly deprived of adequate

mothering, who becomes acutely aggressive in an effort to punish his environment.

3 *Developmental deviations.* These are deviations in personality or biological development which are considered to be beyond the range of normal variation in that they occur at a time, in a sequence or in a degree not expected for a given age level or stage of development. An example is a significant delay in speech development that is not attributed to deafness, oppositional behavior, elective mutism, brain damage or early childhood psychosis.

4 *Psychoneurotic disorders.* These are defined as unconscious conflicts over the handling of sexual and aggressive impulses which, though removed from awareness by the mechanism of repression, remain active and unresolved. These conflicts are believed to have their genesis in the preschool years. The child's reality testing is not grossly disturbed.

5 *Personality disorders.* These are chronic or fixed pathological traits in the personality structure that usually are not perceived by the child as a source of intrapsychic distress (that is, they are *ego-syntonic*). For developmental reasons these are not commonly in a structured form until a later school-age period. Most personality disorders appear to involve strong fixations in psychosexual and psychosocial development at infancy and early childhood levels, related to original conflicts over dependent wishes, strivings for autonomy, aggressive impulses and sexual differentiation.

6 *Psychotic disorders.* These are characterized by marked pervasive deviations from the behavior that is expected for the child's age. Symptoms may include a severe and continued impairment of emotional relationships with persons, associated with an aloofness and a tendency toward preoccupation with inanimate objects; loss of speech or failure in its development; disturbances in sensory perception; bizarre or stereotyped behavior and motility patterns; marked resistance to change in environment or routine; outbursts of intense and unpredictable panic; absence of a sense of personal identity; and blunted, uneven or fragmented intellectual development.

The GAP classification system includes four additional major categories: psychophysiological disorders, brain syndromes, mental retardation, and other disorders. These are not frequently used in classifying emotionally disturbed children.

While the GAP system is praised as being more sensitive to the "fluidity of children's behavior" and to the "developmental significance of symptoms" (Early & Behar, 1978), it has been criticized for its heavy psychoanalytic orientation and for its lack of specificity in its descriptions of diagnostic criteria. A study by Freedman (1971) illustrated the types of problems arising from this lack of specificity; he reported only .59 inter-rater reliability in classifying major GAP categories.

Arriving at a diagnosis, be it educational or psychiatric, is only an intermediate step to beginning an intervention. Data collected during the diagnostic process provide a baseline against which future behavior can be compared. Effectiveness of the intervention can be determined by comparing current behavior to the behavior reported during the diagnostic process. When progress is not being made, intervention plans can be changed and evaluated. In this manner, diagnosis is only the first step in an ongoing evaluation activity. Data about the child and his family are constantly being gathered and evaluated during the intervention phase. Plans are formed, confirmed and changed continuously on that basis. If diagnoses become ends in themselves, they become stigmatizing and harmful rather than prescriptive.

SUMMARY

From this brief review of techinques used for screening, identification and diagnosis, it is clear that there are many approaches to answering the questions, what is the problem? and why is it there?. There are also many answers to the question, what should be done? The differences in points of view may be attributed to the mission, the discipline, and the philosophical orientation of the professionals in the setting in which behavior is observed.

The concept of the least intrusive psychological assessment provides guidance in deciding how to proceed with an evaluation, especially in an educational setting. Briefly stated, this concept suggests that one should start an evaluation with a technique that minimizes intrusion upon the child and, as is necessary, moves inward toward more inferential and personally focused techniques.

Following this approach, one would start an evaluation by observing the child in his classroom. This technique provides a great deal of data with minimal psychological intrusion. Sometimes observational data suggest environmental adjustments, and when these are made the problem disappears. No further assessment is needed. If, however, no environmental changes are indicated or if, after environmental factors are manipulated, the problem persists, additional data should be gathered.

The direction of this data-gathering process is determined by observations of the child. For example, children who appear hyperactive and easily distracted, even after environmental adaptations, may require assessment of cognitive and perceptual motor functioning in order to address the question of organic disorder. A detailed developmental history might be gathered to augment the test results. If no support for organic origin is found or if other problems are also noted, personality testing may be indicated. For children with excessive anxiety and fears, the source of these troubles may be studied. Assessment of the child's inner life and self-perceptions may be needed. Often multiple problems are observed, in which case each problem should be carefully investigated with the appropriate techniques.

Investigation into the child's disturbance leads to a conclusion about the nature of both the child's and the family's problems. This conclusion or classification affects others' expectations for the child. For example, a teacher who believes that a child has a psychoneurological deficit may interpret the child's messy handwriting as a result of this deficit rather than as a form of passive-aggressive noncompliance. General diagnostic information helps in formulating assumptions about the cause of behavior and the nature of the intervention, but it does not help in determining specific educational interventions. This information is gained from educational assessments.

Within the evaluation process, the role of the evaluator is critical. The evaluator, not the test or technique, makes decisions about the meaning of test results. The evaluator makes inferences about the meaning and significance of the child's behavior. The evaluator also determines what to report and how to present the data. Since evaluations done in school become part of the child's educational record, inferential statements, especially about the child's inner life or the family's role in the problem, should be minimized because they are subject to evaluator biases. Erroneous information about children or their families could be very detrimental. Furthermore, children's inner conflicts and the family's dynamics can and do change. When information about them is included in a permanent record, they can be misinterpreted and misunderstood.

The evaluator has a responsibility to help the child and family learn from the evaluation and feel hopeful that their problems can be mastered. The purpose of an evaluation study is "to know another human being, but it is not just knowing in objective terms: it is empathetic knowing so that the child who is thus known will, as a result of the process, feel more accepted, understood, and to the extent he can, more trusting" (Morse, 1979, p. 9).

DISCUSSION QUESTIONS

1. P.L. 94-142 mandates that all handicapped children be identified. Discuss the advantages and disadvantages of conducting systematic screening procedures in a school system.
2. Compare data that one might get from behavior checklists and observation scales with data from interviews, self-report and projective instruments.
3. What role should teachers have in screening, identification and diagnostic procedures?
4. Discuss problems encountered in identifying and evaluating emotionally disturbed children.

REFERENCES

Achenbach, T. M. The classification of children's psychiatric symptoms: A factor-analytic study. *Psychological Monographs*, 1966, *80* (Whole No. 615).

Adelman, H. S. Predicting psycho-educational problems in childhood. *Behavioral Disorders*, 1978, *3*, 148–159.

American Psychiatric Association. *Diagnostic and statistical manual* (Vol. 3). Washington, D.C.: American Psychiatric Association, 1979.

Bakwin, H., & Bakwin, R. *Behavior disorders in children*. Philadelphia, Pa.: Saunders, 1960.

Beck, S. J. *Rorschach's test* (Vol. 1, Basic processes). New York: Grune & Stratton, 1944.

Beery K. E., & Buktenica, M. *Developmental test of visual-motor integration*. Chicago: Follett, 1967.

Bellak, L. *The thematic apperception test and the child's apperception test in clinical use*. New York: Grune & Stratton, 1954.

Bender, L. *A visual motor Gestalt test and its clinical use* (American Orthopsychiatric Association Research Monograph, No. 3). New York: American Orthopsychiatric Association, 1938.

Bloom, R. B., Shea, R. J., & Eun, B. The Piers-Harris self-concept scale: Norms for behaviorally disordered children. *Psychology in the Schools*, 1979, *16*, 483–487.

Blum G. *The Blacky pictures: Manual of instructions*. New York: Psychological Corporation, 1950.

Bower, E. M. Social and emotional problems in the classroom. *Children*, 1957, *4*, 143–147.

Bower, E. M. *Early identification of emotionally handicapped children in school* (1st ed.). Springfield, Ill.: Charles C Thomas, 1960.

Bower, E. M. *Early identification of emotionally handicapped children in school* (2nd ed.). Springfield, Ill.: Charles C Thomas, 1969.

Brown, L. L., & Hammill, D. D. *Behavior rating profile: An ecological approach to behavioral assessment.* Austin, Tex.: PRO-ED, 1978.

Burks, H. F. *Burks' behavior rating scales.* Los Angeles, Calif.: Western Psychological Services, 1977.

Buros, O. (Ed.). *The mental measurements yearbook.* Highland Park, N.J.: Gryphon Press, 1978.

Cohen, H., & Weil, G. R. *Tasks of emotional development.* Lexington, Mass.: D. C. Heath, 1971.

Coie, J. D., & Pennington, B. F. Children's perceptions of deviance and disorder. *Child Development*, 1976, *47*, 407–413.

Cooke, T. P., & Apolloni, T. Developing positive emotional behaviors: A study in training and generalization effects. *Journal of Applied Behavior Analysis*, 1976, *9*, 65–78.

Coopersmith, S. A method for determining types of self-esteem. *Journal of Abnormal and Social Psychology*, 1959, *59*, 87–94.

Cowen, E. L., Pederson, A., Babigian, H., Izzo, L. D., & Trost, M. A. Long-term follow-up of early detected vulnerable children. *Journal of Consulting and Clinical Psychology*, 1973, *41*, 438–446.

Davids, A., & Parenti, A. N. Time orientation and interpersonal relations of emotionally disturbed and normal children. *Journal of Abnormal and Social Psychology*, 1958, *57*, 299–305.

Davis, W. E. A comparison of teacher referral and pupil self-referral measures relative to perceived school adjustment. *Psychology in the Schools*, 1978, *15*, 22–26.

Early B., & Behar, L. *A review of several diagnostic classification systems in child mental health.* Raleigh, N. C.: Division of Mental Health, Mental Retardation and Substance Abuse, North Carolina Department of Human Resources, 1978.

Exner, J. *The Rorschach: A comprehensive system.* New York: John Wiley & Sons, 1974.

Fitzgerald, G. E. The use of objective observational data in the identification of emotionally disabled pupils. In C. Smith (Ed.), *The identification of emotionally disabled pupils: Data and decision making.* Des Moines, Iowa: Department of Public Instruction, 1979.

Freedman, M. Reliability study of psychiatric diagnosis in childhood and adolescence. *Journal of Child Psychology and Psychiatry*, 1971, *12*, 43–54.

French, J. L. *Pictorial test of intelligence* Boston, Mass.: Houghton Mifflin, 1964.

Frostig, M., Maslow, P., Lefever, D. W., & Whittlesey, J. R. The Marianne Frostig developmental test of visual perception: 1963 standardization. Palo Alto, Calif.: Consulting Psychologists Press, 1964.

Glidewell, J., & Swallow, C. *The prevalence of maladjustment in the elementary schools.* Chicago: University of Chicago Press, 1968.

Gordon, I. J. *Studying the child in school.* New York: John Wiley & Sons, 1966.

Greenwood, C. R., Walker, H. M., & Hops, H. Issues in social interaction/withdrawal assessment. *Exceptional Children*, 1977, *43*, 490–499.

Group for the Advancement of Psychiatry. *Psychopathological disorders in childhood: Theoretical considerations and a proposed classification.* New York: Group for the Advancement of Psychiatry, 1969.

Halpern, F. *A clinical approach to children's Rorschachs.* New York: Grune & Stratton, 1953.

Hammer, E. F. *The house-tree-person (H-T-P) clinical research manual.* Los Angeles, Calif.: Western Psychological Services, 1972.

Harris, D. B. *Children's drawings as measures of intellectual maturity.* New York: Harcourt, Brace & World, 1963.

Harris, W. J., Drummond, R. J., & Schultz, E. W. An investigation of relationships between teachers' ratings of behavior and children's personality traits. *Journal of Abnormal Child Psychology*, 1977, *5*, 43–52.

Harth, R., & Glavin, J. P. Validity of teacher rating as a subtest for screening emotionally disturbed children. *Exceptional Children*, 1971, *37*, 605–606.

Hewett, F. M., & Taylor, F. D. *The emotionally disturbed child in the classroom: The orchestration of success* (2nd ed.). Boston, Mass.: Allyn & Bacon, 1980.

Hewett, L. E., & Jenkins, R. L. *Fundamental patterns of maladjustment: The dynamics of their origin.* Springfield, Ill.: State of Illinois, 1946.

Hiskey, M. Hiskey-Nebraska test of learning aptitude. Lincoln, Neb.: Union College Press, 1966.

Hobbs, N. *The futures of children.* San Francisco, Calif.: Jossey-Bass, 1975.

Hoffman, E., Marsden, G., & Kalter, N. Children's understanding of their emotionally disturbed peers: A replication. *Journal of Clinical Psychology*, 1977, *33*, 949–953.

Kaplan, H. K., & Kaufman, I. Sociometric status and behaviors of emotionally disturbed children. *Psychology in the Schools*, 1978, *15*, 8–15.

Kauffman, J. M. *Characteristics of children's behavior disorders.* Columbus, Ohio: Charles E. Merrill, 1977.

Kelly, T. J., Bullock, L. M. & Dykes, M. K. Behavioral disorders: Teachers perceptions. *Exceptional Children*, 1977, *43*, 316–318.

Kessler, J. W. *Psychopathology of childhood.* Englewood Cliffs, N.J.: Prentice-Hall, 1966.

Kirschenbaum, D. S., Marsh, M. E., & Devoge, J. B. The effectiveness of a mass screening procedure in an early intervention program. *Psychology in the Schools*, 1977, *14*, 400–406.

Klopfer, R., & Kelley, D. *The Rorschach technique.* Yonkers, N.Y.: World Book, 1942.

Lambert, N. M., Hartsough, C. S., & Bower, E. M. *A process for early identification of emotionally disturbed children.* Monterey, Calif.: Publishers Test Service, 1979.

Leiter, R., & Arthur, G. Leiter international performance scale and the Arthur adaptation. Chicago: C. H. Stoelting, 1969.

Lillie, D. L. Screening. In L. Cross & K. Goin (Eds.), *Identifying handicapped children: A guide to casefinding, screening, diagnosis, assessment, and evaluation.* New York: Walker, 1977.

Lobitz, G. K., & Johnson, S. M. Normal versus deviant children. *Journal of Abnormal Child Psychology*, 1975, *3*, 353–374.

Long, N. J., Cook, A. R., Evans, E. D., Kerr, J., Linke, L. A., Neubauer, B., & Payne, D. C. Groups in perspective: A new sociometric technique for classroom teachers. *Bulletin of the School of Education, Indiana University*, 1962, *38*, 1–112.

McCarthy, D. McCarthy scales of children's abilities. New York: Psychological Corporation, 1972.

Mercer, J., & Lewis, J. F. SOMPA: System of multicultural pluralistic assessment. New York: The Psychological Corporation, 1977.

Miller, L. C. Louisville behavior checklist. Los Angeles, Calif.: Western Psychological Services, 1977.

Miller, L. E. Setting analysis data in the identification of emotionally disabled pupils. In C. Smith (Ed.), *The identification of emotionally disabled pupils: Data and decision making.* Des Moines, Iowa: Iowa Department of Public Instruction, 1979.

Mischel, W. *Personality and assessment.* New York: John Wiley & Sons, 1968.

Moos, R. H. *Evaluating educational environments.* San Francisco, Calif.: Jossey-Bass, 1979.

Morse, W. C. The educational implications of differential diagnosis. In H. W. Harshman (Ed.), *Educating the emotionally disturbed: A book of readings.* New York: Thomas Y. Crowell, 1969.

Morse, W. C. Emotionally handicapped: Problems of identification and definition.

Proceedings of the Conference on Emotionally Handicapped Pupils: Total IEP Implementation Now and the Future, Raleigh, N.C., November 1978.

Murray, H. A. Thematic apperception test. Cambridge, Mass.: Harvard University Press, 1943.

Nelson, C. M. Techniques for screening conduct disturbed children. *Exceptional Children*, 1971, *37*, 501–507.

Newcomer, P.L. *Understanding and teaching emotionally disturbed children.* Boston, Mass.: Allyn & Bacon, 1980.

Newman, R. G. Conveying essential messages to the emotionally disturbed at school. *Exceptional Children*, 1961, *28*, 199–204.

Novak, D. W. Children's reactions to emotional disturbance in imaginary peers. *Journal of Consulting and Clinical Psychology*, 1974, *42*, 462.

Ogdon, D. P. *Psychodiagnostics and personality assessment: A handbook* (2nd ed.). Los Angeles, Calif.: Western Psychological Services, 1975.

Olson, J., Algozzine, B., & Schmid, R. E. Mild, moderate and severe emotional handicap: An empty distinction? *Behavior Disorders*, 1980, *5*, 96–101.

Peed, S., Roberts, M., & Forehand, R. Evaluation of the effectiveness of a standardized parent training program in altering the interaction of mothers and their noncompliant children. *Behavior Modification*, 1977, *1*, 323–350.

Peterson, D. R. Behavior problems of middle childhood. *Journal of Consulting Psychology*, 1961, *25*, 205–209.

Peterson, D. R., & Quay, H. C. Behavior problem checklist. New Brunswick, N. J.: School of Professional Psychology, Rutgers University, Busch Campus, 1979.

Piers, E. V. Manual for the Piers-Harris children's self concept scale. Nashville, Tenn.: Counselor Recordings and Tests, 1969.

Piers, E. V., & Harris, D. B. *The Piers-Harris children's self concept scale.* Nashville, Tenn.: Counselor Recordings and Tests, 1969.

Quay, H. C. Measuring dimensions of deviant behavior: The behavior problem checklist. *Journal of Abnormal Child Psychology*, 1977, *5*, 277–287.

Quay, H. C. Some basic considerations in the education of emotionally disturbed children. *Exceptional Children*, 1963, *30*, 27–31.

Redl, F. *When we deal with children: Selected writings.* New York: Free Press, 1966.

Roach, E. F., & Kephart, M. C. The Purdue perceptual-motor survey. Columbus, Ohio: Charles E. Merrill, 1966.

Rolf, J. E. Peer status and the directionality of symptomatic behavior: Prime social competence predictors of outcome for vulnerable children. *American Journal of Orthopsychiatry*, 1976, *46*, 74–88.

Rorschach, H. *Psychodiagnostics.* New York: Grune & Stratton, 1942.

Ross, A. O. *Psychological disorders of children: A behavioral approach to theory, research, and therapy* (2nd ed.). New York: McGraw-Hill, 1980.

Ross, D. C. Poor school achievement: A psychiatric study and classification. *Clinical Pediatrics*, 1966, *5*, 109–117.

Rutter, M. A children's behavior questionnaire for completion by teachers: Preliminary findings. *Journal of Child Psychology and Psychiatry*, 1967, *8*, 1–11.

Salvia, J., & Ysseldyke, J. E. *Assessment in special and remedial education.* Boston, Mass.: Houghton Mifflin, 1978.

Sattler, J. M. *Assessment of children's intelligence.* Philadelphia, Pa.: W. B. Saunders, 1974.

Shea, R. M. *Teaching children and youth with behavior disorders.* St. Louis, Mo.: C. V. Mosby, 1978.

Shepherd, M., Oppenheim, A. N., & Mitchell, S. Childhood behavior disorders and the child-guidance clinic: An epidemiological study. *Journal of Child Psychology and Psychiatry*, 1966, *7*, 39–52.

Shepp, M. S. The use of the clinical interview in the assessment of self concept and affective state. In C. Smith (Ed.), *The identification of emotionally disabled pupils: Data and decision making.* Des Moines, Iowa: Iowa Department of Public Instruction, 1979.

Sibley, S. A., Abbott, M. S., & Cooper, B. P. Modification of the classroom behavior of a disadvantaged kindergarten boy by social reinforcement and isolation. *Journal of Experimental Child Psychology,* 1969, *7,* 203–219.

Spaulding, R. L. *The coping analysis schedule for educational settings (CASES).* Paper presented at the annual meeting of the American Educational Research Association, New Orleans, 1973. (ERIC Document Reproduction Service No. ED 066 246)

Stenner, A. J., & Katzenmeyer, W. G. Self-observation scales. Durham, N.C.: National Testing Service, 1974.

Swenson, C. H. Empirical evaluations of human figure drawings: 1957–1966. *Psychological Bulletin,* 1968, 29, 555–571.

Terman, L. M., & Merrill, M. A. Stanford-Binet intelligence scale (3rd revision). Boston: Houghton Mifflin, 1960.

Walker, H. M. Walker problem behavior identification checklist. Los Angeles, Calif.: Western Psychological Services, 1970.

Wechsler, D. Wechsler intelligence scale for children—revised (WISC–R). New York: Psychological Corporation, 1974.

Werkman, S. L. The psychiatric diagnostic interview with children. *American Journal of Orthopsychiatry,* 1965, *35,* 764–771.

Wirt, R. D., Lachar, D., Klinedinst, J. K., & Sear, P. D. *Multidimensional description of child personality: A manual for the personality inventory for children.* Los Angeles, Calif.: Western Psychological Services, 1977.

Wood, F. H., & Johnson, A. Coopersmith Self-esteem inventory scores for boys with severe behavior problems. *Exceptional Children,* 1972, *38,* 739.

Wood, M. M. *Developmental theory: A textbook for teachers as therapists for emotionally disturbed young children.* Baltimore, Md.: University Park Press, 1975.

Yellott, A. W., Liem, G. R., & Cowen, E. L. Relationship among measures of adjustment, sociometric status and achievement in third graders. *Psychology in the Schools,* 1969, *6,* 315–321.

Section Two

Perspectives

EMOTIONAL DISTURBANCE is a complex problem often involving many aspects of a child's life. Educational practice should be informed by the best understanding of the problems of emotional disturbance available.

The teacher must understand emotional disturbance in a way that helps him plan and implement an appropriate educational program for the child. Several theoretical perspectives have been developed that have practical value to teachers. Some perspectives are especially helpful in understanding abberations in the growth and development of children which are associated with emotional disturbance. Other perspectives are more helpful in understanding the role of the culture, the immediate environment and the interactions between the individual and his social setting. Some theories are useful primarily as a way of thinking about the problems of disturbance while other theories have more specific technical value in defining and changing the behaviors that are troubling or disturbing.

While each one of these perspectives has certain strengths and weaknesses, considered together they offer an intellectually rich foundation for understanding behavior. Understood clearly and used carefully, they provide an important basis for educational planning and programming.

In Section Two, six basic theoretical perspectives are described. They are described primarily in terms of their practical value to teachers. The discussion of theoretical perspectives in Section Two provides the basis for the more specific discussions of teaching emotionally disturbed children in Section Three.

Section Two includes the following chapters:

5 Psychodynamic Theory and Practice
6 Organic Theories
7 Behavior Theory and Practice
8 Ecological Theory and Practice
9 Sociological Theory and Practice
10 Cultural Theory and Practice

5
Psychodynamic Theory and Practice

main points

1 Psychodynamic theory views the development of the student's sense of self and autonomy as the central organizing principle of humanistic education.

2 Psychodynamic theory and education have influenced each other mutually and beneficially since the early 1900s.

3 A central theme of normal development, from the psychodynamic point of view, is the child's acquisition of a sense of trust of others, confidence in herself, and the ability to be curious and take initiative in order to learn about the self, significant others and the inanimate world.

4 The child's confidence, initiative, and ability to learn and perform develop out of the caretaking environment and the child's innate potentials acting in combination.

5 Emotional disturbance occurs when a child experiences persistent developmental lags or excessive, prolonged subjective distress, such as anxiety or depression.

6 A student's developmental lags and subjective distress are usually associated with distorted perceptions of the self and others which are transferred to the classroom environment.

7 A careful diagnostic study of the student and the student's environment is crucial to discovering the primary locus of the emotional disturbance which in turn determines the appropriate treatment.

8 A wide range of psychodynamic consultation and treatment modalities are available to assist students and their caretakers and teachers. These modalities may occur in training settings, schools, clinics and hospitals.

This chapter was written by **Charles Keith**, M.D., Duke University.

PSYCHODYNAMIC theory is the study of the dynamics of the human psyche or mind. Most current psychodynamic schools of thought grew out of psychoanalytic theory and all share certain basic principles. A central principle of psychodynamic theory as applied to education is that the child's psychic life is the nodal point of education. Thus, the ultimate usefulness of any educational practice depends on its ability to enhance the forward progression of the child's psychic life.

What is this psychic life of the child? It consists of the child's beliefs about herself in relation to others and to work tasks; the child's moral values, dreams and fantasies; the child's sense of mastery and competency, and a collection of past feelings, experiences and relationships which have crystallized into a character with unique coping styles. This psychic life is both conscious and unconscious; it is for the most part experienced as being inside oneself. But while it is felt to be private and inner, at the same time it is constantly being played out in the public realm including the classroom (Berlin & Szurek, 1965; Bower & Hollister, 1967; Brenner, 1973; Cameron, 1963; Ekstein & Motto, 1969; Jones, 1962; Kessler, 1966).

Psychodynamic theory and education have had a reciprocal impact on each other for over six decades. Though the influence of psychodynamic theories has waxed and waned as other personality theories have moved across the stage of education, its place within educational psychology remains secure due to its emphasis on (a) the child's autonomy and positive sense of self, (b) the child's perception of the world and the tasks of learning and (c) the child's developmental forces and symbolic mental processes which may enhance or interfere with learning and performance.

Psychodynamic theory began in the 1890s with the seminal discoveries of Sigmund Freud (Jones, 1953). Though Freud said he discovered nothing about children that nurses and mothers had not known for centuries, he presented to the startled scientific and educational world the news that the child's mind is not what most adults had wanted to believe. He described how the normal child has intense bodily needs and wishes, more passionate than those experienced in adult life. These needs are reinforced by the normal magical and egocentric thinking of childhood which makes the child experience her own needs as the center of her being and the pivot of her world. Most alarming, though certainly not new, was Freud's description of the child's sexual and aggressive needs and wishes (Freud, 1966a; Freud, 1966b). Freud's discoveries helped to usher in a new era of appreciation of the child's inner mental life. A new respect and understanding of the child were also reflected in the major social reforms of the era, such as child labor laws, school attendance laws, settlement house programs, the creation of juvenile courts, and the inauguration of school social work (Levine & Levine, 1970). Dewey (Levitt, 1960), Montessori (1964) and others were breathing new life into educational philosophy and practice. Nearly every facet of the child's life in the Western world was affected by this revolution in the care and understanding of the child in the early decades of this century.

With the discovery of the child's unreasoning guilt and excessive repression of sexual and aggressive urges, early psychodynamic clinicians worked with educators to create repression- and guilt-free schools. (See Wiener

[1967] for a description of Tolstoi's guilt-free school prior to Freud.) Some of these early experiments were doomed to failure unless directed by unusually gifted teachers. One reason many failed was that some guilt and repression was found to be necessary for a child's normal development and academic learning, a fact ruefully noted by Freud (1966c). These early, collaborative educational efforts, however, drew many gifted educators such as Anna Freud (1979), Aichhorn (1955), Fleischman (1967), Erikson (1959), and Redl (1966) into the psychodynamic movement. These pioneers retained their interest in education and built many bridges of understanding between psychodynamic theory and education through their prolific writings and work with educators (Ekstein, 1969).

In the 1930s and 1940s, psychodynamic clinicians became more aware of the role of the child's caretakers, usually the mother and later the teacher, in shaping the child's character, providing structure and "taming" the child's tumultuous drives (Cameron, 1963). Also, these were the years when child psychology came of age, particularly in the cognitive sphere. Psychodynamic theory and educational psychology recognized the importance of the child's naturally unfolding cognitive and intellectual abilities and how these shape and determine a child's perception of the world (Anderson, 1956; Flavell, 1963; Piaget, 1962; Watson, 1953).

Normal Development: The Psychodynamic View

Before examining the emotionally disturbed child's development from a psychodynamic perspective, we will look at the development of the normal child. According to psychodynamic theory there are few qualitative differences between normal and emotionally disturbed children. Most of the differences are quantitive. For example, a disturbed child may have excessive, prolonged fears, perhaps lasting months or years, about monsters or robbers entering the bedroom at night whereas in the normal child, these fears might exist for a few weeks and disappear with parental reassurance.

In presenting this scheme of normal development, several crucial assumptions will be made. First, it will be assumed the child described has an intact central nervous system and normal physical growth and development. Though children who are significantly damaged in their brains or bodies undergo the same psychological stages of development as normal children, a discussion of the complexities of the interaction between psyche and soma in these cases lies outside the scope of this chapter (Kessler, 1966; Kessler, Smith & McKinnon, 1976).

Another important assumption, for this discussion, is that the children described were born and raised in an "average expectable environment," which means that they have a parent who has enough interest, sense of parental responsibility and personal resources to give emotionally to the child. Thus, we will not be dealing in this chapter with children who have been severely brutalized, abandoned, starved or disadvantaged by extreme poverty. Children who grow up under these cruel conditions go through a similar sequence of developmental stages as do children from more benign environments. Their problems, however, often call for special interventions which, again, would take us beyond the scope of this chapter (Graffagnino,

Bucknam, Orgun & Leve, 1970; Mattick & Murphy, 1973; Meers, 1970; Pavendstedt, 1967).

The narrower scope of this discussion is fitting since the majority of emotionally disturbed pupils in the average classroom are those who have an average expectable environment and who stray quantitatively from the normal scheme of development. On a nationwide basis, the neurologically damaged and severely deprived child are statistically a small minority, though of course their problems loom large in education.

A guiding principle in the psychodynamic developmental scheme is the concept of *epigenesis* (Erikson, 1959). This term was borrowed from embryology. The concept grew out of the finding that injury to a part of the embryo hampers or prevents the development of future body parts which include the damaged part in their developmental sequence. The earlier the damage to the embryo the more future body parts are affected. As applied to human development, the epigenetic concept means that one developmental stage must be completed successfully enough to allow the next developmental stage to unfold and so on through the developmental sequence eventually leading to adulthood. The earlier and more massive the trauma or damage to the young child or infant, the more difficult it is for the subsequent developmental stages to unfold and be successfully completed. The fact that many individuals can surmount and master problems traceable to unfavorable earlier developmental periods through inner strengths, changes in life circumstances and therapy points to the strength and complexity of the human psyche but does not invalidate the epigenetic concept in human development. (For an alternate viewpoint, see Kagan, Kearsley & Zelazo [1978]).

This epigenetic concept underlies organized efforts such as infant stimulation programs and teenage pregnancy projects which are designed to prevent early developmental and emotional difficulties. These programs have won widespread but superficial acceptance; generally our society has not been fully committed to the principle of prevention and the concentration of resources on early child care.

Stage 1: The Early Mother-Infant Matrix

The human infant is the most dependent and helpless of all young mammals. This fact underscores the crucial importance of the early caretaking environment which supplies all that the infant needs for survival, growth and humanization. The early caretaking matrix and the infant who develops within this environment make up the first extrauterine ecosystem, the two elements acting on each other reciprocally. To acknowledge the importance of environment, however, is not the same as saying that the infant is born a tabula rasa. Each infant enters the extrauterine world with its own unique set of coping styles. Some infants are passive, some active; some are quiet, some loud. These innate patterns have been called by various names such as basic temperament (Thomas, Birch, & Chess, 1968), activity patterns (Fries & Woolf, 1953), or autonomous ego structures (Hartmann, 1958).

In recent years, it has been shown that infants also have a surprising repertoire of perceptual and communicative skills, though, again, sensitive mothers have always known this. Infants only a few days old can detect and show preference for complicated visual patterns and can distinguish their caretaker from strangers, as detected by changes in their heart and respiratory rates when the caretaker approaches for a feeding. Tiny infants move in rhythm to the inflections in their mother's voice. Not surprisingly, infants are most responsive perceptually to the external world after a satisfying feeding and when not in a state of marked bodily tension. A tense, crying, unsatisfied infant has trouble scanning and taking in the world about him. Thus, adequate maternal* care increases the opportunity for the infant to contemplate, perceive, take in information and to exercise his inborn skills (Kagan, Kearsley & Zelazo, 1978). The attachment that derives from these early learning experiences between the infant and mother in the first few hours or days of life has been called *bonding*, a concept roughly analogous to *imprinting* in certain animals. Failure to achieve satisfactory bonding has been shown to have detrimental effects throughout the child's early developmental stages (Klaus & Kennel, 1979).

This very early learning about the world becomes connected in the infant's mind with a satisfied feeling state if the caretaker has performed well. Though it is always risky to impute feelings and states of mind to the infant, our empathic observations suggest that the normal, sufficiently contented infant develops a sense of confidence and trust in himself and the caretaking world which allows the infant to enjoy learning and performing (Erikson, 1959).

Piaget and his students have outlined in detail some of these early forms of intelligence which are subsumed under the rubric sensori-motor stage of development. The following vignette illustrates a learning task at this stage:

> At five months, while he is trying to grasp a doll suspended from the crib, the child strikes it by chance. After his initial surprise at the result, he repeats the striking movement rather than trying to grasp the doll, and at the same time looks with interest at the doll; then he systematically practices "striking to make the doll swing again." (Wolff, 1960, p. 84)

The infant is practicing on the world and learning that he can make things happen. Of course, all of this depends on the mother being present physically and emotionally to provide the props and a sufficiently good holding environment. The infant "believes" he is really making things happen though, in truth, the mother is making it possible. The "good enough" mother realizes and accepts this, and enjoys the infant's egocentric activities (Winnicott, 1965). In these first few weeks and months of life are present all the necessary ingredients of successful learning, performing and teaching in later school life.

Stage 2: The Autonomous Self

If learning in Stage 1 has been successful, the infant is ready to move on to the next phase of development in which the central task is to define

---

*In this chapter, the word *maternal* connotes the principal caretaker, be it biological mother, father, relative, day-care supervisor, or housekeeper. Increasingly in our society, the primary maternal figure is not the biological mother.

oneself as an individual separate from the primary caretaker. In Stage 1 the infant shows little sign of distinguishing herself from the caretaker; but Stage 2 marks a forward thrust into autonomy and selfhood. The developments which make this possible are the onset of crawling and walking around 8–12 months of age, the increase in cognitive skills such as the ability to conceive an object having a separate existence from oneself (Piaget, 1962), and the vital maternal support and care which encourages exploration away from the mother but not so far that the toddler cannot readily return, both physically and emotionally, when anxious and in need of refueling (Mahler, 1975). This heady plunge into the world is accompanied by the onset of language and several major, formidable learning tasks. As every parent knows, two central educational issues for the toddler are learning to respect the word *no* and learning to control bladder and bowels, which in our society usually occurs around 18–24 months. Thus, with the newfound freedom of movement and expressive language, the toddler paradoxically must learn for the first time to limit her natural impulses. In other words, for the infant to gain something through learning, she must also relinquish something, a basic pedagogical principle and stumbling block for many children.

Learning problems make their appearance during this stage if the child and the maternal caretaker-cum-educator develop too many conflicts within themselves and in their relationship. There is no precise formula for the optimal learning environment for the young child, but generally it must include the proper balance of love and firmness. Too much guilt, anxiety, hostility or indifference in the caretaker can keep him from being realistically firm, instructive and nurturing to the toddler who is struggling to become socialized. Similarly, too much fear, hostility and anxiety in the child, such as anxiety about the mother's absence, can inhibit the child's nascent sense of competence and skill growth.

Another development is occurring at this stage which can help to explain how later learning problems develop. During this early stage, the infant or toddler is taking in and laying down mental representations in her mind of the innumerable daily interactions with the maternal caretaker as a representative of the external world. The child takes in the world via the mother in a process called *internalization*, which provides the child with the necessary building blocks of her inner psychic life. All children have good and bad experiences. The more normal the child, the more predominant are the good mental representations laid down in her mind. Similarly, the more disturbed the child, the more one finds negatively tinged representations. These mental representations are the eyeglasses through which the growing child views the world. In order to live in the real world, the child must develop methods of integrating her inner world with the demands of the external world. She does so by developing her own unique combination of coping skills, habits and defense mechanisms (Freud, A., 1936).

These marvelously complex coping skills and defenses can be adaptive or maladaptive. For instance, a two-year-old child may overcome a fear of receiving injections from a doctor by lining up dolls or playmates and giving them play shots with great panache. Another child might try to cope with this fear of injections by becoming afraid of people who wear white uniforms and refusing to enter any building reminding her of a doctor's office. Clearly the former child's coping style would be considered more adaptive and could lead to further advances in other related social and play skills. The latter child has developed a less adaptive coping style which could in turn lead to further social isolation.

Many of these coping skills, such as the child playing out fears in order to master them (Peller, 1954), are rather obvious and easily explainable from common sense. Other coping skills and defense mechanisms, however, are much harder to understand. Many coping devices or defenses disguise the true state of affairs within the child's mind so that what appears on the surface is really not what the child is experiencing inside. In this situation caretakers and teachers can become easily confused and misled. For example, a child who is fearful of being hurt or attacked by others will sometimes adapt to this fear by becoming like the attacker, a defense called *identification with the aggressor* (Freud, A., 1936). Such a child often becomes super-tough, combative and pugnacious. An aggressive response to such a child may only increase the child's underlying fear and spur him on to more attacking behavior. What is needed instead is an understanding of his underlying terror. A strategy of verbalizing fears or reducing the sources of fear will lessen the child's attacking stance. Taking defenses at face value rather than understanding how they function to protect a child from inner and outer anxieties and fears is one of the most common reasons for the frustration and misunderstanding on the part of parents, educators and therapists.

By age 2-3 the young child has clearly become separate in her own mind from her caretaker and has developed an inner psychic life with elaborate coping skills and defenses of her own making. The normal child of this age can take care of many of her bodily functions and explore and learn about her immediate environment. Of course, she is still quite dependent on adults and will remain so for many years. Also, magical thinking, in which the thought equals the deed, and egocentrism still abound, which lead the child to distort and misunderstand events in her life. For example, if a child's parent dies or disappears, the child will almost universally blame herself due to her egocentric and magical thinking. The child's reasoning goes something like this, "My parent is gone because I am bad. It is my fault. If I were good and lovable, my parent would have stayed with me." This type of thinking, quite normal for a child of age 2-3, is the main reason why early parent loss creates such a high risk for future problems (Furman, 1974; Nagera, 1970; Wallerstein & Kelly, 1975).

Stage 3: Sexual Identity and Conscience

Up to now, the child knows he or she is a boy or girl or, in other words, each has developed a *gender identity* and has assumed many of the cultural characteristics of a boy or girl. The child's psychic life, however, has been taken up by such matters as autonomy, controlling oneself and practicing language. As far as we know, a child prior to the age of 2 or 3 does not think much about himself or herself as a boy or girl but, instead, learns the cultural role through basic, conditioning processes. Around age 3-4, however, a dramatic change takes place as both the girl and the boy develop wishes and fantasies about what it means to be a girl or boy, particularly from the sexual-genital point of view. As with other forms of development, growth in this stage does not occur in a vacuum but in relation to the father and mother. If a child does not have one or both parents, fantasy parents are created in the child's mind. These fantasy parents are usually inflated to superhuman proportions by the child's magical thinking which if left unchecked by reality experiences can create many problems for the child (Neubauer, 1960).

Children in this phase of learning about oneself as a sexual person become intensely aware of their genitals as pleasurable organs and are avidly curious about the genitals of the opposite sex. For instance, boys and girls may ask why girls do not have penises, and they may create stories of badness and punishment to account for the absence of a penis in girls. Their avid interest in anatomy is matched by their curiosity about babies and how they are made, grow within the mother and arrive on the scene, though the baby's actual arrival is often greeted with mixed feelings by the older child, who feels displaced. Within the normal child's tender love relationship for each parent, possessive sexual feelings toward the opposite-sex parent arise, along with rivalrous, hostile feelings toward the same-sex parent. Children's passions at this age are the most intense they will ever experience (Brenner, 1973). Understandably, children experience much psychic conflict because of their rivalrous, competitive feelings for the parent of the same sex and the sexual longings for the opposite-sex parent. This constellation of feelings and fears that all children have toward their parents has been called the *Oedipus complex*, a name derived from the play *Oedipus Rex* by Sophocles in which a man unknowingly slays his father and marries his mother. Boys, for example, frequently tell their mothers that they wish daddy would not come back from work or a trip so that they could marry and take care of mother. The normal parent finds this amusing and knows that the boy also loves the father and that this stage will pass.

The normal child finally resolves these conflicts through the development of conscience, which reaches its peak around age 5–7 (Hoffman, 1970). The hostile, competitive feelings toward the parent of the same sex are turned against the self so that the child now experiences guilt, or the pangs of conscience, and believes that such hostile thoughts and wishes are bad. Likewise, the child's sexual possessiveness toward the opposite-sex parent is pushed into the unconscious mind by the defense mechanism of repression which is reinforced by the pressures of conscience. Of course, only the unacceptable hostile and sexual wishes and thoughts toward the parents should be repressed, leaving the child free to express love and friendship toward both parents in everyday family life. This repression should not be so excessive and widespread that the child's intense curosity, possessiveness and competitiveness also go underground into the unconscious and are not available to the child as he prepares to enter school. If this occurs, the child is in danger of becoming one of the many pupils who appear to be uninterested in learning and afraid to compete in the classroom, suffering from what Erikson calls a sense of inferiority (Erikson, 1959). The normal child retains an acceptable sense of initiative which allows her to feel safe in exhibiting her skills to explore the mysteries of school subjects and to create and produce in the classroom.

For an in-depth review of research concerning the development of moral values and the conscience see the chapter "Moral Development" in Hoffman (1970). Hoffman masterfully discusses the theories of Piaget, Kohlberg, Freud and others in this area.

Stage 4: Industriousness and the Social Self

Around age 6–7, with the development of conscience and repression of the Oedipus complex, the boy and girl undergo dramatic changes. They become much less preoccupied with sexual matters and what their parents are doing, which allows them to turn their curiosity and mental energy toward school tasks. This crucial developmental fact explains why most children in our Western culture are ready for the structured classroom setting around age 6. It also explains, in part, why early attempts at formal academics usually fail. Of course, as any first grade teacher knows, sexual interests do not disappear entirely but become quiescent and relatively latent; hence the term *latency period* for the years between ages 6–11 (Erikson, 1959; Sarnoff, 1976).

The normal child's character structure and defense mechanisms become much more solidified and resistant to regressive pressures. Children in the developmental phase of latency become interested in rules, learn to enjoy habitual ways of doing things and appreciate adult structure as long as it allows some freedom of thinking and does not reinforce their already strong sense of guilt. Their motor and cognitive skills have advanced so that they can manipulate tools and, as Erikson says, enjoy a sense of industry. Industriousness for the latency-age child is analogous to that activity in adult economic life. The child gains pleasure from making and producing in the classroom. The rewards come from the teacher and peers and from satisfying one's inner ego ideals, which can be defined as "what one wants to be." Child development observers have postulated a competency drive or instinct to master which is also satisfied when the child works successfully (White, 1963).

As the child progresses through the latency years, his conscience becomes less rigid. Hence, he is less preoccupied with right and wrong and fears of blame. The child moving into late latency (ages 9–11) develops more give and take, learns to compromise and accepts responsibility for wrongdoing.

Throughout the latency years, boys and girls prefer their free play to be with their own sex. This helps to reduce sexual stimulation which the latency child experiences as a source of anxiety and an interference with work tasks.

The latency period also includes a major step forward in the child's conceptual skills which Piaget has described as the stage of concrete operations. To illustrate, a third grade teacher shows his pupils models of three tigers and three elephants. He asks, "Are there more animals or more tigers here?" Most of the class should answer, "More animals," since tigers are a subclass of animals. This seemingly simple cognitive task, however, is not mastered by most children until age 7–8. These emerging classification and conceptual skills can only be used for productive learning in the classroom if the child's general development is proceeding well.

Throughout the latency years, boys and girls prefer their free play to be with their own sex.

Emotional Disturbance and Learning: The Psychodynamic View

Using the normal developmental scheme as a reference point, we can define emotional disturbance as a disorder that arises when something goes wrong developmentally for too long. All children, of course, suffer from brief emotional disturbances in which they feel guilty, anxious and inhibited in their work (MacFarlane, Allen & Horzik, 1954). Hence, it is important to keep in mind the distinction between brief and "too long." This is not too difficult for the perceptive teacher who has the opportunity to work with the child over the weeks and months of the school year. More specifically, emotional disturbance can be conceptualized according to objective or subjective criteria.

Conceptualizing Disturbance in the Classroom

Objective criteria. Emotional disturbance may occur when the child strays too far from the normal developmental sequence for too long a time (Freud, A., 1966). Sometimes problems arise when development proceeds too rapidly, for example, when a child undergoes pubescence at an unusually early age. Much more commonly, however, emotional problems ensue from lags in development. A child at age 8, for instance, is normally expected to show features of latency-age development as described in the normal developmental scheme. Some children age 8–9, however, behave more like a younger oedipal child; they may be preoccupied with wooing the teacher and gaining his attention through seductiveness and age-inappropriate sexual behavior. Often this interferes with their ability to concentrate on the learning tasks within the classroom.

Subjective criteria. From a subjective point of view, a child may not experience a developmental lag but, instead, experiences too much internal suffering and distress which goes on for too long. The depressed child and the obsessive child, for example, would both be regarded, by this criterion, as emotionally disturbed. Depression is common in childhood (Rie, 1966). It can be manifested through a sad, forlorn look, preoccupation with death or injury, lackluster performance or actual self-destructive behavior, which is more common in children than we often realize. The obsessive child often has above-average intelligence, but instead of applying her intelligence to schoolwork she may become obsessed in thinking about decisions. These children may appear quite unsure when making up their minds on schoolwork and play activities, may erase their written work innumerable times trying to find just the right word, may appear rigid with themselves and others, and have trouble showing the usual range of emotional expression (Freud, A., 1966).

With both the objective and subjective criteria, the child is the "experiencer," the carrier of the developmental imbalances and internal suffering. The psychodynamic clinician is cautious about using parent or teacher complaints to define emotional disturbance. For example, many psychodynamic clinicians have concerns about the frequent diagnosis of hyperactivity which is often based primarily on teacher rating scales. According to this perspective, the child's development and personal experience are the final determiners in a decision about emotional disturbance (Rhodes & Paul, 1978). Parent and teacher observations and concerns are invaluable indicators of the child's relationship with significant others, but these observations and concerns can also lead the clinician astray since parents and teachers have their own modes of perceiving. A child can be mislabeled on the basis of parental, teacher, family or school needs.

Childhood emotional disturbance in the classroom can be most clearly conceptualized if the child is in an "average expectable classroom," analogous to the "average expectable family" we hope the child was born into. The more unaverage the classroom, the more a teacher or school system's needs intrude on the pupil's normal developmental progression (Snow, 1969). For example, elementary counselors often note that particular teachers refer a large number of children for counseling from their classrooms. Too many referrals from a classroom may signal that the classroom teacher is in distress and needs assistance in handling her classroom or perhaps has an interfering personal problem. In such a situation, therapeutic efforts ideally should be directed to the teacher's problem, though, of course, the children could still have problems in their own right in such a classroom. Fortunately, the majority of classrooms are "average expectable." This means that they are not ideal, nor will they ever be, but that they fall within a broad range of normal teaching and organizational styles which make up a typical public school.

The ups and downs of a child's life are experienced in the context of a relationship to an important caretaker.

Internalization and Transference

What happens when a child lags developmentally for too long or suffers too much anxiety, guilt, depression or other internal stress? Remember that all children, especially the very young, experience developmental lags or excessive painful feelings from time to time. These ups and downs of life are experienced within the context of a relationship with someone important, usually the mother, father, siblings, caretakers or extended family. These all-important people try to help the child learn, become less anxious and move forward in development. At the same time, however, these important people may block the child's learning and increase her distress because of their own particular limitations or blind spots resulting from their past development and their own unique life experiences. In the hundreds of daily, caretaking interactions, the child lays down mental representations in her mind about herself and these caretaking people. For instance, one child may develop a belief that her mother is usually there to help her when she is frightened. Another child, however, may develop the belief that mother is not available and develop predominantly angry feelings around the mental representation of the mother. One child may think of fathers as generally safe and kind, and another child may believe that fathers are scary or angry.

With all children there is normally a mixture of good and bad mental representations. The more normal the child, the greater the preponderance of good representations. In the emotionally disturbed child a preponderance of negative, hostile and fearful feelings develop in connection with these important mental representations, which are compounded by the child's own intense needs and magical thinking. These internalized beliefs in turn set up expectations within the child's mind about how others in the world will behave. A vicious spiral can result when a child's expectations lead the adult to fulfill these expectations, particularly when the adult is struggling with the same issues as the child is. Thus, a great danger in emotional disturbance is that these spirals become internalized and built into the mind in a semipermanent fashion; the emotionally disturbed child comes to believe that she is mean, or bad, or anxious, or a poor performer, and lives out these patterns with others outside the family. This process has been described as *transference*, which means simply that the child transfers past beliefs and experiences onto new people and situations. Normal children also transfer, but they transfer generally positive expectations for themselves and others onto new situations and, hence, their transferences are usually not thought of as a problem. Notice that in this description of the emotionally disturbed child, we have intentionally stayed away from diagnostic categories, important as they are, and have focused on emotional disturbance as a process.

What happens when an emotionally disturbed child enters the average, expectable classroom? The internalized beliefs about the self and others are transferred onto the significant people in the classroom, primarily the teacher but often including fellow pupils and the learning tasks set forth for the child in the classroom (Baron, 1960). If the teacher and enough of the pupils have primarily positive outlooks or transferences, the emotionally disturbed child's transferences seem out of place and incongruent with the goals, tasks and working relationships necessary for the functioning of a normal classroom (Pearson, 1952).

Consider the immature child who has insufficiently entered the latency period and is still struggling with the mother over control of his bodily functions, such as bowel training or speech. This child may set up the same struggles with the classroom teacher, the mother's representation in the classroom. Such a child will quickly seem out of place and out of step with his peers who for the most part will already have worked through these issues and be more interested in pleasing the teacher by doing good work and receiving realistic praise from the teacher.

Another child, experiencing more internalized suffering, might exhibit performance inhibition or depression. Many of these children have come to believe that performing and being competitive is hostile and destructive. They feel they deserve to be punished, either by others or by suffering the pangs of guilt from their conscience. These children may become quite anxious when asked to perform or, if the problem is sufficiently severe, may act dumb. This particular problem is probably at the root of most elementary school failures, particularly in boys. The developmental lag these children suffer is not so easily observable, namely, the persistence of magical thinking by which they view their performance in the classroom as magically hurting someone else or themselves. The internal suffering arises out of the guilt and secondary depression from their poor performance which is viewed negatively by others.

Emotionally disturbed children who are prone to live or act out their transferences in the classroom often draw their teachers into pitfalls. Even very good teachers may unwittingly become drawn into the transference and either act it out with the pupil or react defensively against it. Compliance with a child's transference occurs frequently in the very common situation of the class clown, who is most often a boy. This child is often intelligent and lovable in a distressing sort of way, and usually manages to be the focus of banter and laughter through his classroom antics. The teacher can sense the hostile provocativeness behind this clowning facade and often senses that she is being set up continually by the clowning pupil. Some teachers, however, find themselves unwittingly cooperating with the clowning, teasing the child in provocative ways such as saying, "Well, guess who's done it again." In other situations, a teacher may react defensively to a child's transference. When a child may view the teacher as a hostile, noncaring maternal figure, the teacher may find herself becoming irritated or angry with the child who doesn't seem to appreciate her good teaching qualities. If the teacher finds this response in herself unacceptable, she may become excessively loving and kind toward the pupil in order to demonstrate that she is not mean or uncaring but is actually very nice and loving. Needless to say, teachers who cooperate with a child's transference or react defensively to it will have trouble maintaining the proper teaching stance.

The goal of the teacher is to recognize the child's transference for what it is, to view it as a signal for help, to utilize it for classroom interventions with the pupil, and to keep the transference from pulling him off of the proper teaching stance. Recognizing a child's transference and not reacting to it blindly can by itself be a powerful intervention. Many children who show emotional disturbance in the classroom have experienced faulty, blind reactions from important figures in the past and present life. For a teacher to maintain his teaching perspective and not get caught up in the transference is often for these children a new experience which can lead to personality change and educational growth. In clinical parlance, it is called a *corrective emotional experience* when a child expects and wants, consciously or unconsciously, a particular response from an important person or situation but, instead, gets another, often unexpected, response. The experience has surprise value and can spur the child to productive learning and relating in the classroom.

An emotionally disturbed child may perform poorly in most classes or even for several years in a row, then suddenly hit it off with a particular teacher; his performance improves for that class or school year and sometimes thereafter. These teachers are thought of having an undefinable charisma for certain pupils (Pederson, 1978). One partial explanation for their success is that they probably have the intuitive ability to detect these transferences from emotionally disturbed pupils and are not pushed off base by them. (By now, the reader may have noticed that many psychodynamic concepts can be recouched in terms of behavioral conditioning. In this example, not rewarding a negative, maladaptive transference might lead to its reduction. The good teacher intuitively rewards positive transferences.)

Referral and Teacher Intervention

The preceding discussion gives us some guidelines to the oft-asked question, when is the best time to refer a pupil for outside help? Assuming an average expectable teacher and classroom environment, the best time to ask for outside help is when the teacher has worked for a sufficiently long period of time with the child utilizing his best teaching skills and has concluded that the progress has not been sufficient. Some teachers believe that a child should be referred as soon as a problem arises, but this early referral may prevent the teacher from understanding the transference and working with the child in the classroom. Referring a child can become a subtle form of extrusion even though the child usually remains in the classroom while receiving outside help. The danger here is that the teacher will ignore the emotional problems of the referred child. Of course, there are a number of children whose emotional distress is obvious and who need referral when the problem is first noted. But after a referral, it is important that the teacher remain interested in working with the child's problems and look upon the referral as an opportunity to develop new insights rather than a chance to have someone else take over or take away the problem.

Take the following case, for example. Masturbation by both boys and girls is a relatively common issue in elementary classrooms. Having approached a consultant, a teacher stated that a girl in her second grade was obviously masturbating in her seat to the point that it was distracting to the teacher and the girl's peers and was interferring with her concentration. The teacher felt certain that this was a problem requiring referral and was out of his domain. Hence, he was surprised when the consultant asked what he had tried so far to help the girl with her problem. There followed a discussion of whether it was possible or even proper for a teacher to address such a problem with a classroom pupil. When the two concluded that it is all right for the teacher to address any issue which is interferring with a child's learning in the classroom, the consultant suggested that the teacher go back and talk with the child about the masturbatory activity to make sure the child was consciously aware of what she was doing and to suggest that she might do this at home in privacy rather than in the classroom.

In addition to wondering to what extent they should get involved with a child's emotional problems, some teachers hold the belief that there is a specific solution to those problems. They may want to be told specifically what to do with particular children in their classrooms. By focusing on the teachers' knowledge of their pupils, psychodynamic clinicians try to assist teachers to gain insight into their own techniques rather than offering a list of "how to's" which may have little relevance in the particular classroom environment. Such "how to" lists may foster a teacher's sense of inferiority and prevent him from using his own skills and classroom techniques. These techniques emerge and become usable when a teacher feels that he understands a situation, a child, or a problem more clearly (Berlin & Szurek, 1965). Average and better-than-average classroom teachers usually have a large repertoire of learned and intuitive techniques but are often hesitant to use them because of their own anxieties about a child with problems or a belief that it is not proper for them to be actively involved with an emotionally disturbed pupil. This is the greatest danger of labeling a child as emotionally disturbed: not that the child will be physically extruded from the classroom (only a minority are) but that the teacher will not feel free to work with the child so labeled. Being told specifically what to do by a consultant is sometimes misread by the teacher as a subtle suggestion that he not act and be himself with the child. It may be that what he is told to do is not really suitable for him and his teaching style. Once teachers feel free to say what is really on their minds about the pupil in question, they can come up with creative ideas to help the child and can create a climate for change and growth in the classroom. If a teacher remains fixated on the level of "tell me how to do it," this may indicate that he is not developing in his role professionally.

Teachers and all those who work with children must be constantly aware of the natural impulse to cure or rescue the child. This has been called the "rescue fantasy" by clinicians. The teacher's main goal in the regular classroom is to free up and protect the child's learning process. This focus on protecting and fostering learning helps keep the teacher from wandering into areas of the child's emotional life, such as relationships with parents, that are not clearly related to learning. Delving into a child's relationship with a parent can stir up tumultuous, anxious feelings and fantasies which the child may then attach to the teacher. In the child's mind, the teacher may then be viewed as a parent and some of the advantages of the relatively neutral, objective teaching role will be lost.

The following vignette illustrates how a teacher was able to help ensure that both he and the child focused on educational tasks, and not family problems, in the classroom. A third grade boy enters the classroom each morning distraught, unkempt, and lashes out at those about him. The teacher is aware that this pupil is bringing anxiety and distress from his home environment into the classroom. The parents have declined the recommendation that they seek professional help for their family problems. As with all children with emotional problems in the classroom, the teacher must continue to work with him whether or not the child or the parents are seeing counselors, mental health clinicians or other outside professionals. Rather than becoming involved with the boy's family problems, the teacher worked out a plan that allowed him to leave his problems at the door. By talking with the boy for a minute or two after he got off the school bus he could appraise how the student was feeling, what kind of morning it was going to be in the classroom and whether he would be able to remain on top of his problems. Or, at the classroom door the teacher would chat with the boy a moment ot two while the other children filed past. In this way the teacher was helping this boy build a psychic wall between his problems at home and the classroom where he needed to have his mind more at ease in order to concentrate on the learning tasks.

Misconceptions about Psychodynamic Theory

With the preceding skeletal outline of the psychodynamic development of the normal child and emotionally disturbed child freshly in mind, we can address several common misconceptions which educators often have and which appear in some educational texts. In reviewing these misconceptions, we will see how important the distinction is between theory and how some people put a theory into practice. All the following misconceptions have been stated and practiced by psychodynamic clinicians. Fortunately, theory does not stand or fall by how it is put into practice.

Misconception #1: Psychodynamic theory merely seeks to diagnose and label

Diagnoses and labels are not ends in themselves but are merely general summations of one's detailed understanding of a child's development and how the child is currently functioning internally and in relation to the external world. The use of labels implies that there are important differences between, for instance, a child disgnosed as *autistic* and another child diagnosed as *psychoneurotic*. By analogy it is important to know whether a child with a bad cough has tuberculosis or a cold. A diagnosis is the main heading of a more detailed outline. The various outlines are based on data and observations collected over time and organized to form a scientifically valid conceptual scheme.

Of course, diagnoses do not automatically tell us what to do to help a child since in treatment or in educating one must constantly move from a general conceptual scheme into the concrete world of motivation, individuality and the thorny issue of what is realistic and what isn't. Knowing that a car is a Ford is vital in order to fix it and order the right parts but it does not tell you what to do. Thus, a label by itself is not enough, but it does convey important information. Even people who recognize the value of labels, however, may fear that people will be reduced to their labels, or stereotyped according to them. For example, a child's race might not be mentioned in a treatment conference for fear it might "label the child." But leaving out such a vital piece of information may end up doing the child a disservice. The same principle applies to outlawing the use of IQ tests. Some wish to discard diagnostic understanding entirely because of its past misuses and replace it with other schemes which are often related more to administrative expedience than the child's needs. Such schemes appeal because of their simplicity but are unlikely to further our understanding of the child.

Misconception #2: Psychodynamic theory places too much emphasis on the intrapsychic life of the child

In one textbook, psychodynamic theory was depicted by a picture of a child surrounded by arrows pointing out from his body to represent his interactions with the outside world; these arrows were cut off, leaving the child appearing as if in a vacuum. This diagram was intended to show that psychodynamic theory focuses only on the inner workings of the child's mind and pays no attention to the child's external world. The developmental scheme outlined earlier should help to dispel this notion. There is no fetus without a surrounding mother; there is no infant without a holding, caretaking environment; there is no aggressive or sexual wish without someone or something in the real world who is or once was a target of the wish; there is no real learning without a teacher. Currently, educational theorists are scrutinizing the educational ecosystems of the child and their potential for good or harm (Mortimore, Ansten, Rutter, & Mangham, 1979). Likewise, in recent decades, psychodynamic theorists have focused on the child's interaction with the caretaking environment (Winnicott, 1965).

Misconception #3: Psychodynamic theory places the burden of change on the child rather than the system

As a blanket statement, this is incorrect. It would be unethical and unrealistic to prescribe treatment for a child because she is upset at having to spend seven hours a day in a destructive classroom, or the rest of the day in a grossly destructive home, without taking steps to improve the child's environment. On the other hand, in the reality of everday life some situations cannot be changed sufficiently, so emotionally disturbed children may have to be helped to adapt to a less-than-perfect situation. More commonly a child has problems with an adequate classroom or family setting because of her distorted perceptions of the external world. The child in this situation may be asked to change her perceptions through some type of therapy or educational intervention while the external world essentially holds steady. Clearly what is called for is a thorough diagnostic understanding of where the problem is and where the potential for change lies. The assumption that only one part of a system must always assume responsibility for change is a simplistic notion in a complicated world. This notion can actually depreciate the potential for change within the child. Often responsibility is equated with blame by the parties involved. To develop a sense of responsibility for oneself and one's actions is a worthy goal. To confuse it with being blamed or criticized may deprive a child or a parent of a crucial and necessary developmental step.

Misconception #4: Psychodynamic theory places too much emphasis on the past

The developmental approach we have outlined illustrates how the past is only known and lived out in the present. Understanding how the past is being lived out in the present permits one to take steps to work with the child in the here and now in order to eventually alter the child's perception of her past life.

Educational and Therapeutic Interventions

Many of the techniques and interventions described in this section are practiced by clinicians and educators from diverse schools of thought.

Psychodynamic clinicians, however, carry out these interventions in a manner that reflects the psychodynamic point of view. Many of these interventions can be carried out in educational settings and some are preferably performed there (Stickney, 1968).

Interventions in Educational Settings

Teacher training. Psychodynamically oriented teacher training programs stress the acquisition of self-knowledge and understanding the meaning of behavior. Through small-group seminars, tutorials and case study approaches, all of which require a low teacher-student ratio, teacher trainees have the opportunity to understand more about themselves and discover what a powerful tool this approach can be in the classroom.

Learning techniques for interviewing parents and pupils are also emphasized in psychodynamic teacher training programs. At times, teachers and parents blame each other for a student's problem. This common, destructive spiral can often be interrupted by a teacher who feels confident and nondefensive in talking with the parents (Lightfoot, 1978).

How to talk with pupils in a noncritical, open-ended fashion and yet maintain a focus on the immediate problem is a valuable technique which can be learned by teachers. This technique has been called the *life space interview,* a term first used by Redl (1959). The focus of the interview is on helping the child articulate and conceptualize the issues going on in her immediate life space. The teacher helps the child reach a preliminary closure to the problem, and the agreed upon course of action is verbalized. Usually the interview is most effective when it is carried out in physical and temporal proximity to the problem. In other words, the teacher talks with the child whenever and wherever the trouble occurs.

Interventions in the regular classroom. Because teachers function as caregivers, authorities, group leaders and providers of information, they have the opportunity to foster the child's learning processes and to protect them from outside interference which includes the emotionally troubled child's turbulent affects and distorted thinking. The classroom teacher has a wide range of techniques available, assuming he has both inner and outer permission to carry them out. Some of the techniques are reassurance, clarification, educative correction of distorted thinking and the teaching of normal behavioral responses to peers and authority and to the pupil's learning tasks. These techniques make up a powerful set of tools at the teacher's command (Bower, 1967). Specific teaching strategies are described in more detail in Chapters 11–14, and in Rhodes and Tracy (1974) and Long, Morse, and Newman (1980).

Therapeutic tutoring and other specialized techniques. Therapeutic tutoring involves a teacher or special educator working with a child or small group of children over a period of time to help the child understand what is interferring with the academic learning process (Templeton, Sperry & Prentice, 1967). For instance, if a child begins to daydream and look away or becomes stubborn each time a teacher presents an appropriate learning task, the teacher can talk to the child about her response and eventually the child can understand what fears are making her turn away from performing. This technique is often practiced intuitively by gifted teachers but for most it requires special training. Therapeutic tutoring is distinct from psychotherapy. Therapeutic tutoring maintains a constant focus on the learning and performing in the classroom and whatever interferes with it, whereas psychotherapy is more open-ended and delves into the child's perceptions of past relationships and her fears and fantasies about them.

Consultation. Psychodynamic consultation within a school setting has been going on for several decades (Berlin & Szurek, 1965; Caplan, 1970; Newman, 1967). Consultants try to help teachers to understand themselves better in their work with students, parents and colleagues; they avoid providing specific "how to" lists which may inadvertently foster continued dependence on others and reinforce a teacher's already sagging self-esteem. Psychodynamic consultation often requires a period of many weeks or months before a trusting, comfortable relationship is established between the consultant and the teacher. This trust can become a powerful force for change in the individual teacher, his peer group and sometimes even the entire school environment. Because such consultation emphasizes the teacher's own enhanced sense of self and helps him feel more confident about his work, consultation sessions usually center on the teacher's own presentation of his work with pupils. This approach helps to keep the focus on the learning process in the classroom and prevents the sessions from wandering into the teacher's personal life.

Clinical psychotherapeutic work in school settings. Carrying out clinical or therapeutic work in the child's school setting has both pros and cons. Some professionals are concerned that the roles of the teacher and the mental health clinicians will merge, with the mental health clinician becoming swallowed up in the school system. With agreed-upon safeguards, this need not be a problem. In rural school settings where there are large geographical distances between mental health facilities and schools, mental health clinicians may travel to school settings on a regular basis to provide diagnostic and treatment services in the school setting. If the school system and the clinic are comfortable with each other and are not caught up in administrative or territorial issues, treatment programs for children can often be worked out in school settings.

Treatment Modalities in Clinical Settings

All recommendations for treatment are based on diagnostic evaluation. The purpose of a diagnostic evaluation is not to place a label on a child or family. Diagnosis is actually short-term treatment in which the clinician, parents and the child establish a working relationship, agree on what the problems are and then set up a realistic treatment program. In a well-conducted diagnostic evaluation, the child and her family gain a new perspective on themselves and their situation. A diagnostic evaluation that does not go well often leaves the parents and the child feeling that they didn't learn anything and that the clinician was not in tune with them. A well-conducted diagnostic evaluation is a challenging, formidable task. It is carried out by a child psychiatrist, psychologist, social worker or other clinic personnel through regular meetings with the child, the parents or the family. Sometimes two or more clinicians work with the child and family; at other times one clinician performs the diagnostic evaluation alone. Sometimes psychological testing may be done to help elucidate personality patterns and conflicts in the child or parents; most clinics try to do psychological testing selectively rather than routinely. The diagnostic evaluation concludes with the important interpretive phase in which the clinician pulls together his impressions and findings in lay language for the parents and the child and then makes recommendations for further treatment, or no treatment if none is indicated. The clinician hopes that the parents and the child have been gaining insight throughout the diagnostic evaluation so that his findings will not come as a bolt out of the blue. Many evaluations include telephone conversations or school visits with educators and talks with the child's pediatrician, social service caseworker or other agency people involved with the family and child. In these multiple communications maintaining confidentiality appropriate to the case is important yet at the same time clinicians must have the freedom to talk with school personnel, pediatricians or caseworkers in a frank manner, to ask questions, to share impressions and to obtain relevant information. Nowadays, complicated forms are signed to provide legal safeguards. The best safeguard of all is mutual trust among the parties involved.

For any treatment to be successful, both the parents and the child must believe it will work and that they have the emotional strength to utilize it. Often treatment recommendations are made in the face of parental or child anxieties, doubts and resistances which may drive the parents to seek advice and consultation elsewhere. Deciding on a treatment program is a major decision for the child and parents since it usually involves a large commitment of their emotions, finances and time. They often feel that accepting the treatment program is an admission that they have been bad parents or have a bad child and that they will now be liable to criticism from others and from their own consciences. Thus, an important task of the clinician is to help the parents and the child achieve a receptive frame of mind before making recommendations.

Once a child, parents or family have completed a diagnostic evaluation and a specific treatment is recommended, then comes the problem of matching the treatment proposed with what is actually available in a particular community. Treatment is available through two primary sources. First, there are publicly funded mental health clinics and training institutions in which the treatment staff is paid by tax monies. Fees for services are usually charged in these facilities, but because salaries and operating expenses come from other sources, the patient's fees can be scaled to fit the family's income and living style. For low-income families, the fees can range down to very low amounts such as $1 a session. One might wonder why such fees are even charged when the administrative expenses in collecting such a low fee are greater than the amount of the fee obtained. It is generally felt in our society that paying for services engenders the client's respect for the treatment modality. The other principal source of treatment for children and families is in the private sector in which the treating personnel receive much or all of their income from fees paid by the patient. These private facilities and practitioners tend to be used predominantly by middle- and upper-income socioeconomic groups or those who have adequate insurance programs.

In most settings, whether public or private, treatment is usually carried out by individuals from a variety of mental health disciplines. In other words, psychologists treat children and families in addition to performing psychological tests. Likewise, many social workers treat children as well as work with parents. In recent years, increasing numbers of graduate-level educators have been working in mental health clinics. What treatment modalities are available in a particular community depends not only on the sources of funds and personnel available but also on the particular background, training and interests of the therapists. Some clinics and private facilities are predominantly psychodynamically oriented, others behaviorally, and many are combinations of several schools of thought.

A major problem within the mental health field today, as within education, is to maintain quality of care through the upgrading of staff quality and continued training of clinic personnel. Both public clinics and private facilities vary widely in the quality of care provided. Unfortunately, many communities and school systems are handicapped by not having well-trained child mental health facilities available to them.

Individual psychotherapy. In this treatment modality, the child usually meets once or twice weekly with a therapist. In child analysis, a more intense form of psychotherapy, the child and the analyst meet four times weekly. In psychodynamic psychotherapy, the child usually initiates each session by talking or playing out whatever is on her mind. Since this talking or playing usually reveals the child's fears and defenses against these fears, the therapist is in a position to gently, and at the child's pace, put these wishes, fears and maladaptive defenses into words. Through this working together the child develops her own observing capacity, and the therapist assists the child to gain insight into and better mastery over conflicts that were interferring with the child's development and performance in school. Since it is very important to move at the child's own speed to allow the child maximum autonomy in the therapeutic process, individual therapy usually requires long periods of time, often one, two, or more years. Specific problems can be worked through in short-term individual psychotherapy, lasting from a few weeks to a few months. More general character or personality problems, however, usually require longer periods of time since any significant change in a child requires time and repetitive working through of the problems. The length of time required by psychotherapy is sometimes puzzling and discouraging to schoolteachers who must continue to work with the child in the classroom while therapy is taking hold (Cooper & Wanerman, 1977).

Parent therapy. Many types of parent therapy are conducted in clinics today. These include parent effectiveness groups, open-ended group work with parents and instructional sessions concerning parenting techniques. One important type of parent therapy involves the parents working with the child's therapist while the child is undergoing individual therapy (Sperling, 1979). One or both parents' support is necessary for any type of child therapy to exist and be successful. In parent therapy, the parents are free to bring up their concerns about their child's therapy and any doubts or criticisms they may have of the therapist and the therapeutic process. The purpose is to help the parents put into words any resistances or anxieties they may be developing about the child's therapy. It is almost universal that when any child undergoes individual therapy conflicts which usually involve the parents are brought into the open. Thus, the child's problems reverberate in child-parent and the parent-parent relationships; parents need an arena for verbalizing their feelings so that they will not pile up to destructive proportions and threaten the child's therapy.

In some parent work, the therapist also provides instructions or suggestions to the parents concerning their techniques of child rearing. However, experience has shown that these specific suggestions are often not too successful until the parents have the opportunity to work through some of their own resistances and fears in their relationship with their child. Almost all parents initially take recommendations for therapeutic work with their children as criticism of their parenting. School personnel are sometimes approached by parents who have concerns about what the clinician has told them about their child's problems and their relationship to their child's learning difficulties. When this happens, it is extremely important for the teacher to hear out the parents' concerns and, assuming the teacher has confidence in the clinician or clinic working with the parents, he can gently guide the parents back to the therapist and encourage the parents to put into words their concerns about their child's therapy. Sometimes, parent therapy is recommended as the sole treatment modality, though more often it is recommended in conjunction with child psychotherapy. Parent therapy in conjunction with child psychotherapy usually continues throughout the course of the child's therapy, though in the later stages parents may be seen less often as a child assumes more and more responsibility for her own improvement.

Group therapy with children. In group therapy with children a therapist, or sometimes two co-therapists, meets with a group of children, usually numbering around eight, since experience has shown that this is usually the maximum number of group participants that can effectively work together. The younger the children, the more the group focuses on activities which the children and therapist engage in together and talk about. The older the child, particularly as they enter adolescence, the more group therapies are focused on talking rather than playing and physical activity (Kraft, 1979). This principle applies to all types of child therapy. The younger the child the more the therapist works with play and play metaphors; the older the child, particularly in adolescence, the more the therapist and patient can talk directly about problems.

Group therapy necessarily must focus on the group interactional processes and is particularly helpful when a child's problems center around her relationship with peers. Since the group interactional processes are so important in group therapy, it is crucial that group therapists select a proper mix of children so that they can interact productively, maintain some group cohesiveness and have problems which are sufficiently similar. Some groups have a specific focus and the group work is highly structured by the therapist; other groups are more open-ended and the children talk spontaneously and bring in their own activities.

Family therapy. In the past two decades, family therapy has become an increasingly important treatment modality (Lewis, 1979). In family therapy, the focus is on the interactional relationships between the parents, child and siblings. Since many, if not most, learning and emotional problems arise in the context of conflictual, family relationships, the child often becomes the carrier of the family problems. The general goal of family therapy is to help the family achieve insight into how they are handling family problems so that a particular child is not made a scapegoat for the family conflicts. Through family awareness, the child is freed to pursue her own interests while the other family members, usually the parents, work out their problems between themselves. If problems have become firmly internalized within an individual in the family under treatment, then individual psychotherapy must sometimes be taken up; at other times, the child's problems clear up through family therapy alone. Family therapy is a powerful treatment modality for children since the child is normally quite dependent upon the parents in our culture. Some observers, however, are concerned that at times family therapy can focus on the interactional problems of the parents and the child can slip into the background. How to include the child as an active member of family therapy is an issue under discussion among family therapists today.

Educational Programs in Clinical Settings

Just as clinical treatment modalities and facilities can be located in regular educational settings, therapeutic educational programs can exist in clinical facilities. These programs include therapeutic tutoring, special classrooms usually involving a small number of children and therapeutically trained, clinically oriented teachers, educational activity groups and consulting liaison teachers operating out of a clinical facility (Berkowitz & Rothman, 1960). One advantage of these therapeutic educational activities within clinical settings is that they are free from the usual pressures in public school systems. Thus, the teachers are often freer to do their own programming and are not bound by some of the restrictions found in public schools. At the same time, however, therapeutic educational activities in clinic settings take place in physical isolation from a normal school environment, and role conflicts between teachers and other professional disciplines can develop in a clinic setting. In the historical development of clinical settings in our country, teachers were often the last professionals to join the clinic staff and hence are sometimes viewed as junior members. In recent years, however, special educational and therapeutic educational teachers have become accepted in many clinical settings as peers of professionals in the traditional disciplines.

Day treatment programs. Many children, parents and families require more than can be supplied in the usual outpatient treatment modalities. At the same time, they may not require inpatient hospitalization 24 hours a day, seven days a week. Their needs, in many cases, have been met by day treatment programs.

Within the past 25 years, concurrent with the community mental health center movement, intermediate programs have sprung up in many localities. In these programs, the child can participate in specialized school settings and group activities during the day and return to his home in the evening or on the weekends. Often these children are having considerable difficulty functioning within the regular school classroom but are not sufficiently disturbed to require separation from their neighborhood and families for long periods of time. Sometimes such programs have been difficult to establish because the usual model for hospitalization in our country has been round-the-clock, full-time hospital care. The skyrocketing cost of inpatient hospitalization, however, has forced many communities to look at intermediate, day programs in a more favorable light.

Day programs may consist of only two or three hours a day of school or structured play activities with other children to full eight-hour days of complete schooling and after-school recreational activities. In many clinical settings where sufficient treatment staff are available, the children in day programs also participate in individual and group psychotherapy while the parents and families are often involved in parent therapy or family therapy. One advantage of day treatment programs is that the child may return to her home and neighborhood in the afternoons and evenings, thereby minimizing the harmful effects of extrusion (see Chapter 8).

Inpatient hospitalization. The hospitalization of children has come under considerable criticism in the past decade due to some actual abuses and fears of civil libertarians that a child's rights may be deprived unfairly. Another criticism is that the harmful effects a child may suffer by the extrusion process may outweigh any benefits obtained by hospitalization. Though such criticisms are sometimes valid, the fact remains that the children's psychiatric hospital, if well run with adequately trained and supervised staff, has a valuable and necessary place in the spectrum of child mental health services. Hospitalization is important when removing the child for a period of time would allow all parties involved—the child, parents and siblings—to work on their mutual problems without having to deal with the destructiveness of their usual daily interactions. A well run, adequately staffed children's psychiatric hospital has the full complement of teachers, housemothers, recreational workers, psychologists, social workers and occupational therapists, who can, in effect, supply most of the emotional and physical needs of the child. A child may be hospitalized briefly for a diagnostic evaluation and return to her community for outpatient or day treatment. When it is felt that continued hospitalization is important for the child and the family, the child may remain for longer periods of time ranging from a few months to several years. In most hospital settings, the parents visit with their child regularly or take her home for weekends and holiday visits. Most children's psychiatric hospitals require that the parents be strong enough to support the treatment and to participate actively in parent therapy.

If the parents are not motivated, or perhaps not even available, hospital treatment facilities are often less likely to accept the child. Such children at times do better in group home or orphanages in which they may live for long periods of time. In recent decades, some group homes and orphanages for children have been closed due to fears that the children would be harmed by prolonged institutionalization. Though some of these facilities did not benefit the children they housed, it is unfortunate that orphanages acquired a bad name since many children are best served in such institutions. Currently there is a trend in this country to clearly distinguish group homes and orphanages from psychiatric hospitals. Hospitalization implies active treatment which is time-limited, usually involving some family support for the child. Commitment to an orphanage, however, often implies that parents are not available or not fit to take care of their children. Thus, orphanages and group home function *in loco parentis*, and children stay until they reach young adulthood. Children in group homes and orphanages are educated within the facility or, if capable, attend nearby public schools.

Drug therapy. In general, the use of drugs to treat childhood emotional problems is not as widespread or thought to be as effective as with adults. Tranquilizers such as Thorazine for a psychotic episode or anti-anxiety drugs such as Valium for anxiety attacks are sometimes prescribed for children for brief periods of time to help them through acute crises. Dexedrine and Ritalin have been prescribed extensively for the symptom of hyperactivity. Psychodynamic clinicians have had misgivings about the use of drugs with children, maintaining that drugs are often prescribed in lieu of a careful understanding of a child's problems. Through proper understanding of a child's problems and supplying the necessary environmental support, education and therapeutic treatment, most children respond without the necessity for drugs. Furthermore, some drugs have harmful side effects if taken over long periods of time. If properly used, however, within the context of a thoughtful therapeutic program, drugs can provide a valuable treatment adjunct (Gadow, 1980).

SUMMARY

Psychodynamic theory emphasizes the importance of understanding the individual child, how the child's mental life progresses through developmental stages and how emotional problems arising from developmental difficulties are manifest in the classroom. Through knowledge of these developmental processes and self-awareness, the teacher can bring a wide range of teaching strategies into the regular classroom to assist the emotionally disturbed student by walling off and freeing his learning from emotional problems.

The treatment modalities used by psychodynamically oriented child mental health clinicians complement classroom teaching. Though clinicians and teachers use different techniques and may have different short-term goals, both have the same ultimate goal for the emotionally disturbed child: namely to assist the child to achieve inner freedom in order to learn and to resume normal development.

DISCUSSION QUESTIONS

1. Describe the principle viewpoints of the psychodynamic theory of development.
2. How are these viewpoints relevant to the classroom setting?
3. How are these viewpoints similar to and different from the tenets of the other personality theories described in this text?
4. Define emotional disturbance from the psychodynamic point of view.
5. Describe five ways that emotional disturbance can be manifested in the regular classroom setting. How might these emotional disturbances have arisen in the child's development?
6. What are some of the important roles and functions served by the mother and father in the development of the child? How are these different from the role and function of the teacher in the classroom? How are they the same?
7. Describe five ways that clinicians and teachers can work together to understand and help an emotionally disturbed child in the classroom.
8. List three classroom techniques that a teacher can use to assist an emotionally disturbed student and discuss each technique from the psychodynamic viewpoint.
9. What is *transference* and why is it important for the teacher to be aware of his reactions to it?
10. Describe three treatment modalities and what types of children and families might best use each modality.

REFERENCES

Aichhorn, A. *Wayward youth.* New York: Meridian Books, 1955.

Anderson, J. Child development: An historical perspective. *Child Development*, 1956, *27*, 181–196.

Baron, S. Transference and countertransference in the classroom. *Psychoanalysis and the Psychoanalytic Review,* 1960, *47*, 76–96.

Berkowitz, P. H., & Rothman, E. P. *The disturbed child.* New York: New York University Press, 1960.

Berlin, I. N. & Szurek, S. Z. *Learning and its disorders.* Science and Behavior Books, 1965.

Berlin, I. N. Some learning experiences as a psychiatric consultant. In I. N. Berlin, & S. Z. Szurek (Eds), *Learning and its disdorders.* Science and Behavior Books, 1965.

Bower, E., & Hollister, W. G. (Eds.). *Behavioral science frontiers in education.* New York: John Wiley & Sons, 1967.

Brenner, C. *An elementary textbook of psychoanalysis* (Rev. ed.). New York: International Universities Press, 1973.

Cameron, N. *Personality development and psychopathology.* Boston: Houghton Mifflin, 1963.

Caplan, G. *Theory and practice of mental health consultation.* New York: Basic Books, 1970.

Cooper, S., & Wanerman, L. *Children in treatment.* New York: Brunner/Mazel, 1977.

Ekstein, R. Psychoanalysis and education: A historical account. In R. Ekstein & R. Motto (Eds). *From learning for love to love of learning.* New York: Brunner/Mazel, 1969.

Ekstein, R., & Motto, R. (Eds.). *From learning for love to love of learning.* New York: Brunner/Mazel, 1969.

Erikson, E. *Identity and the life cycle.* Psychological issues (Vol. 1). New York: International Universities Press, 1959.

Flavell, J. H. *The developmental psychology of Jean Piaget.* Litton Educational, 1963.
Fleischman, O. *Delinquency and child guidance: Selected papers of A. Aichhorn.* Menninger Foundation Monograph Series (Vol. 1). New York: International Universities Press, 1967.
Freud, A. *The Ego and the mechanisms of defense.* New York: International Universities Press, 1936.
Freud, A. *Normality and pathology in childhood: Assessments of development.* New York: International Universities Press, 1966.
Freud, A. Obsessional neurosis: A summary of psychoanalytic views as presented at the congress. *International Journal of Psychoanalysis,* 1966, *47,* 116–122.
Freud, A. Psychoanalysis and education. *Psychoanalytic Study of the Child,* 1966, *47,* 116–122.
Freud, A. *Psychoanalysis for teachers and parents.* New York: W. W. Norton, 1979.
Freud, S. Analysis of a phobia in a five year old boy. In J. Strachey (Ed.), Standard edition of the complete psychological works of Sigmund Freud (Vol. 10). London: Hogarth Press and Institute of Psychoanalysis, 1966. (a)
Freud, S. Civilization and its discontents. In J. Strachey (Ed.), *Standard edition of the complete psychological works of Sigmund Freud* (Vol. 21). London: Hogarth Press and Institute of Psychoanalysis, 1966. (b)
Freud, S. Three Essays on the theory of sexuality. In J. Strachey (Ed.), *Standard edition of the complete psychological works of Sigmund Freud* (Vol. 7). London: Hogarth Press and Institute of Psychoanalysis, 1966. (c)
Fries, M., & Woolf, P. Some hypotheses on the role of congenital activity type in personality development. *Psychoanalytic study of the child,* 1953, *8,* 47–54.
Furman, E. *A child's parent dies: Studies in childhood bereavement.* New Haven, Conn.: Yale University Press, 1974.
Gadow, K. *Children on medication.* Reston, Va., Council for Exceptional Children, 1980.
Graffagnino, P. N., Bucknam, F. G., Orgun, I. N., & Leve, R. M. Psychotherapy for latency-age children in an inner-city therapeutic school. *American Journal of Psychiatry,* 1970, *127,* 86–94.
Hartmann, H. *Ego psychology and the problem of adaptation.* New York: International Universities Press, 1958.
Hoffman, M. *Carmichael's manual of child psychology* (P. Mussen, Ed.). New York: John Wiley & Sons, 1970, *2,* 261–361.
Jones, E. *The life and work of Sigmund Freud* (Vol. 3). New York: Basic Books, 1953.
Jones, R. The role of self-knowledge in the educative process. *Harvard Educational Review,* 1962, *32,* 200–209.
Kagan, J., Kearsley, R., & Zelazo, P. *Infancy.* Cambridge, Mass.: Harvard University Press, 1978.
Kessler, J. *Psychopathology of childhood.* Englewood, N.J., Prentice-Hall, 1966.
Kessler, J., Smith, E., & McKinnon, R. Psychotherapy with mentally retarded children. *Psychoanalytic Study of the Child,* 1976, *31,* 493–514.
Klaus, M., & Kennel, J. Early mother-infant contact: Effects on the mother and infant. *Bulletin of the Menninger Clinic,* 1979, *43,* 69–78.
Kraft, I. Group therapy. In J. Noshpitz, (Ed.), *Basic Handbook of Child Psychiatry.* New York: Basic Books, 1979.
Levine, M., & Levine, A. *A Social History of Helping Services.* New York: Meredith Corporation, 1970.
Levitt, M. *Freud and Dewey on the nature of man.* New York: Philosophical Library, 1960.
Lewis, M. (Ed.). Family therapy in child psychiatry. *Journal American Academy of Child Psychiatry,* 1979, *18,* 1–102.

Lightfoot, S. *Worlds apart: Relationship between families and schools.* New York: Basic Books, 1978.

Long, N. J., Morse, W. C., & Newman, R. G. (Eds.). Conflict in the classroom (4th ed.). Belmont, Calif.: Wadsworth, 1980.

MacFarlane, J. W., Allen, L., & Horzik, M. P. *A developmental study of the behavior problems of normal children between 21 months and 14 years.* Berkeley, University of California Press, 1954.

Mahler, M. *The psychological birth of the human infant.* New York: Basic Books, 1975.

Mattick, I., & Murphy, L. Cognitive disturbances in young children. In S. Sapir, & A. Nitzberg (Eds.), *Children with learning problems: Readings in a developmental-interaction approach.* New York: Brunner/Mazel, 1973.

Meers, D. R. Contributions of a ghetto culture to symptom formation. *Psychoanalytic Study of the Child*, 1970, *25*, 209–230.

Montessori, M. *The Montessori method.* New York: Schocken Books, 1964.

Mortimore, P., Ansten, J., Rutter, M., & Mangham, B. *Fifteen thousand hours.* Cambridge, Mass.: Harvard University Press, 1979.

Nagera, H. Children's reactions to the death of important objects: A developmental approach. *Psychoanalytic Study of the Child*, 1970, *25*, 360–400.

Neubauer, P. The one parent child and his oedipal development. *Psychoanalytic Study of the Child*, 1960, *15*, 286–309.

Newman, R. *Psychological consultation in the schools.* New York: Basic Books, 1967.

Pavendstedt, E. *The drifters: Children of disorganized lower-class families.* Boston: Little, Brown, 1967.

Pearson, G. A survey of learning difficulties in children. *Psychoanalytic Study of the Child*, 1952, *7*, 322–385.

Pederson, E., Faucher, T. A., & Eaton, W. A new perspective on the effects of first grade teachers on children's subsequent adult status. *Harvard Educational Review*, 1978, *48*, 1–31.

Peller, L. Libidinal phases, ego development and play. *Psychoanalytic Study of the Child*, 1954, *9*, 178–198.

Piaget, J. The stages of intellectual development. *Bulletin of the Menninger Clinic*, 1962, *26*, 120–128.

Redl, F. The life space interview: 1. Strategy and techniques of life space interview. *American Journal of Psychotherapy*, 1959, *29*, 1–18.

Redl. F. *When we deal with children: Selected writings.* New York: Free Press, 1966.

Rhodes, W. C., & Paul, J. L. *Emotionally disturbed and deviant children.* Englewood Cliffs, N. J.: Prentice-Hall, 1978.

Rhodes, W. C., & Tracy, M. *A Study of Child Variance.* Ann Arbor: University of Michigan Press, 1974.

Rie, H. E. Depression in childhood: A survey of some pertinent contributions. *Journal of the American Academy of Child Psychiatry*, 1966, *5*. 653–685.

Sarnoff, C. *Latency.* New York: Jason Aronson, 1976.

Snow, R. Unfinished pygmalion. *Contemporary Psychology*, 1969, *14*, 197–199.

Sperling, E. Parent counseling and therapy. In J. Noshpitz (Ed.), *Basic Handbook of Child Psychiatry* (Vol. 3). New York: Basic Books, 1979.

Stickney, S. Schools are our community mental health centers. *American Journal of Psychiatry*, 1968, *124*, 101–108.

Templeton, R. G., Sperry, B., & Prentice, N. Therapeutic tutoring of children with psychogenic learning problems. *Journal of the American Academy of Child Psychiatry*, 1967, *6*, 464–477.

Thomas, A., Birch, H. G., & Chess, S. *Temperament and behavior disorders in children.* New York: New York University Press, 1968.

Wallerstein, J., & Kelly, J. The effects of parental divorce. *Journal of American Academy of Child Psychiatry*, 1975, *14*, 600–616.

Watson, R. A brief history of clinical psychology. *Psychological Bulletin*, 1953, *50*, 321–346.
White, R. W. *Ego and reality in psychoanalytic theory.* Psychological Issues. (Vol. 131). New York: International Universities Press, 1963.
Wiener, L. *Tolstoi on Education.* Chicago: University of Chicago Press, 1967.
Winnicott, D. W. *Maturational processes and the facilitating environment.* New York: International Universities press, 1965.
Wolff, P. *The developmental psychologies of Jean Piaget and Psychoanalysis. Psychological Issues* (Vol. 11). New York: New York University Press, 1960.

6
Organic Theories

main points

1. From the organic point of view, emotional disturbances are observable behavioral expressions of some malfunction of the central nervous system (CNS). The malfunction could be directly or indirectly observable.

2. There are essentially two types of organic factor theories related to emotional disturbance. Traditional approaches are based on the notion of some underlying defect (primarily organic) which is responsible for pathological symptoms. Recent organic theories point to certain developmental lags which result in emotional immaturity. Both approaches cite a cluster of behavioral traits which have an organic basis, which are general and which are more or less resistant to modification through environmental manipulations.

3. The theories used to explain organic defects have focused variously on heredity, temperament, drugs, nutrition, food additives and neurological dysfunction.

4. Developmental organic theories attribute developmental delays to a subtle lack of integrity of the central nervous system which places the child at risk for developmental problems. Important organic theories of development include the Doman-Delacato theory, Kephart's perceptual-motor learning theory, Getman's physiology of readiness theory, Ayres's theory of sensory integration and Frostig's developmental theory.

5. The organic defect theories recommend that neurologically impaired children be treated through medical intervention, remedial education, and early intervention and prevention.

6. Developmental theories recommend that neurologically impaired children receive specific training to compensate for or remove the disability. The research does not support the notion that this training has a direct effect on educational skills.

7. The assessment of organic impairment is difficult due to the individual child's response biases, the developmental status of the child and the need to sample a wide variety of behaviors over time.

8. Research leading to practical implications has been hindered by the following facts: (a) the focus has been on brain injury rather than the positive aspects of the child's behavior, (b) most of the children studied have been institutionalized and therefore have restricted developmental and environmental histories, and (c) most neurologically impaired children have been on drugs, and the drug's interaction with neurological development has rarely been studied.

9. The organic factor theories are important and useful in pursuing research with neurologically impaired children, but they are currently inadequate for use in planning classroom activities.

This chapter was written by **Stephen R. Schroeder** and **Carolyn S. Schroeder**, University of North Carolina at Chapel Hill.

THIS CHAPTER will review some of the biologically based definitions, theories and symptomatology of mental disorders which may underly emotional disturbance. It will also analyze some of the approaches to teaching the emotionally disturbed which are based on these theories. We will look at teaching practices to see how—and if—the research on organic theories is applicable to the classroom. Parts of this chapter may be difficult for readers who have no background in the study of neurology, or brain function. Nevertheless, the teacher of emotionally handicapped children should know the rudiments of organic theories in order to evaluate critically which of today's teaching practices and materials are likely to be useful and which are not. Many educational programs in use today are based on organic theories which are grounded in only a limited amount of sound research. The teacher of emotionally handicapped children needs some guidelines to sort fact from fiction in order to be effective with children who have emotional problems with organic bases. For this reason this chapter is written at the introductory level and a glossary of terms is provided. We also recommend as companion reading an introductory text on neurology by Gardner (1975).

Organic Definitions of Emotional Disturbance

From the organic point of view, emotional disturbances are observable behavioral expressions of some malfunction of the central nervous system (CNS). Sometimes the malfunction can be observed rather directly, for example, in sensory disorders like hearing loss; in other cases it is observed indirectly and remotely, for example in neurochemical processes involved in psychotic disorders. All of these processes are affected by the child's heredity and environment. The primary subject of analysis is, however, always the CNS processes of the child. The task of analysis is to specify the relationships between symptoms (behavioral manifestations, and the underlying CNS processes.

This medical model puts a heavy emphasis on diagnosis and classification of symptoms in order to describe the child's pathology, its severity, its etiology, and the child's prognosis for recovery. These classification systems have served us well in the past. With the recognition that not all emotional problems fit into a neat classification scheme, however, the classification systems have evolved. The older *Diagnostic and Statistical Manual* (DSM II) of the American Psychiatric Association (1968) and the *International Classification* (1968) of the World Health Organization stress personality defects and disease processes. The recently revised DSM III (1979), on the other hand, stresses developmental disorders in a multiaxial classification system with five dimensions or axes.

The advantage of a multiaxial scheme is that it can provide symptom description, developmental data, biological bases, and relevant environmental factors that are on a continuum that is not outdated as new advances in the field are made. Specific diagnostic criteria are used as guides so that reliability of diagnosis can be checked. The first three axes or dimensions, which constitute an official diagnostic evaluation are Clinical Syndromes,

Personality Disorders and Specific Developmental Disorders, and Physical Disorders and Conditions. The remaining two axes, Severity of Psychosocial Stressors and Highest Level of Adaptive Functioning for the Past Year, take into account setting factors and are useful for planning treatment and predicting outcome. In this more elaborate classification system of DSM III, which reflects the current state of the art, emotional disturbance is not considered an entity in itself, but one of the criteria for defining certain mental disorders on a multidimensional scale. This is a far more sophisticated approach than has been used in previous classification systems, although its clinical utility remains to be proven.

There are essentially two types of organic or biological theory related to emotional disturbance: theories of defect and theories of development. More traditional approaches have been based on the notion of some underlying defect (primarily organic) which is responsible for pathological symptoms (Strauss & Lehtinen, 1947). More recent organic theories point to certain developmental lags which result in emotional immaturity. Both approaches imply a cluster of behavioral traits which have an organic basis, which are general and which are more or less resistant to modification through environmental manipulations. It is not possible to review thoroughly each theory and all of the more than 10,000 references to research in this area in the past 10 years. We will look at only the major theories which have had a significant impact on teaching emotionally disturbed children.

Biological Defect Theories

Genetic Theories

Genetic theories of emotional disturbance stress the influence of a person's inherited genetic makeup on the behavior a person manifests. Whether a genetic trait is expressed or not depends on its penetrance, its degree of dominance over other traits and expressivity, the degree to which the trait is manifested. Penetrance and expressivity are products of the interaction of heredity and environment. A full spectrum of opinions on the relative contributions of heredity and environment has emerged over the years. At one extreme, sociobiologists like Lorenz (1966) and E. O. Wilson (1975) have proposed that sociocultural motivational and behavioral patterns are shaped directly by heredity. At the other extreme, Szasz (1961) asserts that mental illness is a myth shaped totally by the culture. To a great extent such diversity of opinion can be traced to two methodological problems. First, in any classification system, such as in DSM III, groupings are not homogeneous; therefore, only a loose relationship will be found between the behavior a person manifests and a given identified genetic marker of a particular emotional disorder. Second, by its nature human genetic research methodology must be post hoc and for the most part correlational, not causal. Experimental human genetic research is a highly volatile and controversial topic on ethical grounds, as witness the current furor over recombinant DNA research.

There are basically two methods used for studying hereditary influences on the development of mental illness: (a) comparing the degree of correspondence of family pedigrees to those found in the general population; and (b) comparing concordance of characteristics among twins, either fraternal or identical, reared together or reared apart. For both of these methodologies, selecting a representative subject sample and accounting for comparable environmental experiences in early life are key issues where most of the studies are weak. In spite of these problems, a good deal of evidence has accumulated to support genetic influences in emotional disturbances. Unfortunately, none of the genetic theories accounts adequately for the way genetic makeup exhibits itself in the complex and subtle behavioral patterns that appear in the classroom. Thus most of the genetic theories are important for research purposes but as yet have little practical value.

To see how genetic explanations have been applied to mental disorders, we can look at the case of schizophrenia, which has been examined more closely than other mental illnesses. The simplest theory of genetic influence in schizophrenia is that emotional disturbance is caused by a *major dominant gene* (Böök, 1953; Schulz, 1940) or a *major recessive gene* (Kallmann, 1938). Others (Schulz, 1940; Penrose, 1953) assume that most persons carry a number of pathologic genes which, when combined, produce a particular type of schizophrenia. This *clustering of minor genes* may yield some phenotypic trait, such as delusions of thought. Whether the trait is expressed or not depends on the presence of compensatory favorable genes or favorable environment experiences. Each of these hypotheses has been supported in the literature. More recent, sophisticated, genetic analyses (Elston & Stewart, 1971; Elston, Namboodiri, Spence & Rainer, 1978) seem to favor the single- or few-gene hypotheses mostly because the many-gene theory is too imprecise to be testable. The theory of major-gene heredity implies a disease concept of psychopathology. For example, schizophrenia is assumed to have a different hereditary makeup than affective disorders; and neurosis and psychosis are believed to be different disease entities which lead to different heredity-environment interactions. The genetic analysis of mental illness does have implications for classroom teaching. Certain types of schizophrenia, for instance, are *process* disorders; that is, they are more closely linked to heredity, have more serious symptoms, earlier onset and a poorer prognosis for recovery. *Reactive* schizophrenics, on the other hand, have mild symptoms, acute onset, good prognosis and no genetic predisposition. This distinction has been useful in many diagnostic systems (Rutter, 1978), although its genetic underpinnings are still largely speculative.

Temperament Theory

Temperament theory (Thomas & Chess, 1977), as compared to genetic theories, is based generally on the notion that certain constitutional factors are inherited, but these factors, it is believed, rely heavily on the environment for their expression. *Temperament* refers to behavioral style. It is a phenomenological term that emphasizes *how* a child's behavior patterns emerge rather than *why* they occur or *what* their content is and the child's abilities are. Thomas and Chess (1977) have been observing several cohorts of children, beginning with the New York Longitudinal Study in 1956, and following them into adulthood. They have been able to identify nine categories of temperament which endured throughout childhood: activity level, rhythmicity (regularity), approach or withdrawal, adaptability, threshold of responsiveness, intensity of reaction, quality of mood, distractibility, and attention span and persistence.

Three temperamental types which have functional significance have emerged from factor analyses of these temperamental traits: (a) the *Easy Child* (40% of the sample), characterized by regularity, positive approach responses to new stimuli, adaptability to change, moderately intense mood and high tolerance for frustration; (b) the *Difficult Child* (10% of the sample), with irregular biological functions, negative withdrawal, poor adaptability to change, intense mood expression, and frequent negativism; and (c) the *Slow-to-Warm-Up Child* (15% of the sample), a mix of the first two, but one who eventually adapts satisfactorily. The remaining 35% of the sample were too variable to fit into these clusters.

If these typologies eventually hold up with further research, they could be helpful in pinpointing antecedents of emotional symptoms. Based on research done so far, it appears that whether or not a child shows particular symptoms of emotional disturbance or behavioral disorder is related more to sociocultural variables like socioeconomic status (SES) and parental demands than to temperament. The form of the behavior taken by a symptom when it emerges, however, is highly related to the child's temperamental characteristics. For example, when reacting to frustration, the Difficult Child reacts with negativism and tantrums, the Easy Child tries a different solution to the problem that has previously been effective in a different situation, and the Slow-to-Warm-Up Child withdraws, clings to the parent and refuses to move.

The Chess and Thomas conceptual scheme of temperament is useful as long as we remember that none of these temperament types is unchangeable. Prospective studies of early risk indices of later emotional adjustment have generally failed to demonstrate good predictive validity (Sameroff & Chandler, 1974). Perhaps this is due to geneticists' inability to closely link genetic makeup and behavioral patterns. Or perhaps it is simply due to the ecological complexity of the child's environment which shapes his "temperament" (see Chapter 8). At present this is a moot argument.

Neuropsychopharmacological Theories

The astounding growth of research in this area during the past decade has been due primarily to the accidental discovery of LSD-25, which simulates emotional disturbance, and the discovery of the clinical utility of certain drugs (e.g., phenothiazines, tricyclic antidepressants, MAO inhibitors) as antipsychotic drugs. These discoveries raised new hope for treatment, deinstitutionalization, even cure of emotional disturbance which totally revolutionized the traditionally psychodynamic field of psychiatry into a discipline which now had a scientifically rigorous component (Lipton, DiMascio & Killam, 1978). A natural sequel was to pursue the study of mechanisms of emotional disturbance as disturbances or defects in nerve pathways. Numerous pathways, which were differentially sensitive to specific chemicals, were mapped. In this respect the dopamine receptor pathways, which have been implicated in the antipsychotic effects of some major tranquilizers (e.g., Thorazine, Mellaril, Haldol), are the systems which have received most study.

The dopamine receptor (DA) hypothesis of schizophrenia suggests that this disorder is due to a malfunction of one or more DA systems of the brain which is corrected by the appropriate dosage of an antipsychotic drug. Most of this evidence comes from studies of animals. Much of this neuroanatomical and neuropharmacological experimentation would not be permissable with humans. Unfortunately, animal models of psychosis can only mimic their human counterparts (Bunney & Aghajanian, 1978). The human clinical research support for the DA hypothesis is not strong. An alternative explanation of the therapeutic effects of antipsychotic drugs is that, through action on DA neurons, they correct an imbalance in the central nervous system by correcting malfunctions of other *non*-DA systems. As yet the type of neuron being innervated by dopamine has not been isolated, so its mechanism of action is not fully understood. Nevertheless, the next decade is likely to see some exciting breakthroughs in the use of psychotropic medications. For instance, DA receptor sensitivity can be modified by changing its synthesis or by blocking the DA receptor pharmacologically, which has been shown to affect favorably the abnormal behaviors of animals in whom schizophrenic symptoms had been experimentally induced (Friedhoff & Alpert, 1978). What this means for the teacher in the classroom is that the appropriate dosage level for psychotropic drugs will be more easily determined in the future, side effects will be reduced, interactions with other drugs, such as seizure medications, will be understood more clearly, and a child's supersensitivity to a drug during drug "holidays" will be controllable. Thus, the beneficial effects of the drugs will be maximized while their negative effects will be reduced.

Theories of Nutritional Disorder

Nutrition is certainly one of the most controversial subjects in the study of emotional disturbances. Many toxic substances, such as metals like zinc, iron and perhaps even lead, when ingested at appropriately low levels serve a healthful function in the diet. But when they are ingested in large doses, they may cause behavioral aberrations, even gross brain damage and death. Moderately elevated levels have been implicated in hyperactivity. The toxic effects of lead exposure on the nervous system and behavior is a complex topic that has been reviewed thoroughly in the EPA document *Air Quality Criteria for Lead* (1977) and recently by Rutter (1980). The role of malnutrition and social disadvantage on depression and personality disorders is reviewed exhaustively by Birch and Gussow (1970). Two recent, highly publicized and controversial topics in relating nutrition to emotional disturbance are (a) the relation of vitamin deficiency to emotional disorders and of megavitamin therapy to their remediation and (b) the relation of food additives to hyperactivity.

Vitamin deficiencies, of riboflavin, ascorbic acid and pyridoxine, for example, have long been known to produce neurological and psychiatric

A number of experimental studies have supported the hypothesis that food additives are related to hyperactivity.

deficits (Peterman & Goodhart, 1954). Psychosis based on calcium deficiency has responded to treatment with foods from the vitamin D group (Coleman & Brown, 1976; Gertner, Hodsman & Neuberger, 1976). Also, in 1952 before psychotropic drugs were available, vitamin B_3 was used as a valuable adjunct to electroconvulsive shock therapy and barbiturates (Lipton, Bann, Kane, Levine, Mosher & Wittenborn, 1973) in treating schizophrenic persons.

The rationale for using massive doses of vitamins (megavitamin therapy) originally was that vitamin B_3 reduced the formation of psychosis-producing substances (adrenochrome and adrenolutin) (Hoffer, 1964). More recently, the case has been made (Hoffer, 1970) that schizophrenia is an incipient form of pellagra, a disease caused by lack of niacin, which requires massive doses of the vitamin because the schizophrenic patient is unable to synthesize it naturally. Pauling (1968) and Hawkins and Pauling (1973) have made a sweeping case for the role of vitamins in mental disorders which has stirred up a great deal of controversy. They suggest that some forms of mental illness are due to vitamin deficiencies occurring even in ordinarily adequate diets. Such deficiencies could be due to a genetic defect in which the body fails to produce the vitamin and requires exceptionally large doses of vitamins to replace it. This field of study is called orthomolecular psychiatry.

Orthomolecular psychiatry has since become a whole school of thought which vigorously opposes other forms of treatment for mental illness, such as psychotherapy or behavioral therapy. Orthomolecular psychiatry is "the treatment of mental disease by the provision of the optimum molecular environment for the mind, especially the optimum concentration of substances normally present in the body" (Pauling, 1968). Schizophrenias are seen as biochemical aberrations which can be cured by the correct combination of high doses of niacin or niacinamide, ascorbic acid, pyridoxine, Vitamin E, thyroid and vitamin B_{12}; low-sugar and cereal-free diets; daily physical exercise; and lithium, phenothiazines and other commonly used tranquilizers and antidepressants.

Advocates of megavitamin therapy were initially modest about their claims, supporting them with research. Lately, however, they have become more militant and doctrinaire, claiming success in the treatment of hyperactive children, childhood autism, alcoholism, arthritis, hyperlipidemia, geriatric problems, and even some forms of neurosis and depression (Cott, 1969, 1971; Hoffer, 1967, 1971a, 1971b). The controversy became so heated that the American Psychiatric Association in 1973 appointed a blue-ribbon task force to review the research on megavitamin and orthomolecular therapy. The task force concluded that the effectiveness of megavitamin therapy is not strongly supported by the available research, the theoretical rationale for it is inadequate, many of its successes appear to be due to placebo effects, and the research supporting megavitamin therapy lacks credibility because controlled experimentation has not been scientifically adequate. Thus, while its usefulness has not been disproven, its claims of effectiveness are greatly exaggerated. Most of the definitive research remains to be done (Siva Sankar, 1979). Meanwhile the dangers of vitamin dependency require that megavitamin therapy be conducted only under a physician's supervision.

Theories about Food Additives

Food additives and their relationship to hyperactivity are another very controversial topic. Food itself, of course, is a chemical compound made up of carbohydrates, proteins, fats, minerals, vitamins, antioxidants, thickeners, emulsifiers, colors, flavors, pesticides, drugs, environmental toxins and intentional additives for preservation, enrichment and palatability. Additives, such as spices and sweeteners, have been used since early human history. But in the last century the number of chemical additives has expanded to over 3000 comprising over 1 billion pounds of additives and a $750 million a year industry by 1980. Over half of all foods produced in the U.S. contain additives, which works out to an intake of about 6 pounds per capita per year (Abrams, Schultz, Margen & Ogar, 1979). The use of food additives in the U.S. is pervasive.

Basically there are two hypotheses about the relationship of food additives to behavior problems. The first (Abrams et al., 1979) is that behavior problems, and especially hyperactivity, are due to food allergies which develop in the course of exposure to food additives and affect the immune system. The second hypothesis is that a certain percentage of children are born with a supersensitivity to certain chemicals in the environment, usually foods (Feingold, 1975). The more chemicals are added to our food supply, the more children exhibit these allergies. Treatment under both hypotheses consists of a strict elimination diet, with new foods being added slowly so as not to permit relapse. Feingold (1975) claims success in about 50% of cases. Several clinical reports state dramatic results in 30% to 80% of cases (Brenner, 1977; Cook & Woodhill, 1976). Experimental research is very difficult in this area because there are so many confounding covariants that need to be controlled. Enough well-controlled, double-blind studies have been conducted, however, to support the view that food additives are related to hyperactivity (Swanson & Kinsbourne, 1980; Weiss, Williams, Margen, Abrams, Caan, Citron, Cox, McKibben, Ogar, & Schultz, 1980). Which additives, what doses and which children are most critical are questions which are likely to occupy researchers in this area in the near future.

Neurological Dysfunction Theory

Studies of children with gross neurological impairments reveal higher rates of behavior disorders than studies of normal children. In the most thorough epidemiological survey done in the U.K. (Rutter, Tizard, & Whitmore, 1970), whose sample was representative of children in the U.S., psychiatric disorders, especially childhood psychosis and hyperactivity, were found to be five times as frequent among children with epileptic conditions than among the general population.

In the case of gross neurological impairments, the location of structural brain damage or extent of tissue destruction is only loosely related to behavioral symptoms. In children interpretation of the consequences of brain injury is complicated by the developmental plasticity of the central nervous system. In some cases, loss of function can be compensated for with age, while in other cases age brings increasingly severe aberrations, as in degenerative diseases like Tay-Sachs disease, an enzyme defect, or Schilder's disease, where progressive demyelinization of neurons occurs.

Organic brain syndromes, which are well-defined patterns of gross neurological impairment, can be acute or chronic, progressive or stationary, manifested at the time of injury or later after a symptom-free interval. They have been observed, sometimes but not always, to accompany certain infections, exposure to toxic levels of poisons like lead or mercury, head trauma, congenital malformations, neonatal anoxia, brain tumors, epilepsy and a variety of metabolic disorders (Chess & Hassibi, 1978). Acute symptoms range from mild confusion to total stupor and coma; disorientation toward objects, people and places; illusions, hallucinations, delirium, agitation and panic. Chronic symptoms include intellectual impairment, memory loss, perseveration, attention deficits, loss of impulse control, affect regulation, hyperactivity and hypoactivity. In other words, the symptomatology is so broad and unsystematic that it cannot be used to generate a prescription for treatment that the teacher can use. The presence of these symptoms, however, can alert the teacher to the possibility of brain damage. For preventive purposes it is important to know that some subgroups of the population, such as infants and young children, are more vulnerable than others and that the neurological effects can be worsened by social, economic and educational practices, depending on the nature of the damage and the context in which it occurs (Baumeister & MacLean, 1979).

Gross neurological impairments are usually considered to lie along a continuum which has at its moderate end a more diffuse form of *minimal brain damage* (MBD). In order to understand the degree of confusion that surrounds the term MBD, we need to see it in its historical context. Modern-day usage of the term dates back to the work of Strauss and Lehtinen (1947), who were interested in classifying brain-damaged (exogenous) and familial (endogenous) retardation. They extrapolated from research findings with brain-damaged World War I soldiers that many soldiers exhibited subtle behavioral deficits for which no neuropathy could be identified. These manifestations, later called the "Strauss syndrome," were hyperactivity, inattentiveness, impulsivity, emotional lability (instability), poor motor coordination and disturbances of perception. Thus a neurological syndrome based on a *lack* of observable neural damage was born, and it has been invoked ever since to explain a variety of unexplainable problems. When the concept of learning disabilities was introduced by Kirk in 1963 (see Senf, 1973, for review) MBD became the neural basis for learning disabilities. A similar concept emerged in a commissioned study by the National Institute of Neurological Diseases and Stroke (Clements, 1966): "Minimal brain dysfuction syndrome [refers to] children of near average, average, or above average intelligence with certain learning or behavioral disabilities ranging from mild to severe, which are associated with deviations of function of the central nervous system" (p. 9).

The list of behavioral symptoms associated with MBD grew and grew. By 1971 over a hundred symptoms presumed to be diagnostic of MBD had been catalogued (Wender, 1971), none of which clustered into groups when factor analyzed (Routh & Roberts, 1972). The focus of MBD research then shifted to one of its major aspects, namely, the "hyperkinetic syndrome," the official term used in DSM II in 1968. As research into the hyperkinetic syndrome developed, however, the same diagnostic problems emerged, so that the focus in DSM III (1979) is on "attentional disorders," with or without hyperactivity. In the next decade, a new name for the same behavioral manifestations is likely to emerge, but researchers will probably be no closer to finding reliable neurological referents than Goldstein was with his war veterans over 50 years ago. While behavior symptoms observed in the Strauss syndrome serve as signals of disturbance for the classroom teacher, recommendations for educational practices based on neurology alone are unwarranted at this time. As Bateman (1973) has noted, "Medical classifications such as MBD are as irrelevant to educational practices as educational classifications are to medical practice." The two classifications are meaningful only when the referents are understood from both perspectives.

The new discipline of neuropsychology (Reitan, 1966, 1974) is dedicated to a more careful scientific specification of clinically significant brain-behavior relationships. The Halstead-Reitan test battery is sufficiently sensitive to allow specific statements about level of impairment and locus of some brain lesions. The new electrophysiological techniques for studying brainstem-evoked responses (Galbraith, Gliddon, & Busk, 1978) and cortical-evoked potentials (see Karrer, 1978 for review) give us new hope for localizing brain functions that may be related to specific behavioral deficits. This new science is called *neurometrics* (John, 1977). So Strauss's early work may not have been in vain, although neuropsychology is still in its infancy. Caution must be exercised against generalizing prematurely from the very modest base of firm knowledge that exists in this area.

Developmental Theories of Brain Damage

Developmental theories of brain damage have emerged since, and probably as the result of, the birth of the notions of learning disabilities and minimal brain dysfunction. Central to their conceptualization is that developmental delays reflect a subtle lack of integrity of the central nervous system which places the child at risk for developmental problems. Removing these disabilities or compensating for them through specific types of training removes the risk and thereby promotes appropriate development in all areas. If the child does not build upon earlier skills or fails to negotiate an appropriate stage of development, disharmony in different developmental areas, or scatter of ability levels, will occur and lead to emotional problems. One can see how this type of post hoc neurological explanation nicely fits the medical model for MBD. Unfortunately, as we shall see, it widely oversteps the bounds of research done in this area.

The Doman-Delacato Theory of Neurological Organization

The basic notion of the Delacato (1966) theory is that specific levels of the brain mediate discrete motor functions. Specific locomotor tasks are believed to affect these areas (midbrain, pons, medulla, cortex) which in turn affect perception and cognition specifically related to these CNS areas. Since many cognitive functions of the brain are lateralized in the two hemispheres of the cerebral cortex, the most important task then is to establish cerebral dominance. It is believed that cognitive functions such as speech, receptive language and selective visual attention are improved by a cerebral dominance which can be learned by training in unilateral handedness, monocular eye dominance exercises and so on. Auditory experience, such as hearing and sound localization, because it is mediated by the nondominant cerebral hemisphere, is eliminated because it is presumed to interfere with establishment of dominance in the other hemisphere, such as speech function. Dominance training is encouraged by unilateral eye-hand–eye-ear exercises. Delacato also emphasizes motor patterning, a reenactment of developmental motor sequences, such as crawling. There is practically no empirical validation of this concept or the claims of success made (Harris, 1968; Robbins and Glass, 1968).

Delacato's theory of organization of neural function has unanimously been rejected by neurologists because it lacks support from neuroanatomical research (Whitsell, 1967).

Kephart's Perceptual-Motor Learning Theory

Kephart's approach (Dunsing & Kephart, 1965) emphasizes motor development. Motor movements develop into more complex movement patterns and then into generalized movement patterns which set the stage for "internalized motor generalizations." These provide the basic perceptual-cognitive structure which makes possible meaningful organization, interpretation and manipulation of the world. Thus intellectual function is a copy of motor acts which precede and are prerequisite for intelligent behavior. Some of these motor generalizations are

1. *Posture and balance.* Response to gravity is necessary for adequate spatial judgments.
2. *Locomotor activity.* Movement helps the child learn about the dynamics of his relationships to objects and things.
3. *Contact.* Skills involving manipulation aid in awareness of objects, shapes and textures.
4. *Receipt and propulsion.* Throwing and catching, for example, teach perception of velocity, size and distance.
5. *Body image.* Awareness of one's location and orientation relative to other people and objects allows movement through space in various media.
6. *Laterality-coordination of body asymmetry.* This allows perception of directionality and object placement. (Training in laterality helps to remedy reading and printing reversal problems, for instance.)

Studies on the relationship between perceptual-motor deficits and intelligence suggest restrictions on many of Kephart's motor generalizations. For instance, Ayres's (1965) factor analytic study of perceptual-motor abilities found that directionality was not related to identification of left and right body parts. Smith and Smith (1962) showed that many visual-perceptual attributes develop rather independently. Thus the suggestion that motor learning influences perceptual cognitive development must be qualified. In a factorial study of the development of mental abilities at least six perceptual-motor attributes were differentiated by the age of six months, but early motor responsiveness was not predictive of IQ at the age of 8 years. Thus Kephart's view that early motor performance predicts later intellectual development must also be qualified. Some of Kephart's sensory-motor training techniques, such as ocular coordination exercises, which are supposed to be related to better reading competency have failed to prove useful (Brown, 1968; Lawson, 1968).

Some research (Brown, 1968) has suggested that Kephart's methods may improve the specific perceptual-motor function that is the focus of training. But while the techniques may be useful for training motor skills used in cognition, the assertion that all cognitive function depends on perceptual-motor development is not warranted by the facts. Witness, for example, the cognitive development of paralytics and paraplegic individuals. After an in-depth review of the research, Hammill (1972) concluded that it has not yet been demonstrated that perceptual-motor training facilitates school learning.

Getman's Physiology of Readiness Theory

Getman's theory (1965) is concerned mainly with visual-motor development. Like Kephart he assumes that movement is the basis of all intellectual development: "Thoughts which do not get into the muscles never fully possess the mind!" (Getman, 1963, p. 21). Being an optometrist, he stresses vision. Six developmental stages through which a child must progressively pass are

1 *General movement patterns.* Primary locomotor activities and movements of the hands and eyes in coordination.
2 *Special movement patterns of action.* The use of body parts to manipulate objects.
3 *Eye movement skills.* Necessary for quick and efficient visual exploration.
4 *Communication patterns to replace action.* Learning to use visual and movement experiences to communicate.
5 *Visualization patterns.* Discrimination, recognition, visual imagery.
6 *Visual-perceptual organization.* Interpretation, understanding and concept formation.

Getman's theory is a *motor-copy theory*: the percept is an internal representation of the motor movement (Gibson, 1969). Visual and visual-motor exercises are purported to enhance progress through these developmental stages. Implicit in the stage concept is the notion that perceptual activity can only be trained when the child is "ready." Premature training leads to perceptual problems. Perceptual deficits in one area cause deficits in other areas. Most of Getman's training procedures are visual-motor exercises since he contends that 90% of learning occurs through visual processes. This, however, is essentially an unprovable assertion. It is probably true that some children fail to learn because of visual problems, but it is not true of the general population. Similarly, overcoming a visual deficit will not automatically result in remediation of the learning problem. In a factor analytic study of children with reading disabilities visual problems were not found to be significantly related to reading retardation (Lawson, 1968). Eye defects, however, can aggravate a learning disorder or impede response to remediation.

Like Kephart's theory, Getman's contention that perceptual-motor development must progress through the stages he describes has little research support. His training methods, however, probably do improve performance in the specific areas where they are applied. How this relates to the emotional and intellectual development of the learning disabled child remains to be discovered.

Ayres's Theory of Sensory Integration

Ayres's theory of sensory integration (1972, 1979) is another widely used theory of MBD, as are Kephart's and Getman's. Her theory of neural integration is based primarily on the work of two neuroanatomists, Sherrington (1906) and Herrick (1956), who considered cognitive abilities a product of an evolving motor organism responding to environmental demands. Actions of the body affect the evolution of the mind, not vice versa. Integration is the end product of organizing processes of the brain. The interaction and coordination of these processes enhances the adaptiveness of an individual's response. In learning and perception the CNS provides this integrative function, according to Ayres, through four processes: intersensory interaction, centrifugal influences, modification through feedback, and balancing excitatory and depressant neural activity.

1 *Intersensory integration* is the brain's way of associating information from the different senses, such as seeing and hearing. It is a major evolutionary trend across species in neural processes. Integration occurs at all levels of the central nervous system through convergence of neural impulses from several sources on common pathways and centers in the brain and by modulation of sensory input to corresponding areas of the cerebral cortex. Convergence of brain pathways results both in facilitative and selective information processing through the interaction of excitatory and inhibitory neurons. The capacity to perceive depends greatly on intersensory integration. Thus a multisensory approach to remediation is espoused to enhance integrative processes. Massive sensory load, however, may cause disruption.

2 The brain also can regulate its own sensory input through *centrifugal influences*. Each neural impulse has an arousal function as well as the associative function which occurs during intersensory integration. The reticular activating system, which projects to many specific areas of the brain, acts to control arousal and attention to a stimulus by raising or lowering its threshold of perceptibility. Clinical signs of deficits of inhibition occur in brain damage. Inhibition can be controlled by programming afferent stimuli (neural impulses traveling toward the cerebral cortex) which have central inhibiting effects, such as positioning the body so that certain reflex activities cannot occur, or by eliciting simple adaptive responses which are easily integrated, such as scooter games to promote balance.

3 *Feedback* is controlled mainly through the proprioceptive systems to provide continuous information on the effects of action. Thus vision is important in the development of motor skills. Tactile, kinesthetic and vestibular perception are necessary for visual perception of real and apparent motion. Feedback also regulates input through the selective inhibition of neural impulses to the brain. For instance, for a child to successfully place a peg in a hole, coordinated visual, tactile, and motor feedback is needed to guide the peg properly. An obvious example where these feedback relations are disrupted is cerebral palsy.

4 *Balance of excitatory and inhibitory functions* is important for maturation of the brain. Inhibition of central nervous system activity is of two types: those that inhibit the response to afferent input and those that inhibit afferent input itself. The first type of dysfunction is observed clinically when reflex activity fails to mature with age in the total sensory-motor system. Purposeful sensory-motor activity is thereby inhibited. For instance, sitting and walking in childhood may be delayed if primitive reflexes occurring during infancy are not inhibited. The second type of dysfunction results in problems of homeostasis and central excitatory states, such as lethargy and hyperactivity. The disorders are largely related to regulation of the reticular activating system which controls "afferent bombardment" of the brain necessary for interpretation of sensory information at the cerebral cortex.

Practical application of these principles centers around observation of postural and other reflexes (e.g., erectness and muscle tone), equilibrium reactions (e.g., responses to gravity), CNS excitability (e.g., activity level and distractibility), perception in all sense modalities (e.g., visual acuity) and motor planning (e.g., goal-directed activity). Deficits in these areas are thought to be related directly to neural mechanisms. Treatment is assumed to modify the four integrative neural processes. This is done mainly by controlled environmental stimulation which presumably results in afferent neural activity important for an adaptive or purposeful motor response. For instance, light touch stimuli are used to "stimulate the ascending reticular activating system." Stimulation of the vestibular system and somatosensory system is achieved by gross motion (e.g., rolling, crawling, tumbling, sliding, climbing, riding prone on a wheeled scooter). Adaptive responses elicited are of two types: motor responses which require motor planning and those integrated primarily at subcortical levels (e.g., gravitation). Motor planning is more adaptive and more difficult because focus of attention and increased effort are required. Thus providing even more challenging motor acts enhances sensory-motor integration. Obstacle courses, stunts, competitive games are recommended. Treatment of more primitive motor reflex functions which interfere with development (e.g., tonic neck and labyrinthine reflexes) can be influenced by engaging in activity which is the reverse of the reflex being facilitated by afferent input. Thus scooter games inhibit postural reflexes.

Ayres concludes by noting that the role of sensory integrative processes is limited. Thus in a child with normal sensory-motor development, training will probably not enhance cognitive or perceptual development as much as it will with children who have learning disabilities. But it has been used with a wide variety of children: emotionally disturbed (Weeks, 1979), the schizophrenic (King, 1974), the autistic (Ayres, 1979), and even the profoundly retarded self-injurious child (Bittick, Fleeman, & Bright, 1978; Lemke & Mitchell, 1972).

Ayres's theory and training methods have gained wide acceptance among occupational therapists, but the theory has not received empirical validation because it is essentially untestable in its present form. It is not sufficient to infer alterations in specific neural functions from the observations of the behavior alone. Such inferences need to be strengthened from neurophysiological and neuroanatomical research.

In this connection, Ayres' interpretation of neurophysiological data leaves the impression that the sensory integrative processes she describes are based on proven theories of neural function, when this is anything but the case. First, the bulk of the neurophysiological data is based on work with animals, especially the rat, cat, rabbit and monkey. Important neuroanatomical differences between and within species make generalization to humans very tenuous (Doty, 1970). Second, the neural mechanisms of sensory interaction in humans are mostly speculative. As Buser (1970) notes, the most that can be said about them is that they are there. They probably modulate and participate in input and are correlated with attentive states but how they work together is largely unknown.

There are several other questions raised by Ayres's neuropsychological interpretation which are left unanswered. As noted previously, it remains to be discovered how sensory-motor training enhances cognitive development. It has not been shown how reflex activity inhibits development of more adaptive and purposeful motor activity. Indeed the converse may be just as true. The relation of feedback, especially the brain mechanisms of reward and punishment, to sensory-motor integration has not been examined adequately on the neurophysiological level to draw conclusions about humans.

The behavior of the children in Ayres's training procedures can be explained by alternative theories on a behavioral level alone. The necessity of postulating influence by neural mechanisms is questionable until appropriate data exist. Behavioral research on specific sensory and sensory-motor interaction in children with perceptual-motor dysfunction is practically nonexistent. Thus, while the Ayres's diagnostic and training procedures may be very useful, their utility is not necessarily related to her theory of sensory integration.

Frostig's Developmental Theory

Frostig's (1968) theory is essentially a developmental stage theory. For the average child, specific developmental functions are learned at different age levels in a definite sequential pattern. Dysfunction arises as a result of an imbalance in developmental levels of abilities, i.e. developmental lags. The developmental sequence she describes is very similar to that of Inhelder and Piaget (1964). Growth occurs in five major areas: sensory-motor abilities, language, perception, thought processes, and emotions and social behavior. Emotionally disturbed children are evaluated and given training in the appropriate area. Several standard psychometric instruments are used.

In the *sensory-motor phase* the child discovers the world by simultaneously applying all his senses and moving to explore the environment. Children with dysfunction fail to integrate sensory and motor experiences and cannot perceive the outside world adequately. Disability in the sensory-motor phase often leads to later learning problems. Training for muscular control, coordination and regularity in gross and fine motor sequences often helps these children. The normal teaching of other academic skills, however, need not be delayed until sensory-motor dysfunction is compensated for. In the sensory-motor area physical education training helps to develop endurance, strength, agility, speed, flexibility, balance, coordination, rhythm, laterality and knowledge of direction. Training may also focus on body awareness, fine motor skills and eye movements.

The *language phase* begins around the second year of life. Language allows transcendence of the immediate environment, permits conceptualization and communication of the "not-present" and accelerates social development. Frostig's language training program is based on the Illinois Test of Psycholinguistic Abilities (Kirk & Kirk, 1971), a standardized test that is assumed to measure 12 discrete psycholinguistic abilities thought to be important for language development and academic achievement.

The *perceptual phase* lasts from about 4 to 7 years of age. In this phase the child tries to understand the world directly, perceptually and intuitively. Training of perception encourages visual motor coordination, figure-ground perception, constancy of perception, perception of position in space, and perception of spatial relationships. These are performed in two-dimensional and three-dimensional space and within and across sense modalities.

The phase of development of higher cognitive processes begins at age 6 or 7. The child seeks to verify observations and find causal relationships, compares, analyzes and makes inferences in a systematic fashion. At age 11–13 thought processes become more abstract, and the child begins to think like an adult. Deficits at this phase are often the result of lags in earlier phases. Thus difficulty in spatial perception may impair the learning of mathematical concepts.

To develop the higher cognitive processes, the training methods of Levi (1966) are espoused. Formation and generalization of concepts are taught by sorting tasks, visual memory tasks, and coding and decoding tasks. In designing curricula Frostig emphasizes motivation, establishing learning sets, defining specific goals, maintaining progress through feedback (reinforcement), regulating the tempo of progress, sequencing the curriculum components and structuring the classroom situation.

Emotional development and social adjustment mature more gradually and change throughout life. Emotional disturbances are treated through parental counseling and psychotherapy; the necessary tools for developing social skills, such as language, are taught.

Frostig's theory is certainly the broadest in scope of all the psychoneurological theories we have examined. It is also closer to the facts of development as known presently. Like Piaget's theory it is eclectic and it makes few assumptions about the interrelatedness of the various phases of development or the causes of developmental lags. Training is aimed at achieving maximum competence in each area.

Frostig's program has been criticized for its eclecticism. The use of psychometric diagnostic instruments and a shotgun approach to remediation have left some researchers wondering whether her programs of testing and remediation are representative of how a particular capability is normally used (Black, 1974; Hammill, 1972). Lack of adequate data, however, prevents conclusions on this point.

Instructional Issues

That classroom behavior is mediated by the brain and neurological dysfunction adversely affects classroom performance is an obvious but not particularly enlightening statement. In order to draw any conclusions from this fact for classroom practice, we have to relate the nature, extent, timing and source of brain malfunction to the social and educational factors that contribute to the complex dynamics of good classroom teaching. The child in this context is a total biological system whose performance depends jointly on the integrity of his nervous system *and* environmental experience. As we shall see, however, few firm educational conclusions can be drawn from organic theories.

Compensatory Educational Approaches based on Defect Theories

Symptom reduction through medical intervention. The assumption of this approach is that neurologically impaired children are basically different from normal children and therefore should be educated differently. Performance demands should be minimized in their areas of dysfunction, and their strengths should be strengthened. This notion was the basis for Strauss's suggestion that brain-damaged children should be taught under conditions of reduced stimulation. It has been the rationale for the search for the XYY chromosome which allegedly is responsible for aggressive behavior (Jacobs, Brunton, Melville, Brittain & McClemont, 1965). An example of more timely significance is the widespread use of Ritalin in treating hyperactivity. This stimulant drug is thought to have the paradoxical effect of calming down a hyperactive child. In fact, Wender (1971) has suggested that this paradoxical response to a stimulant drug be a criterion for defining hyperactivity. This circular reasoning assumes that a "hyperkinetic syndrome" involves a defective neurotransmitter system which is corrected by the drug. There is very little concrete evidence for this, however. As we find out more about the pharmacology, especially with respect to brain metabolism, of these drugs, we are finding that no "paradoxical" response exists. In fact, all children and adults probably are "responders," but the effective dose for each person varies as a function of a variety of conditions (Gualtieri, Breese, Wargin, Kanoy, Hawk & Schroeder, in press). Generally, it is not possible to predict which child's classroom performance will be improved by Ritalin without a controlled clinical trial, even though we know from group data that, overall, Ritalin is a very effective adjunct in managing hyperactivity (Gittleman-Klein, Klein, Abikoff, Katz, Gloisten & Kates, 1976).

Remedial education. The basic assumption of this approach is that neurological dysfunction causes a "scatter of abilities." The remedial approach is typified by the psychoeducational approach of Kirk and Kirk (1971) and best exemplified in the test they constructed, The Illinois Test of Psycholinguistic Abilities (ITPA) (Kirk, McCarthy & Kirk, 1968). Cruickshank (1966, 1977) also maintains that learning disabilities reflect neural dysfunctions. For example, letter inversions or reversals represent disorders of "figure-ground relationships," and dysphasia may reflect an underlying "language disorder."

Remedial approaches seem to work best when a program addresses a specific disability. The notion of "teaching to the disability" has a certain face validity and practical value. The theoretical underpinnings that have guided the practice, however, have only equivocal research support (see Schroeder, Schroeder & Davine, 1978 for a review). The teacher may find these specific remedial techniques more useful as an additional resource in her instructional repertoire than as a set of guidelines that need to be followed religiously.

Early intervention and prevention. In a sense, everyone who has a disability can be postulated to have a neurological deficit. The key question is, just how much developmental plasticity is there in the brain? The idea that remediation is most likely to occur through early intervention is subject to dispute as noted at a recent conference sponsored by the President's Committee on Mental Retardation (Tjossem, 1976). There are basically three dimensions along which neurological deficits must be considered: (a) the developmental age at which it occurred, (b) the structural changes in the CNS that have resulted and (c) how changes are expressed behaviorally over time. Younger people tend to be more vulnerable than older ones. Studies of brain-damaged and wounded adults (Penfield & Roberts, 1959; Teuber, Battersby & Bender, 1960) suggest that their deficits are very specific, with other functions remaining intact. By contrast, the effects of brain damage in children are more diffuse and severe. Neurological dysfunction in early childhood yields a much poorer prognosis for adaptations or the development of compensatory mechanisms through learning. Hebb (1942) concludes that fully intact brain function is necessary for intellectual development, but not nearly so important for maintenance of skills already attained. Isaacson (1975) has called recovery from early brain damage a myth. A thorough examination of the research literature supports his contention. This, however, does not mean that brain-damaged children cannot be taught. The similarities between brain-damaged children and other children who do not exhibit the symptoms of brain damage far outweigh their differences (Gallagher, 1966). Nevertheless, the goals of early intervention programs must be set realistically, given our limited knowledge of brain-behavior relationships in child development.

Issues Related to Developmental Theories

The theories of development we have examined involve several assumptions about development which have been aptly labeled "classic false issues" (Gibson, 1969).

Learning or maturation? Some theories of development consider maturation and learning as autonomous processes, the former being a function of biological inheritance and the latter being a function of environmental experience. It is clear that both biology and environment have a role in development, but trends in development always emerge as the product of both. There is no either-or issue. Therefore, teaching concepts based on maturation such as reading readiness are not appropriate; the important point of reference is the current abilities the child manifests.

Perception or action? Which comes first? Current motor theories imply that action has priority. But in fact, production often follows perception. For instance, speech sounds are often discriminated long before they can be reproduced. Forms, particularly diagonals, can be discriminated before they can be produced. Motor training in these cases does not facilitate reproduction, but discrimination training does (Maccoby & Bee, 1965; Olson, 1968). Perceptual and physical performance activities have different developmental histories. They serve different purposes for the organism: perceptual activities provide information from the environment; performance provides feedback on actions of the organism. The issue of whether actions must precede perception is thus a pseudo-issue.

Part or whole? Which comes first? Does the organism develop from global perceptions to more differentiated percepts or vice versa? It depends on what is considered part or whole. The comprehending of structure in the world is a developmental trend but so is responsiveness to critical, specific sets of stimuli.

Does perception lead to inference? Does the organism form general rules based on individual percepts? How this question is answered dictates whether a child learns better under conditions of information redundancy or impoverishment. Some argue that as we learn more cognitive activities we need to perceive less. The basic question is whether the brain compares new percepts with neural templates of old percepts already represented in the brain. The argument is speculative. In the active practice of perception, stimulus redundancy and impoverishment sometimes enhance and sometimes inhibit accuracy. The issue is, therefore, empirical, and not deducible from current theories.

Stages or transitions? Many developmental theories involve progressions through stages and transitions. Characteristic rates of change in development are posited. Many facets of change in development imply that there are significant milestones of growth, but there are just as many trends in development that have been found to be continuous. It is a question of research strategy. The researcher fixated on developmental stages often comes to concentrate on their immutability and neglects complex interactions in development. At this point the stage concept becomes more of an explanatory theory to be defended than a description of developmental processes.

Does remediation automatically enhance development? Probably, the most serious weakness of all of the developmental theories of neurological impairment is the assumption that brain damage can be treated as a unitary concept. Once a sensory or motor deficit is remediated, it is inferred that social-emotional and cognitive development can proceed normally. Longitudinal research, however, has consistently yielded results which do not confirm this position (Chess & Hassibi, 1978). Knowing that a child is "difficult" early in life is not very predictive of how he will be as an adult because so many mitigating environmental circumstances can intervene. The classic example, again, is hyperactivity. Research has shown repeatedly that it is not a unitary but a multidimensional concept (Routh, 1978) which, in many cases, is even specific to a particular social situation or environment (Barkley, 1979).

The symptoms of MBD are also the same symptoms used for other childhood disorders, e.g. conduct disorders (Sandberg, Rutter & Taylor, 1978 for review). From the teacher's standpoint, this state of affairs makes programming difficult. Indeed some dismayed educators have come to conclude that any program for MBD which includes individual attention and parental involvement is as good as any other (Bettman, Stern, Whitsell & Goffman, 1967).

Methodological Issues

There are a number of issues which the teacher needs to keep in mind when interpreting the results of assessment and research based on organic theories.

Assessment Issues

There are several assessment issues which deserve careful consideration if one is to be confident that he is really sampling the behavior of the child which he wants to study. In psychometric types of assessment, tests are often administered in uncontrolled environments, and the amount of behavior sampled is usually small. Thus interpretation is often difficult because of poor test reliability and validity, and inferences about performance level seem to bear little relation to the actual behavior observed. Psychometric tests provide a useful screening function but do not give detailed information on the degree of deficit in an individual. Controlled laboratory assessment requires much more elaborate instrumentation, and, though not without its difficulties, such assessment does allow for simpler and more direct interpretation of performance.

Neuropsychological assessment tools are inadequate. Most of these assessment instruments are of marginal use for brain-damaged children because they cannot assess adequately developmental trends or morphological changes following brain damage (see Baumeister & MacLean, 1979, for review). Also, specific response biases of the neurologically impaired to specific assessment methods are often overlooked. Developmental functions should be assessed with multiple methods applied by an interdisciplinary team.

Research Issues

Research on educating brain-damaged children focuses mostly on brain injury. Little attention is given to the positive aspects of what children can do.

The heterogeneity of the brain-damaged population makes generalization based on the studies in this area difficult. Another problem is that the most carefully researched neurologically impaired children are institutionalized. The research sample is biased toward children who have a restricted developmental and environmental history. Finally, drug histories and their interactions with neurological development have rarely been examined. Yet neurologically impaired children are the very children most likely to receive chronic pharmacotherapy with potent drugs.

SUMMARY

Much of our thinking about curriculum design for the neurologically impaired child where no apparent neuropathology exists (MBD) has been shaped by the behaviors of the Strauss Syndrome, such as hyperactivity, inattentiveness, impulsivity, emotional instability, poor motor coordination and disturbances of perception. For instance, conventional wisdom is that an MBD child should be taught under conditions of reduced stimulation because of easy distractibility, but research has shown that this approach depends on the nature of the distracting stimulus. Hyperactive children imitate high-activity level models (Kasper & Lowenstein, 1971) and perform better alone on individualized token systems (Jenkens, Gorrafa & Griffiths, 1972). But they also respond better to variegated and multisensory stimuli when on task (Anderson & Levin, 1976; Forehand & Baumeister, 1970; Zentall & Zentall, 1976). One would think that a highly structured self-contained classroom would be better than an open classroom but the available research shows just the opposite (Flynn & Rapoport, 1976; Jacob, O'Leary & Rosenblad, 1978). In effect, the theories covered in this chapter have had little say about the practical aspects of managing the neurologically impaired child.

A social skills model of competence training seems to be one method worth further investigation. Routh and Mesibov (1980) have reviewed the social competence literature and the research on long-term follow-up of brain-damaged and MBD children into adulthood. They have proposed three dimensions of social competence to be trained:

1 *Intelligence vs. skill deficits.* For example, rather than remediating language deficits, train reading skills related to marketable job skills.
2 *Responsible behavior vs. conduct problems.* For example, instead of eliminating disruptive behaviors, emphasize self-control, and social and ethical values.
3 *Social participation vs. personality problems.* Instead of remediating skill deficits and training docility to the exclusion of everything else, work also on self-esteem, peer relations and social adjustment.

This educational model has practical value to the teacher in planning for the brain-damaged or MBD student. The organic model is an important and useful research tool, but as currently practiced it is clearly inadequate for planning classroom activities.

We wish to acknowledge NICHD Grant #HD-10570,, NIEHS Grant #ES-01104; USPHS Grant #HD-03110; MCH Project 916 to the Division for Disorders of Development and Learning. The research assistance of **Marsha Stephens** is also gratefully acknowledged.

DISCUSSION QUESTIONS

1. Discuss an emotional disturbance from an organic point of view.
2. Name the two types of organic theory related to emotional disturbance and compare the approaches.
3. Choose a specific organic defect theory and describe (a) its basic theory, (b) the treatment that would follow from the theory, and (c) the general research findings rejecting or supporting the theory.
4. Choose a specific developmental organic theory and describe (a) its basic theory, (b) the treatment that would follow from the theory, and (c) the general research findings rejecting or supporting the theory.
5. Describe a teaching practice that is widely used with neurologically impaired children and discuss the validity of the approach based on research evidence.

REFERENCES

Abrams, B. R., Schultz, S. R., Margen, S., & Ogar, D. A. Perspectives in clinical research: A review of research controversies surrounding the Feingold diet. *Family and Community Health*, 1979, *4*, 93–113.

Air quality criteria for lead. Washington, D.C.: U.S. Environmental Protection Agency, 1977 (EPA L00/8-77-017).

Anderson, D. R., & Levin, S. R. Young children's attention to "Sesame Street." *Child Development*, 1976, *47*, 806–811.

Ayres, A. J. Patterns of perceptual-motor dysfunction in children: A factor analytic study. *Perceptual and Motor Skills*, 1965, *20*, 335–368.

Ayres, A. J. *Sensory integration and learning disorders.* Los Angeles, Calif.: Western Psychological Services, 1972.

Ayres, A. J. *Sensory integration and the child.* Los Angeles, Calif.: Western Psychological Services, 1979.

Barkley, R. A. Recent developments in research on hyperactivity. *Journal of Pediatric Psychology*, 1979, *3*, 158–163.

Bateman, B. D. Educational implications of minimal brain dysfunction. *Annals of the New York Academy of Sciences*, 1973, *205*, 245–250.

Baumeister, A. A., & MacLean, W. Brain damage and mental retardation. In N. R. Ellis (Ed.), *Handbook of mental deficiency* (2nd ed.). New York: Lawrence Erlbaum, 1979.

Bettman, J. W., Stern, E. L., Whitsell, L. J., & Goffmann, H. F. Cerebral dominance in developmental dyslexia: Role of ophthalmologist. *Archives of Opthalmology*, 1967, *78*, 722–729.

Birch, H. G., & Gussow, J. D. *Disadvantaged children: Health, nutrition, and school failure.* New York: Harcourt, Brace & World, 1970.

Bittick, K., Fleeman, W., & Bright, T. *The reduction of self-injurious behavior utilizing sensory integration techniques.* Paper presented at the Gatlinburg Conference on Mental Retardation, Gatlinburg, Tennessee, March 1978.

Black, R. W. Achievement test performance of high- and low-perceiving learning disabled children. *Journal of Learning Disabilities*, 1974, *7*, 178–182.

Böök, J. A. Schizophrenia as a gene mutation. *Acta Genetica*, 1953, *4*, 133–139.

Brenner, A. A study of the efficacy of the Feingold diet on hyperkinetic children. *Clinical Pediatrics*, 1977, *16*, 652–656.

Brown, R. *The effects of a perceptual-motor education program on perceptual-motor skills and reading readiness.* St. Louis, Mo.: American Association for Health, Physical Education and Recreation, 1968.

Bunney, B. S., & Aghajanian, G. K. Mesolimbic and mesocortical dopaminergic systems: Physiology and pharmacology. In M. A. Lipton, A. D. Mascio & K. Killman (Eds.), *Psychopharmacology: A generation of progress.* New York: Raven Press, 1978.

Buser, P. Non-specific visual projections. In R. Young & D. Lindsley (Eds.), *Early experiences and visual information processing in perceptual and reading disorders.* Washington, D.C.: National Academy of Sciences, 1970.

Chess, S., & Hassibi, H. *Principles and practice of child psychiatry.* New York: Plenum Press, 1978.

Clements, S. *Minimal brain dysfunction in children* (NINDS Monograph No. 3, U.S. Public Health Service Publication No. 1415). Washington, D.C.: U.S. Government Printing Office, 1966.

Coleman, M., & Brown, W. M. Apparent reversal of a familial syndrome of seizures and later dementia by administration of vitamin D. In D. V. Siva Sankar (Ed.), *Psychopharmacology of childhood.* Westbury, Mass.: PJD Publications, 1976.

Cook, P. S., & Woodhill, J. M. The Feingold dietary treatment of the hyperkinetic syndrome. *Medical Journal of Australia,* 1976, *2,* 85–89.

Cott, A. Treating schizophrenic children. *Schizophrenia,* 1969, *1,* 44–49.

Cott, A. Orthomolecular approach to the treatment of learning disabilities. *Schizophrenia,* 1971, *3,* 95–105.

Cruickshank, W. M. (Ed.). *The teacher of brain-injured children: A discussion of the bases for competency.* Syracuse, N.Y.: Syracuse University Press, 1966.

Cruickshank, W. M. *The learning disabled child in school, home and community* (Rev. ed.). Syracuse, N.Y.: Syracuse University Press, 1977.

Delacato, C. *Neurological organization and reading.* Springfield, Ill.: Charles C Thomas, 1966.

Diagnostic and Statistical Manual of Mental Disorders (DSM II) (2nd ed.). Washington, D.C.: American Psychiatric Association, 1968.

Diagnostic and Statistical Manual of Mental Disorders (DSM III) (3rd ed.). Washington, D.C.: American Psychiatric Association, 1979.

Doty, R. Modulation of visual input by brain-stem systems. In F. Young & D. Lindsley (Eds.), *Early experience and visual information processing in perceptual and reading disorders.* Washington, D.C.: National Academy of Sciences, 1970.

Dunsing, J., & Kephart, N. Motor generalizations in space and time. In J. Hellmuth (Ed.), *Learning disorders* (Vol. 1). Seattle, Wash.: Special Child Publications, 1965.

Elston, R. C., Namboodiri, K. K., Spence, M. A., & Rainer, J. D. A genetic study of schizophrenia pedigrees: II One-locus hypotheses. *Neuropsychobiology,* 1978, *4,* 193–206.

Elston, R. C., & Stewart, J. A general model for the genetic analysis of pedegree data. *Human Heredity,* 1971, *21,* 523–542.

Feingold, B. *Why your child is hyperactive.* New York: Random House, 1975.

Flynn, N. M., & Rapoport, J. L. Hyperactivity in open and traditional classroom environments. *Journal of Special Education,* 1976, *10,* 285–290.

Forehand, R., & Baumeister, A. A. Effects of variations in auditory-visual stimulation on activity levels of severe mental retardates. *American Journal of Mental Deficiency,* 1970, *74,* 470–474.

Friedhoff, A. H., & Alpert, M. Receptor sensitivity modification as a potential treatment. In M. A. Lipton, A. DiMascio & K. Killman (Eds.), *Psychopharmacology: A generation of progress.* New York: Raven Press, 1978.

Frostig, M. Education for children with learning disabilities. In H. Myklebust (Ed.), *Progress in learning disabilities* (Vol. 1). New York: Grune & Stratton, 1968.

Galbraith, G. C., Gliddon, H. B., & Busk, J. Electro-physiological studies of mental retardation. In R. Karrer (Ed.), *Developmental psychophysiology of mental retardation.* Springfield, Ill.: Charles C Thomas, 1978.

Gallagher, J. J. Children with developmental imbalances: A psychoeducational definition. In W. W. Cruickshank (Ed.), *The teacher of brain-injured children.* Syracuse, N.Y.: Syracuse University Press, 1966.

Gardiner, E. N. *Fundamentals of neurology.* Philadelphia, Pa.: Saunders, 1975.

Gertner, J. M., Hodsman, A. B., & Neuberger, J. N. 1-alpha-hydroxychol-calciferol in the treatment of hypocalcemic psychosis. *Clinical Endrocrinology,* 1976, *5,* 539–544.

Getman, G. N. *The physiology of readiness experiment.* Minneapolis, Minn.: Programs to Accelerate School Success, 1963.

Getman, G. The visuomotor complex in the acquisition of learning skills. In J. Hellmuth (Ed.), *Learning disorders* (Vol. 1). Seattle, Wash.: Special Child Publications, 1965.

Gibson, E. J. *Principles of perceptual learning and development.* New York: Appleton-Century-Crofts, 1969.

Gittelman-Klein, R., Klein, D. F., Abikoff, H., Katz, S., Gloisten, A. C., & Kates, W. Relative efficacy of methylphenidate and behavior modification in hyperkinetic children: An interim report. *Journal of Abnormal Child Psychology,* 1976, *4,* 361–379.

Gualtieri, C. T., Breese, G., Wargin, R., Kanoy, R., Hawk, B., & Schroeder, S. Preliminary studies in the pharmacology and metabolism of methylphenidate. *American Journal of Psychiatry,* in press.

Hammill, D. D. Training visual perceptual processes. *Journal of Learning Disabilities,* 1972, *5,* 552–559.

Harley, J. P., Matthews, C. G., & Eichman, O. Hyperkinesis and food additives: Testing the Feingold hypothesis. *Pediatrics,* 1978, *61,* 818–828.

Harris, A. Diagnosis and remedial instruction in reading. *NSSE Yearbook.* Chicago, Ill.: University of Chicago Press, 1968.

Hawkins, D. R., & Pauling, L. *Orthomolecular psychiatry.* San Francisco, Calif.: Freeman, 1973.

Hebb, D. D. The effect of early and late brain damage upon test scores, the nature of normal adult intelligence. *Proceedings of the American Philosophical Society,* 1942, *85,* 275–292.

Herrick, C. J. *The evolution of human nature.* Austin, Tx.: University of Texas Press, 1956.

Hoffer, A. The adrenochrome theory of schizophrenia: A review. *Diseases of the Nervous System,* 1964, *25,* 173–178.

Hoffer, A. *A program for treating schizaphrenia and other conditions using megavitamin therapy.* Saskatoon, Modern Press, 1967.

Hoffer, A. Vitamin B_3 dependent child. *Schizophrenia,* 1971, *3,* 107–113.(a)

Hoffer, A. Megavitamin B_3 therapy for schizophrenia. *Canadian Psychiatric Association Journal,* 1971, *16,* 499–504.(b)

Inhelder, B., & Piaget, J. *The early growth of logic in the child.* New York: Harper & Row, 1964.

Isaacson, R. L. The myth of recovery from early brain damage. In N. R. Ellis (Ed.), *Aberrant development in infancy: Human and animal studies.* Hillsdale, N.J.: Lawrence Erlbaum Associates, 1975.

Jacob, R. G., O'Leary, K. D., & Rosenblad, C. Formal and informal classroom settings: Effects on hyperactivity. *Journal of Abnormal Child Psychology,* 1978, *6,* 47–59.

Jacobs, P. A., Brunton, M., Melville, M. M., Brittain, R. P., & McClemont, W. F. Aggressive behavior, mental subnormality and the XYY male. *Nature,* 1965, *208,* 1351.

Jenkins, J. R., Gorrafa, S., & Griffiths, S. Another look at isolation effects. *American Journal of Mental Deficiency*, 1972, *76*, 591–593.
John, E. R. Neurometrics. *Science*, 1977, *196*, 1393–1410.
Kallmann, F. J. *The genetics of schizophrenia.* New York: J. J. Augustin, 1938.
Karrer, R. (Ed.) *Developmental psychophysiology of mental retardation.* Springfield, Ill.: Charles C Thomas, 1978.
Kaspar, J. C., & Lowenstein, R. The effect of social interaction on activity levels in six- to eight-year-old boys. *Child Development*, 1971, *42*, 1294–1298.
King, L. J. A sensory-integrative approach to schizophrenia. *American Journal of Occupational Therapy*, 1974, *28*, 529–535.
Kirk, S. A., & Kirk, W. *Psycholinguistic learning disabilities: Diagnosis and remediation.* Urbana, Ill.: University of Illinois Press, 1971.
Kirk, S. A., McCarthy, J. J., & Kirk, W. The Illinois Test of Psycholinguistic Abilities: Examiner's Manual. Urbana: University of Illinois Press, 1968.
Lawson, L. Ophthalmological factors in learning disabilities. In H. Myklebust (Ed.), *Progress in learning disabilities* (Vol. 1). New York: Grune & Stratton, 1968.
Lemke, H., & Mitchell, R. Controlling the behavior of a profoundly retarded child. *American Journal of Occupational Therapy*, 1972, *26*, 261–264.
Levi, A. Remedial techniques in disorders in concept formation. *Journal of Special Education*, 1966, *1*, 3–8.
Lipton, M. A., Bann, T. A., Kane, F. J., Levine, J., Mosher, L. R., & Wittenborn, R. *Megavitamin and orthomolecular therapy in psychiatry.* Washington, D.C.: American Psychiatric Association, 1973.
Lipton, M. A., DiMascio, A., & Killam, K. Introduction and historical overview. In M. A. Lipton, A. DiMascio, & K. Killam (Eds.), *Psychopharmacology: A generation of progress.* New York: Raven Press, 1978.
Lorenz, K. Z. *On aggression.* London: Methuen, 1966.
Maccoby, E., & Bee, H. Some speculations concerning the lag between perceiving and performing. *Child Development*, 1965, *36*, 367–378.
Manual of the international statistical classification of diseases, injuries, and causes of death (Vol. 1). Geneva: World Health Organization, 1977.
Mulick, J. A., & Schroeder, S. R. Research relating to management of antisocial behavior in mentally retarded persons. *Psychological Record*, 1980, In press.
Olson, D. From perceiving to performing the diagonal. *Ontario Journal of Educational Research*, 1968, *10*, 171–179.
Pauling, L. Orthomolecular psychiatry. *Science*, 1968, *160*, 265–271.
Penfield, W. & Roberts, L. *Speech and brain mechanisms.* Princeton, N.J.: Princeton University Press, 1959.
Penrose, L. S. The genetic background of common diseases. *Acta Genetica*, 1953, *4*, 257–265.
Peterman, R. H., & Goodhart, R. S. Current status of vitamin therapy in nervous and mental disease. *Journal of Clinical Nutrition*, 1954, *2*, 11–21.
Reitan, R. M. A research program on the psychological effects of brain lesions in human beings. In N. R. Ellis (Ed.), *International review of research in mental retardation* (Vol. 1). New York: Academic Press, 1966.
Reitan, R. M. Methodological problems in clinical neuropsychology. In R. M. Reitan & L. A. Davison (Eds.), *Clinical neuropsychology: Current status and application.* New York: John Wiley & Sons, 1974.
Robbins, M., & Glass, G. The Doman-Delacato rationale: A critical analysis. In J. Hellmuth (Ed.), *Educational therapy* (Vol. 2). Seattle, Wash.: Special Child Publications, 1968.
Routh, D. K. Hyperactivity. In P. Magrab (Ed.), *Psychological management of pediatric problems* (Vol. 2). Baltimore, Md.: University Park Press, 1978.

Routh, D. K., & Mesibov, G. B. Psychological and environmental intervention: Toward social competence. In H. E. Rie & E. D. Rie (Eds.), *Handbook of minimal brain dysfunctions: A critical view*. New York: John Wiley & Sons, 1980.

Routh, D. K., & Roberts, R. D. Minimal brain dysfunction in children: Failure to find evidence for a behavioral syndrome. *Psychological Reports,* 1972, 31, 307–314.

Rutter, M. Diagnosis and definition. In M. Rutter & E. Schopler (Eds.), *Autism: A reappraisal of concepts and treatment*. New York: Plenum Press, 1978.

Rutter, M. Raised lead levels and impaired cognitive/behavioral functioning: A review of the evidence. *Developmental Medicine and Child Neurology,* 1980, 22, Supplement No. 42.

Rutter, M., Tizard, J., & Whtmore, K. *Education, health, and behavior*. New York: John Wiley & Sons, 1970.

Sameroff, A., & Chandler, M. Reproductive risk and the continuum of caretaking casualty. In F. D. Horowitz, M. Hetherington, S. Scarr-Salapatck, & G. Siegel (Eds.), *Review of child development research* (Vol. 4). Chicago: University of Chicago Press, 1974.

Sandberg, S. T., Rutter, M., & Taylor, E. Hyperkinetic disorders in psychiatric clinic attenders. *Developmental Medicine and Child Neurology,* 1978, 20, 279–299.

Schroeder, C. S., Schroeder, S. R., & Davine, M. Learning disabilities: Assessment and management of reading problems. In B. Wolman, J. Egan, & A. O. Ross (Eds.), *Handbook of treatment of mental disorders in childhood and adolescence*. Englewood Cliffs, N.J.: Prentice-Hall, 1978.

Schulz, B. Kinder manisch-depressiven und anderer Affektiv psychotischer Elternpaare. *Zeitschrift Neurologie,* 1940, 169, 311–328.

Senf, G. Learning disabilities. In S. Grossman (Ed.), *Pediatric Clinics of North America,* 1973, 20, 607–640.

Sherrington, C. *The integrative action of the nervous system*. New Haven, Conn.: Yale University Press, 1906.

Siva Sankar, D. V. Plasma levels of folates, riboflavin, Vitamin B_6, and ascorbate in severely disturbed children. *Journal of Autism and Developmental Disorders,* 1979, 73–82.

Smith, K., & Smith, W. *Perception and motion*. Philadelphia, Pa.: Saunders, 1962.

Strauss, A. A., & Lehtinen, L. E. *Psychopathology and education in the brain-injured child*. New York: Grune & Stratton, 1947.

Swanson, J. M., & Kinsbourne, M. Food dyes impair performance of hyperactive children on a laboratory learning test. *Science,* 1980, 207, 1485–1486.

Szasz, T. S. *The myth of mental illness*. New York: Hoeber-Harper, 1961.

Teuber, H. L., Battersby, W. S., & Bender, M. B. *Visual field defects after penetrating missile wounds of the brain*. Cambridge, Mass. Harvard University Press, 1960.

Thomas, A., & Chess, S. *Temperament and development*. New York: Brunner/Mazel, 1977.

Tjossem, T. (Ed.) *Intervention strategies for high risk infants and young children*. Baltimore, Md.: University Park Press, 1976.

Weeks, Z. Effects of vestibular stimulation on mentally retarded, emotionally disturbed, and learning-disabled individuals. *American Journal of Occupational Therapy,* 1979, 33, 450–457.

Weiss, B., Williams, J. H., Margen, S., Abrams, B., Caan, B., Citron, L. J., Cox, C., McKibben, J., Ogar, D., & Schultz, S. Behavioral responses to artificial food colors. *Science,* 1980, 207, 1487–1489.

Wender, P. *Minimal brain dysfunction in children*. New York: Wiley-Interscience, 1971.

Whitsell, L. Delacato's "neurological organization": A medical appraisal. *California School Health,* 1967, 3, 1–13.

Wilson, E. O. *Sociobiology: The new synthesis.* Cambridge, Mass.: Harvard University Press, 1975.

Zentall, S. S., & Zentall, T. R. Activity and task performance of hyperactive children as a function of environmental stimulation. *Journal of Consulting and Clinical Psychology,* 1976, *44,* 693–697.

Glossary of Terms for Chapter 6

Ablation. Surgical removal of body tissue.

Afferent. Conducting neural impulses inward toward the cerebral cortex.

Cerebral Cortex. The surface layer of gray matter of the brain associated with higher mental processes.

Cerebral Dominance. The normal tendency for one cerebral hemisphere of the brain to be better developed than the other in certain functions, such as speech and handedness.

Deafferentation. The process of interrupting afferent nerve (sensory) fibers (e.g., by surgically cutting them.)

Delusion. A false belief maintained despite objective evidence to the contary.

Demyelinization. Loss of myelin from nerve sheaths or nerve tracts, which results in atrophy of neurons and decreased central nervous system functioning.

Dominant Gene. A hereditary unit which is capable of being expressed as a visible trait in the presence of a different gene which is not expressed behaviorally.

Electroconvulsive Therapy (ECT). A form of biological treatment in which an electric current is passed through the brain to produce a convulsion.

Factor Analysis. A multivariate statistical method which is used in the analysis of tables, or matrices of correlations. These correlations are reduced to a smaller cluster of variables, called factors, which can then be interpreted. For instance, the concept of intelligence consists of several such factors called abilities.

Gene. A submicroscopic unit of inheritance within the chromosome.

Genotype. The hereditary constitution of an organism resulting from its particular combination of genes.

Hallucination. A perception that has no basis in external reality.

Homeostasis. A state of the body in which optimal constancy and balance of physiological processes is maintained.

Hyperlipidemia. A disease characterized by an excess of fatty substances in the blood.

Innervate. To stimulate a neuron.

Kinesthetic. Related to the sensation of movement, either from receptors in muscle and joint, or from the vestibular apparatus of the inner ear.

Labyrinthine Reflex. A reflex initiated by stimulation of the vestibular apparatus of the inner ear resulting in pallor, nausea, vomiting and postural changes.

Monoamine Oxidase (MAO) Inhibitors. A class of psychotropic drugs used primarily to elevate the mood of severely depressed patients. Examples are Marplan, Niamid, Nardil, Parnate.

Neuron. An individual nerve cell which acts as part of brain circuits which convey information in the nervous system.

Neuropsychopharmacology. The branch of medical science which studies the effects of drugs on nervous and mental disorders.

Phenotype. The sum total of genetically influenced visible traits which characterize the members of a group. The visible expression of a genotype.

Phenothiazine. A class of tranquilizing drugs used in the treatment of severe mental illness (e.g., schizophrenia). The two most widely used phenothiazines are Thorazine and Mellaril.

Placebo Effect. A therapeutic result of a theoretically inert treatment (e.g., a sugar pill instead of a drug) used as a control for a client's expectations about the effectiveness of the treatment.

Process Schizophrenia. Schizophrenia whose underlying causes are believed to be an organic brain disorder, which is usually gradual in onset, gets progressively worse and does not remit.

Proprioceptive. Receiving stimuli produced by tension in body tissues, such as muscles.

Reactive Schizophrenia. Schizophrenia that is believed to be provoked primarily by environmental causes. It usually has a rapid onset, brief duration and good chance of recovery.

Recessive Gene. A genetic characteristic which is not expressed in the presence of a dominant gene.

Reticular Formation. An area in the midbrain containing a diffuse network of neurons connecting all levels of the brain known to be involved in maintaining and controlling alertness and arousal. The Reticular Activating System (RAS), as it is sometimes called, is believed to be the relay station for coordinating neural impulses among lower and higher centers in the brain.

Schizophrenia. A group of severe pathological behavior patterns associated with thought disorders and detached coping strategies, delusions and hallucinations.

Somatosensory. Pertaining to bodily sensation (e.g., touch).

Tactile. Relating to the sense of touch.

Tay-Sachs Disease. A genetically transmitted disease of the nervous system occurring predominantly in children of Eastern Jewish ancestry in which there is progressive spasticity, convulsions and visual impairment.

Tonic Neck Reflex. A motor postural reflex seen normally in young infants and thereafter in patients with damage to the midbrain and above. Rotation or deviation of the head causes extension of the limbs on the same side as the chin and flexion in the opposite extremities and relaxation of the lower limbs. Flexing the head forward causes the opposite pattern.

Tricyclic Antidepressants. A class of psychotropic drugs used in treating depression. Examples are Tofranil, Elavil, Aventyl.

Vestibular. Related to the sense organ in the inner ear which aides in movement and balance.

7
Behavior Theory and Practice

main points

1 Behavior theory as applied to clinical and educational work is a general orientation that uses an experimental problem-solving approach to skill development and behavior problems.

2 The behavioral approach to treatment and education consists essentially of four steps: (a) defining desired and undesired behavior in objective terms, (b) assessing the behaviors in question using observational techniques, (c) using intervention methods based primarily on learning principles, and (d) evaluating the effectiveness of the treatment program using observational techniques.

3 Behaviorists view inappropriate or "abnormal" behavior as learned and maintained in the same way as appropriate or "normal" behavior. Behavior is the result of a person's interaction with his environment.

4 The principles of how behavior is learned are essential to understanding a behavioral approach to treatment. The three most basic types of learning are respondent conditioning, operant conditioning and observational learning.

5 Respondent conditioning, sometimes called Pavlovian or classical conditioning, is a form of learning in which an unconditioned stimulus (e.g., food in mouth) which elicits an unconditioned response (e.g., chewing and swallowing) is paired with a neutral stimulus (e.g., a bell) which comes to serve as a conditioned stimulus that elicits a conditioned response (e.g., chewing without food) similar to the unconditioned response (chewing and swallowing with food). Examples of treatment techniques that rely heavily on respondent conditioning are systematic desensitization, cognitive behavior modification and biofeedback.

6 The basic principle of operant conditioning is that behavior is a function of its consequences. The likelihood of a behavior increasing or decreasing under certain stimulus conditions is a function of the consequences of that behavior. Treatment procedures focus on the consequences of behavior as well as the influence of ecological variables.

7 Observational learning, also called modeling, imitation or vicarious learning, plays a key role in socialization. Three important effects of observational learning are (a) the observer can learn new behaviors previously not in his repertoire, (b) the observer's behavior may be inhibited or *disinhibited* by watching a model, and (c) previously learned behavior can be facilitated by watching a model. Treatment techniques based primarily on observational learning are used to desensitize fear, train social skills and teach new behaviors.

8 Assessment is an ongoing process in the behavioral approach which

---

This chapter was written by **Carolyn S. Schroeder** and **Stephen R. Schroeder**, University of North Carolina at Chapel Hill.

focuses on observable behavior. The social context, as well as the specifics of the described behavior, is taken into consideration.

9 Behaviorists do not have a comprehensive classification system for psychological disorders. The limited state of knowledge about the significance of particular variables in the development, treatment and prognoses of most behavior clusters limits the usefulness of any classification system.

10 Behavior theory's departure from traditional views of personality and treatment techniques has given rise to criticism and misconceptions. While no one approach to deviant behavior can provide all of the answers to questions of the etiology, treatment and prognoses of deviant behavior, the behavioral approach has proven to be an appropriate and viable thereuptic method.

BEHAVIOR theory as applied to clinical and educational work can best be defined as a general orientation that uses an experimental problem-solving approach to the areas of skill development and behavior problems. The principles derived from learning and other psychological experimentation are used to teach new behaviors, increase appropriate behavior or decrease inappropriate behavior. A behavioral approach to treatment involves essentially four steps: (a) defining desired and undesired behavior in objective, observable terms, (b) assessing the behaviors in question using observational techniques, (c) using intervention methods based primarily on learning principles, and (d) evaluating the effectiveness of the treatment program using observational techniques. A behavioral approach is also concerned with effecting behavior change that is socially significant (Kazdin, 1975). Behavior therapists, and hopefully all therapists regardless of orientation, are interested in helping an individual function more effectively in his environment. The terms *behavior therapy* and *behavior modification* are used to describe the practical application of a behavioral approach to change or create new behavior.

Elements of Behavioral Theory

Personality Development

Behaviorists define personality as the sum total of an individual's behavior and describe it as the likelihood of an individual to behave in similar ways to a variety of situations that comprise his day-to-day living (Goldfried & Kent, 1972). The focus is on what the person *does* in various situations. No reference is made to global traits that "make" a person behave in a particular way. This point of view is in sharp contrast to most traditional views of personality that assume a person's actions are expressions of certain underlying motives, needs, drives, defenses and traits. Behaviorists contend that a person learns to behave in a certain way through interaction with the environment. They recognize that the individual inherits certain physical traits and a unique biochemical makeup which could help or hinder his interaction with the environment, but it is this interaction that determines behavior (Bijou, 1970). The interaction between environment and biological endowment has been likened to the development of a river (Rutter, 1975). The lake provides the river with its main source of water, but the river is changed and altered by minerals, pollution, additional tributaries and so on that it encounters along its course. Each interaction of the river with the environment is influenced by the last interaction.

The child's use of his potential for various types of behavior, then, will in the final analysis be determined by past social learning, the current environmental situation and the environmental consequences of behavior. Behavior patterns such as stubbornness, bad temper, leadership and friendliness are not inherited; rather, they are the result of the individual's interaction with his environment. The individual has *learned* to behave in a particular way. What a person does is the focus of the behaviorist rather than what he is or has. The observation that a child races around whenever he comes into the classroom is more important to understanding the child than saying he *is* active or *has* hyperactivity.

Normal vs. Abnormal Behavior

According to the behavioral approach, most behaviors, with the exception of simple reflexes, are learned. When a functional relationship between a stimulus in the environment and a person's response occurs, learning has taken place. For example, shortly after birth, a child learns that crying will bring relief to hunger or discomfort. Likewise, the child who gets what he wants by throwing a tantrum has learned this behavior as a result of its effect on the environment. Thus, behavior labeled *abnormal* is learned and maintained in the same way as behavior labeled *normal*. The abnormality of the behavior is inferred from the degree to which the behavior deviates from the expected social norms (Scheff, 1966). Therefore, at any given time, a particular culture or society, or the subjective judgment of a particular person, can set the criteria for behavior being judged as abnormal or normal. This notion of abnormality is expressed in the following behavioral definition of a psychological disorder:

A psychological disorder is said to be present when a child emits behavior that deviates from an arbitrary and relative social norm in that it occurs with a frequency or intensity that authoritative adults in the child's environment judge, under the circumstances, to be too high or too low. (Ross, 1980, p. 19)

The task of the behaviorist is to assess the conditions under which the desired or undesired behavior occurs or does not occur and to determine what changes in the environment or the child's behavior can help the child learn the more socially adaptive responses. The abnormal or undesired behavior can most often be accounted for by past learning experiences or the failure to receive or profit from various learning experiences.

Types of Learning

The behavioral definition of learning is a relatively permanent change in behavior as a result of practice. Because of the stress on permanence, learning is differentiated from other practice effects like habituation or adaptation and from changes explained by motivational factors like temperament and incentives. By identifying practice as a key condition for learning, the effects of heredity and maturation are excluded. Learning research and theory occupies a key role in psychology, but for our purposes only the principles essential to understanding the behavioral approach to the treatment of emotional disturbance will be discussed. The three most basic types of learning are *respondent conditioning* (sometimes called Pavlovian or classical conditioning), *operant conditioning* (sometimes called instrumental conditioning) and *observational learning* (also called imitation learning).

Respondent conditioning. In the United States interest in the use of conditioning with humans began with Pavlov's 1906 Huxley lecture published in *Science* under the title, "The scientific investigation of the psychical faculties or processes in higher animals." The initial discovery of the importance of respondent conditioning in the "mental hygiene of the school child," however, was made by a graduate student, Florence Mateer, who was taking a course from W. H. Burnham on this topic at Clark University in 1913. Her experiments constitute the pioneer study of conditioning in this country (Kimble, 1961). While trying to condition very young children, she accidentally discovered that placing a bandage over the child's eyes immediately before feeding readily elicited chewing and swallowing response *before* food was presented. The words of her dissertation in 1918 testify in a contemporary fashion to learning patterns which many teachers have observed repeatedly since then.

> The great significance of the method came to me all at once about the fourth or fifth day of my first experiments with Phil, in 1914. I learned that even acceptance of a test posture, or entrance into the experimental laboratory, was a conditioning factor and that these and other casual environmental factors had to be unconditioned through disuse before any arbitrary conditioning factor might be used as predetermined in a planned procedure. Even with babies who could not sit up, the bandage was a conditioning factor, as valuable as other stimuli in

evoking response. Neither Bekhterev or Krasnogorski prepared me for this, and, though I had read Pavlov, it took personal experience to show how significant the minutiae of an experimental setting must be.

Mateer's experiment is an excellent example of respondent conditioning. Food in the mouth was an *unconditioned stimulus* which reliably elicited the *unconditioned responses* of chewing and swallowing. By temporally pairing a bandage over the eyes with the presentation of the unconditioned stimulus (food in the mouth), the bandage came to serve as a *conditioned stimulus* which itself elicited a *conditioned response* (mouthing and chewing without food) which was very similar to the original *unconditioned response* (the actual mouthing and chewing of food). Mateer also noticed that Phil *generalized* the conditioned response; that is, he also swallowed and chewed in the presence of other stimuli, such as assuming the test posture and entering the laboratory. These generalized responses had to be unconditioned, or *extinguished*, through disuse. In other words, the experimenter had to make sure that these stimuli were never paired with food in the mouth before the conditioned stimulus (bandage) was *discriminated* by the subject so that only it elicited the conditioned response (chewing).

There are many more important elements to respondent conditioning, but Mateer's experiment contains the essentials: (a) elicitation of a conditioned response by a conditioned stimulus by repeatedly pairing it with the presentation of an unconditioned stimulus which reliably has been eliciting an unconditioned response; (b) discrimination learning by extinction of the conditioned response to generalized conditioned stimuli. These processes have lawful, or predictable, relationships to one another which are relevant to a wide variety of behaviors. There are several types of behavioral treatment today which rely heavily on respondent conditioning, such as systematic desensitization (Wolpe, 1969), cognitive behavior modification, (Meichenbaum, 1977), biofeedback training (Budzynski & Stoyva, 1969) and aversion therapies (Rachman & Teasdale, 1969). The general term *behavior therapy* is often used to describe treatment based primarily on respondent conditioning.

Operant conditioning. Among early Pavlovians no distinction was originally made between classical and operant conditioning. The latter term, which was originally known as *instrumental conditioning*, derived from the work of Thorndike as early as 1898. It was used to emphasize that instrumental conditioning differs from classical Pavlovian procedures in that the subject's behavior is instrumental in producing reward (reinforcement) or avoidance of punishment. But it was Skinner (1938) who made the most forceful case for distinguishing respondent and operant conditioning. Respondent conditioning, he points out, occurs basically by association whereas operant conditioning is under the control of reinforcement. Also, respondent conditioning operates mainly on autonomic responses, whereas operant conditioning works with other responses. Each type of conditioning is subject to a different set of laws. Another unique feature of operant conditioning is that behavioral law can be examined without reference to other organismic concepts such as temperament and can be analyzed as single cases in free-responding situations. Skinner's approach was unorthodox at the time it was introduced. It took 25 years before it began to have a strong impact on learning theory.

The basic principle of operant conditioning is that behavior is a function of its consequences. A person is presented with a stimulus which may be followed by a response; the response may have consequences which themselves act as a stimulus to repeat the sequence at the next opportunity. This consequence is then said to reinforce the connection between the original stimulus and response, that is, increase the probability of its recurrence. If the consequence of the response decreases the probability of its recurrence, then the original stimulus is called a *punisher*. Note that no inference is made that the punisher is *aversive*, or noxious. Behaviorists disagree on whether punishers need to be aversive. The problem seems to be a technical one because some aversive events increase behavior probabilities.

In operant conditioning a discriminative stimulus is a stimulus that has a higher probability of being followed by the conditioned response when it is present than do other stimuli. Likewise, when the discriminative stimulus is absent, the conditioned response is not likely to occur. When this set of relationships prevails, the occurrence of the response is said to be *contingent* upon the presence of the stimulus, and the behavior thus generated is called *operant behavior*. Operants, or behavioral outcomes, themselves can be contingent stimuli for other operants so that, with the help of generalization, huge chains of behavior, or habits, can be formed. Skinner used this notion of *chaining* in his analysis of language (1957).

The basic components of operant conditioning used in behavior therapy are

1 *Positive reinforcement.* Presentation of a stimulus that increases the probability of a response.
2 *Punishment.* Presentation of a strong stimulus that decreases the probability of a response.
3 *Negative reinforcement or avoidance conditioning.* Increasing the probability of a response that removes or avoids an aversive stimulus.
4 *Extinction.* Decreasing the probability of a response by noncontingent withdrawal of a previously reinforcing stimulus.
5 *Time-out.* Decreasing the probability of a response by contingent withdrawal of a previously reinforcing stimulus.
6 *Differential reinforcement of other behavior (DRO).* Decreasing the probability of a response by reinforcing the omission of it.
7 *Satiation.* Decreasing the probability of a response by reinforcing it excessively.

Sometimes a combination of the above procedures is more effective than any one alone. The therapy of overcorrection (Foxx, 1978), for example, has two components: gradual guidance, stopping the undesirable behavior and physically prompting desired behavior, and restitution, repairing the disrupted environment to better than its original condition. But these behaviors probably involve punishment, avoidance and time-out, as well as other components. Thus each basic component in operant conditioning actually represents a class of procedures with many variations that can be adapted to a particular child's problem in a particular setting.

Until recently, operant conditioning forms of behavior therapy have focused almost exclusively on managing the consequences of behavior. Currently the influence of ecological variables (Chapter 8), which in operant terminology comprise the area of differential stimulus control, is receiving more attention (Schroeder, Mulick & Schroeder, 1979).

Observational learning. Observational learning has been studied under a variety of labels: modeling, imitation, vicarious learning, identification, copying, social facilitation, contagion, and role playing. Behavior theorists disagree as to whether it represents a form of learning separate from operant conditioning (Baer & Sherman, 1964; Bandura, 1969; Miller & Dollard, 1941). According to the operant formulation, the necessary conditions for learning through modeling are positive reinforcement for matching the correct responses of a model during a series of initially random, trial-and-error responses. The person is then differentially reinforced for matching the stimulus pattern generated by his own responses to the appropriate modeling cues (Baer & Sherman, 1964). Divergent cue matching goes unreinforced and, therefore, drops out. This operant analysis of imitation, however, does not account completely for imitation in which the observer does not overtly perform the model's responses during acquisition, in which rewards are not administered either to the model or to the observer, or in which the first appearance of the newly learned response may be delayed for weeks or months (Bandura, 1969). The position that observational learning should be distinguished from classical and operant conditioning is currently the prevailing view.

Observational learning, or modeling, plays a key role in socialization. Three main effects of modeling can be distinguished: (a) the observer can learn new behaviors previously not in his repertoire; (b) the observer's behavior may be inhibited or disinhibited by watching a model; and (c) previously learned behaviors can be facilitated by watching a model. In all of these effects the distinction between *learning* and *performance* is important. An observer may learn the response on one trial without reinforcement of any kind but may need to be reinforced in order to perform it.

Some of the factors which affect observational learning are differential reinforcement and punishment of the model; similarity of the observer to the model; status, prestige, power or expertise of the model; observation of several models versus only one model; and whether the responses to be modeled are motor, cognitive, attitudinal or emotional responses (Bandura, 1977a). Observational learning can be a very effective therapeutic technique under the appropriate circumstances to desensitize fears, train social skills and teach new behavior (Kazdin, 1974; Meichenbaum, 1971; Rachman, 1972).

The three types of conditioning are not fundamentally different; they are just different forms of the same basic process. What distinguishes one type of learning from the others is that the learning process responds differently to manipulation by some experimental variables. In a given learning situation, respondent, observational and operant processes are likely to overlap. It is impossible, for example, to perform a purely operant conditioning sequence. When reinforcement occurs, there is always a chance for the responses to reinforcement to become classically conditioned to conditioned stimuli (cues) present at the time. By the same token, it is very difficult to isolate a pure example of classical conditioning, since the conditioned response usually has some effect on the probability of recurrence of the unconditioned stimulus. In the complex interactions occurring in the classroom, all forms of learning may occur in a single teaching episode. For instance, a severe reprimand in class by the teacher might simultaneously punish a student's undesirable operant response (e.g., talking out), elicit a conditioned emotional fear response whenever the teacher is subsequently near the offending student, and serve as a model for the student of a method for dealing with the same behavior of another child. Behavioral analysis can be a complex and potent method for analyzing classroom learning and performance.

Variables to be Assessed

Behavioral assessment has received a great deal of attention in the past several years with the development of two journals, *Journal of Behavioral Assessment* and *Behavioral Assessment*, and several handbooks (Hersen & Bellack, 1976; Ciminero, Calhoun & Adams, 1977) devoted exclusively to this area. In these works readers can find in-depth analyses of assessment techniques and procedures. In this section we will examine the relevant child and environmental variables that should be assessed when planning a behavioral program.

Assessment is an ongoing process in a behavioral approach that not only determines if there is a problem but also generates hypotheses about what is maintaining the behavior, what treatment would be appropriate, and when treatment goals are met. Assessment is also used to evaluate the long-term effectiveness of a treatment program. The first step in assessment is the description of the problem behavior(s) in objective, concrete observable terms. The behavior should be defined in specific terms that allow it to be reliably observed and counted. The use of descriptors such as "lazy" have to be translated into specific behaviors such as "the child does not get out of bed until 10:00," or "he refuses to take the garbage out." Only when the desired and undesired behaviors (target behaviors) are described objectively can one determine if the behavior is indeed deviant and what environmental variables are controlling and maintaining the behavior.

When the behavior is brought to the attention of the professional, it is often assumed that there must be a problem and that the problem will warrant treatment. Children are particularly vulnerable to this assumption since they rarely have a choice in the referral process. Usually the parent, teacher or some other adult states a complaint or concern about a child's behavior. Therefore, it is important to determine if the adult's complaint or concern is a valid reflection of the child's behavior (Ross, 1980). In a study using parent questionnaires, home and clinic observations of clinic and nonclinic populations factors other than the child's behavior were found to

Describing behavior in objective, concrete, observable terms is the first step in behavior assessment.

contribute to the parents' labeling a child as deviant and seeking clinic help (Forehand, King, Peed & Yoder, 1975). Low parental tolerance, high expectations for child behavior, marital distress and other family problems played a major role in the parents' perceptions of their child's behavior. Assessment of these variables is imperative before embarking on a program to change the child's behavior. Social context, as well as the specifics of the desired behavior, should be taken into consideration.

A number of criteria that take into account child and environment variables have been used to determine whether a behavior is deviant (Rutter, 1975):

1 Age and sex appropriateness
2 Persistence
3 Life circumstances
4 Sociocultural setting
5 Extent of disturbance
6 Type of behavior
7 Severity and frequency of behavior
8 Change in behavior
9 Situation specificity of the behavior

Behavior should also be assessed in terms of the social restrictions it places on the child, its interference with development, the suffering it is causing the child and the effect it is having on others in the environment. The addition of the physical state of the child rounds out this list of variables that should be given serious consideration in the assessment process. Methods that behaviorists use to assess these variables include parent interviews, parent questionnaires, observation of the behavior in the clinic, home, school or any other setting in which the behavior primarily occurs, observation of parent-child interactions or teacher-child interactions, parent observations and self-observations by the teacher, parent or child. These assessment methods focus on the conditions under which the behavior occurs, the consequences of the behavior and the frequency, duration and intensity of the behavior. In working with children, it is especially important also to gather information on the child's physical, cognitive, social and emotional developmental level. Standardized tests that give normative data on children at different ages can be very helpful in this assessment. Observation of other children who are not seen as having a problem can also help to define what behavior is appropriate in a given situation.

At the conclusion of a thorough assessment, some questions are generated about the behavior. Is it a developmental problem? Are parental expectations, attitudes or beliefs appropriate for the social situation, the age and development level of the child? Are there environmental conditions contributing to the perception of the behavior or setting conditions for the behavior? Should the child be referred for a medical evaluation? Are the consequences of the behavior creating a problem for the child, parents or environment? The data gathered to answer these questions should provide information for defining how the behavior is deviant and for selecting treatment techniques. The continued assessment of the behavior and environment will determine the short- and long-term effectiveness of the program.

Classification of Psychological Disorders

The purpose of a diagnostic label or classification system for psychological disorders is to group together children who have similar behaviors so that the study and understanding of the etiology, treatment and prognosis of the behavior can be more effective. In effect, labels help to classify, sort and put order into our worlds. With psychological or behavioral disorders, one looks for behaviors that "go together," that is, for the common denominators in the described behaviors of a group of children. To have meaning one category of behavior has to be differentiated from another category in terms of sex distribution, age of onset, association with other problems, etiology, response to treatment, outcome and so on (Rutter, 1975). The labels *hyperactive, autistic, school phobic*, and *mildly retarded* should each describe the behavior of a group of children who have similar problems and are distinctly different from other groups of children. Unfortunately, our limited knowledge of the significance of particular variables in the development, treatment and prognosis of most behavior clusters limits the usefulness of any classification system (Quay, 1972).

While labels and classification systems are important in studying and communicating about particular problem behaviors, their true meaning and their limitations often get lost in our daily use of them. Once a classification system is in use, we often forget, or simply ignore, the fact that there may be little experimental evidence to support a particular classification. Labels take on a life and meaning of their own. Soon they are used to *explain* the reason why a child is behaving in a certain way rather than to *describe* the behavior. The child is said to run around the room *because* he is "hyperactive." A child does not do his school work *because* he has "poor motivation". People use labels to assign reasons for the child's behavior and fail to look at environmental influences on the behavior. While there may, indeed, be a biological basis for the behavior, as with, for example, the self-biting or gnawing associated with Lesch-Nyhan syndrome (Nyhan, Johnson & Kaufman, 1980), such occurrences are rare. Even when physical correlates are found, it is the environmental influences that must usually be manipulated to effect change. Many responses previously considered involuntary, even seizures, high blood pressure and pain, have been altered by the environmental consequences which follow them (Katz & Zlutnick, 1975). In short, labels do not give adequate information about the uniqueness of a child or his environment, and they do not provide guidance in dealing with the behavior. In fact, the assigning of a label often takes the place of dealing with the behavior. Instead of helping a child change his behavior, we say, "Johnny can't go to school because he's retarded" or, "Mary cannot be in a regular class because she is hyperactive." Such statements imply that little can be done about behavior but accept it. The "accepting" environment then ensures the continuation of the behavior.

Behaviorists do not have a comprehensive classification system for psychological disorders. The difficulties in developing such a system are obvious, given the behavioral focus on the individual's unique interaction with the environment. Any classification system would have to take into account client and environment variables without setting universal criteria for what would be called abnormal behavior. A broad and flexible classification system has been proposed by Goldfried and Davison (1976). They outline five general ways in which behaviors can be seen as deviant. Difficulties can be the result of one or more of the following:

1 Poor stimulus control of the behavior
2 A deficient behavioral repertoire
3 A behavioral repertoire that others find aversive
4 A deficient incentive system
5 An aversive self-reinforcing system

Poor stimulus control of behavior means that the child responds inappropriately to social cues or has maladaptive emotional responses to some environmental stimuli. In the first instance, the child may have the appropriate behavioral repertoire, but he uses it at the wrong time or place. For example, when a teacher is talking with a visitor, a child might take this as a cue to talk, walk around the room and stop working. Likewise, a child is often accidentally taught not to respond to appropriate stimuli. Many children do not respond to the first calmly stated request to be quiet because neither positive nor negative consequences follow the children's response. When the teacher finally starts to count to 10, the children learn that they had better respond or negative consequences will follow! In the second type of difficulty with stimulus control, intense aversive emotional reactions are elicited by objectively innocuous cues. The child starts screaming when he sees a dog, or a quiz sets the stage for a stomachache or vomiting. These and other emotional reactions may be classically conditioned to stimuli either by direct or by vicarious social learning experiences.

A child with a *deficient behavior repertoire* lacks the skills needed to deal with situational demands. For example, a child may have never learned to chat socially with other children or may not know how to organize his time wisely. This skill deficit problem is often complicated by aversive consequences such as ridicule and rejection which results in negative subjective attitudes such as lack of confidence and anxiety (Goldfried & Davison, 1976).

A child with an *aversive behavioral repertoire* exhibits behaviors which are harmful or bothersome to others. The person with a problem in this category knows what to say or do but is excessive; for example, he talks very loudly or acts overly aggressive. Or he exhibits behavior that is simply annoying to those around him; for example, he may wipe his nose with his hand or stand too close when talking to people.

Difficulties that arise from a *deficient incentive system* are a result of the reinforcing consequences of the behavior. The individual's incentive system may be deficient or inappropriate, or the consequences available in the environment may be creating the problem. A person with a deficient incentive system does not respond to incentives such as approval or disapproval which usually control other people's behavior. Or, the incentive system itself could be maladaptive in that the consequences sought, for example, drugs or certain sexual practices, are harmful or disapproved of by society. The environment can also present conflicting incentive systems whereby a behavior is labeled inappropriate but inadvertently rewarded. For example, a mother may say her child should go to school yet indulge the child when he stays home. Incentive systems could also be lacking or unavailable to a person. For example, divorce often means the loss of a once available source of reinforcement for children.

A child with an *aversive self-reinforcing system* does not reinforce his own behavior. If a person views his behavior as continually inadequate or sets excessively high standards for himself, then he is unlikely to be able to reward himself even when performance is adequate.

Goldfried & Davison's (1976) classification system for categorizing maladaptive behavior within a social learning context provides some guidelines for a behavioral analysis of deviant behavior. A person may have behaviors that fall into several categories, or a problem behavior may be complex enough to fall into more than one category. In either case, the system helps pinpoint those client and environmental variables that should be the targets of treatment.

Classroom Intervention Strategies
Strategies Based on Respondent Conditioning

Respondent conditioning plays a major role in classroom learning. It is clearly recognized in behavioral interventions involving relaxation training, a technique originally pioneered by a physician (Jacobson, 1929). The basic notion in relaxation training is that anxiety can be inhibited by eliciting an incompatible state, namely, muscle relaxation. Just what all of the essential ingredients in relaxation therapy are is still a subject of research, but variations of this technique have been applied extensively with children. For example, it has been used to desensitize school phobia and other fears, in "stress inoculation training" with aggressive delinquent girls, to control psychosomatic asthma attacks, to control generalized anxiety attacks, that is, the fear of becoming overly anxious, and to cope with stressful situations, such as fainting in the school nurse's office.

The study by Lazarus, Davison and Polefka (1965) is a good example of a multi-modal treatment of a 9-year-old school phobic boy. First, a hierarchy of feared stimuli in the school situation was identified. Then the child was exposed to these school-related stimuli in gradually more difficult steps, while incompatible anxiety-reducing stimuli were presented. Initially, the boy accompanied the therapist to the empty school on Sunday, than after school hours. Next, the two stayed briefly to chat with the teacher. Within a week the boy could stay in class a whole morning with the therapist outside the classroom door. During this period attending school was reinforced, while reinforcements (attention) for staying home were reduced. This basic procedure was replicated in another study with fifty children (Kennedy, 1965). Insistence on school attendance is an essential component in treatments for school phobia since in phobia successful avoidance of the feared stimulus (fear reduction) is itself reinforcing and may perpetuate the fear. In some cases, forced exposure promotes rapid extinction. Forced exposure has been used successfully with school phobia (Smith & Sharpe, 1970) and fear of the dark (Leitenberg & Callahan, 1973), but it should be used judiciously since in some cases it could actually increase the fear.

Relaxation techniques have been used less frequently with children because deep muscle relaxation training is believed to be difficult for young children. One study (Schroeder, Peterson, Solomon & Artley, 1977), however, demonstrated successful biofeedback muscle relaxation training with two profoundly retarded boys. So this notion may be a myth that has not been adequately investigated.

Strategies Based on Operant Conditioning

Most classroom learning occurs in the operant conditioning paradigm. The individual educational plan (IEP) is the prime example of a situation where contingent relationships exist among students, teachers, parents and supporting educational personnel. Low-frequency behaviors need to be increased, new skills need to be learned, and some inappropriate behaviors need to be supplanted by other more socially acceptable behaviors. These goals can be achieved through positive reinforcement, extinction and punishment.

Positive reinforcement techniques. A *positive reinforcer* refers to a stimulus which, when followed by a response, increases the probablity of recurrence of that response. Defining it in this way may seem circular, but not necessarily, if the reinforcer is also able to increase other responses in other situations.

What variables can be used to maximize the effectiveness of positive reinforcers? Delay of reinforcement is an important variable, particularly with emotionally disturbed children. When a new response is being shaped, immediate reward may be necessary; but it is desirable to build in tolerance for delay as soon as possible. Delay of reward often interacts with the magnitude or amount or frequency of reward. One paradigm for studying the development of self-control and moral judgment in children (Mischel, 1974) is to see if they will tolerate a longer delay for a larger reward. Younger, more immature children choose the smaller, more immediate reward (Anderson, 1978). On the other hand, excessive amount of reward leads to satiation and decreases its value. The quality of a reward, taste for example, can make a difference. For instance, Premack (1965) showed that a previously nonpreferred reward can be reinforcing simply because the subject has become satiated on other preferred reinforcers. A continuous schedule of reinforcement usually produces a conditioned response more reliably than an intermittent schedule. Intermittent schedules, however, are usually more characteristic of natural reinforcement contingencies as they occur in the enviornment.

What types of reinforcers can be used in the classroom? Food and other consumables can be very potent reinforcers in the classroom. Some disadvantages of consumables, however, are that they are often not available in naturally occurring social settings, they run the risk of satiation, they are difficult to dispense immediately, especially to a group, and they disrupt the flow of a teaching episode while the child is distracted by consuming them. In most situations social reinforcers, such as hugs, pats, praise, smiles, attention and nods of approval, may be less potent but more functional. With social reinforcers, the teacher must remember that these are conditioned responses which are learned differently by each child. Touches and eye contact may not be reinforcing for some withdrawn children or for hyperactive children whose problem is paying attention to the teacher. In some cases information feedback may be sufficiently reinforcing, but with socially maladapted children it usually needs to be accompanied by social reinforcement, such as teacher approval. Tokens, or symbolic reinforcers, such as poker chips or points, that can be turned in later for a desired reward, can often be used very effectively with individuals or groups in the classroom. They are economical, tangible, not satiable, and they help train children to tolerate delay of reinforcement.

When all of the members of the class are using token systems, a token economy emerges, which often takes on many of the properties of a regular economy (Schroeder & Barrera, 1976a, 1976b). Group contingencies, management of the economy to regulate inflation, and supply and demand become important in assessing the value of tokens. Token economies can be a very potent shaping tool (Ayllon & Azrin, 1968; Kazdin, 1977). In fact, legal questions have been raised as to whether the amount of control exerted is justified by the therapeutic gains achieved (Wexler, 1974). Others (Levine & Fasnacht, 1974) have alleged that token reinforcement leads to "token learning"; that is, the use of tokens may depress behaviors which are intrinsically rewarding. The evidence is that in a properly operated token economy this is definitely not the case (Deiker & Matson, 1979; Schroeder & Barrera, 1976a, 1976b). Clients learn not only to earn tokens, they learn how to use them economically, as people ordinarily do, and they do not become "dependent" on tokens.

Some additional methods for structuring occasions for reinforcement in student programs are priming, reinforcer sampling, group contingencies, and contingency contracting. *Priming* refers to procedures which initiate early steps in a chain of responses. Often when shaping a completely new response, the teacher may have to prompt the student to get him started. For example, if a child is learning to control his anger toward another youngster, the teacher might physically prompt him to move away from the other child by a light touch on the arm. Such priming may also facilitate learning later in the sequence. Of course, prompts need to be faded out after criterion is met. *Reinforcer sampling* may be necessary when students are likely to become satiated on reinforcers. Often the range of permissible reinforcers is restricted in the school setting. Occasionally, the teacher may have to reevaluate the value of reinforcers by recording the ones which children are still working for. This can be done by offering them a reinforcer menu and allowing them to choose the ones they prefer (Ayllon & Azrin, 1968). *Group contingencies*, or consequences dependent on the group's response, have also been found to be very effective in the classroom. Some examples are the "timer game" (Wolf, Hanley, King, Lachowicz & Giles, 1970), peer review (Phillips, 1968) and peer reinforcement (Axelrod, Hall, & Maxwell, 1972). Care must be taken, however, that peer pressure does not get out of hand when group standards are set and reinforced. *Contingency contracting* in the classroom (Homme, Csanyi, Gonzales & Rechs, 1969) specifies, formally and in writing, the relationship between behavior and its consequences. The five key elements are detailed privileges and obligations, readily observable behaviors, sanctions for failure, bonus clauses for consistent compliance, and explicit methods for monitoring rate of reinforcers given and received. Contracts are a very useful tool familiar to most teachers of the emotionally disturbed.

Differential reinforcement techniques. Reinforcement can be used to decrease undesirable behaviors by differentially rewarding other (DRO) behaviors. For instance, discipline problems in a classroom of fifth grade boys were reduced by reinforcing correct performance on written assignments (Ayllon & Roberts, 1974). Also, in a classroom for the learning disabled low rates of inappropriate behaviors (DRL) were reinforced by reinforcing average pause times between misbehaviors (Deitz, Slack, Schwarzmueller, Willander, Weatherly & Hilliard, 1978). This procedure is sometimes called *omission training*. It assumes that other behavior performed at the time of reinforcement gets differentially reinforced. If an incompatible behavior is not specified, however, the student is reinforced for doing nothing. Specifying appropriate alternative behaviors to be reinforced makes DRO more effective (Tarpley & Schroeder, 1979).

Extinction techniques. Extinction techniques consist of noncontingently withdrawing reinforcement from a previously reinforced response. This applies also to classically conditioned responses, as in the previously cited example of school phobia as well as behaviors learned from observing a model. In general, positively reinforced, operantly conditioned responses are more resistant to extinction than classically conditioned or modeled responses. In the case of negatively reinforced responses, however, the classically conditioned emotional responses are more resistant to extinction than the operantly conditioned responses or modeled responses. For example if a child completes his work only under threat of punishment or to stop being nagged and then associates angry emotional responses with this situation, these angry responses will be more difficult to extinguish than operantly conditioned or modeled responses. Classical conditioning of emotional responses is considered the mechanism for formation of phobias, which was originally the stimulus for Wolpe's (1958) development of systematic desensitization.

On the surface it may appear that extinction of inappropriate behavior is a simple procedure to implement, but this is far from the case in an uncontrolled setting like a classroom. First, all of the reinforcers maintaining the behavior must be correctly identified, and second, everyone in the child's environment must consistently and completely withdraw *all* reinforcement for the inappropriate behavior. Otherwise, the behavior will be intermittently reinforced and spontaneous recovery will recur. Sometimes, ignoring the inappropriate behavior of one student in a group is a tall order. When extinction is alleged not to work in such situations, it is important first to ask whether it is being implemented thoroughly. Sometimes extinction has side effects, such as anger and aggression. To be performed effectively, extinction procedures require a careful behavioral analysis and application.

Punishment and negative reinforcement techniques. *Punishment* refers to the presentation of a stimulus which is correlated with a decrease in the probability of the behavior that follows it. Punishment can occur by the presentation of an aversive event (e.g., slap, reprimand, frown) or by the contingent withdrawal of a reinforcing event (e.g., time-out, response cost, fines). For example, a child is fined for every problem he misses or he is removed from the group every time he hits another child. *Negative reinforcement* refers to the withdrawal of a stimulus which leads to an *increase* in behavior (usually avoidance). For example, a child completes an assignment to avoid staying in after school. Negative reinforcement, or avoidance conditioning is considered in the long run to be the least effective technique for decreasing undesirable behavior or developing new appropriate behaviors, although it is used extensively in teaching practice.

The effectiveness of punishment is affected by its intensity, manner of delivery (abrupt versus gradual), delay, schedule (continuous versus intermittent), source of reinforcement, timing and sequence in the response chain, and the presence of alternative reinforced responses. In general, punishment is most effective when it is intense and when it is applied abruptly, immediately and on a continuous schedule to a response that currently is not being reinforced. It should also be introduced early in a response chain and in the presence of alternative responses that are being positively reinforced (Azrin & Holz, 1966).

Punishment has some potential side effects that the teacher must beware of—conditioned anxiety responses, avoidance of or aggression toward the teacher by the child, and modeling of punishment by the child. Also, the teacher may be negatively reinforced by the child for being punitive; for example, the teacher might avoid requiring certain behaviors in order to avoid the child's negative response. By and large, however, these fears are unfounded if punishment is administered with careful planning and for well-specified behaviors (Harris & Ersner-Hershfield, 1978). The primary criticism of punishment is that it only inhibits behaviors and does not necessarily promote desirable behaviors. It is rarely justified unless it is done in the context of appropriate positively reinforcing circumstances.

Response suppression by punishment is usually durable, that is, it may be maintained for months. Spontaneous recovery often occurs; but when the punishment is reintroduced, suppression is more rapid. The punishment situation, however, is usually highly discriminated by the student and suppression may not generalize to other settings or persons unless it is specifically programmed.

Avoidance conditioning or negative reinforcement. This technique has been used to build prosocial behaviors (approaches, hugs, kisses) and inhibit a variety of inappropriate behaviors (Lovaas, Schaeffer & Simmons, 1965). In severely autistic twins, for example, when rocking was stopped, electric shock was terminated. Prosocial contacts increased as rocking and aggression were suppressed. Suppression of the rocking behavior lasted for over 10 months but eventually the behavior returned. Reinstatement of the contingency with a decrease in the behavior occurred after only one shock treatment. Again, little generalization of prosocial responses beyond the therapist and setting was achieved. Nurses' single-blind ratings, however, indicated an increase in dependency on adults, responsiveness to adults, affection seeking, happiness and contentment, and a decrease in pathological behaviors, such as anxiety and fear.

Understandably, there is a great reluctance to do research on avoidance conditioning because it is regarded as too intrusive. Yet behavior management by threat and avoidance is probably a widely used classroom technique and should be researched more carefully.

Time-out. The removal of a positive reinforcement contingent upon some undesirable behavior is probably the most frequent form of punishment used by the teacher. Actually, different social situations define a variety of types of time-out.

1 *Contingent observation*. Contingently attending to desirable and undesirable behavior without removing the subject.
2 *Withdrawal time-out*. Leaving the subject's environment contingent upon undesirable behavior.
3 *Exclusion time-out*. Not allowing the subject to participate in time-in activities.
4 *Seclusion time-out*. Removing the client to a restricted separate enclosure.

5 *Contigent restraint time-out.* Tying or holding the client down plus withdrawal, exclusion or seclusion.

6 *Response cost.* Removing a valued possession, such as a token, from the client contingently.

A number of the relevant variables in time-out have been cited (MacDonough & Forehand, 1973) most of which have not been investigated. In a review of the time-out literature (Forehand & Baumeister, 1976) durations of time-out between 5 and 30 minutes have been found to be most effective. Whether time-out duration has an important influence on effectiveness, however, has been questioned. The main effect of time-out may be disruption of an ongoing chain of inappropriate behavior, and effective duration may interact with other variables, such as inhibition of responses during time-out, contingent release and the reinforcing nature of the time-in environment.

The relationship of time-in to time-out is graphically illustrated in two experiments (Solnick, Rincover & Peterson, 1977; Williams, Rojahn, Eckerman & Schroeder, 1980). The former study found that a fixed 10-second withdrawal time-out for tantrums by an autistic girl increased tantrums because the child could self-stimulate during time-out. When self-stimulation during time-out was contingently restrained, tantrums dropped out. In the second study a 90-second, fixed-duration withdrawal time-out for spitting and self-injurious behavior in a classroom of retarded boys resulted in an increase in these behaviors both in time-in and time-out. But when time-in was enriched by contingent music, stimulating musical toys and copious praise for playing, the same time-out decreased both behaviors dramatically. The strong influence of environmental context raises some classical issues about what the effective ingredient in time-out really is. Is time-out effective because it is aversive (Willoughby, 1969) or does it merely give the subject a chance to choose his source of reinforcers in the Premackian sense? The difficulty arises because it is impossible to untangle the effects of time-out and the effects of reinforcement or punishment during time-in (Leitenberg, 1965).

Strategies Based on Observational Learning

Vicarious reinforcement, extinction and punishment all occur in the classroom. Children who hear praise given to other children improve their own behavior to increase the likelihood that they too will be reinforced. Children also respond to observed extinction and punishment (Kounin, 1970). If children observe that no reinforcement, or punishment, follows certain behaviors, they are less likely to engage in those behaviors. Behavioral rehearsal, or role playing, has been useful in desensitization training, assertion training and social skills training (Goldfried & Davison, 1976). Role playing in group settings has several advantages: social interactions can be realistically stimulated; each student's progress can serve a modeling function for other members of the group; and the social pressures in such settings encourage students to try out their newly learned behaviors.

Self-control, which should be the ultimate goal of all conditioning techniques, is largely based on modeling and conditioned reinforcers. *Self-control* means that a person can reinforce himself for behaviors which he has selected himself. Some examples are covering one's mouth to avoid yawning, leaving the room to avoid a fight, setting an alarm clock to wake up early, not smoking to avoid cancer and jogging to stay healthy. In most cases there is a considerable time lag between the positive consequences and the negative consequences of one's actions. In early life children's behavior is controlled largely by external standards, such as the rules of parents and teachers. The goal of self-control is for the individual to adhere to standards which are self-imposed and maintained by one's own rewards and punishments. This concept has alternately been referred to as "self-efficacy" (Bandura, 1977) and "self-competence" (Routh & Mesibov, 1980).

Modeling is very important to the development of self-control because standards are largely adopted from observed models (Bandura & Kupers, 1964; Mischel & Leibert, 1966). According to Kazdin (1975), self-control patterns can be trained by five different techniques:

1 *Stimulus control.* Practicing specific responses to specific stimuli.
2 *Self-observation.* Monitoring one's own performance.
3 *Self-reinforcement and self-punishment.* Selecting one's own consequences for one's actions via vicarious reinforcement and rehearsal.
4 *Self-instruction.* Prompting oneself to develop and maintain behaviors.
5 *Alternate response training.* Engaging in responses which interfere with or replace the response to be controlled or eliminated.

One of the main advantages of self-control training techniques is their range and ease of applicability. For example, they have been used with disturbed children in an experiment in which hyperactive children who were in the habit of making impulsive errors were trained in methodical work habits (Meichenbaum & Goodman, 1971). First, the experimenter modeled the tasks while continually instructing himself aloud with questions about the task, answers to these questions, planning his actions, guiding his actions, and finally reinforcing himself. Then students imitated the model, first instructing themselves aloud but later doing so without vocalizing or moving their lips. This type of self-instruction resulted in a reduction of impulsive errors compared to those of an untrained control group.

Self-control techniques have also been used with aggressive students. With the "turtle technique" (Robin, Schneider & Dolnick, 1976), students imagine they are turtles withdrawing into their shells, practice muscle relaxation and use a problem-solving approach to generate alternative prosocial responses. *A Turtle Manual* explains how to apply the technique (Schneider & Robin, 1973).

The exact nature of self-control is not as yet clearly understood. Several theories have been put forth to explain how it works, and the importance of external reinforcers and role models has been debated (Stuart, 1972). But clearly a child can be trained to manage a great deal of his own behavior without constant external controls. Conditioning programs that contain a high degree of external control should always include plans for fading the controls and moving toward self-control. This involves the technology of generalization and maintenance training (Stokes & Baer, 1977).

Misconceptions about the Behavioral Approach to Treatment

Behavior theory's departure from traditional views of personality and treatment techniques was a direct challenge to many long-held beliefs about deviant behaviors. It is natural that questions about the behavioral approach to treatment should be asked and that misunderstandings should arise. At this time, no one approach to deviant behavior can provide all of the answers to questions about the etiology, treatment and prognosis of deviant behavior. In the past 20 years, however, the behavioral approach has proven itself to be an appropriate and viable therapeutic method. Nevertheless, certain misconceptions persist.

Some critics maintain that behavior therapy, or behavior modification, offers nothing different from other therapeutic approaches to changing behavior. While learning that involves the use of positive and negative reinforcement, extinction and punishment, is common in everyday life, the behavioral approach involves the systematic and consistent application of psychological principles to behavior problems. The response to be developed or changed is objectively defined and observed, and the intervention program is based on a systematic manipulation of environmental variables. The effects of the intervention are also carefully observed and evaluated. This is distinctly different from the random use of learning principles that occurs in our everyday lives. Although the behaviorist approaches deviant behavior with a framework for ordering the complex data about the individual and environment, the knowledge of how to use basic psychological principles to bring about change is far from simple. A great deal of therapeutic experience and creativity is necessary to translate the principles of behavior to the clinical situation (Goldfried & Davison, 1976). The goals of behavior therapy, or behavior modification, are not unlike Freud's goals of helping people love and work, but the methods of reaching those goals are distinctly different.

A common misperception is that behavior therapists ignore the past. Behaviorists regard past learning experiences as very important in determining the way a person responds to his environment, but rarely do the same conditions under which the behavior was learned and maintained exist at the current time. While the past is seen as important and information on personal history is gathered, the focus of the treatment is on the variables affecting the current behavior and on providing the client with new learning experiences. Behaviorists have also been accused of ignoring private events such as thoughts or feelings. Behavior therapists, themselves, have disagreed about this issue, and therefore where behaviorists stand on this issue has not always been clear. Behaviorally oriented professionals do not deny the existence of such private events as thoughts or feelings, but they look for observable correlates of these behaviors (Ross, 1980). The words people put to their thoughts and feelings often do not coincide with their observable behavior; the behaviorist cautions that these subjective statements are not always reliable correlates of what a person *does*. Statements regarding anger, joy and frustration should not be accepted without some support from observable behavior.

Manipulation and *coercion* are words that often come up in connection with behavior modification. The goal of the behavioral approach, however, and hopefully of any type of therapeutic intervention, is to allow the client greater self-control. Clients seek or, in the case of children, are brought to the attention of a professional because they are not able to control certain aspects of their lives. That behavior therapists are effective in changing behavior does not mean that the client is not actively involved in the change process. The behaviorist's systematic approach to changing behavior clearly indicates that there is no attempt to coerce people into doing things they don't want to do. It is probably because behavior therapists take some of the mystery out of therapeutic intervention that some people see the approach as manipulative in a coercive sense. The behaviorist teaches adaptive skills by relying on the systematic use of positive reinforcers rather than aversive consequences.

Another common misperception is that reinforcement is a form of bribery. Some people see the use of reinforcement to increase a behavior as "buying" the person in order to get him to perform a behavior. *Bribery*, however, refers to the illicit use of rewards and gifts to influence someone to do something they should not be doing. The behavioral therapist's use of reinforcement is to reward behavior that is socially desirable. The desired behavior is usually at a low level or nonexistent, and the systematic use of reinforcement is intended to strengthen the behavior. The goal should always be to use naturally occurring reinforcers, such as more time with other children for improved social skills or more time on the playground for efficient and accurate completion of work. Extrinsic rewards or rewards not usually available in a particular situation, such as food, tokens or activities, are often necessary to increase a particular child's behavior, but these should always be faded back to the reinforcers that would naturally follow a particular behavior. By now, the reader should understand that people don't do things because they "should"; rather, they learn under certain conditions to engage in certain behaviors because of the consequences.

Another concern with the behavior approach is that children will refuse to do anything unless they are specifically rewarded. Actually, this rarely happens, but when it does it is usually because the parent or teacher has inadvertently reinforced the manipulative response. For example, if a child is told, "If you stop crying, you may have ice cream," he quickly learns that crying will set the stage for getting what he wants (Kazdin, 1975). Another possible reason for a child refusing to do things unless rewarded could be that he is getting only a very low level of reinforcement for other behaviors.

Teachers sometimes fear that reinforcing one child might increase the negative behavior of another child in order to get a reward. This concern is often voiced by teachers when a number of children in a class are on individual programs or only one child in a large class is receiving special rewards for increasing desired behavior. Such an increase in negative behavior has been reported in a classroom (O'Leary, Paulos & Devine, 1972), but in general there has been little evidence to support this concern. Again, if the reinforcement level is generally high in the classroom, this is less likely to occur. On the other hand, reinforcing one child has been reported to have positive side effects on the behavior of other children (Bolstad & Johnson, 1972; Broden, Bruce, Mitchell, Carter & Hall, 1970). One way to avoid this potential problem is to have the target child's performance result in extra reinforcement for the entire group (Kazdin, 1975). In this way, all of the children are rewarded for a child's improved behavior, and they, in turn, are more likely to reinforce and encourage the child's behavior.

SUMMARY

The behavioral approach is a general orientation to the clinical and educational work that uses an experimental problem-solving approach to the areas of skill development and behavior problems. Behavior, whether it is labeled normal or abnormal, is believed to be learned and maintained by the same principles. The strength of the behavioral approach lies in its insistence on defining problems in an objective manner so that they can be systematically observed and treated. The principles involved in three types of learning—classical conditioning, operant conditioning and observational learning—were described and related to intervention strategies in the classroom setting. The specific strategies, for example a token system or the use of a time-out program, are less important than the scientific approach that is employed by the behaviorist which enables new methods to be tested and, consequently, new information to be generated. In essence, a behavior therapist employs an ever-changing and self-correcting approach to the treatment of deviant behavior.

DISCUSSION QUESTIONS

1. Define behavior theory as applied to clinical and educational work. Give the four steps in the behavioral approach.
2. Describe a behaviorist's view of personality and abnormal behavior and compare it with traditional views of personality and abnormal behavior. How do these views affect the approach to treatment taken by behaviorists and more traditional therapists?
3. Define *learning* and list the three basic types of learning discussed in this chapter. Give examples of each type of learning in the classroom.
4. Select four components of operant conditioning and, using hypothetical behavior problems, describe how each of the operant components could be used to develop new skills or change behavior in the classroom.
5. Describe the assessment process of the behavioral approach. Name at least four methods a behaviorist could use in assessing a problem behavior.
6. Give a behaviorist's response to the charge that (a) behavior therapists ignore the past, (b) behavior therapy is coercive, (c) rewarding behavior causes children to refuse to do anything unless a reward follows, and (d) if one child is reinforced, another child might increase his negative behavior to get a reward.

We wish to acknowledge NICHD Grant #Hd-10570, NIEHS Grant #ES-01104, USPHS Grant #HD-03110 and MCH Project 916 to the Division for Disorders of Development and Learning. Becky Conover's critical reading of the manuscript is also gratefully acknowledged.

REFERENCES

Anderson, W. A comparison of self-distraction with self-verbalization under moralistic vs. instrumental rationales in a delay of gratification paradigm. *Cognitive Therapy and Research*, 1978, *2*, 299–303.

Axelrod, S., Hall, R. V., & Maxwell, A. Use of peer attention to increase study behavior. *Behavior Therapy*, 1972, *3*, 349–351.

Ayllon, T., & Azrin, N. H. *The token economy*. New York: Appleton-Century-Crofts, 1968.

Ayllon, T., & Roberts, M. Eliminating discipline problems by strengthening academic performance. *Journal of Applied Behavior Analysis*, 1974, *2*, 71–76.

Azrin, N. H., & Holz, W. C. Punishment. In W. K. Honig (Ed.), *Operant behavior: Areas of research and application*. New York: Appleton-Century-Crofts, 1966.

Baer, D. M., & Sherman, J. A. Reinforcement control of generalized imitation in young children. *Journal of Experimental Child Psychology*, 1964, *1*, 37–49.

Bandura, A. *Principles of behavior modification*. New York: Holt, Rinehart & Winston, 1969.

Bandura, A. *Social learning theory*. Englewood Cliffs, N.J.: Prentice-Hall, 1977. (a)

Bandura, A. Self-efficacy: Toward a unifying theory of behavior change. *Psychological Review*, 1977, *84*, 191–215. (b)

Bandura, A., & Kupers, C. J. Transmission of patterns of self-reinforcement through modeling. *Journal of Abnormal and Social Psychology*, 1964, *69*, 1–9.

Bijou, S. What psychology has to offer education—now. *Journal of Applied Behavior Analysis*, 1970, *3*, 63–71.

Bolstad, O. D., & Johnson, S. M. Self-regulation in the modification of disruptive behavior. *Journal of Applied Behavior Analysis*, 1972, *5*, 443–454.

Broden, M., Bruce, C., Mitchell, M. A., Carter, V., & Hall, R. V. Effects of teacher attention on attending behavior of two boys at adjacent desks. *Journal of Applied Behavior Analysis*, 1970, *3*, 199–203.

Budzynski, T. H., & Stoyva, J. M. An instrument for producing deep muscle relaxation by means of analog information feedback, *Journal of Applied Behavior Analysis*, 1969, *2*, 231–238.

Ciminero, A. R., Calhoun, K. S., & Adams, H. E. (Eds.), *Handbook of behavioral assessment*. New York: John Wiley & Sons, 1977.

Deiker, T., & Matson, J. L. Internal control and success orientation in a token economy for emotionally disturbed adolescents. *Adolescence*, 1979, *14*, 215–220.

Deitz, S. M., Slack, D. J., Schwarzmueller, E. B., Wilander, A. P., Weatherly, T. J., & Hilliard, G. Reducing inappropriate behavior in special classrooms by reinforcing average interresponse times: Interval DRL. *Behavior Therapy*, 1978, *9*, 37–46.

Forehand, R., & Baumeister, A. A. Deceleration of aberrant behavior among retarded individuals. In M. Hersen, R. M. Eisler & P. M. Miller (Eds.), *Progress in Behavior Modification* (Vol. 2). New York: Academic Press, 1976.

Forehand, R., King, H. E., Peed, S., & Yoder, P. Mother-child interactions: Comparisons of a non-compliant clinic group and non-clinic group. *Behavior, Research and Therapy*, 1975, *13*, 79–84.

Foxx, R. M. An overview of overcorrection. *Journal of Pediatric Psychology*, 1978, *3*, 97–101.

Goldfried, M. R., & Davison, G. C. *Clinical behavior therapy*. New York: Holt, Rinehart & Winston, 1976.

Goldfried, M. R., & Kent, R. N. Traditional versus behavioral personality assessment: A comparison of methodological and theoretical assumptions. *Psychological Bulletin*, 1972, *77*, 409–420.

Harris, S., & Ersner-Hershfield, R. Behavioral suppression of seriously disruptive behavior in psychotic and retarded patients: A review of punishment and its alternatives. *Psychological Bulletin*, 1978, *85*, 1352–1375.

Hersen, M., & Bellack, A. S. (Eds.). *Behavioral assessment*. New York: Pergamon Press, 1976.

Homme, L., Csanyi, A., Gonzales, M., & Rechs, J. *How to use contingency contracting in the classroom*. Champaign, Ill.: Research Press, 1969.

Jacobson, E. *Progressive relaxation*. Chicago, Ill.: University of Chicago Press, 1929.

Katz, R. C., & Zlutnick, S. (Eds.). *Behavior therapy and health care: Principles and applications*. New York: Pergamon Press, 1975.

Kazdin, A. E. The effect of response cost in suppressing behavior in a prepsychotic retardate. *Journal of Behavior Therapy and Experimental Psychiatry*, 1971, *2*, 137–140.

Kazdin, A. E. Covert modeling, model similarity, and reduction of avoidance behavior. *Behavior Therapy*, 1974, *5*, 325–340.

Kazdin, A. E. *Behavioral modification in applied settings*. Homewood, Ill.: Dorsey Press, 1975.

Kazdin, A. E. *The token economy: A review and evaluation*. New York: Plenum Press, 1977.

Kennedy, W. A. School phobia: Rapid treatment of fifty cases. *Journal of Abnormal Psychology*, 1965, *70*, 285–289.

Kimble, G. A. *Hilgard and Marquis conditioning and learning*. New York: Appleton-Century-Crofts, 1961.

Kounin, J. S. *Discipline and group management in classrooms*. New York: Holt, Rinehart & Winston, 1970.

Lazarus, A. A., Davison, G. C., & Polefka, D. Classical and operant factors in the treatment of a school phobia. *Journal of Abnormal Psychology*, 1965, *70*, 225–229.

Leitenberg, H. W. Is time-out from positive reinforcement an aversive event? *Psychological Bulletin*, 1965, *64*, 428–441.

Leitenberg, H. W., & Callahan, E. J. Reinforced practice and reduction of different kinds of fears in adults and children. *Behavior Research and Therapy*, 1973, *11*, 19–30.

Levine, F. M., & Fasnacht, G. Token rewards may lead to token learning. *American Psychologist*, 1974, *29*, 816–820.

Lovaas, O. I., Schaeffer, R., & Simmons, J. Q. Experimental studies in childhood schizophrenia: Building social behavior in autistic children by the use of electric shock. *Journal of Experimental Research in Personality*, 1965, *1*, 99–109.

MacDonough, T., & Forehand, R. Response-contingent time-out: Important parameters in behavior modification with children. *Journal of Behavior Therapy and Experimental Psychiatry*, 1973, *4*, 231–236.

Mateer, F. *Child behavior: A critical and experimental study of young children by the method of conditioned reflexes*. Boston: Badger, 1918.

Meichenbaum, D. H. Examination of model characteristics in reducing avoidance behavior. *Journal of Personality and Social Psychology*, 1971, *17*, 298–307.

Meichenbaum, D. H. *Cognitive-behavior modification: An integrative approach*. New York: Plenum Press, 1977.

Miller, N. E., & Dollard, J. *Social learning and imitation*. New Haven, Conn.: Yale University Press, 1941.

Mischel, W. Processes in delay of gratification. In L. Berkowitz (Ed.), *Advances in experimental social psychology* (Vol. 7). New York: Academic Press, 1974.

Mischel, W., & Leibert, R. M. Effects of discrepancies between observed and imposed reward criteria on their acquisition and transmission. *Journal of Personality and Social Psychology*, 1966, *3*, 45–53.

Nyhan, W., Johnson, H. G., Kaufman, I. A., & Jones, K. L. Serotonergic approaches to the modification of behavior in the Lesch-Nyhan Syndrome. *Journal of Applied Research in Mental Retardation*, 1980.

O'Leary, K. D., Paulos, R. W., & Devine, O. T. Tangible reinforcers: Bonus or bribes? *Journal of Consulting and Clinical Psychology*, 1972, *38*, 1–8.

Phillips, E. L. Achievement Place: Token reinforcement procedures in a home-style rehabilitation setting for "pre-delinquent" boys. *Journal of Applied Behavior Analysis*, 1968, *1*, 213–223.

Premack, D. Reinforcement theory. In D. Levine (Ed.), *Nebraska symposium on motivation*. Lincoln, Neb.: University of Nebraska Press, 1965.

Quay, H. C. Patterns of aggression, withdrawal, and immaturity. In H. Quay & J. S. Werry (Eds.), *Psychopathological disorders of childhood*. New York: John Wiley & Sons, 1972.

Rachman, S. Clinical applications of observational learning, imitation, and modeling. *Behavior Therapy*, 1972, *3*, 379–397.

Rachman, S., & Teasdale, J. *Aversion therapy and behaviour disorders*. Coral Gables, Fla.: University of Miami Press, 1969.

Robin, A., Schneider, M., & Dolnick, M. The turtle technique: An extended case study of self-control in the classroom. *Psychology in the Schools*, 1976, *13*, 449–453.

Ross, A. O. *Psychological disorders of children*. New York: McGraw-Hill Company, 1980.

Routh, D. K., & Mesibov, G. B. Psychological and environmental intervention: Toward social competence. In H. E. Rie & E. D. Rie (Eds.), *Handbook of minimal brain dysfunctions: A critical view*. New York: John Wiley & Sons, 1980.

Rutter, M. *Helping troubled children*. New York: Plenum Press, 1975.

Scheff, T. J. *Being mentally ill: A sociological theory*. Chicago: Aldine, 1966.

Schneider, M., & Robin, A. *Turtle manual*. Unpublished manuscript, 1973.

Schroeder, S., & Barrera, F. How token economy earnings are spent. *Mental Retardation*, 1976, *14*, 20–24. (a)

Schroeder, S., & Barrera, F. Effects of price manipulations on elasticity of demand by the retarded in a sheltered workshop token economy. *American Journal of Mental Deficiency*, 1976, *81*, 172–180. (b)

Schroeder, S. R., Mulick, J. A., & Schroeder, C. S. Management of severe behavior problems of the retarded. In N. R. Ellis (Ed.), *Handbook of mental deficiency* (2nd ed.). New York: Lawrence Erlbaum, 1979.

Schroeder, S. R., Peterson, C., Solomon, L., & Artley, J. EMG feedback and the contingent restraint of self-injurious behavior among the retarded: Two case illustrations. *Behavior Therapy*, 1977, *8*, 738–741.

Skinner, B. F. *The behavior of organisms*. New York: Appleton-Century-Crofts, 1938.

Skinner, B. F. *Verbal behavior*. New York: Appleton-Century-Crofts, 1957.

Smith, R. E., & Sharpe, T. M. Treatment of a school phobia with implosive therapy. *Journal of Consulting and Clinical Psychology*, 1970, *35*, 239–243.

Solnick, J. V., Rincover, A., & Peterson, C. R. Some determinants of the reinforcing and punishing effects of time-out. *Journal of Applied Behavior Analysis*, 1977, *10*, 415–424.

Stokes, T. F., & Baer, D. M. An implicit technology of generalization. *Journal of Applied Behavior Analysis*, 1977, *10*, 349–367.

Stuart, R. B. Situational versus self-control. In R. D. Rubin, H. Fensterheim, J. D. Henderson & L. P. Ullmann (Eds.), *Advances in behavior therapy*. New York: Academic Press, 1972.

Tarpley, H. D., & Schroeder, S. R. Comparison of DRO and DRI on rate of suppression of self-injurious behavior. *American Journal of Mental Deficiency*, 1979, *84*, 188–194.

Wexler, D. B. Token and taboo: Behavior modification, token economics, and the law. In C. M. Franks & G. T. Wilson (Eds.), *Annual review of behavior therapy* (Vol. 2). New York: Brunner/Mazel, 1974.

Williams, J. R., Rojahn, J., Eckerman, D. A., & Schroeder, S. R. An ecological analysis of time-out. Unpublished manuscript, 1980.

Willoughby, R. H. The effects of time-out from positive reinforcement on the operant behavior of preschool children. *Journal of Experimental Child Psychology*, 1969, *7*, 299–313.

Wilson, G. T., & Davison, G. C. Processes of fear reduction in systematic desensitization: Animal studies. *Psychological Bulletin*, 1971, *76*, 1–14.

Wolf, M. M., Hanley, E. L., King, L. A., Lachowicz, J., & Giles, D. K. The timer-game: A variable interval contingency for the management of out-of-seat behavior. *Exceptional Children*, 1970, *37*, 113–117.

Wolpe, J. *Psychotherapy by reciprocal inhibition.* Stanford Calif.: Stanford University Press, 1958.

Wolpe, J. *The practice of behavior therapy.* New York: Pergamon Press, 1969.

8
Ecological Theory and Practice

main points

1 Disturbance is a condition in which the components of an ecosystem are so much out of harmony that the stability of the environment is threatened.

2 The classroom, school and community are important ecosystems in which the process of defining, identifying, labeling and treating disturbance occurs as a product of the discordant interactions between the components of the ecosystem.

3 The child or the environment may be the primary or initiating source of disturbance, resulting in chronic, negative interactions, that is, a "poor fit" between the child and the environment.

4 Ecological interventions have in common the goal of adapting the "fit" between the setting and behavior.

5 Interventions based on different theoretical perspectives may be used to achieve ecological goals.

6 The special educator can be a key ecological intervenor in the role of consultant, professional resource for staff development, service broker or advocate.

7 The ecological perspective resists traditional classification systems.

8 All interventions have ecological significance.

ACCORDING to psychodynamic, psychoneurological and behavioral theories (Chapters 5, 6 and 7) emotional disturbance is viewed primarily as a problem in the lives of individual children—in their physical, psychological or behavioral selves. In ecological and sociological theories (Chapters 8 and 9) disturbance is regarded as a phenomenon created by social or cultural forces outside the individual. In this chapter we will examine the ecological view of emotional disturbance. Emotional disturbance, according to this view, exists neither within individuals nor outside of individuals, but rather in the interaction between the individual and her surroundings.

Basic to the ecological perspective is the assumption that no behavior is inherently "disturbed." One must look at the behavior in context before making a judgment of pathology. Disturbance is the result of a mismatch between individuals and the context they are in. Change the individual,

---

This chapter was written by **Mark D. Montgomery,** University of North Carolina at Charlotte, and **James L. Paul,** University of North Carolina at Chapel Hill.

change the context, or change both, and the disturbance may be reduced or eliminated.

The ecological perspective on emotional disturbance has its roots in several disciplines. Among the theoretical contributors to this perspective are anthropologists (Kluckholm, 1944; Mead, 1961) who pointed out the reciprocal relationships between individuals and their environment, and the relative nature of deviance. Sociologists, such as Faris and Dunham (1939), contributed to this perspective by describing how pathological environments may create mental disorders. Out of the biophysical tradition, Thomas, Chess, and Birch (1968) examined and reported the interactions between individual traits and environmental response. They identified temperamental differences in infants that seemed to lead to deviant behavior only under certain environmental conditions. Lewin (1951), a psychologist, worked on the interactions between individuals and environments, and coined the term "ecological psychology." Other psychologists (Gump, Schoggern & Redl 1963; Kounin, Fueson & Norton, 1966; Barker, 1968), using "naturalistic inquiry" techniques, began to study the behavior of children in various settings, such as the classrooms, the summer camp and the home. They documented the power of environments to affect behavior, including "disturbed" behavior.

Rhodes (1967) is perhaps the individual most responsible for the application of the ecological perspective to the problem of emotional disturbance. Rhodes's principles of "ecological management" and the ecological principles of re-education developed by Hobbs (1966) place the special educator in a unique position. The special educator, from an ecological perspective, attempts to intervene not only with the disturbed student but also with significant other people in the environment.

This chapter introduces some of the concepts that are used by the ecologist (particularly the human or social ecologist), looks at some of the ways in which the environment can be disturbed and the effects that this disturbance has on the components of the environment, and presents some of the intervention strategies that are based on ecological concepts.

Ecological Concepts

For the ecologist, the most global unit of study is the ecosystem—a set of living and non-living components, existing at a particular time in a particular space, which are related to each other, as well as to space and time. Components include all physical objects and organisms within the ecosystem. Time involves not only the familiar clock time but also events, schedules and calendar time. Space refers to the physical location as well as psychological territory.

Before going any further, let us try to apply these terms to a familiar ecosystem—the classroom. If we were to take an inventory of the classroom from an ecological point of view, we might list the following:

Components: desks, books, children, teacher, aide, papers, tables, chairs, flags, pencil sharpener, sink, aquarium

Time: 9:45 a.m., Tuesday, December 21, day before holidays, two days after a major fire in the neighborhood, reading time

Space: 20' x 30' room, walls painted light green, windows along one wall, fluorescent lighting, beige carpet, located at opposite end of hall from the principal's office, used by a third grade class, south side of building

In addition to these static elements, the classroom ecosystem has dynamic aspects. Participants in the environment engage in activities. These occur within activity settings. In fact, a day in the classroom can be visualized as a series of activity settings: welcome, getting ready (includes collecting milk money, taking attendance), Pledge of Allegiance, sharing time, reading time, group time and so on until it is time to go home. Each activity setting is characterized by regular participants, behaviors and expectations. Between each activity is a period of transition.

Of course the classroom does not exist in total isolation from the rest of the school. Since there may be 20 or 30 classrooms in a school, routines are established to maintain a sense of order within the ecosystem of the school. Not only are there everyday routines for activities such as beginning the day, going to lunch, assemblies and leaving the building but there are special routines for library time, fire drills and the like. In order for these routines to be carried out in an orderly fashion, covenants are established among the teachers, the principal and staff. These covenants, or mutual expectations (sometimes formalized into written rules and schedules), ensure a common purpose that helps routines flow smoothly. Regular and orderly relationships also exist between teachers, teachers and aides, teachers and the principal, and other school staff people.

The school exists within the ecosystem of the community. Thus, some components of the community have relationships with elements of the school. Parents are part of the school and also part of other segments of the community. Likewise the mail carrier, the city bus driver, the telephone repairer are all components of the school and the community simultaneously. Various ecological units that are in constant and regular relationship to each other can be conceived of as a network. In the area of emotional disturbance, for instance, the school, mental health center, social service agency and the family are often considered to be a network, cooperating (ideally) for the benefit of the emotionally disturbed child.

The ecosystem is not something separate from individuals. Children do not exist *within* an ecosystem; they are *part of* the ecosystem. Each individual occupies a niche, a psychological place that is comfortable to her and to the rest of the ecosystem.

The ecological view is grounded in two basic principles. First, *ecosystems seek equilibrium.* Ecosystems are composed of so many elements, so delicately arranged that permanent equilibrium is almost never achieved. Yet the system seeks it and achieves it temporarily. When the various components of an ecosystem are so out of harmony that the stability of the environment is seriously threatened, the ecologist speaks of disturbance.

Ecological disturbance can be resolved, and the various components brought into equilibrium through four processes: adaptation, assimilation, expulsion and succession. Adaptation occurs when one component changes or is changed so that it better fits the rest of the ecosystem. When adaptation does not occur, and the disturbance continues, the ecosystem may either assimilate the disturbing element by establishing a new niche for it or expel it from the system altogether. Finally, if the disturbing element cannot be adapted, assimilated or expelled, ecological succession takes place; that is, the total ecosystem is altered in some basic way, with concomitant changes in relationships and expectations. For example, if Johnny is a "behavior problem" in Mrs. Smith's room (let's say he won't stay in his seat) several strategies are available to Mrs. Smith. She may modify Johnny's behavior (adaptation), put him in the corner (assimilation) or send him to the principal's office (expulsion). Or, Mrs. Smith could create a classroom where staying in one's seat is not necessary (succession).

The second principle of ecology is, components of ecosystems are interrelated. Each component of the environment affects and is affected by every other component of the same environment. Changes in one component necessitate changes in every other and, thus, in the ecosystem as a whole.

Ecological Research

Investigators into the ecology of human settings have devised a number of techniques for gathering information. Most of these techniques were designed to ensure, through quantification, the accuracy of observations. Among these techniques are observation scales, chronicles, specimen records and questionnaires.

Numerous checklists and coding schemes have been developed to be applied to a variety of ecological phenomena. Most are keyed to behavior. In these *observation scales* checks, or some other coding symbol, are used to record the occurrence of a specific behavior, such as hand raising or being out of one's seat. After a great deal of observation, patterns, relationships and sequences emerge for analysis. Many observation systems are keyed to interactions between students or between teachers and students. One of the most famous was developed by Flanders (1966). It is designed to record the relationships between various kinds of "teacher talk" and "student talk." Observation scales have become increasingly complex. A system developed by Stallings (1980) employs a number of categories to describe a teacher's interactions with the class. The observation data are coded and fed into a computer which constructs a profile of the teacher's classroom behavior. This profile can then be compared to the profiles of teachers of proven effectiveness. Detailed descriptions of various observation scales are to be found in *Mirrors for Behavior* (Simon & Boyer, 1974).

Several variations on the chronicle, developed by Gump (1964), have been used to observe behavior in natural settings. The *chronicle* is a running record of the activities that occur in an environment. The observer writes down, at each activity change, the participants, location and other pertinent information. The result is a detailed record of the ongoing flow of behavior and contexts.

A *specimen record* is a verbal or visual description of ongoing activities, including the behavior of participants in a particular setting. The use of audiovisual equipment to record ecological phenomena is increasing. Videotaping, combined with tape-recording of environments, yields a rich supply of data for analysis. Another piece of equipment used is a dictation silencer ("Stenomask"). The observer comments into the mask on the events going on in the setting, and the comments are then transcribed. These specimen records can be analyzed repeatedly in different ways. Wright (1960) and Barker (1968) pioneered the use of the specimen record for studying children in their natural environments.

Many *questionnaires* have been developed by investigators into the ecology of groups. Typically, these ask the subject questions about her relationships, perceptions or attitudes. The purpose of these surveys is to elicit the individual's perceptions of environmental components. From such information the investigator can describe how participants in the ecosystem are affected by other participants or by other aspects of the environment.

Ecosystems: Units of Analysis

The ecological investigator analyses an ecosystem in various *frames*, or at various levels. The classroom, the school or the community may become the frame within which ecological phenomena are viewed.

The Classroom as an Ecosystem

The classroom is the immediate context for most student behavior, including disturbing behavior. Naturally, a great deal of ecological research has used this ecosystem as the unit of study. Investigators into the ecology of classrooms have turned their attention to a variety of phenomena.

Teacher-student interactions. The relationship between teachers and students is a basic feature of classroom life. In 1938, Lippitt and White (1958) examined one dimension of this relationship in a study of leadership style. Into artificially constructed groups of children they introduced adults with one of two leadership styles, authoritarian or democratic. The groups were given tasks to accomplish under the direction of the adults. The results suggested that the style displayed by the leader has an effect on the group's productivity and cohesiveness. For instance, the democratic group experienced less hostility and aggression, created fewer scapegoats and felt more cohesion than did the group under the authoritarian leader.

More recent investigations into the relationship between teachers and students have also suggested that this relationship affects classroom behavior. Three factors that might be associated with authoritarian classrooms—competition, high teacher control and harsh reprimanding—have been associated with disruptive or antisocial behavior. In a study of the effects of different kinds of teacher reprimands, soft reprimands were found to be more effective with disruptive students (O'Leary, Kaufman, Kass & Drabman, 1970). In a study of student absenteeism (Moos & Moos,

1978) classes that were rated high in teacher control and competitiveness experienced more absenteeism than those rated low. Competitiveness may be an inevitable result of classroom grouping (Crockenberg & Bryant, 1978.) When children are assigned to groups given arbitary codes (e.g., Red Team, Blue Team), they tend to become less sociable and more aggressive with those in other groups.

The ecological differences between special and regular programs for emotionally disturbed preschoolers have been studied (Pastor & Swap, 1978). Among the differences in teacher-child relationships, they found that there was more interpretation of rules and behavioral expectations in special classes but that there was more ignoring of inappropriate behavior in regular programs. They also found that there was no difference in the amount of structure in the two kinds of settings.

The behavioral expectations implicit in an environment are often set by, or at least communicated by, the teacher. Rosenthal and Jacobson (1968), in the classic *Pygmalion in the Classroom,* examined the effect of this teacher expectancy on academic achievement. They concluded that teachers communicate their expectations to children and that children tend to conform to them. Thorndike (1968) has noted methodological problems with this research; the conclusions may not have been supported by the data though the power of teacher expectancy, he believes, is logically plausible. In studying "transgressions" in classrooms, Marwit, Marwit, and Walker (1978) found that a student's race and physical attractiveness can affect the teacher's judgment of the seriousness of a behavior offense. In at least one instance (White, 1975), it has been demonstrated that perceptions of emotionally disturbed children held by teachers can be modified through teacher training. "Hyperactive" can be seen as "active," "aggressive" can be seen as "energetic," and so forth. Thus, the expectations and perceptions held by teachers have an effect on whether a child will be seen as disturbed and, perhaps, whether the child will see herself as disturbed.

Student-student interactions. That students affect each others' classroom behavior has long been recognized in the schools. Lewin, Lippitt, and White (1939) were among the first to describe the differences in behavior that are attributable to different patterns of child interaction. They found, for instance, that certain kinds of experimentally created interaction, such as adult-encouraged competition for scarce rewards, would inevitably result in aggressive behavior.

Recent attempts have been made to utilize student relationships to promote the successful integration of emotionally disturbed children. In one study (Guralnick, 1976) non-handicapped children acted as confederates of the teacher, modeling appropriate behavior for their mildly disturbed peers. This technique was reported to be successful in improving the disturbed children's social behavior. An interesting variation of this approach (Graubard & Rosenberg, 1974) used disturbed children themselves as intervention agents. The disturbed children were enlisted to help their teacher modify the behavior of normal classmates. In the process the disturbed children's own behavior changed. In both of these examples, not only was the behavior of individuals changed but the overall pattern of interactions was modified. Johnson (1981) has summarized the importance of student-student interactions in nine propositions:

1. Peer relationships influence educational aspirations and achievement.
2. Peer relationships contribute to the socialization of values, attitudes, and ways of perceiving the world.
3. Peer relationships are prognostic indicators of future psychological health.
4. It is within peer relationships that students learn the social competencies necessary to reduce social isolation.
5. Peer relationships influence the occurrence or non-occurrence of potential problem behaviors in adolescence such as the use of illegal drugs.
6. Peer relationships provide a context in which children learn to master aggressive impulses.
7. Peer relationships contribute to the development of the sex-role identity.
8. Peer relationships contribute to the emergence of perspective-taking abilities.
9. Peer relationships influence attitudes toward school. (pp. 5–6)

Structure. The effects of different kinds of classroom structure on deviant behaviors has been examined. A study (O'Connor, Stuck & Wyne, 1979) of children who were not staying "on task" in class found that a highly structured special class was effective in increasing academic achievement. This environment, specially designed to eliminate distractions and reward productiveness, produced increases in task behavior that were maintained after the children returned to regular classes. While it appears that a highly structured environment may result in changes in individual behavior, there is some doubt as to whether these changes are maintained after the intervention is complete. A study by O'Leary and Schneider (1977), for instance, suggests that short-term intervention gains in problem behavior are lost fairly quickly after the disturbed child is reintegrated into a regular classroom. This study seems to indicate that the power of the classroom ecology is so great that it can overwhelm whatever change has occurred in an individual's behavior.

Another recent study (Axelrod, Hall & Tams, 1979) also points to the effects of structure on classroom behavior. The investigators compared the behavior patterns in classes where children were seated in clusters with those where children were in rows and columns. "Talking out" behavior was increased in the cluster-seating condition while "study" was increased in the rows-and-columns condition. Thus, changes in individual behavior achieved during intervention may be maintained in the regular classroom, if that environment is sufficiently and appropriately structured.

Other writers have advocated less, rather than more, structure. Knoblock (1973) asserts that the "open" classroom is the setting most appropriate for emotionally disturbed children. This kind of classroom, characterized by a flexible physical and temporal environment, a student-centered curriculum and a minimum of arbitrary rules, will produce, according to its proponents, children who are more responsible and responsive, less hostile and disturbing. Investigations into the benefits of open classes for emotionally disturbed children indicate that they have at least one advantage: they are

When the physical structure of the classroom is rigid, deviant behavior may be more noticeable and hence more disturbing.

environments where deviant behavior is more easily tolerated. In one study comparing open and traditional classes, deviant behavior was less noticeable and therefore less disturbing in the open classes (Flynn & Rapoport, 1976).

Thus, it is not clear whether a highly structured environment, designed to minimize deviant behaviors, or an open classroom, designed to tolerate a wider range of behaviors, is preferable. The question is as much a philosophical as an empirical one. The benefits reported by advocates of both more and less structure for emotionally disturbed children reflect the interactive nature of ecological interventions. One may elect to minimize deviance within individuals or create an environment more tolerant of deviance. Either approach is appropriate from this perspective.

The School as an Ecosystem

The ecosystem of the school, like that of the classroom, is made up of many interacting components. The aspects of the school environment which are significant for the understanding of emotional disturbance are discussed in the following sections.

Behavior settings. The school is not a monolithic environment. It includes a variety of behavior settings: regular classrooms, special classrooms, the media center, hallways, the cafeteria, administrative offices, the playground and others. The impact of these different settings on individual and group behavior has not been adequately studied. The previously mentioned study (O'Leary & Schneider, 1977), in which the gains made with "conduct problem" children in a short-term intervention program were lost when the children returned to their regular classrooms, led the authors to conclude that the environment of the regular classroom was so different from that of the special classroom that the new behavioral repertoire, gained during intervention, was not seen by the children as applicable to the new situation. This sort of evidence has been used to advocate keeping disturbed children in special classes, thereby protecting them from having to adjust to the environment of the regular classroom (Silverman, 1979).

Teacher relationships. The way in which teachers relate to one another has an effect on the way in which teachers relate to children seen as being emotionally disturbed. The presence or absence of interprofessional support, of formalized "team teaching" relationships and the like can provide or deny teachers resources for dealing with problem situations in classrooms. The relationship between the classroom teacher and the special education teacher is also important because this relationship usually affects the level and type of services provided to disturbed children. This relationship is often difficult to establish and maintain (Montgomery, 1979).

Organization and philosophy. To the extent that schools differ in their organization and philosophical orientation, one can expect differences in the way teachers and administrators respond to deviant children. Ellison and Trickett (1978), for instance, compared the satisfaction of students with traditional and alternative schools. They found that satisfaction in traditional schools was related to the perceived similarity of students to their teachers whereas satisfaction in alternative schools was related to students' relationships with peers.

Special programs. The types of special intervention programs existing in a school affect the ecology of the school. Not only will such programs (e.g., resource rooms, volunteer programs) have an impact on the children being directly served, they will affect the curriculum and scheduling of regular classes. Of particular interest here is the mainstreaming movement and the effects of the integration of handicapped children into regular classrooms. An extremely important factor in the effectiveness of mainstreaming, for instance, is the availability of support services for classroom teachers (Larrivee & Cook, 1979).

Staff development. The impact of in-service education programs for classroom teachers that relate to exceptional children is also of interest. To what extent does such training affect teacher attitude, perception and behavior toward disturbed children? Harasymiw and Horne (1976) conducted a series of mainstreaming workshops for teachers. They found that the workshops made the teachers more willing to work with handicapped children but that teachers' basic attitudes toward the children changed very little.

The School within the Ecosystem of the Community

Just as the classroom exists within the ecosystem of the school, the school operates within the larger context of the community. Accordingly, various investigators (Redl, 1959; Hobbs, 1966; Rhodes, 1967) have examined the interplay between the school and other elements in the community.

Location. Differences between schools in rural and urban settings have been examined as they relate to differences in organizational climate and classroom practices. In one study of classrooms of schools in urban and rural settings (Randhawa & Michayluk, 1975) rural school classrooms were found to be more competitive and disorganized while their urban counterparts were found to be more challenging and better equipped. Another study (Garbino, Burston, Raber, Russell & Crouter, 1978) compared the social relationships of pre-adolescents in urban, suburban and rural schools. Relationships with peers and adults varied in the three types of communities. For example, relationships with family members and teachers were more significant for rural children than for suburban and urban children. Peers were the most significant models for urban children.

Parental involvement. Parents can be involved in school life in several ways. Parents are required by law to be invited to participate in the programs for their handicapped children. Attempts have also been made to include parents in treatment plans, either as recipients of therapy or training, or as ancillary service providers (Glenurick & Barocas, 1979; Brown, 1980). Participation of parents in IEP-writing conferences has been increased through parent training and the presence of an advocate on the IEP committee (Goldstein et al., 1980).

Service networks. The relationships between the school and other service agencies in the community have also been explored. The interplay between the school, the mental health system, social services and other agencies forms a network that has a potential impact on the overall treatment and education of the emotionally disturbed child.

Ecological Disturbance

The Child as Disturbing Agent

The simplest way to view the emotionally disturbed child through the ecological lens is to see her as an irritant. Like a thorn in the side, or a pebble in a shoe, the child is seen as a disruptive force, disturbing to the ongoing flow of activities in the classroom and to the orderly relationships established between the teacher and the students. The solution to this sort of disturbance is to help (or require) the child to adapt to the setting. This is done through one or many of the behavioral, psychological or medical interventions described elsewhere in this volume.

If intervention is successful, the child adapts to the setting so that she is no longer disturbed or disturbing. If, on the other hand, the child is not completely adapted, she may be expelled from the setting and put in a special environment for therapy; then the child must find a special niche within the special setting.

There are several deviant niches available to the child. There is the "class clown," intentionally or unintentionally providing amusement for other students and, perhaps, for the teacher. The "black sheep" is always expected to be verbally defiant, rebellious and always in trouble. The "crybaby" is a child who is expected to express constant and extreme dismay, fear or hurt. The "scapegoat" is blamed for bad things that happen in or to the class but is expected to be good-natured about her persecution.

These niches exist because they serve the ecology. They are useful ways of venting or redirecting tension that could be harmful to the equilibrium of the ecosystem. For instance, the class clown, black sheep and crybaby often express emotions that many of their classmates feel. Rather than risk the general disruption that might result if all students began to joke, rebel or complain, the ecology of the classroom allows certain individuals to take on these special functions. The unfortunate result is that, in the process of fulfilling this function, "emotionally disturbed" children often doom themselves.

The Disturbing Environment

Sometimes the child that we think of as being disturbed is, in fact, the symptom rather than the cause of ecological disturbance. Such disturbance could be the result of several kinds of circumstances.

1. *Conditions within classrooms.* Public school classrooms can contain conditions which promote negative feelings and behaviors. Among these conditions are competition, inappropriate or irrelevant academic requirements, autocratic or permissive teaching style, excessive structuring, lack of structure, overstimulation and understimulation. While most children are able and willing to tolerate these conditions, there are some children who are not. Many of these children become labeled *emotionally disturbed*. Emotionally disturbed children are often those who are unable to adapt to the conditions within classrooms.
2. *Dissonance between environments.* Children who are expected to adapt to radically different demands in different settings are in particular jeopardy. Sometimes the conflicting demands of the home and the school, or the regular class and the resource room, are too much for children to handle.
3. *Poor fit between the behavior and the environment.* Every child has a set of skills, attitudes, perceptions and values. These attributes combine to

produce characteristic ways of behaving—of dealing with others, reacting to conflicts and responding to environmental forces. As long as the child is in an environment that is appropriate to her attributes and tolerates her behavior, there is a good fit and disturbance is minimized. In an environment that makes inappropriate demands upon the child, however, she may react negatively, through aggression or withdrawal, for example. It is then that the child begins to be seen as emotionally disturbed.

Ecological Interventions

Since the mid 1960s, professionals have worked to develop programs based on the idea that emotional disturbance is an interactive problem characterized by disharmony between the child and her environment (Hobbs, 1966; Rhodes, 1967). Most interventions for emotionally disturbed children prior to the 1960s, and indeed throughout the 1960s, were directed primarily at the child. Many interventions were based on the assumption that the problem was either in the child (usually) or in the environment. Classical therapists recognized the complexity of social forces interacting to produce psychopathology in the child, although their interventions could not always practically address the environmental issues and circumstances. Work with parents and with families was recognized as important, as shown by the fact that a member of the clinical mental health treatment team, usually the social worker, assumed responsibility for working with parents.

The ecological perspective encourages the development of interventions that seek to reduce the interactive disharmony directly by focusing on the child and the environment simultaneously. The distinctive feature of the ecological intervention is that, while a major portion of the disharmony may in fact come from the child or the environment, there is a simultaneous focus on change in the child and the environment to produce harmony in the exchange between the two.

Many interventions based on the ecological perspective have been developed. Morse and Smith (1980) provide one of the most cogent reviews of ecological strategies. They point out that, while ecological interventions have in common the goal of adapting the fit between the setting and behavior, the procedures vary depending on the target of the intervention (child, setting or perception of the child's behavior) and the theoretical perspective of the intervenor. They also argue that psychodynamic, behavioral, organic and sociological techniques may be used to achieve ecological goals.

Morse and Smith classify ecological interventions into three areas. The first is interventions within artificial residential settings. Examples of this type of intervention are the "psychoeducateur" program developed in French Canada and Project ReEd, which will be described in more detail in the next section.

The second category of ecological interventions is intervention in natural community settings. Morse and Smith, in their review, describe the Provo and Silverlake experiments (Empey & Rabow, 1961; Empey & Lubeck, 1961), alternatives to incarceration for delinquent boys age 15 to 18, as examples. They also describe family interaction (Vogel & Bell, 1960) and social network interventions (Attneave, 1976). The family is used as the entry point for interventions and people beyond the immediate family, including a social network of those who have close ties with family members, are brought together in one place to work on interaction patterns. Other examples of interventions in natural community settings include community network therapy (Gatti & Coleman, 1976), advocacy within systems (Paul, Neufeld & Pelosi, 1977) and community special education (Apter, 1977).

Community special education, described by Apter as "an application of ecological theory," illustrates the scope of ecological interventions. The development of community education depends on the acceptance of certain basic principles: lifelong learning, more efficient use of community facilities including schools, increased community participation in making educational decisions, increased educational program options for children and adults, recognition that the school does not own education and recognition that the totality of a person's education must be addressed by research and program development activities.

The third type of ecological intervention is intervention in public school settings. Morse and Smith identify five types of ecological interventions in school settings and provide examples. These include using students as behavior change agents (Graubard & Rosenburg, 1974), life space interviewing (Redl, 1971), physical space interventions (Hewett, 1968; Bednar & Haviland, 1969), classroom management interventions (Smith & Smith, 1975) and expanding the teacher's role (Morse, 1967; Rhodes, 1970). (These ecological interventions are described in Chapter 11 on curriculum, Chapter 12 on behavior management and Chapter 13 on educational methods.)

Research on school ecosystems points not so much to the effectiveness of specific interventions but rather to principles of human ecology.

1. *Changes can be made in ecosystems.* One clear conclusion can be drawn from the literature on educational ecosystems: constructive change is possible.
2. *Change in one component of an ecosystem affects all other components of that ecosystem.* Whether one changes the seating pattern in a classroom, the behavior of an individual child or the information held by parents, the overall ecology of the classroom or school will be affected.
3. *Many ecological changes affect noncompliant behavior of children.* The more harmonious the classroom environment, the more smoothly coordinated the various behavior settings of the school and the more cooperative the various elements of the community service network, the less disturbing are noncompliant behaviors.
4. *The special educator plays a vital role in creating or directing change.* Whether by modifying the classroom environment, providing staff development or consultation to teachers or conducting a public awareness campaign, the special educator is in a central position in the ecosystem of the emotionally disturbed child.

The ecological perspective provides a rather broad philosophical base for the development of interventions. In the next section, we will examine in detail one major ecological intervention to illustrate the principles involved. The example selected for review is historically significant because it has laid the groundwork nationally for the development of programs based on the ecological view of emotional disturbance. This program, called Project ReEducation (ReEd), was developed by Hobbs in the early 1960s.

Project ReEducation

Project ReEd was developed in response to the growing recognition in the late 1950s that a radical departure from traditional definitions and intervention strategies was necessary in order to meet the needs of emotionally disturbed children. Several factors contributed to the decision to try what Hobbs (1966) called a "bold new approach": research (Albee, 1956) which revealed the inadequate number of mental health specialists and the futility of trying to retrain traditional mental health professionals; heightened public awareness of the plight of children in adult psychiatric wards in hospitals; long waiting lists for mental health services; expensive private psychiatric services; and the experiences of parents of emotionally disturbed children seeking unsuccessfully to find services for their children.

Hobbs took his lead from the "educateur" program in France and Canada and the school psychology program in Scotland. He and his colleagues created a new social institution for emotionally disturbed children which incorporates some of the features of short-term residential care and private residential schools. The philosophy, curriculum, intervention strategies and organizational arrangement, however, were new.

The ecological view of disturbance developed and advocated under the ReEducation Program sees the problem as "a crisis in the exchange between a culture bearer (the teacher) and a culture violator (the child)" (Rhodes, 1967). The task is, therefore, not to treat the child, or to blame the parents or the teachers, but rather to simultaneously improve the adaptive behavior of the child and increase the tolerance threshold and supportive competence of parents, teachers and others in the child's environment. This approach involves teaching the child how to act appropriately in different situations while at the same time helping teachers and parents understand their own reactions to the child and ways in which their behavior can facilitate the child's positive adaptation.

Two of the major features of the ReEd Program are development of an educationally relevant definition of the problem of disturbance to replace the then-prevalent psychiatric definition and training of teachers to provide the primary interventions for the child. A new role called the "teacher-counselor" has been developed to serve as the primary, front-line staff person in a specialized short-term residential center or school for these children.

The first ReEd center, Cumberland House, opened in Nashville, Tennessee in 1962. Less than a year later, the second center, Wright School (also called the North Carolina ReEd Center) opened in Durham, North Carolina. These two demonstration centers continue to operate and are used as models for other programs that have developed in other parts of the country.

Project ReEd was developed to serve the needs of young children, age 6 to 12, with emotional problems. Its mission is not to cure children but rather to modify symptoms and alleviate stress in the home, school and community in as short a time as possible. Hobbs and his colleagues accepted the fact that disturbed children were upsetting and disturbing to teachers, parents and others and that the disturbed responses the children elicited tended to reinforce and maintain their disturbing or discordant behavior. A major goal of ReEducation is, therefore, to interrupt this negative behavior cycle and create the possibility of more positive relationships between the child and her environments.

Educational philosophy. While Project ReEd draws concepts and intervention strategies from a variety of disciplines, its perspective is primarily educational. The child is viewed as having learned ways of behaving that are self-defeating, and she can be taught to behave in a way that will be more personally satisfying and fulfilling. There developed, therefore, the concept of the 24-hour day in a residential program where the teacher-counselor's job was, as Hobbs described it, to "teach, teach, teach." This heavy emphasis on teaching was new. Education had generally been secondary in importance to other forms of therapy. In psychiatric hospitals, for example, traditional psychotherapy provided on a one-to-one or on a small-group basis, along with the therapeutic milieu, was regarded as the primary source of gain. In the traditional psychiatric view, the child's education was something that had to wait until she was able to use and benefit from an educational program. Hobbs adopted the view that education cannot wait. The primary staff of the residential centers, therefore, are teacher-counselors with a background and training as teachers.

The residential school staff. Project ReEd accepted the view that in many instances, moving the child to a new environment for a short period of time is necessary to allow one person to work intensively with the child while simultaneously someone else works with the school, home and community. The child is expected to stay in the residential school for no more than four months. While there, she may go home on weekends. The staff of the school usually includes teacher-counselors, a liaison teacher-counselor and a director. While ReEd programs vary slightly in their staffing patterns and role definitions, the philosophies and practical concepts are similar.

The concepts of teaching and counseling are combined in the primary child-care role in the school—the *teacher-counselor*. This person is someone who has been trained, and preferably is experienced, as a teacher and who also has been trained to understand and modify disturbed and disturbing behavior.

While the specific staffing patterns within the school have changed over time, generally a teacher-counselor is responsible for the children 24 hours a day. Most typically, two teacher-counselors are responsible for a group of eight children on a 24-hours-per-day basis. One is the "day teacher-counselor" and the other the "night teacher-counselor." The day teacher-counselor functions much like a teacher in a public school in that he has a classroom and works with the children as students during the day using a prescribed curriculum. The night teacher-counselor, on the other hand, is responsible more for group work and the participation of the child in a wide range of activities designed to help the children learn about themselves and others and how to more constructively participate in the social life of a community.

The role of consultants has been important since the beginning of Project ReEd. Child psychiatrists, psychiatric social workers and clinical child psychologists have consulted with the teacher-counselors rather than intervened directly with the children. The consultation focuses on the needs of the children with whom the teachers work and effective strategies for working with them. Consultants have also been used to provide support to the teacher-counselors in fulfilling this personally demanding and difficult role.

The *liaison teacher-counselor* is a key professional role developed in the ReEd program. The liaison teacher-counselor has responsibility for helping the home, school and community understand the child according to her diagnosis and for developing effective alliances between them on behalf of the child. He also has responsibility for helping members of an ecosystem "conceptionalize what keeps the system from working, [and to help] identify sources of discord, modify behaviors, mobilize resources required to achieve shared goals, and acquire the capacity to deal with excessive discord in the future" (Hobbs, 1979, p. 23). The liaison teacher-counselor's responsibilities fall into two major areas: school, and home and community.

The liaison teacher-counselor coordinates activities between the residential ReEd school program and the child's public school. A person with a background in education often fills this role because he understands the organization, roles, procedures, policies and curriculum of the public school.

After collecting information about the child's performance in public school, the liaison teacher-counselor contributes that information to the intake conference at the ReEd school where a decision is made regarding the admission of a child. The liaison teacher-counselor is interested in the child's career in the school: What is her social, psychological and medical history? How has she performed academically? How have the teachers perceived the child? What have been the child's strengths as well as weaknesses in the school?

The liaison teacher-counselor is interested in this information not only in order to assess the nature of the child's problem and how problems have been manifested in school but also to find the resources in the school that can be used in developing a plan for the child's re-entry into the school after a short-term placement in the ReEd center. As a link between the ReEd school and the child's public school, the liaison teacher-counselor keeps the public school informed of the child's progress and helps the school plan for the child's return. The liasion teacher-counselor then follows up with the school to evaluate the re-entry and to act as consultant regarding the child's educational program and, where needed, strategies for working with the child's behavior.

The child is seen in the context of the school, home and community, and the liaison teacher-counselor collects information about the child's functioning in the home and community. This aspect of the liaison teacher-counselor's job involves professional activities similar to those associated with psychiatric social work. In some instances, psychiatric social workers have occupied this role in ReEd schools.

The liaison teacher-counselor participates as a member of the intake staff at the ReEd center which evaluates the appropriateness of the child's placement in the center, develops plans and strategies for the child's re-entry into the home and community, and serves as a catalytic agent for the re-entry process. The liaison teacher-counselor keeps the parents informed of the child's progress in the ReEd school and at home on weekends. He also assists the parents in getting access to and making use of services they or the child may need in the community. Parents are recognized as very important allies or partners of the ReEd staff throughout the program (Reed, 1978).

An important function of liaison teacher-counselors is to work with the mental health and other service delivery agencies within the child's community to assist them in providing the services the family needs. Their aim is to make the home and community more responsive and more helpful to the child. The practical support by community service agencies of the child and family reduces the likelihood of failure in the child's future interactions in the home and community. Parents are not necessarily aware of the services available to them in their own community. Frequently, too, more than one service is needed, and the existing services do not necessarily work in concert. Help in coordination of services for a particular family, therefore, is often needed. The thrust of the ReEd program is to raise the threshold of tolerance of the school, home and community to increase the likelihood of the child's success there. This means readying the supportive resources of the school, home and community, and creating a supportive and responsive system that will work on problems over time.

In his review of the programmatic developments and progress in ReEd over the past 20 years, Hobbs (1979) emphasizes the importance of the Ecological Assessment and Enablement Plan as a tool of the liaison teacher-counselor. This plan is "a procedure to facilitate the definition of shared objectives, to specify what behaviors should be changed and what resources mobilized, to assign responsibility for accomplishing particular objectives, to track the progress of the system's reorganization, and to assess the outcome of the effort" (p. 23). The term *enablement* rather than *treatment* or *intervention* is used in the title of this plan because the concept of enabling more accurately reflects the facilitating and consulting function of the liaison teacher-counselor who helps make the ecosystem work on its own.

The director of the ReEd school is typically a person with an education or social work background. This person must be able to administer the ReEducation program and facilitate the constructive interactions between the ReEd school and its staff, the emotionally disturbed child, and the child's family, school and community. The director has a key role in interpreting the program philosophy, policies and procedures to the professional mental health and education community. ReEd remains a relatively small program that must compete with larger, more established programs for limited state dollars. Priorities for service and training must be established within the

ReEd program where the principles of reeducation can be disseminated and yet the quality of services maintained at a high level. The dissemination and training functions require the expenditure of scarce resources which may be needed in the service program.

A disadvantage which ReEd administrators work under is the absence of research to guide many programmatic decisions. For which children is the ReEd program most effective? What criteria are most relevant in the selection of teacher-counselors? How can teacher-counselors be trained most effectively and efficiently? What are the most effective staffing patterns? What are the most effective educational interventions? What is the best approach to evaluating the program? These and many other questions are often guided by impressions or tentative conclusions based on experience. Knowledge about reeducation is accumulating however; some of it is derived from the perceptive analysis of 20 years of experience (Hobbs, 1979), some of it from systematic research (Weinstein, 1969, 1974; Monson, 1980; Hurth, 1981, Lane, 1981).

ReEducation principles and psychological strategies. Hobbs (1966) has identified 12 basic psychological strategies or principles upon which the work with individual children in the ReEducation program and their families, school and communities is based.

1. The here and now, the present is emphasized, rather than the past or future. Life is to be lived now.
2. Time is an ally. The child's growth and her developmental momentum are important resources to the teacher who is interested, for example, in behavioral and attitudinal changes.
3. Trust between the child and adult is the precondition for effective work with the child. It is the starting point for reeducation.
4. Competence is important. The "teach, teach, teach" philosophy is aimed at helping the child learn how to do something well. Skills that are important in school are developed.
5. Symptoms are important in their own right and are worked on directly. This position deviates from the psychodynamic view that behavior is an outer manifestation of an inner reality and that when the inner reality or dynamic that is producing the behavior is changed, behavioral change will follow. While reeducation does not deny the inner reality or the dynamic integrity of psychological processes, it identifies more with behavioral theory in viewing behavior as a definable entity and an appropriate object for intervention. ReEd differs from the psychodynamic view primarily with regard to strategies and assumptions regarding change.
6. Behavior can be cognitively dominated by the child. The child can be in charge of her own behavior and act voluntarily and purposefully to change that behavior. Further, the child need not understand the motives, needs or origins of problematic behavior in order to change it. This assumption underscores the importance of the educational process in behavior change, and also the importance of clarifying and teaching values.

Trust between the child and adult is a prerequisite for learning.

7 Feelings are important. Teaching a child how to recognize, label, describe and share feelings in appropriate ways is a very important feature of the reeducation philosophy. While emotionally disturbed children do need to learn to control or express more appropriately certain feelings, the child also needs to develop relationships in which positive feelings can be nurtured and expressed.
8 The group is very important to the child. It is a source of learning for the child and, hence, a powerful tool, if understood and appropriately used, for the teacher in working with the child.
9 Ceremony and ritual can provide a stable, consistent, predictable and orderly structure in the environment that is of educational benefit of the child.
10 The physical body is important in the child's self-concept. Hobbs calls the body the "armature of the self."
11 Many resources are available in any community for children and youth, but those resources must be used appropriately. Communities vary widely in the impact they have on the growth and development of children. The amount and quality of public and private professional and social resources also vary. Every child, however, lives in a community of some sort and needs the general resources it offers. Children with behavior disorders are often excluded from Little League baseball, scouts, church groups and other activities in which their peers are involved because of their inability to get along with others. Ecological planning involves getting the child into activities such as these in such a way that success is more likely than failure. For example, a child might join a group that has an adult leader who

has the particular strengths needed to help the child make a positive social adjustment.
12. A child must know joy. Childhood depression is, of course, the major problem for many emotionally disturbed children. Bower (1960) has noted, in particular, the quality of sadness in many of these children. The ReEducation program emphasizes that children need to have something positive to look forward to. There is no single or simple prescription for creating an experience that will give the child a sense of joy, but the attitudes of teacher-counselors, the techniques for managing behavior, the curriculum—indeed the overall philosophy of the program—must work toward this goal.

The ReEd program has been evaluated since its beginning at several levels, from policies to intervention strategies. Overall, the results have been positive and encouraging (Weinstein, 1969, 1974; Whitaker, 1979; Hobbs, 1979). While the evaluation continues and new interventions are being developed or existing ones adopted for use within the context of ReEd, the value of the approach, and the soundness of the philosophy and ideas upon which it is based, is widely accepted.

The Special Educator as Ecological Intervenor

In addition to employing ecological interventions in the classroom, the special educator may play several roles within the ecosystems of the school and community. Among these are consultant, advocate, staff developer, and service broker. In each of these roles the special educator has an opportunity to affect not just the emotionally disturbed child but also other components of the disturbed environment—teachers, administrators, parents and other service providers.

Consultation. The teacher-consultant, in advising the teacher of a class that includes emotionally disturbed children, attempts to modify the ecology of the classroom in order to improve the fit between the emotionally disturbed child and other components of the ecosystem. While the consultant may not personally hold an ecological perspective, he provides services which inevitably affect the relationships between the student, her teachers, peers and parents. The consultant should keep in mind the following considerations.

1. *Consultation is a relationship.* Various writers (McKenzie, Egrer, Knight, Perelman, Schneider & Garvin, 1970; Prouty, 1970) have described the relationship between the consultant and the teacher. Essential features are a peer rather than a leader-follower relationship, and an ongoing, rather than temporary, basis for working with teacher-identified problems.
2. *Consultation is a process.* Like all processes, the consultation process occurs in stages: first comes referral, whereby the teacher asks for assistance; then information collection, in which the consultant, through observation, interview or assessment, gathers information on

the case; then prescription, in which the consultant makes suggestions to the teacher; then implementation and follow-up, in which the teacher tries the suggested ideas with the consultant's assistance; and finally, evaluation, in which the teacher decides whether or not the presenting problem has been successfully addressed.

3 *Consultation requires skills that are different from those involved in teaching.* The consultant must not only be competent in methods and materials of instruction, assessment techniques and management strategies but must also be able to communicate, in a nonthreatening way, with teachers who are experiencing classroom problems. The consultant must have the ability to listen actively, to clarify teacher concerns, to make suggestions tactfully and to be persistent in following up with teachers.

4 *Consultation is emotionally draining.* Several facts of school life make teacher consultation a stress-filled activity. It involves going into teachers' classrooms, suggesting a variety of ideas to teachers who are themselves experienced, presenting and defending a service that is unfamiliar to teachers and principals, managing a variety of cases simultaneously and trying to get teachers to modify their classroom organization, methods of instruction and expectations for the performance of their students.

5 *Consultation can be a valuable service.* The impact of consultation services may be greater than the impact of direct intervention with children. Consultation is a form of staff development. By increasing the teacher's skills in dealing with a problem, the consultant is setting off a "ripple effect" whereby the teacher may be better able to deal with a number of child problems rather than just the problems of an individual child.

6 *Consultation can work.* Despite the difficulties in instituting a consultation program, strategies have been developed by teacher-consultants over the years that can realize the promise that this service holds (Montgomery, 1978; Newman, 1967).

Staff development. In order for the ecosystem of the school or the classroom to become more responsive to the needs of the emotionally disturbed, behaviors and attitudes of teachers and administrators may need to be changed. Staff development activities, such as workshops, are one way of accomplishing these changes. The specialist in emotional disturbance often plays a key role in staff development.

Staff development in special education is usually controlled at the school level by the principal and at the school system level by the special education supervisor. In planning a workshop or series of workshops, therefore, the consultant should get the permission, and if possible, the support of either the principal or the supervisor. In planning a staff development activity, the following steps are important:

1 *Determine a need.* Either formally, through a questionnaire, or informally, through talking with teachers, get an idea of what information or skills teachers need.

2 *Survey resources.* Decide who will be responsible for planning the activity, for preparing materials, for providing refreshments and so on. Find out what funds, if any, are available.
3 *Plan the activity.* What are the objectives? What approaches (e.g., lecture, simulation) will be most effective in reaching the objective? How long will it take? In the planning stage consider who your audience will be (e.g., teachers, administrators). Also provide a mechanism for evaluation and follow-up. How will you know that the objectives have been met? How can you determine the long-range effects of the experience?
4 *Schedule the activity.* Keep in mind the audience. Should it be on teacher planning days? after school? on Saturdays?

Service brokerage. The special educator is in a unique position to act as a broker for services provided by other subsystems within the school, as well as by other agencies in the community. Such brokerage can begin in the school-based committee. The special teacher, who is often called upon to coordinate the writing of the emotionally disturbed child's Individualized Education Program (IEP), can help bring the services of the guidance counselor, school psychologist, administrators, social workers, parents and others into a coordinated effort on behalf of the referred child. In addition, the special educator may be in a position to seek assistance from other agencies (e.g., mental health, social services) who offer needed services. Again the goal is to coordinate these efforts.

The IEP becomes the point of reference for all of these services. Therefore, the IEP must reflect all of the needs of the emotionally disturbed child. By having one person responsible for orchestrating needed services, duplications and gaps in service can be reduced or eliminated. In order to make this brokerage effective, the special educator should become aware of the variety of services available to the emotionally disturbed child. He should understand the types of services provided, know how to gain access to these services and should have a contact person for each service or program.

Advocacy. Special educators have, for a long time, functioned as advocates for identified groups of children with special needs (Biklen, 1976). Much of the progress to date in special education has come about because parents and professionals have provided information to, and exerted pressure on, decision makers. Some of the activities subsumed under the general heading of "advocacy" are listed below.

1 *Awareness.* Through the use of media and personal contacts, advocates try to make the public in general, professionals in various human service agencies, and decision makers aware of the needs of the handicapped.
2 *Information.* Special interest groups of parents and professionals provide information on characteristics of the emotionally disturbed, their legal rights and other information that would assist professionals and decision makers in developing or improving programs.

3 *Lobbying*. Advocates also try to persuade agency administrators and legislators to improve the quality of programs for the emotionally disturbed. By pointing out inadequacies in existing services and suggesting steps for improvement, the advocate attempts to influence decision makers to give a high priority to this group of children.
4 *Litigation*. Some advocacy groups have retained lawyers to pursue legal action on behalf of handicapped children. Sometimes this involves the development of a class action suit, whereby children receive legal remedy through the courts when it is thought their rights have been violated.
5 *Consumerism*. Advocates also try to provide parents of emotionally disturbed children with information of various kinds. This can include information on legal rights, educational, vocational or psychological services available to them, and information on parent groups active in the community.

Advocacy is, in some cases, a formalized function. Many states have advocacy councils to provide the kinds of services listed above. In other situations, individuals are hired by service agencies to act as advocates for clients.

Some special educators take on advocacy activities as part of their professional role. Thus, a resource room teacher might decide to make the school faculty more aware of the needs of the emotionally disturbed child, provide information on classroom management techniques, lobby with administrators for more services or resources or participate with parents in seeking a due process hearing to resolve conflicts with the school regarding the program for a child. A word of warning is appropriate here: working for change from within the school system may put the special educator in an adversarial stance with regard to his employer. The danger here is obvious.

The Problem of Classification

The ecological intervenor views disturbance as existing within the total environment of the child—a child who may be the cause or the result of that disturbance. In conceptualizing the problem, the intervenor examines not only the whole child but also the various settings through which the child moves—the home, the classroom, the agency, the neighborhood and so on. Only through this process can the intervenor derive a true picture of the nature of the disturbance.

Having arrived at a diagnosis of the ecological disturbance, the intervenor begins to determine which ecological modifications would reduce or eliminate the disturbance. The intervention might take the form of therapy for the child, alterations in the classroom structure, counseling for the parents or any of a variety of other modifications in one or more elements of the ecosystem of the classroom, school or service network.

The ecological orientation toward the problem of disturbance resists the traditional forms of classification. To say that a child *is* disturbed, or that she *has* a disorder, locates the disturbance within the individual. What is needed is a way of thinking about, and talking about, disturbance that locates the disturbance within the ecosystem. One attempt in this direction has been made by Prieto and Rutherford (1977). Their assessment of disturbance combines ecological theory and principles of applied behavioral analysis and proceeds through the following steps:

1. *Collect "niche breadth" information.* The teacher examines the niches that the child occupies during the day and makes a judgment as to which of these niches are positive and which are negative. For example, the teacher may observe that the child is not disturbing in math, science or language arts, and also is not disturbing in interactions with other teachers or the principal. The child is disturbing in reading, on the playground, in the halls and in the cafeteria. Thus the niches occupied by the child in these latter behavior settings are negative.
2. *Establish "ecological baseline."* In this step the teacher observes to find out more about the negative occurrences. The antecedents and consequences of the problem, the time, the location and the frequency of the events are noted on an ecological baseline card.
3. *Define the problem.* Using the niche breadth and the ecological baseline data, the teacher can then describe the disturbance as an ecological phenomenon, taking into account not only the individual characteristics of the child but also the interactions between that child and his or her environment.

One of the problems with "conceptual models" or "perspectives" is that one is tempted to see them as categories within which things "fit." Things (e.g., interventions, conditions, theories) do not "fit" into perspectives. Rather, perspectives are used to view such things. Any perspective can be used to view any theory, condition or intervention.

Therefore, the ecological perspective can be brought to bear on any of the interventions that are described in this book, for all interventions have ecological significance. For instance, when one employs behavior modification techniques, one is essentially making modifications in the environment. Although it is hoped, of course, that these environmental changes will have the effect of changing the behavior of the individual emotionally disturbed child, it is the environment that is being directly manipulated. Likewise, group or individual therapy, by introducing a new activity setting in the child's day, has ecological significance. Biophysical interventions involve changes in the micro-ecosystem inside the individual child; sociologists and anthropologists, on the other hand, attempt to understand the "macro-ecosystem" of the society and culture.

The ecological perspective, then, might better be considered a lens rather than a model, a lens that focuses on the reciprocal nature of persons and their environments.

SUMMARY

The ecological perspective invites one to view the child against a backdrop of varying settings and within a context of intricate relationships. Viewing the child in isolation from the setting or the relationships is tempting. It seems somehow more clinically pure to strip the child of the context, to devote full attention to the individual. In this way, we think, we can more clearly see the disturbed child and hence "the problem." From the ecological standpoint, however, taking the child out of the environment makes it impossible to view, or to address, the problem because the problem exists within the enviornment of which the child is an integral component.

In a sense the ecological perspective allows us to make maximum use of the information gleaned from each of the other perspectives. One must, after all, have an understanding of the organic, psychological and behavioral characteristics of the disturbed (or disturbing) child. Similarly, one must be aware of the social and cultural context within which the child lives. But it is the ecological perspective that sheds maximum light upon the interaction between the child with certain characteristics and the context with certain expectations. And it is in this interaction that the human ecologists attempt to design a solution to the problem of emotional disturbance.

Once we learn to see disturbance through the ecological perspective our approach to remediation is altered. No longer can we be content to act solely upon the individual child. Now we must act simultaneously on the child, the family, the peer group and the teachers. Thus, the special educator's role can no longer be that of an isolated clinician, modifying the behavior or feelings of an individual child. Now the special educator can take on a variety of other responsibilities: serving as a team member on IEP-writing committees, consulting with parents and other teachers, working cooperatively with representatives of other agencies and upholding the rights of children in the larger context of our society.

DISCUSSION QUESTIONS

1. How much should a teacher know about the life of an emotionally disturbed child? What kinds of information about home life, hobbies and so on would you want to have? How could such information help you to design a program? Is it possible to know too much about the life of a child outside of school?
2. What would be an ideal setting for teaching an emotionally disturbed child? How would you determine, for an individual child, what kind of setting would be most appropriate?
3. Reading a book in a burning house might be considered "disturbed" while reading a book in a library might not be. For each of the following behaviors, think of a situation where the behavior would be considered "disturbed" and a situation where it would be considered "normal": (a) singing, (b) rocking back and forth, (c) laughing, (d) throwing rocks, (e) slapping somebody, (f) talking to oneself.
4. What kinds of behaviors would be most disturbing to a classroom? What is the role of the teacher of the emotionally disturbed in dealing with these behaviors? What measures could a teacher take to prevent or reduce the occurrence of these behaviors?

REFERENCES

Albee, G. W. *Mental health manpower trends.* New York: Basic Books, 1956.

Apter, Steven. J. Applications of ecological theory: Toward a community special education model. *Exceptional Children,* 1977, *43,* 366–373.

Attneave, C. L. Social networks as the unit of intervention. In P. Guerin (Ed.), *Family therapy: Theory and practice.* New York: Garner, 1976.

Axelrod, S., Hall, R. V., & Tams, A. Comparison of two common classroom seating arrangements. *Academic Therapy,* 1979, *15*(1), 29–36.

Barker, R. C. *Ecological psychology: Concepts and methods for studying the environment of human behavior.* Stanford, Calif.: Stanford University Press, 1968.

Bednar, M. J., & Haviland, D. S. *The role of the physical environment in the education of children with learning disabilities.* Troy, N.Y.: Center for Architectural Research, Rensselaer Polytechnic Institute, 1969.

Biklen, D. Advocacy comes of age. *Exceptional Children,* 1976, *42,* 308–313.

Bower, E. M. *Early identification of emotionally handicapped children in schools.* Springfield, Ill.: Charles C. Thomas, 1960.

Brown, G. Parents in the classroom. In N.J. Long, W. C. Morse & R. G. Newman (Eds.), *Conflict in the classroom* (4th ed.) Belmont, Calif.: Wadsworth, 1980.

Crockenberg, S., & Bryant, B. Socialization: The "implicit curriculum" of learning environments. *Journal of Research and Development in Education,* 1978, *12*(1), 67–78.

Ellison, T. A., & Trickett, E. J. Environmental structure and the perceived similarity-satisfaction relationships: Traditional and alternative schools. *Journal of Personality,* 1978, *46,* 57–71.

Empey, L. T., & Lubeck, S. *Silverlake experiment: Testing delinquency theory and community intervention.* Chicago: Aldine, 1961.

Empey, L. T., & Rabow, J. The Provo experiment in delinquency rehabilitation. *American Sociological Review,* 1961, *26,* 679–695.

Faris, R., & Dunham, H. *Mental disorders in urban areas.* Chicago: University of Chicago Press, 1939.

Flanders, N. *Interaction analysis in the classroom: A manual for observers.* Ann Arbor: School of Education, University of Michigan, 1966.

Flynn, N. M., & Rapoport, J. L. Hyperactivity in open and traditional classroom environments. *Journal of Special Education,* 1976, *10*(3), 285–290.

Garbino, J., Burston, N., Raber, S., Russell, R., & Crouter, A. The social maps of children approaching adolescence: Studying the ecology of youth development. *Journal of Youth and Adolescence,* 1978, *7*(4), 417–427.

Gatti, F., & Coleman, C. Community network therapy: An approach to aiding families with troubled children. *Ortho 46,* 1976, *4,* 608–617.

Glenurick, D., & Barocas, R. Training impulsive children in verbal self-control by use of natural change agents. *Journal of Special Education,* 1979, *13,* 387–398.

Goldstein, S., Strickland, B., Turnbull, A., & Curry, L. Observational analysis of the IEP conference. *Exceptional Children,* 1980, *46,* 278–286.

Graubard, P., & Rosenberg, H. *Classrooms that work.* New York: E. P. Dutton, 1974.

Gump, P. V. Environmental guidance of the classroom behavioral system. In B. Biddle & W. S. Ellena (Eds.), *Contemporary research on teacher effectiveness.* New York: Holt, Rinehart & Winston, 1964.

Gump, P. V., Schoggen, P., & Redl, F. The behavior of the same child in different milieus. In R. E. Barker (Ed.), *The stream of behavior.* New York: Meredith, 1963.

Guralnick, M. J. The value of integrating handicapped and non-handicapped preschool children. *American Journal of Orthopsychiatry,* 1976, *46,* 236–245.

Harasymiw, S., & Horne, M. Teacher attitude toward handicapped children and regular class integration. *Journal of Special Education,* 1976, *10,* 393–400.

Hewett, F. M. *The emotionally disturbed child in the classroom.* Boston: Allyn & Bacon, 1968.

Hobbs, N. Helping disturbed children: Psychological and ecological strategies. *American Psychologist,* 1966, *2,* 1105–1115.

Hobbs, N. *Helping disturbed children: Psychological and ecological strategies, II; Project Re-ed, Twenty Years Later.* Nashville, Tenn.: Center for the Study of Families and Children, Vanderbilt Institute for Public Policy Studies, Vanderbilt University, 1979.

Hurth, J. L. *The day teacher-counselor role at Wright School.* Unpublished doctoral dissertation, University of North Carolina at Chapel Hill, 1981.

Johnson, D. W. Student-student interaction: The neglected variable in education. *Educational Researcher*, 1981, *10*, 5–10.

Kluckholm, C. *Navaho witchcraft.* Cambridge, Mass.: Peabody Museum, 1944.

Knoblock, P. Open education for emotionally disturbed children. *Exceptional Children*, 1973, *39*, 358–366.

Kounin, J., Fueson, W., & Norton, A. Managing emotionally disturbed children in regular classrooms. *Journal of Educational Psychology*, 1966, *57*, 1–13.

Lane, Grace. *Moral education of emotionally handicapped children.* Unpublished doctoral dissertation, University of North Carolina at Chapel Hill, 1981.

Larrivee, B., & Cook, L. Mainstreaming: A study of the variables affecting teacher attitude. *Journal of Special Education*, 1979, *13*(3), 315–324.

Lewin, K. Psychological ecology. In D. Cartwright (Ed.), *Field theory in social science.* New York: Harper & Row, 1951.

Lewin, K., Lippitt, R., & White, R. Patterns of aggressive behavior in experimentally created social climates. *Journal of Social Psychology.* 1939, *10*, 271–299.

Lippitt, R., & White, R. An experimental study of leadership and group life. In E. E. Maccoby, T. M. Newcomb & E. L. Hartley (Eds.), *Readings in social psychology* (3rd ed.). New York: Holt, 1958.

Marwit, K., Marwit, S., & Walker, E. Effects of student race and physical attractiveness on teachers' judgments of transgressions. *Journal of Educational Psychology*, 1978, *70*, 911–915.

McKenzie, H. S., Egrer, A., Knight, M., Perelman, P., Schneider, B., & Garvin, J. Training consulting teachers to assist elementary teachers in the management and education of handicapped children. *Exceptional Children*, 1970, *37*(2), 137–144.

Mead, M. (Ed.). *Cooperation to competition among primitive peoples.* Boston: Beacon Press, 1961.

Monson, L. B. *The social understanding and social behaviors of emotionally disturbed and non-disturbed children.* Unpublished doctoral dissertation, University of North Carolina at Chapel Hill, 1980.

Montgomery, M. D. *An ethnography of an elementary school resource room program.* Unpublished doctoral dissertation, University of North Carolina at Chapel Hill, 1979.

Montgomery, M. D. The special educator as consultant: Some strategies. *Teaching Exceptional Children*, 1978, *10*, 110–112.

Moos, R. H., & Moos, B. S. Classroom social climate and student absences and grades. *Journal of Educational Psychology*, 1978, *70*(2), 263–269.

Morse, W. C. Enhancing the classroom teacher's mental health function. In E. L. Cowen, E. A. Gardner & M. Zax (Eds.), *Emergent approaches to mental health problems.* New York: Appleton-Century-Crofts, 1967.

Morse, W., & Smith J. *Understanding child variance.* Reston, Va.: Council for Exceptional Children, 1980.

Newman, R. *Psychological consultation in schools.* New York: Basic Books, 1967.

O'Connor, P., Stuck, G., & Wyne, M. Effects of a short-term intervention resource room program on task orientation and achievement. *Journal of Special Education*, 1979, *13*, 375–385.

O'Leary, K., Kaufman, K., Kass, R., & Drabman, R. The effects of loud and soft reprimands on the behavior of disruptive students. *Exceptional Children*, 1970, *37*(2), 145–155.

O'Leary, S., & Schneider, M. Special class placement for conduct problem children. *Exceptional Children*, 1977, *44*, 24–30.

Pastor, D. L., & Swap, S. M. An ecological study of emotionally disturbed preschoolers in special and regular classes. *Exceptional Children*, 1978, *45*, 203–215.

Paul, J. L., Neufeld, G. R., & Pelosi, J. *Advocacy within the system.* Syracuse, N. Y.: Syracuse University Press, 1977.

Prieto, A., & Rutherford, R. An ecological assessment technique for behaviorally disordered and learning disabled children. *Journal of Behavior Disorders*, 1977, *2*, 169–75.

Prouty, R. Diagnostic teaching: A modest proposal. *Elementary School Journal*, 1970, *70*, 265–270.

Randhawa, B. S., & Michayluk, J. O. Learning environment in rural and urban classrooms. *American Educational Research Journal*, 1975, *12*(3), 265–285.

Redl, F. *Mental hygiene and teaching.* New York: Harcourt, Brace & World, 1959.

Redl, F. The concept of the life space interview. In N. J. Long, W. C. Morse & R. G. Newman (Eds.), *Conflict in the classroom: The education of children with problems.* Belmont, Calif.: Wadsworth, 1971.

Reed, Jeanne W. Parents/re-ed: Partners in re-education. *Council for Children with Behavior Disorders*, 1978, *3*(2), 92–94.

Rhodes, W. C. The disturbing child: A problem of ecological management. *Exceptional Children*, 1967, *33*(7), 449–455.

Rhodes, W. C. A community participation analysis of emotional disturbance. *Exceptional Children*, 1970, *36*, 309–314.

Rosenthal, R., & Jacobson, L. *Pygmalion in the classroom.* New York: Holt, 1968.

Silverman, M. Beyond the mainstream: The special needs of the chronic child patient. *American Journal of Orthopsychiatry*, 1979, *49*, 62–68.

Simon, A., & Boyer, E. *Mirrors for behavior.* Wyncote, Pa.: Communication Materials Center, 1974.

Smith, J. M., & Smith, D. E. P. *Classroom management.* New York: Random House, 1975.

Stallings, J. A. *Allocated academic learning time revisited, or Beyond time on task.* Paper presented at annual meeting of the American Educational Research Association, Boston, April 1980.

Thomas, A., Chess, S., & Birch, H. *Temperament and behavior disorders in children.* New York: New York University Press, 1968.

Thorndike, R. L. Review. *American Educational Research Journal*, 1968, *5*, 708–711.

Vogel, E. F., & Bell, N. W. The emotionally disturbed child as the family scapegoat. In N. W. Bell & E. F. Vogel (Eds.), *A modern introduction to the family.* Glencoe, Ill.: Free Press, 1960.

Weinstein, L. Project Re-ed schools for emotionally disturbed children: Effectiveness as viewed by referring agencies, parents and teachers. *Exceptional Children*, 1969, *35*(9), 703–711.

Weinstein, L. *Evaluation of a program for re-educating disturbed children: A follow-up comparison with untreated children.* Washington, D.C.: U.S. Department of Health, Education and Welfare, 1974.

Whitaker, J. K. *Caring for troubled children.* San Francisco, Calif.: Jossey-Bass, 1979.

White, K. Final evaluation report. Raleigh, N. C.: State Department of Public Instruction, 1975. Project CASCADE: ESEA, Title III.

Wright, H. F. Observational child study. In P. H. Mussen (Ed.), *Handbook of research methods in child development.* New York: John Wiley & Sons, 1960.

9
Sociological Theory and Practice

main points

1. Deviance involves the violation of social rules and the meaning those in authority give to the violations.

2. Emotional disturbance applies not only to what goes on within the self; it also applies to what goes on between self and others. The sociological perspective on emotional disturbance focuses primarily on the nature of rule violation, social controls imposed by institutions and persons in authority and the social relationships between the individual rule violator and others.

3. The meaning given to a rule-breaking incident and the assumptions made about the rule breaker will directly shape how the incident will be treated.

4. The likelihood that those in authority will resort to formal control depends on the ability or willingness of the offender to engage in appropriate corrective action. Two of the more important forms of corrective action are confession and contrition.

5. Labels affect the way persons behave toward each other. The behavior of individuals as well as the performance expectations of organizations contribute to the labeling process. *Emotionally disturbed* is a label applied to individuals who at some level threaten our shared view of the social nature of man.

6. While teachers may be able to do little about the way society is organized, they can do a great deal to affect the way classrooms are organized and the relationships that exist within classrooms.

7. The sociological perspective is especially helpful to teachers in understanding the problems of emotional disturbance and evaluating their interventions.

This chapter was written by **Phillip C. Schlechty** and **James L. Paul**, University of North Carolina at Chapel Hill.

REGARDLESS of etiology, persons who become identified as emotionally disturbed have been judged by persons who occupy positions of authority to be behaving in ways that are dysfunctional to themselves, to others or to both self and others. Sometimes this judgment is made by persons whose authority is based on training and special knowledge (e.g., psychiatrists). At other times, the judgment is made by people who have less well-established claims to special knowledge concerning pyschopathology but who are, nonetheless, in a position to make their judgments count (e.g., teachers and judges). Thus, emotional disturbance, like many other handicapping mental and physical conditions, is not solely the property of the person judged to be suffering from the condition. Emotional disturbance also has to do with the judgments and perceptions of others. Those who have special training are not always the best diagnosticians. The identification of emotionally disturbed children by teachers has been found to be relatively reliable because they have a broad normative frame of reference (Bower, 1969). In either case, those who are capable of making the judgment that one is "emotionally disturbed" count have the recognized right to make such judgments.

Furthermore, whether or not a particular pattern of behavior is defined as aberrant or as a sign of pathology depends on the meaning given the situation in which the behavior occurs as well as on the behavior itself. For example, nations make heroes of men who throw themselves on hand grenades in the midst of battle. Under other conditions such behavior would be defined as insane. In sum, emotional disturbance has to do not only with what goes on *within self;* it also has to do with what goes on *between self and others.*

Sociology, as a discipline, is explicitly concerned with what takes place between self and others, that is, human relationships, patterns of interaction, the nature of social roles and how social rules are established and maintained (Wilson, 1971). Thus, the field of sociology is concerned with many of the same kinds of phenomena that concern teachers who are called upon to deal with youngsters identified as emotionally disturbed. It seems appropriate, therefore, to ask, what does the sociologist have to say to those who deal with emotionally disturbed children?

The purpose of this chapter is to present sociological concepts that may be useful in better understanding the nature and effects of emotional disturbance in the school. The reader, however, should view the concepts presented as illustrative rather than exhaustive. Sociologists employ many ideas that will not be mentioned here but which might be useful to explore if one were interested in gaining a better understanding of the social nature of emotional disturbance. For example, sociologists have long been concerned with the link between aberrant human behavior and the ways in which groups and societies are structured. Some go so far as to suggest that many forms of human behavior that appear to be highly individualistic in nature and origin, such as suicide (Durkheim, 1951), may have as much to do with the way societies are organized as with the peculiar biographies of individuals.

A classroom teacher can do very little about the way society is organized. A teacher can, however, do a great deal about the way classrooms are organized and the ways in which relationships between and among children and adults are established and maintained in school.

In this chapter we will look at social phenomena over which teachers and those who work in schools can exercise some control. Specifically, we will examine the ways in which social control is established and maintained in schools and the ways in which those who violate school and classroom rules are perceived and responded to. Central to this discussion, are the ideas of social control and social deviance, and the conflict between individual rights and society's expectations.

Social Control in the School

For human society to exist, individuals must behave in ways that are generally predictable and expected by others. Without such dependability, the young would not be nurtured, the dead would not be buried and human interaction could not proceed. In order for human behavior to be channeled in a way that assures that most people will behave in a dependable fashion, societies and groups exercise social control.

The primary mechanism by which social control is maintained is self-control (Goffman, 1971). Self-control depends on the fact that group members know what they are to do, are capable of doing it and value the requirements placed on them and therefore make these requirements a part of themselves; that is, they internalize them. For example, one of the aims of primary education is to develop student skills in working in group settings and the value of cooperative action. Kindergarten teachers often give attention to direct instruction regarding such matters. High school teachers assume (sometimes mistakenly) that the students they teach know how to work in groups and rely on peer pressure to enforce rules related to cooperative group action.

A second means of social control is informal control. In the classroom informal control is usually manifested as corrective feedback, gentle reminders (sometimes expressed humorously) or instruction. For example, a teacher may scold a child for being tardy to class. Corrective feedback is constantly occurring in all groups. Indeed, many sociologists view informal control as the basic means by which instruction and social learning occurs (Parsons, 1951).

A final mechanism by which social control is maintained is through the application of formal sanctions and official disapproval. For example, if a child's tardiness persists, the child may be sent to the principal's office or assigned detention.

Given the nature of schools and children, self-control is always less available as a control mechanism than it is in other organizations. The reason is that children are not fully socialized. Indeed, one of the functions of school is to teach children new and increasingly complex rules and to create conditions in which self-control will be enhanced. This does not mean that children are incapable of self-control, only that the degree to which self-control can be counted on to maintain order in schools is always less than in adult organizations, because adult organizations are made up of participants who

Social order in the school depends on the compliance of participants who are not fully socialized.

have been more fully socialized. This fact has important consequences for schools and for children, as will be shown later.

In many ways the structure of schools directly parallels other types of formal organizations, such as hospitals and factories. Schools, however, have several unique features. First, only in schools are the relatively young (students) and the relatively old (teachers and other adults) forced into daily interaction outside of the context of primary group relationships (the family) and the social bonds and sentiments that group engenders and supports. Second, only in schools is social order dependent upon the compliance of a membership comprised predominantly of persons who have not yet learned those things they need to know in order to comply, or if they have learned them, they have not made them their own, that is, internalized them.

These two features combine in a way that makes social control in schools uniquely problematic and the fear of loss of control one of the primary fears teachers and administrators harbor as they carry out their tasks in schools. This situation has been summarized by Waller (1967).

> It is not enough to point out that the school is a despotism. It is a despotism in a state of perilous equilibrium. It is a despotism threatened from within and exposed to regulation and interference from without. It is a despotism capable of being overturned in a moment, exposed to the instant loss of its stability and its prestige. It is a despotism demanded by the community of parents, but specially limited by them as to the techniques which it may use for the maintenance of a

stable social order. It is a despotism resting upon children, at once the most tractable and the most unstable members of the community.

There may be some who, seeing the solid brick of school buildings, the rows of nicely regimented children sitting stiff and well-behaved in the classroom or marching briskly through the halls, will doubt that the school is in a state of unstable equilibrium. A school may in fact maintain a high morale through a period of years, so that its record in the eyes of the community is marred by no untoward incident. But how many schools are there with a teaching body of more than—let us say—ten teachers, in which there is not one teacher who is in imminent danger of losing his position because of poor discipline? How many such schools in which no teacher's discipline has broken down within the last three years? How many school executives would dare to plan a great mass meeting of students at which no teachers would be present or easily available in case of disorder? (p. 10)

Though Waller's characterization may be ideologically repugnant to some, and it may be somewhat dated, the fact that teachers and parents see social control as one of the primary problems confronting schools is beyond doubt.

Broadly speaking, the term *deviance* refers to a condition in which some person or group violates a social rule, or social norm, and this violation is addressed by persons who have the authority to impose sanctions, for example, by inflicting punishment. Thus, social deviance involves not only violation of a rule; it also involves others seeing the violation and deeming the violation to be of sufficient importance to act toward it in some negative way. For a person to be considered deviant, then, it is not sufficient to know that the person has violated a rule; one must also know what meaning others, especially others who have authority, give to the rule violation.

The Social Meaning of Behavior

Behavior in itself has no meaning. Rather, the meaning behavior has is constructed, or negotiated, in interaction. The way meaning is assigned to behavior will depend on the structure of relationships that occur between those who are involved in the negotiation. Furthermore, the meaning assigned to any item of behavior, or set of behaviors, will in part be shaped by prior meanings and understandings that have been negotiated or learned in other interactions. For example, at the present point in reading this chapter, most readers are probably willing to accept that the authors' intent is to write a serious piece. Some may even believe that the authors have something worthwhile to say. There are a number of ways in which the symbol system surrounding the reading of this chapter encourages such a definition.

First, this chapter is in a book that is sold by a commercial publisher which has a vested interest in being taken seriously. Whether or not the reader has consciously considered this fact, it is understood and taken into account in giving meaning to the words written here. Second, the reader probably was assigned to read this chapter as a part of a course of study that is expressly committed to the proposition that the study of emotional disturbance is a serious business. Thus, in approaching this chapter the reader has been encouraged to see the authors' behavior as a serious endeavor. Finally, the language pattern used so far has conveyed that the authors' intent is serious and scholarly. Suppose the introduction had been written in the following way:

> Grab a chair and hold onto your seat. We're going to tell you some stuff you need to know if you are going to work with emotionally disturbed kids. Now the first thing you need to know is that the word emotional disturbance is a euphemistic term for being a little bit crazy, and schools, like families and churches, can't really live with crazy folks. So what society does is (a) find ways to make them respectable (for example, make the crazies into priests) or (b) find ways not to take them into account (for example, separate the crazies from the normals and put the crazies in insane asylums—or, if you prefer, mental institutions.)

Given this latter style of writing, the reader would probably be asking, "Are these authors really serious, or is this a joke?" In more technical terms, what is being asked is, "Is my definition of the situation appropriate? Is the meaning I am giving the behavior the appropriate one? What, indeed, is going on here?"

From this illustration one can see that the reader does have some power to give meaning to the authors' behavior (in the broadest sense, to label it), but the behavior in itself shapes the meaning the reader is likely to give it. Furthermore, even if the reader should label the authors crackpots, charlatans or incompetents, the label is unlikely to stick because most of the readers of this book will be university students who are not sufficiently initiated into the group to be acknowledged as having power to impose meaning. On the other hand, reviewers in professional journals, especially reviewers who are held in high regard by sociologists, could do the authors' reputations some minor harm by labeling this work "a serious violation of the norms of scholarship." Even if this should happen, however, the authors would likely be given the chance to rebut the criticism and thus renegotiate, or try to renegotiate, the meaning.

Thus, some persons, such as teachers and judges, by virtue of the position they hold in a group are more likely to successfully label a rule violator as deviant than are others, but the person whose behavior gives rise to the label contributes to the process and to the negotiations surrounding the process. "Social groups create deviance by making rules whose infraction constitutes deviance, and by applying these rules to particular people and labeling them as outsiders" (Becker, 1963, p. 9).

Rules

All organizations and groups have social rules, ways of doing things, norms. Such rules vary one from the other in numerous ways. For example, rules vary in their content: some rules refer to how things should be done (technical rules), some refer to standards of taste, or beauty (aesthetic rules) and some refer to standards of what is good and bad (moral rules).

Rules also differ with regard to whom they apply. For example, some rules apply only to a small segment of a group or organization, though all members of the group may know about the rule and uphold it. For example, in the Catholic church the norm of celibacy applies only to members of the clergy, but most, if not all, Catholics know about the rule. Such rules are referred to by sociologists as *speciality norms* (Williams, 1960).

Other rules, however, apply to all members of the group. These are referred to as *universal norms* (Williams, 1960). For example, the requirement that all drivers in the United States drive on the right-hand side of the road is a universal norm. It is not, however, a norm that is upheld in England. From this example, it should be clear that the universality of a norm can only be determined after the group of interest has been identified. For example, celibacy could be considered a universal norm if one were to limit one's attention to Catholic priests as a group.

Williams (1960) suggests that variance in norms, or rules, can be conceptualized along four dimensions: (a) how the norms are distributed throughout the group, (b) how the norms are transmitted, (c) how the norms are enforced, and (d) the pattern of conformity that adheres to the norms. To illustrate the first dimension, most elementary students would be shocked at the behavior teachers consider to be appropriate in the teachers' lounge. This norm is one that only a few people in the group (school) know about. The knowledge of a norm, as well as the applicability of a norm, can be distributed in different ways throughout the group.

Some norms are transmitted consciously, and formal agencies are assigned the responsibility of transmitting the norms, while other norms are taken for granted and transmitted in less formal, though not less important, ways. For example, in some schools administrators require teachers to instruct youngsters about "school rules." The rules referred to are generally those that are officially recognized and codified, such as rules regarding tardiness and proper decorum in the restrooms. Other rules are more likely to be transmitted by members of the group, or by teachers, only to those who are observed to violate the rules. For example, one generally learns the proper signs and euphemisms for gaining access to the restroom by making mistakes, or observing others making mistakes, and by otherwise being given corrective feedback.

Variance in the ways norms are enforced is rather easy to illustrate. Some rules are consistently and routinely enforced while other rules are enforced only sporadically or on special occasions. For instance, in schools teachers and administrators commonly are much more attentive to certain rules at the beginning of the school year than they are at other times of the year, or are much more consistent and rigid in enforcing rules related to politeness and manners when visitors are present.

Finally, the cliche that "rules are made to be broken" has more than a bit of truth in it, for in all social groups there are rules about breaking rules as well as rules which can never be broken with impunity. Certain classes of persons can break some rules with impunity, even though the rule applies to them, and other classes of persons must obey all the time. Teachers, for example, are more free to be late to class than are students. Thus, patterns of conformity—who conforms, how many persons try to conform, how much conformity is expected, and so on—vary considerably from rule to rule as well as from group to group and organization to organization.

The study of rules and rule-related behavior, whether in schools or elsewhere, is a complex and complicated task. One needs to understand what rules have been stated, but one needs also to understand those rules that are so taken for granted, or those rules that are so emotionally loaded or refer to subjects that are so embarrassing, that they are never mentioned though routinely enforced. Furthermore, one must understand who, or what group and what parties, conforms to what rules. One must also understand which rules, even though they are formally stated, do not apply to anyone in the group.

If this is a complex and confusing topic to a student armed with at least some concepts that permit him to organize experience, think how much more complex the task is for a child. Yet, much of a child's success in school is determined by the child's ability to understand what people really mean when they state a rule, what unstated rules he must obey and all of the subtle shadings and nuances of rule-related behavior that are never mentioned but which always are present.

The Problematic Nature of Rule Breaking

Schools as social agencies can be defined as expressly designed to instruct the young in the rules (norms and values) embedded in the culture, to provide them with experiences, or skills, that will enable them to conform to these rules and to foster attitudes and beliefs that support these rules. Such a definition must take into account technical rules (how to solve a particular kind of math problem) as well as aesthetic rules (what constitutes beautiful art) and moral rules (what are the duties of a good citizen). Furthermore, it must take into account conventions and customs (how to feel when the national anthem is played, when the school alma mater is sung and so on). Such a view suggests that the school is an agency of cultural transmission, as well as a social agency intended to teach skills and academic "knowledge."

Given this view of schools, we can see that the meanings that can be given to episodes of rule breaking in the school are numerous. For example, one meaning that could be given to a rule-breaking incident is that the offending child is ignorant of the rule. Another meaning could be that the child knows the rule but lacks the ability or skills to conform. Still another interpretation could be that the child knows the rule and chooses to break it. Rule-breaking might also be a sign that the child has elected to conform to a competing or alternative rule. For example, children are taught to be loyal to their peers and also to be honest! Does honesty require one to reject other children who cheat? If so, does a child who rejects a cheater violate rules related to loyalty?

The meaning that is given to a rule-breaking incident will directly shape how the incident will be treated. If, for example, the meaning that is given suggests the child is ignorant of the rule, the situation is likely to be defined as a condition calling for some type of instruction. If the meaning suggests rebellion, however, it is likely that some more formal control mechanism will be brought into play or that the intensity of informal correction, such as scolding, will be increased.

In schools, as in other social settings, the corrective cycle does not begin until a rule or expectation has been violated or gone unsatisfied. In school, as elsewhere, the hoped-for corrective action is self-control. Self-control suggests that the person refrains from improper, rule-violating, behavior. The child is his own police officer. But there is more, for self-control also suggests that the persons who find themselves acting improperly admit their offense and take whatever action is necessary to assure others they can and will support the rule in the future (Goffman, 1971).

In schools, where children are being constantly confronted with new norms and increasingly complex expectations, a considerable amount of rule-breaking behavior is to be expected. Usually, this rule-breaking behavior is taken as "normal" and treated as a situation calling for corrective feedback, that is, the exercise of informal control. As Goffman observes, however, control exercised from the outside, both formal and informal, is intended to awaken "corrective action from within" (1971). The likelihood that those in authority will resort to formal control depends, in part, on the ability or willingness of the offender to engage in appropriate corrective action. Two of the more important forms of corrective action are confession and contrition. *Confession* is the act of acknowledging the legitimacy of the rule and that one has transgressed the rule either wittingly or unwittingly. *Contrition* refers to actions and behaviors that signal the offender's willingness to undertake whatever reparative work is needed to assure others that he accepts the rule and is not likely to transgress the rule in the future.

In schools, children are expected to uphold rules that many do not yet know about or, if they do know about them, do not possess the skill to comply with. Acts of confession and contrition, therefore, are especially important in determining how a rule violation will be interpreted or framed. Knowing how to say one is sorry is a critical skill. Knowing the circumstances under which teachers and other adults will believe one is really sorry—and willing to repair the social damage the violation of a rule has created, or is perceived to have created—is even more important.

What teacher, for example, is unaware of those cases where children who are unable to master a skill are given extra credit for "trying"? What trying suggests is that the child has behaved in a way that symbolizes that he would be willing to uphold the rule, or behave in the expected way, if only he could. Showing that one is working hard, even if the work produces little result, is a form of reparative work. Such work serves to confirm the rule or expectation as legitimate even as it demonstrates that the offending child is unable to comply with the expectation. Furthermore, some children are in a better position to understand the elaborate rituals and subtle meanings associated with confession and contrition than are other children. For example, school children born to middle-class families have learned that they can be forgiven for rule breaking if they are properly contrite and confessional, even before they come to school. This is illustrated by the myth of George Washington and the cherry tree. Lower-class children, on the other hand, may learn that confession is just as likely to bring reprisal from arbitrary adults as it is to bring praise and forgiveness.

In addition, some children come from sociocultural groups that are generally perceived to be more prone to rule breaking than are others. For example, although delinquency is not limited to the lower classes, children from lower-class environments are generally thought to be more likely to run afoul of the law than are middle-class children. Thus, children from lower-class environments are probably going to be required to engage in much more elaborate forms of confession and contrition if they are to convince others they are sincere. Saying one is sorry, and proving one is sorry, are different things.

Labels

Labeling Theory

Over the past two decades, special educators have come to be very impressed with the concept of labeling. The notion of labeling was developed primarily by sociologists concerned with the study of deviant behavior, that is, the study of the violation of social rules, or norms. Historically, those who studied deviance focused on the deviant individual and asked questions about motivation (Why did he do it?) and prognosis (Who is likely to do it? If one has done it once, will one do it again?). Sociologists who approach deviance from a symbolic interactionist's perspective ask a different order of question: What is the nature and meaning of the various labels that signify deviance, such as *delinquent, homosexual, criminal* or *insane*. Do some of these labels carry more negative meaning than others? Do some labels encourage others to view the person who is labeled with pity, while others encourage repulsion or fear? What, for example, are the consequences of being labeled, that is, publicly identified, as *retarded* as opposed to *mentally ill?* (Becker, 1963).

Other questions an interactionist perspective encourages are: Who is in a position to label another and make it stick? That is, who is in a position to call another person deviant, by whatever label, and get others to accept that definition of the person and act toward him in ways that grow out of this meaning? What are the effects of various labels on the self? For example, does a person who is labeled come to accept the meanings about self that are suggested by the label? If so, what are the social processes by which these definitions and redefinitions of self are accomplished? Are some groups or classes of persons more likely to be given a deviant label than others? Why? Indeed, what are the dimensions of the labeling process itself? Under what conditions does a person who manifests a certain behavior, or set of behaviors, come to be a candidate for a deviant label? How is this candidacy confirmed? What happens after confirmation? Is it possible to become "unlabeled"? Do some labels stick better or longer than others? (Becker, 1963).

Clearly such questions are important at a theoretical level. Furthermore, they have intuitive appeal for the practitioner, who has committed her life to working with and for persons who are living at the fringes of the normative order and outside the boundaries of organized group life. Unfortunately, practitioners have often been guilty of applying labeling "theory" narrowly or in selective ways that fail to take into account the broader social nature and function of labels and the labeling process. For example, in the field of education the idea of labeling is often used in such a way as to suggest that labels are nothing more—or less—than a part of a giant conspiracy by middle-class adults to oppress children, especially unfortunate children and children of the unfortunate, namely, the handicapped and the poor.

Persons who are committed to the well-being of youngsters, especially handicapped youngsters, are rightly concerned with the potential harm labels can do to youngsters. Not only can labels establish inappropriate or harmful expectations for children, labels can also stigmatize children for life, not just for school life. Furthermore, the popular understanding of the meaning of a technical label is often vastly different from the understanding professionals have of the term. Thus, a label that is used professionally to convey the need for special treatment, such as *learning disabled*, may mean that the child comes to be viewed by peers and others as unable to learn. Indeed, it may mean that the child comes to see himself as unable to learn.

Labels, however, do help to organize behavior. Schools are organizations, and organizations necessarily place limits on behavior and impose performance expectations on all who participate in them. Without such limits there would, in fact, be no organized social life. Labels are sometimes applied to persons arbitrarily, and some categories of persons are more likely to be arbitrarily labeled than are others. Yet labels are functional as well as dysfunctional. And the behavior being labeled contributes to the labeling process. A society could do away with the label *thief* by doing away with the idea of private property, or the label *adulterer* by refusing to have rules regulating sex, marriage, family and kinship relationships. Also, different societies, groups and organizations have different rules. All of this makes it seem that rules are somewhat arbitary—and they are—but not quite. For such rules do have a logic, a *socio*logic. They have negotiated, shared logic that is worked out in interaction. Without such logic human society is not possible. Indeed, it is in participating in such logic that one becomes human.

The critical question then, is what kinds of humans do we want members of our society to become? As human beings in a particular society we come to understand what labels we will apply, what deviations we will tolerate and what violations will be punished. The label *emotionally disturbed*, therefore, can be understood as a label applied to individuals who, at some level, threaten or challenge our shared view of the social nature of man. It suggests that the rules we accept for our own behavior, and which tell us what is appropriate, good and worthy in our definition of who we are, have been violated.

The Social Meaning of Labels

In the broadest sense labels are neither good nor bad. Rather, they are symbols that have the effect of fostering shared definitions of a particular situation or behavioral episode. Some labels, such as *mentally ill, criminal* and *delinquent*, have negative consequences for the person who is labeled. These kinds of labels encourage others to view any rule-violating behavior the labeled person undertakes in terms of the label given. For example, the child who has been labeled a behavior problem in school is more likely to be

The labeling of a child as a "trouble maker" fosters expectations of rule-violating behavior.

perceived as being rebellious when he forgets to turn in an assignment in class than is the child who has been labeled an honor student. When the honor student fails to turn in an assignment, others are prone to look for extenuating circumstances, quickly accept apologies and see the behavior as forgivable. For the child labeled as a behavior problem, however, rule breaking is expected, and thus the meaning is clear—or so it seems.

Labels, and the expectations they engender, have considerable staying power. A child develops a reputation as a "trouble maker," a "very shy child" and so forth. When the expectations have been made public and institutionalized, the officially labeled child may well be launched in a career characterized by a specified role and relationship with the educational system. Mercer (1973), for example, has described the career of the mentally retarded. The career, which is labeled by the expectations that officially launched it, will tend to be stabilized as the child continues to fulfill those expectations.

While some labels set up circumscribing rules for behavior, certain labels serve to permit persons to violate rules with impunity, rules which, if violated by others, would bring formal sanctions. For example, geniuses are expected to behave, or are more readily forgiven if they behave, in erratic ways.

Thus, labels serve important social functions. Labels permit others to give meaning to behavior that violates norms or that occurs at the fringes of the range of behavior that is expected and required. Labels permit social life to proceed with some sort of order, even when individuals behave in what seems to be disorganized ways. Indeed, it could even be argued that groups and organizations establish their limits or boundaries through the labeling of certain behaviors, or persons. In effect, they are saying that these persons, and the behavior they manifest, are at the edge of the group, if not outsiders.

Thus, the labeled person serves as an object lesson to those inside, or those who want to be inside, of what is normal and what is expected for the group.

The Labeling Process

In school, as in other organizations, children who exercise self-control, children who know how to confess and how to be contrite, are less likely to become involved in the official labeling process than are other children. Of interest, however, is the fact that children's groups often develop negative labels for children who are overcompliant or who are quick to please or who are too able. Gifted children often learn, sometimes in cruel ways, that the biblical rule that one should not hide one's talents is not always to be obeyed, especially when a test is given that is graded "on the curve." Similarly, children who respond well and quickly to informal control mechanisms are not likely to be nominated for some negative label for their rule-breaking behavior.

Some children, however, are less able or less willing than others to conform to certain rules, or are less quick to understand what the rules are. Through rule breaking they become candidates for the labeling process. Of course, not all rule breakers become candidates, and the breaking of just any rule does not automatically make one a candidate. At some point, however, the conduct of a rule-breaking individual comes to the attention of social control agents, such as teachers and administrators, and is defined as conduct about which something should be done. When the behavior is publicly taken into account by those with the power to make labels stick, the official control structure is activated and the labeling process begins.

According to Erikson (1964) the labeling process involves three phases: the confrontation phase, the judgment phase and the placement phase. Each of these phases is of sufficient interest to be considered in some detail here.

Confrontation. Confrontation includes those processes and activities associated with bringing the candidate for deviant labeling to the attention of the official representatives of the community in a way that suggests that here is a person about which "something must be done." Such confrontations sometimes involve a single episode, as when a child is observed masturbating in the classroom. More frequently, however, it involves a series of mini-episodes, where the teacher, playing the role of informal control agent, finds the student unable or unwilling to respond to corrective feedback. Eventually, the teacher begins to take the role of official control agent and sets in motion actions that make the student a candidate for further attention in the system.

Two aspects of the confrontation phase are critical. First, the social control agent, for example the teacher, has considerable influence on the conditions under which confrontation will occur and the behaviors over which confrontation is likely to occur. In schools, especially, most of the rules are established by adults (they are seldom negotiated with children) and adults decide when and under what conditions they will be enforced. Second, the nature of certain rules makes confrontations with some groups or categories of individuals more likely than with other groups or categories. For example, rules regarding personal hygiene are more likely to be violated by children from impoverished families than by children from families of the upper-middle class. Requiring children to do seat work in the late afternoon means that children who are hyperactive, or who have short attention spans, are more likely to break rules than are more docile youngsters. Thus, to understand how and why children come to be labeled as they are, one must understand those who do the labeling as well as those who are labeled since labeling is a reciprocal-interactive process.

Judgment. The judgment phase of the labeling process has to do with those activities associated with developing a verdict or diagnosis. In some fashion social control agents must develop an official meaning for the behavior violation and announce that meaning in a way that makes it stick. In recent years, especially since the enactment of P.L. 94-142, the judgment process used by schools has come under careful scrutiny, and a variety of efforts have been made to rationalize this set of activities. Perhaps even more important is the fact that in the judgment phase the decision is made to give the offender either a label of forgiveness or a label of damnation.

Labels of forgiveness imply that rule violations by the person so labeled ought to be tolerated, accepted or excepted. In effect, labels of forgiveness ask others to uphold specialty norms or to make exceptions for the person being labeled. Illustrations of labels of forgiveness are *learning disabled* and *mentally retarded*. To say one is disabled means that one would do what one should do if one could. To say that one is retarded, means that one is likely to do what others will do, but on a different time schedule or with less proficiency.

Labels of damnation are labels like *delinquent* and *character disordered*. They suggest that there is something wrong with the will or moral nature of the offender. The offender offends because he somehow wills it, not because he cannot do otherwise.

It is not accidental that mental illness, emotional disturbance and demonic possession often get confused in the popular media (e.g., *The Exorcist*). Before behavior variance was explained as mental illness and treated by medical doctors (i.e., up until the 19th century), it was explained as demon possession and witch doctors were primary care agents for those afflicted (Seeley, 1953). Also, while reform in the 1960s placed mental illness in a context broader than medicine and characterized the problem more as one of social adaptation and coping (Szasz, 1961), the educational system still viewed the problem as belonging to the child and placed the burden of responsibility for change upon him. Unlike programs for the mentally retarded, in which the curriculum was modified, or for the sensory or physically handicapped, in which prosthetic technology helped circumvent the disability to make it possible for the child to use the regular curriculum, emotionally disturbed children were expected to change. Prior to the mainstreaming movement, which emphasized the need for some curriculum modifications for handicapped children in the regular classroom, the special class for the emotionally disturbed had as its goal the re-entry of the child into an unmodified regular curriculum (Trippe, 1963). Not surprisingly, special educators in the 1970s substituted the label *emotionally handicapped* for *emotionally disturbed*, since *handicapped* suggests the possibility of understandable exception to the universal rule. Handicapped people would comply if they could, or so they are seen. The relabeling of children as emotionally handicapped, first accomplished in California in the 1950s, has been called a reform in special education for emotionally disturbed children (Trippe, 1963).

Placement. Placement is the third phase of the labeling process. Placement refers to those activities associated with redefining the role of the person who is labeled in the social system. Among other things it involves teaching others to behave toward the labeled person in a different way and teaching the labeled person to accept and internalize his new position. In all of these a variety of social mechanisms may be set in motion that *cause* the condition that has been judged to be the case, that is, the self-fulfilling prophecy (Merton, 1968) and deviant career development take over. For example, the handicapped child may come to understand that because he is handicapped, less is expected, so he does less. The emotionally disturbed child may learn that he is expected to have temper tantrums in class so he continues this behavior. Furthermore, on those days that the labeled child behaves normally, his behavior may be considered abnormal. The emotionally disturbed child who disturbs no one for a full school day is said to have had a good day, but the normal child is not said to have had a good day under similar circumstances.

Practical Implications of the Sociological Perspective

The sociological perspective described here is perhaps most useful as a way to think about the nature of emotional disturbance and how one intervenes to change it. That is, while the sociological view suggests certain approaches to intervention, it does not offer obvious and specific prescriptions. It is more helpful to the practitioner as a means for understanding the nature of the problem being considered (Morse & Smith, 1980) and for evaluating the interventions that seek to address it.

What You Expect Is What You Get

Teachers should be very careful about how they use and what they contribute to the child's permanent record. The child is constantly changing as a function of his genetic blueprint of development, and the social setting, including the adults, the curriculum, the tasks, the peer group, and so on, is a powerful determinant of the child's behavior. Therefore, the teacher must realize that the child's behavior and the problems labeled as emotional disturbance can change. The written word in the child's permanent record and the spoken word in informal communication between teachers in the school, however, tend to crystallize expectations from teacher to teacher; that is, they help teachers know "what they are in for" with a particular child.

Expectations have a powerful influence on behavior. A child's reputation can precede him and, in fact, reinforce a deviant career. Changing expectations should therefore be an important part of the planned programmatic intervention for the child. The teacher should consciously expect appropriate behavior as a part of her strategy for working with the child. While she must be prepared to deal with inappropriate behavior when it occurs, expecting inappropriate behavior simply increases by a large factor the likelihood that inappropriate behavior will occur. The teacher is in a key position to intervene in this cycle of negative behavior–negative expectation–negative behavior. Pappanikou and Spears (1977) describe this negative behavior cycle in more detail. They point out the necessity of interrupting the negative cycle with positive experiences. This can involve, for example, assigning a task which the teacher is certain the child can succeed at, which he can be rewarded for and which he can feel good about.

The teacher must expect appropriate behavior and reward it accordingly. To expect inappropriate behavior from the child "because he has always acted that way" is to contribute directly to the likelihood that he always will. What you expect is likely to be what you get.

Rules, Roles and Emotional Disturbance

The sociological view encourages the teacher to evaluate carefully the nature of the rules that govern behavior in the classroom and in the school and the ways in which social control is maintained. Viewing emotional disturbance as rule-breaking behavior leads one logically to examine carefully the rules that are broken as well as the rule breaker.

Rules define relationships and the ways in which one participates in relationships in part defines emotional disturbance. Social order, however is impossible without rules. It is unreasonable, therefore, to argue that the problem is that rules exist. Rather, the problem is likely to be in the nature of the rules. The question is, do the rules reasonably take into account the variety of human natures that exist in a society and the plurality of talents that are to be fostered and valued by that society? Or do the rules suggest a more limited view of human nature? The democratic ethos requires that the rules we establish enhance the capacity of all to succeed. At the very least, democracy requires that no one be precluded from the opportunity to succeed in some way. That is what is meant by the often stated phrase "respect for the dignity and worth of the human individual."

We are not suggesting here that the rules of basketball, for example, should be changed so that the physically handicapped child can compete on equal terms with the tall and the athletic. What we are suggesting is that new "games" with different rules can be constructed to make success possible for many who cannot now succeed. By expanding the role structure of classrooms and by expecting more types of performance, teachers can bring into the group many who are now excluded and many who now fail when they are included.

The teacher should realize that there are different kinds of rules and some rules are more important than others. Some rules, for example, have to do with the safety of children in the classroom, and those rules must be clear and firmly enforced. These rules are not the same as rules governing participation in class discussions, proper care of one's books, punctuality in arriving to class, or where to write one's name on a paper before it is turned in. Furthermore, rules related to safety and rules related to classroom procedures and decorum are different from rules justified by moral principles, such as honesty. Cheating on a test or lying are examples of violating a moral principle.

The teacher, of course, must consider the nature and seriousness of the rule that is broken, the consistency with which it is broken and whether or not there is a pattern to the rule-breaking behavior. For example, some children may consistently break rules related to classroom decorum or procedures because they have habits of behaving otherwise and they forget what is required in this particular situation. Some children may not entirely understand the rule even though some teachers have been heard to say, "I've told you three times this week." These same children may not consider breaking moral or safety rules. Other students may show impeccable classroom behavior while the teacher is present but consistently create problems in the class when the teacher is absent; they may manipulate other children in devious ways that get those children into trouble, or they may constantly be untruthful with the teacher about what is going on. Many patterns of rule breaking are possible.

From a psychological perspective these different patterns of behavior are the result of differences in the character structures of the children and may, in fact, be evidence of other defective or psychopathological processes. From a sociological perspective these patterns can be explained by the types of rules that are broken are different. Neither of these perspectives is correct to the exclusion of the other. Each suggests different interventions, however.

From the sociological perspective, it is important that the teacher understand what effect a behavior (or an intervention) has on the structure and order maintained in the classroom and the school. What is placed in jeopardy? Since the teacher is in charge of the social order of the classroom, how does she feel about the child changing it? How does the teacher feel about spontaneous behavior for which permission has not been given or behavior that defies the teacher's authority, for example, ignoring the teacher's request that all students work quietly at their desks.

The teacher needs to assess to what extent she is in control of the classroom and needs to know how she feels about behavior that challenges that control. A teacher who is comfortable with herself as a teacher and feels herself to be in charge in the classroom is more likely to be flexible and resourceful in responding to emotionally disturbed children than a teacher who is anxious and unsure of herself as a teacher. Many emotionally handicapped children, like many other children who are not handicapped, function well in a clear, consistent well-managed structure. Being "in control," however, is not just a function of how highly structured the classroom is. The teacher needs to recognize the interaction of "the child's problem" with the social order of the classroom and with her own feelings about that interaction.

The teacher's work with the child in the classroom can be enhanced by enforcing different rules according to their importance. In a play therapy room the therapist may have only one rule; that is, the child cannot injure himself or the therapist. In a classroom, which is infinitely more complex as a social setting, more rules are needed. Those rules, however, are not all equally important. The breaking of some rules will result in the removal of the child from the classroom. The breaking of other rules may be ignored by the teacher and not cause the teacher any difficulty. Differential enforcement of rules is not necessarily inconsistent. The pattern of rule enforcement will depend on the teacher and the child involved.

Planned ignoring is a strategy that can be effective in extinguishing some behavior for some children. Children can understand and accept the teacher ignoring a certain child's problem behavior as long as the teacher is in charge and the ignoring is (and is perceived to be) a deliberate act of the teacher. In other words, the teacher is in charge in permitting the child to break a rule of minor significance. This does not weaken the teacher's position; in fact, it can strengthen it. In situations like this other students in the classroom may become a source of support for the rule and may provide peer pressure for the child to comply.

Finally, in considering the nature of rules and ways they relate to emotional disturbance in the classroom, one has to consider the potential value of emotional disturbance in the social setting in which it is identified. A sociological perspective suggests that being "emotionally disturbed" is a learned response and that interacting with persons who behave in ways that are likely to be labeled as disturbed benefits the group and those in authority. Rules and labels are vital aspects of human life in groups and without them the group could not exist. Rules define the human group; without outsiders there could be no insiders. In this sense at least, those who misbehave provide the group with a means of defining itself. The critical question is how to define the rules without excluding people who could meaningfully contribute to the life and vitality of our shared social experience. Deviations can represent creative alternatives to accepted behavior. Though often deviation, especially in a democracy, should be valued, because deviation is a part of the vital experimentation that is essential to progressive social action.

Complexity of Labeling

The sociological perspective suggests that the simple paradigm of "seek, find, identify (label), and treat" is misleading when applied to the problem of emotional disturbance. The identification and labeling process is inextricably related to the rules of the setting in which the problem is "found" and the values and power of the finder and the labeler. Emotional disturbance is not like a malignant tumor on which a biopsy can be performed. With a tumor tissue pathology can be analyzed, a diagnosis of disease can be made and a particular treatment can be recommended on the basis of the diagnosis. The clinical determination that a child is emotionally disturbed, however, does not imply the presence of an entity and the absence of other entities. It is, rather, a professional judgment that a child's failure to perform in customary ways in normal social settings is a result of the emotional weaknesses or inabilities of the child. The expectations, values and rules operating in the social setting of the classroom, therefore, become important in defining the problem labeled *emotional disturbance*.

From a sociological perspective, the incidence of emotional disturbance in schools could be reduced by altering the structure of relationships that occur in schools. For example, the reason some children cannot "keep their place" in school may be that their place is too confining or restraining. Indeed, the most psychologically healthy persons in some kinds of organizations may be those who cannot, or refuse to, keep their place. Places can be insane as well as people (Goffman, 1971). Where is it written, for example, that emotional health is defined by one's willingness to do meaningless work or passionately embrace boring tasks? Is it always the case that resistance to authority is a sign of emotional disturbance? Is one emotionally disturbed because one withdraws from a race one cannot win? Who are the rules for, anyway? What view of human nature and human ability do the rules imply?

A sociological view of emotional disturbance in schools encourages one to consider the possibility that the values and behavior of rule makers and rule enforcers may have as much to do with the incidence and effects of emotional disturbance in schools as does the behavior of children who eventually come to be labeled as emotionally disturbed. It may be, for example, that rule-breaking behavior on the part of girls, or middle-class children, is viewed differently by teachers than are the behaviors of boys or lower-class children. Perhaps it is because of teacher values that so many more poor children become labeled emotionally disturbed than do children of the affluent (Hollingshead & Redlich, 1958). Or, it may be that lower-class children break rules that teachers value more. For example, lower-class children may be more likely to break rules that have moral content (e.g., one *ought* to be obedient to the demands of adults). The breaking of moral rules, in turn, is more likely lead one to a confrontation with the system than is the violation of aesthetic or technical norms.

Delabeling children. Teachers and other support personnel in the school need to be aware of the power of labels, especially the negative impact of what has been called here labels of damnation. The process by which labels are assigned and remain assigned to a child is very important. When that process results in a label such as *emotional disturbance*, the social order of the setting in which the child was identified has been taken as given. Yet changes within the setting could change the pattern of the behavior of some children to the extent that a special label would not be required. The evaluation of potential for change in the classroom to improve the child's success in it should be a continuous process. The child's behavior and the setting, and consequently the interaction between the two, can be expected to change, and the necessity for a label at some future time may no longer exist.

The school needs to give as much attention to delabeling as to the process by which children acquire labels. Because of the weight of the label, and the social-political and technical-professional process by which labels are assigned, attention needs to be given to the process of canceling the label. Such a process would logically be attached to the periodic evaluation of the child specified in the IEP. Just as the re-evaluation of the child is specified, a policy could be adopted requiring the label to be reassigned based on the findings of follow-up evaluations. In reality, this amounts to no more than requiring the diagnosis to be updated and reconfirmed, since labeling is only one part of the diagnostic process.

Doing without labels. Closely related to the notion of delabeling children is a proposal for no labeling (Hobbs, 1979). Hobbs suggests that the differences between emotionally disturbed children, and indeed all handicapped children, are much more impressive and compelling than their similarities. Furthermore, he recognizes the problems built into the existing social and bureaucratic system by which children acquire labels. Since labeling is a process for grouping children for the purposes of allocating resources and providing services, Hobbs argues that it is possible and desirable to omit labels altogether. Computer technology is now available to handle the large amounts of data on individual children and it is possible, therefore, to group children for specific service needs and let the nature of the service be labeled rather than the child. This proposal has strong appeal. It is consistent with the policy of integrating handicapped children into the mainstream and of programming for children on the basis of specific needs. Services have been arranged in such a way that the child with special needs in a certain area had to be assumed to have special needs in all areas. On the contrary, a child considered to be emotionally disturbed is not necessarily weak in all subject areas and is not necessarily unable to work and play successfully with other children in all situations. Special class placement for such children treats them as if they were disabled in all areas. Considering and programming for the child's specific deficits obviously has the corollary benefit of keeping the child involved in the regular curriculum with his normal peer group in areas where the child can succeed. Hobbs' suggestion, therefore, that we label services rather than children has considerable merit in the context of a sociological perspective.

Values Clarification

Another important intervention, or set of interventions, from a sociological perspective has to do with clarifying, and making students and the teacher aware of, the values that are operating the classroom (see Chapter 14). Role playing and socio-drama are particularly important classroom techniques because they help the children and the teacher understand the values and social processes at work in the classroom and encourage them to consider alternative solutions to problems. These procedures can help the teacher clarify the emotional component of certain interactions in the class and help students understand the meaning of certain activities for their classmates. Role-playing situations, for example, may highlight a difference of opinion that must be resolved or different values that are competing for acceptance as the right course of behavior. Group discussions of the basis of rules that govern the classroom is another example.

Empathy, taking the role of another, is an important social-psychological ability that children develop under normal circumstances. It is, however, a complex psychological process and some children learn it late, if at all. Many emotionally disturbed children behave in ways that can be considered thoughtless, punitive, sadistic or otherwise socially insensitive. They do not appear to internalize the rules or the values of society. These children are especially difficult for the teacher to work with in the classroom.

A wide range of group methods are available to teachers to help children learn about the social dynamics that govern human behavior. Helping children to listen and read and thereby understand, to talk and write and thereby be understood, and to function effectively as members of a group are basic goals of education. From a sociological perspective these are primary interventions that affect the nature and quality of relationships in the classroom and, hence, the incidence of manifest disturbance or disturbing behaviors. (Special teaching strategies for accomplishing these goals are discussed in Chapters 13 and 14.)

Shared Accountability

There has been an important shift in attitude among parents and professionals regarding the accountability for behavior problems of children and the emotional difficulties that may ensue from those problems. While historically the blame has at different times been directed at the parents, for "not raising the child right," or the teacher, for not teaching the child well, there has been a move to recognize the complexity of behavior and the value of having all important adults working together in the interest of assisting the child with whatever problem he may have. Several strategies have been developed in the 1970s that reflect this attitude. Some of these are discussed below.

Advocacy. During the past decade advocacy has become an important strategy for improving the quality of services for handicapped children (Paul, Neufeld & Pelosi, 1977; Biklen, 1976). Some advocacy activities are operated from outside the service delivery system in order to be able to challenge the activities and, if necessary, confront the authority structure within a service system. The value of advocacy from outside the system is that it reduces the likelihood of a conflict of interest; the exclusive interest of the advocate is that of the handicapped child who has a particular need. Advocacy activities are also conducted within service delivery systems—in schools, communities and residential institutions (Paul et al., 1977).

In the present context, anything the teacher can do to avoid making unilateral decisions in the classroom expresses an advocacy attitude. One approach to this is involving students in deciding what the rules will be and what the consequences will be for students who break the rules. Sharing some responsibility for control in the classroom with students can be helpful to the teacher and the students (see Chapters 12 and 13).

In the typical classroom the rules of behavior are set early and arbitrarily by the teacher (Sarason, Grossman, & Zitnay, 1972). Cheney and Morse, however, have stated that from a psychodynamic point of view "the participation of pupils in the evolution of the code and working through issues is therapeutic" (1972). From a sociological perspective this strategy alters the pattern of relationships in the classroom by sharing responsibility for what occurs in contrast to exclusive teacher responsibility.

IEP development. A clear illustration of how relationships in schools can be altered in ways that affect the incidence and effects of emotional disturbance in schools is P.L. 94-142. It could be argued, in fact, that P.L. 94-142 has fundamentally altered the structure of relationships between the child, the child's parents and school personnel by formally bestowing upon families authority with respect to the school which prevailing customs had denied them. The expectation that the school will be responsive to the needs of individual children is now buttressed with the legal mandate that schools must be responsive. If successfully implemented, P.L. 94-142 could represent one of the most fundamental alterations to occur in the structure of relationships between children and schools in the history of American education.

P.L. 94-142 contains two important provisions which affect the decision-making and accountability structure. One provision is the development of the individual education plan (IEP). Decisions regarding the evaluation of the child and the individual program, including placement when special placement is indicated, must involve and have the support of the child's parents or guardian (see Chapter 2). Their participation in the IEP development and evaluation is important from a sociological perspective. The sharing of responsibility between the home and school for the special treatment of a child and the assigning of labels, when labeling occurs, has altered important traditional relationships in the school. The changed relationships will affect the treatment and could affect the incidence of emotional disturbance. Thus, the social as well as professional dimensions of the process of labeling are substantially altered by including the parents.

Due process. The due process provision of P.L. 94-142 has also altered the process by which children are labeled and placed. Some children have been stigmatized because of racial, ethnic and social class differences (Johnson, 1969). Considerable research has documented biases in placement having to do more with cultural factors than with factors related to the special educational needs of children (Mercer, 1973). In fact, successful litigation by parents and parent organizations charging cultural bias in the assessment and placement of children, inequality of educational opportunity in tracking systems and specialized placements, and due process violations in placement decisions was an important force that led to the passage of P.L. 94-142. The protection of the rights of children and parents to due process in decisions that affect their membership and participation in the social mainstream of the educational system is, from a sociological perspective, a key provision because it substantially alters the rights and privileges in the social relationships in the school.

Mental Health Consultation

Consultation is a basic intervention strategy that recognizes a sociological perspective. The focus is on providing assistance to the teacher or other change agents who represent and mediate the social values of a particular system, such as the public school.

In school environment interventions, the child behavior consultant works with teachers, nurses, principals and others in the school who work with children (Wagnor, 1972). The consultant strives to enhance the classroom teacher's function in nurturing mental health and to help teachers to develop more effective strategies for managing behavior and to employ sound psychological principles in teaching. While the child behavior consultant's input may be primarily psychological in nature and focused on understanding and working with individual children and groups, the goal of the consultation is to change the knowledge, attitudes and skills of the teacher.

The most practical implications of the sociological perspective perhaps have more to do with the prevention of emotional disturbance than with its treatment. With an understanding of the social dynamics of a classroom and the nature of emotional disturbance as an interactive problem between an individual and his social settings, the teacher can intervene to prevent chronic behavioral problems that lead to the institutional displacement of children (e.g., labeling, special placement). With the knowledge that the problem is not simply the child's problem the teacher is free to explore alternative organizations of the physical and social space of the classroom. Understanding that the child's problem does not necessarily require the specialized individual treatment of a mental health professional, the teacher can, and in fact should, try to effect changes in the child's relationship with the classroom environment which will inevitably change the problem which may be labeled *emotional disturbance*.

The sociological perspective has practical value also for mental health professionals in approaching their work with children in schools. Providing mental health consultation to teachers can have a major impact on the incidence of emotional disturbance in schools. If teachers understand more about the nature of emotional disturbance and alternative approaches for working with children in the classroom, they may be able to work with problems at an earlier stage of development and prevent occurrence of problems. Mental health consultation to schools is a much more efficient strategy for mental health professionals, from the standpoint of public health, than individual treatment.

SUMMARY

The sociological perspective of emotional disturbance places emphasis on the socially discordant aspect of behavior. Emotional disturbance is a form of social deviance and, therefore, should be understood in relation to the social rules that are broken and the institutional controls used to obtain conformity. Many environmental factors, such as the social significance attributed to rule breaking behavior and the labels assigned to the rule breaker, affect the treatment the child receives and the way he is dealt with educationally. The sociological perspective is important to teachers in calling attention to the role of the educational setting (classroom and school) in defining emotional disturbance and in specifying appropriate educational interventions.

DISCUSSION QUESTIONS

1. The view is developed in this chapter that *emotionally disturbed* is a label applied to individuals who, at some level, threaten our shared view of the social nature of man. How does this view apply to the teacher's work in the classroom and the school?

2. Labeling of children who violate social norms is a defensible process in an educational system. What arguments could support this proposition? What arguments could refute this proposition?
3. What are the most important aspects of social control that relate to the teacher's role in working with children labeled *emotionally disturbed?* What are some examples, from a sociological perspective, of ways the teacher can influence the labeling and educational management of emotionally disturbed children?

REFERENCES

Becker, H. S. *Outsiders: Studies in the sociology of deviance.* New York: Free Press, 1963.

Biklen, D. Advocacy comes of age. *Exceptional Children*, 1976, *42*, 308–313.

Bower, E. M. *Early identification of emotionally handicapped children in school.* Springfield, Ill.: Charles C Thomas, 1969.

Cheney C., & Morse, W. C. Psychodynamic interventions in emotional disturbance. In W. C. Rhodes & M. L. Tracy (Eds.), *A study of child variance* (Vol. 2). Ann Arbor: University of Michigan Press, 1972.

Durkheim, E. *Suicide: A study in sociology.* (S. Simpson, Trans.) Glencoe, Ill.: Free Press, 1951.

Erikson, K. T. Notes on the sociology of deviance. In H. S. Becker (Ed.), *The other side.* New York: Free Press, 1964.

Goffman, E. *Relations in public.* New York: Harper & Row, 1971.

Hobbs, N. *Helping disturbed children: Psychological and ecological strategies, II: Project Re-ed, Twenty Years Later.* Nashville, Tenn.: Center for the Study of Families and Children, Vanderbilt Institute for Public Policy Studies, Vanderbilt University, 1979.

Hollingshead, A. B., & Redlich, F. C. *Social class and mental illness.* New York: John Wiley & Sons, 1958.

Johnson, J. J. Special education and the inner city: A challenge for the future or another means of cooling the mark out? *Journal of Special Education*, 1969, *3*, 241–251.

Mercer, J. *Labeling the mentally retarded.* Riverside: University of California Press, 1973.

Merton, R. K. *Social theory and social structure.* New York: Free Press, 1968.

Morse, W. & Smith, J. *Understanding child variance.* Reston, Va.: Council for Exceptional Children, 1980.

Pappanikou, A. J., & Spears, J. J. The educational system. In A. J. Pappanikou & J. L. Paul (Eds.), *Mainstreaming emotionally disturbed children.* Syracuse, N.Y.: Syracuse University Press, 1977.

Parsons, T. *The social system.* New York: Free Press, 1951.

Paul, J. L., Neufeld, G. R., & Pelosi, J. *Advocacy within the system.* Syracuse, N.Y.: Syracuse University Press, 1977.

Sarason, S. B., Grossman, F., & Zitnay, G. *The creation of a community setting.* Syracuse, N. Y.: Syracuse University Press, 1972.

Seeley, J. R. Social values, the mental health movement and mental health. *Annals of the American Academy of Political and Social Science*, 1953, *286*, 15–24.

Szasz. T. S. *The myth of mental illness.* New York: Dell Books, 1961.

Trippe, M. Conceptual problems in research on educational provisions for disturbed children. *Exceptional Children*, 1963, *29*, 400–406.

Wagnor, M. Environmental interventions in emotional disturbance. In W. C. Rhodes & M. L. Tracy (Eds.), *A study of child variance* (Vol. 2). Ann Arbor: University of Michigan Press, 1972.

Waller, W. *The sociology of teaching.* New York: John Wiley & Sons, 1967.
Williams, R. M., Jr. *American society: A sociological interpretation* (2nd ed.). New York: Alfred A. Knopf, 1960.
Wilson, E. K. *Sociology: rules, roles and relationships.* Homewood, Ill.: Dorsey Press, 1971.

10
Cultural Theory and Practice

main points

1 Our culture has a pervasive effect on the way we see things, the value we place on things and the beliefs we hold.

2 The school is not only part of a culture but partly a culture in and of itself.

3 Special education exists within, and must operate according to, the culture of the school.

4 The culture of the school affects the way in which we view emotional disturbance, the beliefs we hold about emotionally disturbed children and our approaches to intervention.

5 Interventions may be pro-cultural or counter-cultural.

6 *Pro-cultural* interventions are designed to "cure" the emotionally disturbed child, changing her to fit into the culture as it exists.

7 *Counter-cultural* interventions are designed to bring about changes in the existing culture, reducing the need to change individual children.

8 The choice between the pro-cultural and counter-cultural approaches is made every day by every teacher of emotionally disturbed children.

IN *A Study of Child Variance* (Rhodes & Tracy, 1975) the different theories of emotional disturbance are described in terms of the conceptual models on which they are based. A number of writers, however, are not credited with a model at all but are rather loosely lumped together under the "counter-cultural perspective."

This chapter describes a model that gives some conceptual integrity to the various positions of the "counter-theorists." This model is termed the *cultural model* because it looks at the values and basic perceptions that our culture tries to transmit. What the counter-theorists have in common is a skepticism about those perceptions and values; and in some cases they have alternatives to suggest.

This chapter does not contain a great many "how to's" but, rather, presents the reader with a perspective that can be turned upon the school, and upon any service intervention. The cultural perspective looks at the uses to which interventions are put rather than the interventions themselves. The

---

This chapter was written by **Mark D. Montgomery**, University of North Carolina at Charlotte.

cultural perspective is included in this text on educational methods for emotionally disturbed children not so much because of the unique classroom methods it suggests as for the dimension it adds to our understanding of the meaning of disturbance.

The reader should not approach this chapter expecting to find a theoretical perspective that has been developed apart from other perspectives. This chapter addresses issues and topics common to the theoretical perspectives that have been discussed previously. Cultural theory is similar to ecological and sociological theory in its rejection of individual function or dysfunction as a basis for explaining deviance. Because of this similarity there is some overlap among these perspectives. Cultural theory, however, is unique in focusing attention on cultural significance of interventions—their symbolic nature and the values they maintain or challenge.

Rather than asking, "What is disturbance and how do you deal with it educationally?" this chapter asks, "What does it suggest about our culture that we have defined disturbance and intervened in the lives of people labeled disturbed as we have?"

Cultural Views of Disturbance

Since civilized life began there have been people who, for one reason or another, have not fit into the culture into which they were born. These people have been called, at different times and in different places, witches, heretics, rebels, weirdos, nuts, misfits, crackpots, eccentrics, perverts and oddballs; they have been burned at the stake, institutionalized, stoned, ridiculed, even pitied. What they have in common is their violation of the rules, disregard for the values or indifference to the beliefs of the larger culture. Unable to tolerate this non-belonging, the culture attempts to modify the individuals' thinking, or failing that, to eliminate them.

What Is Culture?

Culture, in simplest terms, is shared meaning, the combination of all those beliefs, values and perceptions that a given group of people hold in common. Different cultures are defined by differences in meanings. Thus, an individual who believes that evil spirits cause mental illness, or who perceives polygamy as the natural form of marriage, or who values racial segregation, is by this definition in a different culture from someone who believes that poor parenting causes mental illness, or that monogamy is the only true form of marriage, or that racial integration is desirable.

Anthropologists have divided the concept of culture into a number of components. *Customs*, or behavioral regularities, combine meaning and value; they define "normal," "expected," "right" or "correct" behavior. Thus customs form part of the cultural value structure.

Violations of custom may be tolerated up to a point, but will eventually bring down negative *sanctions*, or punishments, upon the violator. Sanctions may be informal, such as ridicule, or formal, such as incarceration. Some breaches of custom are considered particularly odious. These *taboos*, such as murder, are almost always met with severe sanctions.

One of the ways that culture is maintained is through ritual—largely self-affirmatory, symbolic sets of activities. *Symbols* may be either physical (e.g., a flag) or behavioral (e.g., saluting the flag). A common understanding of cultural symbols allows for clear communication between cultural members. That is, cultural members must share understanding of the significance of various phenomena (e.g., "low IQ" or "acting out"). This shared perception makes intracultural communication, or *symbolic interactions*, possible (Meltzer, Petras & Reynolds, 1975). In general, cultural members share the same "common sense," the same assumptions about the human condition and beliefs about "the good life."

Consider the following sketch of a problem situation in the school:

> Several years ago in a high school in a rural area, it became popular, among the black males in the school, to wear hats all day long—usually crocheted or knitted caps in black, green and red, or with pom-poms hanging from the side. This practice prompted the principal to issue an official proclamation banning the wearing of hats in school. He said that the school should enforce "proper attire," and that it was not proper for gentlemen to wear hats inside.
>
> The reaction among the students was immediate and explosive. Many students began to make a point of breaking the new rule. In addition, students who had previously not worn hats, girls and white boys, started to wear all sorts of outlandish hats in an apparent act of defiance. A real problem had now arisen.

How do we understand a situation like this? We could see it as a behavioral problem and look for ways to modify the hat-wearing behavior through the use of rewards and punishments. Or we could see it as a psychological problem, focus on the attitudes of the students, and try to deal with their rebellious feelings.

Neither of these perspectives helps us to adequately understand and deal with the problem. Even the ecological and sociological perspectives, through examination of group dynamics, peer pressure and patterns of deviance, cannot give us a complete picture of the situation. It is the cultural perspective that allows us to view the problem most clearly. The hat had become a symbol. It was banned by the school power structure as a symbol of the young, black, male subculture. It was just as vehemently supported by the students as a symbolic affirmation of students' rights, and served as a rallying point for them.

How Does Culture Affect Us?

The effects of our culture on us are so pervasive and so subtle that they are often ignored. Take, for instance, the cultural rules involved in riding an elevator. It is common knowledge (i.e., cultural rule) that one stay as far away from the other people in the elevator as possible, that one look straight ahead or at the floor indicator and that there be no serious conversation. These rules are so much a part of our culture, so taken for granted, that we hardly think of them as rules at all. It is only when a fellow rider looks deeply into our eyes or stands looking toward the back of the elevator, for instance, that we get a feeling that something is wrong, that a rule has been violated. We begin to feel uncomfortable in the situation because we no longer understand the rules. We also begin to feel afraid of, or hostile toward, the person breaking the rules.

Not only does culture affect our behavior in elevators and in other places, it also affects our perceptions. If you were shown a figure like this: T , you would probably see it as a *T* with a missing space in the vertical segment. You have been exposed to so many *T*s that you quite involuntarily fill in the missing space. Somebody from a different culture, one where a different set of symbols is used, would not be so likely to see a *T*.

Culture also affects the way in which we organize our social perceptions. In fact, one of the ways in which we demonstrate our membership in, or allegiance to, a particular cultural group is to see things or interpret things in a way characteristic of that group. For instance, seeing a connection between big business, corrupt politicians, military spending and the John Birch Society might be a way of demonstrating membership in a particular subculture.

The difference between culture and attitude is one of degree. If a single person holds a particular view, it is probably an attitude. When most or all people in a certain situation hold the same or nearly the same view, it is culture. For example, the fact that teachers in 1932, 1968 and 1979 and in Detroit, London and Yokohama held similar views of "inappropriate behavior in class" illustrates the effects of the culture of the school, not just individual attitudes.

Often the psychological perspective takes the place of the cultural view. Consider the following description of an "attitude" change:

> On a television talk show a reformed alcoholic was talking about the benefits of a rehabilitation program he had been involved in. He said that the most significant thing about the program was that it had given him "a new attitude."

What had really happened in this example was that the man had been enculturated into a new group, one that had non-drinking as one of its values. His attitude change was in reality the adoption of a new set of cultural standards, a new way of looking at the world.

What Are the Functions of Culture?

The functions of culture fall under four main headings.

1 *Continuity*. Culture enables us to live in a relatively stable condition. Customs, symbols and rituals change at a slow enough pace that most of us are able to keep up without a great deal of trouble. Our children grow up in a culture that is not radically different from that in which we grew up.
2 *Communication*. Continuity makes communication between individuals possible, even across generations. Our culture provides us with a "definition of situations" (McHugh, 1968). We all know what being "in school" or "in trouble" or "in love" means. Thus we can all share in and communicate about these situations. We also share

Symbolically, time-out is a way of isolating individuals who violate the cultural rules of the school.

symbols, making symbolic interaction possible. The handshake, the frown, the report card—all are symbols for which we have a shared meaning.

3 *Prescription.* Our culture tells us what is right. Whether formally (as through laws) or informally (as through sermons), cultural rules are conveyed to us from infancy. For most of us, these rules for correct behavior are soon internalized to the point where we no longer think of them as rules at all, but rather as self-evident standards of behavior.

4 *Proscription.* Being able to identify sinners, outsiders and enemies is important to the culture, and to us as cultural members. Individuals who violate cultural rules are punished. Depending on the nature of the offense, this punishment may take any of several forms: *extermination*, actually killing the culprit; *exclusion*, expelling the individual from the culture; *isolation*, shutting the culprit up in a special place; or *helping*, curing, teaching or fixing the individual. All of these strategies require that the violator first be labeled and stigmatized in some way.

When something or somebody has been defined as an exception, there must be something else, at least in our perceptions, to which this something or someone is an exception. The phenomenological precept, "The exception proves the rule," means that by defining one case as an exception, you are implicitly postulating a rule.

This expression also works in reverse: "The rule proves the exception." Once we establish norms—the way that most things are—we create abnormality. When we say, for instance, that most three-year-olds can speak, we are also saying, implicitly, that not to speak at age three is abnormal. All exceptions, then, including exceptional children, are created by us, by our unquestioned assumption that there is a normal way that children ought to be.

How Do We Study Culture?

Learning our own cultural reality is easy. In fact, it happens, for most of us, without our even trying. We are naturally *enculturated* from birth. By the way in which we are brought up, we automatically learn to adopt the way of life of those around us.

When anthropologists attempt to recreate this process of enculturation, they immerse themselves in the day-to-day life of the culture being studied. This is called *participant observation*. They try to avoid any preconceptions about the culture and allow themselves to be taught by the people they are observing. By reflecting on the process of enculturation as it happens to them, anthropologists come to feel what the subjects feel and to see the way they see.

Several clues are available to cultural investigators to help them understand the culture they are studying:

1. *Language*. The way that cultural members use words gives the investigator insight into the structure of the culture. For instance, consider the following situation:

   (The teacher's lounge) Mrs. Smith and Mr. Jones are discussing Tommy, one of Mrs. Smith's students. "I don't know what's the matter with him. He just doesn't belong in the third grade. Mr. Jones asks, "What's his problem?" "I don't know," says Mrs. Smith, "he just can't do anything!"

   This brief interchange reveals several aspects of the school culture. First, both teachers refer to the "problem" as being owned by or inside of Tommy. Thus, Tommy is a defective individual, damaged or incomplete. He doesn't "fit" the school, which is a second assumption. The school is stable. Individuals must accommodate themselves to it. Those who succeed are fine, but those who cannot or will not are "problems."

2. *Technology and artifacts*. The objects that exist in a culture provide information to the anthropologist. The existence of boys' and girls' bathrooms tells something about the way in which schools deal with sex. The existence of report cards tells about the value placed upon achievement and competition. Wooden paddles can be used as evidence of the culture's valuing of docility and obedience.

3. *Organization*. The anthropologist is interested in the ways in which cultural members are grouped and the ways in which they relate to each other. Special classes, scheduled exercise periods, reading groups, principals' offices—all are organizational structures that yield evidence about the culture of the school.

The anthropologist, through observations as well as through interviews, attempts to answer some of the following questions:

What things are taken for granted by cultural members?
What are the rules by which cultural members live?
What are some of the symbols that have significance for cultural members?
What are some of the rituals that cultural members engage in?
How do cultural members decide who is an insider and who is an outsider?
What ways of acting do cultural members consider "bad," "evil," or "weird"?
How are rule breakers punished?
What are some of the perceived classes, types or categories of people within a culture?

The Culture of the School

The traditional image of the anthropologist is a pith-helmeted explorer who treks into the darkest reaches of another continent in order to study the strange and exotic habits of some obscure tribe living in the Stone Age. While it is true that some anthropologists do, in fact, study primitive cultures, a large number prefer to examine our own culture. Many investigators, in fact, have brought anthropological methodology to bear upon the culture of the school.

In a sense, it is easier for anthropologists to study an alien culture than to study the American school. By entering a culture without preconceived ideas, the anthropologist can be enculturated in the same way that a child is. He need only be free from ethnocentricity (the tendency to judge everything by one's own standards) in order to learn about the culture being entered.

The problem for those of us who study the culture of the American school is that, as products of the school culture, we have difficulty seeing it clearly. We tend to see cultural assumptions as basic facts of life. For instance, most of us take it for granted that school lasts for about 6 hours per day, for about 180 days per year. It is difficult for us to see that this sort of scheduling is arbitrary, that there is nothing natural about it. We are so wrapped up in the school culture, we have a hard time studying it objectively.

Various investigators have, however, delineated some of the predominant themes of the school's culture.

Being a Teacher

The perceptions of teaching held by teachers have been subjected to some direct investigation. Waller (1932) reported that teachers saw their primary role as executives: "The teacher is the representation of the established order; as such he must be ready to force conformity and enforce discipline" (p. 325). More recent investigators (Jersild, 1955; Knoblock & Goldstein, 1971), making use of in-depth interviews, have focused on themes of frustration, isolation, anxiety and loneliness expressed by teachers.

The cross-cultural study conducted by Edman (1968) found striking similarities in the self-perceptions of teachers around the world. The primary goal of the elementary school was agreed upon, by teachers from Detroit to Yokohama, as being the teaching of reading and writing. There was also a great deal of agreement on issues ranging from class control to professional organizations; from preferred methods of in-service training to reasons for low student achievement.

Teachers learn how to perceive teaching. They are enculturated, socialized to see things as a teacher does. This process is essentially an informal one (Eddy, 1969; Lortie, 1975). While the recruit is learning the instrumental aspects of the job, such as methods and materials, the values, customs and beliefs of teachers are being absorbed as well. This often subliminal learning forms the basis of assumptions, common understandings or "theories in use" (Argyris, 1952) that affect every aspect of a teacher's professional life.

Textbooks on teaching (Combs, Blume, Newman & Wass, 1974; Seaberg, 1974) characterize the teaching experience as joyful, hectic, frustrating and satisfying all at the same time. The good teacher is depicted as concerned, hard-working, imaginative, clean, independent and loving. All interference with teaching is to be avoided, whether it be the performance of clerical duties, visits from administrators or the giving of standardized tests. Teaching is seen as a challenging, yet rewarding, profession.

A less inspiring picture of teaching is drawn by some. Jersild (1955) depicts teaching as a lonely position, isolated from others, filled with anxiety and self-doubt. The theme of teacher isolation is repeated by others, and supplemented by views of hostility, anomie and disillusionment (Henry, 1963; Knoblock & Goldstein, 1971).

Another perspective comes from sociologists and anthropologists who have examined the school. Some have taken the position that teaching, rather than being a profession, is often a form of caretaking or babysitting. This "holding pen" function of schools is seen as one of the major, albeit latent, functions of the educational institution (Henry, 1963; Pettitt, 1970; Schlechty, 1976).

An additional perspective on teaching is held by many educational critics. Some of them have characterized teachers as humorless, autocratic, insensitive, arrogant and rigid. Teachers, they say, see themselves as assembly-line workers, manufacturing products that are designed to be as standardized, docile and externally oriented as themselves.

Relationships with Colleagues

One of the functions of culture is to establish rules governing human relationships. In the school, the conduct of teachers with respect to others is highly controlled. This is especially true of relationships between adults.

The first rule of teacher-teacher relationships seems to be not to interfere. It is a severe breach of propriety, and considered unprofessional, for one teacher to interfere with or speak critically of another teacher's teaching. Such actions are considered to pose a challenge to the teacher's authority (Becker, 1953). Given the importance placed upon this authority (Lortie, 1975; Schlechty, 1976), such a challenge would be serious indeed.

Ritualized patterns of behavior, therefore, have developed to avoid conflicts between teachers. In team teaching situations, for instance, teachers learn not to interfere with each others' territory (temporal and spatial) by dividing up, rather than sharing, their joint responsibilities (Bredo, 1977).

Most of the information on relationships between teachers and specialists comes from textbooks. Thus, textbooks for teachers tell what kinds of services they can expect from the guidance counselor, school psychologist or specialist. On the other side, textbooks for guidance counselors, school psychologists and specialists are generally collections of suggested practices.

Interviews with teachers suggest dissatisfaction with special services. Added paperwork involved with receiving special services and the inaccessibility of specialists themselves are two common complaints. An underlying cause of this disaffection, however, seems to be a general distrust, among classroom teachers, for anyone who is not in their position (Sarason, 1971). Clearly, teachers feel that only teachers understand teaching.

This fact seems to be recognized by authors of textbooks on consulting with teachers (Dinkmeyer & Carlson, 1973; Brown & Brown, 1975). Consultants are encouraged to develop empathy with the teacher-consultee, to try to take on the teacher's perspective. One study on consultation with teachers (Miller, 1974) examined the preferences of classroom teachers for three different consultation "modes": behavioral, psychodynamic and nondirective. Teachers stated preference for a nondirective, Rogerian-type, consultation relationship.

Comparisons

Comparisons form an important part of the culture of education, particularly when it comes to special education. The existence of "exceptional" or "special" children is the result of comparisons having been made between these children and "normal" or "regular" children. Just as we learn, as children, to discriminate between squares and triangles, we learn as teachers to discriminate between the "normal," the "learning disabled" and the "emotionally disturbed."

The Responsibilities of Children

Teachers tend to feel that children owe them certain things. They want children to come to them with a desire to learn, with certain prerequisite skills, from a home that values education and with a willingness to be obedient to all adults. Teachers also feel that they have a right to expect these things. When a child comes in who does not display the proper set of characteristics, or values, the teacher feels cheated. While the teacher may intellectually acknowledge that the problem is in the system (as in the case of socially promoting a child not academically prepared for the next grade), it is often the child who must suffer the heat of the teacher's anger and frustration.

That children have a potential and that a child should live up to her potential is taken for granted among educators. In discussing a fourth grade child considered to be gifted, a teacher complained that she should be doing much better. "After all," he said, "she has an IQ of 155! She should be at the seventh or eighth grade level at least." The "problem" was that the child was performing only one and a half years above her grade placement. The teacher was trying to figure out how he could get the child to work up to her potential.

The notion of potential is so compelling that teachers are sometimes led into ridiculous positions. Take, for instance, the psychological evaluation on a child who was reported to be "working above his potential"!

Cultural Aspects of Special Education

"Problem" Students

The notion that some students are "problems" has long been part of the culture of the school (Waller, 1932). Generally, teachers believe in "discipline problems" and "slow learners." Children who are difficult to control, posing a direct threat to the teacher's authority, are usually considered to be the most pressing problems. While several approaches have been suggested for establishing, maintaining or regaining control over students (Carter, 1972), implicit in each is the notion that the teacher needs to define the situation in class as a situation in which the teacher is in control.

Slow students pose a different sort of threat to teachers. A teacher's rewards for teaching are largely the psychic rewards that come from seeing learning take place in students. A student whose achievement is slower is able to give fewer of these rewards. In addition, slow students are seen as requiring more time than regular students, further reducing the teacher's ability to interact, and receive rewards from, other more capable students (Warren, 1975). This last view, incidentally, seems to be refuted by Brophy and Good (1970), who determined that slower students are not given as much time with the teacher as regular or fast students. This may be a situation where the cultural reality (i.e., slower students take up more time) is in conflict with "objective" reality (i.e., slower students take up less time).

Special Education as an Ideology

Exceptionality is a human concept and thus a phenomenological issue; that is, it is a matter of perception. Programs designed to deal with children with special needs reflect a particular perspective on the nature of exceptionality (Rhodes & Tracy, 1975; Rhodes & Paul, 1978).

Ryan (1971) speaks of two major perspectives on special education: the exceptionalistic and the universalistic. From the *exceptionalistic perspective*, special education should be for special children; those who act differently and learn differently, it is believed, *are* different from regular students. Special services should be added on to existing regular programs. From the *universalistic perspective*, special education should add a new dimension to all programs. All students are seen as varying on numerous dimensions, with no sharp delineation between "normal" and "special." Echoing Ryan, Lilly (1970) submits that the goal of special education is to deal with "exceptional school situations" (p. 48), to modify regular programs, making them more appropriate for a wider range of students.

The universalistic perspective is becoming more popular among special educators. The result is the mainstreaming movement, with an emphasis on change in the regular classroom for the benefit of children with special needs. One potential barrier to mainstreaming is the exceptionalistic perspective of classroom teachers. According to Sarason (1971), "Segregation of problem children is the prepotent response to the professional and personal dilemmas that teachers face" (p. 156). Teachers are likely to feel that they are unprepared to handle "special" children, but to ask for consultation from a specialist is to risk loss of prestige among the faculty or authority over students.

Special educators have sold the exceptionalistic perspective to classroom teachers. Implicitly and explicitly the message has been that "special" education for "special" children should involve "special" methods and materials, which can only be learned from "special" courses which lead to "special" certification and degrees. Certainly, today, many special educators have given up the exceptionalistic perspective in favor of the universalistic. The problem is that many teachers still hold the exceptionalistic perspective that they bought years ago.

The problems associated with differing perspectives on exceptional children have rarely surfaced in textbooks on special education. Prospective resource room teachers, for instance, are encouraged to be helpful, to seek and to offer cooperation (Wiederholt, Hammill & Brown, 1978). Rarely is any attention given to the difficulties inherent in implementing a mainstreaming program. The message is that most teachers will be tractable but that a few "traditional" teachers may offer resistance (again, the psychological perspective). Most textbooks seem to be unaware of the cultural realities of schools that threaten well-intentioned innovation.

Ritual and Symbol in Special Education

The certification process. This elaborate series of events has many of the aspects of ritual. It is, after all, very explicitly codified by laws and regulations. What is more, the exact nature of the ritual is known only to those who are in special education. Classroom teachers, parents, and in many cases principals, must depend on the specialist to guide the way through the ritual.

The process is generally divided up into a number of subrituals which are orchestrated by the special education teacher, much as any other rite of initiation. The referral form is completed using some of the many words familiar to classroom teachers, such as "behavior problem" and "short attention span." This referral is turned over to the psychologist who redefines the teacher's perceptions. By using magic words such as "aggressive," "acting out" and "anxious," he is qualifying the candidate for admission into special education. At the school-based and placement committee meetings, the various specialists, along with symbolic members, such as parents and classroom teachers, go through an elaborate process in order to satisfy the requirements of the regulations and "meet the needs" of the child. The result of the meeting, assuming that the candidate is not found to be "unqualified," is a symbolic tattooing, in which the candidate, now an initiate, is assigned a label and a duly authorized Individualized Education Program. Some of the symbols of special education membership are the "little bus," the IEP, the label, the special class, the special grading system, the special diploma and the confidential folder.

Categories and labels. Categorizing and labeling people may be an integral part of human nature. Certainly young children seem to apply a variety of labels to others: "dummy," "naughty," "smart" are part of most kindergarteners' lexicons. Among adults the use of labels is even more evident: "women's libber," "red-neck," "male chauvinist" are frequently heard descriptions of people.

It is interesting to note that labels are almost exclusively used on people who are considered to be "not-like-us." For instance, it is not uncommon for white teachers, when referring to a child from a racial minority, to make mention of that fact even if it has nothing to do with the conversation: "One of my black boys told the funniest joke to the class yesterday."

One area that has not yet been fully explored by cultural investigators is the meaning of labels. Some of the questions to be asked are

1 Do classroom teachers distinguish between "emotionally disturbed," "mentally retarded" and "learning disabled"?
2 Do special teachers attach different meanings to "emotionally disturbed," "behavior disordered," "socially maladjusted" and so on?
3 Do teachers' understandings of labels change with more information on the characteristics of the groups being labeled?
4 Are there other, unofficial, categories of children in the perceptions of teachers?
5 If so, are the categories shared by all teachers, or are there differences between special and classroom teachers, elementary and secondary school teachers?

The Cultural View of Emotional Disturbance

The terms we use to describe the phenomenon of emotional disturbance give us several clues to its place within the culture. The fact there is a term for it is an indication that we think it exists. We think of it as a condition, one that some people have and some do not. It is an internal condition; that is, it exists within the individual.

Beyond these few common understandings, however, there is little agreement. When one investigator examines a "behavior disorder" and another looks at a "personality disorder" and still another studies "social maladjustment," are they seeing the same thing? Probably not. One study, for instance, found that no fewer than 21 terms have been used for what we are choosing to call here "emotional disturbance" (Hirshoren & Heller, 1979). The fact is that this phenomenon is a mixed bag of conditions, traits, behaviors and interactions. What's more, they change appearance before your eyes when seen in different ecological, social and cultural contexts.

The culturally significant fact is that, even though no one condition called "emotional disturbance" exists, we continue to operate as if it did. We have established elaborate diagnostic procedures, fancy classifications and a multitude of treatment programs, in order to justify the existence of this "condition."

Our culture has assigned a number of meanings to the phenomenon (or phenomena) of emotional disturbance. Each meaning tends to evoke in us a different feeling that determines the way in which we deal with the "problem." Some of the common views of emotional disturbance are summarized below.

1 *Emotional disturbance as a sickness.* In many ways, children seen as emotionally disturbed are considered to be afflicted with a disease. For one thing, they are separated from those of us who are not so afflicted, much as a child with chicken pox would be. Second, they are given certain kinds of "treatment" for their condition. Such treatment is, of course, aimed at a cure, the goal being emotional "health."

2 *Emotional disturbance as a tragedy.* It is considered a sad thing to be emotionally disturbed. Whether or not the children in question consider themselves to be so, the rest of us are prone to think of them as miserable. We tend to think that the children wish that they were not disturbed since we ourselves imagine that we would be unhappy if we were in their position.

3 *Emotional disturbance as cultural deprivation.* When a child is raised in a home that we consider to be culturally depriving, we tend to have pity on him: "It's not Johnny's fault," we say, "he comes from a rotten home. He doesn't know any better." These kids are somehow more worthy than kids from "good homes" who should know better. We also tend to think that the emotionally disturbed child from a rotten home is easier to deal with than those from good homes. All we have to do, after all, is show the child how we do things, just as we might show a savage, and he will adopt the ways of our culture. It is an insidious form of ethnocentricity that makes us consider anyone from another culture to be culturally deprived. It is a process Ryan (1971) calls "savage discovery."

4 *Emotional disturbance as a sin.* It is important to the culture for individuals to fit in. We are all encouraged to be predictable in our behavior, to act "normally." Historically, those who did not or could not act normally were often considered to be evil, or at least the instruments of evil. Unnatural behavior was attributed to possession by demons or spirits. Today, of course, we no longer believe in demonic possession. We continue, however, to use a sort of language in talking about disturbance that implies a bad or weak character.

"Jane," we might say, "is laden with conflicts." "Her ego has been weakened." "Her behavior carries the seed of a neurosis." And so forth. We might just as well be referring to evil humors.

The reaction of others to a child identified as emotionally disturbed is often one of fear or anger. These are, after all, two reactions of the faithful to sin: fear of contamination and anger at the sinner.

5 *Emotional disturbance as a taboo.* Look at the following list, which was taken from a definition of emotional disturbance (Christianson, 1967). It is a list of behavioral characteristics that, according to the author, suggest emotional disturbance.

Underachievement in school is not related to physiologic or other logical causes.
Chronic displays of unhappiness or depression.
Destroys the property of others.
Frequently lies or boasts.
Relates poorly to peers in cooperative situations.
Daydreams frequently.
Shows unusual anxiety, fearfulness, or tenseness.
Shows a preference for working and playing alone.
Has an unkempt or slovenly appearance.
Tries too hard to please others. (p. 575)

Looked at another way, this could be considered a list of cultural taboos. The violation of one or more of these taboos can result in punishment in the form of therapeutic intervention. Of course we don't think of therapy as punishment, and for us as educators perhaps it really isn't. For the culture, however, therapy is a punitive reaction to taboo behavior—punitive in the sense that it is mandatory and carries with it the threat of punishment if the therapy fails because of the client's lack of cooperation.

A few years ago the principal of an elementary school was visibly uncomfortable as he related a "problem" that he was having. Sam, a third grade boy, had caused quite a stir. It seems that Sam had, sometime during the morning, found a way to put some (in the principal's words) "doo-doo" into the bread dough mixer in the school cafeteria.

Had Sam put mashed potatoes or pudding in the machine, the principal might have considered it a prank, something that Dennis the Menace might do. But because of the taboo surrounding feces, Sam was seen as sick.

6 *Emotional disturbance as an explanation.* Once a child is identified as being emotionally disturbed, we tend to use that fact as a way of explaining his behavior. This "reification of the label" described by Lilly (1970) often releases us from a responsibility for doing anything with the child.

"Why did Sam put feces in the bread mixer?"
"Because he is emotionally disturbed."
Case closed.

7 *Emotional disturbance as a threat.* In relating the story about Sam, the principal stated several times, each time with more feeling, "He just goes berserk, *for no reason!*" It is not unusual for teachers to feel that emotionally disturbed children do not play by our rules. That is, after all, why they are labeled emotionally disturbed in the first place. But when teachers begin to feel that they don't play by any rules at all, that there is no way to understand the children's behavior, a crippling fear can be the result.

8 *Emotional disturbance as an ideology.* Some writers (Szasz, 1974) make the case that emotional disturbance is a political phenomenon. That is, people who do not think the way the rest of us do threaten the power of many of our institutions. If children don't learn conformity, they won't obey the law; if they don't learn materialism, they won't buy new cars and new clothes; if they don't learn obedience, they won't make good workers.

It is convenient for us to think of people with unusual ideas as sick. This allows us to isolate and change them, without ever questioning the cultural values and perceptions that they are rejecting, or the social institutions that create them.

Interventions from the Cultural Perspective

There are no cultural interventions as such. This does not mean that there is nothing to be learned about interventions by using the cultural perspective, for every attempt to deal with emotional disturbance has cultural significance. Such attempts can be divided into two categories; pro-cultural and counter-cultural.

Most intervention strategies are *pro-cultural*. They are designed to fit the individual child into the existing culture of the school, or the larger community. The intervenor, as a representative of this culture, tries to get the emotionally disturbed child to enter, or re-enter, the predominant culture.

Counter-cultural interventions have as their goal not the fitting of the individual into the culture but rather the accommodation of the culture to the individual. Here the intervenor takes the role of change agent, attempting to bring about conditions that will be more nurturant for all children, including those termed emotionally disturbed. From this perspective, it is the culture, not the child, that is sick.

Pro-Cultural Interventions

The predominant approaches to emotional disturbance are pro-cultural in nature, that is, supportive of the existing culture of the school. They are responses of that culture to individuals who have drifted away from or violently rejected the popular version of reality. Any intervention that attempts to cure, remediate, re-educate, socialize or otherwise modify the behavior, perceptions or thinking of an emotionally disturbed child so that she will fit the culture as it is, is a pro-cultural intervention.

Pro-cultural intervenors try to convey the following messages:

1 *The world is the way we, the "helpers," say it is.* A major component of interventions is reality communication. That is, the intervenor attempts to convey to the child the way things really are. Newman (1961), for instance, feels that an important job of the intervenor is to convey "essential messages" to the child. Some of these messages are: "The emotionally disturbed child can learn," "School is a place where gratification exists" and "School is a place where help is available."

   In some cases, "therapeutic environments" for instance, a temporary artificial reality is established. This reality is usually one where the "rules" are clearly and explicitly stated. The hope is that, having learned these rules, the individual will eventually be able to learn the rules of the larger culture.

2 *The emotionally disturbed individual has a distorted, incomplete or alien view of reality.* As a justification for curing, the intervenor points out the error in the child's ways. Often this is done directly, as in directive psychotherapy. Sometimes, however, this process is more subtle. The nondirective therapist may utilize reality testing or life space interviewing to demonstrate to the child her misperceptions.

3 *Everyone would be a lot happier if the child would or could adopt the reality as communicated by the school.* The disturbed child is told, both explicitly and implicitly, that her unhappiness would be relieved if the child would see things our way; that the "Big Brother" she is struggling against is actually a benign helper; that the rest of us are saddened by the child's struggling and would be very happy to see her come back into the fold.

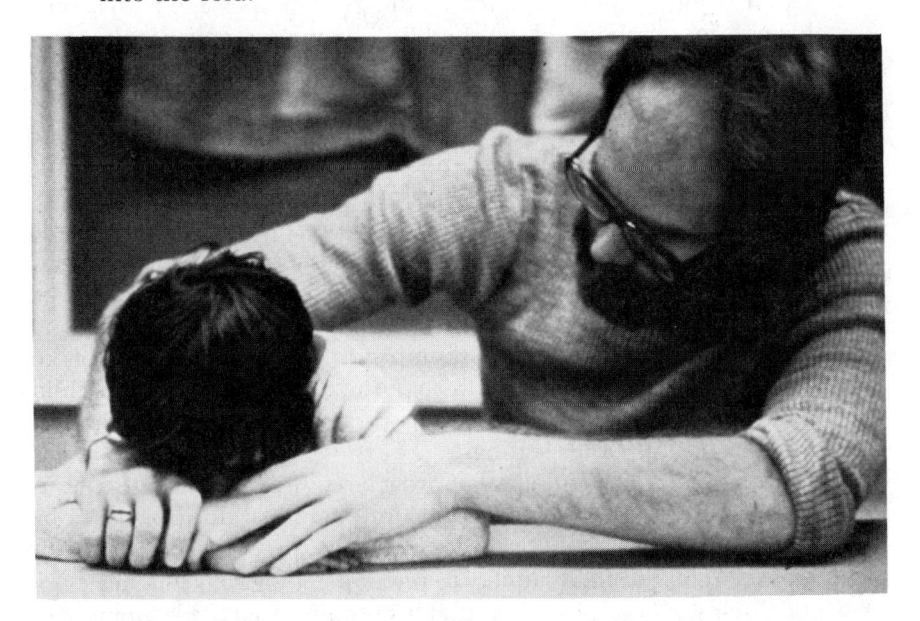

The message behind pro-cultural interventions is that the disturbed child will be happier if she sees reality the way his helpers see it.

4 *We are the road to salvation.* The emotionally disturbed child is made to feel that we hold the cure for her trouble. It is through the child's cooperation with us in our efforts to help that she will achieve acceptance and happiness. Whether the specific intervention is behavior modification, milieu therapy, individual counseling or drugs, the child is assured that it will work if she cooperates.

Some pro-cultural interventions include the following:

1 *Special classes, time-out booths, resource rooms.* These forms of isolation serve a variety of cultural purposes. On the symbolic level, these practices convey the message that the emotionally disturbed child is sick, and therefore must be put into quarantine, at least until she is well. Also on the symbolic level, such isolation communicates to others, particularly the child and her parents, that we are doing something to help. To classroom teachers and to parents of non-handicapped children, we are communicating our willingness to protect normal children from the influence of the emotionally disturbed.

Segregation also has a pragmatic purpose. By putting a child in a controlled, artificial setting we are able to effectively control her reality. By controlling who and what comes into the setting, we control information. When we control information, we can loosen the child's grip on her own version of reality. In the resulting vacuum, we can introduce or re-introduce "the way things really are."

2 *Counseling and token economies.* The goal of these interventions is to alter the perceptions of the child, to get her to "see things our way." This generally involves a charismatic therapist who is able to convince the child to get into the spirit of things. The message is that only through cooperation will the child find happiness, either in the therapeutic setting or on the outside. The setting itself usually contains a variety of symbols (e.g., tokens, circles of chairs, puppets) that the child learns to relate to in a certain way. The child also learns to define the situation as "therapy" or "group" or "time-out."

Once the child has become accustomed to the therapeutic milieu, the therapist begins to mold the child's perceptions. Through role playing, moral dilemmas, art therapy or other means the therapist attempts to show the child the error of her ways and the benefits to be gained from right thinking. Even so-called nondirective counseling has a symbolic function. The therapist in this situation attempts to show the child how relations can be positive. It is hoped that the child will internalize this lesson in therapy and thus alter her perceptions of those around, in other settings.

3 *Drugs and shock.* The biological approach requires that the intervenor, and to some extent the child, consider emotional disturbance to be pathological, with a physical locus. Part of the cure, in fact, might depend upon the child's ability to phenomenologically link her emotional self with her physical self. This requires that the "patient" put herself into the hands of someone attributed with healing powers. In our culture, this person is most often a medical doctor. In other cultures, this person is a witch doctor or shaman. The doctor or shaman impresses the patient with his powers, and convinces the patient that he has the ability to heal the emotional disturbance. Treatment is then applied. Positive changes in the patient are interpreted as being the result of such treatment.

4 *Alternative schools*. Various attempts have been made to establish schools that are different from the public school. Often called "open schools," they have in common an approach that differs from the traditional experience of the public school. Often they purport to promote humanistic values, to teach interpersonal and self-knowledge skills, to foster creativity and individuality. They are pro-cultural in that they leave the dominant culture unchallenged. They serve as an outlet for people with different ideas about education, and as a safety valve against the pressure for change. The school system can demonstrate its progressiveness by pointing to these schools, while keeping economic and administrative control over them. These are not to be confused with "free schools" which are discussed under counter-cultural interventions.

Some Objections to the Culture of the School

Critics of schools have argued for a long time that certain aspects of the way we view education and the way we approach schooling cause or aggravate problem behavior in children. The root of the problem, so they say, is our preoccupation with the goal of schooling—enculturation—at the expense of the goal of education—the development of the individual. Thus, while all statements of school philosophy are full of high-sounding expressions such as "the worth of the individual" and "developing the whole person," the practice of schooling promotes just the opposite—conformity, docility and unquestioning obedience.

In our attempts to standardize the school experience, we have stifled creativity and individuality in teachers. We are constantly searching for the best way to teach, for the most effective way to control behavior, for the most efficient grouping pattern. Teachers who have lost their own individuality are not likely to promote this in children. What is more, the school has become an instrument of only one—the dominant—culture. Success or failure in school is related to the willingness and ability of the individual child to assimilate this normative culture, even if it means denying another culture in the process.

One of the ways that schools maximize this enculturation function is through compulsory attendance. We require children to attend school for a certain amount of time. The compulsory nature of the experience and the way in which we isolate school children from the outside world are strategies commonly used by people we call "brainwashers," because of their effectiveness in controlling thought. We desperately want children to see things our way, so sure are we that it is the "best way."

Schools establish an artificial reality that places emphasis on comparisons between children through competition for grades. In this light, the "back to basics" movement can be seen as an attempt to maximize comparison and competition by concentrating attention on those activities that lend themselves most readily to quantification and standardization.

Also, artificial standards are erected for classroom behavior. Many behaviors that would be acceptable outside (e.g., talking, moving around, chewing gum, cursing) are forbidden in school. Having established arbitrary rules for social behavior, we are assured of a certain number of failures. The arbitrariness of school rules seems to be designed to teach children that rules (and teachers) are to be obeyed without question, even at the expense of individual freedom. In fact, there are very few areas in which children may exercise any free will, except in their freedom to obey or to defy rules.

Once a child decides to defy authority, or is incapable of obeying, official mechanisms come into play. The child becomes a "problem." She may be pitied, feared or hated, but she must be changed. The child's "wrong thinking" must be altered. She must be taught "right thinking." This mind alteration is, we say, for the child's own good and protection, although it is for our own good and for our protection that we change the child. If the child needs protection, it is from us.

Thus, say the critics (Kozol; Holt, 1972), we create "problems," that is, problem children. We do this by establishing a large, all-powerful arbitrary system that attempts to homogenize our children and by calling those children who resist this process "problems."

Counter-Cultural Interventions

Indirect intervention—the change agent. This kind of intervention is described in Chapter 8 as ecological. A consultant or advocate attempts, through working with the child, the teacher, the home and the school administration, to resolve a problem situation.

Consultation and advocacy are considered here as counter-cultural interventions for several reasons. First, the notion of working with situations rather than with children runs counter to the accepted idea of problems being inside children. Second, the change agent, by attempting to modify other aspects of the situation (particularly teachers), is violating another important cultural rule—that one teacher does not interfere with another's teaching. A related rule is that the curriculum is stable. By suggesting changes in curriculum and scheduling, the consultant or advocate is entering into counter-cultural territory.

This is, by the way, dangerous territory. A teacher who attempts to disrupt the culture of the school is asking for trouble. Great care must be taken in order to avoid becoming an outcast (Montgomery, 1978). The potential benefits of change in schools are, however, enormous. By changing the way teachers see students, the curriculum, parents, the principal, each other and themselves, the consultant or advocate can affect the lives of many more people than could be touched through direct intervention alone.

Legislation and litigation. Laws are one of the ways in which cultural values are formalized and translated into action. Each law, and the attending litigation, is a statement by cultural leaders (politicians) regarding lawful or rightful behavior. Legislation carries the possibility of cultural change. As the product of our official cultural leaders, a law has validity. The effects of laws may be slow in being realized but are probably inevitable.

P. L. 94-142 was written as a civil rights law. It spelled out the constitutional right of every child, including the handicapped, to share equally in the educational enterprise. Couched in concepts and language that few would argue with—"equal rights," "due process," "appropriate education"—the law attempts to alter the way in which we view the handicapped. The message is no longer "Pity the handicapped" but "Handicapped people have rights." No longer are the handicapped asking for charity; they are now demanding service. The law reinforces this new view of the handicapped and as such is a potential instrument of cultural change.

So far this potential has not been realized. Many school systems are still at the level of grudging compliance with the letter of the law and lack a commitment to its spirit. This is understandable since the law also carries some implicit messages about special education: that children "have" handicaps, that more special services will help, that labeling is a necessary preconditioning to appropriate education, and so on.

Free schools. Unlike alternative schools which are under the control of the public school system, the "free school" is a real alternative. Typically instituted by groups of parents, these schools obtain only minimal support from the school system. They are often run by teachers without some of the credentials valued by the public school, or even by parents themselves. The curriculum usually varies from that of the public school; it may include atypical courses such as meditation, backpacking or gardening, for instance. The most radical feature of the free school, and the greatest threat to the public school, is its rejection of many of the values associated with traditional schooling. The highest priority is given to freeing the individual child from the pressures of conformity, unquestioning obedience, unnatural behavioral demands and competition—all fundamental to the public school.

Doing away with school. Some educational critics (Illich, 1970) have suggested that schools are so bad, so harmful to children, so disturbing that they should be eliminated. The premise is usually that schools as they now exist are instruments of a society that is increasingly authoritarian, and that by perpetuating this authoritarianism schools are antithetical to the healthy growth of children. Given the fact that schools are political entities, and therefore tied to the society that creates them, the only hope, according to the critics, is to take the schools away from the government and give them to the people.

Media and symbols. Various attempts have been made to raise the consciousness of the public concerning handicapped individuals in the society. This usually occurs through the manipulation of symbols. Generally, one or both of the following is included: (a) a poster child, that is, a symbolic representation of a typical retarded, disturbed or impaired person, and (b) a testimonial from either a celebrity, a parent or a professional with whom the audience can identify. The message is that this child needs help, and that people like you are trying to help; therefore, you should try to help. The media, perhaps, will also be used to take the public consciousness to the next step: the realization that children don't need to be treated fairly because of their handicaps, but that they need to be treated fairly because they are human beings.

Books. One of the ways in which people with ideas try to influence others is by writing books, such as the one you are reading. While most textbooks on schools are pro-cultural, aimed at maintaining the tradition of schools, many educational critics, such as Holt, Kozol, Postman and Weingartner, have attempted to suggest changes in the culture of the school through their writings.

The Culture of the School: Prospects for Change

Many of the people mentioned in this chapter have been referred to as "counter-theorists" (Rhodes & Tracy, 1975). This term expresses the main misconception surrounding this perspective, that it is anti-school. While some of the critics (e.g., Illich) see little hope for school reform, it does not follow that the cultural perspective is one based upon negativism. On the contrary, a critic is likely to be a true idealist, having a clear idea of what schools could or should be. The negativism is typically aimed toward the practice, rather than the ideals, of education. Of course, it would be a mistake to think of the cultural perspective as the exclusive domain of educational critics. This perspective is simply a tool, a lens for looking at the values, myths, symbols, taboos, rituals and beliefs that surround us. It may be used to promote, challenge or simply observe the culture.

Most often, people who are interested in changing a large system such as the public schools decide that it is too difficult to effect change. Having made this decision, such individuals either give up and go along with whatever the system dictates or leave the system and search for someplace else to go, another job to do. A few people, however, recognizing the difficulties of change, are still willing to stay within the system and continue to work for that change. These people are change agents.

Change agents have several characteristics in common which give them a chance, albeit a slim one, to bring about positive changes in the way in which schools do business. Among these characteristics are

1 *Dissatisfaction with the status quo.* This is basic. Unless one feels that the way things are is not good enough, there is no motivation for change. Change agents consider the statement "We could do better" not just a platitude but a mandate for action.
2 *An agenda.* Whether it is a hidden or a public one, change agents have an agenda, a set of goals, a list of things to do. Most teachers are reluctant to have personal goals. "What right have I," they say, "to have goals for my school or my school system? That's the principal's place." Change agents feel entitled to have goals and are willing to work to attain them.

3 *Willingness to take risks.* Change always involves danger. Particularly in schools, extremely conservative organizations, change is seen as a threat to the stability of the power structure. Individuals who try to make changes are considered dangerous and are treated accordingly. That is why many change agents work subversively within the system, hiding their agenda, dealing with people subtly and with great tact to bring about the ends they want. Of course subversion carries with it danger, just as open confrontation does, for nothing is considered more odious than a teacher who is sneaky.
4 *Knowledge of power, and the ability to use it.* Change agents know that schools are political systems, and that the only way to change them is through the exercise of power. Recognizing this, the agent of change attempts to gain access to some of the power within the school, and to use it.
5 *Clarity of values.* Going counter to the prevalent values of the school is not an easy thing to do. Most people, after all, are proponents of the status quo; they have internalized the values dictated by the predominant power structure. It is extremely difficult, in the face of almost total disagreement, to maintain the desire for change and a clear vision of what that change would look like.
6 *Energy.* Nobody in schools is hired to make changes. People are hired to keep things the same. It requires a great deal of energy, therefore, to take it upon oneself to work for change.

It is not easy to say whether or not there is any future in challenging the culture of the schools. After all, the progressive movement of the 1930s, the math and science movements of the early 1960s, the humanistic movement of the late 1960s, and the "back to basics" movement of the 1970s have all left the schools relatively untouched. The culture of the school was able to absorb these movements and not change very much. And most of the critics of traditional schools, from Dewey to Illich, Neill to Holt, have written their books, been read and ignored. Most of the special, innovative projects last only as long as there is federal money to support them. Idealistic young teachers enter the profession, try to change things, are disillusioned or anesthetized. All in all, there is not much room for optimism if one is looking for change.

There will always be change agents, however, individuals who demand improvement and are willing to work for it. It is those people who have a chance to make a difference, and for whom this chapter was written.

SUMMARY

The cultural perspective is, in a sense, a perspective on ourselves. It is focused not so much on the emotionally disturbed child as on our reactions to such children: the fear, disgust, pity, anger, concern, amusement, hate or love that we as adults feel toward children who do not or cannot see things our way. We may hide our feelings toward the children, clothing them in clinical jargon, behavior management systems or therapeutic techniques, but it is those feelings that determine our response to the problem of disturbance.

The two basic responses described in this chapter, the pro-cultural and the counter-cultural, seem to be fundamentally incompatible. Every bit of energy aimed toward "curing" the child (i.e., fitting her into the culture) adds power to the status quo, tacitly endorsing the rightness of the way things are. Conversely, any energy turned toward changing the culture does little, in the short run, to make the lives of children-seen-as-disturbed any more pleasant or productive.

The issue of emotional disturbance from the cultural perspective is this: the culture must maintain certain standards of behavior if it is to offer any stability from generation to generation. At the same time, flexibility in those standards and a greater tolerance for deviance are necessary if the culture is to adapt to the increasing diversity of its membership and to grow in its capability to discover novel solutions to old problems.

DISCUSSION QUESTIONS

1. How could the technique of counseling be both a pro-cultural and a counter-cultural intervention?
2. How are handicapped children portrayed in the media?
3. Mary Ann, an upper-middle-class teenager, was convinced by the Great Boffo, the leader of a religious cult, to join his group. While living with this group, she was taught to reject the "thought control" that had been imposed on her by her parents. She became "enlightened" through what her parents later called "brainwashing." Three months later, Mary Ann was kidnapped by her parents. She was then "de-programmed" through techniques similar to those used by the Great Boffo.

    In what ways was Mary Ann treated as emotionally disturbed by Boffo? By her parents? What is the difference between brainwashing and enlightenment?
4. Mark, age 8, attends a special class for the emotionally disturbed and takes Ritalin each day. This drug has the effect of calming him down and making him more pleasant to be around. Janice, age 20, attends a teacher's college and smokes marijuana every day. This drug has the effect of calming her down and making her more pleasant to be around. In what ways are these instances of drug use similar and in what ways are they different?

FOR FURTHER READING

The teachings of Don Juan, Carlos Castaneda. A book that leads the reader through the experience of culture shock.

Between teacher and child, Haim Ginott. A gentle book by a gentle man; his approach, while simple and down to earth, involves a radical change in the way we view children.

The underachieving school, John Holt. Another radical approach; not as upbeat as Postman and Weingartner, but more intense and compelling.

Brave new world, Aldous Huxley. By looking at the logical extension of some of our cultural values, the reader can question their merit.

Deschooling America, Ivan Illich. Illich suggests that doing away with schools as we know them may be the only answer to school problems.

Summerhill, A. S. Neill. The classic description of a free school that works.

Teaching as a subversive activity, Neil Postman and Charles Weingartner. A taste of radical thinking; their views are presented with humor and uplifting optimism.

Blaming the victim, William Ryan. Ryan proposes a radically different way of viewing "unfortunates."

The culture of school and the problem of change, Seymour Sarason. An anthropological perspective on the schools.
Crisis in the classroom, Charles E. Silverman. A perspective on some of the practices in schools that are harmful to children, and some of the alternatives.
The myth of mental illness, Thomas Szasz. A radical examination of our assumptions about insanity and emotional disturbance.
The sociology of teaching, Willard Waller. A historical perspective on the realities of school life.

REFERENCES

Argyris, C. Diagnosing defenses against the outsider. *Journal of Social Issues*, 1952, *8*, 24–34.
Becker, H. S. The teacher in the authority system of the public school. *Journal of Educational Psychology*. 1953, *27*, 128–141.
Bredo, E. Collaborative relations among elementary school teachers. *Sociology of Education*, 1977, *50*, 300–309.
Brophy, J. E. & Good. T. L. Teachers' communication of differential expectations for children's classroom performance. *Journal of Educational Psychology,* 1970, *61*, 365–374.
Brown, D., & Brown, S. T. *Consulting with elementary school teachers*. Boston: Houghton Mifflin, 1975.
Carter, R. D. *Help! These kids are driving me crazy*. Champaign, Ill.: Research Press, 1972.
Christianson, T. A method of identifying maladjusted children in the classroom. *Mental Hygiene*, 1967, *5*, 574–575.
Combs, A. W., Blume, R. A., Newman, A. J., & Wass, H. L. *The professional education of teachers*. Boston: Allyn & Bacon, 1974.
Dinkmeyer, D., & Carlson, J. *Consulting*. Columbus, Ohio: Charles E. Merrill, 1973.
Eddy, E. M. *Becoming a teacher*. New York: Teachers College Press, 1969.
Edman, M. *A self-image of primary school teachers*. Detroit, Mich.: Wayne State University Press, 1968.
Henry, J. *Culture against man*. New York: Random House, 1963.
Hirshoren, A., & Heller, G. G. Programs for adolescents with behavior disorders: The state of the art. *Journal of Special Education*, 1979, *13*(3), 275–281.
Holt, J. *Freedom and beyond*. New York: Dell, 1972.
Illich, I. *Deschooling society*. New York: Harper & Row, 1970.
Jersild, A. T. *When teachers face themselves*. New York: Teachers College Press, 1955.
Knoblock, P., & Goldstein, A. P. *The lonely teacher*. Boston: Allyn & Bacon, 1971.
Kozol, J. *Death at an early age*. New York: Houghton Mifflin, 1972.
Lilly, M. S. Special education: A teapot in a tempest. *Exceptional Children*, 1970, *37*, 43–49.
Lortie, D. C. *Schoolteacher*. Chicago: University of Chicago Press, 1975.
McHugh, P. *Defining the situation*. Indianapolis, Ind.: Bobbs-Merrill, 1968.
Meltzer, B. N., Petras, J. W., & Reynolds, L. T. *Symbolic interactionism*. London: Routledge & Kegan Paul, 1975.
Miller, J. Consumer response to theoretical role models in school psychology. *Journal of School Psychology*, 1974, *12*, 310–317.
Montgomery, M. D. The special educator as consultant—some strategies. *Teaching Exceptional Children*, 1978, *10*(4), 110–112.

Newman, R. G. Conveying essential messages to the emotionally disturbed child at school. *Exceptional Children*, 1961, *28*, 199–204.
Pettitt, G. A. *Prisoners of culture*. New York: Charles Scribner's Sons, 1970.
Rhodes, W. C., & Paul, J. L. *Emotionally disturbed and deviant children: new views and approaches*. Englewood Cliffs, N.J.: Prentice-Hall, 1978.
Rhodes, W. C., & Tracy, M. *A study of child variance*. Ann Arbor: University of Michigan Press, 1975.
Ryan, W. *Blaming the victim*. New York: Vintage Books, 1971.
Sarason, S. *The culture of the school and the problem of change*. Boston: Allyn & Bacon, 1971.
Schlechty, P. C. *Teaching and social behavior*. Boston: Allyn & Bacon, 1976.
Seaberg, D. I. *The four faces of teaching*. Pacific Palisades, Calif.: Goodyear, 1974.
Szasz, T. S. *The myth of mental illness*. New York: Harper & Row, 1974.
Waller, W. W. *The sociology of teaching*. New York: John Wiley & Sons, 1932.
Warren, R. L. Context and isolation: The teaching experience in an elementary school. *Human Organization*, 1975, *34*(2), 139–148.
Wiederholt, J. L., Hammill, D. D., & Brown, V. *The resource teacher: A guide to effective practices*. Boston: Allyn & Bacon, 1978.

Section Three

Teaching Approaches

THIS SECTION provides specific information about approaches to teaching emotionally disturbed and behavior disordered children in the classroom.

In order for a teacher to be able to teach these children, she must be able to manage and motivate behavior so that success in learning is possible for the child. The teacher wants to intervene positively in situations that are distracting or otherwise working against an organized educational setting. The teacher must create a curriculum and choose teaching methods that have a high likelihood of succeeding. This involves practical decisions about what to do in the classroom and how to go about it.

The day-to-day problems faced by the teacher of emotionally disturbed children are many and complex. The teacher needs a broad intellectual base for thinking about why approach A may work better than approach B with a particular child. The well-trained teacher will be aware of the kinds of questions to ask about children in the classroom—disturbed and disturbing—and alternative ways to answer those questions. The teacher's choices about teaching methods should reflect awareness of reasonable options. In making these choices the teacher does not necessarily decide that one theoretical perspective is better than or more appropriate than another in a particular situation, although that may sometimes be the case. Rather, the teacher's decisions about instruction, curriculum and behavior management should reflect an informed and creative integration of ideas about the nature of the problem and how to address it. Thus, an eclectic perspective that makes use of existing theories and knowledge about behavior and social settings is the best guide for teaching. The teacher is an integrator and synthesizer of ideas and information whose educational practices are informed by that synthesis. The synthesis changes as the problems to be understood and addressed change.

Section Three presents practical methods for teachers to use in the management of behavior and in instruction. These methods draw their rational support from the theoretical perspectives presented in Section Two. Specific teaching and behavior management strategies are presented, based on an integrative perspective. The guidance offered to the teacher is in the form of examples that can be adapted to the teacher's individual classroom. The examples can be adjusted to the teacher's own individual style, values, beliefs and situation. The array of suggestions will give the teacher an idea of the range of techniques from which she can choose as an informed decision maker.

Section Three includes the following chapters:

11 Curriculum Design and Educational Programming
12 Behavior Management
13 Educational Methods
14 Affective Education

11

Curriculum Design and Educational Programming

main points

1 Emotionally disturbed children can and should be expected to learn. They are not fragile creatures, hurt by expectations to achieve; rather they are children, like all children, who need help and support in the process of growth and development.

2 Problems in learning do not automatically disappear as emotional problems improve; therefore, learning and emotional problems must be dealt with concomitantly.

3 Achievement and success breed confidence and growth in self-esteem. Central to a curriculum for emotionally disturbed children should be a mechanism for ensuring that children experience success. With success, it is generally believed that children will have the confidence to undertake new challenges.

4 Increased competence contributes to adaptive functioning. As children acquire new skills, they are more capable and less deviant.

5 The nature of the teacher-student relationship has considerable influence upon the success of any curriculum or educational program.

6 Curricula for the emotionally disturbed must be individualized. Because emotionally disturbed children are such a heterogeneous group, each child's social, emotional and academic needs must be individually considered.

7 Curricula for emotionally disturbed children should be carefully planned and organized in accord with individual children's needs. The development of programs should not be haphazard.

8 While the content and methods of curricula for emotionally disturbed children do vary, most emphasize techniques for managing behavior, coping with motivational forces and providing remedial instruction in academic areas.

9 Since there is relatively little comparative data on the various curricular approaches and since no one technique works for all teachers with all children all of the time, approaches from various theories of behavior should be used.

This chapter was written by **Betty C. Epanchin**, University of North Carolina at Chapel Hill, and **Virginia J. Dickens**, Fayetteville State University.

CURRICULUM is a course of study, the framework of an educational program. It is the structure upon which educational planning rests and one of the primary vehicles for meeting educational goals.

It is defined variously in both general and special education. Some authors view curriculum as broad and all-inclusive while others restrict its scope to academic content or specific activities. For example, Rhodes (1963) defines curriculum as the "twenty-four hour teaching-learning transaction conducted between the teacher and the learner" (p. 1). In contrast to the broad definition of Rhodes is the more narrowly focused definition of Hewett and Taylor (1980). They define curriculum as "any lesson, activity or assignment given to the child which is directed toward assisting him in achieving competence" (p. 108).

Both approaches to definition, the broad and the narrow, have advantages and disadvantages. A broad definition holds schools accountable for learning that takes place in incidental encounters throughout the school day as well as during organized classroom experiences. While undoubtedly learning does occur throughout the day, it is difficult, if not impossible, to plan and specify objectives for all behaviors and to evaluate with confidence all aspects of the day. Conversely, if curriculum is only the academic content to be taught, the scope of the curriculum is more manageable; however, it is difficult, and maybe impossible, to obtain agreement on what the content should be.

In addition to differences in opinion about the scope of curriculum, there are also differences in opinion about what should be included. Stephens (1977) maintains that "teaching methods and curriculum are separate areas in instruction, although each influences the other. Methods represent the how. These are instructional approaches. Curriculum, however, is the what—the content to be taught" (p. 93). Ekstein and Motto (1969) take a different view. They maintain that "the concept of curriculum does not simply contain the thought of the goal to be reached at the end of the school term but also conveys the idea of a process leading to it. The means-and-end discussions, the subject-versus-method controversies, focus on but two inseparable sides of the same coin" (p. 48).

Although many authors stress the importance of methods or process, their views differ with respect to which methods are most effective or therapeutic. These differences stem from different theoretical positions and consequently are evaluated by different criteria. As a result, comparison between models is difficult.

In this chapter we will review critical components of educational programming which affect curriculum, describe systems and techniques for individualizing curriculum, and outline steps for designing a curriculum for emotionally disturbed children.

Components of Educational Programming that Affect Curriculum

Curriculum does not exist in a vacuum. Rather, it is determined, at least to a large extent, by the educational system in which it is used, by the teachers who choose and interpret it and by the children for whom it is designed. Furthermore, the success of a curriculum depends, to a large extent, upon the educational system's expectations for it and upon how effectively the teacher uses it. These are variables from which curriculum cannot be extricated and, therefore, must be considered when issues of curriculum and educational programming are discussed.

The Educational System

Purpose of the educational program. In our society the function of education is to help prepare children for adulthood by contributing to their socialization, their learning of our cultural heritage and their acquisition of skills necessary to function in society. The purpose of curriculum is to present the content and methods needed to carry out this mission.

With emotionally disturbed children, education serves an even broader function because, in order to provide these children with experiences which will help them adjust to society, remedial and therapeutic interventions are needed in many spheres of functioning. Education is a means both of helping children learn the requisite new skills and of re-experiencing old conflicts in new, more growth-supporting ways. It is a normalizing force in the lives of emotionally disturbed children because it is an experience common to all children and one which requires accommodation and adjustment to norms. By meeting the expectations of school, children learn what they can do, what their limits are and how others view their accomplishments. These experiences contribute to the child's life adjustment. Curriculum, therefore, is a means of providing for academic and social development; it is also a means through which personal problems are treated.

Education and curriculum have not always been viewed as having such a potentially positive role in the lives of disturbed children. In the early part of this century many viewed education as a repressive, damaging force in the lives of children. Progressive educators of the day, often trained within the theoretical framework of early psychoanalytic thinking, were critical of Victorian society's suppressive, rigid mores and espoused the belief that education should liberate children's instincts and minimize the trauma of limits. Therefore, it was believed that parents and teachers should allow children to grow and develop in a permissive, accepting atmosphere.

In 1931, when explaining why psychoanalysts acquired such beliefs, Anna Freud observed that the early psychoanalysts learned to view education "from its worst side" because the analyst "is engaged in the therapeutic work of resolving such inhibitions and disturbances in the (child's) development" (quoted in Ekstein and Motto, 1969, p. 8). And, indeed, therapists do tend to hear the child's side of the problem, the child's view of school. Although sometimes children's views are horrifyingly accurate, often they contain the child's distortions of the situation—distortions born out of fear, anger and self-doubt. Lacking evidence to counter the children's fears, clinicians and teachers often came to believe the children's view that school was repressive and harmful. They believed that the demands to achieve in school would overwhelm the inadequate egos of emotionally disturbed children. This fear persisted in the literature at least into the 1950s and, even today, is expressed in schools when concern about expecting disturbed children to work and to conform is voiced.

Gradually, however, educators and clinicians began to see education as having a wider purpose than that of simply freeing instincts. Anna Freud, speaking to this issue, suggested that there should be at each developmental stage in the child's life "the right proportion of instinct gratification and instinct restriction" (in Ekstein and Motto, 1969, pp. 8–9). While it is difficult to determine what Freud thinks the correct proportion of success and frustration should be, she clearly is acknowledging the constructive aspects of control and the potentially destructive aspects of indulgence.

Carl Fenichel, founder of the League School, the first day school for severely disturbed children, addressed this issue.

> At the beginning, we believed that our teachers should play a permissive and relatively unstructured "therapeutic" role that permitted their children the freedom to ventilate hostilities, aggressions, and primitive drives until basic intra-physic conflicts were "worked-through" and resolved. We assumed this was what mentally ill children with weak, fragile egos and strong, over-whelming conflicts needed.
>
> Our children taught us otherwise. We learned that disorganized children need someone to organize their world for them. We began to realize that disturbed children fear their own loss of control and need protection against their own impulses; that what they needed were teachers who knew how to limit as well as to accept them. We learned the need for a highly organized program of education and training that could bring order, stability, and direction to minds that are disorganized, unstable, and unpredictable. (Fenichel, 1971, pp. 339–402)

Gradually clinicians learned that the education of emotionally disturbed children could not be postponed until their therapy was finished. The problems in learning, that so many emotionally disturbed children have, did not disappear as their emotional problems improved. In fact, for many children as they grew older and further behind their age mates, new problems arose that appeared to be related to their academic retardation. Furthermore, children who had not been having academic problems developed them if their schooling was not maintained.

Today, while most intervention programs view education as having a critical role in therapeutic programming, the nature of this role does vary. For example, curricula designed for use with emotionally disturbed children in public schools who receive no outside therapy must provide for these children's emotional, social and academic needs. Teachers need to consciously plan activities that will facilitate growth and development in the affective domain and that will allow the children opportunities to work on their problems. In contrast, in residential programs where children are in therapy or therapy-like activities much of the day, curricula may be more traditionally academic. In such a program, the responsibility for therapeutic intervention is divided among several aspects of the program. It is the function of the school program to provide a neutral, normalizing influence in the child's life. It is the function of therapy to focus on the child's inner life in an effort to help the child resolve conflict.

This is not meant to imply that teachers in the public schools should also be therapists or that teachers who work in conjunction with therapeutic teams are not therapeutic and should not deal with affective issues. Teachers in public schools are teachers who teach academic subjects as well as social skills, problem-solving techniques, awareness of affective states and so on. The scope of what they need to teach is broader because they are being asked to provide the child's only treatment. How they provide the treatment, however, is by teaching, not by "therapy." In contrast, a teacher on a treatment team needs to understand the nature of the child's problem but usually deals with it on a here-and-now, manifest level that focuses upon academic content (Blom, 1969). In both settings, therefore, education is therapeutic, that is, beneficial to the child. How that end result is accomplished, however, varies and, as a result, so does the curriculum.

Legislative mandate. Today there is another system-level factor that has an impact on curriculum, namely legislation. Embedded in P.L. 94-142 is the mandate that educational programming for handicapped children be monitored, individualized and comprehensive. Through this legislation an effort is being made to ensure that programming and services for handicapped children are modified and changed as children grow and develop; that curricula be tailored to the needs of individual children; and that curricula focus upon children's total functioning, not just their academic performance. In spite of the fact that educators have encountered numerous problems in implementing this legislation, the intent of P.L. 94-142 is very appropriate.

In order to program for emotionally disturbed children, teachers need to be willing and able to devise education plans for individual children, to change and modify these plans as the children develop and to plan for experiences that promote social, emotional and cognitive growth. Superficially, such a curriculum may look very much like the standard curriculum; upon close scrutiny, however, it is clear that careful attention has been given to individual children's abilities, interests, likes, dislikes, fears and foibles. As these change, so does the curriculum. Such careful matching of learning experiences with individual children cannot be haphazard.

The Teacher

Teachers of the emotionally disturbed are usually responsible for designing, adapting or choosing curricular materials; therefore, in this role they exert considerable influence over curriculum. Yet, they have an even more fundamental role of translating, using and applying the curriculum.

For some time educators have voiced the belief that the nature of the relationship established between the teacher and the child is the most important ingredient in the successful teaching of these children. For example, in 1907 Miss Julia Richman, superintendent of the district in which a probationary school for the "truant, delinquent, and incorrigible" was located, wrote in her annual report to the New York City Board of Education:

It must be understood, however, that tactfulness, sympathy, patience and personal magnetism on the part of the teacher are the first essentials for success in this work. As these attributes are often found in men and women not pedagogically sound along other lines, the task of making skillful teachers of such material is not always easy. (Berkowitz & Rothman, 1967, pp. 9–10)

Wanda Wright, first principal of the school at Bellevue Hospital, saw the success of the curriculum as almost totally dependent upon the teacher. She believed that the smooth operation of the program depended upon the children's acceptance of their teacher, their attitude toward their teacher and their respect for her knowledge and ability to teach. Wright (1967) states "With these factors present it matters little what is taught. This is not to say subject matter is not important, but rather that it is of primary importance for the children to feel they are learning whatever the subject matter" (p. 109). This view is echoed by Morse (1979) with regard to a self-control curriculum; "Who and how the teaching is done can well be more important in the way the child learns self-control than the curriculum in abstract. This is the confounding element in teaching in general and in affective education in particular" (p. 84).

In explaining why the teacher-student relationship is so important, Ekstein and Motto (1969) maintain that children learn to care about and identify with their teacher and her values. Among the values which children incorporate are the teacher's love of knowledge and learning. As the children grow and develop, they move from learning because of love for the teacher (i.e., wishing to please) to loving learning itself; the value of learning is incorporated and becomes intrinsically motivating. In Ekstein and Motto's words this process is the transition from "learning for love to love of learning." Similarly, Long, Morse, and Newman (1980) note that "pupils learn through a process of unconscious identification with significant adults in their lives. This means the teacher's personal appearance, attitudes, and behavior are important factors in teaching which must be evaluated continuously" (p. 280).

In placing so much emphasis on the teacher-student relationship or on the role of the teacher in the learning process, emphasis is also being placed on methods—on how the teacher helps the child believe that success is possible, on how the teacher makes learning seem important and fun and on how the teacher makes school appear inviting and pleasant to the child. Ekstein and Motto (1969) view the curriculum as an "external organizer that facilitates the learning process" because it "is the bridge between the teacher and the learner" (p. 57). In this analogy it is how the teacher helps the child cross the bridge that is most important.

Specifying the nature of a good relationship is difficult, however, because it varies with different pairs of teachers and children. Furthermore, relationships are intangible and thereby hard to define concretely. Nonetheless, when a good relationship exists, an atmosphere conducive to learning is created. The following conditions are critical elements in creating this type of relationship:

1 *The teacher and student regard each other positively.* Children need to feel valued and safe. They need to be able to trust that their teacher will

respect and accept their efforts and not ridicule or expose their mistakes. Quite simply, they need to believe that their teacher likes them. This condition of positive regard is often most accurately assessed by how the teacher feels toward the child. If the teacher does not genuinely like at least some qualities of the child, it is highly unlikely that the child will feel valued.

2 *The teacher conveys a purposeful attitude toward learning and achieving.* Many emotionally disturbed children dislike school and are vigilant in their search for ways to avoid school work and learning. If teachers are not invested in learning and in teaching, they may unwittingly support the child's resistances and thereby indirectly convey either that learning is not important or that the teacher does not believe the child can do the work.

3 *The teacher shows a willingness and ability to deal with problems and conflicts.* When dealing with emotionally disturbed children, few good teacher-student relationships blossom spontaneously. In order to develop such a relationship the teacher often must demonstrate to the children that their fears and anxieties can be mastered and are comprehensible. This means being able and willing to confront problems directly when they arise and to help children successfully find resolutions.

4 *The teacher is confident and personally secure.* Since many emotionally disturbed children oppose all efforts to help them learn new skills and attitudes, it is easy to become discouraged. Teachers who lack confidence in their ability to teach or who need a great deal of approval from their students are likely to lose their helping and objective view of the child. Teachers need to maintain a relatively objective attitude toward the child and the methods being used with the child in order to assess what is going wrong, to seek outside advice when needed and to plan different strategies when indicated.

The Children

In discussing curriculum for the emotionally disturbed, Morse (1969) states, "There is one point universally agreed upon by special teachers: the program must be individualized (p. 345)." He attributes this need for individualization to the children. "Each child is a school unto himself" (p. 345). There are bright and academically talented children who use academic involvement as an escape from the world of people, a world in which they feel inadequate. There are children whose thinking is concrete and language skills are poor. They are significantly behind their age mates academically and have little tolerance for the frustrations encountered in school work. Still other children present complex pictures of physiological deficits which are compounded by motivational problems and excessive dependency on their environment. Consequently, curriculum must be individualized both in method and content.

For example, with the bright child who is socially isolated, attention needs to be given to teaching the child ways to interact. As a means of providing emotional support to the child, stories about other shy and inhibited people might be assigned. The child might be asked to be a peer tutor, or rewards might be given for social interaction and limits set on the amount of time the child can spend in solitary academic work.

For the child who has little tolerance for frustration and is academically behind his age mates, even a remedial educational program may need to be adapted in order to provide the child with extensive success experiences. Only after the child has had sufficient emotional support through academic successes might the actual remediation program be started. Even then, the remedial program may need to be paced slowly in order to match the child's ability to tolerate frustrations.

For the child with physiological deficits, the teacher may need to teach the child about his problems as well as offer remedial instruction in academic areas. Using such an approach might be indicated as a means of helping the child become more accepting of himself. If the child learns more about the problem and how other people cope with it, he also can learn strategies to help himself deal with the problems.

Not only must curriculum be geared to remediating children's emotional and academic problems, it must also be geared to children's *normal*, developmental needs. Attention should be given to what is appropriate for children at a particular age or developmental level. Background experiences and personal interests should be considered as well.

Individualizing Curriculum

Individualizing Academic Content

Given the practical, humanistic and legislative mandates that point to the use of an individualized approach to curriculum for the emotionally disturbed, one must ask, how is this done? What techniques or approaches are used in order to meet individual children's needs?

In order to answer these questions, one must first specify what *individualization* is. It is, most importantly, an attitude of viewing a class of children as individual people with individual needs, wishes, fears, likes, dislikes and abilities. This does not mean that teachers who individualize do not believe in the force of the group. On the contrary, group life, as a force in the classroom that affects individuals, must be carefully considered, along with many other elements that impinge upon individuals. Successful individualization requires the teacher to know and to value each individual. In a classroom that is truly individualized, teachers do not stop with the observation that Karen seems preoccupied. They want to know if or how they can help. Individualization is the antithesis of indifference.

Individualization also requires that the teacher have a system for organizing and managing the classroom so that individual children's needs can be accommodated in a natural way. Teachers try not to plan, and certainly not to repeat, activities that embarrass or defeat an individual.

The term individualization has sometimes inappropriately been understood to mean individual tutoring. Teachers do not have to tutor children individually in order to individualize, although this technique is frequently used during portions of the school day. Teachers do, however, have to think about and plan for each child's needs. With some groups, individualization may be accomplished within the group at all times, while with other groups, in order to individualize, teachers may need to have children working independently during a large portion of the day. Again, it depends upon the teacher, the children and the system.

A variety of approaches are described in the literature for individualizing instruction. Also, a variety of techniques are described which help teachers plan for and accommodate to individual children's emotional and social needs.

Learning centers. Learning centers are places in the classroom where materials and instructions for certain activities are arranged so that children can go to the center and independently carry out an assignment. While learning centers can be used in a variety of ways, they are especially useful as substitutes for seat work, that is, as an interesting way for children to gain additional practice or to delve into enrichment activities or as an instant alternative when an activity is not going well for a particular child.

In a learning center the stage is already set. Children may go to the center, get their instructions, carry out the activity and record their progress. Sometimes learning centers are set up so that teacher and aide have little contact with the child and sometimes centers are set up so that adults or other children guide and other children help. Hewett and Taylor (1980) draw upon this concept extensively in their orchestrated classroom.

Instructional units. Instructional units are another means by which the curriculum can be individualized. In this approach, children are assigned the same topic to study and given assignments that are to be completed within the same amount of time but the assignments are all different. Some are shorter and less complex than others. Different standards for evaluation may be used. Organizationally this approach resembles a study group with each member having a different part to contribute. In determining individual children's assignments, factors such as the child's functioning level, attention span and specific interests are considered in relation to the available materials.

For example, when teaching an instructional unit, the teacher starts by choosing a general topic that is of interest to the children. A variety of materials (e.g., books, worksheets, filmstrips, records) on different levels are collected. A group of children are assigned the overall topic. For example, a topic could be "Describe life in a Cherokee Indian village." With such an assignment, each child contributes to the total product. An artistic nonreader might illustrate reports done by more verbally oriented students. A poor reader might gather information from a filmstrip and record rather than from books. Easily distracted children who have difficulty staying on task might be assigned the task of making Indian clothes or replicas of teepees rather than being expected to read a great deal of information. It is often helpful for these children to have an assignment that keeps them constantly busy motorically as well as cognitively.

In sequential tutoring the teacher moves from student to student, giving help as needed on individualized seat work.

This approach is particularly suited to social studies, science, health and some math (e.g., measurement and Roman numerals) lessons although it may be used with other subject areas. The structure of this approach not only enables the teacher to individualize instruction but also to teach children how to work in groups. Lee (1971) describes the "enterprise unit" in the ReEd curriculum (see Chapter 8). This concept utilizes the basic design of an instructional unit but is initiated by the children's spontaneously expressed interests. Slagle (1969) advocates the use of "naturalized" and "actualized" teaching in the ReEd curriculum. Naturalized teaching involves the use of the "real world as a teaching tool" (p. 34) whenever possible. Actualized teaching is providing experiences which give children a chance to apply concepts or to utilize skills that they have just learned. For example, after studying fractions in the morning mathematics class, the children might have a cooking lesson in the afternoon which requires the use of fractions, such as making half a recipe. Both naturalized and actualized teaching fit easily into a unit approach.

Sequential tutoring. Sequential tutoring is another approach to individualization. This is a means of providing individual tutoring within a group. Children are given individualized seat work and, as they work, teachers tutor individual children. The tutoring takes place as teachers rotate from student to student, giving help as needed, or as children take their work to the teacher who is stationed at a desk. In the latter approach, children may seek teacher help when needed either for clarification of their assignment or in order to obtain a new assignment.

Seat work for individual children usually varies a great deal. Some children may have assignment sheets on which directions are given for work in a textbook or workbook. Other children may have manila folders in which there are worksheets and workbooks for them to complete. Still other children may be expected to use some type of teaching machine such as the Language Master, the Cyclo-teacher or electronic game machines. Some teachers have found programmed texts to be particularly useful during sequential tutoring times because children can have immediate feedback as they work.

Sequential tutoring is a popular approach to individualization. Morse, Cutler, and Fink (1964) found in their survey of public school classes for the emotionally disturbed that individual work was the rule. Except during social studies, "the classroom pattern was teacher-pupil one-to-one while free activity or seat work went on for the others" (p. 58). They noted, however, that sequential tutoring had shortcomings. When the teacher rotated from child to child a "continual nagging, competitive" process tended to develop. "The sight of children receiving the teacher's response while others were denied it except for a periodic turn upset many youngsters in this feast or famine arrangement" (Morse et al., 1964, p. 76). Brendtro and Stern (1967) advocate that the teacher be stationed at a desk and children come to the teacher. With this arrangement, they believe, childen are not distracted by the teacher's wanderings, and they may feel less resistant to receiving help since they initiate the interaction. Also, teacher attention is contingent upon completion of work, not upon having trouble. Children do not receive immediate feedback with this approach, however. Furthermore, no matter how carefully planned, individual seat work usually is not as stimulating and as intriguing as other learning approaches. Hence, if overused, it may contribute to children becoming bored, distracted and, therefore, disruptive. Morse et al. observe that the teacher who is able to use this technique successfully is the teacher who can "give split attention, providing something minimally necessary for all while providing maximally for the one" (p. 75–76).

Peer and cross-age tutoring. Peer or cross-age tutoring is another form of tutoring which teachers can utilize as a means of providing children with individual instruction. Children are trained and supervised by a teacher to teach younger children or to teach classmates. When intra-class tutoring is used, teachers need to be careful to give all children a chance to teach. If only the best students are allowed to tutor, a type of elitism may be condoned. Poor students may be able to drill other students in spelling or to teach other children an athletic skill. Turnbull and Schulz (1979) suggest the use of a classroom resource bank as a means of initiating peer teaching. In this technique, students interview each other in order to find out what talents and skills individual children have. A class directory is developed which lists and gives information about each class member. When help is needed, the directory is a resource.

Contracting. In this procedure a contract is developed between teacher and child (usually), or between teacher and group, or child and child. These

When intra-class peer tutoring is used to individualize instruction, all children should be given a chance to teach.

contracts may be determined by the teacher completely, may be mutually developed by teacher and student or may have some teacher-determined and some student-determined elements. Nonetheless, the contract is a written agreement between two parties that specifies what is expected of each party. Teachers may use contracts to outline individual assignments for a period, for a day or even for a week. Contracts often specify not only what work is expected but also what behavior is desired (see Chapter 12 for additional discussion of behavioral contracting).

Frequently contracts are tied to reward systems. For example, if Rachel finishes her contract within the week or at a specified quality level, she earns a predetermined reward. Since many emotionally disturbed children are prone to interpreting situations that are personally disappointing as unfair, predetermined contracts are particularly helpful. The conditions are clearly specified at the outset and, therefore, the potential for distorting the situation is reduced.

Task analysis. This procedure is currently receiving a great deal of attention in special education. In their survey of public school classes for the emotionally disturbed, Morse et al. (1964) report that in most classrooms the standard curriculum was used "though on a more corrective teaching basis with rate, level, and particularly the expectation reduced" (p. 57). Although a comparable far-reaching survey has not been done in recent years, this practice still seems to be the most typical approach. Since one of the overriding objectives of working with most emotionally disturbed children is to help them adjust to regular classroom situations, the mastery of standard content and the use of common curricular materials is indicated whenever possible.

Task analysis can be very helpful in adjusting the rate, level and expectation of the curriculum. When content is too complex or too streamlined for particular children, teachers can use task analysis to clarify and truncate information and skills so that children can succeed. In task analysis the teacher identifies components of the required task and then teaches each component. For example, if a child is having difficulty learning how to regroup and borrow, the teacher may need to replace the standard materials with teacher-made ones that give the child an opportunity to learn components of regrouping before he tackles the total process. In effect, this enables the teacher to alter both the rate and expectation of the child's performance. (See Chapter 13 for more discussion of task analysis).

Precision teaching. This approach, developed by Ogden Lindsley, is a systematic way of teaching and evaluating progress. According to Howell, Kaplan, and O'Connell (1979), precision teaching "is best used when a teacher wants to gain knowledge and desires to apply technology as an aid to developing a more individualized program" (p. 143).

In this approach specific educational objectives are determined on the basis of assessment data. Children's work is frequently and carefully monitored, and precise data about their progress are plotted on a semilogarithmic chart. Progress, or lack of progress, may be readily seen. The data can be further analyzed to yield a rate of progress. This rate of progress enables teachers to project when a child is likely to master a particular objective. This approach, therefore, allows teachers to look at children's current functioning, to predict their future functioning and to project time lines for future achievement.

For additional reading on individualizing instruction, see the following, Blackburn and Powell (1976), Charles (1980), De Risi and Butz (1975), Dunn and Dunn (1972), Homme, Csanyi, Gonzales, and Rechs (1970), Kourilsky and Barry (1973), Kunzelmann, Cohen, Hulten, Martin, and Mingo (1970) and *Teaching Exceptional Children* (Spring, 1971).

Individualizing for Social and Emotional Needs

The primary purpose of individualizing for social and emotional needs is to enable children to feel and be perceived as successful and like the other children. In order to do this, teachers must have knowledge of, and be sensitive to, individual children's problems. Based upon this understanding, teachers can make minor adjustments in their curriculum plans that accommodate individual children's needs while not calling attention to their differences and problems. Such modifications usually are only necessary until the children become familiar and secure with the setting and teacher. Once a good teacher-student relationship is established and once a child starts deriving pleasure from achieving, the teacher does not have to be so wary of the child being threatened or bored. This does not mean, however, that teachers can stop being concerned about making the curriculum relevant and appealing. Almost all children benefit from such programming. It does mean that teachers usually can raise expectations and expect children to be more trusting and more secure once a good teacher-student relationship develops.

The following practices can be helpful in accommodating individual children's emotional and social needs.

Plan lessons that are appealing and exciting. For unmotivated, oppositional children, high-interest activities can allow them to save face and give up their anti-school stance. For these children, field trips, games, concrete rewards, special privileges or unusual projects may be necessary in order to engage them in learning and achieving. For other children, predictable, structured, familiar activities are most appealing. Novel lessons and field trips may be distressing. The teacher must discover what type of activities engage each child and see that they are frequently included in the daily schedule.

Avoid reminders of past failures. Books which were used in previous classes and which have the grade level clearly marked on them are constant reminders to children far behind their age mates of personal inadequacies and failures. New and different materials are usually more desirable.

Be sensitive to the appearance of materials. Many children glance at an assignment and if it appears to be more than they believe they can do, they reject it immediately. For them it may be psychologically safer to reject the work as "dumb" than to risk confirmation that they are "dumb." It is often wise, therefore, at least initially to make individual worksheets with fewer problems on them. In doing this, however, the teacher also needs to guard against making it too easy. If it looks too much like "baby work," the child is also likely to reject it.

Pay close attention to the content of materials. Because children often have strong positive and negative emotional reactions to the content of material they read, the teacher should carefully consider its potential impact. For the child who excels in athletics but has much difficulty academically, stories about athletic heroes' struggles can be very encouraging. On the other hand, emotionally charged stories which expose the child's fears may elicit the child's standard defense, and thus may be inappropriate reading material. (See Chapter 14 for a discussion of how reading materials may be used in helping children deal with their feelings.)

Reading is not the only area in which content should be considered. With a volatile group of pre-adolescent boys, who have many concerns about their sexual identity, a unit on sexual development may be very helpful. If, however, the content is not carefully paced and presented, students may find it too stimulating and as a result become disruptive. Teachers, however, should not resort to using only sterile, emotionally neutral content. On the contrary, exciting relevant materials are recommended as long as the child can integrate them. The point is that the teacher should try to anticipate how the child will react to content and screen out materials that may be too emotionally loaded and too stimulating. In addition, the teacher should try to find material of particular interest to the child.

Build in repetition and err on the side of being easy. With successful learners it is often wise to encourage them to try assignments which are slightly above their functional level. With unsuccessful learners, however, it is often better to give them work which they can quickly and successfully master. Children with long histories of failure often give up without trying or become easily frustrated with challenges. Overlearning, therefore, is often recommended, at least until the child gains more confidence in his ability to achieve. Stiles (1980) describes teaching an 8-year-old nonreader to read by carefully pacing the child's assignments so that he always believed he could do the work. Her account is an excellent example of how a teacher succeeded in helping an oppositional nonreader learn to read by blending an understanding of the child's fears about reading with a knowledge of the reading process. During this teaching-learning process Stiles consistently followed the child's cues about what he felt he could master. By allowing the child repeated successes, she helped him gain confidence in himself and his ability to read.

Allow the children some control over their schoolwork. Many emotionally disturbed children have a need for control. Psychodynamic writers postulate many reasons why children have this need but most writers agree that, regardless of the reason, it is a defense against vulnerability. If one controls others, one is less likely to feel helpless, to be subjected to hurt inflicted by others. When teachers counter children's attempts to control by imposing more control, the struggle usually ends in the teacher's defeat. If teachers use all their authority and power, the children's immediate rebellion may be squelched, but their feelings about being squelched may not disappear. Indeed, their resentment often intensifies. When teachers are not able to control children, teachers often feel threatened and frustrated. They may no longer be able to set a good example for conflict resolution. If children realize that they can control their teacher, they may actually become frightened by that power. Children generally find security in adults who are secure in their authority and, therefore, able to sidestep control struggles.

Giving children choices allows them to feel in control. Without threat to the teacher's control, children can decide upon the order of assignments and perhaps which one of several assignments shall be finished. Children may also be permitted to correct their work, to chart their progress, to vote on activities and to help select units of study. Rather than seeing children's attempts to control as a threat to authority, teachers may view such behavior as an effort to be autonomous and not vulnerable. Teachers can then help to channel the children's energy into productive, cooperative behavior.

Keep the child actively involved. Many emotionally disturbed children are highly susceptible to boredom. Many others are vulnerable to distractions both from the environment and from their own thoughts and concerns. It is especially important, therefore, that the teacher counter the potential for distraction and boredom by planning short, high-interest, novel lessons. Lectures, and even some demonstrations, can be disastrous, especially if the children are sitting close to each other or have pencils, papers or other supplies. Games, or other forms of sugar-coating, and tasks which require the child to watch, listen and do something are usually more successful. For example, when teaching the geographic location of a state, rather than pointing out neighboring states on a map or merely telling the child the names of border states, the teacher might give the class a worksheet on which there is an outline of all states. Using a master map, the teacher may point out neighboring states and have the children color and label the border states.

Use simple, straightforward, neutral language. Many emotionally disturbed children have marked deficits in communication skills. Anxious children often cannot remember a list of instructions, and disorganized children often have trouble with sequences. It may be necessary therefore to give directions at each step of an activity rather than all at once. Excess verbiage, complex or difficult terminology and emotionally loaded words all tend to increase the child's anxiety. When this happens, the child acts out, withdraws or becomes more disorganized. The teacher, therefore, must pay careful attention to the impact of language. An illustration of this is found in the story of the 7-year-old boy, who after a week of being in a residential treatment center was still having difficulty following routines and adjusting to expectations. Finally, in response to his teacher's reminder, "Follow instructions," he replied, "I don't know instructions. I've been trying to find him all week."

This amusing anecdote illustrates the importance of appropriate communication, and also underscores the difficulty of meeting individual children's needs. As Kauffman (1980) observes, "American public schools have not been smashing successes at individualized education programming in the past, even though they have mouthed the words and given assent to the idea" (p. 523). A great deal of skill in both interpersonal relations and educational programming, as well as careful, thorough planning for many details, is required in order to effectively individualize.

Steps for Designing a Curriculum for Emotionally Disturbed Children

In planning and refining a curriculum for individual children, the teacher needs to follow these general procedures.

Specify the nature of the child's social, behavioral and affective problems. These problems need to be described in specific operational terms whenever possible. To say that Joshua has a poor self-concept is to say very little. It is too global and therefore is not prescriptively useful. To say that he seems to lack confidence in his ability to learn to read is more useful.

Especially when paired with background data and observation of current behavior, such a statement is useful when planning an educational program.

Formulate hypotheses as to why these problems exist. Interventions should never be haphazard. We need to back up interventions with reasons and the reasons we cite grow out of the way we conceptualize problems. For example, if we observe Karen in class, and see that every time she cries she gets the teacher's attention, we may hypothesize that she has learned that crying gets the teacher's attention. We attribute the problematic behavior to learning and prescribe an intervention that helps the child learn more adaptive behavior.

This process of thinking through possible causes of the problem helps the teacher to choose the most appropriate intervention. Causal statements should always be viewed as hypotheses, however. We never know unequivocally why a condition exists. We can only observe factors that are associated with a problem. Then we can formulate hypotheses about what contributes to the problem and we can test our ideas. Because the factors that are associated with emotional problems are so complex, it is wise to focus on specific and immediate factors when identifying causes. When causal statements focus on specific factors, there is usually a constructive course of action to follow.

Determine the child's current level of academic functioning. In order to have a complete picture of the child's current academic functioning, two types of assessment are needed. The first, norm-referenced testing, is typically done during the diagnostic evaluation. It involves comparing a child's performance on a test with that of a representative sample of his age mates to determine whether the child has a learning deficit. The second type of assessment, criterion-referenced testing, is typically done by the teacher to determine what specific skills the child has mastered. This type of assessment is particularly helpful in establishing instructional objectives.

Determine in what way and to what extent the child's emotional problems affect his academic performance. While it is generally agreed that emotions and learning interact, the extent of this interaction remains a controversy. It seems to vary from child to child and to be a function of the severity of the child's problems. There are depressed children who lack energy and motivation to perform in school; there are psychotic children whose thoughts are so disordered that abstract learning is almost impossible; and there are angry, inhibited children whose fury at what seems to them to be unfair expectations is expressed through passive-aggressive noncompliance (i.e., not achieving). In each case the issues vary but in each an understanding of the interaction between affect and cognition is important.

Analyze the rate at which the child has been learning academic content. The rate of learning formula was first described by Libaw, Berres, and Coleman (1962). By determining the child's rate of learning, the teacher knows what the child has been doing and, therefore, has a guide as to what she may reasonably expect in the future. Rate of learning may be computed by using the following formula:

$$\frac{\text{current level of functioning}}{\text{number of years in school}} = \text{rate of learning}$$

The current level of functioning may be obtained from the grade equivalent score on a norm-referenced test. The number of years of school is expressed in decimals with September being the first month. For example, a child tested in April in his fourth year of school would have been in school 4.8 years.

If a child is progressing more slowly than his peers, the rate of learning will be less than 1. If the child is functioning at grade expectancy or better, the rate of learning will be 1 or greater than 1. The smaller the number, the greater the deficit; however, as the child progresses through school, any rate of learning less than 1 becomes more of a problem. For example, a child who is tested in March of the first grade with a .7 rate of learning is approximately five months behind what is expected for average first graders. Theoretically he has learned 70% of the standard curriculum. In February of the fifth grade, however, a .7 rate of learning means the child is approximately a year and a half behind his peers.

Obviously, rate of learning is an estimate of progress. There is considerable variation in the content tested by specific achievement tests and in the content taught by particular school systems (Jenkins & Pany, 1978). These variations do affect a child's rate of learning. Additionally, the child's intellectual ability should be considered. Children whose ability is below average usually should not be expected to progress as quickly as children with above-average ability. Again, however, the validity of the test results must be carefully considered. Many emotionally disturbed children function erratically on tests; hence, their IQ scores are often not considered to be indicative of their potential ability.

Nonetheless, when rate of learning and IQ are both considered, the teacher has data to use in projecting how much content in a given time period a child may be able to learn. Rate of learning can also be used to monitor a child's progress. If a child's rate of learning increases after a child is placed in a special classroom, the teacher has reason to believe the program is benefiting the child.

Carefully study the curriculum content which the child must eventually learn in order to fit into the mainstream. Often the standard curriculum must be adapted to individual children's needs. Some children need more repetition than typically occurs in regular classrooms. Some need specific skills taught in smaller, more concrete increments. Others benefit from faster pacing. For still others, certain parts of the curriculum may need to be omitted. In order to meet children's individual needs, teachers must be thoroughly familiar with curriculum content. For example, Fred, an oppositional boy who has not been motivated to learn, decides that he wants to catch up with his classmates in school. Naturally, his teacher wants to support his working toward this goal, but he currently is functioning three years behind his classmates. After studying the child, the teacher believes that Fred's negative attitude and lack of motivation are the primary causes of his learning problems rather than any specific learning disabilities. Given these problems, Fred's teacher hypothesizes that success in learning and clear evidence of progress toward his goal will be important elements in the ultimate reaching of his goal. After studying the math content which Fred must master in order to be on grade level, his teacher sees many possible shortcuts. She teaches skills in sequence but bypasses much of the practice work included in most textbooks. As soon as Fred is able to successfully complete five examples of a specific skill, he is allowed to advance to another skill. In so doing, Fred is able to feel encouraged by his rapid progress.

Project long-term goals which seem feasible and appropriate for the child. One of the ultimate goals for most emotionally disturbed children is to function effectively in the mainstream. In order to help a child achieve this, long-term goals need to be developed that minimize the differences between the emotionally disturbed child and his peers as efficiently and effectively as possible. Academic as well as social, behavioral and affective goals are needed.

Devise short-term instructional objectives for each long-term goal. Short-term instructional objectives should outline the hierarchy of skills to be taught as a means of reaching each long-term goal. The task analysis process discussed earlier in this chapter is useful when formulating short-term instructional objectives.

Plan activities and assignments that correspond to each instructional objective. Creativity pays great dividends in this process because high-interest and diverse activities and assignments are well received.

An effort should be made to plan activities that reflect individual children's special interests and that include a variety of instructional settings, such as quiet seat work, one-to-one tutoring, small-group instruction, large-group instruction and active games. Additionally, before teaching an activity, teachers should try it themselves to be certain that it is feasible, that it is neither too easy nor too difficult and that it is presented in the proper sequence.

Develop specific lesson plans. The lesson plan should include not only the instructional objective being taught but also the specific activities, materials and means of evaluation. The teacher should also consider behavior management strategies she will use and the readiness of the classroom. The necessary equipment and supplies must be available and in good working order.

In addition to the regular lesson plans, teachers need to plan alternative activities because frequently a lesson goes more quickly than anticipated or is not well received. Insisting that children complete an activity when it is not working may be inviting trouble. Consequently, teachers need to be alert to potential distress or boredom and be willing to move on to another activity.

An exception to this recommendation is when a teacher insists that a child complete an assignment in order to help the child learn that he *can,* in fact, do the work. This, however, is very different from insisting children do something just because it was planned and is next in the sequence.

Constantly evaluate. Be willing to reformulate ideas as children learn and change. Sound educational decisions are based on the actual documented performance of children as well as the teacher's feelings about how learning is taking place. Evaluation should occur each time a lesson or unit is taught to ascertain whether the objective was reached. This evaluation can take many forms, including observation, teacher-made criterion-referenced tests and formal assessment tools. Evaluation should be ongoing so that any changes in the choice of goals, objectives, activities or methods can be based on actual evaluation data. These data should be recorded on graphs, charts or some type of daily record. Many children benefit from seeing their performance on these visual charts and even from collecting and charting data.

SUMMARY

Curriculum is the vehicle through which teachers intervene in the lives of emotionally disturbed children. Because the term *curriculum* is ambiguous and because interventions are conceptualized in so many different ways, a generally accepted curriculum does not exist. Teachers do tend to agree, however, that long-term curriculum planning is important, that individualization in the classroom is necessary and that teaching plans must include some means of evaluating instruction. In addition, practitioners generally believe that the curriculum for emotionally disturbed children should serve yet another function—a therapeutic one. Through the curriculum teachers can introduce content that is emotionally relevant to a child. As the child masters the content, the child may also grapple with problems that are causing him distress. For this reason curriculum is a critical factor in successful intervention, but it is certainly not the only one. Teachers, systems and children, in addition to the curriculum, determine the appropriateness or inappropriateness of an intervention.

DISCUSSION QUESTIONS

1. Develop a rationale for the need to individualize curricula for emotionally disturbed children.
2. Describe four techniques for individualizing curricula. What are the advantages and disadvantages of each technique?
3. Outline an appropriate process for a teacher to follow when planning a curriculum for emotionally disturbed children.

REFERENCES

Berkowitz, P. H., & Rothman, E. P. *Public education for disturbed children in New York City: Application and theory.* Springfield, Ill.: Charles C Thomas, 1967.

Blackburn, J. E., & Powell, W. C. *One at a time all at once: The creative teacher's guide to individualizing instruction without anarchy.* Pacific Palisades, Calif.: Goodyear, 1976.

Blom, G. E. The concept "perceptually handicapped": Its assets and limitations. *Seminars in Psychiatry*, 1969, *1*, 253–261.

Brendtro, L. K., & Stern, P. R. A modification in the sequential tutoring of emotionally disturbed children. *Exceptional Children*, 1967, *33*, 517–21.

Charles, C. M. *Individualizing Instruction* (2nd ed.). St. Louis: C. V. Mosby, 1980.

De Risi, W. J., & Butz, G. *Writing behavorial contracts: A case simulation practice manual*. Champaign, Ill.: Research Press, 1975.

Dunn, R., & Dunn, K. *Practical approaches to individualizing instruction: Contracts and other effective teaching strategies*. West Nyack, N.Y.: Parker, 1972.

Ekstein, R., & Motto, R. L. *From learning for love to love of learning*. New York: Brunner/Mazel, 1969.

Fenichel, C. Psycho-educational approaches for seriously disturbed children in the classroom. In N. J. Long, W. C. Morse & R. G. Newman (Eds.), *Conflict in the classroom* (2nd ed.). Belmont, Calif.: Wadsworth, 1971.

Hewett, F. M., & Taylor, F. D. *The emotionally disturbed child in the classroom: The orchestration of success* (2nd ed.). Boston: Allyn & Bacon, 1980.

Homme, L., Csanyi, A., Gonzales, M., & Rechs, J. *How to use contingency contracting in the classroom*. Champaign, Ill.: Research Press, 1970.

Howell, K. W., Kaplan, J. S., & O'Connell, C. Y., *Evaluating exceptional children: A task analysis approach*. Columbus, Ohio: Charles E. Merrill, 1979.

Jenkins, J. R., & Pany, D. Standardized achievement tests: How useful for special education? *Exceptional Children*, 1978, *44*, 448–453.

Kauffman, J. M. Where special education for disturbed children is going: A personal view. *Exceptional Children*, 1980, *46*, 522–527.

Kourilsky, M. L., & Barry, B. F. *Classroom learning centers: A practical guide for teachers*. Los Angeles, Calif.: Educational Research, 1973.

Kunzelmann, H. K., Cohen, M. A., Hulten, W. J., Martin, G. L., & Mingo, A.R., *Precision teaching: An initial training* sequence. Seattle: Special Child Publications, 1970.

Lee, B. Curriculum design: The Re-Education approach. In N. J. Long, W. C. Morse & R. G. Newman (Eds.), *Conflict in the classroom* (2nd ed.). Belmont, Calif.: Wadsworth, 1971.

Libaw, F., Berres, F., & Coleman, J. C. A new method for evaluating the effectiveness of treatment of learning difficulties. *Journal of Educational Research*, 1962, *55*, 582–584.

Long, N. J., Morse, W. C., & Newman, R. G. *Conflict in the classroom*: The education of emotionally disturbed children (4th ed.). Belmont, Calif.: Wadsworth, 1980.

Morse, W. C. Educational designs. In H. W. Harshman (Ed.), *Educating the emotionally disturbed: A book of readings*. New York: Thomas Y. Crowell, 1969.

Morse, W. C. Self-control: The Fagen-Long curriculum. *Behavioral Disorders*, 1979, *4*, 83–91.

Morse, W. C., Cutler, R. L., & Fink, A. H. *Public school classes for the emotionally handicapped: A research analysis*. Washington, D.C.: Council for Exceptional Children, 1964.

Rhodes, W. C. Curriculum. Paper presented at North Carolina Re-Ed Meeting, Durham, January 1963.

Slagle, R. Overview of curriculum. *Mind over matter*, 1969, *14*, 26.

Stephens, T. M. *Teaching skills to children with learning and behavior disorders*. Columbus, Ohio: Charles E. Merrill, 1977.

Stiles, C. A strategy for teaching remedial reading: I'm not gonna read and you can't make me! In N. J. Long, W. C. Morse & R. G. Newman (Eds.). *Conflict in the classroom: The education of emotionally disturbed children* (4th ed.). Belmont, Calif.: Wadsworth, 1980.

Teaching Exceptional Children, 1971, *3* (entire issue).

Turnbull, A. P., & Schultz, J. B. *Mainstreaming handicapped students: A guide for the classroom teacher.* Boston: Allyn & Bacon, 1979.

Wright, W. G. The Bellevue psychiatric hospital school. In P. H. Berkowitz & E. P. Rothman (Eds.). *Public education for disturbed children in New York City: Application and theory.* Springfield, Ill.: Charles C Thomas, 1967.

12
Behavior Management

main points

1 Prevention and neutralization are the best approaches to behavior management.

2 A good student-teacher relationship is the foundation upon which effective behavior management is based.

3 Proactive planning is essential to effective behavior management because it helps teachers be prepared to deal with the unexpected.

4 Continua of consequences are helpful when implementing systems of behavior management.

5 Behavioral contingencies and verbal processing are both effective interventions that can be used in the same classroom even though they stem from different philosophical perspectives.

6 Teachers should consider carefully their reasons for choosing various interventions.

7 If teachers use time-out, seclusion or physical restraint for dealing with extremely disruptive behavior, they need to understand local regulations, document their actions and review their behavior to see what else could have been tried.

THE SKILLFUL MANAGEMENT of disruptive, inappropriate problem behavior presents a constant challenge to the teacher of emotionally handicapped children. These children frequently display behaviors which threaten, anger, discourage and shock teachers. If teachers respond to the problematic behaviors constructively, the children are likely to learn new values and ways of behaving, and thus gain control over themselves. If, however, teachers respond to problem behavior in a destructive, counterproductive fashion, children's negative views of school, of their abilities and of themselves are verified once again.

Clearly the daily decisions about what to do, when and how are critically important in creating a therapeutic, growth-supporting environment. Such decisions are often very difficult for at least two reasons. The first one has to do with teacher self-management. Teachers must be in control of their own feelings in order to manage problem behavior constructively. An angry

---

This chapter was written by **Betty C. Epanchin**, University of North Carolina at Chapel Hill.

retort to an angry child or an uncertain pause when a child starts to throw books merely adds fuel to the fire; whereas a calm confrontation, a firm limit or a quick redirection may defuse the problem. This is not to say that teachers should not have feelings about children and their behavior. Naturally, teachers may get angry and frustrated and discouraged with children. The challenge for the teacher is how to manage one's own feelings so that one can be helpful.

The second reason why making daily management decisions is difficult is that teachers have no readily apparent gauge of effectiveness. Rarely can a teacher determine immediately whether or not a particular intervention was successful. The following episode, so typical in a class for emotionally disturbed children, illustrates this point. Mrs. Moore limits Ann from earning free time because she tore up a worksheet. Ann reacts angrily and sulks for the rest of the morning. Her work goes undone and her morning seems wasted. Mrs. Moore is left with questions about whether there was a way of managing her behavior that would have helped her return to work or whether it was helpful to Ann to see once again that her teacher has set limits on her inappropriate behaviors regardless of her reactions. These questions cannot be answered until one knows what happens the next time and at other subsequent times when the child feels like ripping up her work. Did knowing that limits would follow diminish the frequency of the child's behavior? One also needs to know how the child perceived and understood the conflict. Did she feel the teacher was picking on her, or did she consciously or unconsciously wonder whether the teacher was afraid of her?

Even when the child's behavior begins to reflect a pattern, explanations of the pattern are rarely indisputable. For example, the teacher may chart the frequency of disruptions and see that the child's outbursts are not as frequent. This, however, may not alleviate the teacher's doubts altogether because he still may wonder whether the child's newly acquired control will be maintained in other settings.

In this chapter we will outline conditions for effective behavior management, look at strategies for preventing behavior problems, discuss methods of enforcing expectations and describe techniques for dealing with a child who is "out of control."

Conditions for Effective Behavior Management

The System's Support

Effective behavior management does not occur in a vacuum. In order to establish an effective system for managing and dealing with behavior, teachers need to understand and to be understood by the system in which they work. They need to know what they can expect and what is expected of them. They need answers to questions such as, what type of back-up personnel are available when children are out of control? what type of coverage is possible when they need to collaborate with other teachers? what resources are available when additional help is needed for a particular child? and perhaps most importantly, how much supervision and consultation is available?

Likewise, the system needs answers to questions such as, what can be expected of emotionally disturbed children? how should people react when a child throws a temper tantrum in the cafeteria? what types of children should be in a class for the emotionally disturbed?

If questions such as these are not clarified, the mission of the program remains unclear. Important behavior management decisions will be difficult to make and conflicts among staff members are likely to develop. Differences of opinion are often personalized and teacher "burn-out" is likely to increase. Given these potential difficulties, programs are well advised to allot time for program-level planning. (See Chapter 3 for further discussion of working with educational systems.)

The Teacher-Student Relationship

In addition to clarifying their relationship with the system in which they work, teachers need to establish a productive, working relationship with the children in their class. When children feel that their teacher does not care about them, is incompetent or insecure, is distant and alien, or does not understand, they are likely to be on the offensive continually. Rather than allow their teacher to actualize their fears of being exposed or hurt, the children may disrupt the class, refuse to cooperate, provoke the teacher or display a myriad of other disturbing behaviors.

When children care about their teacher, however, they want to please the teacher and meet his expectations. They try to cooperate, and they are more likely to accept the teacher's appraisal of a problem situation. They trust their teacher as a person and as an authority. These are conditions necessary for children to be able to perceive school and the teacher in a positive manner. Children's positive regard for school and their teacher is the necessary foundation for effective behavior management. (See Chapter 11 for additional discussion of the teacher-student relationship.)

Preventing Behavior Problems

The best approach to problem behavior is preventing it from ever occurring; short of total prevention the best alternative is redirecting and neutralizing emerging problem behavior. In order to do this teachers need to anticipate potential problems, plan ways of avoiding them and be alert to developing storms.

Unfortunately, very little research has been conducted on situational antecedents of problem behavior. An *antecedent* event is defined as a condition that either sets the stage for behavior to occur or actually prompts its occurrence (Walker, 1979). Walker notes

> We are often much more concerned with the consequences supplied to behavior than we are with the situations that actually prompt its occurrence. If we were more sensitive to such situations and conditions, it would be possible to prevent the occurrence of inappropriate or undesirable behavior in many instances. (pp. 43–44)

As children enter this classroom, they check in at the "roll call" board where daily classroom jobs are announced and assignments can be picked up.

Although there is little research on preventive strategies, the clinical literature consistently refers to certain settings and practices as being hazardous for many emotionally disturbed children. Some that are frequently noted are unstructured activities, transition times, inconsistent use of rewards and punishment, frustrating or boring academic tasks, competitive games, unpredictable teacher reactions, unclear expectations and highly stimulating environments and activities. The following suggestions are presented as means of avoiding problems altogether.

Arrange the room to fit instructional objectives. The physical appearance and organization of a classroom undoubtedly affects children's behavior. A classroom that is unkempt conveys the impression that the teacher is, at best, indifferent to the setting and to the occupants of the setting, whereas a classroom that is clean and inviting conveys a sense of welcome. Bettelheim (1974) maintains that the nicer and more attractive the surroundings at the school are, the less deliberate or careless destruction is done by the children.

Likewise, the arrangement of space within a classroom conveys expectations of what should occur. A bookcase filled with books and placed in a quiet corner with small comfortable chairs or pillows nearby suggests that children are expected to relax and read there. With time, children learn what is expected behaviorally in various settings. When planning curriculum objectives, it is important for the teacher to follow through by giving attention to the room arrangement and how it facilitates or hinders particular activities.

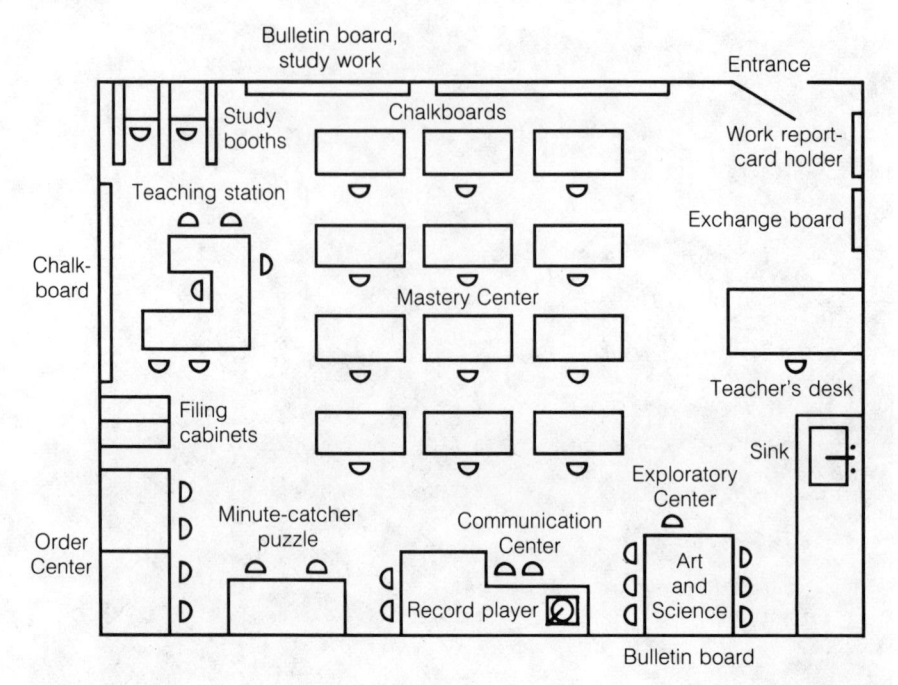

12.1 **Classroom Floorplan for a Class for Emotionally Handicapped Children**

Hewett and Taylor (1980) present an example of a classroom floorplan designed to fit curriculum tasks (See Figure 12.1). The center of the room is designated as the Mastery Center. It consists of student desks, a teaching station and two study booths. Academic tasks are normally done in this area. Around the perimeter of the room are various activity centers that facilitate carrying out of instructional objectives. For example, the Communication Center features games and activities that minimize competition and encourage waiting one's turn. The Exploratory Center offers art and science activities. It is located near the sink to allow activities requiring water as well as to make cleanup easier. The Order Center, which consists of two tables and a storage cabinet, is located in a corner of the room which is designed to minimize distractions. In this center students who are learning basic student behaviors (e.g., paying attention, following directions, completing assignments) may engage in assigned tasks such as working on puzzles, matching shapes and cutting out pictures. The work report-card holder and the exchange board are located just inside the door. Here students pick up their daily work assignments, and completed work is exchanged for rewards. Locating these fixtures near the door allows the child to receive her assignment as soon as she enters the door and before she becomes involved in problem situations.

Other authors (Gallagher, 1979; Stephens, Hartman & Lucas, 1978) suggest floorplans for use in classes for emotionally handicapped children.

Note. From *The Emotionally Disturbed Child in the Classroom: The Orchestration of Success* (2nd ed.) by F. M. Hewett and F. D. Taylor. Copyright 1980. Reprinted by Permission.

Although they differ in particular details, all emphasize the importance of paying attention to room arrangement when planning instructional activities.

Plan interesting, appealing and appropriate work. Individualized instruction (Chapter 11) is an important aspect of preventing behavior problems. When children are frustrated or bored with their school work, they are easily distracted and likely to have difficulties. For this reason one of the single most effective preventive techniques is providing each child with work that is interesting and that can be successfully completed.

Have the classroom ready for use. Before starting each day, teachers should check equipment and supplies that are to be used during the day to be certain they are in good working order and ready to use. Making children wait while the projector bulb is changed is creating a fertile situation for problems to develop. Giving children pencils with dull or broken points means that children may roam around the room on their way to sharpen the pencil. Such situations frequently result in problems which could have been prevented with better planning.

Maintain predictable schedules. Especially at the beginning of the school year, predictable daily schedules can reduce children's stress by helping them anticipate what comes next. Gallagher (1979) recommends the following daily scheduling techniques as aids in carrying out activities:

   a. Provide each student with a daily schedule.
   b. Alternate high-probability tasks with low-probability tasks [e.g., schedule less preferred tasks before more preferred tasks].
   c. Schedule work that can be finished by the end of the school day.
   d. Plan for leeway time.
   e. Require students to complete one task before beginning another.
   f. Provide time reminders.
   g. Don't assign additional work if tasks are completed ahead of schedules. [Otherwise the teacher conveys the message that when work is finished early, more is given.]
   h. Plan ahead and anticipate student needs.
   i. Establish expectations in advance and do not introduce unexpected activities.
   j. Include feedback and evaluative marks with a student's daily schedule.
   k. Provide positive feedback. (pp. 244–250)

In addition to helping children know what to expect, developing daily schedules for each child helps teachers plan the small but critically important details of each day. This procedure also provides a basis for keeping a record of what each child does daily.

Give specific and clear directions. Lovitt and Smith (1972) speculate that, on the basis of their observations of teachers in a regular fourth grade class and in a small class for exceptional children, teachers give between 260 and 620 instructions in one day. In spite of the frequency with which this technique is used, very little exists in the experimental literature on the effectiveness of instructions.

In conveying any type of behavioral expectation it is critical that the teacher specify in brief, clear terms exactly what is expected and under what circumstances. For example, "Act your age" may convey very little constructive information to a 10-year-old, immature boy; most likely, however, the boy would sense a rebuke. It would be more helpful to give the instruction "Do 10 problems by yourself before asking for help" or "Keep your thumb out of your mouth during recess."

Kounin and Gump (1958) conducted a study which demonstrates the importance of using instructive directions. They developed a strategy for ending pupil misbehavior and returning the pupil to work simultaneously. This strategy involved having the teacher define with clarity the child's misbehavior and then give the child the appropriate standard of behavior. For example, "Edward, stop bothering Susan and work on your story or read your library book" tells Edward what not to do as well as what is expected. This strategy was found to be useful in returning distracted students to order without reducing educational efficiency. It does not slow down the academic program. On the contrary, it can encourage the rest of the class to continue their work. When teachers clarify what kind of behavior they object to and what kind of behavior they expect, pupils who are watching and listening respond with increased conformance and decreased nonconformance, a phenomena described as the "ripple effect."

Not only should teachers use clear, precise terms when explaining but they may also need to model or demonstrate what they expect. If, for example, the teacher uses the technique of turning off the lights to gain the children's attention, he will probably want to explain the technique and then have a practice session or demonstrate with a few children what behavior is expected when the lights go off.

Establish routines. Routines are clearly established ways of operating that define what the classroom expectations are and how they should be met. They help the teacher organize and control the antecedents of behavior. For emotionally handicapped children, who are particularly vulnerable in unstructured and transitional times, routines can provide structure and security. For the teacher who feels exhausted by continual squabbles about who goes first and who has the biggest pencil, routines can help bypass such issues.

Routines are most needed during times of stress. The wise teacher spends time with each new group of students to establish routines of operation. Transition times and unstructured activities in particular require routines. Examples of times when routines may be needed are when children are moving from one setting to another, obtaining supplies, sharpening pencils, going to the bathroom, getting water, getting help from the teacher, finding a seat in the reading group, auditorium or cafeteria, and putting on outdoor clothes.

A careful distinction needs to be made between routines and rules. Routines are ways of operating (social habits) within the classroom, but exceptions or changes may be tolerated when appropriate. Rules, on the other hand, are akin to good laws. They apply to everyone at all times. If violated, negative consequences result. As children learn appropriate social behavior the teacher can relax somewhat and allow spontaneous activities without chaos ensuing. Transgression of rules, however, is always serious.

Set up a few rules for everyone and enforce them consistently. Rules are like good laws: they apply to all children all the time, they can be consistently enforced, and the transgression of a rule is always a serious offense.

Obviously, rules should be fair and reasonable, and in order to be consistently enforced, there should be a reasonably small number of them. If possible, they should be displayed in a clearly visible place in the classroom so children can see them at all times, and they should be stated in a positive and instructive manner whenever possible. If a rule is more clearly stated as what not to do rather than what to do, however, the negative version may be more appropriate. For example, in one class a teacher listed among the rules the following, "We respect each other." The first grade children did not understand what that meant operationally, so it became necessary to spell it out more clearly, "We do not hit each other," "We do not tear up other children's things," and so on.

By distinguishing between rules and routines, the teacher sets up a continuum of expectations that allows flexibility and helps prevent excessive punishment. For example, among the list of class rules one often sees "We raise our hands when we want to talk," followed by "We do not hit each other." The consequences of violating the two should not be the same, yet the teacher presents them as equally important. In so doing, the teacher undercuts the absolute importance of not hitting classmates. Raising hands should be considered a classroom routine, a way of operating in the class. Teachers can and should remind children that hand-raising is expected. When children fail to comply, ignoring or mild reprimanding, not a more severe punishment, is usually an appropriate response.

Many authors recommend involving children in the process of setting up rules and developing routines. Although not experimentally validated, this technique may help in teaching children what is expected and elicit their support and cooperation. When using this approach the teacher should be forewarned that some emotionally disturbed children tend to suggest very punitive rules. The teacher must exercise some control over the discussion and guide students toward adopting positive rules and positive consequences.

The effectiveness of a rule is dramatically affected by the consequences that back it up (Walker, 1979). Rules alone produce minimal or no effect on child behavior, especially when dealing with "acting-out" aggressive children. Hence, developing rules that can be consistently enforced is imperative.

Neutralizing Potential Problems

Preventive techniques include not only structuring and organizing the classroom so that problems do not get started but also detoxifying and deflating potential problem situations. Redl and Wineman (1957) propose the following techniques for managing surface behavior:

1. *Planned ignoring.* This technique is useful when the teacher recognizes that the behavior is being used by the child for its "goating" value and will gradually dissipate if left unchallenged. This technique is appropriate for potentially dangerous or disruptive behaviors or for children who lack the self-control to calm down.
2. *Signal interference.* The teacher signals to the child by waving a finger or a slight frown, when trouble is developing. For children who do not think of the consequences of their behavior, signals can be helpful in getting them to think before they act.
3. *Proximity and touch control.* Standing near a child, pointing to a place on the book, putting a hand on the child's shoulder—all are means of calming the child and of reminding her that the adult cares.
4. *Involvement in interest relationships.* Engaging a child in a discussion about a topic of interest helps to subvert boredom and revitalize positive energies.
5. *Hypodermic affection.* Especially younger and more disturbed children need frequent demonstrations that the teacher cares. By providing such attention the teacher can help a child who is wavering on the brink of becoming disruptive retain control.
6. *Tension decontamination through humor.* Skillful kidding can be helpful in diverting problems and in allowing the child a face-saving out when tension is building.
7. *Hurdle help.* Providing immediate, on-the-spot assistance to a child in whom tension is building can help her cope with the frustration of the task at hand. For example, when a teacher sees that a child who has little tolerance for frustration is having trouble with some arithmetic problems, the teacher may decide to assist the child rather than risk the child losing control.
8. *Interpretation as interference.* The teacher can help the child understand the meaning of a situation which she has misinterpreted. He can talk with the child about why the teacher acted as he did and why the child behaved as she did.
9. *Regrouping.* Making temporary changes in a group can reduce friction among the members.
10. *Restructuring.* At times the teacher can choose to abandon an activity, no matter how appealing he may think it is when it is not being well-received by the group.
11. *Direct appeal.* Sometimes an honest appeal, "Hey, I'm really tired. Please cooperate!" is sufficient in stopping problem behavior, particularly when the children like the adult.
12. *Limiting space and tools.* When the teacher perceives that something has excessive seductive value for children, it is better to limit it rather than let the children walk into a situation that the teacher believes the children cannot handle.
13. *Antiseptic bouncing.* If a child has reached a state where less intrusive techniques are not working, simply removing her from the group

for a few minutes may help her get control. If the child has the control and the self-awareness to realize that unless she gets away from the class she will lose control, the child can remove herself from the situation in order to cool off.

Enforcing Behavioral Expectations

A structured, supportive environment is only the first step in setting up an effective behavior management system. Although preventive techniques are very important, they are useless without a back-up system. Effective techniques for enforcing expectations must exist in order for the expectations to have meaning. Telling Marie to finish her work is futile if Marie knows that nothing will happen whether she does or does not do the work.

Enforcement techniques may be classified in two ways: (a) reward and punishment or (b) verbal processing. Obviously, these two approaches frequently overlap, but they stem from different theoretical perspectives and their goals are somewhat different. When the teacher chooses to give a specific reward or punishment, the intent often, though not always, is control. When the objective is control, the teacher wants the behavior either to recur or to stop. An immediate response is desired and this is an efficient technique for getting the desired results. Certainly generalization is also a concern, but at the moment the teacher usually is most concerned about the results.

If, however, a verbal processing technique is used, the teacher generally has another objective in mind. The teacher wants to help children reflect on their behavior, think about different alternative behaviors and learn more about themselves. Though change in behavior is certainly desired, an immediate response is not required.

Both of these approaches have been demonstrated to be effective. They can be used by the same teacher in the same classroom, provided that the teacher has the proper knowledge base. The choice of which to use must be based upon considerations of what will be most effective, what is feasible under the present circumstances and which technique is the teacher most comfortable using?

Systems of Reward and Punishment

If the teacher decides to use a system of reward and punishment, the following guidelines should be kept in mind.

Be positive and constructive. There are numerous ways in which the teacher can focus upon teaching adaptive, appropriate behavior rather than relying solely upon punishment to do away with a behavior. Teaching children a substitute for maladaptive behavior, providing role models, modeling desired behavior and giving direct instruction are all ways of helping children learn new, more appropriate behaviors. This is not meant to imply that punishment should not be used. Walker (1979) states:

> One clear finding seems to be emerging from research on the use of positive reinforcement and punishment techniques in applied settings. That is, reward-

ing and punishing techniques applied in combination generally produce immediate and dramatic change in behavior that usually exceeds that which would be produced by either one in isolation. Further, the more deviant and disruptive a child's behavior, the more likely it is that reinforcement and punishment will be required to change the child's overall behavior. (p. 48)

Consider carefully the message conveyed by a consequence. In a study (Hewett, 1978) of work with deprived, delinquent children, taking away points for not meeting expectations upset and angered the children whereas increasing the number of points necessary to earn rewards was seen as a fair consequence that challenged them. Another example of the importance of the message conveyed is found in the practice of reverse punishment. When a child is having a lot of difficulty in school, he is removed from school and works on getting back to school. The reward is being in school rather than being punished continually by being excluded.

Use a variety of consequences. Any reward or punishment may lose its potency if overused. It is very easy for a teacher to gradually increase the use of a particular consequence when it works. The consequence is reinforcing not only to the child but also to the teacher. If a particular consequence produces the desired effect, the teacher is more likely to try it again. Unfortunately, this is an insidious process and over time the consequence may lose its effectiveness.

The teacher should clearly understand the chosen technique and should be comfortable with it. The teacher who believes giving rewards is a form of bribery neither understands nor feels comfortable with the technique; therefore, that teacher should not use the technique. Likewise, teachers who believe time-out is unkind should not use it; and teachers who fear a particular child's aggressive outburts should not undertake a system of reward and punishment that is likely to provoke aggressive outbursts (Spaulding, 1978; Kuypers, Becker & O'Leary, 1968).

Intervene quickly and consistently. The strength of a consequence is undoubtedly enhanced when the teacher administers it immediately and nonambivalently. Teachers who are uncertain and inconsistent about disciplining are not likely to convey clear messages about what they expect of the children. As a result the children's misbehavior is likely to escalate.

The punishment should fit the crime and the reward the accomplishment. If a control technique is used that is too harsh or unfair, the child will probably become angrier and more alienated. "It would hardly do to gain the control and lose the student" (Gnagey, 1968, p. 32). If the reward is not in proportion to the accomplishment, the child may become suspicious of the teacher's sincerity. Also, when the consequence is not of sufficient magnitude, behavior change is unlikely. In fact, a number of studies (Thomas, Becker & Armstrong, 1968; Madsen, Becker, Thomas, Koser & Plager, 1970; and Sibley, Abbott & Cooper, 1969) have reported that teacher disapproval responses actually increased inappropriate behaviors.

Be willing to compromise. Admitting a mistake, saying that one is sorry and working out a mutually acceptable solution can be a very wise reaction. Honesty and fairness go a long way with almost all children. If the teacher sees that part of a child's problem is teacher induced, an apology and compromise can be most effective in securing cooperation.

Consider both group and individual consequences when planning a program. The impact of the group upon an individual should not be underestimated. Some children seem more responsive to peer feedback than to teacher feedback. Group contingencies, or combinations of group and individual contingencies, are reported to be at least as powerful as individual contingencies (Walker, 1979).

A number of investigators have used peer contingencies in behavior change projects. For example, Solomon and Wahler (1973) trained peers to dispense rewards effectively; Patterson (1965) had a target child earn rewards for himself as well as for his classmates by achieving and behaving appropriately in class; and Carlson, Arnold, Becker, and Madsen (1968) rewarded children for ignoring a classmate's temper tantrums and punished children for attending to the tantrums. Blackham and Silberman (1980) suggest placing both the offender and the reinforcer in time-out when peers reinforce the undersirable behavior of each other.

Plan for growth and development. At the beginning of the year the teacher must often rely on concrete rewards and a great deal of structure in order to achieve the desired behavior; however, as the children learn what is expected, become more secure in the classroom and develop positive relationships with the teacher, less structure is needed and social praise or mild disapproval may be effective. Also, over time children can learn to monitor their own behavior and exhibit greater self-control. When planning systems of enforcing expectations, the teacher should anticipate greater student self-control and self-direction. The teacher's role should move from enforcing limits and dispensing consequences to helping children control themselves.

Children and teachers alike should continually evaluate themselves and their program. Children need to learn to monitor their behavior. Reviewing children's daily behaviors in order to determine which ones earn points and which ones do not is a way of teaching and enforcing behavioral expectations. It helps children gauge their progress and establish goals for themselves. Likewise, if teachers monitor their behavior management plans carefully, they can determine whether or not an intervention is making a difference and whether the children are ready for modifications in the program. Without such monitoring even the best of behavior management plans become stale. Behavior management is not a static process.

The teacher, then, needs a variety of appropriate rewarding and punishing consequences that are fair and reasonable and that range in magnitude. The two continua that are described in this section illustrate the range of possible consequences available to teachers. The effectiveness of these consequences will vary in different settings with different teachers and with different children; therefore teachers must create their own continua in accord with their needs.

Continuum of rewards. Stephens (1977) describes what he calls a "reinforcement menu" (see Figure 12.2). The menu ranges from concrete, tangible, highly potent rewards to naturally occurring, intrinsic rewards. The categories are ranked in order of desirability for classroom instruction. Stephens recommends that teachers use the highest ranked category of reward wherever possible and that students should progress from needed rewards towards less tangible rewards as they become internally motivated to behave and perform properly.

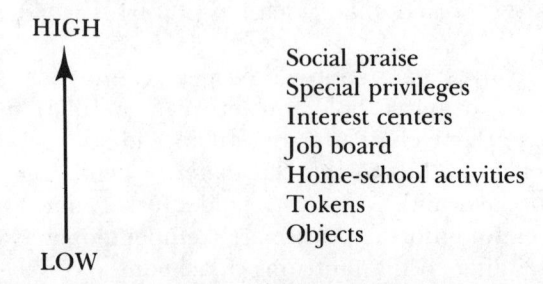

```
HIGH
 ↑         Social praise
 |         Special privileges
 |         Interest centers
 |         Job board
 |         Home-school activities
 |         Tokens
 |         Objects
LOW
```

Note. From *Teaching Skills to Children with Learning and Behavior Disorders* by T. M. Stephens. Copyright 1977 by Charles E. Merrill. Reprinted by permission.

12.2 Hierarchy of Categories in the "Reinforcement Menu"

At the lowest level, objects, children are given concrete objects contingent upon desired behavior, which may or may not have been specified through contingency contracting. In contingency contracting the teacher and child agree upon a contract that specifies what the consequences will be for specific behaviors. Examples of objects given directly as rewards are M&M's, peanuts and pretzels. This level is typically necessary only for the very young or severely disturbed child.

At the next level, tokens are given when the child displays the desired behavior. Tokens are seen as a step up on the progression because they are an interim recognition of achievement. In themselves, they are not rewarding but they do represent tangible rewards. The tokens may be given directly or through contingency contracting. The use of tokens is fairly widespread, largely because teacher-administered praise alone is not always an effective reinforcer for emotionally disturbed children.

Home-school activities are next on the hierarchy. These activities are usually implemented through contingency contracting and are usually initiated by a conference with the child's parents. During the conference the plan, rationale and expected results are discussed. Such a system can be very effective in helping the child to gain new skills and behaviors, and in helping the parents to use more constructive techniques in interacting with their child around school-related issues. The teacher must be certain, however, that the parents understand the rationale and method of implementation. In some homes of emotionally disturbed children such systems backfire, usually because the parents do not understand the rationale for such an intervention or because the parents are convinced that "their method" is better. Once the behaviors that were targeted in the home-school activities have improved, the teacher, child and parents may discontinue the program.

The four remaining rewards on Stephens's reinforcement menu are employed everyday in many classrooms. The important point with these practices is to use them systematically, deliberately and consistently.

The job board involves the use of classroom jobs as rewards. These may be administered through direct reinforcement or contingency contracting. If contingency contracting is used, Stephens suggests that the teacher designate more jobs than there are children so every child has a choice. Types of jobs that one might include are

Storing audiovisual materials	Stapling papers
Setting up projector	Running errands
Setting up screen	Answering phone
Closing shades	Patroling crosswalks
Operating lights	Leading lines
Caring for pets or plants	Collecting materials
Decorating room	Erasing board

Interest centers are areas where students may explore and pursue their curiosities during off-task time. In these activities children should be managed through contingency contracting. Advantages of this category of rewards are (a) they help organize teachers and classrooms; (b) they provide students with a variety of activity choices; (c) they provide a structured break in the work; and (d) they provide opportunities for students to learn to work and play together. (See Chapter 11 for a discussion of interest centers.)

Special privileges are desirable tasks that children may earn the right to perform. They may be administered through direct reinforcement or through contingency contracting. Types of activities suggested for this category are

For individual children	*For a group of children*
Choosing a seat for a particular time	Having a class Coke break or party
	Extra time at recess
Free time	Playing games
Leading a discussion	Watching a movie
Visiting the principal	Taking a field trip

The highest category, social praise, includes written comments, evaluation marks and other forms of recognition such as displaying children's papers on a bulletin board and verbal social approval. Written social praise may be administered directly or by contingency contracting. Verbal social praise is usually administered directly and often paired with written praise. Stephens includes in the category of social praise positive proximity (eating with children, standing beside them, touching them and shaking hands), positive physical expression (smiling, cheering, clapping hands, signaling V for victory), and spoken and written feedback.

When teachers use a continuum such as Stephens's reinforcement menu with emotionally disturbed children, they may find it necessary to start with objects and tokens. Over time these can be substituted with jobs, work in an interest center, special privileges or social praise—all of which are naturally occurring, frequently used rewards in most classrooms. Moving children up the reinforcement continuum is one way that teachers can prepare emotionally disturbed children to function in the mainstream.

Continuum of Punishments. With children whose behavior is very disruptive and deviant, rewards alone may not be sufficient. The teacher, therefore, needs to consider what types of aversive consequences may be appropriately used.

Forness (1978) has organized a hierarchy of aversives that move from the severe and externally administered to the mild and internally felt (see Figure 12.3). Within each category there are levels of punishing responses. Forness recommends that the lowest-order aversives should be viewed as a means of helping children develop to a higher level of functioning. He also underscores the importance of a relationship with the child, noting that once a teacher has developed a good relationship with a child, the teacher may only need to use the milder aversives.

Self-disappointment
↑
Negative feedback
↑
Ignoring
↑
Reprimands
↑
Time-out
↑
Seclusion

Note. From "Developmental Programming for the Use of Aversive Procedures in a Hospital School" by Steven R. Forness, in *Punishment and Aversive Stimulation in Special Education*, F. H. Wood and K. C. Lakin, (Eds.). Copyright 1978 by F. H. Wood and K. C. Lakin. Reproduced by permission of the author.

12.3 Developmental Outline of Aversives

Seclusion, according to Forness, involves placing children by themselves in a room. Types, or levels, of seclusion include asking a child if she needs to go to the study room (the least severe form of seclusion), telling her to go to the study room, asking if she needs to go to the quiet room (time-out room), telling her to go to the quiet room and forcing her to go to the quiet room. Additional levels of seclusion include removing the child from the classroom area (to the ward or to the principal's office) and then completely removing her from school (the most severe form of seclusion).

Time-out, in this hierarchy, involves removing children from the immediate activity but not necessarily placing them in seclusion. Types or levels of time-out include turning the child's chair away from the group, having the child go to another area within the room (with or without restraint from the teacher or the aide), having the child sit in the hall, having her sit at her desk without materials, time-out from activity (children observe but cannot participate) and time-out from earning rewards.

Reprimands are defined as "admonitions to cease maladaptive or initiate appropriate behaviors" (Forness, 1978, p. 94). Forness suggests that reprimands are most effective when they come from a person the child wants to please and when they are used early in the sequence of disruptive behavior. As has previously been noted, repeated reprimands tend not to be effective.

O'Leary, Kaufman, Kass, and Drabman (1970) found that most teacher reprimands were loud in nature and could be heard by other children in the class. They also found that when teachers used reprimands audible only to the pupil in question, the frequency of disruptive behavior declined in most children. O'Leary et al. maintain that soft reprimands model desired behavior and can have a calming effect, whereas loud ones can make children jumpy. The authors note that to give a soft reprimand, one must be physically close. This means attention and interest is shown to individual children, a technique that is more positive than a shout from someone far away who's busy with something else.

The category of ignoring consists of both passive and active ignoring. In active ignoring teachers actually turn away from the offending child, whereas with passive ignoring, teachers simply do not acknowledge the problem behavior. They may act as if it went unnoticed and do nothing, or they may repeat their instructions.

This technique, much like Redl's "planned ignoring," is often appropriately used with emotionally disturbed children when they balk at assignments. Instead of responding to children's complaints such as "This is dumb!" or "I can't do this," teachers either act as though they did not hear the child and do nothing or they repeat the directions for doing the work. When using this technique, however, teachers must be careful. When inappropriate behavior begins to escalate, teachers may need to use more stringent punishment quickly.

Negative feedback and self-disappointment are considered by Forness (1978) to reflect more mature motivational processes and a high level of intrinsic motivation. "Although both levels are somewhat dependent on feedback from external sources, they are still transactions essentially between a child and his sense of his own performance" (p. 89).

When teaching emotionally disturbed children, teachers may need to start with the more severe aversives until children learn what is expected, but with time the more naturally occurring punishments may be sufficient. For additional information on how to pair rewards and punishment, the reader is referred to Walker (1979) and Blackham and Silberman (1980).

Using seclusion and time-out. Although time-out and seclusion are widely used forms of punishment, they are easily abused. When used inappropriately, they have been the topic of considerable controversy. Gast and Nelson (1977) have formulated guidelines for using time-out in the classroom.

If a seclusion time-out is to be employed, the time-out room should:
  a. be at least six by six feet in size;
  b. be properly lighted (preferably recessed lights with the switch outside the room);
  c. be properly ventilated;
  d. be free of objects and fixtures with which a child could harm himself;
  e. provide the means by which an adult can continuously monitor—visually and aurally—the student's behavior;
  f. *not* be locked—a latch on the door should be used only as needed and only with careful monitoring. (p. 464)

Some states also require that time-out rooms be constructed from nonflammable materials in order to meet fire regulations for insurance purposes.

Records should be kept whenever time-out is used. According to Gast and Nelson (1977) the records should include the following information:

  a. the student's name;
  b. the episode resulting in student's placement in time-out (behavior, activity, other students involved, staff person, etc.);
  c. time of day the student was placed in time-out;
  d. time of day the student was released from time-out;
  e. the total time in time-out;
  f. the type of time-out (contingent observation, exclusion time-out, or seclusion time-out);
  g. the student's behavior in time-out. (pp. 464–465)

Techniques for using time-out and seclusion vary somewhat depending upon state or local laws and upon the theoretical perspective of the person setting the policies. Most policies, however, are similar to the one Gast and Nelson recommend. The following guidelines are typical:

1 Avoid lengthy verbal explanations as to why the student is being placed in time-out. Behaviors resulting in time-out should be clearly explained prior to implementing the time-out program. When a child needs to go to time-out, the teacher, if he says anything at all, should be brief and to the point. For example, he might say, "David, go to time-out because you grabbed Jane's toy."

2 Identify those behaviors, if any, that will result in a warning before time-out is implemented. These generally are behaviors that rarely occur, are not extremely disruptive and previously have not been defined explicitly.

3 To maximize opportunities for self-control, students should be given the opportunity to take their own time-out after receiving the instruction from the teacher. If after 5 to 10 seconds, however, children do not respond to teachers' instructions, teachers may physically move children to the time-out area. For high intensity behavior (e.g., kicking, screaming), children should be escorted immediately to time-out.

When teachers doubt they can control a particular child, they should never try to physically remove that child. If an aide or additional help is not readily available, teachers must rely on alternative strategies such as re-evaluating the reinforcers in the classroom and possibly taking away a valued object or privilege contingent upon a behavior. Other alternatives may include reinforcing other children for ignoring disruptive behaviors or reassigning the uncontrollable student to a teacher who can manage highly aggressive and resistant behavior.

4 The duration of each time-out period should be brief. Gast and Nelson (1977) believe that 1 to 5 minutes should be sufficient most of the time. They maintain that time-out periods exceeding 15 minutes are unlikely to serve the purpose for which they are intended (i.e., temporary withholding of positive reinforcement).

5 Release from time-out should be made contingent upon the student's behavior while in time-out. For example, children in time-out may be required to behave appropriately for 1 minute before they can be released. When using such a policy teachers need to monitor carefully because if children are required to stay in time-out for longer periods, the continued punishment often seems to anger them and they may become disruptive once more. One-minute egg timers have been useful devices in monitoring time-out. When the child settles down, the teacher starts the timer, and when the sand is through the glass or when the bell rings, the child can leave.

In closing this section on time-out procedures, it is important to re-emphasize that time-out is effective only when children want to be *in*, not *out*, of the classroom. A classroom that is reinforcing does not have to be a constant flurry of creative and inviting activities, but it does need to be a setting in which the children feel secure, cared for and successful. In order to help children feel this way, the teacher must know and understand each child in the room.

Verbal Processing

One of the most frequently used classroom techniques for dealing with children's behavior problems is classroom discussion, or verbal processing. Teachers discuss with students reasons for being late, for not completing homework and for being preoccupied, but if these discussion are not conducted skillfully, little may be accomplished. Verbal processing appears, at least initially, to be a straightforward and easy technique. As any seasoned teacher can attest, however, it is not simple. In order to effectively conduct a discussion about a child's problems, the teacher needs to have basic skills and knowledge in verbal processing as well as a clear understanding of the child's problems and the setting's requirements. Effective verbal processing is not an accident; it is the result of clear and careful thought and skill. Several approaches to verbal processing have been suggested to help teachers manage behavior problems.

Life space interviewing. In 1959, Fritz Redl introduced the phrase "life space interview," or LSI, to describe a reality-oriented, here-and-now interview that teachers can productively conduct in the classroom. He suggested two broad goals for conducting an LSI. They were the "clinical exploitation of life events" and "emotional first aid." "Clinical exploitation of life events" means using the here-and-now routine occurrences as material for helping children gain insight into their problems and learn new ways of coping. Examples of exploiting life events include dealing with children's distortions of a social situation, helping children become aware of their maladaptive attitudes and teaching children new problem-solving skills. Providing "emotional first aid" involves functioning as an alter ego or supplying the child with needed direction, organization and control. Giving emotional support to children who are overwhelmed by intense feelings or who are frustrated by daily annoyances is an example of emotional first aid.

De Magistris and Imber (1980) observed a number of differences between an LSI and a typical classroom discussion. In many classroom discussions the children's behavior was criticized immediately, and little attention was directed toward understanding the children's perception of a specific incident. LSIs were usually conducted in a private setting with the people directly involved being the only ones present. Classroom discussions, in contrast, usually took place in front of an entire class. During an LSI teachers usually tried to help students understand how the group affected them. This rarely happened in classroom discussions. Classroom discussions frequently ended with the teacher and child in a stand-off or with the child being punished for inappropriate behavior. When an LSI was used, the child was generally given the responsibility or helped to take the responsibility for generating alternatives.

Since Redl first introduced the concept, the goals or purpose of the LSI have been expanded so that now the phrase includes a wide array of verbal interventions that aid in behavior management or contribute to children's understanding of themselves and their behavior.

To maximize the potential of an LSI Redl (1959) suggests the teacher consider the following factors before undertaking one:

1 *Is there sufficient time?* To start a serious discussion 5 minutes before the school bus comes is to ensure that the discussion will be rushed and probably be less productive.
2 *Is the child in the right frame of mind?* The child must be psychologically ready to enter into a discussion. When a child is acutely upset, she is not in a condition to calmly consider the situation. Likewise, once a child has settled down and put the problem out of her mind, bringing up the problem again may reactivate her fury.
3 *Is the teacher in the right frame of mind?* When a teacher is still recovering from fury triggered by a child's outburst, it is clearly not a good time to initiate an LSI. The teacher's own feelings would interfere.
4 *Is the setting appropriate?* Airing private issues in public can make the child uncomfortable and can interfere with the interview and the teacher-student relationship. Likewise, conducting an interview in a highly stimulating environment may prove to be too distracting to the youngster.

5 *Is the issue closely related to other issues the child is presently working on?* To bombard children with all their problems at once is likely to overwhelm them and accomplish nothing. Problems should be raised one at a time and in a carefully considered sequence.

6 *Is the issue one that the child is psychologically ready to understand?* To focus upon issues that a child is firmly defended against is to risk either antagonizing the child or being dismissed by her as incompetent. The problem must be "close to consciousness." Underlying this issue is the belief that people understand and remember selectively; hence, issues should be raised when children are ready to understand.

In an effort to provide teachers with guidelines for how to conduct an LSI, Morse (1980) suggests seven steps to follow. These parallel the steps that are frequently suggested for conducting a clinical interview. The main differences have to do with the reality, here-and-now focus on specific classroom events as compared to more general personality problems.

1. The teacher should start by finding out how the child (or the group) perceived the event which precipitated the LSI.
2. The teacher should learn also whether the child sees the event as an isolated event; if so, it hardly merits a great deal of attention. If the teacher sees it as a central issue and the child does not, the teacher must begin to focus with the child on other similar episodes so that with time the child understands its significance.
3. After learning how the child perceived the event, the teacher clarifies what really happened, in a non-evaluative manner. As the event is reconstructed, concomitant feelings and impulses are recognized.
4. Throughout the LSI, but particularly as the child's distortions are challenged, the teacher strives to convey a feeling of acceptance to the child. The teacher tries to convey to the child the right to be heard without condoning the problem behavior. An attempt is made to respond to the feelings behind the defense rather than to counterattack the defenses.
5. As a strategy for helping the child learn better ways of dealing with similar situations, the implications or logical consequences of her behavior are explored in a nonpunitive, nonjudgmental way.
6. The next phase is a period in which the teacher looks for sources of motivation to change in the child. The constant question in the teacher's thoughts is, "What can I do to help the child change?"
7. After motivation to change is examined, the interview may be concluded. If the child has not arrived at a resolution, the teacher explains reality limits in a neutral, nonmoralistic way. If a plan can be worked out for resolving the problem or for preventing similar problems in the future, steps are taken in that direction. Before agreeing to the plan, the teacher should feel confident that the plan will be successful.

In life space interviewing the teacher should not force the situation. While it is true that confrontation may ultimately be necessary, it is wiser to

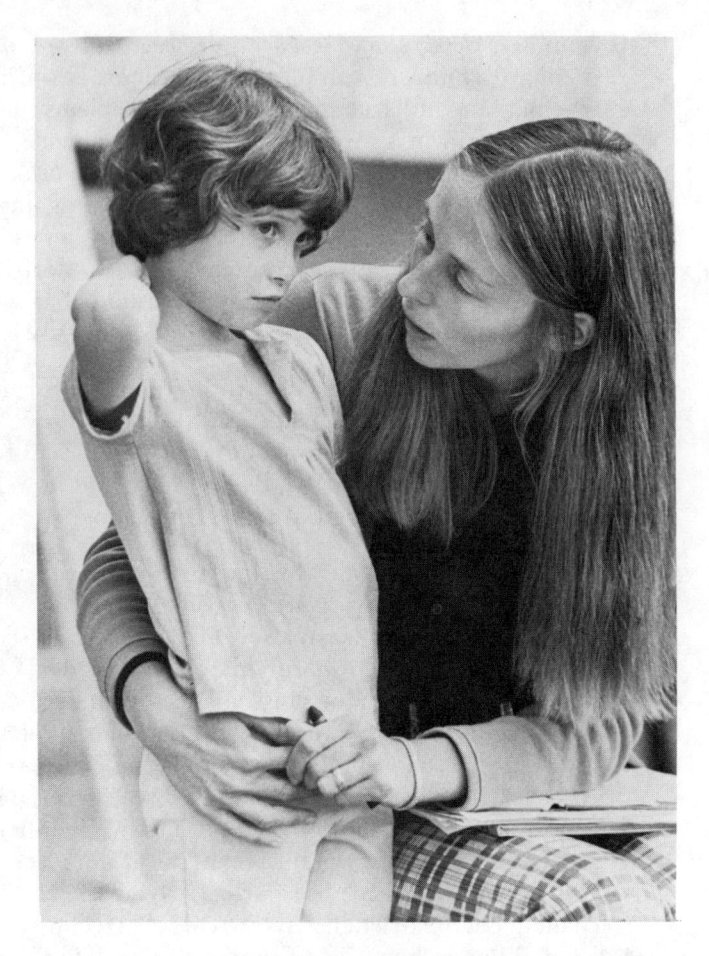

In a life space interview, the teacher lets the child know he has a right to be heard without condoning the problem behavior.

allow children time to resolve the issue themselves. As Bettelheim (1950) points out,

> We are most anxious to strengthen the child's ego, to enhance his self-respect, his feelings of adequacy, to convince him that he is able to understand, to change and control his own action. Nothing is more conducive to developing these attitudes than the conviction that one can figure out by oneself just what motivates one, and nothing is more deflating than to have to think that others can understand the mainspring of one's innermost behavior either better or sooner than oneself. (p. 152)

Whenever possible, it is better to help the children learn how to understand their feelings and behaviors rather than have someone try and force insight. For this reason another one of Bettelheim's suggestions is helpful.

> Therefore, we do not use our hunches, or information received from parents, for example, unless the child has first informed us of it, or we not only think, but

really know what goes on. But once he has told us about it, we feel free to make use of it at appropriate moments, even if the child has forgotten it, because such information has become part of our relation, is now common and no longer a private possession. (p. 152)

The LSI, therefore, is very much like the clinical interview. Many of the same skills are used and much of the same content is dealt with, but there are also important differences. The LSI is generally precipitated by a specific event in the classroom whereas the clinical interview is begun when the agreed-upon hour arrives. The teacher generally keeps the focus of an LSI on the here and now, the patterns of behavior, emotions and events seen in the classroom during the time that teacher and student are together. The therapist, in contrast, often encourages the child to reflect on relationships at home and on past events or feelings as a means of eliciting evidence of the conflict with which to work. Both the teacher and the therapist, however, are helping children to work on their conflicts and problems.

LSI interventions have been shown to be effective. De Magistris and Imber (1980) used a behavioral assessment procedure to evaluate the effectiveness of the LSI with behaviorally disordered adolescents in a residential treatment facility.

LSI interventions were highly effective in generating decreases in maladaptive behavior ranging from 31 percent to 72 percent. . . . Not only did subjects begin to accept the reality of the negative effects of their undesirable behaviors, but they also began to generate alternative solutions to problems. Clearly, the familiar "blame the other guy" syndrome was less evident as the intervention phase progressed. (p. 23)

Teacher effectiveness training. Another approach to conducting discussions about problems in the classroom has been suggested by Gordon (1975). This system, known as the "No-Lose Method," is a process of working through conflicts from beginning to end. The steps in this method are (a) defining the problem, (b) generating possible solutions, (c) evaluating the solutions, (d) deciding which solution is best, (e) determining how to implement the decision, and (f) assessing how well the solution solved the problem. This approach may be used with groups or with individuals, but in order to use this method, the teacher must have a good relationship with students and possess good communication skills.

Listening is a critical component of constructive talk. Gordon describes two types of listening. *Passive listening* includes silent listening, that is, verbal or nonverbal acknowledgment responses (e.g., nods, smiles, "Uh-huh") and verbal encouragement to continue (e.g., "That's interesting," "Do you want to go on?"). *Active listening* is the process of decoding a student's uniquely coded message and then trying to give feedback.

Gordon provides the following as an example of active listening. The student complains, "This school sure isn't as good as my last one. The kids there were friendly." The teacher hypothesizes that the student feels lonely and left out; therefore, the teacher responds, "You feel pretty left out here?" The student's agreement confirmed that the teacher had correctly heard and decoded the child's message. This process is akin to Morse's recommendation that teachers not counterattack defenses. Had the teacher become defensive and replied, "Why, that is a great school—the kids are known for being friendly," the teacher would have been responding to the literal meaning of defensive behavior, or counterattacking a defense.

Gordon also stresses the importance of determining who "owns" the problem. If the student owns the problem, Gordon believes that the teacher should become a counselor, so to speak, and help the student deal with the problem, primarily through active and passive listening. If the teacher "owns" the problem, Gordon recommends confronting the student with an "I-message."

I-messages consist of three parts: a description of what is causing the problem, a description of the tangible effect of the behavior and identification of the resulting feelings. An example is: "When art supplies are not put up after they are used in the art center, I have to do it and it takes a lot of time. This upsets me, especially when I'm in a hurry."

The advantage of an I-message, according to Gordon, is that it helps keep the responsibility for the problem where it belongs and, by not accusing the child, it helps prevent the child from becoming defensive. This, in turn, helps the child hear the message and discuss the problem rationally. Gordon maintains that by using an I-message the teacher usually elicits the student's feelings. When this happens, the teacher should listen actively.

Finally, in describing effective communication, Gordon (1975) presents what he calls the "Dirty Dozen," 12 roadblocks to effective communication. He maintains that these 12 kinds of messages inhibit or block two-way communication, and without two-way communication, it is not possible, he believes, to help students with their problems. The "Dirty Dozen" are

1. Ordering, commanding, directing. Example: "You stop complaining and get your work done."
2. Warning, threatening. Example: "You'd better get on the ball if you expect to get a good grade in this class."
3. Moralizing, preaching, giving "shoulds" and "oughts." Example: "You know it's your job to study when you come to school. You should leave your personal problems at home where they belong."
4. Advising, offering solutions or suggestions. Example: "The thing for you to do is to work out a better time schedule. Then you'll be able to get all your work done."
5. Teaching, lecturing, giving logical arguments. Example: "Let's look at the facts. You better remember there are only 34 more days of school to complete that assignment."
6. Judging, criticizing, disagreeing, blaming. Example: "You're just plain lazy or you're a big procrastinator."
7. Name-calling, stereotyping, labeling. Example: "You're acting like a fourth grader, not like someone almost ready for high school."
8. Interpreting, analyzing, diagnosing. Example : "You're just trying to get out of doing that assignment."
9. Praising, agreeing, giving positive evaluations. Example: "You're really a very competent young man. I'm sure you'll figure how to get it done somehow."

10. Reassuring, sympathizing, consoling, supporting. Example: "You're not the only one who ever felt that way about tough assignments, too. Besides, it won't seem hard when you get into it."
11. Questioning, probing, interrogating, cross-examining. Examples: "Do you think the assignment was too hard?" "How much time did you spend on it?" "Why did you wait so long to ask for help?" "How many hours have you put in on it?"
12. Withdrawing, distracting, being sarcastic, humoring, diverting. Examples: "Come on, let's talk about something more pleasant." "Now isn't the time." "Let's get back to our lesson." "Seems like someone got up on the wrong side of the bed this morning." (pp. 48–49. Reprinted with permission from the book *Teacher Effectiveness Training* by Thomas Gordon, copyright 1975. Published by David McKay Co., Inc.)

Other writers, notably Ginott (1971), Glasser (1969) and Dreikurs (1968), have also developed techniques for communicating with children in the classroom. Ginott (1971) advocates "congruent communication," which he believes enables teachers to communicate with students about problems without attacking the student. In this approach to verbal processing, teachers convey the message "I like you but I don't like what you are doing." By using congruent communication Ginott believes teachers can be helpful, accepting and constantly aware of their impact upon children.

Glasser (1965) developed a technique for problem solving which he calls "reality therapy." He then applied this technique in school situations. He maintains that people's past experiences influence but do not determine their present functioning, that people have choices about how they behave and that the teacher's role is to help children make wise choices.

Dreikurs (1968) proposes a model for disciplining children that relies upon the use of logical and natural consequences. He views consequences as actions that naturally and logically follow behavior. Good behavior results in rewards, and unacceptable behavior causes unpleasant consequences. Dreikurs sees children's misbehavior as stemming from mistaken goals (e.g., gaining attention). In his approach teachers are responsible for helping children acquire better, more adaptive goals and ways of behaving.

All of these writers present approaches that help teachers recognize and understand patterns of maladaptive behavior in children because it is critical that teachers do not perpetuate the maladaptive patterns by reacting as people in the past have reacted. Whatever technique is used it is important that teachers find a way to respond to emotionally disturbed children in a way that conveys both the belief that the child has the ability to behave appropriately and the expectation that the child can acquire better ways of behaving.

Clearly effective verbal processing is a complex process. It requires of the teacher a technical knowledge of interpersonal dynamics, but it also requires personal qualities such as sensitivity to others and the ability to empathize. If a classroom discussion is conducted in a judgmental or intrusive manner, it may create more problems for the teacher, but if it is conducted appropriately, it can cement the student-teacher relationship. The use of appropriate verbal processing techniques can contribute to emotional growth in children as well as to an effective behavior management system.

Dealing with "Out-of-Control" Behavior

No chapter on behavior management is complete without a discussion of managing "out-of-control" behavior. This phrase refers to the behavior of children who are distraught, acutely upset and unable to control themselves during the peak of their outbursts. Redl and Wineman (1957) describe such children as ones whose ego has obviously gone AWOL.

> The children who hate and at the same time show severe ego disturbances will invariably be given to violent fits of rage, accompanied by a total loss of control, from time to time. They will hit, bite, kick, throw anything within their reach, spit, scream, swear, and accompany all this by disjointed and meaningless movements of lashing out at things or people "without apparent reason." In short, their organism will show a totality of destructiveness with a totality of abandon comparable only to the fits of rage of the little baby in the crib. Such behavior may turn up "spontaneously" from "within" at any time, or it may be the reaction to something in their surroundings that "brought it on." (p. 451)

Clearly when children's emotional outbursts reach such acute proportions, routine disciplinary measures are not appropriate or useful because these techniques are premised on the belief that children are in control, that with some cues they can control themselves. When dealing with children who are out of control, such an expectation may be unreasonable. Such children may need more than the usual help from the environment in order to get back on top of their emotions. When children are acutely upset, teachers may need to function as alter egos or to provide the children with the control they are missing. This may be done in a number of ways. The choice of intervention depends on a variety of factors such as the age and size of the children, the children's ability to use the help of others and the philosophical orientation of the program.

Basically three approaches are available for dealing with children who are out of control: isolation of the child from everyone, removal of the child from the group but with an adult present, and physical restraint of the child by an adult. All three of these techniques are seen as temporary interventions that are used only until the child acquires control.

Isolation

An example of the use of isolation, or seclusion, is found in the Forness (1978) account of working with a 9-year-old aggressive boy at the UCLA Neuropsychiatric Institute School. The child had a history of parental abandonment and rejection. Although he was functioning at grade level academically, his behavior was characterized by aggressive outbursts and fits of temper directed at both teachers and peers. At one point he slammed a classroom door, breaking the teacher's finger in two places. His outbursts were not always predictable but seemed related to episodes of real or perceived rejection.

The intervention program that was used in dealing with his extreme behavior reflects the behavioral orientation of the program. That orientation was based on the following assumptions: the classroom should be positively reinforcing to the child; seclusion is removing the child from positive reinforcement; and the child is capable of self-control. The program described by Forness (1978) involved using progressively more intense forms of seclusion until the child's behavior improved. In the order in which they were used the levels of seclusion were

1. Encouraging the boy to voluntarily go to the study room
2. Providing a warning
3. Having the boy stay in an unlocked time-out room for 5 to 10 minutes
4. Having the boy stay in a locked seclusion room for 5 to 20 minutes with release contingent upon quiet behavior for two minutes prior to release
5. Having the boy removed from the classroom and sent to the ward security room
6. Excluding him from school

At each of the first four levels, if the child's aggressive behavior desisted, he was allowed to return to the classroom activities. At the fifth level, once he had calmed down, he was allowed to return to his room on the ward until the next scheduled activity outside of school. At the sixth level, depending on the seriousness of his infraction, he was excluded from school for a 24-hour period. Throughout the period of using seclusion, teachers were encouraged to increase their level of positive interaction with the boy and, whenever possible, to engage in debriefing sessions with him after outbursts. The object of these sessions was to help him learn more appropriate techniques for dealing with his behavior.

Removal from the Group with an Adult

The second approach to dealing with out-of-control behavior involves the teacher or another adult leaving the classroom with the child and staying with the child until the force of the emotional outburst diminishes. The decision to stay with the child may be determined by the teacher's philosophical orientation, but it also should be determined by pragmatic issues such as how the child responds to isolation, whether the child poses a physical threat to the teacher or to herself and how receptive the child is to others' help.

The child with whom the teacher almost always stays is the child whose panic is intensified by isolation or the child who retreats into autistic-like withdrawal when isolated. Such children regress further if isolated. Some even become self-injurious. With such children the teacher stays merely to maintain contact and to comfort, if possible. Some welcome being held, much like a very young child, while others are bothered by physical contact. Until the child begins to calm down, reasoning or discussion is out of the question. Once this begins to happen, however, the teacher may be able to review the incident and essentially conduct a life space interview, if it is deemed appropriate.

Josselyn (1955) warns against petting or reassuring children during the peak of their outburst because such behavior may intensify their rage.

> When the time arrives, the child will ask for comfort. Often he will not ask for it verbally but by bodily language. The sobbing changes tone. His vituperative attack loses force. His body rigidity lessens. (p. 303)

When teachers notice these changes in the child, it is time to comfort. Josselyn also believes that the adult's role is to help children regain control of their "transiently overwhelmed egos" (p. 305) and to re-establish communication with the child. She does not believe that children should be punished for losing control but neither should adults rescind limits that precipitated the loss of control. She maintains that children must learn to accept limits and disappointment but should not be punished for being immature.

Physical Restraint

The third approach to dealing with out-of-control behavior is physical restraint. This technique should be used *only* when teachers feel secure in being able to hold the child and when a child is physically lashing out at her environment with such intensity that the teacher fears that the child or someone in the classroom will be hurt. If a child is physically attacking the environment and the teacher is uncertain about his ability to hold the child, the teacher should send for help or find some means of avoiding direct confrontation. If, however, the child is young and the teacher feels capable of both restraining the child and managing his own feelings, the teacher may hold the child in order to prevent a continued assault on the environment.

This technique, referred to as a "therapeutic hold" in some settings, involves crossing the child's arms in front of the body and holding the arms from behind. The intent is to prevent children from hurting themselves and others, but if used improperly, children can be hurt. At no time should such a procedure involve counteraggression on the part of the teacher. Furthermore, as soon as is possible, the teacher should release the child. It could be argued that the therapeutic hold is unnatural and overpowering. Because of these characteristics, it provides a negative model. When the teacher overpowers the child, the teacher is providing a model of solving problems with force. A more natural way of containing the child's aggressive behavior may appear less overpowering.

In discussing physical restraint Redl and Wineman (1957) suggest that the adult talk soothingly to the child in a low voice, using primarily content-empty words. At no time should the adult seriously believe the content of the child's explosion. During such outbursts children often lash out at favorite adults, calling them every derogatory name that they can summon.

Such outbursts can be frightening to children and teacher alike. They present intense challenges to the teacher's self-control, poise under fire and ability to think and react reasonably during a crisis. If handled well, however, both during and after the outburst, such episodes can be very therapeutic for the child. By going through such crises, the child often acquires increased self-control and trust in the ability of others to help.

Choosing an Approach

In determining which of these approaches to use, the teacher should consider several issues. First, the teacher must be comfortable with whatever technique is chosen. When dealing with high-intensity behavior, the teacher needs to be calm, firm and self-assured. If the teacher is uncomfortable with the technique, he will find it very difficult to convey confidence and security.

In addition to the teacher's beliefs, the child's needs must be considered. Sometimes, a child's behavior intensifies in the presence of other people, especially when a person present is the target of her anger. With these children, the teacher may use isolation, giving the child some choice in the matter if possible. For example, he might ask, "Can you settle down, or do you need to go out?" Other children may react with autistic-like withdrawal. For these children, isolation is not appropriate. Also, for children who panic, isolation is generally not appropriate, although it may be effective in stopping the behavior. Furthermore, some children are comforted by physical contact while others cannot tolerate it. Obviously, the use of physical restraint or the therapeutic hold must be determined by the child's reactions.

Given the dangers inherent in the use of physical contact, one might wonder whether it is ever justified. Perhaps the only basis on which this technique is consistently justified is the protection of property and people. By restraining the child and thereby preventing destruction, the teacher may interrupt an assault on the environment which later would cause the child to feel guilty and remorseful.

Since the techniques of seclusion and physical restraint are controversial, teachers using either technique should be thoroughly familiar with the rules and regulations governing seclusion and restraint in their state. These regulations vary from state to state and from LEA (local education agency) to LEA but some general issues are common.

When teachers try to physically restrain a child, they risk a struggle. The child could be hurt, and should this happen, the teacher might be liable to charges of assault. In such cases the courts have generally been concerned with the question of "reasonableness." Kallan (1971) lists four criteria for determining reasonableness:

1 Was the rule that was being enforced reasonable?
2 Considering the student's offense, was the form and extent of the force used reasonable?
3 Considering the student's age and physical condition, was the force reasonable?
4 Did the teacher act without malice or ill will toward the child?

In at least two states (Maine and New Jersey), lawmakers have differentiated between corporal punishment and physical restraint. Physical restraint is permitted when used for preventing injury to people or property. This distinction may become more common in the future (Wood & Lakin, 1978). Nevertheless, if teachers use physical restraint they should be aware that not only are they modeling an aggressive approach to solving problems, they may also be risking their safety and the child's safety. When children are hurt by a teacher, the teacher is in an awkward, if not liable, position.

No state forbides the use of seclusion as a disciplinary technique in the public schools (Wood & Lakin, 1978). This technique when used in institutions, however, has been reviewed by the courts (*Wyatt* v. *Stickney*, 1972; *Morales* v. *Turman*, 1974). In these cases the central issue was not the institution's right to use the procedure; rather, the issue centered on whether the technique was used appropriately, that is, not excessively. If teachers follow the guidelines set forth by Gast and Nelson (pp. 457–467), they will be acting in accord with the guidelines set forth by the courts.

SUMMARY

Prevention and early neutralization of behavior problems are the best approaches to managing the behavior of emotionally disturbed children. It is always easier for the teacher and for the child to anticipate trouble and avoid it than it is to deal with the aftermath of fury and despair. A program in which careful and sensitive attention is given to children's individual academic and behavioral needs, to teachers' emotional well-being and to the nature of the demands in the setting will help prevent and neutralize behavior problems.

Even in the most carefully planned programs, however, problems will arise; therefore teachers must be prepared to deal with them. Most problem behavior is within the child's control, that is, with the proper motivation the child can stop the undesired behavior. For this reason, rewards for desired behavior balanced with clear and predictable limits for undesired behavior are effective interventions. Especially when the teacher's objective is to help the child learn about herself and why she behaves as she does, verbal processing is also an effective technique.

If, however, the child is not able to control her problem behavior, the teacher must be prepared to help the child regain control. Isolation, quiet support and presence, and physical restraint are all ways of managing out-of-control behavior. These techniques, however, are appropriate only during crises. They should be used infrequently and always with the aim of helping the child regain control.

The teacher's role in these processes is a central one. Not only must teachers organize and plan in order to prevent problems from arising, they also must carefully monitor their own emotions in order to be effective when problems do arise. The purpose of behavior management techniques is not merely to gain control of children but to help children gain control of themselves so that they can function as students and as productive members of a class.

DISCUSSION QUESTIONS

1. Analyze a "live" classroom to determine what measures are being taken to prevent behavior problems.
2. Observe a class for one hour and then specify the behaviors that are essential in a productive classroom. What rewards could be used to promote the occurrence of these behaviors?

3. After observing in a classroom, list 10 problem behaviors that occurred frequently and then think of consequences that might be appropriate for each.
4. Transcribe a discussion between a teacher and a child that was aimed at dealing with a problem. Analyze the problem-solving techniques.
5. How are time-out and antiseptic bouncing alike and how are they different?
6. Develop a set of guidelines for dealing with children who are extremely disruptive or upset.

REFERENCES

Bettelheim, B. *Love is not enough.* New York: Free Press, 1950.

Bettelheim, B. *A home for the heart.* New York: Alfred A. Knopf, 1974.

Blackham, G. J., & Silberman, A. *Modification of child and adolescent behavior* (3rd ed.). Belmont, Calif.: Wadsworth, 1980.

Carlson, C. S., Arnold, C. R., Becker, W. C., & Madsen, C. H. The elimination of tantrum behavior of a child in an elementary classroom. *Behavior Research and Therapy*, 1968, *6*, 117–119.

De Magistris, R. J., & Imber, S. C. The effects of life space interviewing on academic and social performance of behaviorally disordered children. *Behavior Disorders*, 1980, *6*, 12–25.

Dreikurs, R. *Psychology in the classroom: A manual for teachers* (2nd ed.). New York: Harper & Row, 1968.

Forness, S. R. Developmental programming for the use of aversive procedures in a hospital school. In F. H. Wood & K. C. Lakin (Eds.), *Punishment and aversive stimulation in special education: Legal, theoretical and practical issues in their use with emotionally disturbed children and youth.* Minneapolis: University of Minnesota Press, 1978.

Gallagher, P. A. *Teaching students with behavior disorders: Techniques for classroom instruction.* Denver, Colo.: Love, 1979.

Gast, D. L., & Nelson, C. M. Legal and ethical considerations for the use of timeout in special education settings. *The Journal of Special Education*, 1977, *11*, 457–467.

Ginott, H. *Teacher and child.* New York: Macmillan, 1971.

Glasser, W. *Reality therapy: A new approach to psychiatry.* New York, Harper & Row, 1965.

Glasser, W. *Schools without failure.* New York: Harper & Row, 1969.

Gnagey, W. J. *The psychology of discipline in the classroom.* New York: Macmillan, 1968.

Gordon, T. *Teacher effectiveness training.* New York: David McKay, 1974.

Hewett, F. M. Punishment and educational programs for behaviorally disordered and emotionally disturbed children and youth: A personal perspective. In F. H. Wood & K. C. Lakin (Eds.), *Punishment and aversive stimulation in special education: Legal, theoretical and practical issues in their use with emotionally disturbed children and youth.* Minneapolis: University of Minnesota Press, 1978.

Hewett, F. M., & Taylor, F. D. *The emotionally disturbed child in the classroom: The orchestration of success* (2nd ed.). Boston: Allyn & Bacon, 1980.

Josselyn, I. *The happy child.* New York: Random House, 1955.

Kallan, L. *Teachers' rights and liabilities under the law.* New York: Arco, 1971.

Kounin, J. S., & Gump, P. V. The ripple effect in discipline. *The Elementary School Journal*, 1958, *59*, 158–162.

Kuypers, D. S., Becker, W. C., & O'Leary, K. D. How to make a token system fail. *Exceptional Children*, 1968, *35*, 101–109.

Lovitt, T. C., & Smith, J. O. Effects of instructions on an individual's verbal behavior. *Exceptional Children*, 1972, *38*, 685–693.

Madsen, C. H., Becker, W. C., Thomas, D. R., Koser, L., & Plager, E. An analysis of the reinforcing function of "sit-down" commands. In R. K. Parker (Ed.), *Readings in educational psychology.* Boston: Allyn & Bacon, 1970.

Morse, W. C. Worksheet on life space interviewing. In N. J. Long, W. C. Morse & R. G. Newman (Eds.). *Conflict in the classroom: The education of emotionally disturbed children* (4th ed.). Belmont, Calif.: Wadsworth, 1980.

Morales v. *Turman,* 364 F. Supplement 166 (E.D. Texas, 1973).

O'Leary, K. D., Kaufman, K., Kass, R. E., & Drabman, R. The effects of loud and soft reprimands on the behavior of disruptive students. *Exceptional Children,* 1970, *37,* 145–155.

Patterson, G. R. An application of conditioning techniques to the control of a hyperactive child. In L. P. Ullman & L. Krasner (Eds.), *Case studies in behavior modification.* New York: Holt, Rinehart & Winston, 1965.

Redl, F. *Mental hygiene and teaching.* New York: Harcourt, Brace & World, 1959.

Redl, F., & Wineman, D. *The aggressive child.* New York: Free Press, 1957.

Sibley, S. A., Abbott, M. S., & Cooper, B. P. Modification of the classroom behavior of a disadvantaged kindergarten boy by social reinforcement and isolation. *Journal of Experimental Child Psychology,* 1969, *1,* 203–219.

Solomon, R. W., & Wahler, R. G. Peer reinforcement control of classroom problem behavior. *Journal of Applied Behavior Analysis,* 1973, *6,* 49–56.

Spaulding, R. L. Control of deviancy in the classroom as a consequence of ego-enhancing behavior management techniques. *Journal of Research and Development in Education,* 1978, *11,* 39–52.

Stephens, T. M. *Teaching skills to children with learning and behavior disorders.* Columbus, Ohio: Charles E. Merrill, 1977.

Stephens, T. M., Hartman, A. C., & Lucas, V. H. *Teaching children basic skills: A curriculum handbook.* Columbus, Ohio: Charles E. Merrill, 1978.

Thomas, D. R., Becker, W. C., & Armstrong, M. Production and elimination of disruptive classroom behavior by systematically varying teacher's behavior. *Journal of Applied Behavior Analysis,* 1968, *1,* 35–45.

Walker, H. M. *The acting-out child: Coping with classroom disruption.* Boston: Allyn & Bacon, 1979.

Wyatt v. *Stickney.* 344 F. Supplement 400 (M.D. Alabama, 1972).

13
Educational Methods

main points

1 P.L. 94-142 contains the legislative mandate that educational programs for emotionally disturbed children be individualized.

2 Many emotionally disturbed children have problems in learning or achieving that must be dealt with educationally.

3 An understanding of the child's emotional problems and how they affect the child's ability to perform in each subject or skill area is necessary for developing teaching sequences and choosing educational methods and materials.

4 Prior to teaching a subject, the teacher needs to be aware of the internal organization of each subject or skill area so that material is presented in a logical, sequential, hierarchical manner.

5 Each academic skill can be broken down, through task analysis, into a set of component subskills which the teacher should be aware of when planning teaching sequences.

6 Teaching sequences for academic skills should be carefully planned and based on an assessment of the specific skills the child possesses.

LEARNING and achieving are critical tasks in childhood but tasks which are difficult for a majority of emotionally disturbed children. In a review of the literature, Kauffman (1977) reports that "the results of research now lead to the conclusion that most mildly and moderately disturbed children are academically deficient even when it is taken into account that their mental ages are typically slightly below those of their chronological age mates.... few severely and profoundly disturbed children are found to be academically competent" (p. 122). Teaching methods, therefore, usually reflect a strong remedial approach.

No specific teaching methods, however, are uniquely suited to emotionally disturbed children as opposed to other types of exceptional children or normal children. Instructional approaches do vary considerably, but they vary on the basis of each individual child's unique learning characteristics, some of which are affected by emotions.

This chapter was written by **Virginia J. Dickens**, Fayetteville State University, and **Betty C. Epanchin**, University of North Carolina at Chapel Hill.

Some emotionally disturbed children are so anxious that their thinking is constricted. Others are so disruptive that learning is prevented. Still others are so disorganized and disoriented that their learning is erratic and disjointed. Teaching these children does require particular attention to emotional and motivational factors. It requires blending sound educational technology with knowledge of the child's conflicts, fears, wishes, interests, abilities and disabilities in such a way that the child is able to understand and master the learning situation. The following three case studies illustrate how this is done.

Mark is an 8-year-old boy referred to a special class for emotionally disturbed children because his mother was concerned about his immaturity and learning problems. After a thorough evaluation the special services committee in his school concurred with his mother that Mark was excessively constricted, inhibited and anxious. Even after the evaluation, however, it was not clear why he was having learning problems. He was placed in the special class for academic work. His teacher formulated an IEP that included remedial work in reading and math. The teaching materials included stories about children and how they felt in various circumstances. In addition, the teacher tried whenever possible to give Mark psychological permission to express his feelings. For example, one day when the teacher was very late getting to him, she said, "I'm sorry I'm late. If I had to wait as long as you've had to wait, I'd be upset. Are you a little upset?" On another day when a child ripped his paper off the bulletin board, she said, "It's too bad about your paper! That upsets me!"

Gradually Mark began to express his feelings and as he did it became increasingly apparent that once he vented his frustrations and concerns, he could learn and produce more efficiently. With this realization the teacher began to teach Mark about himself—about how he behaved and how he could monitor himself.

Elizabeth was a 6-year-old girl who earned intelligence scores in the mid 70s but who was thought to be capable of higher functioning because of her performance profile on various subtests. Both her parents and kindergarten teacher described a variety of unusual problems: she was terrified of machine noises; she had a host of imaginary friends; she was afraid of other children and therefore avoided them when in a group of children; her speech was bizarre and stereotypic at times; and she was easily upset by changes in her environment. Academically, she was easily discouraged, had little confidence in her ability to achieve and was deficient in many basic readiness skills.

In Elizabeth's case, the more unstructured her learning environment, the more disordered her thought processes seemed to become. Overt discussions of her fears and problems appeared to compound her confusion. Intervention strategies that emphasized predictability, a structured environment and remedial skills were planned. Little overt attention was given to emotions.

Michael was a 10-year-old twin from a family fraught with social and emotional problems. His mother was twice divorced, an alchoholic and unemployed. The family was comprised of five children born within six years, and all had mild to major problems. Michael was referred because of aggressive behavior (hitting classmates, frequent fights and a quick temper) as well as learning problems.

After careful evaluation he was reported to be of at least average intelligence with no apparent specific learning problems. The evaluators hypothesized that he was immature and lacked many readiness skills (emotional and academic) when he entered school. Understandably he had experienced repeated failure. The intervention program had a strong developmental emphasis, stressing acquisition of basic readiness and academic skills. In addition, care was taken to use age- and interest-appropriate materials which would capture his attention.

Although the emotional, social and academic needs of emotionally disturbed children may be met in very different ways, with the advent of P.L. 94-142 a format for educational planning common to all handicapped children who receive special education has emerged. This format is the Individualized Education Program, or IEP. P.L. 94-142 specifies that the IEP should contain the following seven elements:

1. A documentation of the student's current level of educational performance.
2. Annual goals or the attainments expected by the end of the school year.
3. Short-term objectives, stated in instructional terms, which are the immediate steps leading to the mastery of annual goals.
4. Documentation of the particular special education and related services provided to the child.
5. An indication of the extent of time a child will participate in the regular education program.
6. Projected dates for initiating services and the anticipated duration of services.
7. Evaluation procedures and schedules for determining mastery of short-term objectives at least on an annual basis. (Turnbull, Strickland & Brantley, 1978, p. 5)

The IEP, therefore, is a document which requires systematic and long-range planning for the child's education as opposed to the day-by-day or week-at-a-time planning which occurred frequently in the past. According to Turnbull et al., this latter type of planning is comparable to traveling in a car with no preset route, destination or idea when to end the trip. Such an approach to educational programming results in a curriculum that lacks continuity, has no clear objectives and is not properly individualized.

In order for the IEP to effectively meet the child's individual needs, a plan must be outlined for specifically identifying those needs, translating those needs into educational objectives, teaching the needed skills in a systematic, well-planned manner and evaluating progress on an ongoing basis. Such a plan is outlined below.

First, the child should be tested with a criterion-referenced test or observed in order to gather very specific information as to what tasks the child can and cannot perform in the subject area at hand. These test results must then be translated into very specific educational objectives. These objectives will guide the development of teaching sequences to correct problems or develop new skills. The objectives should be behavioral in nature and speak equally to the performance to be required, the conditions under which the performance will be carried out and the degree of correctness required of the performance.

Next, the educational objectives are analyzed into their component parts (task analysis); the subskills needed to perform the objectives in question are listed. The skills within each list should be ordered from lowest to highest as needed to accomplish the objective. Teaching sequences are then developed which use the information uncovered in the diagnostic process. The specific skills which the child lacks or needs to improve should be addressed. The teaching methods chosen should allow for the most efficient skill development for a particular child based on observed progress. To keep track of the child's progress the teacher keeps an ongoing record of child performance in the learning situation. Any changes in methods or objectives should be based on the performance data.

This chapter on educational methods emphasizes the basic skills of language arts and arithmetic because much of the learning in the various content areas rests on these skills. In addition, these skills must be established if the child is to become an independent adult (Hawisher & Calhoun, 1978). The suggested teaching methods are based on a developmental perspective. Since no one set of methods has been demonstrated to be effective for all teachers with all children in all settings, the most prevalent practices are reviewed.

Readiness

Before children can learn the basic academic skills of reading, writing and arithmetic, they must be ready to learn. They must have acquired some basic skills which are necessary for more advanced performance. For example, before a child is ready to read, the child must be able to distinguish one letter from another, remember different letter sounds, remember how letters are grouped and have a basic understanding of word meanings.

Over the years there has been a great deal of controversy in the educational literature about what skills are really prerequisites to learning in school. This controversy has been stimulated by repeated observations that some children acquire more advanced academic skills even though they have deficits in the areas presumed to be prerequisites. For example, some children have learned to read even though they had major visual discrimination problems. Although this controversy has not been resolved, most educators agree that teachers should help young children develop readiness skills. Children do not have to be totally proficient in a readiness skill, however, in order to learn higher level skills. An inordinate amount of attention to readiness skills is generally not considered necessary once the child is past 7 years of age.

The list of conditions and skills thought to be necessary for optimal academic learning is varied and long. Some of the important skills are visual discrimination, auditory discrimination, motor skills, mental and reasoning abilities, appropriate prior experiences, language skills, emotional readiness and academic survival skills.

Readiness and the Emotionally Disturbed Child

Many emotionally disturbed children are described by their teachers as immature. Early-latency-age emotionally disturbed children, in particular, often lag behind their age mates in academic readiness skills. Why this is so is not clear. Psychotic, thought-disordered children frequently have impairments in visual perception, auditory and visual discrimination, directional orientation, cognitive functioning and conceptual organization (Mack, 1979; Baker, 1979). Acting-out, aggressive children often start school with deficits in impulse control, social skills and educational-related experiences. For these children, and for other emotionally disturbed children who are lacking in basic readiness skills, pre-academic training helps the child start school successfully.

Assessing Readiness Skills

Many of the readiness skills are assessed during early childhood, in preschool or kindergarten, although in some cases the assessment may come later. Among the instruments used to assess readiness skills are rating scales (Novack, Bonaventura, & Merenda, 1972) and the School Readiness Survey (Jordan & Massey, 1969). Additional tests of an informal screening nature include Pre-reading Screening Procedures (Slingerland, 1969) and Program for the Early Identification of Learning Disabilities (Petersen, 1970). The latter is a good general reference for teachers. Teachers may also wish to devise their own readiness checklist after the one illustrated in Wallace and Larsen (1978, pp. 170–171).

Teaching Readiness Skills

Visual discrimination. Visual discrimination is the ability to distinguish one object from another by sight. It is necessary for many academic skills, such as telling one letter or word from another in reading. An inordinate amount of time should not be spent on training visual discrimination skills to the detriment of other readiness or academic skills. Children need to be taught to distinguish between and to match increasingly smaller, increasingly less concrete objects until they are actually discriminating between and matching letters, words, numbers or symbols. For example, the child could practice matching and discrimination by progressing through the following series:

Large, identical concrete objects (balls, toys)
Smaller identical concrete objects (small toys, geometric-shaped blocks)
Large, identical pictures and shapes
Smaller, identical pictures and shapes
Large symbols on paper (geometric shapes, stars)
Smaller symbols on paper (lines, squiggles)
Letters
Numbers
Words

Auditory discrimination. Auditory discrimination is the ability to distinguish one sound from another. It is necessary for monitoring the different speech sounds, words and sentences heard in the learning situation. Auditory discrimination seems to be a vital skill for phonics analysis in reading. In learning auditory discrimination, the child should be presented with increasingly fine discrimination tasks until he is actually distinguishing between or matching speech sounds, words, numbers and sentences. Training activities in auditory matching or discrimination could progress through the following series:

> Gross, artificially produced sounds (noisemakers, blocks)
> Gross environmental sounds (car horns, door slams)
> Softer artificially produced sounds (soft footsteps, quiet hand claps)
> Softer environmental sounds (bird calls, wind sounds)
> Sentences
> Speech words
> Numbers
> Isolated speech sounds

Motor skills. Adequate motor skills include the ability to move eyes in a left to right direction across a page, the ability to hold a book and turn pages, the ability to hold and manipulate a pencil and so on. Of course, academic progress can take place when the child lacks such abilities but is assisted by special prosthetic devices. In most emotionally disturbed children, movement abilities are intact and simply need to be verified or trained. Training should flow from gross movements to finer physical or optical movements. For example, a child can practice holding a large ball, a large box and later a book. For children with poor motor control and strength, however, the reverse order may be needed; the child needs to move from holding small, light objects to heavier, larger objects to a book. Optical training, if necessary, can include eye tracking in a left to right movement (as across a page) in increasingly finer units. Another related motor skill is the ability to keep one's place on the page when reading or following along as another reads. This is a difficult concentration task for some emotionally disturbed children due to problems of poor attention and distractibility.

Mental and reasoning abilities. The child's mental and reasoning abilities for learning need to be verified. Highly disorganized and disoriented children (overtly psychotic) may be excluded from academic activities initially; many of these children, however, are eventually able to accomplish academic skills to some degree, and some quite well. A teacher needs to know whether the child can follow a sequence, think in logical patterns, remember simple information long enough to act upon it and so on. If the child is found to be deficient in his reasoning abilities, teaching sequences can be designed to address specific skills.

Some of the component skills involved in thinking clearly are:

1 *Detecting relationships.* Give the child similar objects (e.g., two dolls) and ask him to point out how they are alike or different.
2 *Sequencing.* Have the child arrange a series of simple story pictures in correct order.

3. *Logical thinking.* Have the child tell why fish cannot fly or trees cannot walk.
4. *Remembering.* Have the child repeat increasingly long lists of words or numbers. Have him recall facts from a recent story.

This list of components of mental and reasoning abilities is only partial. For additional discussion see Alley and Deshler (1979) and Lillie (1975).

Experience. Adequate experience is the basis for the development of intelligence and language. Children whose backgrounds include few educationally relevant experiences or over-exposure to stress and emotional deprivation are severely limited in their ability to interact with their environments and to express themselves in spoken or written language. A child must have enough knowledge to operate within the school environment. If a teacher determines that, due to deprivation from whatever source, the child has inadequate experience, she must try to fill this void. She may provide carefully structured experiences, such as field trips and visits to arts events. After these experiences, the teacher should then review the experiences with the child to ensure that they have been beneficial. Such experience-stimulation programs may be undertaken as part of a general language development process (see pp. 367–368).

Language skills. Appropriate language skills for academic learning include the ability to produce and understand oral language. Minuchin, Dollarhide, and Graubard (1969) studied the communication patterns of a group of emotionally disturbed, delinquent youngsters and noted that these children had "a style of communication in which people do not expect to be heard and therefore assert themselves by yelling" (p. 384). They explain:

> There is a lack of training in elaboration of questions to gather information or garner the nuances of degree. There is also a lack of training in developing themes to their logical conclusion, and there is no closure on conflicts. This communication style can be entirely adequate for the transactions of gross power and nurturing relationships, but it is insufficient to deal with chronic and subtle conflicts requiring the search for, ordering of, and sharing of different or new information. (p. 384)

Children with these problems need to learn the usefulness of language. Practice with thinking before they speak, asking pertinent questions and carrying a discussion to its logical conclusion is helpful.

Emotional readiness. Before the child is ready to engage in academic learning, a certain degree of emotional maturity is required. The child must have developed an interest in the outside world, some emotional separation from home and parents, and a desire to master aspects of the environment. The child also must be able to tolerate limits from others and to wait for what he wants, or delay gratification. He needs to have acquired a basic awareness of self—what he can and cannot do—and some social skills. For example, the child who is not ready to learn to read responds to the question "Don't you want to read like other children?" by asking, "Why should I? What's in it for me? . . . if he has not already discovered the satisfaction of acquiring a new skill through work, no answer you give will have meaning" (Kessler, 1966, p. 210).

So many emotionally disturbed children do not see how learning and achieving can benefit or interest them. Consequently, teachers often must start by helping the child learn "what's in it for him." This process is a complicated one. It involves helping the child develop the motivation to learn through identification with the teacher and her values; it involves creating an environment that rewards learning and achieving; and it involves teaching and demonstrating the relevance of an education. Chapters 11, 12 and 14 describe techniques that are useful for helping a child develop the emotional readiness to learn. But emotional readiness to learn cannot be separated from academic readiness. A child must develop the requisite academic skills for success so that learning can become intrinsically rewarding; hence, emotional readiness is developed as academic skills are required.

Classroom survival skills. Such skills as ability to attend to a task, follow directions and follow a classroom routine can have a significant effect on whether a child is successful in the learning setting. Not only can survival skills such as attending and working be learned but this learning can also affect academic achievement (Cobb & Hops, 1973).

For the emotionally disturbed child who already has problems with distractibility, whose inner conflicts leave little time for attention to directions and whose disorientation or need to defy authority make it difficult to follow established routines, survival skills may be lacking. The teacher may need to delay concentration on the more traditional academic tasks until survival skills are developed in the child. For example, following directions may be taught in a practical, task-analyzed fashion by having the child perform increasingly more complex tasks in a step-by-step manner. Likewise, children may also need to be taught to follow routines. Both of these skills may be taught as a part of the behavior management system as well as during academic lessons.

Additional Resources

Commercial materials which may be helpful for developing readiness skills include Learning to Think Series (Science Research Associates), Concept Builders with Write and See (Appleton-Century-Crofts) and I Want to Learn Program (Follett Educational Corporation).

Additional reading on developing readiness skills may be found in Carrillo (1971), Durkin (1978) and Spache and Spache (1977).

Language Arts

Language arts is a broad term which includes some of the most vital academic, social and life skills children acquire. These skills include listening, speaking, reading, writing, handwriting and spelling.

Hierarchies of how language develops in normal children provide guidance when teaching language to the emotionally disturbed (Bartel & Bryen,

1978). In order of acquisition, a child normally develops the abilities to listen, to speak, to read and to write. (Lerner, 1976; Turnbull & Schulz, 1979). This is the basic hierarchy of language skill development. Writing may be further subdivided into the functional writing tools of handwriting and spelling as well as conceptual writing.

Evidence points to the existence of an inner language in the child which may act as a training ground for acquiring competence in the higher-level language skills. It is this inner language that forms the connection between thinking and speaking in the very young child. Inner language itself is an unobservable phenomena, the existence of which must be inferred from other higher-order language performances (Myklebust, 1964; Vygotsky, 1962; Wallace & Larsen, 1978). Unobservable or nonexpressive language skills are by no means educationally irrelevant, however.

Language is intimately linked to one's ability to think and learn (Erb & Mercer, 1979). Therefore, learning appropriate language is important in helping the emotionally handicapped child approach normalcy. Although the language development process remains unclear, several assumptions are widely accepted. First, language skills are learned performances (Bartel & Bryen, 1978). Second, language develops in a stage-like, hierarchical fashion (Turnbull & Schulz, 1979). Third, certain abilities must be present prior to appropriate language development in the child. These include the ability to perceive things that exist in one's environment and the ability to use an organized system of communication (language) for responding to and representing those things perceived (Bloom, 1970). Fourth, speech and personality mutually influence each other (Verville, 1968).

On the basis of the evidence available in language research it can be determined that (a) language is teachable; (b) language can be task analyzed; (c) language competence requires certain preliminary skills; and (d) language and emotions interact and this effect must be considered.

Listening

Listening is perhaps the most basic language skill. Language is taken in receptively and understood before it is acted upon or expressed (Lerner, 1976; Wallace & Larsen, 1978). Listening is essential to success in most school situations since the student spends about half of the school day listening (Wilt, 1957).

Listening skills may be categorized in a number of ways. Generally, they can be broken down into abilities such as attending, literal comprehension of words and sentences (as in following directions and gathering details), auditory memory, critical evaluation of spoken material (as in detecting propaganda and separating fact from opinion), and appreciation of spoken material (as in detecting mood, tone and rhythms) (Alley & Deshler, 1979).

Listening and the Emotionally Disturbed Child

Inattentiveness, distractibility and a short attention span are behavior problems frequently cited as characteristic of emotionally disturbed children. In some children these problems seem to be related to organic problems which are presumed to affect the child's ability to listen. In other children it is hypothesized that their high levels of anxiety or depression interfere with their ability to listen; their capacity to listen is intact, but they are distracted by their emotional turmoil. Regardless of etiology, these behaviors cripple the child in the classroom. He either misses information altogether or he acquires it in a piecemeal fashion.

Children with these problems often respond well to interventions such as counseling or medication, but in addition, they need to be taught how to listen and they need help in focusing and sustaining their attention (Swift & Spivack, 1974). Without such remedial help many emotionally disturbed children fall further behind their classmates academically.

Assessing Listening and Receptive Language Skills

In order to determine whether a child possesses adequate listening and receptive language skills, the teacher may use a number of informal, classroom-adaptable assessment tools. One format for measuring spoken language comprehension assesses the ability to respond to spoken language when not facing the speaker and the ability to attend promptly, and with purpose, to spoken language (Berry, 1969). Another format is a listening checklist which allows children to assess points such as proper positioning and appropriate mental preparation for good listening (Kopp, 1967). Additional assessment tools in listening and receptive language skills are cited in Wallace and Larsen (1978).

Teaching Listening Skills

Poor listening skills can be improved. According to Alley and Deshler (1979) "there is considerable evidence to indicate that instruction in listening leads to improvement in listening performance" (p. 277).

Attending. For some students, the teacher may need to begin a listening program by teaching a child how to attend. The following techniques are helpful:

1 Signal to the child when it is time to attend. For example, call his name, touch him, point on his page (Turnbull & Schulz, 1979).
2 Highlight important aspects of the situation to which the child should attend. For example, tell him, "Listen carefully to the instructions."
3 Emphasize important stimuli when developing teaching sequences. For example, use bright colors on the parts of the learning materials on which the child is expected to focus.

Comprehending. If no problems are noted in the child's attending, higher-level listening skills may still be deficient. Assuming auditory acuity and perception are intact (and one should not assume this without evidence), children need to be taught good listening skills in an overt fashion in order to become purposeful, and therefore effective, listeners (Turnbull & Schulz, 1979). Among the goals of listening are remembering, evaluating and appreciating (Alley & Deshler, 1979).

The teacher may first break down simple listening comprehension skills into the component parts and develop teaching sequences for each part. A suggested breakdown is presented by Alley and Deshler (1979).

Listening Comprehension (literal)
a. Understanding the relationship of details to main ideas
b. Following directions
c. Following the sequence of the message
d. Listening for details
e. Listening to a question with an intent to answer
f. Repeating what has been heard (p. 282)

An example of a teaching sequence for following directions would be to give increasingly complex commands or directions. Also, the teacher can ask the child to repeat directions, and to respond to one direction, then two directions, then a series of directions (Turnbull & Schulz, 1979).

While developing good listening habits, there is ample opportunity to build receptive language vocabulary at the same time. This can be done through storytelling activities. Taking "let's imagine" trips is a listening-oriented experience. In this activity the teacher talks the class through the sights and sounds, tastes and smells of a new place. Although there may be no immediate feedback from children, such activities can be very valuable in building stores of inner information which can be used later in expressive language.

Remembering. After the development of lower-level listening skills, which in themselves can greatly enhance a child's academic performance, more sophisticated listening intervention may be needed. Strategies for improving memory may need to be taught. Memory strategies are important because they help ensure that what is listened to is retained. These strategies include rehearsal or repetition of material to be retained, clustering material under organizing categories and coding the information to be retained through mnemonic devices.

Evaluating. Some emotionally disturbed students hear what they expect to hear. Therefore, overt teaching of higher listening skills such as evaluating the truth and worth of what is heard can be an important skill to develop. By so doing the students gain some control over their environment and are better able to make their own judgments and decisions. Students should have ample opportunity to practice making judgments with plenty of teacher guidance. For example, students can listen to recordings of mock television commercials in the classroom and evaluate their persuasive content. Following this, students could be encouraged to listen closely to commercials at home and bring comments regarding their persuasive content back to the classroom for discussion.

Appreciating. Listening for appreciation is a high-level skill which can provide some emotionally disturbed children with outlets and activities that will help lessen personal conflicts. Some background information should usually precede listening of this sort. In order to appreciate a poetry reading, the student needs to be informed in an enthuasiastic and interesting way about poetry and the particular poet. The same is true for listening to music or a public speech.

Additional Resources

A number of commercial materials are available to help the teacher develop good listening skills in her students. Among these are Sound—Order—Sense: A Developmental Program in Auditory Perception (Follett Educational Corporation), Learn to Listen (Mafex Associates, Inc.) and Junior Listen-Hear Program (Follett Educational Corporation).

Additional reading on developing listening skills may be found in Lundsteen (1979), Russell and Russell (1959) and Wilt (1957).

Speaking

Spoken language, an expressive language skill, is the next highest level of language development. Observation and research have revealed that spoken language develops in a stage-like process beginning shortly after birth. Early utterances of the infant are limited to reflex vocalizations. By the time a child is 6 years old, however, he has usually acquired the sound and language system of English. Mastery of the ways of putting words together to form sentences, and thus ideas, may continue up to and even beyond the teen years (Lerner, 1976; Erb & Mercer, 1979). By being familiar with the milestones of normal speech development, the teacher can better develop or correct spoken language in the emotionally disturbed child. Such developmental milestones are depicted in chart form in Bartel and Bryen (1978) and Smith (1974).

Spoken language can be broken down into the component parts of phonology, morphology, syntax, semantics and pragmatics. Specific problems in spoken-language development may occur in any one or a number of these categories. Spoken language problems can also manifest themselves in more general ways. For example, a child may be nonverbal, may use an incomprehensible spoken language or may communicate poorly (Schiefelbusch, Ruder & Bricker, 1976). A particularly troublesome language problem which may be first noticed in the child's spoken language but which may also be manifested in other areas of language development (such as conceptual writing) is language delay. This problem is sometimes categorized as a severe form of incomprehensible language.

Characteristics of language-delayed children are (a) phrase production that is unusually childish, (b) language use without apparent purpose, (c) lack of sufficient speech or language production and (d) deficient concept development and labeling ability (Scofield, 1978). Language delay has been explained by a variety of factors, such as lack of environmental stimulation and inability to respond to environmental stimulation. Whether the cause for such delay lies within the environment or within the child is probably irrelevant at the point of remediation, assuming any sensory acuity problems have been identified.

Speaking and the Emotionally Disturbed Child

The development of appropriate spoken language is a complex process for all children. Although many emotionally disturbed children have deficient communication skills, it is often impossible to determine whether the language skill deficit appeared prior to the emotional disturbance or after, so closely do language and the emotions interact. After all, language is the means by which one's inner life is revealed. When children are in turmoil, speech often reflects their conflict. Likewise, children who lack adequate skills in speaking experience problems as a result of their disability (Cantwell, 1977). When they are not able to communicate effectively, they often get anxious which further interferes with their functioning. Stutterers may be the most obvious example of this. Although stuttering may not be caused by emotional problems, it does seem to be exacerbated by anxiety. The anticipation of failure seems to evoke fragmentation of speech and increased tension (Hoffman, 1979).

The types and severity of language problems seen in emotionally disturbed children vary considerably. Children diagnosed as elective mutes presumably can speak but they choose not to. Many clinicians believe that their refusal to communicate is a way of exerting control and expressing anger (Hoffman, 1979). Psychotic children often have severe speech and language problems. "Their vocal quality is often loud, high-pitched, and without intonation. Connotative expressions, formed by appropriate rhythm, articulation, stress and volume are often not employed" (Mack, 1979, p. 64). Additionally, the speech of many psychotic children is often garbled, confused and nonsensical. A child repeatedly greeting her teacher in a singsong voice by saying, "Do the stars come out at night?" is an example of the absurd speech that is typical of some psychotic, thought-disordered children.

Much more frequently seen are children who speak indistinctly at times, who occasionally use words inappropriately, who have difficulty expressing their needs and most particularly their feelings, whose speech development was slow and who are having trouble academically. When other psychological problems are also present such as excessive dependency or inhibition of aggression, some clinicians see the speech and learning problems as symptomatic of the child's emotional problems. Others believe that the child has learning disabilities which cause the child to feel inadequate and to be overly dependent or inhibited.

Often teachers must work with such children for a period of time before they are able to sort out the problems. It may not be necessary to specify whether the problem is an emotional one or a language disability as long as the child is making progress academically. If, however, the child is not progressing, teachers may need to employ alternative interventions such as counseling, life space interviewing, therapeutic tutoring and affective education, in addition to remedial education.

Assessing Speaking Skills

Wallace and Larsen (1978) cite a number of informal language assessment tools for the area of spoken language. These include a form for assessing the linguistic skills of phonology, semantics and syntax (Berry, 1969). This form gives attention to aspects of spoken language such as vocabulary and sentence form. Language scales which examine spoken and receptive language adequacy are offered by Goodman and Hammill (The Basic Schools Skills Inventory, 1975), Mecham (The Verbal Language Development Scale, 1959) and Zimmerman, Steiner, and Watt (Preschool Language Scales, 1969). An additional tool which can be used to analyze a language sample taken from the child is the Developmental Sentence Analysis (Lee, 1974).

Teaching Speaking Skills

Spoken language is the foundation on which reading and writing skills are later developed. Therefore, this skill area is often given special attention in remediation programs. Remediation of spoken language problems takes many forms depending on the nature and severity of the problem. Severe language delays, for example, may require a broad developmental approach to help the child acquire basic language usage. One language training program for language-deficient students features phases such as sound imitation, noun and verb imitation, noun and verb production, and phrase imitation and production (Bricker, Ruder & Vincent, 1976). Another approach, developed by Fitzgerald (1966) for the deaf, helps in teaching children correct sentence structure. A word of caution is in order here. When encouraging the child to use language, the teacher needs to be careful not to push the emotionally disturbed child too much. Many such children respond negatively to demands.

Language experience. One technique which works very well as a language stimulator and model is the *language experience approach* (Allen, 1976; Stauffer, 1970). It is useful for children with many types of language handicaps. The approach is briefly summarized in the following steps.

1. *Set up an experience.* Either take advantage of a naturally occurring event or plan a special language-stimulation outing. Take the children on a field trip or walk, or engage them in some special classroom activity (such as dyeing Easter eggs). Be sure to prepare the children ahead of time by teaching them new concepts or vocabulary that they will need and then follow up on the preparation by pointing out essential concepts and vocabulary as they come up during the experience.
2. *Reinforce the experience.* Upon return from or completion of the experience, reinforce what has been encountered with a time of "planned remembering." Discuss systematically the events of the experience using pictures and play drama to help the children remember.

3 *Provide any necessary language.* Using pictures, word cards, sentence strips and so on, supply any language needed during the planned remembering stage.
4 *Ask children to retell the experience.* As the teacher elicits oral experience from the children, sentences are written on an experience chart as they are spoken. Again, the teacher supplies any needed words. This written version can be used for many purposes such as grammatical correction exercises, development of a word list for reading or spelling, or copying into an experience book.
5 *Have children tell or write a related story.* This gives children a chance to generalize and expand current knowledge by telling (or later writing) a related story using some of the same concepts and vocabulary as in the original experience story.

This approach is especially useful for developing language skills in the child who is "turned off" or threatened by more structured, school-like activities. It can also be easily structured around student interest.

Linguistic skills. Many children, unlike the language-delayed child, exhibit language problems of a narrow, specific nature. Problems can arise in any of the linguistic skill areas (phonology, morphology, syntax, semantics, pragmatics) which allow the child to master the sound, structure, meaning and social systems of English. Problems in these areas may be attacked through exercises and games which present models and give practice in the specific areas of deficiency (Erb & Mercer, 1979). Helpful commercial materials include Lessons in Syntax (Educational Activities, Inc.), Parts of Speech (Teaching Resources Corporation) and Peabody Articulation Cards (American Guidance Service).

Whenever specific remedial exercises are being applied to language problems, the teacher should make use of the basic principles of educational psychology.

1 Prepare children to receive language teaching experiences.
2 Use clear prompts, models and cues to ensure that the child participates in and understands the language experience.
3 Reinforce appropriately any correct responses by the child to help ensure recurrence of the response.
4 Refer to the language experience in as many ways and contexts as possible to ensure maximum generalization and transfer of learning.
5 Give as many opportunities to practice newly acquired language skills as possible in order to encourage mastery (this usually takes many more practice opportunities than expected).

Additional Resources

Commercial materials which may prove valuable to the teacher in working with the language-deficient child include Matrix Games For Young Children (Appleton-Century-Crofts), Distar I, II, III (Science Research

Associates), GOAL: Language Development-Games Oriented Activity for Learning (Milton Bradley), Language Master, Language Stimulator Program (Bell & Howell), The Peabody Language Development Kits (American Guidance Service), and Language Training for Adolescents (Educators Publishing Service).

Additional reading in language development and teaching may be found in Bangs (1968), Lamb (1971) and Wiig and Semel (1976).

Reading

After spoken language, reading is the next skill acquired in the language arts developmental sequence. The reading process has been defined, conceptualized, and programmed by many authors. Generally, reading is regarded as both a word identification (or decoding) process as well as a comprehension (or encoding) process. Word identification skills include phonic analysis, structural analysis, sight word recognition and context analysis. Comprehension skills include identifying the main idea of a paragraph, contrasting main idea with details, identifying literal facts, interpreting the author's meaning and character's actions or thoughts, and evaluating the author's meaning and character's actions or thoughts. There are many subskills in each of these skill areas, some of which will be discussed later in the chapter.

Reading and the Emotionally Disturbed Child

A number of investigators have looked at the extent of reading deficits in emotionally disturbed, elementary-age children. Findings have ranged from no differences in the reading achievement of normal and disturbed children to significant and marked differences.

Reading problems may be more prevalent in certain types of disorders. In a study on the relationship between reading achievement and behavior disorders, Graubard (1971) found that the higher the child's score on the conduct dimension of a behavior checklist, the greater the reading retardation. Also, a number of other investigators have reported a high incidence of reading failure in delinquent, conduct-disordered populations. The relationship between reading and emotional handicaps is far from clear, however. Historically, difficulties in learning to read were attributed to "emotional disturbance due to child rearing practices" (Kauffman & Hallahan, 1976). Over time, however, a number of other factors have also been cited, such as poor teaching, environmental factors and neurological factors.

Three major groupings in reading retardation have been identified (Rabinovitch & Ingram, 1962). The first group is said to exhibit *primary reading retardation*. The capacity to learn to read is impaired in this group of children because of biological causes. These children show disturbed neurological organization but not brain damage. Another group has suffered *brain injury with resultant reading retardation*. The reading problems of this group are believed to result from brain damage which has been established in the medical history. A third group exhibits *secondary reading retardation*. The capacity to learn to read is intact in these children, but because of negativism, depression, anxiety, emotional blocking, psychosis, limited educational opportunities or other external factors, these children either are not reading or are not reading at their expected level.

In the psychodynamically oriented clinical literature, considerable attention has been given to the secondary reading retardation group. The reading problems of these children are often described as reading inhibitions. Theoretically, the inhibition serves to allay anxiety or avoid conflict. For most children who are starting school beginning to read symbolizes growing up. For children fearful of being autonomous and independent, reading can be threatening. Such children may undo all efforts to teach them to read because, it is hypothesized, their unconscious conflicts interfere with their ability to learn.

Another commonly cited cause of learning inhibitions in the psychodynamically oriented literature is a fear of aggression (Sperry, Staver, Reiner & Ulrich, 1958). According to this perspective, children who do not learn to differentiate between assertion and hurtful aggression often try to inhibit all assertive activities. Learning is mastering, an assertive activity; hence, for some children a conflict emerges. Fear of success, of failure and of competition also are cited as causes of learning inhibitions (Kessler, 1966; Pearson, 1952).

While reading and learning inhibitions have received considerable attention in the psychodynamic literature, how pervasive these problems are is difficult to determine. The psychiatric literature tends to focus on individual cases and their individual dynamics; educational literature focuses on groups of children who are reading failures but not on the dynamics of the individual. For the teacher the important issue is not to establish the prevalence of reading inhibitions but to understand how emotions, specifically conflictive emotions, may interfere with reading.

Assessing Reading Skills

A number of criterion-referenced and informal measures can be used to pinpoint reading difficulties. Some widely used examples of criterion-referenced testing and teaching materials for reading are Brigance Diagnostic Inventory of Basic Skills (Curriculum Associates, Inc.), Read-On (Random House) and Skills Monitoring System—Reading (Harcourt Brace Jovanovich). Criterion-referenced and informal assessment techniques for the skill areas of word identification (analysis) and comprehension include the Wisconsin Tests of Reading Skill Development: Word Attack and Comprehension (Kamm, Miles, Van Blaricom, Harris & Stewart, 1972, Ekwall's (1970) checklist, which checks for errors such as omissions, repetitions and substitutions and Critical Reading Skills Checklist (Wallace & Larsen, 1978), which checks for skills such as the ability to anticipate outcomes and analyze character. Graded reading passages followed by questions may also be used to ascertain reading and comprehension level. Additional tests which can provide direct information on the reading performance of problem readers are the Prescriptive Reading Inventory (CTB, McGraw-Hill) and the Reading Miscue Inventory (Goodman & Burke, 1972).

Teaching Reading: The Major Approaches

Professionals disagree on the exact nature of the reading process and, therefore, on the appropriate approach to teaching reading skills. Several major approaches to reading are currently recognized. An excellent, easily digested review of these approaches is provided by Miller (1977).

The basal reader approach. The basal reader approach is one of the oldest and most familiar reading methods. Basal readers are graded reading texts primarily featuring narrative stories and sometimes accompanied by student workbooks. Newer basal series may also come with supplements such as games and cassettes. In a basal program, children are often grouped according to reading ability. Lessons usually consist of "development of a background of experiences for the story, presentation of new vocabulary terms, guided silent reading, purposeful oral reading, extending skill development, and enriching experiences" (Miller, 1977, p. 65). The recognition of sight words and the use of picture context clues are usually stressed as word identification methods prior to phonic analysis. Also the emphasis on reading comprehension starts early.

Modern basal series are frequently praised for making use of a variety of word recognition and comprehension techniques and for the systematic and sequential way in which reading skills are presented. This is the approach used most frequently in the public schools. For some emotionally handicapped children the basal reading approach may be contraindicated because the books remind the children of past failures.

In the past, basal readers were soundly criticized for introducing vocabulary so slowly (Miller, 1977). Critics charged that this held children back and prevented them from acquiring a reading vocabulary that matched their already substantial spoken vocabulary. More recent basal reading series have made efforts to remedy this problem. Examples of two basal reader programs are The Bank Street Readers (Macmillan) and the New Open Highways (Scott, Foresman).

The phonics approach. The phonics approach is actually an umbrella term covering several similar approaches to reading. In general, phonics programs are early supplemental reading programs. Although many other reading approaches contain phonics components, the major emphasis in phonics programs is to teach children to pronounce new words by teaching rules of sound-letter relationships.

There are at least two philosophies for teaching the sound-letter relationships. In the analytic phonics approach children begin by examining whole words and move on to examining sounds within syllables of the word. In the synthetic approach, children produce isolated sounds within words and then blend those into the whole word. Many phonics programs advocate

In the synthetic phonics approach, children learn to produce separate sounds within words and then blend the sounds into a whole word.

delay of emphasis on comprehension until after a child has a good grasp of decoding or word pronunciation skills.

Phonics programs have been praised because they allow a child to acquire sounding-out skills which can be used to figure out unfamiliar words somewhat independently. Many emotionally disturbed children are either over- or under-dependent in their relationship to school work. Such children need to achieve a balance between autonomy and dependence in subjects such as reading. Programs that start with a phonics emphasis encourage such a balance. The child's skills are built using generally psychologically neutral reading rules and materials. Reading matter is not as apt to be loaded with reading passages which stir up old failures and conflicts at school or home.

An additional advantage of the early phonics approach for the emotionally disturbed child is that phonics programs usually emphasize oral reading. Silent reading is stressed in many basal programs. Many emotionally handicapped children find it extremely difficult to concentrate when reading silently, perhaps because of inner turmoil, upsetting reading material or distractions in the room. Generally they are able to concentrate more effectively when reading out loud.

A number of research studies (Bleismer & Yarborough, 1965; Gurren & Hughes, 1965) have suggested that early phonics programs promote better reading achievement in the early grades. Critics of this approach state that the research regarding the efficacy of phonics is inconclusive and the superiority of the "phonics first" programs unsubstantiated. They point out that not all of the studies used control groups and that children who were taught with a strong, early emphasis on phonics did not necessarily become superior readers in all areas. The programs have also been accused of developing noncomprehending "word callers." Phonics programs include the Open Court Reading Program (Open Court Publishing Company) and Distar Reading (Science Research Associates).

The linguistic approach. The linguistic approach to teaching reading, again, is an umbrella for a number of reading methods which differ in varying degrees. Basically, the linquistic approaches apply the study of language to the reading process. Because there are subsets of linguists who stress different aspects of language, there are various linguistic approaches to reading. For example, phonologists are interested in the sounds of reading, structuralists in the structure of reading language, and psycholinguists in the psychological aspects of language and reading. In the phonological approaches, decoding is generally emphasized initially, and comprehension may not be stressed at all in early reading. Phonological reading materials are not easily distinguished from phonics materials. In phonological linguistics, pronunciation is often taught by comparing and contrasting spelling patterns within words or nonsense words, as in the following consonant-vowel combinations.

CVC	CVCV
not	note
vot	vote
pot	pote
fot	fote

Some simple sight words may be also be taught early in the program.

Structuralists have influenced the teaching of reading primarily by applying their ideas to basal series as opposed to developing programs of their own. This linguistic approach emphasizes oral reading of complete sentences in the early stages of reading. Sentences to be read may be introduced according to their conformity to particular sentence patterns defined by the structuralists. For example, a Pattern I sentence consists of the following:

Noun Marker	Noun	Verb	Adverb
The	girl	played	happily.

Psycholinguists, too, have applied their ideas to existing programs; they have not developed reading programs of their own. This group is interested in how language, reading and psychology interact.

Strong points of the linguistic approach in general are its demonstrated usefulness and success with older reading-disabled students and its contribution to improvement of basal readers. The approach has been criticized because it sometimes employs reading material which is uninteresting and because it does not emphasize comprehension skills early. Two linguistically oriented series are the Harper & Row Linguistic Series and the Structural Reading Series (The L. W. Singer Company).

The language experience approach. A fourth common reading approach is the language experience approach. In this approach, the readers undergo an experience (planned or perhaps incidental) which is then translated by the teacher into written format. The translation often follows eliciting the story out loud from the class. The teacher then uses this written format as a stimulus for having children read aloud, answer comprehension questions, practice phonics skills and so forth. (The language experience approach is discussed further in Manarino, 1980).

An obvious advantage of this approach is that it utilizes the child's own language and experiences for reading, thus maximizing motivation. It also helps the child to see the interrelationships between spoken and written language. A drawback of the approach is the time involved in the process of eliciting the material before it can be read. A more serious drawback, perhaps, is the sometimes nonsequential nature of the presentation or exposure to particular reading skills. Materials representing this approach include Language Experiences in Reading (Encyclopaedia Britannica Educational Corporation) and Language Experience Activities (Houghton Mifflin).

Other approaches to reading. A number of other specialized approaches to reading have very unique characteristics. For example, the *rebus approach* to reading utilizes pictures in the place of some words in a sentence, as in

The 🕴 drove his 🚗 to town.

A commercially available rebus program is the Peabody Rebus Reading Program (American Guidance Service). This is an interesting approach for children but the reading process may be slower to develop when the children eventually replace the pictures with words.

Another unique approach to reading is the use of the *initial teaching alphabet* (i.t.a.) (Mazurkiewicz & Tanyzer, 1966), a modification of traditional English orthography (the written alphabet) which corresponds more closely to spoken English. The i.t.a. utilizes 44 written symbols to correspond to the sounds of spoken English. For example:

$$ae = pl\underline{a}ce$$
$$th = \underline{th}row$$

This alphabet is used to spell words encountered by the child in a reading program. While the use of the i.t.a. makes spelling and pronunciation more uniform, it may also confuse the child when the switch is made to traditional spelling patterns.

A third unique approach to reading is offered by the proponents of the *multi-sensory reading methods*. In these methods, the emphasis is on using more than one sensory modality to acquire reading skills. An example is a program advocated by Grace Fernald (1943) which combines the use of the visual, auditory, kinesthetic and tactual modalities, commonly called the VAKT method. The VAKT approach is valuable because it does not limit the ways in which a child may gather information. Such an approach, however, may prove cumbersome if all senses are consistently addressed. Two other multi-sensory programs are presented in Gillingham and Stillman (1970) and Spalding and Spalding (1962).

A technique considered to be multi-sensory in nature which is used with very disabled readers is the *neurological impress method* (Heckelman, 1969). It features unison reading by the teacher and the child in hopes that "the auditory process of feedback from the reader's own voice and the voice of someone else reading the same material establishes a new learning process" (Lerner, 1976, p. 245).

This review of common approaches to teaching reading is representative rather than exhaustive. Unfortunately, no single approach has been found to work best overall. In addition, much of the research is marred by problems of research design and control. Perhaps this control problem is due to the fact that the children are so different; this element of heterogeneity, even within a particular special population, is very difficult to control. More emphasis needs to be placed on determining specifically what types of children are suited to what particular processes in reading (Gillespie-Silver, 1979).

Since no one program works best with all emotionally disturbed children all of the time (Orlando, 1973), the best strategy for teachers is to know the techniques of many approaches thoroughly and to build a repertoire of solid skills representing a variety of philosophies. These may then be used as the particular child and situation require. Still, the teacher may be wondering, "Out of the variety of approaches, which should I try first with a particular child?" The most appropriate guides are those of time and effectiveness. Choose the approach which seems to allow the particular child to acquire reading skills as quickly and efficiently as possible so that he can proceed in other reading-related learning areas. Generally, Haring and Bateman (1977) suggest that the further away the child is from mastering the objective, the more beneficial a structured, deductive approach is. Conversely, the closer the child is to mastering the objective, the more beneficial an inductive approach is. Thus, the more reading disabled the child is, the more structured the approach needs to be.

As noted earlier, reading skills are usually separated into decoding (word identification or analysis) skills and comprehension skills. While these categories form neat divisions for educational analysis, it is essential to remember that no skill alone is enough to be called reading. If the skills are not taught, ultimately, in an integrated fashion, the resulting product will be an inefficient reader.

Decoding or word identification. In this subskill of reading, the emphasis is on allowing children to find the keys to unlock printed symbols on paper so that words can be pronounced correctly and thus matched with the spoken vocabularies already acquired by school-age children. Decoding is involved in a number of specific reading skills, such as phonic analysis, structural analysis and sight word recognition.

Phonic analysis is the ability to match the written form of letters and words to the spoken form by means of rules learned about sound-symbol relationships. Acquiring these skills is complicated by the fact that the English language has only 26 letters to represent approximately 44 speech sounds. Therefore, situations occur frequently in which one symbol (or set of symbols) can represent many sounds, or one sound can be spelled in many different ways. Certain sound-symbol relationships occur in enough situations, however, to justify the teaching of rules for them (Clymer, 1963; Emans, 1967).

Some of the phonic elements which may be taught systematically to children in the form of rules are consonant sounds, vowel sounds, blending, digraphs and diphthongs. Suggestions for teaching these elements are found in Heilman (1976), Hull (1976) and Johnson and Pearson (1978). Helpful teaching materials include Distar Reading (Science Research Associates), Phonovisual (Phonovisual Products) and Schoolhouse Word Attack (Science Research Associates).

Structural analysis in reading has been defined as "a skill through which children determine the meaning of an unfamiliar printed word by examining its meaningful parts" (Johnson & Pearson, 1978, p. 80). These parts are called morphemes, and they are the smallest meaningful parts of words. Morphemes include components such as root words, prefixes, suffixes, inflectional endings (plurals, possessives, verb tenses and comparisons), compound words and contractions. Sometimes principles of syllabication and the use of accents are also taught as part of structural analysis. Fairly uniform and consistent language rules have developed around the use of each of the morphological components. Additional reading in the area of structural analysis includes Dawson (1971), Durkin (1976) and Miller (1977). Useful materials include Learning Structural Analysis (Hampden Publications, Inc.) and Supportive Reading Skills (Dexter & Westbrook, Ltd.).

Sight word recognition means many things to teachers depending on their preferred orientation to reading. Sight words are words which do not follow rules and which, therefore, cannot be "sounded out." Many of these words appear quite frequently in reading material and thus must be memorized. Examples of such words are *what, done, some,* and *once.* A number of sight word lists have been developed which the teacher can use in teaching sight word recognition (Dolch, 1941; Fry, 1972). Other sight word lists can be found in Dawson (1971) and Dallmann, Rouch, Chang and Deboer (1974).

Johnson and Pearson (1978) offer a five-level strategy for teaching sight vocabularies or any new words to the child. In these five steps the child (a) sees the word (and hears it spoken), (b) discusses the word in terms of how it may relate to the child, (c) uses the word in sentences or forms synonyms for it, (d) defines the word in his own words and (e) writes the word in isolation and context. Not all of these steps can be applied to every sight word (e.g., *for* is difficult to discuss), but the overall strategy can be applied to all words.

Context analysis, or the use of context clues in reading, has been defined as "obtaining the meaning, and less often the pronunciation, of an unknown word by examining its context, nearby sentences, the entire paragraph, or the entire passage" (Miller, 1977, p. 185). This skill is a useful one if there are only a limited number of unknown words in the passage.

A number of authors (Emans, 1971; Herber, 1978; Miller, 1977) have presented classification systems for context clues which might be used to develop teaching sequences. A simple but useful hierarchical breakdown of types of clues is offered by Emans and Fisher (1967). These clues, presented in a step-by-step fashion, can be used to acquaint children with the idea of filling in missing or omitted information in a sentence. In one set of suggested exercises children must figure out a missing word under each of the following conditions:

1 The teacher supplies only the missing cononants
2 The teacher gives the child a choice between four words
3 The teacher supplies the first and last letters
4 The teacher tells the length of the word
5 The teacher gives only the beginning letter
6 The teacher allows no clues apart from the existing context

For additional information on context analysis see Durkin (1976) and Burns and Roe (1976).

When teaching children to use context clues to figure out unknown words in a sentence, guessing can be a problem. Children are great guessers, and given the opportunity (such as a chance to "guess" a word from its context) they may produce numerous miscellaneous "answers," many of which may be totally inappropriate. For example, impulsive children who want to get out of school as quickly as possible or anxious children who fear failure in dealing with the actual words may depend too much on context for word recognition. They may try to bluff word recognition from the picture context rather then concentrating on reading the passage itself, perhaps because they fear failure in dealing with the actual words. The instructor must be careful to avoid such guessing sessions by having children make only educated guesses based on *strategies* of information gathering (such as the list of guidelines above). In addition, the instructor may have to handle word bluffers by eliminating texts with pictures initially.

Comprehension. Reading comprehension, or reading with understanding, is the point behind reading instruction. Only at this level does the child begin to use reading as a vehicle for gathering information or entertainment. For children who are easily disorganized and for children who impulsively rush through material in a disjointed fashion, training in reading comprehension may be of particular value. It can help the children become more competent individuals.

There is little agreement on the models and skills that comprise the area of reading comprehension. Therefore, the teacher must decide on an operational definition of comprehension, complete with component learning tasks around which she can build instructional sequences for the classroom. A number of models or hierarchies of the comprehension process have been offered (Barrett, 1976; Clymer, 1963; Duffy & Sherman, 1972). While some of these comprehension skills classification systems are quite detailed, the teacher of the child with reading problems can often choose a more simple hierarchy of skills to begin developing reading comprehension. According to one simplified version (Herber, 1978) reading comprehension is a process comprised of three levels: literal comprehension, interpretive comprehension and applied comprehension. At the *literal level* "the reader examines the words of the author and determines what is being said, what information is being presented" (p. 40). At the *interpretive level* "the reader looks for relationships among statements within the materials, and from these intrinsic relationships derives various meanings" (p. 40). At the *applied level* the reader uses information gained at the previous two levels "and applies it to other knowledge she already possesses, thereby deepening the understanding" (p. 40). Some researchers, however, do not agree with such a discrete-skills approach to teaching comprehension but favor a more generalized approach.

Another method which is often used to help develop comprehension is called the Cloze procedure. Cloze procedures may differ according to the particular purpose for which they are used, but generally the child fills in missing words from a passage using context to help him. This process is similar to the use of context clues to aid in word recognition. The Cloze procedure is a very structured method of requiring comprehension and therefore may be particularly useful with the emotionally disturbed child who responds well to structure. For more information on the use of the Cloze procedure see Taylor (1953).

Another strategy for helping the child comprehend is the use of questions. Questions should be designed to elicit answers at various levels of comprehension. The teacher can elicit correct responses initially by providing students with models or guides as to what form the answers should take or what information the answers should contain. This gives the student a strategy for answering. Without a strategy, a question intended to elicit a response at a comprehension level on which the child is unaccustomed to answering might produce frustration or incorrect answers automatically (Herber, 1978). Questioning is also discussed in Herber and Nelson (1975) and Sanders (1966).

In addition to the process of comprehension itself, the content of the reading material being comprehended needs to be considered. Many emotionally disturbed children resist materials that are clearly nothing more than reading exercises. They find them pointless and boring. The teacher may have to circumvent this attitude by surrounding these children with opportunities for reading skill development without their knowing it. This can be accomplished by providing material that students perceive as highly interesting, sometimes of low reading difficulty, such as The Interesting Reading Series (Follett Educational Corporation) and Wildlife Adventure Series (Field Educational Publications).

Attention also must be given to reading content because certain subjects may have an undesirable impact on some students. Some children are overly stimulated by sensational and violent subjects (e.g., sharks, tigers). Other children react aversively to stories of normal family life because theirs has been chaotic. On the other hand, shy and withdrawn children may benefit from success stories featuring people with similar problems. Teachers need to monitor constantly the effect of reading material on these kinds of students and make changes in reading content as necessary. In some cases the teacher may even wish to create teacher-made materials for reading. Often teacher-made (or even child-made) materials appeal to emotionally disturbed children because they are personalized and not from a book which has aroused fear or hatred. Additional reading resources in comprehension are Burns and Roe (1976), Dallmann et al., (1974) and Pearson and Johnson (1978). Commercial materials include Specific Skills Series (Barnell Loft) and the SRA Skills Series: Comprehension (Science Research Associates).

Reading for survival. A subject which has received much attention in the competency testing movement is reading survival skills. Survival reading covers reading which is required to be an informed consumer, get and hold a job, use a bank and so on. Materials which teach reading survival skills include What's Happening? Newspaper Reading Skills (Associated Press), Real People at Work—Supplemental Reading Skills (Changing Times Education Service) and Reading for Survival in Today's Society (Adams, Flowers & Woods, 1978).

Additional Resources

Extensive lists of reading materials and resources are available in Hammill and Bartel (1978), Hawisher and Calhoun (1978), Swanson and Reinert (1979), and Turnbull and Schulz (1979). For more information on teaching reading skills see Adams et al. (1978), Burns and Broman (1975), Engelmann (1969), Gillespie-Silver (1979) and Spache and Spache (1977).

Conceptual Writing

Following reading, writing is generally considered to be the next language skill to be acquired developmentally. Writing involves at least three basic skills: the ability to express oneself through written language (conceptual writing), the ability to form and space letters (handwriting) and the ability to form words (spelling).

Conceptual writing requires the ability to develop an idea in a logical, sequential manner, to record ideas in acceptable format and to evaluate and revise one's work as necessary. Written material may be functional (e.g., reports) or creative (e.g., stories) in nature. Written language may be broken down into the same linguistic categories as spoken language—morphology, syntax, semantics, pragmatics and spelling (for phonology).

Conceptual Writing and the Emotionally Disturbed Child

Conceptual writing includes a number of tasks which pose problems for many youngsters. Some emotionally disturbed children have a great deal of difficulty organizing and developing their ideas. They may lack organizational skills or they may be threatened by the revelatory nature of writing. As Tate and Evans (1977) point out, spontaneous speech requires little self-conscious reflection, but written expression requires that one be acutely aware of what is being expressed. Some children may have difficulty with the solitary nature of this task. They may be easily distracted or they may have difficulty persevering. Still others may be unable to tolerate evaluation of their work. Many children have trouble separating criticism of their work from criticism of themselves. In spite of these problems writing is an area which should not be avoided or de-emphasized. A strong relationship exists between written expressive language and reading (Hammill & McNutt, 1980). Moreover, "children want to be able to express themselves" (d'Alelio, 1980, p. 318). Written expression is both a valuable academic tool and a gratifying and appropriate means of self-expression.

Assessing Conceptual Writing Skills

Informal assessment of written conceptual language which is useful to the classroom planner is reviewed by Wallace and Larsen (1978). These authors offer a chart of written expression skills such as organization, word choice and usage for recording teacher observations of students' work. Error analysis charts of more mechanical aspects of writing such as punctuation (Burns, 1974; Furness, 1960) and capitalization are presented by Wallace and Larsen.

Teaching Conceptual Writing Skills

The writing process can be said to consist of three stages: prewriting, writing and postwriting (Andreason, Cadenhead, Havens, Riley & Tyra, 1980). Rather than merely assign a topic and expect children to write about it, the teacher can help children think and plan before they write. This is especially important when teaching emotionally disturbed children who need a lot of structure and support. The following guidelines are useful when planning writing assignments:

1. Reserve sufficient time to allow for reflection before writing.
2. Communicate clearly the expectations for the composition.
3. Provide a writing stimulus that is meaningful to children.
4. Communicate the purposes for writing, including consideration of the audience.
5. Encourage reflection and visualization through discussion and questioning.
6. Encourage organization of ideas, including the jotting down of important words and phrases. (Andreason et al., p. 251)

The teacher's chief responsibility during the writing phase is to be available for assistance. The teacher should be involved in writing at the same time the children are in order to emphasize the value of the activity.

The goal of postwriting is to have children become independent evaluators of their work. This can be a difficult stage for children who are highly sensitive to criticism. The following suggestions for postwriting are particularly relevant when teaching emotionally disturbed children:

1. Allow sufficient time for reflection about the writing.
2. Look for strengths as well as things to consider changing, and concentrate on changes to be made rather than errors to be corrected.
3. Pay attention to the things that affect meaning.
4. Provide direct instruction in proofreading.
5. Link the postwriting experience to instruction in writing and language skills. (Andreason et al., p. 252)

According to another view (Cartwright, 1967) conceptual writing has four components: (a) Fluency (how much written language is produced?), (b) vocabulary (how many different words are used?), (c) structure (how correct are the mechanics of the writing, such as grammar, capitalization, punctuation?) and (d) content (how accurate is the content? what are the ideas? how is the content organized?) When developing or correcting written expressive skills in emotionally disturbed children, activities related to these components may be useful.

To teach fluency, the teacher can start by giving the children an interesting picture and ask them to describe it. The teacher may need to do a lot of prompting before the children are able to give an organized, thorough description. After oral descriptions, the teacher may have the children finish sentences about the picture. For example, the teacher provides the subject and verb and the children fill in the descriptors. Next, the teacher may have the children write about the picture, with the teacher providing specific directions for the overall structure. When children reach the level where they can express their thoughts on paper, even minimally, regular times to write may be scheduled. During these times everyone should write something. The product is not graded or evaluated. The point is to encourage fluency. Kohl (1967), Tate and Evans (1977) and d'Alelio (1980) describe ideas for stimulating reluctant writers. All emphasize the need to help these children over the hurdles of self-consciousness and fear of failure.

Vocabulary can be developed through a structured program. This program may be developed in units by choosing vocabulary related to specific areas, such as holidays or sports. To keep children interested, new vocabulary words should be drawn from areas of particular interest or relevance to the child.

When teaching the structure of language, the teacher needs to make it relevant and interesting. Punctuation, capitalization and grammar can seem very dry and irrelevant; therefore, the teacher may first have to help children see why they are needed. A fun exercise to demonstrate this point is to give them a short story in which all the punctuation and paragraphing have been left out. While trying to unravel the meaning, they also must apply structure skills. To proceed in his understanding of structure, the child may also need to develop language competency through written exercises in fluency and vocabulary.

Teaching content awareness can take several forms. When teaching accuracy, the teacher can ask children to write short articles for the class newspaper about specific topics which require the use of specific facts. Help them see why it is important that all the facts be correct before they are put in

Children can become more fluent writers with regular writing sessions that do not involve evaluation.

the newspaper. When helping children learn to express their ideas, the teacher should provide interesting and thought-provoking materials (some affective curriculum exercises are very appropriate). Ask the children to express their opinions in writing. Then evaluate the essays not for content but for the logic of thought. Organization is a more difficult task for these children. Teaching them how to develop an outline or how to analyze a paragraph can help them learn how to organize their thoughts. If such activities can be demonstrated to be useful to them personally, the children usually will invest themselves in learning how to do it.

Clearly, when teaching expressive skills structure and direction should be provided in a nonjudgmental manner. Without this helpful guidance many children either do not try to learn how to write or they try but get disorganized, discouraged and give up.

Additional Resources

Commercial language programs which are useful for teaching or remediating written language include Michigan Language Program (Random House), Wilson's Initial Syntax Program (Educators Publishing Service) and The Writing Center (Holt, Rinehart & Winston).

Additional reading on written language problems may be found in Glaus (1965), Meyers and Torrance (1965) and O'Donnell and Duncan (1980).

Handwriting

Handwriting is considered to be a supportive writing skill. The component tasks of handwriting include general legibility, letter form and size, spacing, alignment, slant and speed (Burns, 1962). Additional components of handwriting competency are line quality (or the appropriate amount of pressure exerted in writing) and hand and body position. Each of these components is applicable to manuscript or cursive writing.

Handwriting and the Emotionally Disturbed Child

Because feeling states are often revealed through handwriting, handwriting is another skill area in which some children's emotional problems can affect their academic progress. Impulsive children may race through their work; consequently their handwriting may be sloppy. Children with poor motor coordination often find handwriting to be a difficult task. Insecure and anxious children are often reluctant to have their handwriting understood for fear they will be wrong. Their writing may be small and hard to read.

Whatever the difficulty, the teacher should try to determine what role, if any, a child's emotional problems may have in his handwriting problems and then choose teaching strategies accordingly. For example, if the child is using poor handwriting as a means of opposing authority, the teacher may elect to ignore the handwriting and thereby avoid a control struggle. The natural consequences of poor handwriting may provide the child with the motivation to improve. If a child earns a poor grade on a spelling test due to illegibility or if his peers ridicule his handwriting, he may become more concerned about how he writes. If, on the other hand, a child is very disorganized and lacking many skills, the teacher may decide to work on handwriting as another means of providing organization and skill development.

Assessing Handwriting Skills

In the assessment of handwriting for classroom remediation the teacher can draw on the error-analysis charts offered by Wallace and Larsen (1978). Among the kinds of problems they list are problems with slant and spacing (Greene & Petty, 1967) and problems with malformed letters (Newland, 1932; Pressy & Pressy, 1927), for instance, an *a* which resembles an *o*, or a *g* which resembles a *y*. The Basic School Skills Inventory (Goodman & Hammill, 1975) also has a handwriting section which helps the teacher assess the child's printing of first and last names and the ability to write in a straight line. Such error-analysis sheets may also be shared with students to aid them in checking for their own writing errors.

Teaching Handwriting Skills

Because handwriting is a support skill and not essential to most learning activities, teachers need to guard against spending an inordinate amount of time developing exquisite handwriting to the detriment of more vital skills. Children only need to be able to use the medium efficiently and without feeling worried or embarrassed about the written product.

Handwriting authorities have suggested a number of general guidelines for forming handwriting teaching sequences (Burns, 1962). The teacher should provide students with a proper model, not fancy and elaborate but simple and readable. Handwriting instruction should occupy from 10 to 15 minutes of the teaching day in the primary grades. In the intermediate grades, the weekly total can be the same as for primary grades, but practice can be longer and more spaced. Self-monitoring and improvement skills should be nurtured in children so that they can assume early responsibility for their own progress and feedback. Generally, feedback and correction should be as specific and graphic as possible. The use of a correcting pen in a contrasting color highlights corrections. Models and suggestions for improvement should always be available. A program which provides immediate feedback to children is Handwriting with Write and See (Lyons & Carnahan).

For the emotionally disturbed child, correction of errors may be a highly charged issue. While feedback and correction of errors are important aspects of teaching writing, the teacher needs to be sensitive to what the children can tolerate. Self-evaluations may be preferable to teacher evaluation.

For children who need a developmental program because they have not acquired basic handwriting competence, the following teaching sequence is suggested:

1. Choose carefully an order of letters to be presented or remediated. Useful sequences can be found in Burns (1962) and Hammill and Poplin (1978).
2. Develop or acquire a task-analyzed method for having children reproduce these letters based on the ability of the child and his particular needs. The teaching sequence should use the concept of progressive approximation toward successful production: tracing letters, connecting dotted lines to form letters, copying letters from close models and copying letters from the board or from charts.
3. Develop a sequence for working on handwriting skills beyond letter production, such as spacing, alignment, slant. Children's handwriting behavior can be shaped into correct production by using specially lined and spaced paper or at a higher level by using guides or rules.
4. Ensure a smooth transition from manuscript to cursive writing by giving extra care and attention to this time. Spend additional time discussing the differences between manuscript and cursive writing; give additional practice in connecting strokes between letters; and give particular emphasis to common trouble spots in cursive writing such as the *br* combination and the *oe* combination.
5. For children who have a great deal of difficulty with handwriting in general, careful thought may be given to the form of handwriting that is taught. Some children may learn manuscript writing early and never switch to cursive. Others may learn cursive writing early and

never use manuscript. The form of the handwriting matters much less than the efficiency with which the form is eventually used.

For the emotionally handicapped student who has already acquired truly illegible handwriting, the teacher can consider several approaches, again according to student ability, degree of the problem and time available.

1 Work only on remediating the most obvious and most illegible trouble spots. This requires scrutinizing the child's writing on a letter-by-letter, component-by-component basis.
2 Take the student back through a developmental program, as outlined above, in order to relearn incorrect production.
3 Provide an alternative method for expressive language production. For example, let the child switch from cursive writing back to manuscript, allow the child to use a typewriter or have the child tape-record what he wishes to say.

Practice material. While some handwriting practice consists of drill on isolated letters, words or other components (e.g., connective strokes), children also need practice in using integrated skills in connected written material. These practice sessions are excellent opportunities for acquiring skills in other areas while also practicing handwriting. Practice activities can include having children make up their own stories, copy poems of their choosing, write letters to interesting people and keep a personal journal. A commercial program for developing handwriting and creative writing simultaneously is Creative Growth with Handwriting (Zaner-Bloser).

Additional Resources

Additional handwriting teaching aides include Cursive Handwriting Development (Teaching Resources Corporation) and Manuscript Workbook (Zaner-Bloser).

Sources which provide teaching ideas for developing and remediating handwriting include Burns (1962), Larson (1968) and *Academic Therapy* (Fall 1968, entire issue).

Spelling

At least two prerequisite abilities need to be present before one can be considered a competent written speller. The most basic skill is the ability to form letters correctly. This is primarily a handwriting skill. Second, the child must know how these letters fit together to form words. This process is rooted in one's ability to understand and use the rules of sound and letter relationships which govern the English language (Wallace & Larsen, 1978).

Spelling and the Emotionally Disturbed Child

Very little research has been done that focuses on spelling deficits in the emotionally disturbed. Kitano (1959) compared the frequency and types of spelling errors made by children in regular classes and in classes for the emotionally disturbed. Emotionally disturbed children made significantly more errors, and the types of errors they made were different from those of children in the regular classes. The errors of the normal children were usually due to difficulty with the English language whereas errors made by the emotionally disturbed children were usually due to "refusals" or "unrecognizable spelling."

Glavin and DeGirolamo (1970) replicated and extended Kitano's study. They equated children in regular classes with children in classes for the emotionally disturbed on the basis of socioeconomic status, chronological age, IQ and spelling scores. They, too, found that emotionally disturbed children made more total errors and more "refusal" or "unrecognizable spelling" errors; however, there were no differences between the groups in errors made because of irregularities in the English language. In addition they found that withdrawn, anxious children tended to attempt to conform by writing unrecognizable spelling words whereas conduct-problem children were overtly rebellious and frequently refused to write the word. Again, the evidence suggests that emotional problems exacerbate spelling problems for emotionally handicapped children.

Assessing Spelling Skills

Assessment of spelling performance which yields specific information useful for classroom remediation planning is available with the use of a number of instruments cited by Wallace and Larsen (1978). One commercially published test which places its test components within a scope-and-sequence chart for the teacher's reference convenience is Spellmaster (Cohen & Abrams, 1974). Informal spelling techniques are provided by Brueckner and Bond (1966) with observational spelling guidelines, by Partoll (1976) with a spelling error checklist, and by Edington (1968) with a list of spelling error patterns.

Teaching Spelling Skills

Historically, English spelling was not thought to be sufficiently governed by rules of sound-letter relationships to warrant the teaching of such rules. Research by Hanna, Hanna, Hodges and Rudorf (1966), however, has suggested that this is not the case. In many instances, the teaching of sound-letter relationship rules heightens spelling ability significantly.

In an excellent review of the current status of spelling instruction, Graham and Miller (1979) present a list of teaching theories which are supported by spelling research. The following procedures were upheld by their research:

1. Pre-testing, allowing study time and then post-testing spelling words rather than simply allowing study time and then testing
2. Presenting spelling study words in a list rather than in sentence or paragraph content form
3. Devoting 60–75 minutes per week to classroom teaching of spelling

Some procedures that were not upheld by the reviewed research are

1 Air-writing new spelling words for practice
2 Concentrating study on difficult-to-spell areas within words
3 Rewriting spelling words to aid memory

Common approaches to teaching spelling. At least three common approaches to teaching spelling are currently in use (Turnbull & Schulz, 1979). These approaches are not always mutually exclusive in that some spelling programs may contain characteristics of other approaches.

The first approach and one often used traditionally by basal spelling series is the graded word list approach. In this approach, words are often presented in list fashion and words are chosen based on frequency of use. Graham and Miller (1979) report that as few as 100 words make up 50% of a child's written vocabulary. In addition, they cite research indicating that "a basic spelling vocabulary of 2,800 to 3,000 well-selected words should form the core of the spelling program" (p. 4). The Basic Goals in Spelling (McGraw-Hill) is a spelling program that includes words chosen according to frequency of use (it also emphasizes sound-symbol relationships). In addition, the teacher can teach directly from lists of frequently used words such as the Dolch (E. W. Dolch, compiler) list of the 2,000 Commonest Words for Spelling (Garrard Press). An advantage of this approach is that the words taught are often needed by children. A disadvantage is that the words on the lists may have to be memorized for spelling much as sight words are memorized in reading.

A second approach to spelling new words employs linguistic rules. Phonological spelling rules have to do with sound-letter relationships. These rules have proven to be consistent for predicting the spelling of words (Hanna et al., 1966). Additional rules drawn from phonics reading programs may be useful for predicting word pronunciation. Morphological spelling rules emphasize the spelling of word parts which carry meaning on their own. Various rules cover spellings of prefixes, suffixes, inflectional endings and so forth. Programs which feature linguistic approaches to spelling include *Word Book Spelling Series* (Lyons & Carnahan) and the *Magic World of Dr. Spello* (McGraw-Hill). Linguistic approaches to spelling may aid the child in becoming more of an independent speller once basic rules are learned. On the other hand, rules must be carefully chosen for teaching so that one doesn't waste time teaching seldom used rules. Also, some children balk at the task of memorizing set rules.

A third approach to spelling instruction teaches children to spell environmental "survival words." Such word lists may be drawn from the child's general surroundings or from specific job-related occupational needs. A survey of the child's immediate environment is taken to discover the words the child must be able to read and spell in order to get along in that environment. Examples of such words are traffic safety guides, common warning labels, common directions on products, words designating locations of needed public facilities and words used on application forms. Two lists which represent the survival approach are offered by Schilit and Caldwell (1980) for occupational words and Wilson (1963) for essential environmental words. An obvious advantage of this approach lies in its immediate and lasting application to the actual life of the learner. Again, the onus is on the teacher to develop lists if appropriate ones are not available and to develop teaching sequences and materials to accompany the lists. This approach might be useful as a "last resort" for older handicapped youths who have failed to master other rule-oriented approaches. For the emotionally disturbed child who finds school irrelevant to his life and needs, this approach allows the teacher to tailor the child's spelling words to fit his particular situation.

The best approach to designing a program to teach or correct spelling problems is to combine appropriate techniques from each of the above approaches. The spelling teacher will also want to incorporate research-based teaching principles into the program, as reviewed earlier. Teachers will want to make preparations to offer adequate practice sessions and study periods, either group or individual.

Study methods. Generally the best study method for spelling acquisition is not a student-designed study method but rather one structured by the teacher for the student (Graham & Miller, 1979). "An effective word study method concentrates on the whole word and requires careful pronunciation, visual imagery, auditory and/or kinesthetic reinforcement, and systematic recall" (p. 10). According to Graham and Miller, the most helpful technique for good spelling acquisition offers the child an opportunity to self-correct incorrect words directly upon completing the test. This approach also allows students to appraise difficult words and difficult parts of words. For the emotionally disturbed child who feels a strong need to be in control of his environment, self-correction may be particularly useful because it allows the child to take responsibility for and do something about his errors. This, too, might be the best time to employ word study techniques on the words missed as the student corrects his own paper.

Games are a legitimate way to get students interested in spelling. The teacher should not overlook games in her efforts to make spelling learning and practice as stimulating as possible. Games must always be used judiciously, but they can be a palatable way for children to practice and transfer new skills. Familiar games such as "Word Mastermind" and "Hangman" can be used to help children learn word problem-solving strategies (Marino, 1980). Another source for word games is a kit entitled *Spelling Games* (Milton Bradley).

Compensatory method. For the child who seems unable to gain spelling competence after much time has been spent and many approaches have been tried, the dictionary can be a valuable aid. When the problem truly becomes one of building compensation skills in a child who cannot or does not consistently spell well, the use of the dictionary will need to be taught in a practical, structured way. The first step involves convincing the student of the importance of using a dictionary to compensate for the spelling deficits which both he and the teacher know exist. Once the child understands the reason for using the dictionary, the teacher will want to structure teaching sequences designed to develop the child's ability to look up words when unable to spell them. Correct spelling of initial sounds in words and correct spelling of initial syllables should be stressed. A useful compensatory tool might also be *The Bad Speller's Dictionary* (Kreirsky & Linfield, 1963) which presents, in dictionary format, words as they are commonly misspelled.

Additional Resources

Additional spelling materials which the teacher may wish to investigate are Reading Road to Spelling (Harper & Row) and Spelling Word Power Lab (Science Research Associates).

Additional readings in the area of teaching spelling are available in Hanna, Hodges, and Hanna (1971), Shaw (1971) and *Academic Therapy Quarterly* (Fall 1967, entire issue).

Arithmetic

The basic skills making up the area of arithmetic have been described or listed slightly differently by every writer on the subject. The teacher seeking guidelines for developing teaching sequences will want to consider the following skill areas: readiness skills, computational skills, time, money, measurement and problem-solving skills.

Arithmetic readiness skills, likewise, are described differently by different authors (Bartel, 1978; Wallace & Kauffman, 1978). A simple but useful analysis of arithmetic readiness skills is offered by Wallace and Kauffman (1978).

1. Be able to discriminate among different sizes, shapes, and quantities;
2. Understand one-to-one correspondence;
3. Be able to count meaningfully;
4. Be able to order number names and sets. (p. 222)

Additional readiness skills include classification ability, spatial-concept understanding, flexibility, reversibility and conservation (Bartel, 1978).

Arithmetic and the Emotionally Disturbed Child

Arithmetic is an academic area of such difficulty that Bereiter (1968) has surmised every learner would eventually fall victim sooner or later. Emotionally disturbed children are no exception. Although the evidence is certainly not conclusive, several researchers have reported arithmetic to be the area in which emotionally disturbed children have the most difficulty (Bower, 1970; Kauffman, 1977; Stone & Rowley, 1964).

> The larger differences in arithmetic achievement between the emotionally handicapped child and other children may in part be due to the reading difficulties on certain of the arithmetic tests where reading is an integral part of the problem. It is also possible that arithmetic is more abstract and less meaningful to the emotionally handicapped child than it is to other children and it is a skill that requires greater concentration and attentiveness than reading. The learning of mathematics in general may require a greater degree of freedom from anxiety and inner concern than does reading. (Bower, 1970, p. 59)

Mathematics is a subject area which requires more step-by-step instruction, whereas reading is a skill that can be developed independently once the basic word decoding and comprehension skills are in place. Many emotionally disturbed children are psychologically or physically absent from class a great deal of time due to daydreaming, distractedness or disruptive behavior which often results in time-out. Moreover, some of these children have problems with mathematics because they fail to grasp its relevance and applicability (Copeland, 1976). Speaking of behavior-disordered children, Copeland states that "emphasis in the development of mathematical skills must be on the functional. Many of these children are struggling for emotional or social survival and are concerned with those things which are useful to them. They should be taught math skills which have immediate use and, as such, motivational value" (p. 213).

Subject matter that is tedious, irrelevant and hard work is likely to be rejected by many emotionally disturbed children. Children may refuse to do it or, more commonly, they do not put themselves in a position to learn. They make careless mistakes by not attending to details such as signs and decimals; they get distracted; and by not having committed basic facts to memory, they take an inordinate amount of time to do simple procedures. In effect, this makes complicated processes impossible to teach.

Assessing Arithmetic Skills

A number of arithmetic assessment tools are cited by Wallace and Larsen (1978). Two instruments which are somewhat criterion-referenced in nature are the Key Math Diagnostic Arithmetic Test (Connolly, Nachtman, & Pritchett, 1971) and the Diagnostic Tests and Self-Helps in Arithmetic (Brueckner, 1955). The Key Math purports to measure math content, operations and applications. The Diagnostic Tests are sequenced according to skill levels and these are matched with remediational practice sheets.

In addition to the usual global and criterion-referenced assessment measures which pinpoint a child's needs in math, error-analysis techniques have been cited by many authors as an essential form of assessment. It is necessary to know whether the child can perform a specific math skill, but equally important, when he cannot, is why not. A number of authors (Bartel, 1978; Reisman, 1972) present error-analysis charts for computation skills. These include variables such as failing to complete an operation, yielding a partial answer, or failing to regroup. Error analysis can also be applied to word problems (Turnbull & Schulz, 1979). Errors in word problems include errors in word recognition, difficulty in coping required problems and carelessness. Simple handwriting difficulties might also cause a child to lose credit for operations actually carried out correctly.

Teaching Arithmetic Skills

Arithmetic appears to be a curriculum area which lends itself well to task analysis. According to Drucker (1976) "mathematics, more so than any other subject, is a logical and truly sequential subject" (p. 51). As orderly as math seems to be, however, comparatively few remedial math programs are available. Furthermore, as a number of authors (Bartel, 1978; Johnson, 1979) have noted, research dealing with arithmetic and the learning disordered child is scarce.

According to Haring and Eaton (1978) "there is a hierarchy of learning stages through which a child progresses in learning *each* skill" (p. 250). They list the stages as (a) acquisition (the child is beginning to learn the skill), (b) proficiency (the child can perform the skill correctly and fluently), (c) generalization (the child can perform the skill in more than one setting) and (d) adaptation (the child can apply the acquired principle on his own). Lovitt (1978) and Mercer (1979) cite research supporting the following points regarding the acquisition and proficiency stages:

1 Modeling by teachers is helpful.
2 Verbal mediation (saying problem and answer to oneself prior to writing the answer) pays off in the acquisition stage.
3 Making students pay a fee for incorrect answers (cost response) is effective in the acquisition stage.
4 Positive reinforcement is effective if given for correct responses in the proficiency stage.

Readiness. In developing readiness skills for math, regardless of how one defines or approaches readiness, children must acquire a sense of "numberness." Such a sense requires an understanding of what numbers are, what they represent and why they are needed.

In order to help children grasp these concepts the teacher may use what Alpher (1980) calls "whimsical speculation." For example, the teacher may present the following story:

> You are a shepherd in the Land of No-Number. In this country there are no numbers. Each morning you take *all* the village sheep up on the mountain to graze; you watch the sheep all day; and you bring them back to their owners each evening. One day you fall asleep and the sheep wander away while you are sleeping. When you wake up you gather together all the sheep that you see. How do you know whether you have all of them?

Alpher also uses a historical method, that is, children learn about early mathematical systems. Through discussions about numbers most children slowly grasp their utility.

In addition to understanding the function of numbers, children need to feel comfortable with them. They should be given nonthreatening experiences with simple manipulation of numbers before moving on to computational skills. Children also need to grasp firmly the following concepts:

1 One number is said each time a new thing appears (one-to-one correspondence).
2 Things can come in groups (beginning sets).
3 One group of something can have the same number of things in it as another group (sets).

4 One can start with a few things and get more things (counting forward).
5 One can start with many things and lose some things (counting backwards).

Much counting needs to take place, again in hierarchical fashion, such as counting pictures of objects or rote counting with many starting and stopping places. Also needed is practice in counting objects in recognized groups, such as fingers, toes, children in the class. Personalizing this process is often effective. An example of an arithmetic readiness program is Foundations for Mathematics (Teaching Resources Corporation).

Computation skills. Computation skills represent what can be done with and to numbers. Children need to grasp ideas such as the following:

1 Some things can cause numbers to grow larger and some things can cause numbers to grow smaller.
2 There are interrelationships between the computational skills.
3 There are generally two ways to make numbers grow larger (addition and multiplication, which is a fast way of adding).
4 There are generally two ways to make numbers grow smaller (subtraction and division, which is a fast way of subtracting).

Learning computation skills is easier for children if they understand that such skills are really just "number language" ways to solve problems and get answers. Actual verbal word problems need to be interjected often so that children see the point behind these purely numerical manipulations. For example, use daily classroom occurrences to drill children: "I have two pencils here. How many more do I need so that we all will have one?"

The computation skills listed above are often successfully taught to exceptional children by a mastery method consisting of a pre-test, instruction, practice and post-test. The skills comprising each area are specified via task analysis, and a criterion-referenced test is used to determine which skills children know or do not know. Children are then grouped according to levels of achievement with those needing initial teaching in a skill in one group, those needing supervised practice in another group and those needing spaced practice in another. Children in the initial stages of acquisition receive direct teaching and are shown strategies for performing the skill. Children in need of supervised practice in order to reach proficiency are given practice sheets to complete, accompanied by some well-supervised student-to-student drills (e.g., flash cards, drill games). Children in need of spaced practice may also be given drills and allowed to play reinforcing games to maintain skills (Archer & Edgar, 1976). Arithmetic games available for reinforcing basic computation skills include Addo Arithmetic Game (Kenworthy Educational Service) and Multiplication, Division, Addition, Subtraction (Milton Bradley).

Additional hurdles that have to be crossed in teaching basic computation operations are place value and regrouping. Valuable tools here are visual prompts and learning strategies which children can use from one situation to another. Charts can be used to illustrate the steps to follow in regrouping, ice cream sticks can be bundled into groups to illustrate place value, and jingles can be used to help children remember what operations to use.

Fractions. Fractions can be presented as "parts of numbers" that can function in the same way as whole numbers. Children who have problems with abstract concepts often benefit from many concrete, illustrative demonstrations and life-like, "hands-on" experiences prior to doing computations on paper.

The Distar Arithmetic program (Science Research Associates) offers a unique method of teaching fractions. Additional resources include Fractions and Fractional Numbers (Milton Bradley) and Fractions as Easy as Pie (Fisher-Price Toys).

Time, money and measurement skills. Time, money and measurement skills may be included as an extension of computational skills. These skills give one vital information about the world. Again, the place to begin with any of these skill areas is with concrete, hands-on experience; then move on in a task-analyzed fashion to higher levels of understanding and on-paper computations. When beginning to teach these skills, call attention to how the skill is relevant to a particular child. When teaching time, discussions about the time of day or year in which things happen are useful. The teacher can start with statements like "Christmas comes when it is cold," or "We go home in the afternoon." From here, more specific time language, notation and computation skills can be taught, such as days of the week, months of the year, on-paper clock time notations and dates.

Money skills are best introduced after children understand what money does; that is, it allows one to buy and sell. For the child who does not clearly understand this process, the first experiences should involve exposure to buying and selling situations. Next, children can begin to learn in an appropriate sequence the values of coins and bills, the comparability of various combinations of coins and bills, the buying power of coins and bills, computation with money and verbal money problems. Children may be given real-life and simulated experiences in money usage (e.g., playing store, visiting a real restaurant as a class).

Measurement skills, again, need to be taught in the context of real-life situations. Situations can be set up in which children see the need to measure: "How long does this board need to be to make the back of the bird house?" "How far do we have to walk to town?" Gradually, children should be supplied, in an appropriate sequence, with conventional measurement techniques and language (e.g., feet, yards, inches, miles). Again, solving verbal problems in real life should precede on-paper manipulations of measurement problems.

Useful materials for teaching time, money and measurement include Clock Dial (Ideal School Supply Company), History of the Measurement of Length (Visual Education Consultants) and Money Book (Xerox Education Publications). Numerous other materials are listed by Hammill and Bartel (1978).

Verbal problem solving. The verbal problem, linked closely to the child's real life, is the area in which math can make the most sense. Solving verbal problems should be a process introduced not after other math skills but as an integrated part of these skills (Turnbull & Schulz, 1979). The following items represent some of the essential tasks involved in solving verbal problems:

1 Picking out essential information given in the problem, such as how many, how far or how long.
2 Picking out what operation is required to solve the problem. This may involve translating cue words, such as *bought, sold, got, lost, left, more,* into math operations.
3 Checking to see whether all information necessary to solve a problem is given and whether irrelevant or filler information has been given which should be ignored.
4 Translating the verbal problem into a solvable number sentence. For example, the problem, "If John had three balls and he lost one, how many are left?" translates into $3 - 1 = ?$.
5 Checking to see that the answer is reasonable. This may involve using logic. For example, equating "I'll be gone for two weeks" and "I'll be home in 36 days" is illogical. It may also involve overt checking methods such as checking subtraction answers by addition (Wallace & Kauffman, 1978).

Verbal problem solving is also discussed by Bartel (1978).

For some students, intensive attention to arithmetic consumer and survival skills may be needed. Examples of materials which help develop these skills are Everyday Business (e.g., Banking, Buying, Insurance) (Lawson Book Company) and Consumer Education Series (e.g., Understanding Tags and Labels, How to Read Ads) (Interpretive Education/Melton Book Company).

Strategies. When teaching math skills to the handicapped child, practice activities should include as many examples, cues, visual and verbal prompts, and strategies as possible. The teacher should use any measure to make the stimulus items attention-getting and to offer children guides or maps to follow in carrying out operations. Examples of such measures are computation answer charts (for early computing work), number lines, jingles and charts of steps to be followed in carrying out particular operations. Turnbull and Schulz (1979) offer numerous helpful suggestions for adapting the math curriculum for children who have arithmetic-related deficits. The cues, prompts and learning strategies they advocate make arithmetic learning easier for children. Examples are the use of specialized counting systems to aid memory and the use of signals to cue the child when it is time to attend.

Additional Resources

Commercial materials available in the area of arithmetic include Basic Essentials of Math (Steck-Vaughn Company), Basic Mathematics (Educational Activities) and School House Mathematics (Science Research Associates).

For additional reading in teaching arithmetic consult Arena (1970), Bereiter (1968), Johnson (1979) and Reisman (1972).

Choosing and Adapting Teaching Materials

At times, subject materials may have to be adapted for emotionally disturbed children, especially in areas such as science and social studies, but often the primary difficulties are reading level and organization of material. Many students simply have great difficulty reading the text materials and assignments in their different academic subjects. Even if students can read the words, the material is sometimes organized in a way that makes comprehension difficult.

For the teacher concerned with choosing appropriate materials for teaching social studies, science and other content areas, the following criteria are important:

1 *Readability.* Is the text material written at a reading level within the child's range? Are vocabulary level, sentence structure and sentence length comensurate with the reading level of the child? If information about the readability level of a particular text is lacking, a number of readability formulas can be applied which allow the instructor to estimate readability level (Burmeister, 1978; Estes & Vaughan, 1978; Fry, 1977).

2 *Content load.* Does the material present a "reasonable" number of ideas within an appropriate number of words (West, 1978), or is the material overloaded with concepts? How abstractly are the concepts presented? These factors are difficult to determine scientifically and call for careful teacher judgment. Can the children respond to content appropriately or will it be too provocative?

3 *Organization.* Is the material presented in such a way that important main ideas are clearly emphasized as opposed to supporting details? Are sufficient examples given to illustrate ideas? Many textbooks have violated such organizational guidelines (Peters, 1975–76).

4 *Interest and motivational appeal.* Does the material arouse the student's interest in an appropriate way? Is the material presented in such a way that the child is motivated to participate? Again, these factors are best evaluated by teacher judgment and observation of student performance.

Sometimes a particular set of materials is found to be usable but in need of major or minor adaptations because it violates the above or some other criteria. Adaptation is time-consuming but worthwhile, especially if the product can be preserved and reused. Adapting materials may involve the following tasks:

1 *Adjusting readability levels.* Simplify vocabulary level and sentence length and complexity through word-for-word rewriting or by paraphrasing as needed.

2 *Altering concept load.* Cut down on the number of concepts introduced. Provide more concrete examples to offset abstract ideas.
3 *Reorganizing format of material.* Emphasize main ideas; make supporting details clearly subordinate. Provide sufficient examples of concepts discussed.
4 *Using supplements with motivational appeal.* Bring in supporting information and additional examples of interest to the child. Provide pictures, films and so on to support and illustrate textual information.

When adapting materials teachers should remember to adapt not only the lessons but also the assignments. Assignments and questions should be simplified, again using familiar vocabulary and sentence construction. The assignments may need to be adjusted by providing additional structure and guidance to the student (Archer & Edgar, 1976).

Developing Teaching Sequences in Specific Academic Areas

Numerous resources are available to the teacher to help in preparing teaching sequences for developing or working on remediation of academic skills in the emotionally disturbed child. These come in the form of commercially produced teaching materials and skill development programs as well as published texts on teaching academic skills.

For additional reading in the area of choosing and adapting material for use with learning handicapped children see Archer and Edgar (1976), Hawisher and Calhoun (1978), Lambie (1980) and Wilson (1978).

Among the resources available for teaching reading in the content areas are Herber (1978), Estes and Vaughan (1978) and West (1978).

Physical and Leisure Education

In addition to planning for skill development in the basic academic areas, physical education and leisure skills should also be fostered. Through these activities children can learn appropriate and constructive means of expressing themselves, can develop motor and social skills and can acquire a socially acceptable outlet for their frustration or excess energy. Additionally, by developing such skills, children who may never be outstanding academically may excel in athletics or other leisure activities.

As in the traditional skill areas, physical and leisure education require skillful teaching. Readers interested in references focusing on teaching these skills to emotionally disturbed children are referred to: Allen, 1980; Appell, 1979; Chace, 1965; Daniels, 1980; Dreikurs, 1965; Folio & Norman, 1981; Huber, 1980; Lament, 1978; Marlowe, 1980; Ulman, 1965; Windham, Dummer & Fagan, 1980; and Woltmann, 1976.

SUMMARY

Teaching emotionally disturbed children requires a blending of sound educational technology with an understanding of emotionally disturbed children and their individual problems. It is not enough to manage these children or to help them talk about their problems. They also must be taught skills that enable them to fit into the world in which they live. Some need global remediation, others need remediation in specific skills, and others need initial skill development. All of them need the confidence and self-esteem gained from accomplishment.

This effort requires systematic, structured planning for the child's educational experience. The IEP, required by PL 94-142, was mandated as a means of providing handicapped children with this type of planning. When developing an IEP, teachers must assess the child's current level of functioning, project realistic long- and short-term instructional objectives and specify a means of evaluating the child's progress. Emphasis should be placed on skill acquisition in the basic areas of language arts (including reading) and mathematics so that the child will be equipped to return to the mainstream if possible. In order to tailor instruction to individual children, teachers must know a great deal about the children. They must be able to pace and present material so that the children will be interested, invested in learning and successful.

DISCUSSION QUESTIONS

1. In what instances would a child's emotional status directly affect the classroom methods the teacher chooses? Cite several specific examples.
2. What major reading approach might be recommended for the following children and why?
    a. The alienated child who expresses open hostility toward traditional school experiences
    b. The withdrawn, anxious child who seems very unsure of the ability to succeed
3. What are some specific suggestions which would help the arithmetic teacher of the children in question 2 to teach them basic computation skills?
4. What teaching techniques and teacher requirements would be helpful for remediating conceptual language deficits in the disorganized, disoriented child?
5. What adaptations (cite several examples) might have to be made to each of the following for the emotionally disturbed child?
    a. Materials
    b. Grouping techniques
    c. Grading
    d. Method of response

REFERENCES

Adams, A. H., Flowers, A., & Woods, E. E. *Reading for survival in today's society. Volume One, Modules 1–18.* Santa Monica, Calif.: Goodyear, 1978.

Allen, J. I. Jogging can modify disruptive behaviors. *Teaching Exceptional Children*, 1980, *12*, 66–70.

Allen, R. V. *Language experiences in communication.* Boston: Houghton Mifflin, 1976.

Alley, G., & Deshler, D. *Teaching the learning disabled adolescent: Strategies and methods.* Denver Colo.: Love, 1979.

Alpher, R. W. A strategy for teaching remedial mathematics: If I had $1,000,000 . . . . In N. J. Long, W. C. Morse & R. G. Newman (Eds.), *Conflict in the classroom:* The education of emotionally disturbed children (4th ed.). Belmont, Calif.: Wadsworth, 1980.

Andreasen, N., Cadenhead, K., Havens, G., Riley, J. F., & Tyra, D. The child and the composing process. *The Elementary School Journal*, 1980, *80*, 247–253.

Appell, L. S. Enhancing learning and enriching lives: Arts in the education of handicapped children. *Teaching Exceptional Children*, 1979, *11*, 74–76.

Archer, A., & Edgar, E. Teaching academic skills to mildly handicapped children. In S. Lowenbraun & J. Q. Affleck (Eds.), *Teaching mildly handicapped children in regular classes.* Columbus, Ohio: Charles E. Merrill, 1976.

Arena, J. (Ed.). *Building number skills in learning-disabled children.* San Rafael, Calif.: Academic Therapy Press, 1970.

Baker, A. M. Cognitive functioning of psychotic children: A reappraisal. *Exceptional Children*, 1979, *45*, 344–348.

Bangs, T. E. *Language and learning disorders of the pre-academic child.* New York: Appleton-Century-Crofts, 1968.

Barrett, T. Taxonomy of reading comprehension. In R. Smith & T. C. Barrett (Eds.), *Teaching reading in the middle grades.* Reading, Mass.: Addison-Wesley, 1976.

Bartel, N. R. Problems in mathematics achievement. In D. D. Hammill & N.R. Bartel (Eds.), *Teaching children with learning and behavior problems* (2nd ed.). Boston: Allyn & Bacon, 1978.

Bartel, N. R. & Bryen, D. N. Problems in language development. In D.D. Hammill & N.R. Bartel (Eds.), *Teaching children with learning and behavior problems* (2nd ed.). Boston: Allyn & Bacon, 1978.

Beismer, E. P., & Yarborough, B. H. A comparison of ten different beginning reading programs in first grade. *Phi Delta Kappan*, 1965, *46*, 500–504.

Bereiter, C. *Arithmetic and mathematics.* San Rafael, Calif.: Dimensions Publishing, 1968.

Berry, M. *Language disorders of children.* New York: Appleton-Century-Crofts, 1969.

Bloom, L. *Language development: Form and function in emerging grammars* (Research monograph no. 59). Cambridge, Mass.: MIT Press, 1970.

Bower, E. M. *Early identification of emotionally handicapped children in school* (2nd ed.). Springfield, Ill.: Charles C Thomas, 1970.

Bricker, D., Ruder, K. F., & Vincent, L. An intervention strategy for language-deficient children. In N. G. Haring & R. L. Schiefelbusch (Eds.), *Teaching special children.* New York: McGraw-Hill, 1976.

Brueckner, L. J. *Diagnostic tests and self-helps in arithmetic.* Monterey, Calif.: CTB/McGraw-Hill, 1955.

Brueckner, L. J., & Bond, G. L. *The diagnosis and treatment of learning difficulties.* New York: Appleton-Century-Crofts, 1966.

Building handwriting skills. *Academic Therapy*, 1969, 4 (entire issue).

Building spelling skills. *Academic Therapy Quarterly*, 1968, *3*, (entire issue).

Burmeister, L. E. *Reading strategies for middle and secondary school teachers* (2nd ed.). Reading, Mass.: Addison-Wesley, 1978.

Burns, P. C. *Diagnostic teaching of the language arts.* Itasca, Ill.: F. E. Peacock, 1974.

Burns, P. C. *Improving handwriting instruction in elementary schools.* Minneapolis, Minn.: Burgess, 1962.

Burns, P. C., & Broman, B. L. *The language arts in childhood education* (3rd ed.). Chicago: Rand McNally, 1975.

Burns, P. C., Broman, B. L., & Wantling, A. L. *The language arts and childhood education* (2nd ed.). Chicago: Rand McNally, 1971.

Burns, P. C., & Roe, B. D. *Teaching reading in today's elementary schools.* Chicago: Rand McNally, 1976.

Cantwell, D. Psychiatric disorder in children with speech and language retardation. *Archives of General Psychiatry*, 1977, *34*, 588–591.

Carrillo, L. W. *Informal reading readiness experiences* (Rev. ed.). New York: Noble & Noble, 1971.

Cartwright, G. P. *Multivariate analyses of the written language abilities and educable mentally retarded children.* Paper presented at the annual meeting of the American Education Research Association, February 1967.

Chace, M. Dance in growth or treatment settings. In N. J. Long, W. C. Morse & R.G. Newman (Eds.), *Conflict in the classroom: The education of emotionally disturbed children.* Belmont, Calif.: Wadsworth, 1965.

Clymer, T. The utility of phonic generalizations in the primary grades. *The Reading Teacher,* 1963, *16,* 252–258.

Cobb, J. A., & Hops, H. Effects of academic survival skill training in low achieving first graders. *The Journal of Educational Research,* 1973, *67,* 108–113.

Cohen, C., & Abrams, R. *Spellmaster.* Exeter, N. H.: Learnco, 1974.

Connolly, A. J., Nachtman, W., & Pritchett, E. M. *Key Math diagnostic arithmetic test.* Circle Pines, Minn.: American Guidance Service, 1971.

Copeland, R. W. *Mathematics and the elementary teacher* (3rd ed.). Philadelphia, Pa. Saunders, 1976.

d'Alelio, W. A. A strategy for teaching remedial language arts: Creative writing. In N. J. Long, W. C. Morse & R. G. Newman (Eds.), *Conflict in the classroom: The education of emotionally disturbed children* (4th ed.). Belmont, Calif.: Wadsworth, 1980.

Dallmann, M., Rouch, R. L., Chang, L. Y. C., & Deboer, J. J. *The teaching of reading.* New York: Holt, Rinehart & Winston, 1974.

Daniels, W. D. Tumbling my way to success. In N. J. Long, W. C. Morse & R. G. Newman (Eds.), *Conflict in the classroom: The education of emotionally disturbed children* (4th ed.) Belmont, Calif.: Wadsworth, 1980.

Dawson, M. A. (Ed.). *Teaching word recognition skills.* Newark, Del.: International Reading Association, 1971.

Dolch, E. W. Dolch basic sight vocabulary of 220 words. *Teaching primary reading.* Champaign, Ill.: Garrad Press, 1941.

Dreikurs, R. Music therapy. In N. J. Long, W. C. Morse & R. G. Newman (Eds.), *Conflict in the classroom: The education of emotionally disturbed children.* Belmont, Calif.: Wadsworth, 1965.

Drucker, H. *The organization and management of the resource room: A cookbook approach.* Springfield, Ill.: Charles C Thomas, 1976.

Duffy, G. G., & Sherman, G. B. *Systematic reading instruction.* New York: Harper & Row, 1972.

Durkin, D. *Strategies for identifying words. A workbook for teachers and those preparing to teach.* Boston: Allyn & Bacon, 1976.

Durkin, D. *Teaching them to read.* Boston: Allyn & Bacon, 1978.

Edington, R. "But he spelled them right this morning!" *Academic Therapy Quarterly,* 1968, *3,* 58–59.

Ekwall, E. E. *Locating and correcting reading difficulties.* Columbus, Ohio: Charles E. Merrill, 1970.

Emans, R. The usefulness of phonic generalizations above the primary grades. *The Reading Teacher,* 1967, *20,* 419–425.

Emans, R. Use of context clues. In M. A. Dawson (Ed.), *Teaching word recognition skills.* Newark, Del.: International Reading Association, 1971.

Emans, R., & Fisher, G. M. Teaching the use of context clues. *Elementary English,* 1967, *44,* 243–246.

Engelmann, S. E. *Preventing failure in the primary grades.* Chicago: Science Research Associates, 1969.

Erb, L., & Mercer, C. D. Language disabilities. In C. D. Mercer (Ed.), *Children and adolescents with learning disabilities.* Columbus, Ohio: Charles E. Merrill, 1979.

Estes, T. H., & Vaughan, J. L., Jr. *Reading and learning in the content classroom: Diagnostic and instructional strategies.* Boston: Allyn & Bacon, 1978,

Fernald, G. *Remedial techniques in basic school subjects.* New York: McGraw-Hill, 1943.

Fitzgerald, E. *Straight language for the deaf.* Washington, D.C.: The Volta Bureau, 1966.

Folio, M. R. & Norman, A. Toward more success in mainstreaming: A peer-teacher approach to physical education. *Teaching Exceptional Children*, 1981, *13*, 110–114.

Fry, E. B. Fry's readability graph: Clarification, validity, and extension to level 17. *Journal of Reading*, 1977, *21*, 249.

Fry, E. B. *Reading instruction for classroom and clinic.* New York: McGraw-Hill, 1972.

Furness, E.L. Pupils, pedagogues, and punctuation. *Elementary English*, 1960, *34* 187–189.

Gillespie-Silver, P. *Teaching reading to children with special needs: An ecological approach.* Columbus, Ohio: Charles E. Merrill, 1979.

Gillingham, A., & Stillman, B. *Remedial training for children with specific disability in reading, spelling, and penmanship.* Cambridge, Mass.: Educators Publishing Service, 1970.

Glaus, M. *From thoughts to words.* Champaign, Ill.: National Council of Teachers of English, 1965.

Glavin, J. P., & DeGirolamo, G. Spelling errors of withdrawn and conduct problem children. *Journal of Special Education*, 1970, *4*, 199–204.

Goodman, L., & Hammill, D. D. *The basic school skills inventory.* New York: Follett, 1975.

Goodman, Y. M., & Burke, C. I. *Reading miscue inventory manual: Procedure for diagnosis and remediation.* New York: Macmillan, 1972.

Graham, S., & Miller, L. Spelling research and practice: A unified approach. *Focus on Exceptional Children*, 1979, *12*(2), 1–6.

Graubard, P. S. The relationship between academic achievement and behavior dimensions. *Exceptional Children*, 1971, *37*, 755–757.

Greene, H. A., & Petty, W. T. *Developing language skills in the elementary schools.* Boston: Allyn & Bacon, 1967.

Gurren, L., & Hughes, A. Intensive phonics vs. gradual phonics in beginning reading: A review. *Journal of Educational Research*, 1965, *58*, 339–346.

Hammill, D. D., & Bartel, N. R. *Teaching children with learning and behavior problems.* Boston: Allyn and Bacon, 1978.

Hammill, D. D., & McNutt, G. Language abilities and reading: A review of the literature on their relationship. *Elementary School Journal*, 1980, *80*, 269–277.

Hammill, D. D., & Poplin, M. Problems in writing. In D. D. Hammill & N. R. Bartel (Eds.), *Teaching children with learning and behavior problems* (2nd ed.) Boston: Allyn & Bacon, 1978.

Handwriting: Dysfunction and remedial approaches. *Academic Therapy,* 1968, *4* (1) (entire issue).

Hanna, P. R., Hanna, J. S., Hodges, R. E., & Rudorf, E. H. *Phoneme-grapheme correspondences as cues to spelling improvement.* Washington, D.C.: U.S. Government Printing Office, 1966.

Hanna, P. R., Hodges, R. E., & Hanna, J. S. *Spelling: Structure and strategies.* Boston: Houghton Mifflin, 1971.

Haring, N. G., & Bateman, B. *Teaching the learning disabled child.* Englewood Cliffs, N.J.: Prentice-Hall, 1977.

Haring, N. G., & Eaton, M. D. Conclusion. In N. G. Haring, T. C. Lovitt, M. D. Eaton & C. L. Hansen (Eds.), *The fourth R: Research in the classroom.* Columbus, Ohio: Charles E. Merrill, 1978.

Hawisher, M. F., & Calhoun, M. L. *The resource room: An educational asset for children with special needs.* Columbus, Ohio: Charles E. Merrill, 1978.

Heckelman, R. G. A neurological impress method of remedial reading instruction. *Academic Therapy,* 1969, *4,* 277–282.

Heilman, A. W. *Phonics in proper perspective* (3rd ed.). Columbus, Ohio: Charles E. Merrill, 1976.

Herber, H. L. *Teaching reading in content areas* (2nd ed.). Englewood Cliffs, N.J.: Prentice-Hall, 1978.

Herber, H. L., & Nelson, J. Questioning is not the answer. *Journal of Reading,* 1975, *18,* 512–517.

Hoffman, L. Speech disorders: Stuttering and elective mutism. In M. Josephson & R. Porter (Eds.), *Clinician's handbook of childhood psychopathology.* New York: Jason Aronson, 1979.

Huber, F. A strategy for teaching cooperative games: Let's put back the fun in games for disturbed children. In N. J. Long, W. C. Newman & R. G. Newman (Eds.), *Conflict in the classroom: The education of emotionally disturbed children* (4th ed.). Belmont, Calif.: Wadsworth, 1980.

Hull, M. A. *Phonics for the teacher of reading* (2nd ed.). Columbus, Ohio: Charles E. Merrill, 1976.

Johnson, D. D., & Pearson, P. D. *Teaching reading vocabulary.* New York: Holt, Rinehart & Winston, 1978.

Johnson, S. W. *Arithmetic and learning disabilities: Guidelines for identification and remediation.* Boston: Allyn & Bacon, 1979.

Jordan, F. L., & Massey, J. *School readiness survey* (2nd ed.). Palo Alto, Calif.: Consulting Psychologists Press, 1969.

Kamm, K., Miles, P. J., Van Blaricom, V. L., Harris, M. L., & Stewart, D. M. *Wisconsin tests of reading skill development: Word attack.* Minneapolis, Minn.: National Computer Systems, 1972.

Kauffmann. J. M. *Characteristics of children's behavior disorders.* Columbus, Ohio: Charles E. Merrill, 1977.

Kauffman, J. M., & Hallahan, D. P. *Teaching children with learning disabilities: Personal perspectives.* Columbus, Ohio: Charles E. Merrill, 1976.

Kessler, J. W. *Psychopathology of childhood.* Englewood Cliffs, N.J.: Prentice-Hall, 1966.

Kitano, H. Refusals and illegibilities in the spelling errors of maladjusted children. *Journal of Educational Psychology,* 1959, *50,* 129–131.

Kohl, H. *36 Children.* New York: New American Library, 1967.

Kopp, O. W. The evaluation of oral language activities: Teaching and learning. *Elementary English,* 1967, *44,* 117.

Kreirsky, J., & Linfield, J. *The bad speller's dictionary.* New York: Random House, 1963.

Lamb, P. *Guiding children's language learning.* Dubuque, Iowa: William C. Brown, 1971.

Lambie, R. A. A systematic approach for changing materials, instruction and assignments to meet individual needs. *Focus on Exceptional Children,* *13*(1), 1980, 1–16.

Lament, M. M. Reaching the exceptional student through music in the elementary classroom. *Teaching Exceptional Children,* 1978, *11,* 32–35.

Larson, C. Teaching beginning writing. *Academic Therapy Quarterly,* 1969, *4,* 61–66.

Lee, L. *Developmental sentence analysis.* Evanston, Ill.: Northwestern University Press, 1974.

Lerner, J. W. *Children with learning disabilities* (2nd ed.). Boston: Houghton Mifflin, 1976.

Lillie D. L. *Early childhood education: An individualized approach to developmental instruction.* Chicago: Science Research Associates, 1975.

Lovitt, T. C. Arithmetic. In N. G. Haring, T. C. Lovitt, M. D. Eaton & C. L. Hansen (Eds.) *The fourth R: Research in the classroom.* Columbus, Ohio: Charles E. Merrill, 1978.

Lundsteen, S. W. *Listening: Its impact on reading and the other language arts.* Urbana, Ill.: ERIC Clearinghouse on Reading and Communication Skills, National Institute of Education, 1979.

Mack, J. Childhood psychosis. In M. Josephson & R. Porter (Eds.), *Clinician's handbook of childhood psychopathology.* New York: Jason Aronson, 1979.

Manarino, P. Reading: An integrated approach for the beginner. *Journal of Language Experience,* 1980, *3,* 23–26.

Marino, J. L. What makes a good speller? *Language Arts,* 1980, *57,* 173–177.

Marlowe, M. Games analysis: Designing games for handicapped children. *Teaching Exceptional Children,* 1980, *12,* 48–51.

Mazurkiewicz, A. J., & Tanyzer, H. J. *Early-to-read: i/t/a program.* New York: Alphabet Publications, 1966.

Mecham, M. *The verbal language development scale.* Circle Pines, Minn.: American Guidance Service, 1959.

Mercer, C. D. Arithmetic disabilities. In C. D. Mercer (Ed.), *Children and adolescents with learning disabilities.* Columbus, Ohio: Charles E. Merrill, 1979.

Meyers, R. E., & Torrance, P. *Invitations to speaking and writing creatively.* Boston: Ginn, 1965.

Miller, W. *The first R: Elementary reading today* (2nd ed.). New York: Holt, Rinehart & Winston, 1977.

Minuchin, S., Dollarhide, P.C., & Graubard, P.S. A project to teach learning skills to disturbed delinquent children. In P.S. Graubard (Ed.), *Children against schools.* Chicago: Follett, 1969.

Myklebust, H. *The psychology of deafness* (2nd ed.). New York: Grune & Stratton, 1964.

Newland, T. E. An analytical study of the development of eligibilities in handwriting from the lower grades to adulthood. *Journal of Educational Research,* 1932, *26,* 249–258.

Novack, H.S., Bonaventura, E., & Merenda, P. F. *Manual to accompany Rhode Island pupil identification scale.* Providence, R.I.: Authors, 1972.

O'Donnell, P., & Duncan, K. D. I won't write/but I'll do calligraphy. *The Pointer,* 1980, *24,* 4–11.

Orlando, C. P. Review of the reading research in special education. In L. Mann & D. A. Sabatino (Eds.), *The first review of special education* (Vol. 1). Philadelphia: JSE Press, 1973.

Otto, W., McMenemy, R., & Smith, R. *Corrective and remedial teaching.* Boston: Houghton Mifflin, 1973.

Partoll, S. F. Spelling demonology revisited. *Academic Therapy,* 1976, *11,* 339–348.

Pearson, G. H. J. A survey of learning difficulties in children. *Psychoanalytic Study of the Child,* 1952, *7,* 322–386.

Pearson, P. D., & Johnson, D. D. *Teaching reading comprehension.* New York: Holt, Rinehart & Winston, 1978.

Peters, C. W. The effect of systematic restructuring of materials upon the comprehension process. *Reading Research Quarterly,* 1975–76, *11*(1), 87–111.
Petersen, W. *A program for the early identification of learning disabilities.* Seattle, Wash.: Special Child Publications, 1970.
Pressy, S. L., & Pressy, L. C. Analysis of 300 illegibilities in the handwriting of children and adults. *Educational Research Bulletin,* 1927, *6,* 270–273.
Rabinovitch, R. D., & Ingram, W. Neuropsychiatric considerations in reading retardation. *Reading Teacher,* 1962, *15,* 433–439.
Reisman, F. K. *A guide to the diagnostic teaching of arithmetic.* Columbus, Ohio: Charles E. Merrill, 1972.
Russell, D. H., & Russell, E. F. *Listening aids through the grades.* New York: Teachers College, Columbia University, 1959.
Sanders, N. M. *Classroom questions: What kinds?* New York: Harper & Row, 1966.
Schiefelbusch, R. L., Ruder, K. F., & Bricker, W. A. Training strategies for language-deficient children: An overview. In N. G. Haring & R. L. Schiefelbusch (Eds.), *Teaching special children.* New York: McGraw-Hill, 1976.
Schilit, J., & Caldwell, M. L. A word list of essential career/vocational words for mentally retarded students. *Education and Training of the Mentally Retarded,* 1980, *15,* 113–117.
Scofield, S. J. The language-delayed child in the mainstreamed primary classroom. *Language Arts,* 1978, *55,* 719–723, 732.
Shaw, H. *Spell it right.* New York: Barnes & Noble, 1971.
Slingerland, B. H. *Pre-reading screening procedures.* Cambridge, Mass.: Educators Publishing Service, 1969.
Smith, R. M. *Clinical teaching methods of instruction for the retarded* (2nd ed.). New York: McGraw-Hill, 1974.
Spache, G. D., & Spache, E. B. *Reading in the elementary school* (4th ed.). Bsoton: Allyn & Bacon, 1977.
Spalding, R. B., & Spalding, W. T. *The writing road to reading.* New York: William Morrow, 1962.
Spelling: Diagnosis and remediation. *Academic Therapy Quarterly,* Fall 1967, *3*(1) (entire issue).
Sperry, B., Staver, N., Reiner, B. S., & Ulrich, D. Renunciation and denial in learning difficulties. *American Journal of Orthopsychiatry,* 1958, *38,* 98–111.
Stauffer, R. G. *The language-experience approach to the teaching of reading.* New York: Harper & Row, 1970.
Stiles, C. A strategy for teaching remedial reading: I'm not gonna read and you can't make me! In N. J. Long, W. W. Morse & R. G. Newman (Eds.), *Conflict in the classroom: The education of emotionally disturbed children* (4th ed.). Belmont, Calif.: Wadsworth, 1980.
Stone, F. B., & Rowley, V. N. Educational disability in exceptional children. *Exceptional Children,* 1964, *31,* 423–426.
Swanson, H. L., & Reinert, H. R. *Teaching strategies for children in conflict: Curriculum, methods, and materials.* St. Louis: C. V. Mosby, 1979.
Swift, M. S., & Spivack, G. Therapeutic teaching: A review of teaching methods for behaviorally troubled children. *Journal of Special Education,* 1974, *8,* 259–289.
Tate, F., & Evans, G. *Dealing with inhibitions.* Paper presented at the meeting of the Southeastern Regional American Association of Psychiatric Services for Children, May 1977.
Taylor, W. L. Cloze procedure: A new tool for measuring readability. *Journalism Quarterly* 1953, *30,* 415–433.
Turnbull, A. P., & Schulz, J. B. *Mainstreaming handicapped students: A guide for the classroom teacher.* Boston: Allyn & Bacon, 1979.

Turnbull, A. P., Strickland, B. B., & Brantley, J. C. *Developing and implementing individualized education programs.* Columbus, Ohio: Charles E. Merrill, 1978.

Ulman, E. Art therapy. In N. J. Long, W. C. Morse & R. G. Newman (Eds.), *Conflict in the classroom: The education of emotionally disturbed children.* Belmont, Calif.: Wadsworth, 1965.

Verville, E. *Behavior problems of children.* Philadelphia: Saunders, 1968.

Vygotsky, L. S. *Thought and language.* Cambridge, Mass: MIT Press, 1962.

Wallace, G., & Kauffman, J. M. *Teaching children with learning problems* (2nd ed.). Columbus, Ohio: Charles E. Merrill, 1978.

Wallace G., & Larsen, S. C. *Educational assessment of learning problems: Testing for teaching.* Boston: Allyn & Bacon, 1978.

West, G. B. *Teaching reading skills in content areas: A practical guide to the construction of student exercises* (2nd ed.). Oviedo, Fla.: Sandpiper Press, 1978.

Wiederholt, J. L., Hammill, D. D., & Brown, V. *The resource teacher: A guide to effective practices.* Boston: Allyn & Bacon, 1978.

Wiig, E. H., & Semel, E. M. *Language disabilities in children and adolescents.* Columbus, Ohio: Charles E. Merrill, 1976.

Wilson, C. T. Essential vocabulary: Caution words. *The Reading Teacher*, 1963, *17*(63), 94–96.

Wilson, J. Selecting educational materials and resources. In D. D. Hammill & N. R. Bartel (Eds.), *Teaching children with learning and behavior problems* (2nd. ed.). Boston: Allyn & Bacon, 1978.

Wilt. M. E. *Let's teach listening:* Creative ways in teaching the language arts. (*Leaflet 4*). Champaign, Ill.: National Council of Teachers of English, 1957.

Windham, G. M., Dummer, G. M., & Fagen, S. A. Mainstreaming in physical education: Teacher strategies. *The Pointer*, 1980, *24*, 12–21.

Woltmann, A. G. The use of puppetry in therapy. In N. J. Long, W. C. Morse & R. G. Newman (Eds.), *Conflict in the classroom: The education of emotionally disturbed children* (3rd ed.). Belmont, Calif.: Wadsworth, 1976.

Zimmerman, I., Steiner, V., & Evatt, R. *Preschool language scale.* Columbus, Ohio: Charles E. Merrill, 1969.

14
Affective Education

main points

1 The idea of affective education is not new to general education or to the field of educating the emotionally disturbed.

2 Affective education can be used by teachers as a means of preventing emotional, social or behavioral problems as well as a means of therapeutically intervening in a child's life.

3 In order to be effective, affective education must be part of the total educational program, not an isolated lesson during the day.

4 Little systematic research has been conducted using affective curricula with emotionally disturbed children; therefore, guidelines must be drawn from clinical principles.

5 The approaches to affective education range from teaching cognitive control to simply encouraging the expression of affect. Although not empirically documented, most programs offer something of value to children.

AFFECTIVE EDUCATION is concerned with helping children develop an awareness and understanding of their emotions, values and attitudes by means of constructive educational activities. In general education considerable attention is currently being paid to affective education (Charles, 1980). A number of programs are offered commercially and numerous books and articles have been written that are intended to help teachers promote children's affective development. The affective domain is believed to have a powerful effect on cognitive and behavioral functioning. By helping children learn to deal with this domain more effectively, future mental health problems may be prevented.

The goals of most affective education programs are concerned with increasing children's self-esteem, developing their awareness of themselves in relation to others and improving their interpersonal problem-solving skills. Since these goals are consistent with the identified needs of most

---

This chapter was written by **Betty C. Epanchin,** University of North Carolina at Chapel Hill, and **Lynne B. Monson**, Rutgers—The State University.

emotionally disturbed children, it is somewhat surprising that few, if any, of the commercially available programs have been developed specifically for use with this population. Nonetheless, most of the curricular materials can be adapted easily.

In this chapter we will identify social forces which have promoted the widespread use of affective curricula, look at selected examples of affective curricula, along with the research on the efficacy of affective curricula, and examine techniques for using affective curricula with emotionally disturbed children in the classroom.

The Current Emphasis on Affective Education

Affective education, as it is known in the schools today, is an offshoot of the human potential movement (Chase, 1975). That movement has been greatly influenced by humanistic psychologists such as Arthur Combs, Erich Fromm, Abraham Maslow, Rollo May and Carl Rogers. Common to all of these writers has been an emphasis upon the following beliefs:

1 People have control over their destinies; they are not mere puppets in the hands of environmental or internal forces.
2 People can learn about and gain control over forces which influence their behavior.
3 People can grow toward what Maslow (1970) describes as self-actualization.

During the 1950s and 1960s human growth centers developed throughout the country, among them the National Training Laboratory in Bethel, Maine, Esalen in Big Sur, California, and Oasis in Chicago, Illinois. These centers have as their central purpose helping people become more in control of themselves and their lives. The ideas developed in these and other human growth centers have subsequently been translated into affective curriculum programs for children.

Affective education is not a new area for educators (Morse, Andizzone, Macdonald & Pasick, 1980). Though not always deliberately, teachers have always dealt with children's feelings, attitudes and behavior. Furthermore, in most societies, schools have been and still are seen as responsible for transmitting social values and for training future citizens. In colonial times, for example, one of the primary purposes of education was to be able to read the Bible. The hornbooks of moral adages stressed values of the times such as "Respect thy father and mother." The McGuffy Readers, which dominated educational textbooks for most of the 19th century, also emphasized moral principles.

Unlike the McGuffy Readers, current affective education programs generally encourage children to discover and develop their values and moral principles rather than to accept unquestioningly what is taught. As Morse et al. (1980) suggest, what is new about today's affective education, in addition to the name, is the systematic approach. Guided by psychologically relevant curricula teachers have been given responsibility for the emotional growth of their pupils. These authors cite three social conditions which are creating the need for affective educational programs.

1 *A crisis of personal and social values.* "The amount of aggression, delinquency, unhappiness and self-defeating behavior has raised real questions concerning the ability of the democratic society to maintain itself. When society has a crisis, the schools inherit an obligation. Hence, there is a direct, overt concern with affective education in terms of values clarification, self-control, moral education, and the like. In some cases this supplements home training and in others it does what does not get done in the home" (p. 4).
2 *The recent cultural revolution.* "Getting ahead is no longer all that counts. Life satisfaction competes with socioeconomic upward mobility. Out of this current conflict of values has come a great deal of introspection, both personal and social. This is reflected in certain specific curricula such as values clarification" (pp. 4–5).
3 *The increasing number of children living in "risk" situations.* The conditions in which these children live necessitate that the schools replace some of the "essential psychological ingredients that are missing in a poor home life. . . . teachers are child upbringers, the professional agents of society" (p. 5). Therefore, the responsibility for being the primary stabilizing influence falls upon the school and the teacher.

The pressure for accountability is another factor contributing to the emphasis on affective education in regular education (Divoky, 1975).

> Scratch any one of many affective programs and beneath the surface you'll find a system very concerned about reading scores. The affective route offers a way to attack the old scores bugaboo and, at the same time, hedge your bets. It's hard to fault a program of role playing, self-awareness and counseling if it doesn't raise reading scores and, at the same time, hard to show improved mental health, measurement in that area being a murky business indeed. (p. 22)

Affective programs, thus, seem to be a safe bet. They are thought to enhance achievement, and yet their actual effectiveness is difficult to measure.

Examples of Affective Curricula

The affective programs reviewed in this section were selected according to certain specific criteria. First, the goals of these programs are in keeping with the overall goals of affective education; that is, their professed goals are affective in nature. Second, the curricula reviewed here are used or intended for use by classroom teachers themselves. Third, the child rather than the teacher or setting is the point of intervention. Those techniques primarily intended for teacher training, counselor use or classroom climate improvement are not included. This review of programs is by no means exhaustive and inclusion of a program in this section does not imply that the program is one of the best in the field. This review illustrates the range of strategies followed in affective programs.

A useful distinction can be made between those approaches to affective education with both cognitive and affective content and those with more purely affective content (Vicary, 1976). In the cognitive-affective approach, feelings are explored and discussed throughout the presentation of the basic facts of the academic subject. For example, when studying Columbus's discovery of America, the teacher could introduce into the discussion questions about how Columbus must have felt when facing the unknown or how the students would have felt if they had been in his situation, if they had been a friend of his or if they had been on the Santa Maria. The regular curriculum offers numerous opportunities to integrate children's emotional lives with their cognitive lives.

Curricula that focus primarily on affective content are composed of activities that deal with self-perceptions, feelings or relationships with others. An example of this type of activity is having children think of as many words as possible that connote anger. Once a list is compiled, nuances of the various words can be explored by arranging the words on a continuum from mild annoyance to rage. Another example typical of this approach is having children identify a personal quality or a quality in a classmate that is admirable.

Vicary's (1976) categorization can be extended to incorporate a third type of content. This third category includes programs that focus on developing cognitive processes such as cognitive role taking and problem solving as a way of helping children learn how to deal with their feelings. An example of an activity within this type of curriculum is teaching the child about steps she can follow to guide herself through an academic problem. An approach that stresses cognitive processes is a more structured way to achieve the affective goals of greater self-awareness and interpersonal awareness.

Cognitive-Affective Approaches

Confluent education. Confluent education is "the integration or flowing together of the affective and cognitive elements in individual and group learning" (Brown, 1971, p. 3). Brown is concerned with meshing the thinking and feeling of learning, with personalizing education. In this respect, confluent education falls under the heading of cognitive-affective content. This approach encompasses a number of affective and Gestalt techniques. One technique is the fantasy body trip. In this exercise, the teacher has each group member concentrate on different parts of her body, moving from the toes to the head. Everyone shares the sensations experienced. Then the questions "What is a human being?" and, more specifically, "Who am I?" are explored from scientific, physical education and social studies perspectives. The confluent approach is a direct effort to effect a positive change in the American education system in answer to the rising discontent with the "traditional" classroom approach.

Systematic studies of this approach have not been conducted. Brown (1971) provides anecodotal evidence of significant positive results after incorporating the concept of confluent education in classrooms. Students are described as improving academically and socially as well as becoming increasingly involved in the education process.

Man: A Course of Study (MACOS). Another curriculum combining cognitive and affective material is *Man: A Course of Study (MACOS)* (Dow, 1972). In 1965 Bruner outlined this year-long course for upper elementary- and middle-school-age children around the questions "What is human about being human beings? How did they get that way? How can they be made more so?" The course is classified as a social studies curriculum in which teachers and students "explore together the roots of man's social behavior through the study of selected animal groups and intensive examination of a remote human society very different from our own" (the Netsilik Eskimo). Ethnological films, simulations, games, role playing, books and exercises are used in covering a number of topics, such as adaptation, innate behavior, learning, parental care, aggression, social structure and communication. An atmosphere is generated in which children can openly express their feelings. This curriculum may be adapted very easily for emotionally disturbed children because the distance of the subject matter from the children's immediate living situation may allow for a more open discussion of critical issues such as aggression and parental care.

MACOS was evaluated extensively during the academic years 1967–68 and 1968–69) (Hanley & Moo, 1970). Subjects of this study were fourth, fifth and sixth graders (10% of the children were ungraded) from 176 different urban and suburban classrooms. Fourteen of the classrooms comprised a control group in 1968–69. It was not clear from Hanley and Moo's report whether or not the control classes participated in any type of complementary "special activity" to reduce the likelihood of a Hawthorne effect (behavior change caused solely by participation in a unique program).

Teachers administered the *MACOS* program and were trained in 20 seminar sessions which ran concurrently. Children and teachers were interviewed at three different points during the program; children were given pre-tests and post-tests on information, concepts and attitudes about the program, and classrooms were observed. When the variables of grade, sex, school and socioeconomic status were controlled for, significant gains in learning were reported. Children were particularly enthusiastic about the films, and their interviews demonstrated that they made links between their own feelings and those of the Netsilik Eskimos. Teachers found the manual, the diversity of activities and materials, and the films to be strengths of the program. Active listening, communicating and sharing in group situations were social skills the teachers thought were emphasized. Shortcomings of the study were that the measures were not scored blindly and reliability checks were not made on individual interpretations of the qualitative measures. The control group was used only to observe differences in classroom climate; *MACOS* classes were more student-centered and exhibited more student-to-student interactions.

Values clarification. Values clarification is a systematic attempt to aid children and adolescents in developing a "process of valuing," a process of decision making about personal issues such as career choice, religion, sex, authority and friendship. The process of valuing rather than values themselves are taught (Simon, Howe & Kirschenbaum, 1972). Seven subprocesses comprise the valuing process:

1. Prizing and cherishing
2. Publicly affirming, when appropriate
3. Choosing after consideration of consequences
4. Choosing from alternatives
5. Choosing freely
6. Acting
7. Acting with a pattern, consistency and repetition (p. 19)

The values clarification manual (Simon et al., 1972) offers many practical strategies which may be used at a specific time set aside during the school day or incorporated into standard subject matter. Thus, this approach includes both cognitive-affective and purely affective content.

One strategy representative of values clarification is entitled "Spread of Opinion." Its purpose is to increase children's awareness of the wide range of possible opinions on different issues. An issue (or issues) is selected and groups of five or six are formed. The group's task is to identify five or six possible positions on the controversial issue. Each student chooses one of the positions and writes a paragraph to defend it. These opinions are then shared.

Affective education is closely related to the idea of "personalizing" education. Howe and Howe (1975) set forth four dimensions which need to be considered when personalizing the classroom: human relationships, instruction, curriculum, and classroom organization and management. A number of different humanistic strategies are offered under each heading to facilitate the integration of the cognitive and affective aspects of education. For example, Brown's confluent education is suggested as one method of personalizing instruction.

Simon and O'Rourke (1977) have collected a number of values clarification strategies that are particularly appropriate for emotionally disturbed and learning disabled children. The exercises they suggest promote self-disclosure to others, love, values, parent involvement and so on, and have been found to be successful with exceptional children.

Thirteen research studies on the effectiveness of values clarification strategies have been critically reviewed by Lockwood (1978). The majority of these studies were unpublished doctoral dissertations and manuscripts. Lockwood examined each study for external and internal validity problems, strengths and weaknesses, and then assigned each study a confidence rating based on the study's overall merits. Ten of the 13 studies received merit ratings of "fair," "low" or "none." Major weaknesses included the poor outcome measures, lack of information on treatment duration, misuse of statistics, misinterpretations and no control for teacher effect. Thus, Lockwood concluded that many of the claims made about values clarification strategies were unwarranted in light of research to date. He posits that the only warranted claim about the effects of values clarification is that it may improve reading ability and may positively affect students' classroom behavior. Further research is needed on the differential effects of values clarification related to age, teacher variables and follow-up testing.

Self-control curriculum. Another example of a cognitive-affective curriculum is *Teaching Children Self-Control* by Fagen, Long and Stevens (1975). This program is intended as a guide to teaching "basic enabling skills for self-control." On the basis of observation, literature review and "shared reflection" the authors identified a set of eight core skills which they believe enable an individual to control her behavior. The first four of these rely more on cognitive development while the remaining four are more related to emotional or affective development. The eight skill clusters are:

1. *Selection.* Ability to perceive incoming information accurately
2. *Storage.* Ability to retain the information received
3. *Sequencing and ordering.* Ability to organize actions on the basis of a planned order
4. *Anticipating consequences.* Ability to relate actions to expected outcomes
5. *Appreciating feelings.* Ability to identify and constructively use affective experiences
6. *Managing frustration.* Ability to cope with external obstacles that produce stress
7. *Inhibition and delay.* Ability to postpone or restrain action tendencies
8. *Relaxation.* Ability to reduce internal tension (p. 38)

The curriculum emphasizes the need for "balance" and "interaction" between the cognitive and affective domains. For each skill area the curriculum includes a description of the skill and its components, a rationale for including the skill and a number of games and activities which teach the skill. For example, as part of the sequencing and ordering skill area, time puzzles are suggested. Children indicate what is wrong with sentences such as the following samples:

1. I got up early this morning, had supper, and went to school.
2. During June, July, and August, I wear a heavy coat and gloves to school.
3. I like the fall when the flowers start blooming. (Fagen, Long & Stevens, 1975, p. 26)

This curriculum was described and reviewed extensively in the February 1979 issue of *Behavior Disorders*.

Fagen, Long and Stevens have also developed the *Self-Control Behavior Inventory* (SCBI) (1975) which assesses self-control abilities. This instrument is intended to help teachers identify the areas in which the child is deficient in her self-control curriculum. Dembinsi (1979) investigated the reliability of the SCBI and concluded "the possibilities for their psychoeducational approach to self-control are too promising to go uninvestigated" (p. 142).

Affective Approaches

Bibliotherapy. Bibliotherapy has been defined as "a dynamic, interactive process between reader personality and literature which effects adjustment and growth" (Morgan, 1976, p. 39). Thus it can be regarded as an educational technique with affective content designed to prevent as well as correct emotional problems. The effectiveness of bibliotherapy depends on the child's ability to identify with the situation in the book. Emotional tensions are released, and the child reaches a better understanding of herself (Russell

& Russell, 1979). Follow-up is another key to effectiveness (Morgan, 1976). It is pointless to give a child a book about a known problem if there are no opportunities for follow-up discussion.

Bibliotherapy has been used with disturbed children (Morgan, 1976; Russell & Russell, 1979) and with abused children (Watson, 1980). Russell and Russell (1979) present general guidelines to promote discussion of the material read, activities to follow up reading and suggestions for helping the reader. Fassler (1978) offers suggestions for books and stories to help children cope with feelings and disabilities. Dreyer (1977) lists and describes a number of children's books that deal with childhood problems and concerns. Research studies on the effectiveness of bibliotherapy are still greatly needed.

Group therapy. In group therapy children work through their feelings in a group "where inquiry, support, and interpretation are all utilized appropriately" (Anderson & Marrone, 1977, p. 99). Group therapy has been used in the classroom with "normal" and with emotionally disturbed children. Anderson and Marrone (1977) tried a variety of group and individual procedures to help children become self-aware and to cope with difficult situations. After evaluating the effectiveness of several approaches, they recommend that the psychiatrist or psychologist (or therapeutic team) join the teacher in school and jointly conduct group therapy. In operating group therapy sessions, setting up ground rules (i.e., no hitting) and choosing an appropriate location (i.e., a circle of chairs in the classroom as opposed to being outside) are important. Topics for discussion are generated by the students because "affective working through of difficult problems is not an intellectual exercise; therefore, one cannot predetermine what concerns the children will bring to the group" (p. 102). In a controlled study of 27 children divided equally into three groups matched for age, intelligence and severity of emotional disturbance, children who received group treatment in the classroom were found to make more progress toward their treatment goals than children in individual therapy either within or outside of a school setting. The measurement of their progress and its reliability were not addressed in their report.

Developing Understanding of Self and Others (DUSO) and the Human Development Program (HDP). *DUSO* (Dinkmeyer, 1970) and *HDP* (Bessell & Palomares, 1970) are structured affective programs designed to build children's understanding of self and others. Both are popular classroom curricula for preschool and early elementary-aged children.

Materials for *DUSO* include puppets for role playing, stories and records. The program is arranged in units which have themes such as Understanding and Accepting Self, Understanding Independence, and Understanding Choice and Consequences. Children develop listening, inquiry and discussion skills as they learn about socio-emotional behavior. A set of activities for the week might include a story with some moral, a problem situation, a role-playing situation and a puppet activity, all focusing on one of the unit themes.

Koval and Hales's (1972) research represents the first published study of the *DUSO* program. One experimental and one control class in each of the first three grades of two different schools were included in their sample. The researcher held a 30-minute guidance session using *DUSO* materials once a week for 10 weeks. The control classes remained with their regular teacher. (Thus, there was no control for a Hawthorne effect on the experimental classes.) Experimental class children were found to score higher on the Self-Reliance and Feeling of Belonging subtests of the California Test of Personality.

Several studies, both published and unpublished, of the *DUSO* program in which it was administered by either a teacher or a counselor were reviewed by Medway and Smith (1978). The overall weakness of the studies in their evaluation was the inadequate treatment period (less than three months) in which to expect improvement in constructs such as self-concept.

HDP or the Human Development Program, is more generally known as the "Magic Circle" because 8–13 children are arranged in a circle on the classroom floor to discuss a particular topic. Topics follow the themes of similarities and differences between self and others, one's own abilities and social relationships. In one well-controlled study, the program was administered as part of a number of exercises in human relations to a group of eight third graders, three of whom were identified as having behavior problems (Garner, 1974). A control group of comparable third graders participated in social activities sessions with the same leader; a second control group of fourth graders was also formed. Treatment consisted of three 30-minute sessions for nine weeks. Pre- and post-classroom observations were made. Teachers completed behavior rating scales and students completed self-concept measures. Significant differences favoring the experimental group were found on the behavior rating scale completed by teachers and on the self-concept measure. A follow-up on the durability of these changes is needed.

Studies on the effectiveness of the *HDP* with normal children, most of which are unpublished, have been reviewed by Elardo and Elardo (1976) and Medway and Smith (1978). Both reviews indicate the need for more systematic research on the program. Medway and Smith (1978) comment that few of the studies have reported the amount of training that group leaders received, a critical variable for teachers to consider.

Dimensions of Personality (DOP). This program, developed by Limbacher (1973), is a K–12 program with affective content. The material is organized in a chapter format and includes topics such as "I Can Do It" and "Becoming Myself." A passage is read, students respond orally or by writing in a workbook, and then results are shared. Emotions, groups, awareness, growth, family and peer relations, environment and self-image are all considered. The developmental approach of this program allows it to be easily adapted for exceptional children.

Medway and Smith (1978) report the results of only three studies of the *DOP* program, two of them unpublished. Results were mixed. From their discussion it appears that these *DOP* studies suffer from many of the weaknesses pointed out in other studies, such as inadequate length of treatment and measurement problems. Much more systematic research is needed on this program. Morse et al. (1980) have noted occasional sexist remarks in the stories. This incidental sexism, as long as teachers are aware of it, may be utilized for additional learning.

Focus on Self-Development. Organized into three stages, *Focus on Self Development* (Anderson, Henner & Miner, 1972) is another popular affective education program for kindergarten through sixth grade. The first stage is entitled "Awareness" and is designed particularly for younger children. Self-concept, sensory awareness, socialization, sharing and problem solving are topics included in the program. Materials include films, posters, records and workbooks; activities involve role playing, games, projects and discussions. "Responding" and "Involvement" are the second and third stages. To date, no systematic research on the program has been published or reviewed.

Social Learning Curriculum. Another affective program, whose effectiveness has not been studied, is the *Social Learning Curriculum* (Goldstein, 1974). The uniqueness of this package is that it was originally designed for exceptional children, particularly the mildly retarded. The curriculum contains 16 phases, each of which is broken down into specific subskills. For example, effective communication is subdivided into lessons on understanding the different parts of communication, sending appropriate messages, recognizing nonverbal communication, use of the telephone and so on. Materials include slides, photographs, a cassette and manuals. Discussion, role playing, games, art and music are some of the activities of the program. Included in the curriculum are suggestions for integrating the affective content of this program into academic instruction.

Cognitive Approaches

The following programs deal with improving children's cognitive understanding of social relationships and self as well as with more affective content material.

Toward Affective Development (TAD). This program, developed by Dupont, Gardner, and Brody (1974), was designed to foster both psychological growth (e.g., problem solving) and affective growth. Materials include illustrations, filmstrips, cassettes, posters, shape and object cards, duplicating masters and "feeling" wheels. Games, simulations, role playing, modeling and group discussion are some techniques used in the program. It includes five different sections which deal with issues such as feelings that occur in a social context of antecedents and consequences and the building of peer relations.

Hudgins (1979) conducted a well-designed study of the *TAD* program with 42 to 50 fourth graders. Subjects were randomly assigned to either a control or treatment group. Children in the treatment group were involved in the *TAD* program for 15 minutes a day, 5 days a week, over an 11-week period. Art activities conducted by the same teacher who was administering the *TAD* program served as a control on the Hawthorne effect. Social adjustment and self-concept were measured with several instruments following the treatment period. No differences were found between the two groups regardless of sex or class membership. Hudgins, however, notes that the program leader had no training and that the subjects were generally older than those of other studies of more successful programs. Thus, teacher training and programming in the early grades may be important factors to consider in order to maximize student gains from affective curricula.

Project Aware. The major goals of *Project Aware* (Elardo & Cooper, 1977) are increasing children's role-taking ability and interpersonal problem-solving ability, both of which are cognitive processes. Role-playing of problem situations presented by the teacher and group discussion are the main techniques of the program. In a similar vein, Spivack and Shure (1974) have developed a cognitive approach to solving real-life problems. Their program is designed to increase preschool and kindergarten behavioral adjustment by developing children's social and cognitive problem-solving skills and awareness of consequences. Games and dialogues help children learn the word concepts and cognitive skills necessary for effective peer interaction. Causes ("Why did you take her book?"), consequences ("What might happen when you take her book?") and alternative courses of action ("Can you think of a different way to get to use her book?") are considered.

Project Aware was examined in a study by Elardo and Caldwell (1979). In their experiment 34 children, 9 and 10 years old, were matched by sex, race, age and group IQ scores with 34 control students. Pre-testing was conducted on role taking, generation of alternatives to social problems and class adjustment. Teachers attended five months of inservice training sessions on *Project Aware* and social and cognitive development. Experimental children received two 25-minute discussions per week from November to May. Post-tests were then administered. Results demonstrated that experimental children were more able to generate alternatives to a social problem and were more improved in role-taking ability. Also, teachers gave higher ratings to the experimental children's behavior, though these ratings were not blind. Though strong in its choice of dependent measures and in its basic design, the study did not control for a possible Hawthorne effect.

The Think Aloud classroom program. As a result of several studies which noted that aggressive and normal boys differed not only on a behavioral dimension but also on a cognitive dimension, Camp and Bash (1978) developed the *Think Aloud* classroom program to teach verbal mediation skills.

Using some of Spivack and Shure's (1974) measurement instruments and building on Meichenbaum's (1975) self-control research, Camp, Blom, Hebert, and van Doorninck (1977) evaluated the program when used by resource room teachers for one-half hour daily for eight young boys considered to be aggressive. This strategy involved modeling the cognitive activity one follows when solving interpersonal problems. Camp et al. (1977) reported improvement on pro-social behaviors for the aggressive boys who participated in the program in comparison with untrained aggressive boys.

After completing the program the aggressive boys' performances on several cognitive tests were similar to those of an untrained "normal" group of boys rather than to the untrained aggressive boys. Among the cognitive tests administered were three subtests of the Weschler Intelligence Scale for Children, Revised, the reading test from the Wide Range Achievement Test and Kagan's Matching Familiar Figures Test.

Value education. Another program representative of a cognitive process approach, value education, uses discussion of moral dilemmas and is based on the cognitive-developmental perspective of Kohlberg (Kohlberg & Turiel, 1971). The purpose of programs of this type is to develop the organizational structures which one uses to analyze, interpret and make decisions about interpersonal problems. Their concern is to match the curriculum material with the developmental level of the child, a match they claim is ignored by many curricula. An assumption of Kohlbergian programs is that the development of a cognitive process is contingent on the interaction between already existing cognitive structures and new ideas presented by the environment. Thus, for example, Kohlberg's programs include the discussion of controversial issues and moral dilemmas to stimulate the student's thought processes through the actual experience of others' ideas.

An excellent study of this approach to value education was conducted by Blatt and Kohlberg (1975). The subjects, 132 in number, were divided into 12 different groups. Subjects came from two age groups, 11–12 years and 15–16 years; both white and black children were selected. The treatment groups included ExI (participants in moral discussion led by the researcher using developmental principles), ExII (participants in discussion of moral dilemmas without active adult leadership) and the control group. ExI and ExII attended 45-minute sessions twice a week for nine weeks according to their respective treatment. Pre- and post-tests presenting moral dilemmas were administered. A follow-up was also conducted a little more than one year after the post-test. The general results of the study were that ExI showed a significant increase in moral judgment compared to both control groups (ExII and control) which was still in evidence one year later.

In evaluating 11 studies of the Kohlbergian approach, Lockwood (1978) noted a high confidence rating for the Blatt and Kohlberg (1975) study. Randomization of subjects to the different groups and follow-up testing were noted as its strengths. Only two of the other studies reviewed received a high confidence rating. Rest (1974) presents a number of criticisms of the Kohlberg approach, including the lack of a sequenced curriculum, the paucity of varied materials and the high level of demands placed upon the teacher as group facilitator.

Efficacy of Affective Curricula

"The field is amorphous, the goals and objectives unmeasurable, the rhetoric often incomprehensible" (p. 22). Such is Divoky's (1975) summary of affective education. In many ways such a statement is justified. The problems encountered in evaluating affective programs are many. These problems have been enumerated in a number of excellent review articles (Baskin & Hess, 1980; Medway & Smith, 1978; and Elardo & Elardo, 1976). One major problem in the research is that the amount of affective instruction under review is often not significant; generally, the curriculum is followed for less than one year and not on a daily basis, as recommended by some of the manuals. The training of the group leaders is many times not reported and varies from study to study. As Divoky (1975) points out, many teachers are not trained to deal with the emotion-laden issues that may arise in an affective education session.

Measurement of affective constructs is another major problem. Specifying appropriate affective education objectives and outcome criteria is difficult at best. For example, improved self-esteem is often identified as an objective, but numerous problems are involved in defining and quantifying the construct of self-esteem (Baskin & Hess, 1980). Dependent measures are often not standardized; many times they have been developed by program authors. Consequently, proponents of programs often report positive outcomes. This is not because they have manipulated their results, rather because "everything is going for them, including unintended experimenter influence" (Morse et al., 1980, p. 102).

Validity and reliability problems associated with self-ratings and teacher ratings are prevalent. Subjects may give the socially desirable response rather than a more candid response; some subjects are more comfortable with self-exposure than are others; and some subjects are more aware of feelings than are others. In addition, there may be little relationship between reported self-perception and actual benefit, or between knowing and doing. Children may be sensitized to others' feelings without necessarily feeling better about themselves. Children may develop the ability to make higher-order moral decisions without necessarily behaving differently.

In a great majority of the studies no effort has been made to control for a possible Hawthorne effect or to prevent the confounding effects of teacher and program. Follow-up studies need to be conducted in order to test the endurance of any gains claimed. Therefore, longitudinal studies are in demand.

Almost all of the research studies on affective curricula have been conducted with "normal" subjects. To generalize the findings to emotionally handicapped children may not be appropriate. The role of the teacher is more complicated with the additional concerns of the emotionally disturbed. Thus, controlled research with emotionally disturbed children on the various programs and implementation strategies is needed. In summary, the efficacy of affective education seems to be the greatest when teachers are trained in the use of the materials and when children are introduced to the material in the early grades (Hudgins, 1979). Affective education for exceptional children has yet to be systematically studied.

Using Affective Curricula with Emotionally Disturbed Children

In spite of the paucity of empirical data to guide affective education programs, affective programs are important. For many emotionally disturbed children, the only affective intervention in their lives is that conducted in the classroom. Morse et al. (1980) note, "With our special children, so much is needed that we are obligated to get on with the work. Affective education is the birthright of these youngsters" (p. 105).

Effective affective education is not accidental, however. Teachers, the pivotal persons in providing affective education, must know how and when to intervene. They must understand the children with whom they are working and must be able to establish positive relationships with the children. Yet most teachers are not trained for such an undertaking. They are trained to manage behavior and to deal with curriculum but they are not taught how to deal with feelings—either their own or their students'. The following list provides general guidelines for choosing and using affective programs for emotionally disturbed children.

Integrate formal affective curriculum activities with the regular curriculum. Little personal and social growth occurs when the teacher conducts a lesson on respecting one's classmates but does not see that the expectations presented are carried over into other settings. Affective programs are supplements to the teacher's more general management of affective issues. They are a compilation of activities and materials which aid the teacher in focusing upon affective issues from a cognitive perspective. They are not a substitute for consistently fair, caring and empathetic relationships.

In integrating the formal affective curriculum with the regular curriculum, teachers must give careful thought to their own attitudes and values and to the attitudes, feelings and values that they want to promote in the classroom. Once they have carefully considered their own values and the ones which they want to promote in the classroom, they are in a better position to choose from the variety of available programs. When this procedure is followed, the packaged affective curricula are systematic and organized means of helping children acquire a cognitive understanding of affective issues that occur daily in their classroom.

Match affective objectives and activities with the level of the teacher-student relationship and the level of trust and support in the group. In deciding upon affective curriculum objectives and activities, it is usually wise for the teacher to save personal topics until all persons concerned know each other fairly well. Discussions about one's feelings, one's shortcomings and one's family (when the family is in turmoil) are often topics which children have very intense feelings about. To expect children to discuss such personal topics before they have developed some trust of their teacher and the group is usually unrealistic and insensitive. When children feel that the expectations are intrusive, they do not feel secure and trusting. Furthermore, they characteristically react by misbehaving or by conforming superficially (e.g., they give the "right" answer). For these reasons it is wiser usually to start a group with relatively impersonal, neutral, group-oriented objectives. For example, starting a group with an objective such as being able to discuss the value of rules encourages everyone to think about why rules are set, a worthwhile exercise that does not put anyone "on the spot."

As the children and teacher get to know each other better by sharing more experiences, affective education objectives can be generated naturally

Through "success stories" children can learn to cope with new and frightening situations.

from the daily activities. For example, when several members in the group have difficulty each time new work is assigned, the teacher may decide to use affective curriculum materials as a means of helping the children learn to cope with new experiences. By teaching the children about people's characteristic reactions to new situations, the teacher helps the children learn that many people react to changes with fear and apprehension. Such awareness may aid the children in seeing that their difficulties are not unique to them and not due strictly to their own inadequacies. Once their problems with new activities are seen in a supportive, impersonal light, the children can be helped to develop personal coping strategies for dealing with new activities.

The following sequence of activities might be used when teaching children how to deal with new, threatening situations:

1. Read stories about children or animals who learn to cope with new and frightening situations. *Ira Sleeps Over,* by Waber (1972), for example, is a story about a young boy going to spend his first night away from home. He wants to take his teddy bear with him but fears his friend will think he is a baby.
2. Identify activities frequently done by the group and discuss why group members like familiar activities.
3. Recall activities that once were new to the group and discuss how group members felt when they first started the activities.
4. Ask individual children to specify an activity which in the past they thought was frightening but which they now have mastered. En-

courage discussion of their feelings about having mastered the situation.
5. Have an individual child (but not necessarily the child who has special difficulty with new situations) volunteer to specify a task which she wants to do but about which she is apprehensive.
6. Have all the children brainstorm the worst possible consequences that could happen to the child while learning the new task.
7. Have the children specify the likelihood of each of the consequences really happening.
8. Have the individual child list reasons why it is desirable to learn to do the task. Allow the group to add to the reasons.
9. Encourage an individual child to compare the risks with the benefits. Again, allow group input.
10. If, after weighing the risks and benefits, the child still believes she wants to learn the skill, have the group describe strategies for learning the skill, making certain that they include in the strategies some ideas for coping with anxiety and apprehension.
11. Have the individual child decide which strategy seems most appropriate and appealing.

After such activities, the teacher may ask who else feels apprehensive about new situations. If the children who have been having difficulty do not identify themselves, the teacher may ask each one directly whether she thinks the issue applies to her. The teacher may even say to the child that it may be a problem for her if the child is not forthcoming.

After individual children have identified this as a problem area, the teacher may negotiate strategies individually or in the group to help them cope with new situations. By following such a progression the teacher can use affective curriculum materials to stimulate discussion in needed areas. Discussion may start as part of an affective curriculum activity and end as a life space interview (see Chapter 12).

In open-ended groups where children are continuously being admitted and discharged, progressions such as the one described above may be unrealistic. Nonetheless, the teacher should be mindful of the normal, natural hesitancies of each new child to disclose intensely personal feelings. In such situations, perhaps the best policy is to expect new children to be present during affective education discussions but allow them time to adjust before participating.

Plan for normal developmental needs. Clearly, children of different ages are interested in different activities, respond differently to strong emotions and vary in the nature and focus of their attachments to others. The preference of third and fourth graders to be in same-sex groups stands in contrast to the heterosexual interests of many sixth graders. Likewise, while it may be acceptable for first graders to cry when upset, for sixth graders, who usually are more stoic, it may be extremely embarrassing. While first graders enjoy peer relationships, they are still very dependent on adults. In contrast, although teachers are important to sixth graders, the influence of their peer group is more important.

When choosing affective curriculum materials, therefore, the age-appropriateness of the materials and activities should be evaluated carefully. After all, children with emotional disorders are first and foremost children. The following specific tasks are important for the elementary-age child (Morse et al., 1980):

1. Acquiring an increased sense of self and self-esteem, through realistic, enjoyable, and successful use of the body and the mind.
2. Gaining and using more independent self-direction without too much opposition from adults or too much anxiety.
3. Expanding socially to peer group membership, especially with members of one's own sex; one must find friends.
4. Developing a solid, relevant and satisfying sex role.
5. Expanding one's concept of fair play, rules, and rights of both oneself and others. There is moral growth to accomplish. This is tied to development in logical thought.
6. Developing more self-control to meet the expectations of your age.
7. Exploring new emotional feelings and attachments.

Evaluate the appropriateness of each affective activity for individual children. If an affective lesson is to be successful, every child in the group must be able to do what is expected; yet one of the few certainties in the field of educating emotionally disturbed children is that diversity exists in every group of children. The teacher, therefore, must critically evaluate the appropriateness of each lesson and activity. Each child's ability to deal with the topic, the type of activity and the level of the materials should be considered. Lessons that should be discarded are those in which the content is too difficult, those that have emotionally loaded topics (e.g., discussing the physical size of students when one child is obese and likely to be ostracized) and those that are overly stimulating (e.g., playing the human pretzel game* with a group of children who are prone to having problems when in close physical proximity to their peers). In other words, with emotionally disturbed children the wholesale use of a particular affective curriculum is probably inappropriate.

Fit affective education into the existing school structure. Instead of planning activities that are designed to meet children's needs, some teachers have instituted programs that reflect their own biases. Some have used programs which were helpful to them but which seemed strange to the school, parents or children involved. For example, Divoky (1975) recounts a teacher who was personally very involved in EST (Erhard Seminars Training) and therefore used it in his classes. He reasoned that because it helped him, it would help his students. Such a program, however, could be entirely unsuitable for the children, and it could polarize parents and teachers. Programs should be

---

*The human pretzel game involves the whole class. Someone who likes to solve puzzles volunteers to be the "dectective." The detective leaves the room while the rest of the class joins hands in a circle. Then without breaking contact, they weave themselves over and under each other's arms to become completely tangled. The detective must untangle the group through verbal instructions.

geared to the children's needs in the school setting, not to the teacher's personal needs.

Respect the children's right to privacy. The aim of including affective education in educational programs for the emotionally disturbed is to promote emotional and social development. It should serve to motivate and involve children rather than to scare and alienate them. Trying to force children to talk about their feelings when they do not want to may antagonize and frighten them. While the teacher may be very accurate in seeing that a problem exists, forcing the child to deal with the problem usually alienates the child. The old saying that you can lead a horse to water but not make it drink is apropos. Children (and adults) will deal with their problems when they can and want to do so. Teachers are most helpful, therefore, when they create safe, supportive environments conducive to risk taking, not when they struggle overtly with children.

Teach what the child can and should do rather than criticize what she is doing. In the psychiatric literature, it has often been stated that the symptom is the child's greatest achievement, that problem behavior is a plea for help and that a defense should not be removed until the child has something with which to replace it. All of these assumptions support the approach of re-educating the child before taking away problem behavior (i.e., defensive behavior). In their eagerness to help, teachers sometimes attack children's problems head on. Teachers set goals to change the problems but do not teach the children what they should do instead. When this happens, the children often feel criticized and unliked and the teacher feels frustrated and inadequate.

Occasionally children will continue to behave inappropriately in spite of the teacher's efforts to teach them more appropriate behaviors. Psychodynamically oriented clinicians view many such behaviors as defensive. The behaviors provide the child with a smokescreen, a means of avoiding conflictive and disturbing thoughts and feelings. Theoretically, if the basic problematic feelings and thoughts are not dealt with, the child may continue to resist new behavior repertoires. In such cases, the teacher can help the child by confronting the child with her behavior. I-messages (see Chapter 12) are an effective and tactful means of confrontation. By addressing the child's defense directly, it may be removed, thereby releasing the more basic affect. The teacher then may use "active listening" or LSI techniques to help the child deal with the troublesome feelings.

Know your limitations and use outside resources. Inevitably, when the teacher is using affective curriculum materials with emotionally disturbed children, a situation arises which the teacher feels unable to handle. Children may divulge very personal feelings, they may disclose their involvement in illegal activities or they may describe highly charged family interactions. When responding to such disclosures, the teacher first needs to determine whether the content should be dealt with in a group setting. For example, if a child's participation in illegal activities is discussed, children may get the impression that the behavior is condoned and/or they may become attracted to the behavior. Likewise, if a child discloses a great deal of personal information about his family, the child may regret the revelation later. With so many people sharing the information, keeping the topic out of the discussion in the future may be difficult.

If the teacher decides to continue an emotional discussion, it is important for the teacher to be accepting of the child's feelings. For example, the teacher should reflect the child's thoughts back to her in a nonjudgmental fashion ("Sometimes you worry that your mom really doesn't love you") rather than denying the feelings ("You don't really mean that") or moralizing about them ("You shouldn't feel that way").

When the teacher does not know what to say or what to do or when the teacher feels unqualified to deal with the child's problem, often the best policy is to acknowledge his position honestly ("I really don't know what to say or how to help. Maybe we should talk to someone who can help.") Sometimes the most beneficial action a teacher can take is putting the child in touch with additional resources that can help her deal with her problems. While it is both appropriate and necessary that schools help children deal with their problems, it is unrealistic to expect the schools to do this on their own. Support from family and community must also be available.

SUMMARY

Affective education is a murky area—hard to define, hard to research and hard to teach; yet it is a critical component of educational programming, especially with emotionally disturbed children. Affective programs are not new to the field of education but they are currently receiving renewed attention. Efforts are underway to develop systematic and theoretically sound affective programs for classroom use which will aid teachers in meeting the multitude of needs that emotionally disturbed children have.

In closing, one is reminded of A. A. Milne's introduction to Winnie-the-Pooh:

Here is Edward Bear, coming downstairs now, bump, bump, bump, on the back of his head, behind Christopher Robin. It is, as far as he knows, the only way of coming downstairs, but sometimes he feels that there really is another way, if only he could stop bumping for a moment and think of it. And then he feels that perhaps there isn't.

Affective education is intended to help children stop and think so that they can avoid self-destructive experiences and learn new alternatives. When appropriately used, affective education can provide children and teachers alike with rewarding, growth-promoting experiences; however, like all other interventions, it is not a panacea. It cannot provide a simple solution to complex problems.

DISCUSSION QUESTIONS

1. Which affective education programs might be useful with conduct-disordered, acting-out children and why? Which programs might be useful with anxious, inhibited children and why?
2. Design a study to evaluate one of the programs described in this chapter. Specify instructional objectives, desired outcomes and appropriate devices for measurement.

3. What skills should a teacher possess in order to use affective curricula effectively and why?
4. Of the three types of affective education approaches described in this chapter, which one seems most promising and why?

REFERENCES

Anderson, J. L., Henner, M., & Miner, P. *Focus on self-development.* Chicago: Science Research Associates, 1972.

Anderson, N., & Marrone, R. T. Group therapy for emotionally disturbed children: A key to affective education. *American Journal of Orthopsychiatry,* 1977, *47,* 97–103.

Baskin, E. J., & Hess, R. D. Does affective education work? A review of seven programs. *Journal of School Psychology,* 1980, *18*(1), 40–50.

Bessell, H., & Palomares, V. *Magic Circle/Human Development Program.* San Diego, Calif.: Human Development Training Institute, 1970.

Blatt, M. M., & Kohlberg, L. The effects of classroom moral discussion upon children's level of moral judgment. *Journal of Moral Education,* 1975, *4*(2), 129–161.

Brown, G. I. *Human teaching for human learning: An introduction to confluent education.* New York: Viking Press, 1971.

Camp, B. W., & Bash, M. A. Think Aloud: Group manual (Rev. ed.). Denver, Colo.: University of Colorado Medical School, 1978.

Camp, B. W., Blom, G. E., Herbert, F., & van Doorninck, W. J. "Think Aloud": A program for developing self-control in young aggressive boys. *Journal of Abnormal Child Psychology,* 1977, *5*(2), 157–169.

Charles, C. M. *Individualizing instruction* (2nd ed.). St. Louis: C. V. Mosby, 1980.

Chase, L. *The other side of the report card: A how-to-do-it program for affective education.* Santa Monica, Calif.: Goodyear, 1975.

Dinkmeyer, D. *Developing understanding of self and others.* Circle Pines, Minn.: American Guidance Service, 1970, (D–1,) 1973, (D–2).

Divoky, D. Affective education: Are we going too far? *Learning,* 1975, *4*(2), 20–26.

Dow, P. B. *Materials and strategies for educational innovation 1973.* Cambridge, Mass.: Education Development Center, 1972.

Dreyer, S. L. *The book finder: A guide to children's literature about the needs and problems of youth aged 2–15.* Circle Pines, Minn.: American Guidance Service, 1977.

Dupont, H., Gardner, O., & Brody, D. *Toward Affective Development.* Circle Pines, Minn.: American Guidance Service, 1974.

Elardo, P. T., & Caldwell, B. M. The effects of an experimental social development program on children in the middle childhood period. *Psychology in the Schools,* 1979, *16*(1), 93–100.

Elardo, P. T., & Cooper, M. *AWARE—Activities for social development.* Menlo Park, Calif.: Addison-Wesley, 1977.

Elardo, P. T., & Elardo, R. A critical analysis of social development programs in elementary education. *Journal of School Psychology,* 1976, *14*(2), 118–130.

Fagen, S. A., Long, N. J., & Stevens, J. S. *Teaching children self-control: Preventing emotional and learning problems in the elementary school.* Columbus, Ohio: Charles E. Merrill, 1975.

Fassler, J. *Helping children cope: Mastering stress through books and stories.* New York: Free Press, 1978.

Garner, H. G. Mental health benefits of small group experiences in the affective domain. *The Journal of School Health,* 1974, *44*(6), 314–318.

Goldstein, H. *Social learning curriculum.* Columbus, Ohio: Charles E. Merrill, 1974, (Level I), 1978, (Level II).

Hanley, J. P., & Moo, E. W. *Curiosity, competence, community*. Cambridge, Mass.: Education Development Center, 1970.

Howe, L. W., & Howe, M. M. *Personalizing education*. New York: Hart, 1975.

Hudgins, E. W. Examining the effectiveness of affective education. *Psychology in the Schools*, 1979, *16*(4), 581–585.

Kohlberg, L., & Turiel, E. Moral development and moral education. In G. Lesser (Ed.), *Psychology and educational practice*. Chicago: Scott, Foresman, 1971.

Koval, C. B., & Hales, L. W. The effects of the DUSO Guidance Program on the self-concepts of primary school children. *Child Study Journal*, 1972, *2*(2), 57–61.

Limbacher, W. *Dimensions of personality*. Dayton, Ohio: Pflaum, 1973.

Lockwood, A. L. The effects of values clarification and moral development curricula on school-age subjects: A critical review of recent research. *Review of Educational Research*, 1978, *48*(3), 325–364.

Maslow, A. *Motivation and personality* (2nd ed.). New York: Harper & Row, 1970.

Medway, F. J., & Smith, Jr., R. C. An examination of contemporary elementary school affective education programs. *Psychology in the Schools*, 1978, *15*(2), 260–269.

Meichenbaum, D. Theoretical and treatment implications of development research on verbal control of behavior. *Canadian Psychological Review*, 1975, *16*, 22–27.

Morgan, S. R. Bibliotherapy: A broader concept. *Journal of Clinical Child Psychology*, 1976, *5*, 39–42.

Morse, W. C., Andizzone, J., Macdonald C., & Pasick P. *Affective education for children and youth*. Reston, Va.: Council for Exceptional Children, 1980.

Rest, J. Value education: A review of "Kohlbergian" programs. *Review of Educational Research*, 1974, *44*(2), 241–259.

Russell, A. E., & Russell, W. A. Using bibliotherapy with emotionally disturbed children. *Teaching Exceptional Children*, 1979, *11*(4), 168–169.

Simon, S., Howe, L., & Kirschenbaum, H. *Values clarification*. New York: Hart, 1972.

Simon, S., & O'Rourke, R. *Developing values with exceptional children*. Englewood Cliffs, N.J.: Prentice-Hall, 1977.

Spivack, G., & Shure, M. *Social adjustment of young children*. San Francisco, Calif.: Jossey-Bass, 1974.

Vicary, J. R. Teaching models involving affective education. *The Journal of School Health*, 1976, *46*(7), 392–400.

Waber, G. *Ira sleeps over*. Boston: Houghton Miffin, 1972.

Watson, J. J. Bibliotherapy for abused children. *The School Counselor*, 1980, *27*(3), 204–208.

RESOURCES FOR TEACHING MATERIALS

American Guidance Service, Inc.
Publishers' Building
Circle Pines, MN 55014

Appleton-Century-Crofts
440 Park Avenue South
New York, NY 10016

Associated Press
50 Rockefeller Plaza
New York, NY 10020

Barnell Loft
958 Church Street
Baldwin, NY 11510

Bell & Howell
7100 McCormick Rd.
Chicago, IL 60645

California Test Bureau, A Division of McGraw-Hill
Del Monte Research Park
Monterey, CA 93940

Changing Times Education Service
1729 H Street N.W.
Washington, DC 20006

Curriculum Associates, Inc.
6 Hinshaw Street
Woburn, MA 01801

Dexter & Westbrook, Ltd.
958 Church Street
Rockville Centre, NY 11510

Educational Activities, Inc.
1937 Grand Avenue
Baldwin, NY 11520

Educators Publishing Service
75 Moulton Street
Cambridge, MA 02138

Encyclopedia Britannica Educational Corporation
425 N. Michigan Avenue
Chicago, IL 60611

Field Educational Publications, Inc.
2400 Hanover Street
Palo Alto, CA 94002

Fisher-Price Toys
East Aurora, NY 14052

Follett Educational Corporation
1010 W. Washington Boulevard
Chicago, IL 60607

Garrard Publishing Company
1607 N. Market Street
Champaign, IL 61820

Ginn & Company
191 Spring St.
Lexington, MA 02173

Hampden Publications, Inc.
Box 4873
Baltimore, MD 21211

Harcourt Brace Jovanovich, Inc.
757 Third Avenue
New York, NY 10017

Harper & Row Publishers, Inc.
10 East 53 Street
New York, NY 10022

Holt, Rinehart & Winston, Inc.
383 Madison Avenue
New York, NY 10017

Houghton Mifflin Company
One Beacon Street
Boston, MA 02107

Ideal School Supply Company
11000 South Lavergne Avenue
Oak Lawn, IL 60453

Interpretive Education/Melton Book Company
111 Leslie Street
Dallas, TX 75207

Kenworthy Educational Service
P.O. Box 3031
138 Allen Street
Buffalo, NY 14201

Lawson Book Company
9488 Sara Street
Elk Gove, CA 95624

Lyons & Carnahan Education Publishers
407 E. 25th Street
Chicago, IL 60616

The Macmillan Company
866 Third Avenue
New York, NY 10022

Mafex Associates, Inc.
11 Barron Avenue
Johnstown, PA 16906

McGraw-Hill Book Company
1221 Avenue of the Americas
New York, NY 10020

Milton Bradley Company
74 Park Street
Springfield, MA 01101

Open Court Publishing Company
Box 599
1039 Eighth Street
LaSalle, IL 61401

Phonovisual Products
12216 Parklawn Drive
Rockville, MD 20852

Random House
201 E. 50th Street
New York, NY 10022

Science Research Associates
259 E. Erie Street
Chicago, IL 60611

Scott, Foresman and Company
1900 East Lake Avenue
Glenview, IL 60025

The L. W. Singer Company
201 E. 50th Street
New York, NY 10022

Steck-Vaughn Company
Box 2028
Austin, TX 78767

Teaching Resources Corporation
100 Boylston Street
Boston, MA 02116

Visual Education Consultants
P.O. Box 52
Madison, WI 53701

Xerox Education Publications
Education Center
Columbus, OH 43216

Zaner-Bloser Company
612 N. Park Street
Columbus, OH 43215

Name Index

Abbott, M. S., 100
Abidin, R., 71
Abikoff, H., 171
Abrams, B. R., 161, 162
Abrams, R., 386
Achenbach, T. M., 104, 105
Adams, A. H., 379
Adams, H. E., 193
Adelman, H. S., 95
Aghajanian, G. K., 159
Aichhorn, A., 124
Albee, G. W., 39, 227
Alexander, E., 80
Algozzine, B., 104
Algozzine, R., 7, 9
Allen, J. L., 396
Allen, L., 131
Allen, R. V., 367
Alley, G., 360, 362, 363, 364
Alpert, M., 159
Alpher, R. W., 391
Anderson, J., 124, 415
Anderson, N., 413
Anderson, W. A., 199
Andizzone, J., 407
Andreason, N., 380
Ansten, J., 139
Apolloni, T., 89
Appell, L. S., 396
Apter, S. J., 226
Archer, A., 392, 396
Arena, J., 395
Argyris, C., 277
Arkans, J., 62
Armstrong, M., 332
Arnold, C. R., 333
Arthur, G., 101
Artley, J., 198
Atkinson, L., 54
Attneave, C. L., 226
Axelrod, S., 220
Ayers, D., 63
Ayres, A. J., 165, 167, 168
Ayllon, T., 199, 200
Azrin, N. H., 199, 200, 201

Babigian, H., 92
Baer, D. M., 192, 205
Bailey, D. B., 41
Baker, A. M., 358
Bakin, H., 108
Bakin, R., 108
Bandura, A., 192, 204
Bangs, T. E., 369
Bann, T. A., 160
Barach, R., 80
Barker, R. C., 215, 217
Barkley, R. A., 174
Barocas, R., 80, 223
Baron, S., 134
Barrera, F., 199, 200
Barrett, T., 378
Barry, B. F., 310
Bartel, N. R., 361, 362, 365, 379, 389, 391, 393, 394
Bash, M. A., 416
Baskin, E. J., 418
Bateman, B. D., 163, 375
Battersby, W. S., 172
Baumeister, A. A., 163, 174, 203
Beck, S. J., 108
Becker, H., 42, 68, 249, 253, 278
Becker, W. C., 332, 333
Bednar, M. J., 226

Bee, H., 173
Beery, K. E., 102
Behar, L., 81, 111
Bell, N. W., 226
Bell, R. Q., 21
Bellak, A. S., 193
Bellak, L., 108
Bender, L., 102
Bender, M. B., 172
Bereiter, C., 389, 395
Berkowitz, P. H., 145, 303
Berlin, I. N., 123, 137, 141
Berres, F., 314
Berry, M., 363, 367
Bessell, H., 413
Bettelheim, B., 325, 342
Bettman, J. W., 174
Bijou, S., 188
Biklen, D., 235, 264
Birch, H. G., 125, 159, 215
Bittick, K., 168
Black, R. W., 170
Blackburn, J. E., 310
Blackham, G. J., 333, 337
Blatt, B., 42
Blatt, M., 417
Bleismer, E. P., 373
Blom, G. E., 416
Bloom, L., 362
Bloom, R., 53, 94
Blum, G., 108
Blume, R. A., 277
Bolstad, O. D., 207
Bonaventura, E., 358
Bond, G. L., 386
Böök, J. A., 157
Bower, E. M., 8, 39, 89, 90, 92, 94, 123, 140, 245, 389
Boyer, E., 217
Bredo, E., 70, 278
Breese, G., 171
Brendtro, L. K., 308
Brenner, A., 162
Brenner, C., 123, 129
Bricker, D., 365, 367
Bright, T., 168
Brittain, R. P., 171
Broden, M., 207
Brody, D., 415
Broman, B. L., 379
Brophy, J. E., 279
Brown, D., 278
Brown, G., 80, 223, 409
Brown, L. L., 94
Brown, R., 165
Brown, S. T., 278
Brown, V., 280
Brown, W. M., 160
Bruce, R., 207
Brueckner, L. J., 386, 390
Brunton, M., 171
Bryant, B., 219
Bryen, D. N., 361, 362, 365
Bucknam, F. G., 125
Budzynski, T. H., 190
Buktenica, M., 102
Bullock, L. M., 10, 104
Bunney, B. S., 159
Burke, C. I., 371
Burks, H. F., 101
Burmeister, L. E., 395
Burnham, W. H., 189
Burns, P. C., 377, 379, 380, 383, 384, 385

Buros, O., 102
Burrello, M., 62
Burstow, N., 223
Buser, P., 169
Busk, J., 163
Butz, G., 310

Caan, B., 162
Cadenhead, K., 380
Caldwell, M. L., 387
Calhoun, K. S., 193
Calhoun, M. L., 357, 379, 396
Callahan, E. J., 198
Cameron, N., 123, 124
Camp, B. W., 416
Cantwell, D., 366
Caplan, G., 141
Carlson, C. S., 333
Carlson, J., 278
Carrillo, L. W., 361
Carter, R. D., 279
Carter, V., 207
Cartwright, G. P., 381
Chace, M., 396
Chandler, M., 158
Chang, L. Y., 376
Charles, C. M., 310, 406
Chase, L., 407
Cheney, C., 264
Chess, S., 125, 157, 158, 162, 174, 215
Christianson, T., 283
Christopolos, F., 62
Ciminero, A. R., 193
Citron, L. J., 162
Clements, S., 163
Clymer, T., 376, 378
Cobb, J. A., 361
Cohen, C., 386
Cohen, H., 108
Cohen, M. A., 310
Coleman, C., 226
Coleman, J. C., 314
Coleman, M., 160
Coll, J. D., 92
Combs, A. W., 277
Conners, R., 7
Connolly, A. J., 390
Cook, A. R., 92
Cook, L., 222
Cook, P. S., 162
Cooke, T. P., 89
Coopchik, H., 10, 11
Cooper, B. P., 100
Cooper, M., 416
Cooper, S., 143
Coopersmith, S., 94
Copeland, R. W., 390
Cott, A., 161
Cowen, E. L., 89, 92
Cox, C., 162
Crockenberg, S., 219
Crouter, A., 223
Cruickshank, W. M., 171
Csanyi, A., 200, 310
Cullinan, D., 6, 9
Cutler, R., 62, 308

d'Alelio, W. A., 380, 381
Dallmann, M., 376, 379
Daniels, W. D., 396
Davids, A., 92
Davine, M., 172
Davis, W. E., 89

429

Davison, G. C., 196, 197, 198, 203, 205
Dawson, M. A., 376
Deboer, J. J., 376
DeGirolamo, G., 386
Deiker, T., 200
Deitz, S. M., 200
Delacato, C., 164
De Magistris, R. J., 340, 343
Deno, E., 62
De Risi, W. J., 310
Deshler, D., 360, 362, 363, 364
Deutsch, M., 53
Devine, O. T., 206
Devoge, J. B., 89, 95
Dewey, John, 26
DiMascio, A., 158
Dinkmeyer, D., 278, 413
Divoky, D., 408, 417, 418, 422
Dolch, E. W., 376
Dollard, J., 192
Dollarhide, P. C., 360
Dolnick, M., 204
Donahue, G., 80
Doty, R., 169
Dow, P. B., 410
Drabman, R., 218, 337
Dreikurs, R., 345, 396
Dreyer, S. L., 413
Drucker, H., 390
Drummond, R. J., 90
Duffy, G. G., 378
Dummer, G. M., 396
Duncan, K. D., 382
Dunham, H., 215
Dunn, K., 310
Dunn, L. M., 62
Dunn, R., 310
Dunsing, J., 165
Dupont, H., 415
Durkheim, E., 245
Durkin, D., 361, 376, 377
Dykes, M. K., 10, 104

Early, B., 111
Eaton, M. D., 391
Eckerman, D. A., 203
Eckwall, E. E., 370
Eddy, E. M., 277
Edgar, E., 392, 396
Edman, M., 277
Egner, A., 68
Egrer, A., 233
Ekstein, R., 123, 124, 299, 300, 301, 303
Elardo, P. T., 414, 416, 418
Elardo, R., 414, 418
Ellison, T. A., 222
Elston, R. C., 157
Emans, R., 376, 377
Empey, L. T., 225
Engelmann, S. E., 379
Epstein, M. H., 6, 9
Erb, L., 362, 365, 368
Erikson, E., 124, 125, 126, 129, 130
Erikson, K. T., 256
Ersner-Hershfield, R., 202
Estes, T. H., 395, 396
Eun, B., 94
Evans, E. D., 92
Evans, G., 380, 381
Exner, J., 108

Fagen, S. A., 396, 411, 412
Faris, R., 215
Fasnacht, G., 199
Fassler, J., 413
Feingold, B., 161, 162
Fenichel, C., 301
Fernald, G., 375
Fink, A., 62, 308
Fisher, G. M., 377
Fitzgerald, E., 367
Fitzgerald, G. E., 99
Flanders, N., 217
Flavell, J. H., 124
Fleeman, W., 168
Fleischman, O., 124
Flowers, A., 379
Flynn, N. M., 221
Folio, M. R., 396
Forehand, R., 90, 194, 203
Forness, S. R., 336, 337, 346, 347
Foxx, R. M., 191
Freedman, M., 111
French, J. L., 101
Freud, A., 124, 127, 128, 131, 132, 300, 301
Freud, S., 62, 123, 124, 130, 205
Friedhoff, A. H., 159
Fries, M., 125, 169
Frostig, M., 102
Fry, E. B., 376, 395
Fueson, W., 215
Furman, E., 128
Furness, E. L., 380

Gadow, K., 147
Galbraith, G. C., 163
Gallagher, J. J., 172
Gallagher, P. A., 326, 327
Garbino, J., 223
Gardner, O., 415
Garner, H. G., 414
Garvin, J., 68, 233
Gast, D. L., 337, 338, 339, 350
Gatti, F., 226
Gertner, J. M., 160
Gesten, E., 79
Getman, G. N., 166, 167
Gibson, E. J., 166, 172
Giles, D. K., 200
Gillespie, E., 43
Gillespie-Silver, P., 375, 379
Gillingham, A., 375
Ginott, H., 345
Gittelman-Klein, R., 171
Glass, G., 164
Glasser, W., 345
Glaus, M., 382
Glavin, J. P., 89, 386
Glenurick, D., 80, 223
Gliddon, H. B., 163
Glidewell, J., 89
Gloisten, A. C., 171
Gnagey, W. J., 332
Godfried, M. R., 196, 197
Goffman, E., 39, 246, 252, 262
Goffman, H. F., 174
Goldfried, M. R., 188, 203, 205
Goldstein, A., 79, 276, 277
Goldstein, H., 42, 415
Goldstein, S., 223
Gonzales, M., 200, 310
Good, T. L., 279
Goodhart, R. S., 160

Goodman, L., 367, 383
Goodman, Y. M., 371
Gordon, I. J., 92, 93
Gordon, T., 343, 344
Gove, W., 42
Graffagnino, P. N., 124
Graham, S., 386, 387, 388
Graubard, P. S., 219, 226, 360, 369
Greene, H. A., 383
Greenwood, C. R., 92
Grosenick, J. K., 9, 63, 79
Grossman, F., 264
Gualtieri, C. T., 171
Gump, P. V., 215, 217, 328
Guralnick, M. J., 219
Gurren, L., 373
Gussow, J. D., 159

Hales, L. W., 414
Hall, R. V., 207, 220
Hallahan, D. P., 369
Halpern, F., 108
Hammer, E. F., 109
Hammill, D. D., 94, 165, 170, 280, 367, 379, 380, 383, 384, 393
Hanley, E. L., 200
Hanley, J. P., 410
Hanna, J. S., 386, 387, 389
Hanna, P. R., 386, 387, 389
Harasymiw, S., 63, 223
Harbin, G. L., 41
Haring, N. G., 375, 391
Harris, A., 164
Harris, D. B., 94, 109
Harris, M. J., 370
Harris, S., 202
Harris, W. J., 90
Harth, R., 89
Hartman, A. C., 326
Hartmann, H., 125
Hartsough, C. S., 94
Hassibi, H., 162, 174
Havens, G., 380
Haviland, D. S., 226
Hawisher, M. F., 357, 379, 396
Hawk, B., 171
Hawkins, D. R., 160
Hebb, D. D., 172
Hebert, F., 416
Heckelman, R. G., 375
Heilman, A. W., 376
Heller, G. G., 282
Heller, H., 63
Heller, O., 63
Henner, M., 415
Henry, J., 277
Herber, H. L., 377, 378, 396
Herrick, C. J., 167
Hersen, M., 193
Hess, R. D., 418
Hewett, F. M., 30, 39, 63, 76, 103, 226, 299, 306, 326, 332
Hewitt, L. E., 105
Hilliard, G., 200
Hirshoren, A., 63, 282
Hiskey, M., 101
Hobbs, N., 10, 39, 95, 215, 223, 225, 227, 228, 229, 230, 231, 233, 263
Hodges, R. E., 386, 389
Hodsman, A. B., 160

Name index

Hoffer, A., 160, 161
Hoffman, E., 92
Hoffman, L., 366
Hoffman, M., 129, 130
Hollingshead, A. B., 53, 262
Hollister, W. G., 123
Holt, J., 288, 290
Holz, W. C., 201
Homme, L., 200, 310
Hops, H., 92, 361
Horne, M., 63, 223
Horzik, M. P., 131
Howe, L., 410, 411
Howe, M., 411
Howell, K. W., 310
Huber, F., 396
Hudgins, E. W., 415, 416, 418
Hughes, A., 373
Hull, M. A., 376
Hulten, W. J., 310
Hung, D. W., 81
Huntze, S. L., 9, 63, 79
Hurth, J. L., 231

Iano, R., 63
Illich, I., 289
Imber, S. C., 340, 343
Ingram, W., 369
Inhelder, B., 169
Isaacson, R. L., 172
Izzo, L. D., 92

Jacobs, P. A., 171
Jacobson, E., 198
Jacobson, L., 219
Jenkins, J. R., 315
Jenkins, R. L., 105
Jersild, A. T., 276, 277
John, E. R., 164
Johnson, A., 94
Johnson, D. D., 376, 379, 391, 395
Johnson, D. W., 220
Johnson, H. G., 196
Johnson, J. J., 265
Johnson, S. M., 90, 207
Jones, R., 62, 123
Jordon, F. I., 358
Jordon, L., 42
Josselyn, I., 348

Kagan, J., 125, 126
Kallan, L., 349
Kallmann, F. J., 157
Kalter, N., 92
Kamm, K., 370
Kane, F. J., 160
Kanner, L., 61
Kanoy, R., 171
Kaplan, H. K., 92
Kaplan, J. S., 310
Karrer, R., 164
Kass, R. E., 218, 337
Kates, W., 171
Katz, R. C., 196
Katz, S., 171
Katzenmeyer, W. G., 94
Kaufman, I. A., 92, 196
Kaufman, K., 218, 337
Kauffman, J. M., 6, 10, 104, 313, 354, 369, 389
Kazdin, A. E., 187, 192, 199, 204, 206, 207

Kearsley, R., 125, 126
Kelley, D., 108
Kelly, J., 128
Kelly, T. J., 10, 104
Kennedy, W. A., 198
Kennel, J., 126
Kent, R. N., 188
Kephart, M. C., 102
Kephart, N., 165, 167
Kerr, J., 92
Kessler, J. W., 107, 109, 123, 124, 361, 370
Killam, K., 158
Kilpatrick, D. M., 55
Kimble, G. A., 189
King, H. E., 194
King, L. A., 200
King, L. J., 168
Kinsbourne, M., 162
Kirk, S. A., 163, 170, 171
Kirk, W., 170, 171
Kirschenbaum, D. S., 89, 95
Kirschenbaum, H., 410
Kitano, H., 385, 386
Kitsuse, J., 42
Klaus, M., 126
Klein, D. F., 171
Klinedinst, J. K., 109
Klopfer, B., 108
Kluckholm, C., 215
Knight, M., 68, 233
Knoblock, P., 79, 220, 276, 277
Kohl, H., 381
Kohlberg, L., 130, 417
Kolstoe, O., 62
Koser, L., 332
Kounin, J. S., 203, 215, 328
Kourilsky, M. L., 310
Koval, C. B., 414
Kozol, J., 288, 290
Kreirsky, J., 389
Kroth, R., 80
Kunzelmann, H. K., 310
Kupers, C. J., 204
Kuypers, D. S., 332
Kyriacou, C., 79

Lachar, D., 109
Lachowicz, J., 200
Lakin, K. C., 6, 9
Lamb, P., 369
Lambert, N. M., 94
Lambie, R. A., 396
Lament, M. M., 396
Lamkin, J., 80
Lane, G., 231
Laneve, R., 79
Larrivee, B., 222
Larsen, S. C., 362, 363, 367, 370, 380, 383, 385, 386, 390
Lawson, L., 165, 166
Lazarus, A. A., 198
Lee, B., 307
Lee, L., 367
Lefever, D. W., 102
Lehtinen, L. E., 156, 163
Leibert, R. M., 204
Leitenberg, H. W., 198, 203
Leiter, R., 101
Lemke, H., 168
Lerner, J. W., 362, 365, 375
Leve, R. M., 125
Levi, A., 170

Levine, A., 123
Levine, F. M., 199
Levine, J., 160
Levine, M., 123
Levitt, M., 123
Lewin, K., 27, 215, 219
Lewis, J. F., 41, 101
Lewis, M., 145
Libaw, F., 314
Liem, G. R., 89
Lightfoot, S., 140
Lillie, D. L., 89, 360
Lilly, M. S., 62, 280, 283
Limbacher, W., 414
Lindsley, O., 310
Linfield, J., 389
Linke, L. A., 92
Lippitt, R., 217, 219
Lipton, M. A., 158, 160
Lobitz, G. K., 90
Lockwood, A. L., 411, 417
Long, N. J., 92, 140, 303, 411, 412
Lorenz, K. Z., 156
Lortie, D. C., 277, 278
Lortie, E., 70
Lovaas, O. I., 202
Lovitt, T. C., 327, 391
Lubeck, S., 225
Lucas, V. H., 326
Lundsteen, S. W., 365

Maccoby, E., 173
Macdonald, C., 407
MacDonough, T., 203
MacFarlane, J. W., 131
Mack, J., 358, 366
MacLean, W., 163, 174
MacMillan, D., 63
Madsen, C. H., 332, 333
Mahler, M., 127
Manarino, J. L., 374
Mangham, B., 139
Margen, S., 161, 162
Marino, J. L., 388
Marlowe, M., 396
Marrone, R. T., 413
Marsden, G., 92
Marsh, M. E., 89, 95
Martin, G. L., 310
Marwit, K., 219
Marwit, S., 219
Maslow, A. H., 30
Maslow, P., 102
Massey, J., 358
Mateer, F., 189, 190
Matson, J. L., 200
Mattick, I., 125
Mazurkiewicz, A. J., 374
McCarthy, D., 101
McCarthy, J. J., 171
McClemont, W. F., 171
McKinnon, R., 124
McGettigan, J., 63
McHugh, P., 273
McKenzie, H., 68, 233
McKibben, J., 162
McNutt, G., 380
Mead, M., 215
Mecham, M., 367
Medway, F. J., 414, 418
Meers, D. R., 125

Name index

Meichenbaum, D. H., 190, 192, 204, 416
Meltzer, B. N., 272
Melville, M. M., 171
Mercer, C. D., 362, 365, 368, 391
Mercer, J. R., 10, 41, 54, 101, 265
Merenda, P. F., 358
Merrill, M. A., 101
Merton, R. K., 258
Mesibov, G. B., 204
Meyers, R. E., 382
Michayluk, J. O., 223
Miles, P. J., 370
Miller, J., 278
Miller, L., 386, 387, 388
Miller, L. E., 91, 98
Miller, N. E., 193
Miller, T., 63
Miller, W., 371, 376, 377
Miner, P., 415
Mingo, A. R., 310
Minuchin, S., 360
Mischel, W., 99, 199, 204
Mitchell, M. A., 207
Mitchell, R., 168
Mitchell, S., 91
Monson, L. B., 231
Montessori, M., 123
Montgomery, M. D., 30, 40, 68, 71, 222, 234, 288
Moo, E. W., 410
Moos, B. S., 218
Moos, R. H., 98, 218
Morgan, S. R., 412, 413
Morse, W. C., 10, 11, 39, 62, 63, 80, 105, 140, 225, 226, 258, 264, 303, 304, 308, 309, 341, 343, 407, 415, 418, 419, 422
Mortimore, P., 139
Mosher, L. R., 160
Moss, J., 42
Motto, R., 123, 299, 300, 301, 303
Mulick, J. A., 192
Murphy, L., 81, 125
Murray, H. A., 108
Myklebust, H., 362

Nachtman, W., 390
Nagera, H., 128
Namboodiri, K. K., 157
Nelson, C., 63, 89, 337, 338, 339, 350
Nelson, J., 378
Neubauer, B., 92
Neubauer, P., 129
Neuberger, J. N., 160
Neufeld, G. R., 41, 43, 81, 226, 264
Newman, A. J., 277
Newman, R. G., 104, 140, 141, 234, 285, 303
Norman, A., 396
Northcutt, J., 81
Norton, A., 215
Novak, D. W., 92
Novak, H. S., 358
Nyhan, W., 196

O'Connell, C. Y., 310
O'Connor, P. D., 7, 63, 220
O'Donnell, P., 382

O'Leary, K. D., 206, 218, 220, 222, 332, 337
O'Rourke, R., 411
Ogar, D. A., 161, 162
Ogdon, D. P., 109
Ogletree, E. J. E., 80
Olson, D., 173
Olson, J., 104
Oppenheim, A. N., 91
Orgun, I. N., 125
Orlando, C. P., 375

Palomares, V., 413
Paluszny, M., 20
Pany, D., 315
Pappanikou, A. J., 259
Pappenfort, D., 55
Parenti, A. N., 92
Parsons, T., 246
Partoll, S. F., 386
Pasick, P., 407
Pastor, D. L., 219
Patterson, G. R., 333
Paul, J. L., 21, 29, 41, 43, 44, 55, 81, 132, 226, 264, 279
Pauling, L., 160, 161
Paulos, R. W., 206
Pavendstedt, E., 125
Payne, D. C., 92
Pearson, G., 134, 370
Pearson, P. D., 376, 379
Pederson, A., 92
Pederson, E., 135
Peed, S., 90, 194
Peller, L., 128
Pelosi, J. W., 43, 226, 264
Penfield, W., 172
Pennington, B. F., 92
Penrose, L. S., 157
Perelman, P., 68, 233
Petarsky, D., 55
Peterman, R. H., 160
Peters, C. W., 395
Peterson, C., 198, 203
Peterson, D. R., 90, 105
Peterson, W. A., 358
Petitt, G. A., 277
Petras, J. W., 272
Petty, W. T., 383
Phillips, E. L., 200
Piaget, J., 124, 126, 127, 130, 169, 170
Piers, E. V., 94
Plager, E., 332
Polefka, D., 198
Poplin, M., 384
Powell, W. C., 310
Premack, D., 199
Prentice, N., 140
Pressy, L. C., 383
Pressy, S. C., 383
Prieto, A., 237
Pritchett, E. M., 390
Prouty, R., 68, 233

Quay, H. C., 9, 90, 105, 195

Raber, S., 223
Rabinovitch, R. D., 369
Rabow, J., 225
Rachman, S., 189, 192
Rainer, J. D., 157
Randhawa, B. S., 223

Rapoport, A., 27
Rapoport, J. L.,, 221
Rechs, J., 200, 310
Redl, F., 98, 124, 140, 215, 222, 226, 330, 337, 339, 346, 348
Redlich, F. C., 53, 262
Reichler, R. J., 11
Reiner, B. S., 370
Reinert, H. R., 379
Reing, V., 80
Reisman, F. K., 390, 395
Reitan, R. M., 163
Reld, J. W., 230
Renz, P., 62
Rest, J., 417
Reynolds, L. T., 272
Rhodes, W. C., 29, 37, 39, 43, 49, 55, 132, 140, 215, 222, 225, 226, 227, 270, 279, 290, 299
Richman, J., 302
Rie, H. E., 132
Riley, J. F., 380
Rincover, A., 203
Rivlin, L., 70
Roach, E. F., 102
Robbins, L., 14
Roberts, L., 172
Roberts, M., 90, 164, 200
Roberts, R. D., 163
Robin, A., 204
Roe, B. D., 377, 379
Rojahn, J., 203
Rolf, J. E., 92
Rorschach, H., 108
Rosenberg, H., 219, 226
Rosenthal, R., 219
Ross, A. O., 91, 104, 189, 193, 205
Ross, D. C., 105
Rothenberg, M., 70
Rothman, E. P., 145, 303
Rouch, R. L., 376
Routh, D. K., 163, 174, 204
Rowley, V. N., 389
Rubin, R., 80
Ruder, K. F., 365, 367
Rudorf, E. H., 386
Russell, A. E., 412
Russell, D. H., 365
Russell, E. F., 365
Russell, R., 223
Russell, W. A., 412
Rutherford, R., 237
Rutter, M., 90, 139, 157, 159, 162, 174, 188, 194
Ryan, W., 279, 280, 282

Sabatino, D. A., 9, 63
Salvia, J., 101, 102
Sameroff, A., 158
Sandberg, S. L., 174
Sanders, N. M., 378
Sarason, S., 69, 70, 71, 264, 278, 280
Sarnoff, C., 130
Sattler, J. M., 101
Schaeffer, R., 202
Scheff, T. J., 188
Schiefelbusch, R. L., 365
Schilit, J., 387
Schlechty, P. C., 277, 278
Schmid, R., 7, 104
Schmidt, L., 63

Name index

Schneider, B., 68, 233
Schneider, M., 204, 220, 222
Schoggern, P., 215
Schopler, E., 11
Schroeder, C. S., 172, 192
Schroeder, S., 171, 172, 192, 198, 199, 200, 201
Schultz, E., 62, 90
Schultz, J. B., 308, 362, 363, 364
Schultz, S. R., 161, 162
Schulz, B., 157
Schulz, J. B., 379, 387, 390, 394
Schwarzmueller, E. B., 200
Scofield, S. J., 365
Seaberg, D. I., 277
Sear, P. D., 109
Seeley, J. R., 257
Semel, E. M., 369
Senf, G., 163
Sharpe, T. M., 198
Shaw, H., 389
Shea, R. J., 94
Shepherd, M., 91
Shepp, M. S., 107
Sherman, G. B., 378
Sherman, J. A., 192
Sherrington, C., 167
Shotel, J., 63
Shure, M., 416
Sibley, S. A., 100
Silberman, A., 333, 337
Silverman, M., 222
Simon, A., 217
Simon, S., 410, 411
Simmons, J. Q., 202
Siva Sankar, D. V., 161
Skinner, B. F., 189
Slack, D. J., 200
Slagle, R., 307
Slingerland, B. H., 358
Smith, D. E., 226
Smith, E., 124
Smith, J., 62, 225, 226, 258, 327
Smith, K., 165
Smith, R. C., 414, 418
Smith, R. E., 198
Smith, R. M., 365
Smith, W., 165
Snow, R., 132
Solnick, J. V., 203
Solomon, L., 198
Solomon, R. W., 333
Spache, E. B., 361, 379
Spache, G. D., 361, 379
Spalding, R. B., 375
Spalding, W. T., 375
Spaulding, R. L., 100, 332
Spears, J. J., 259
Spence, M. A., 157
Sperling, E., 144
Sperry, B., 140, 370
Spivack, G., 416
Stallings, J. A., 217
Stauffer, R. G., 367
Staver, N., 370
Stedman, D. J., 41, 81
Steiner, V., 367
Stenner, A. J., 94
Stephans, D., 81
Stephens, T. M., 299, 326, 333
Stern, E. L., 174
Stevens, J. S., 411, 412

Stewart, D. M., 370
Stewart, J., 157
Stickney, S., 140
Stillman, B., 375
Stiles, C., 312
Stokes, T. F., 205
Stone, F. B., 389
Stoyva, J. M., 189
Strauss, A. A., 156, 163, 164, 171
Strickland, B., 46
Stuart, R. B., 204
Stuck, G. B., 63, 220
Sutliffe, J., 79
Swallow, C., 89
Swanson, H. L., 379
Swanson, J. M., 162
Swap, S. M., 219
Swenson, C. H., 109
Szasz, T. S., 39, 156, 257, 284
Szurek, S. Z., 123, 137, 141

Tams, A., 220
Tanyzer, H. J., 374
Tarpley, H. D., 200
Tate, F., 380, 381
Taylor, E., 174
Taylor, F. D., 30, 63, 103, 299, 306, 326
Teasdale, J., 189
Templeton, R. G., 140
Terman, L. M., 101
Teuber, H. L., 172
Thelander, M. J., 81
Thomas, A., 125, 157, 158, 215
Thomas, D. R., 332
Thorndike, R. L., 219
Tipton, G., 81
Tizard, J., 162
Tjossem, T., 172
Torrance, P., 382
Tracy, M., 62, 140, 270, 279, 290
Trickett, E. J., 222
Trippe, M., 257, 258
Trost, M. A., 92
Tuckman, B. W., 73
Turiel, E., 417
Turnbull, A. P., 44, 46, 308, 362, 363, 364, 379, 387, 390, 394
Turnbull, H. R., 44
Tyra, D., 380

Ulman, E., 396
Ulrich, D., 370
Unger, C., 53

Vacc, N., 63
Van Blaricom, V. L., 370
van Doorninck, W. J., 416
Vaughan, J. L. Jr., 395, 396
Verville, E., 362
Vicary, J. R., 409
Vincent, L., 367
Vogel, E. F., 226
Vygotsky, L. S., 362

Waber, G., 420
Wagnor, M., 266
Wahler, R. G., 333
Walker, E., 219
Walker, H. M., 90, 92, 324, 329, 331, 333, 337

Walker, V., 63
Wallace, G., 362, 363, 367, 370, 380, 383, 386, 389, 390
Waller, W., 70, 247, 276, 279
Wallerstein, J., 128
Wanerman, L., 143
Wargin, R., 171
Wass, H. L., 277
Watson, J. J., 413
Watson, R., 124
Weatherly, T. J., 200
Wechsler, D., 101
Weeks, Z., 168
Weil, G. R., 108
Weinstein, L., 76, 231, 233
Weiss, B., 162
Wender, P., 163, 171
Werkman, S. L., 107
West, G. B., 396
Wexler, D. B., 199
Whelan, R. J., 53
Whitaker, J. K., 233
White, K., 219
White, R. W., 130, 218, 219
Whiteman, M., 53
Whitmore, K., 162
Whitsell, L., 164, 174
Whittlesey, J. R., 102
Widerholt, J. L., 63, 280
Wiener, L., 123
Wiig, E. H., 369
Willander, A. P., 200
Williams, J. H., 162
Williams, J. R., 203
Williams, R. M. Jr., 250
Willoughby, R. H., 203
Wilson, C. T., 387
Wilson, E. K., 245
Wilson, E. O., 156
Wilson, J., 396
Wilt, M. E., 362, 365
Windham, M., 396
Wineman, D., 330, 346, 348
Winnicott, D. W., 126, 139
Wirt, R. D., 109
Wittenborn, R., 160
Wolf, M. M., 200
Wolfensberger, W., 44
Wolff, P., 126
Wolpe, J., 189, 201
Woltmann, A. G., 396
Wood, F. H., 6, 9, 10, 94
Wood, M. M., 77, 103
Woodhill, J. M., 162
Woods, E. E., 379
Woolf, P., 125
Wright, B. A., 79
Wright, H. F., 218
Wright, W., 303
Wyne, M. D., 7, 63, 220

Yarborough, B. H., 373
Yellot, A. W., 89
Yoder, P., 194
Ysseldyke, J. E., 101, 102

Zabel, R. H., 10
Zauha, H., 44
Zelazo, P., 125, 126
Zimmerman, I., 367
Zitnay, G., 264
Zlutnick, S., 196

Subject Index

Advocacy, 44–45, 48, 235–36, 264, 288
Affective education, 406–24
Aggression, 104–105
Alternative schools, 287
Anxiety, 105–106
Arithmetic, 389–95
Arthur Adaptation, 101
Auditory acuity, 102
Austin State Hospital, 81
Autism, 20
Aversives, 336–37

Basic Schools Skills Inventory, 367, 383
Behavior, 18, 248–49
  learned, 188–93
Behavior checklists, 90–91, 101
Behavior disorders. *See* Emotional disturbance
Behavior management, 323–50
  aversives, 336–37
  life space interviewing, 339–43
  out-of-control behavior, 346–50
  physical restraint, 348–49
  reinforcement menu, 336–37
  seclusion, 337–39, 346–47
  teacher effectiveness training, 343–46
  time-out, 337–39
Behavior modification, 187, 190, 205, 206
Behavior Problem Checklist, 90
Behavior Rating Profile, 94
Behavior theory, 186–207
Behavioral assessment, 193–95
Bender Viaual Motor Gestalt Test, 102
Bibliotherapy, 412–13
Blacky Test, 108
Bonding, 126
Brain damage, 164–74, 175

Career education teachers, 80–81
Child's Apperception Test (CAT), 108
Children's Behavior Questionnaire, 90
Classical conditioning. *See* Respondent conditioning
Classification System of Psychopathological Disorders in Childhood (GAP), 9, 110–11
Classrooms. *See* Schools; Education; Teachers
Clinical interviews, 106–107
Clinicians. *See* Psychiatrists; Psychologists; Social workers
Community-based services, 41–44
Conditioning
  operant, 189, 190–92, 198–203
  respondent, 189–90, 197–98
Confluent education, 409
Contracting, 308–309
Coping Analysis Schedule for Educational Settings, 100
Corrective emotional experience, 135
Counselors, school, 80, 141, 286
Cultural theory, 270–92
Cumberland House, 227
Curriculum. *See* Education, curriculum

Day treatment programs, 146
Deductive theory, 27
Depression, 132
Developing Understanding of Self and Others (DUSO), 413–14
Developmental Disabilities Services and Facilities Construction Act, 48
Developmental Sentence Analysis, 367
Developmental Test of Visual-Motor Integration (VMI), 102
Developmental Test of Visual Perception, 102
Developmental theories, 169–71, 172–74

Diagnosis
  educational settings, 96–106
  mental health settings, 106–112
Diagnostic and Statistical Manual of Mental Disorders (DSM III), 110, 155, 156, 163
Dimensions of Personality (DOP), 414–15
Doman-Delacato theory, 164–65
Dopamine receptor hypothesis, 159
Drug therapy, 147, 158, 171, 286
DSM III. *See* Diagnostic and Statistical Manual of Mental Disorders

Ecological Assessment and Enablement Plan, 230
Ecological theory, 192, 214–38
Ecosystems, 218–23
Education
  affective, 406–24
  classroom intervention, 197–205
  confluent, 409
  culture of, 276–79, 290–91
  curriculum, 299–317, 408–24
  neurologically impaired, 171–72
  open, 82
  outdoor, 81–82
  remedial, 171–72
  See also Schools; Teachers
Educational methods, 354–97
  arithmetic, 389–95
  language arts, 361–89
  listening, 362–65
  readiness skills, 357–61
  speaking, 365–69
  spelling, 385–89
  teaching materials, 395–96
  writing, 379–85
Educational services, 60–82
  development of, 61–64
Education for All Handicapped Children Act, 45, 63
Emotional development, 170
Emotional disturbance
  affective education, 406–24
  behavior management, 323–50
  behavior theory, 186–207
  biological factors, 156–64
  classification of, 9–10
  cultural model, 270–92
  curriculum for, 299–317, 408–24
  definition of, 4, 5–9, 39–40
  diagnosis of, 96–112
  ecological theory, 214–38
  educational methods, 354–97
  educational services, 11–17, 60–82
  identification of, 96–106
  organic factor theories, 154–75
  parents, role of, 19–22
  psychiatrists, role of, 23–26
  psychodynamic theory, 131–37
  psychologists, role of, 23–26
  screening, 89–96
  social workers, role of, 23–26
  socioeconomic factors, 53–54
  sociological theory, 245–67
  statistics, 10–11
  teachers, role of, 22–27, 30–32
  theory in, 27–29
Epigenesis, 125
Epilepsy, 162

Family therapy, 145
Focus on Self-Development, 415
Food additives, 159, 161–62
Free Schools, 289

Subject index

GAP. *See* Classification System of Psychopathological Disorders in Childhood
Genetics, 156–57
Group theraphy, 144–45, 413
Guess Who Technique, 92, 93

Hallucinations, 13
Halstead-Reitan test, 163
Handwriting. *See* Writing
Hearing. *See* Auditory acuity
Heredity. *See* Genetics
Heuristic theory, 27–28
Hiskey-Nebraska Test of Learning Aptitude, 101
Hospitalization, 50, 146–47
Hospitals, mental, 81
Human Development Program (HDP), 413–14
Human service systems, 37–56
   legal-correctional services, 49, 54–55
   mental health services, 49–52
   religious services, 49, 55
   social welfare services, 49, 52–54
Hyperactivity, 147, 159, 161–62, 171, 174
Hyperkinetic syndrome, 163

Identification, in educational settings, 96–106
IEP. *See* Individual education program
Illinois Test of Psycholinguistic Abilities (ITPA), 170, 171
Imitation learning. *See* Observational learning
Individual education program (IEP), 30, 43, 45, 46, 63, 65, 68, 73, 79, 96, 198, 223, 235, 265, 281, 304–13, 356–57
Individual habilitation plan, 45
Individual program plan, 45
Individual treatment plan, 45
Individual written rehabilitation plans, 45
Infants, 125–26
Instructional units, 306–307
Instrumental conditioning. *See* Operant conditioning
Intelligence testing, 101–102
Internalization, 133–36

Labeling theory, 253–58, 261–63, 281
Language arts, 361–89
Language development, 170
Language experience approach, 367–68
Latency period, 130
League Schools, 301
Learned behavior, 188–93
Learning
   observational, 189, 192–93, 203–205
   rate of, 314–15
Learning centers, 306
Legal-correctional services, 49, 54–55
Leiter International Performance Scale, 101
Lesch-Nyhan syndrome, 196
Life space interview, 140, 339–40
Listening, 362–65
L-J Sociometric Test, 92–93
Louisville Behavior Checklist, 91

MACOS (Man: A Course of Study), 410
Mainstreaming, 44, 62–63, 222, 280
MBD. *See* Minimal brain damage
McCarthy Scales of Children's Abilities, 101
Media, 289
Mental health services, 49–52
Minimal brain damage (MBD), 163, 164, 167, 174, 175. *See also* Brain damage
Minnesota Multiphasic Personality Inventory (MMPI), 109

Multidimensional Description of Child Personality (PIC), 109

National Association of Social Workers (NASW), 52
Neurological impairments, 162–64
Neurometrics, 164
New York Longitudinal Study, 157
No-Lose method, 343–46
Normalization, 44
Nutrition, 159–61

Observational learning, 189, 192–93, 203–205
Oedipus complex, 129–130
Open education, 82
Operant conditioning, 189–92, 198–203
Organic factor theories, 154–75
Orthomolecular psychiatry, 160–61
Outdoor education, 81–82

Parents, 19–22
   intervenor, 79–80
   interviews, 109–110
   involvement in school life, 223
   rights, 46
   screening for emotional disturbance, 90–92
   therapy, 143–44
Pavlovian conditioning. *See* Respondent conditioning
Pellagra, 160
Perceptual-motor learning theory, 102, 165–66
Perceptual phase, 170
Phonics, 371–73
Physical restraint, 348–49
Physiology of readiness theory, 166
Pictoral Test of Intelligence, 101
Piers-Harris Children's Self-Concept, Scale, 94
P.L. 94-103, 45
P.L. 94-142, 8, 15, 27, 37, 41, 43, 45, 46, 63, 65, 68, 78, 80, 89, 96, 257, 265, 289, 302, 356
Precision teaching, 310
Predictive theory, 27, 28
Preschool Language Scales, 94
President's Commission on Mental Retardation, 172
Process for In-School Screening of Emotionally Handicapped Children, 94
Project Aware, 416
Project ReEducation, 61, 225, 227–33, 307
Projective tests, 108
Provo experiment, 225
Psychiatrists, 23–26, 50
Psychodynamic theory, 62, 131–37
Psychoeducateur program, 225
Psychological testing, 107–109
Psychologists, 23–26, 51
Psychotherapy, 143
Punishment, 201–203, 331–37
Purdue Perceptual-Motor Survey, 102

Readiness skills, 357–61
Reading, 358, 369–79
ReEd Schools. *See* Project Reeducation
Referral process, 66–68, 136–37
Reinforcement techniques, 198–203, 333–36
Religious services, 49, 55
Respondent conditioning, 189–90, 197–98
Reward, 331–37
Ritalin, 171
Rorschach Test, 108
Rules, 249–53, 259–61, 329

Schizophrenia, 11, 157, 159, 160, 161
School counselors, 80, 141, 286

Subject index

School Readiness Survey, 358
Schools
 alternative, 287
 classroom floorplans, 325–27
 as ecosystem, 218–25
 free, 289
 social control, 246–48
 See also Education; Teachers
Screening, 89–96
Seclusion, 336–39, 346–47, 350
Self-contained classes. *See* Special classes
Self-control, 204–205, 246, 252
Self-Control Behavior Inventory (SCBI), 412
Self-Esteem Inventory, 94
Self-fulfilling prophecy, 258
Self-Observation Scales, 94
Sensory integration theory, 167–69
Setting analysis, 97–99
Silverlake experiment, 225
Social adjustment, 8, 170
Social Learning Curriculum, 415
Social welfare services, 49, 52–54
Social workers, 23–26, 52, 54
Socioeconomic factors, 53–54
Sociological theory, 245–67
Sociometric testing, 92–93
Speaking, 365–69
Special classes, 73–78, 286
Special education, cultural aspects of, 279–81. *See also* Education
Special schools, 78–79. *See also* Schools
Special services. *See* Human service systems
Special subject teachers, 49, 80, 233–36
Spelling, 385–89
Standard Snellen Wall Chart, 102
Stanford-Binet Intelligence Scale, 101
Strauss syndrome, 163
Students. *See* Education; Schools; Teachers
Supportive services, 68–73
System of Multicultural Pluralistic Assessment (SOMPA), 101

Task analysis, 309–10

Tasks of Emotional Development, 108
Teacher effectiveness training, 343–46
Teachers
 career education, 80–81
 human service systems, 37–38
 identification of emotional disturbance, 22–27, 30–32, 135, 245
 individualized instruction, 305–17
 instructions, 327–29
 intervention, 64–68, 135–37, 233–36
 screening for emotional disturbance, 89–90
 special subject, 49, 80, 233–36
 teacher burnout, 79
 training, 140–41, 276–79, 302–304, 324
 See also Education; Schools
Teaching Children Self-Control, 411
Teaching materials, 395
Temperament, 157–58
Thematic Apperception Test (TAT), 108
Therapeutic tutoring, 140–41
Think Aloud Classroom Program, 416–17
Time-out, 337–39, 347
Toward Affective Development (TAD), 415–16
Transference, 133–36
Tutoring
 therapeutic, 140–41
 peer and cross-age, 308
 sequential, 307–308

Value education, 417
Values clarification, 263–64
Verbal Language Development Scale, 367
Visual acuity, 102
Visual motor development, 166
Vitamins, 159–61

Walker Problem Behavior Identification Checklist, 90
Wechsler Intelligence Scale for Children–Revised (WISC–R), 101
Wright School, 227
Writing, 379–85

MAY 01 1995